T0364811

Ford S-Max and Galaxy Diesel

Owners Workshop Manual

Mark Storey

Models covered

(6299 - 3B2 - 384)

Turbo-diesel: 1.6 litre (1560cc), 1.8 litre (1753cc), 2.0 litre (1997cc) & 2.2 litre (2179cc)

Does NOT cover petrol models or 'Powershift' or automatic transmissions
Does NOT cover new S-MAX and Galaxy ranges introduced July 2015

ISBN **978 1 78521 299 4**

British Library Cataloguing in Publication Data
A catalogue record for this book is available from the British Library.

Printed in India

Haynes Group Limited
Sparkford, Yeovil, Somerset BA22 7JJ, England

Haynes North America, Inc
2801 Townsgate Road, Suite 340, Thousand Oaks, CA 91361

Contents

Contents

REPAIRS AND OVERHAUL

Engine and Associated Systems

Transmission

Brakes and suspension

Body equipment

REFERENCE

Index

The first generation Galaxy model range was introduced to the UK in 1995. This was a joint venture between Ford and the Volkswagen group, but with Volkswagen providing most of the input, the original Galaxy was effectively a rebadged Volkswagen product. The second generation Galaxy (and S-MAX) is a stand alone Ford product with no Volkswagon content.

The second generation Galaxy and first generation S-MAX share an identical floor plan (based on the third generation Mondeo), running gear and engines. The main differences are in size and the interior trim, with the S-MAX being the smaller of the two. Both models feature seven seats, but the S-MAX is described by Ford as a 'sporty' seven seater or 'SAV' (Sports Activity Vehicle). The Galaxy is a more family orientated standard MPV (Multi-Purpose Vehicle).

Both petrol and diesel engines were available from launch, but the sales of the petrol engined models are small in comparison to the diesel engines and are therefore not covered by this manual.

Four sizes of diesel engine are available, with the 1.6, 2.0 and 2.2 litre models being shared by Citroën and Peugeot – a result of joint projects between Ford and PSA (Citroën/ Peugeot's parent company), whilst the 1.8 litre unit is of Ford's own design. All of the engines are four cylinder turbo diesel units. The 1.6 and 1.8 litre engines are SOHC (Single Overhead Camshaft) 8-valve engines. The 2.0 and 2.2 litre units are a 16-valve DOHC design. They incorporate the latest design of direct injection common rail fuel system, with a variable geometry turbocharger, intercooler, catalytic converter and exhaust gas recirculation. Later models have a Diesel Particulate Filter (DPF) fitted.

The transversely-mounted engines drive the front roadwheels through either a five- or six-speed manual transmission with a hydraulically-operated clutch.

The fully-independent suspension is by MacPherson struts and transverse lower arms at the front, with multilink independent suspension at the rear; anti-roll bars are fitted at front and rear.

The vacuum servo-assisted brakes are disc at the front, and either disc or drum at the rear. An electronically-controlled Anti-lock Braking System (ABS) is fitted on all models, with Dynamic Stability and Traction Control System (DSTC) also available.

Power-assisted steering is standard on all models. Air conditioning is fitted to most models. All models have an ergonomically-designed passenger cabin with high levels of safety and comfort for all passengers.

Provided that regular servicing is carried out in accordance with the manufacturer's recommendations, the Focus should prove a reliable and economical car. The engine compartment is well-designed, and most of the items needing frequent attention are easily accessible.

Your Ford Galaxy and S-MAX manual

The aim of this manual is to help you get the best value from your vehicle. It can do so in several ways. It can help you decide what work must be done (even should you choose to get it done by a garage). It will also provide information on routine maintenance and servicing, and give a logical course of action and diagnosis when random faults occur. However, it is hoped that you will use the manual by tackling the work yourself. On simpler jobs it may even be quicker than booking the car into a garage and going there twice, to leave and collect it. Perhaps most important, a lot of money can be saved by avoiding the costs a garage must charge to cover its labour and overheads.

The manual has drawings and descriptions to show the function of the various components so that their layout can be understood. Tasks are described and photographed in a clear step-by-step sequence. The illustrations are numbered by the Section number and paragraph number to which they relate – if there is more than one illustration per paragraph, the sequence is denoted alphabetically.

References to the 'left' or 'right' of the vehicle are in the sense of a person in the driver's seat, facing forwards.

Acknowledgements

Thanks are due to AST tools and Draper Tools Limited, who provided some of the workshop tools, and to all those people at Sparkford who helped in the production of this manual.

We take great pride in the accuracy of information given in this manual, but vehicle manufacturers make alterations and design changes during the production run of a particular vehicle of which they do not inform us. No liability can be accepted by the authors or publishers for loss, damage or injury caused by any errors in, or omissions from, the information given.

Ford S-Max

Ford Galaxy

Working on your car can be dangerous. This page shows just some of the potential risks and hazards, with the aim of creating a safety-conscious attitude.

General hazards

Scalding

• Don't remove the radiator or expansion tank cap while the engine is hot.
• Engine oil, transmission fluid or power steering fluid may also be dangerously hot if the engine has recently been running.

Burning

• Beware of burns from the exhaust system and from any part of the engine. Brake discs and drums can also be extremely hot immediately after use.

Crushing

• When working under or near a raised vehicle, always supplement the jack with axle stands, or use drive-on ramps.

Never venture under a car which is only supported by a jack.
• Take care if loosening or tightening high-torque nuts when the vehicle is on stands. Initial loosening and final tightening should be done with the wheels on the ground.

Fire

• Fuel is highly flammable; fuel vapour is explosive.
• Don't let fuel spill onto a hot engine.
• Do not smoke or allow naked lights (including pilot lights) anywhere near a vehicle being worked on. Also beware of creating sparks (electrically or by use of tools).
• Fuel vapour is heavier than air, so don't work on the fuel system with the vehicle over an inspection pit.
• Another cause of fire is an electrical overload or short-circuit. Take care when repairing or modifying the vehicle wiring.
• Keep a fire extinguisher handy, of a type suitable for use on fuel and electrical fires.

Electric shock

• Ignition HT and Xenon headlight voltages can be dangerous, especially to people with heart problems or a pacemaker. Don't work on or near these systems with the engine running or the ignition switched on.

• Mains voltage is also dangerous. Make sure that any mains-operated equipment is correctly earthed. Mains power points should be protected by a residual current device (RCD) circuit breaker.

Fume or gas intoxication

• Exhaust fumes are poisonous; they can contain carbon monoxide, which is rapidly fatal if inhaled. Never run the engine in a confined space such as a garage with the doors shut.
• Fuel vapour is also poisonous, as are the vapours from some cleaning solvents and paint thinners.

Poisonous or irritant substances

• Avoid skin contact with battery acid and with any fuel, fluid or lubricant, especially antifreeze, brake hydraulic fluid and Diesel fuel. Don't syphon them by mouth. If such a substance is swallowed or gets into the eyes, seek medical advice.
• Prolonged contact with used engine oil can cause skin cancer. Wear gloves or use a barrier cream if necessary. Change out of oil-soaked clothes and do not keep oily rags in your pocket.
• Air conditioning refrigerant forms a poisonous gas if exposed to a naked flame (including a cigarette). It can also cause skin burns on contact.

Asbestos

• Asbestos dust can cause cancer if inhaled or swallowed. Asbestos may be found in gaskets and in brake and clutch linings. When dealing with such components it is safest to assume that they contain asbestos.

Special hazards

Hydrofluoric acid

• This extremely corrosive acid is formed when certain types of synthetic rubber, found in some O-rings, oil seals, fuel hoses etc, are exposed to temperatures above 4000C. The rubber changes into a charred or sticky substance containing the acid. *Once formed, the acid remains dangerous for years. If it gets onto the skin, it may be necessary to amputate the limb concerned.*
• When dealing with a vehicle which has suffered a fire, or with components salvaged from such a vehicle, wear protective gloves and discard them after use.

The battery

• Batteries contain sulphuric acid, which attacks clothing, eyes and skin. Take care when topping-up or carrying the battery.
• The hydrogen gas given off by the battery is highly explosive. Never cause a spark or allow a naked light nearby. Be careful when connecting and disconnecting battery chargers or jump leads.

Air bags

• Air bags can cause injury if they go off accidentally. Take care when removing the steering wheel and trim panels. Special storage instructions may apply.

Diesel injection equipment

• Diesel injection pumps supply fuel at very high pressure. Take care when working on the fuel injectors and fuel pipes.

⚠️ *Warning: Never expose the hands, face or any other part of the body to injector spray; the fuel can penetrate the skin with potentially fatal results.*

Remember...

DO

• Do use eye protection when using power tools, and when working under the vehicle.
• Do wear gloves or use barrier cream to protect your hands when necessary.
• Do get someone to check periodically that all is well when working alone on the vehicle.
• Do keep loose clothing and long hair well out of the way of moving mechanical parts.
• Do remove rings, wristwatch etc, before working on the vehicle – especially the electrical system.
• Do ensure that any lifting or jacking equipment has a safe working load rating adequate for the job.

DON'T

• Don't attempt to lift a heavy component which may be beyond your capability – get assistance.
• Don't rush to finish a job, or take unverified short cuts.
• Don't use ill-fitting tools which may slip and cause injury.
• Don't leave tools or parts lying around where someone can trip over them. Mop up oil and fuel spills at once.
• Don't allow children or pets to play in or near a vehicle being worked on.

The following pages are intended to help in dealing with common roadside emergencies and breakdowns. You will find more detailed fault finding information at the back of the manual, and repair information in the main chapters.

If your car won't start and the starter motor doesn't turn

☐ Open the bonnet and make sure that the battery terminals are clean and tight (unclip the battery cover for access).

☐ Switch on the headlights and try to start the engine. If the headlights go very dim when you'r e trying to start, the battery is probably flat. Get out of trouble by jump starting using a friend's car.

If your car won't start even though the starter motor turns as normal

☐ Is there fuel in the tank?

☐ Has the engine immobiliser been deactivated? This should happen automatically, on inserting the ignition key. However, if a replacement key has been obtained (other than from a Ford dealer), it may not contain the transponder chip necessary to deactivate the system. Even 'proper' replacement keys have to be coded to work properly – a procedure for this is outlined in the vehicle handbook.

☐ Is there moisture on electrical components under the bonnet? Switch off the ignition, then wipe off any obvious dampness with a dry cloth. Remove the plastic cover on the top of the engine (where applicable). Spray a water-repellent aerosol product (WD-40 or equivalent) on ignition and fuel system electrical connectors like those shown in the photos.

A Check the security and condition of the battery connections – unclip and lift the battery cover for access.

B Check the mass airflow sensor wiring plug.

C Check that none of the engine compartment fuses have blown.

Check that all electrical connections are secure (with the ignition switched off). Spray the connector plugs with awater-dispersant spray like WD-40 if you suspect a problem due to damp. Diesel models do not usually suffer from damp startingproblems, but check all visible connector plugs just in case.

Jump starting

 Jump starting will get you out of trouble, but you must correct whatever made the battery go flat in the first place. There are three possibilities:

1 *The battery has been drained by repeated attempts to start, or by leaving the lights on.*

2 *The charging system is not working properly (alternator drivebelt slack or broken, alternator wiring fault or alternator itself faulty).*

3 *The battery itself is at fault (electrolyte low, or battery worn out).*

When jump-starting a car, observe the following precautions:

Note: *Remove the key in case the central locking engages when the jump leads are connected*

✓ Before connecting the booster battery, make sure that the ignition is switched off.
✓ Ensure that all electrical equipment (lights, heater, wipers, etc) is switched off.
✓ Take note of any special precautions printed on the battery case.
✓ Make sure that the booster battery is the same voltage as the discharged one in the vehicle.

✓ If the battery is being jump-started from the battery in another vehicle, the two vehicles MUST NOT TOUCH each other.
✓ Make sure that the transmission is in neutral (or PARK, in the case of automatic transmission).

 Budget jump leads can be a false economy, as they often do not pass enough current to start large capacity or diesel engines. They can also get hot.

1 Connect one end of the red jump lead to the positive (+) terminal of the flat battery

2 Connect the other end of the red lead to the positive (+) terminal of the booster battery.

3 Connect one end of the black jump lead to the negative (-) terminal of the booster battery

4 Connect the other end of the black lead to the to the earth terminal on the left-hand front suspension turret in the engine compartment.

5 Make sure that the jump leads will not come into contact with the fan, drive-belts or other moving parts of the engine.

6 Start the engine using the booster battery and run it at idle speed. Switch on the lights, rear window demister and heater blower motor, then disconnect the jump leads in the reverse order of connection. Turn off the lights etc.

Identifying leaks

Puddles on the garage floor or drive, or obvious wetness under the bonnet or underneath the car, suggest a leak that needs investigating. It can sometimes be difficult to decide where the leak is coming from, especially if an engine undershield is fitted. Leaking oil or fluid can also be blown rearwards by the passage of air under the car, giving a false impression of where the problem lies.

 Warning: Most automotive oils and fluids are poisonous. Wash them off skin, and change out of contaminated clothing, without delay.

 The smell of a fluid leaking from the car may provide a clue to what's leaking. Some fluids are distinctively coloured. It may help to remove the engine undershield, clean the car carefully and to park it over some clean paper overnight as an aid to locating the source of the leak.

Sump oil

Engine oil may leak from the drain plug...

Oil from filter

...or from the base of the oil filter.

Gearbox oil

Gearbox oil can leak from the seals at the inboard ends of the driveshafts.

Antifreeze

Leaking antifreeze often leaves a crystalline deposit like this.

Brake fluid

A leak occurring at a wheel is almost certainly brake fluid.

Power steering fluid

Power steering fluid may leak from the pipe connectors on the steering rack.

Wheel changing

⚠️ *Warning: Do not attempt to repair a flat tyre in a situation where you risk being hit by other traffic. On busy roads, try to stop in a lay-by or a gateway. Be wary of passing traffic while attempting to repair the wheel.*

Preparation

- ☐ When a puncture occurs, stop as soon as it is safe to do so.
- ☐ Park on firm level ground, if possible, and well out of the way of other traffic.
- ☐ Use hazard warning lights if necessary.
- ☐ If you have one, use a warning triangle to alert other drivers of your presence.
- ☐ Apply the handbrake.

Finally . . .

- ☐ If the pressure does not reach around 1.8 bar (26 psi) after 10 minutes the tyre is beyond repair.
- ☐ If the pressure holds, drive for 10 minutes/2 miles and recheck the pressure. If the pressure is less than 1.3 bar or 18 psi the repair has failed.
- ☐ Where the repair has been successful, do not exceed 50 mph and have the tyre replaced at the earliest opportunity.
- ☐ If the repair has failed. Move the vehicle off the highway and call your breakdown service.

3 Ford do not supply a spare wheel for any of the models covered by this manual, instead a small compressor and a bottle of sealant are provided as an emergency fix. Note however that the sealant will not repair tyres that have serious damage and the damaged tyre must be replaced as soon as possible.

Using the tyre sealant

1 The compressor and sealant are stored under the floor behind the driver's seat. Lift up the cover panel.

3 Full instructions are provided on the inside of the compressor lid

4 Whilst many manufacturers offer a space saving emergency wheel (and special tyre) as an option this is not available for the Ford Galaxy or S-Max. The only option for the owner who does not wish to be completely stranded and reliant on one of the breakdown service providers will be to purchase a full size wheel and carry that with them.

2 Remove the thumbwheel screws and lift off the polystyrene cover. Remove the sealant and compressor.

4 Always thoroughly shake the sealant before installing the bottle on the compressor. Connect the compressor to the 12 volt power outlet and inflate the tyre

---

Towing

When all else fails, you may find yourself having to get a tow home – or of course you may be helping somebody else. Long-distance recovery should only be done by a garage or breakdown service. For shorter distances, DIY towing using another car is easy enough, but observe the following points:

- ☐ Use a proper tow-rope – they are not expensive. The vehicle being towed must display an ON TOW sign in its rear window.
- ☐ Always turn the ignition key to the 'On' position when the vehicle is being towed, so that the steering lock is released, and the direction indicator and brake lights work.
- ☐ The towing eye is of the screw-in type, and is found in the tool compartment in the floor behind the driver's seat. The towing eye screws into a threaded hole, accessible after prising out a cover on the right-hand side of the front or rear bumper **(see illustrations)**.

Note: *The towing eye has a left-hand thread – rotate it anti-clockwise to install it.*

- ☐ Before being towed, release the handbrake and make sure the transmission is in neutral.
- ☐ Note that greater-than-usual pedal pressure will be required to operate the brakes, since the vacuum servo unit is only operational with the engine running.

Prise open the cover . . .

- ☐ The driver of the car being towed must keep the tow-rope taut at all times to avoid snatching.
- ☐ Make sure that both drivers know the route before setting off.
- ☐ Only drive at moderate speeds and keep the distance towed to a minimum. Drive smoothly and allow plenty of time for slowing down at junctions.

. . . and install the towing eye

Introduction

There are some very simple checks which need only take a few minutes to carry out, but which could save you a lot of inconvenience and expense.

These require no great skill or special tools, and the small amount of time they take to perform could prove to be very well spent, for example:

☐ Keeping an eye on tyre condition and pressures, will not only help to stop them wearing out prematurely, but could also save your life.

☐ Many breakdowns are caused by electrical problems. Battery-related faults are particularly common, and a quick check on a regular basis will often prevent the majority of these.

☐ If your car develops a brake fluid leak, the first time you might know about it is when your brakes don't work properly. Checking the level regularly will give advance warning of this kind of problem.

☐ If the oil or coolant levels run low, the cost of repairing any engine damage will be far greater than fixing the leak, for example.

Underbonnet check points

◀ 2.0 litre engine (Galaxy)

A *Engine oil level dipstick*

B *Engine oil filler cap*

C *Coolant expansion tank*

D *Brake and clutch fluid reservoir*

E *Power steering fluid reservoir*

F *Screen washer fluid reservoir*

◀ 2.2 litre engine (S-Max)

A *Engine oil level dipstick*

B *Engine oil filler cap*

C *Coolant expansion tank*

D *Brake and clutch fluid reservoir*

E *Power steering fluid reservoir*

F *Screen washer fluid reservoir*

Engine oil level

Before you start
✔ Make sure that the car is on level ground.
✔ Check the oil level before the car is driven, or at least 5 minutes after the engine has been switched off.

 HAYNES HiNT *If the oil is checked immediately after driving the vehicle, some of the oil will remain in the upper engine components, resulting in an inaccurate reading on the dipstick.*

The correct oil
Modern engines place great demands on their oil. It is very important that the correct oil for your car is used (see *Lubricants and fluids*).

Car care
● If you have to add oil frequently, you should check whether you have any oil leaks. Place some clean paper under the car overnight, and check for stains in the morning. If there are no leaks, then the engine may be burning oil.
● Always maintain the level between the upper and lower dipstick marks. If the level is too low, severe engine damage may occur. Oil seal failure may result if the engine is overfilled by adding too much oil.
● If the oil level is high it is possible that diesel fuel has increased the volume (due to bore wash) during the post TDC injection phase, whilst regenerating the particulate filter. Replace the oil and filter if this is the case.

1 The dipstick is located at the front of the engine (see *Underbonnet check points* for exact location). Withdraw the dipstick. Using a clean rag or paper towel, remove all oil from the dipstick.

2 Insert the clean dipstick into the tube as far as it will go, then withdraw it again. Note the oil level on the end of the dipstick, which should be between the MAX and MIN marks. If the oil level is only just above, or below, the MIN mark, topping-up is required.

3 Oil is added through the filler cap. Unscrew the filler cap and top-up the level; a funnel may be useful in reducing spillage.

4 Add the oil slowly, checking the level on the dipstick often, and allowing time for the oil to run to the sump. Add oil until the level is just up to the MAX mark on the dipstick – don't overfill (see *Car care*)

Brake (and clutch) fluid level

Note: *All manual transmission models have a hydraulically-operated clutch, which uses the same fluid as the braking system.*

 Warning: Brake fluid can harm your eyes and damage painted surfaces, so use extreme caution when handling and pouring it.

 Warning: Do not use fluid that has been standing open for some time, as it absorbs moisture from the air, which can cause a dangerous loss of braking effectiveness.

✔ Make sure that your car is on level ground
✔ The fluid level in the reservoir will drop slightly as the brake pads wear down, but the fluid level must never be allowed to drop below the DANGER mark.

Safety first!

● If the reservoir requires repeated topping-up this is an indication of a fluid leak somewhere in the system, which should be investigated immediately.
● If a leak is suspected, the car should not be driven until the braking system has been checked. Never take any risks where brakes are concerned

1 The brake fluid reservoir is located on the right-hand side of the engine compartment.

2 The MAX and MIN marks are indicated on the front and side of the reservoir. The fluid level must be kept between the marks at all times.

3 If topping-up is necessary, first wipe clean the area around the filler cap to prevent dirt entering the hydraulic system. Unscrew the reservoir cap and carefully lift it out of position, holding the wiring connector plug and taking care not to damage the level sender float. Inspect the reservoir; if the fluid is dirty, the hydraulic system should be drained and refilled (see Chapter 1).

4 Carefully add fluid, taking care not to spill it onto the surrounding components. Use only the specified fluid; mixing different types can cause damage to the system. After topping-up to the correct level, securely refit the cap and wipe off any spilt fluid.

Power steering fluid level

Note: *According to Ford, there is no requirement to check the fluid level. However, it may be prudent to check the level every few months or so.*

Before you start

✔ Park the vehicle on level ground.
✔ Set the steering wheel straight-ahead.
✔ The engine should be cold and turned off.

 For the check to be accurate, the steering must not be turned once the engine has been stopped.

Safety first!

● The need for frequent topping-up indicates a leak, which should be investigated immediately.

1 The reservoir is mounted close to the right-hand headlight. The fluid level can be viewed through the reservoir body. It should be between the MIN and MAX marks when the engine is cold. If the level is checked when the engine is running or hot, the level may rise slightly above the MAX mark.

2 If topping-up is necessary, use the specified type of fluid – do not overfill the reservoir. Undo the reservoir cap. Take care not to introduce dirt into the system when topping-up. When the level is correct, securely refit the cap.

Coolant level

 Warning: Do not attempt to remove the expansion tank pressure cap when the engine is hot, as there is a very great risk of scalding. Do not leave open containers of coolant about, as it is poisonous.

Car care

● With a sealed-type cooling system, adding coolant should not be necessary on a regular basis. If frequent topping-up is required, it is likely there is a leak. Check the radiator, all hoses and joint faces for signs of staining or wetness, and rectify as necessary.

● It is important that antifreeze is used in the cooling system all year round, not just during the winter months. Don't top up with water alone, as the antifreeze will become diluted.

1 The coolant level varies with the temperature of the engine and is visible through the expansion tank. When the engine is cold, the coolant level should be between the MAX and MIN marks on the front of the reservoir. When the engine is hot, the level may rise slightly above the MAX mark.

2 If topping-up is necessary, wait until the engine is cold. Slowly unscrew the expansion tank cap, to release any pressure present in the cooling system, and remove it.

3 Add a mixture of water and antifreeze to the expansion tank until the coolant level is halfway between the level marks. Use only the specified antifreeze – if using Ford antifreeze, make sure it is the same type and colour as that already in the system. Refit the cap and tighten it securely.

Battery

Caution: Before carrying out any work on the vehicle battery, read the precautions given in 'Safety First!' at the start of this manual.

✔ Make sure that the battery tray is in good condition, and that the clamp is tight. Any ' white' corrosion on the terminals or surrounding area can be removed with a solution of water and baking soda; thoroughly rinse all cleaned areas with water. Any metal parts damaged by corrosion should be covered with a zinc-based primer, then painted.

✔ Periodically check the charge condition of the battery. On the original-equipment battery, the state of charge is shown by an indicator 'eye' in the top of the battery, which should be green – if the indicator is clear, or red, the battery may need charging or even renewal (see Chapter 5 Section 2).

✔ If the battery is flat, and you need to jump start your vehicle, see *Jump Starting*).

 Battery corrosion can be kept to a minimum by applying a layer of petroleum jelly to the clamps and terminals after they are reconnected.

1 The battery is located in the left-hand rear corner of the engine compartment. The battery must be removed to gain access to the negative (earth) terminal. See Chapter 5 for removal details.

2 Check the tightness of battery clamps to ensure good electrical connections. You should not be able to move them. Also check each cable for cracks and frayed conductors.

3 If corrosion (white, fluffy deposits) is evident, remove the cables from the battery terminals, clean them with asmall wire brush, then refit them. Automotive stores sell a tool for cleaning the battery post …

4 …as well as the battery cable clamps

Tyre condition and pressure

It is very important that tyres are in good condition, and at the correct pressure – having a tyre failure at any speed is highly dangerous.

Tyre wear is influenced by driving style – harsh braking and acceleration, or fast cornering, will all produce more rapid tyre wear. As a general rule, the front tyres wear out faster than the rears. Interchanging the tyres from front to rear ("rotating" the tyres) may result in more even wear. However, if this is completely effective, you may have the expense of replacing all four tyres at once!

Remove any nails or stones embedded in the tread before they penetrate the tyre to cause deflation. If removal of a nail does reveal that the tyre has been punctured, refit the nail so that its point of penetration is marked. Then immediately change the wheel, and have the tyre repaired by a tyre dealer.

Regularly check the tyres for damage in the form of cuts or bulges, especially in the sidewalls. Periodically remove the wheels, and clean any dirt or mud from the inside and outside surfaces. Examine the wheel rims for signs of rusting, corrosion or other damage. Light alloy wheels are easily damaged by "kerbing" whilst parking; steel wheels may also become dented or buckled. A new wheel is very often the only way to overcome severe damage.

New tyres should be balanced when they are fitted, but it may become necessary to re-balance them as they wear, or if the balance weights fitted to the wheel rim should fall off. Unbalanced tyres will wear more quickly, as will the steering and suspension components. Wheel imbalance is normally signified by vibration, particularly at a certain speed (typically around 50 mph). If this vibration is felt only through the steering, then it is likely that just the front wheels need balancing. If, however, the vibration is felt through the whole car, the rear wheels could be out of balance. Wheel balancing should be carried out by a tyre dealer or garage.

1 *Tread Depth - visual check*
The original tyres have tread wear safety bands (B), which will appear when the tread depth reaches approximately 1.6 mm The band positions are indicated by a triangular mark on the tyre sidewall (A).

2 *Tread Depth - manual check*
Alternatively, tread wear can be monitored with a simple, inexpensive device known as a tread depth indicator gauge.

3 *Tyre Pressure Check*
Check the tyre pressures regularly with the tyres cold. Do not adjust the tyre pressures immediately after the vehicle has been used, or an inaccurate setting will result. Tyre pressures are shown on page 0•16.

Tyre tread wear patterns

Shoulder Wear

Underinflation (wear on both sides)
Under-inflation will cause overheating of the tyre, because the tyre will flex too much, and the tread will not sit correctly on the road surface. This will cause a loss of grip and excessive wear, not to mention the danger of sudden tyre failure due to heat build-up.
Check and adjust pressures
Incorrect wheel camber (wear on one side)
Repair or renew suspension parts
Hard cornering
Reduce speed!

Centre Wear

Overinflation
Over-inflation will cause rapid wear of the centre part of the tyre tread, coupled with reduced grip, harsher ride, and the danger of shock damage occurring in the tyre casing.
Check and adjust pressures

If you sometimes have to inflate your car's tyres to the higher pressures specified for maximum load or sustained high speed, don't forget to reduce the pressures to normal afterwards.

Uneven Wear

Front tyres may wear unevenly as a result of wheel misalignment. Most tyre dealers and garages can check and adjust the wheel alignment (or "tracking") for a modest charge.
Incorrect camber or castor
Repair or renew suspension parts
Malfunctioning suspension
Repair or renew suspension parts
Unbalanced wheel
Balance tyres
Incorrect toe setting
Adjust front wheel alignment
Note: *The feathered edge of the tread which typifies toe wear is best checked by feel.*

Washer fluid level

● The windscreen washer reservoir also supplies the tailgate washer jet, where applicable. On models so equipped, the same reservoir also serves the headlight washers.

● Screenwash additives not only keep the windscreen clean during bad weather, they also prevent the washer system freezing in cold weather – which is when you are likely to need it most. Don't top-up using plain water, as the screenwash will become diluted, and will freeze in cold weather.

Caution: On no account use engine coolant antifreeze in the screen washer system – this may damage the paintwork.

1 The washer fluid reservoir filler neck is located in the right-hand rear corner of the engine compartment. The washer level cannot easily be seen. Remove the filler cap, and look down the filler neck – if fluid is not visible, topping-up may be required.

2 When topping-up the reservoir, add a screenwash additive in the quantities recommended on the additive bottle.

Wiper blades

✔ Set the wipers to the service position before fitting the blades. Turn the ignition on and within 3 seconds press the wiper switch down. The blades will park in the upper position.

✔ Only fit good-quality wiper blades.

✔ When removing an old wiper blade, note how it is fitted. Fitting new blades can be a tricky exercise, and noting how the old blade came off can save time.

✔ While the wiper blade is removed, take care not to knock the wiper arm from its locked position, or it could strike the glass.

✔ Offer the new blade into position the same way round as the old one. Ensure that it clicks home securely, otherwise it may come off in use, damaging the glass.

✔ Check the condition of the wiper blades; if they are cracked or show any signs of deterioration, or if the glass swept area is smeared, renew them. Wiper blades should be renewed annually, regardless of their apparent condition.

✔ After replacing the blades the wipers will return to the parked position when the ignition is turned on (models built up to 07/2006) or when the wipers are operated on all later models.

If smearing is still a problem despite fitting new wiper blades, try cleaning the glass with neat screenwash additive or methylated spirit.

1 Check the condition of the wiper blades. If they are cracked or show any signs of deterioration, or if the glass swept area is smeared, renew them. For maximum clarity of vision, wiper blades should be renewed annually as a matter of course.

2 To remove a windscreen wiper blade depress the locking catch...

3 ... pull the blade from the wiper arm

4 To remove the tailgate blade, lift the arm, position the blade at 90° to the arm, and pull the blade from the arm.

Electrical systems

✔ Check all external lights and the horn. Refer to the appropriate Sections of Chapter 12 for details if any of the circuits are found to be inoperative.

✔ Visually check all accessible wiring connectors, harnesses and retaining clips for security, and for signs of chafing or damage.

 HAYNES HiNT *If you need to check your brake lights and indicators unaided, back up to a wall or garage door and operate the lights. The reflected light should show if they are working properly.*

1 If a single indicator light, stop-light or headlight has failed, it is likely that a bulb has blown and will need to be renewed. Refer to Chapter 12 for details. If both stop-lights have failed, it is possible that the switch has failed (see Chapter 9).

2 If more than one indicator light or tail light has failed, it is likely that either a fuse has blown or that there is a fault in the circuit (see Chapter 12). The main fusebox is located below the glovebox on the passenger's side. To access the main fusebox, undo the 2 bolts and pull the trim panel downwards, then undo the two bolts and lower the fusebox from position. Pull the fusebox rearwards and lower it completely. The auxiliary fuse/relay box is located on the left-hand side of the engine compartment – unclip and remove the cover for access. An additional fusebox can be found behind the left-hand load area side panel.

3 To renew a blown fuse, simply pull it out and fit a new fuse of the correct rating (see Chapter 12). Spare fuses, and a fuse removal tool, are provided on the inside of the auxiliary fusebox lid. If the fuse blows again, it is important that you find out why – a complete checking procedure is given in Chapter 12.

Lubricants and fluids

Engine	Multigrade engine oil, viscosity SAE 5W/30 to Ford specification WSS-M2C913-B
Cooling system	Motorcraft SuperPlus antifreeze to Ford specification WSS-M97B44-D
Manual transmission	75W FE oil to Ford specification M2C200-D2
Brake and clutch hydraulic system	Hydraulic fluid to Ford specification WSS-M6C57-A2, Super DOT 4
Power steering	Ford or Motorcraft power steering fluid to Ford specification WSS-M2C204-A2

Tyre pressures (cold)

	Front	Rear
Normal load (up to 3 people)		
215/60 R16	2.4 bars (35 psi)	2.4 bars (35 psi)
225/55 R16	2.4 bars (35 psi)	2.4 bars (35 psi)
225/50 R17	2.4 bars (35 psi)	2.2 bars (32 psi)
235/45 R18	2.4 bars (35 psi)	2.2 bars (32 psi)
Full load (more than 3 people):		
All sizes	2.6 bars (38 psi)	3.1 bars (45 psi)

Note: *Pressures apply to original equipment tyres and may vary if any other make of tyre is fitted. Check with the tyre manufacturer or supplier if any other make is fitted.*

Chapter 1
Routine maintenance and servicing

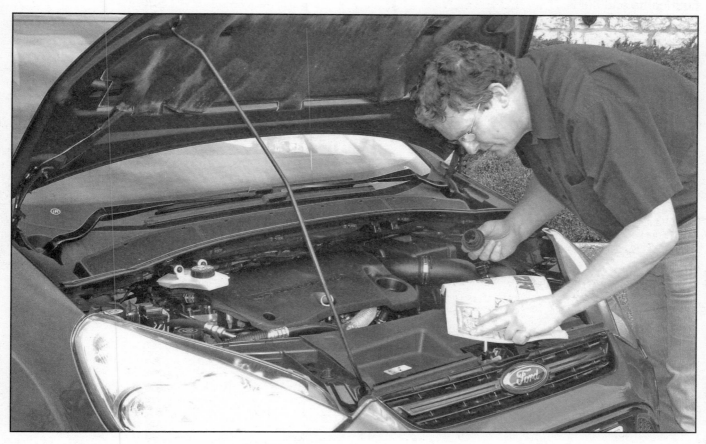

Contents

Degrees of difficulty

| **Easy,** suitable for novice with little experience | | **Fairly easy,** suitable for beginner with some experience | | **Fairly difficult,** suitable for competent DIY mechanic | | **Difficult,** suitable for experienced DIY mechanic | | **Very difficult,** suitable for expert DIY or professional | |

Lubricants and fluids. . . . . Refer to end of *Weekly checks*

Capacities

Engine oil (including filter)
1.6 litre engines	3.8 litres
1.8 litre engines	5.6 litres
2.0 litre engines	5.5 litres
2.2 litre engines	5.9 litres

Cooling system (approximate)
1.6 litre engines	7.3 litres
1.8 litres	8.1 litres
2.0 litre engines	8.4 litres
2.2 litre engines	8.4 litres
Washer fluid reservoir.	3.3 litres
Fuel tank	53.0 litres

Cooling system

Antifreeze mixture:
50% antifreeze	Protection down to –37°C
55% antifreeze	Protection down to –45°C

Note: *Refer to antifreeze manufacturer for latest recommendations.*

Brakes

Friction material minimum thickness:
Brake pads	1.5 mm
Brake shoes	1.0 mm

Torque wrench settings

	Nm	lbf ft
Engine oil drain plug:		
1.6 litre engines	35	26
1.8 litre engines	36	27
2.0 litre engines	34	26
2.2 litre engines	20	15
Engine oil filter housing cap:		
1.6 and 2.0 litre engines	25	18
2.2 litre engines	16	12
1.8 litre engines	Not applicable	
Roadwheel nuts:		
M12 standard nuts	140	103
M12 locking nut with conical washer	110	81
M12 locking nut with one-piece nut	140	103
M14 nuts	170	125

If the vehicle is driven in dusty areas, used to tow a trailer, or driven frequently at slow speeds (idling in traffic) or on short journeys, more frequent maintenance intervals are recommended.

When the vehicle is new, it should be serviced by a dealer service department (or other workshop recognised by the vehicle manufacturer as providing the same standard of service) in order to preserve the warranty. The vehicle manufacturer may reject warranty claims if you are unable to prove that servicing has been carried out as and when specified, using only original equipment parts or parts certified to be of equivalent quality.

Every 250 miles or weekly
- [ ] Refer to Weekly checks.

Every 6000 miles or 6 months, whichever comes first
- [ ] Renew the engine oil and filter (Section 3)

Note: *Ford recommend that the engine oil and filter are changed every 12 500 miles or 12 months. However, oil and filter changes are good for the engine and we recommend that the oil and filter are renewed more frequently, especially if the vehicle is used on a lot of short journeys.*

Every 12 500 miles or 12 months, whichever comes first
In addition to the items listed above, carry out the following:
- [ ] Check the condition of the auxiliary drivebelt (Section 22)
- [ ] Check the operation of the lights and the horn (Section 5)
- [ ] Check under the bonnet for fluid leaks and hose condition (Section 6)
- [ ] Check the condition of the engine compartment wiring (Section 7)
- [ ] Check the condition of the seat belts (Section 8)
- [ ] Check the condition of the brake pads, shoes and discs (Section 9)
- [ ] Check the exhaust system (Section 10)
- [ ] Check the steering and suspension components for condition and security (Section 11)
- [ ] Check the condition of the driveshaft joints and gaiters (Section 12)
- [ ] Check the underbody and all fuel/brake lines (Section 13)
- [ ] Lubricate all hinges and locks (Section 14)
- [ ] Check roadwheel nut tightness (Section 15)
- [ ] Carry out a road test (Section 16)
- [ ] Renew the pollen filter – vehicles with air conditioning (Section 17)*
- [ ] Check and if necessary adjust the handbrake (Section 18)

Note: *If the vehicle is used in dusty conditions, the pollen filter should be renewed more frequently.*

Every 37 500 miles or 3 years, whichever comes first
In addition to the items listed above, carry out the following:
- [ ] Renew the fuel filter (Section 19)
- [ ] Renew the air filter (Section 20)*

*Note: *If the vehicle is used in dusty conditions, the air filter should be renewed more frequently.*

Every 62 500 miles
In addition to the items listed above, carry out the following:
- [ ] Renew the timing belt and tensioner (Section 21)

Note: *The Ford interval for belt renewal is actually at a much higher mileage than this (112 500 miles or 10 years – 1.6 litre engines and 125 000 miles or 10 years – 1.8, 2.0 and 2.2 litre engines). It is strongly recommended, however, that the interval is reduced to 62 500 miles, particularly on vehicles which are subjected to intensive use, ie, mainly short journeys or a lot of stop-start driving. The actual belt renewal interval is therefore very much up to the individual owner, but bear in mind that severe engine damage will result if the belt breaks. Note also that on all engines (except the 1.8 litre) the idlers and tensioner must be replaced at the same time. Replacement of the coolant pump is also highly recommended at this point.*

Every 100 000 miles or 8 years, whichever comes first
- [ ] Renew the auxiliary belt (Section 22)

Every 150 000 miles or 10 years, whichever comes first
- [ ] Renew the fuel pump drive chain/belt (Chapter 2E, Section 9) – 1.8 litre engines only

Every 2 years, regardless of mileage
- [ ] Renew the brake fluid (Section 23)
- [ ] Renew the remote control battery (Section 24)
- [ ] Renew the coolant (Section 25)*

*Note: *If Ford pink/red antifreeze is used, the coolant can then be left indefinitely, providing the strength of the mixture is checked every year. If any antifreeze other than Ford's is to be used, the coolant must be renewed at regular intervals to provide an equivalent degree of protection; the conventional recommendation is to renew the coolant every two years.*

Underbonnet view of a 2.0 litre model

1 Engine oil level dipstick
2 Oil filler cap
3 Coolant expansion tank cap
4 Washer fluid reservoir cap
5 Brake/clutch fluid reservoir cap
6 Air filter element cover
7 Fuel filter
8 Battery
9 Fuse/relay box cover
10 Power steering fluid reservoir

Underbonnet view of a 2.2 litre model

1 Engine oil level dipstick
2 Engine oil filler cap
3 Coolant expansion tank cap
4 Washer fluid reservoir cap
5 Fuel filter
6 Air filter cover
7 Battery cover
8 Fuse/relay box
9 Brake/clutch fluid reservoir cap
10 Power steering fluid reservoir

Front underbody view of a 2.2 litre model – others similar

1 Engine oil sump drain plug
2 Air conditioning compressor
3 Right-hand driveshaft intermediate bearing
4 Lower control arm
5 Track rod end
6 Front subframe
7 Inter cooler pipe
8 Front brake caliper

Rear underbody view

1 Anti-roll bar
2 Shock absorber
3 Front lower control arm
4 Handbrake cable
5 Trailing arm
6 Upper control arm
7 Fuel tank

1 General Information

1 This Chapter is designed to help the home mechanic maintain his/her vehicle for safety, economy, long life and peak performance.

2 The Chapter contains a master maintenance schedule, followed by Sections dealing specifically with each task in the schedule. Visual checks, adjustments, component renewal and other helpful items are included. Refer to the accompanying illustrations of the engine compartment and the underside of the vehicle for the locations of the various components.

3 Servicing your vehicle in accordance with the mileage/time maintenance schedule and the following Sections will provide a planned maintenance programme, which should result in a long and reliable service life. This is a comprehensive plan, so maintaining some items but not others at the specified service intervals will not produce the same results.

4 As you service your vehicle, you will discover that many of the procedures can – and should – be grouped together, because of the particular procedure being performed, or because of the proximity of two otherwise-unrelated components to one another. For example, if the vehicle is raised for any reason, the exhaust can be inspected at the same time as the suspension and steering components.

5 The first step in this maintenance programme is to prepare yourself before the actual work begins. Read through all the Sections relevant to the work to be carried out, then make a list and gather all the parts and tools required. If a problem is encountered, seek advice from a parts specialist, or a dealer service department.

2 Regular maintenance

1 If, from the time the vehicle is new, the routine maintenance schedule is followed closely, and frequent checks are made of fluid levels and high-wear items, as suggested throughout this manual, the engine will be kept in relatively good running condition, and the need for additional work will be minimised.

2 It is possible that there will be times when the engine is running poorly due to the lack of regular maintenance. This is even more likely if a used vehicle, which has not received regular and frequent maintenance checks, is purchased. In such cases, additional work may need to be carried out, outside of the regular maintenance intervals.

3 If engine wear is suspected, a compression test or leakdown test (refer to the relevant part of) will provide valuable information regarding the overall performance of the main internal components. Such a test can be used as a basis to decide on the extent of the work to be carried out. If, for example, a compression or leakdown test indicates serious internal engine wear, conventional maintenance as described in this Chapter will not greatly improve the performance of the engine, and may prove a waste of time and money, unless extensive overhaul work is carried out first.

4 The following series of operations are those most often required to improve the performance of a generally poor-running engine:

Primary operations

a) Clean, inspect and test the battery (refer to 'Weekly checks.').
b) Check all the engine-related fluids (refer to 'Weekly checks.').
c) Check the condition and tension of the auxiliary drivebelt (Section 22).
d) Check the condition of the air filter, and renew if necessary (Section 20).
e) Renew the fuel filter (Section 19).
f) Check the condition of all hoses, and check for fluid leaks (Section 6).

5 If the above operations do not prove fully effective, carry out the following secondary operations:

Secondary operations

6 All items listed under Primary operations, plus the following:

a) Check the charging system (refer to Chapter 5).
b) Check the preheating system (refer to Chapter 5).
c) Check the fuel system (refer to Chapter 4A).

3 Engine oil and filter renewal

1 Frequent oil and filter changes are the most important preventative maintenance procedures which can be undertaken by the DIY owner. As engine oil ages, it becomes diluted and contaminated, which leads to premature engine wear.

2 Before starting this procedure, gather together all the necessary tools and materials. Also make sure that you have plenty of clean rags and newspapers handy, to mop-up any spills. Ideally, the engine oil should be warm, as it will drain more easily, and more built-up sludge will be removed with it. Take care not to touch the exhaust or any other hot parts of the engine when working under the vehicle. To avoid any possibility of scalding, and to protect yourself from possible skin irritants and other harmful contaminants in used engine oils, it is advisable to wear gloves when carrying out this work.

3 Remove the cover from the top of the engine. (see illustrations).

1.6 litre engines

4 Remove the air cleaner assembly as described in Chapter 4A Section 3.

5 Using a socket on an extension bar, undo the oil filter housing cap. Lift the cap up, with the filter element inside it. Discard the filter and the O-ring seal around the circumference of the cap (see illustrations).

3.3a Pull up the cover...

3.3b ... or unbolt it

3.5a The engine oil filter is located at the front, left-hand corner of the cylinder block

3.5b Unscrew the cap and remove it complete with the filter element

3.7 The engine oil filter is located on the rear of the cylinder block, above the right-hand driveshaft

3.10a Disconnect the wiring plug, unclip the fuel pipe, then undo the 4 bolts...

3.10b ...and Torx bolt on the side

Note that there may be another bolt securing the bracket

1.8 litre engines

6 The canister-type oil filter is located on the rear of the engine block. Firmly apply the handbrake, then jack up the front of the vehicle and support it on axle stands (see *Jacking and vehicle support*). Undo the fasteners and remove the engine undershield.

7 Move a container into position under the oil filter, then use an oil filter removal tool if necessary to slacken the filter cartridge initially, then unscrew it by hand the rest of the way **(see illustration)**. Empty the oil from the old filter into the container.

8 Use a clean rag to remove all oil, dirt and sludge from the filter sealing area on the engine.

9 Apply a light coating of clean engine oil to the sealing ring on the new filter, then screw the filter into position on the engine. Tighten the filter firmly by hand only – do not use any tools.

2.0 litre engines

10 Release the wiring harnesses from the cable ties on the fuel filter bracket, then disconnect the filter wiring plug, release the fuel pipe from the clip, undo the bolts at the top and the bolt(s) on the side, then lift up the filter with the bracket, and place it to one side **(see illustrations)**.

11 Using a 27 mm socket on an extension bar, undo the oil filter housing cap. Lift the cap up, with the oil filter inside it. Discard the filter and the O-ring around the circumference of the cap **(see illustrations)**.

2.2 litre engines

12 Firmly apply the handbrake, then jack up the front of the vehicle and support it on axle stands (see *Jacking and vehicle support*). Undo the fasteners and remove the engine undershield.

13 Anticipating some oil spillage unscrew the filter **(see illustration)**.

14 Lift out the filter cap, complete with the oil filter. Pull the filter from the cap and remove

3.10c Lift up the fuel filter and move it to one side

3.11a Undo the oil filter cap...

3.11b ...then lift up the cap with the filter element...

3.11c ...pull the element from the cap...

3.11d ...and discard the O-ring seal

3.13 The oil filter cap viewed from below

3.14a Remove the filter and cap...

3.14b ...and pull the filter from the cap...

3.14c ...and remove the seal

the O-ring seal from the filter cap – dispose of the seal **(see illustrations)**.

All engines

15 If not already done so, firmly apply the handbrake, then jack up the front of the vehicle and support it on axle stands (see *Jacking and vehicle support*). Unscrew the fasteners and remove the plastic undershield below the engine **(see illustration)**.

16 Using a spanner, socket or Allen key as applicable, slacken the drain plug about half a turn **(see illustrations)**. Position the draining container under the drain plug, then remove the plug completely.

17 Allow some time for the oil to drain, noting that it may be necessary to reposition the container as the oil flow slows to a trickle.

18 After all the oil has drained, wipe the drain plug and the sealing washer (where fitted) with a clean rag. Examine the condition of the sealing washer, and renew it if it shows signs of scoring or other damage which may prevent an oil-tight seal (it is generally considered good practice to fit a new washer every time). Clean the area around the drain plug opening, and refit the plug complete with the washer and

3.15 Undo the fasteners and remove the engine undershield

3.16a Engine oil sump drain plug – 1.6 litre engine...

3.16b ...1.8 litre engine...

3.16c ...2.0 litre engine...

3.16d ...and the 2.2 litre engine

3.18a Renew the sump plug sealing washer

3.18b A slightly different sealing washer and sump plug are fitted to some engines

3.25a Fit a new O-ring seal ...

tighten it to the specified torque **(see illustrations)**.
19 Remove the old oil and all tools from under the vehicle and then lower the vehicle to the ground.

1.6 litre engines

20 Ensure the oil filter housing and cap are clean, then fit a new O-ring seal to the cap.
21 Fit the new filter element into the cap, then fit the cap to the housing and tighten it to the specified torque.

2.0 litre engines

22 Ensure the oil filter housing and cap are clean, then fit a new O-ring seal to the cap.
23 Fit the new filter element into the cap, then fit the cap to the housing and tighten it to the specified torque.
24 Position the fuel filter and bracket, then refit the retaining bolts and tighten them securely. Refit the pipe into the clip, reconnect the wiring plug and secure the wiring harnesses to the bracket.

2.2 litre engines

25 Ensure the oil filter housing and cap are clean, then fit a new O-ring seal to the cap **(see illustrations)**.
26 Fit the new filter element into the cap **(see illustration)** then fit the cap to the housing and tighten it to the specified torque.

All engines

27 With the car on level ground, fill the engine, using the correct grade and type of oil (refer to *Weekly checks.* for details of topping-up). An oil can spout or funnel may help to reduce spillage. Pour in half the specified quantity of oil first, then wait a few minutes for the oil to run to the sump.
28 Continue adding oil a small quantity at a time until the level is up to the MIN mark on the dipstick. Adding around 1.0 litre of oil will now bring the level up to the MAX on the dipstick – do not worry if a little too much goes in, as some of the excess will be taken up in filling the oil filter. Refit the dipstick and the filler cap.
29 Start the engine and run it for a few minutes, while checking for leaks around the oil filter seal and the sump drain plug. Note

3.25b ...and lightly oil it

that there may be a delay of a few seconds before the low oil pressure warning light goes out when the engine is first started, as the oil circulates through the new oil filter and the engine oil galleries before the pressure builds-up.
30 Stop the engine, and wait a few minutes for the oil to settle in the sump once more. With the new oil circulated and the filter now completely full, recheck the level on the dipstick, and add more oil as necessary.
31 Jack up and support the front of the vehicle and then refit the engine undershield.
32 Dispose of the used engine oil and the old oil filter safely, with reference to General repair procedures in the Reference section of this manual. Many local recycling points have containers for waste oil with oil filter disposal receptacles alongside.

3.26 Fit the new filter to the cap

4 Fuel filter water draining

1 The fuel filter is located at the front of the engine compartment on 2.0 litre and 2.2 litre models. On 1.6 and 1.8 litre models the filter is located at the left-hand end of the cylinder head. Remove the engine cover from the top of the engine.
2 To improve access on 1.8 litre models, remove the air filter assembly as described in Chapter 4A Section 3.
3 Position a container or cloth beneath the filter, then attach a length of plastic/rubber hose to the drain nipple, with the other end of the hose in a container **(see illustrations)**.
4 Slacken the drain nipple and the top bleed

4.3a Water draining nipple – 1.8 litre models ...

4.3b ...and 2.0 litre models

screw a few turns, and allow the fuel to drain until it appears clean and free from water droplets. Tighten the bleed screw and drain nipple (see illustrations).

5 Remove the hose, and if necessary bleed the fuel system as described in Chapter 4A Section 7.

5 Lights and horn operation check

1 With the ignition switched on where necessary, check the operation of all exterior lights.

2 Check the brake lights with the help of an assistant, or by reversing up close to a reflective door. Make sure that all the rear lights are capable of operating independently, without affecting any of the other lights – for example, switch on as many rear lights as possible, then try the brake lights. If any unusual results are found, this is usually due to an earth fault or other poor connection at that rear light unit.

3 Again with the help of an assistant or using a reflective surface, check as far as possible that the headlights work on both main and dipped beam.

4 Renew any defective bulbs with reference to Chapter 12 specifications.

HAYNES HiNT *Particularly on older vehicles, bulbs can stop working as a result of corrosion build-up on the bulb or its holder – fitting a new bulb may not cure the problem in this instance. When renewing any bulb, if you find any green or white-coloured powdery deposits, these should be cleaned off using emery cloth.*

5 Check the operation of all interior lights, including the glovebox and luggage area illumination lights. Switch on the ignition, and check that all relevant warning lights come on as expected – the vehicle handbook should give details of these. Now start the engine, and check that the appropriate lights go out. When you are next driving at night, check that all the instrument panel and facia lighting works correctly. If any problems are found, refer to Chapter 12.

6 Finally, choose an appropriate time of day to test the operation of the horn.

6 Underbonnet check for fluid leaks and hose condition

⚠️ *Warning: Renewal of air conditioning hoses must only be done after the system has been degassed. Have the system*

4.4a Slacken the bleed screw – 1.6 litre models...

4.4b ...1.8 litre models...

4.4c ...2.0 litre models...

4.4d ...and 2.2 litre models

degassed by a Ford dealer or an air conditioning specialist who will have the equipment to depressurise the system safely.

1 Visually inspect the engine joint faces, gaskets and seals for any signs of water or oil leaks. Pay particular attention to the areas around the cylinder head cover, cylinder head, oil filter and sump joint faces. Bear in mind that, over a period of time, some very slight seepage from these areas is to be expected – what you are really looking for is any indication of a serious leak. Should a leak be found, renew the offending gasket or oil seal by referring to the appropriate Chapters in this manual.

2 High temperatures in the engine compartment can cause the deterioration of the rubber and plastic hoses used for engine, accessory and emission systems operation. Periodic inspection should be made for cracks, loose clamps, material hardening and leaks.

3 When checking the hoses, ensure that all the cable-ties or clips used to retain the hoses are in place, and in good condition. Clips which are broken or missing can lead to chafing of the hoses, pipes or wiring, which could cause more serious problems in the future.

4 Carefully check the large top and bottom radiator hoses, along with the other smaller-diameter cooling system hoses and metal pipes; do not forget the heater hoses/pipes which run from the engine to the bulkhead. Inspect each hose along its entire length, replacing any that is cracked, swollen or shows signs of deterioration. Cracks may become more apparent if the hose is squeezed, and may often be apparent at the hose ends.

5 Make sure that all hose connections are tight. If the large-diameter air hoses from the air cleaner are loose, they will leak air, and upset the engine idle quality. If the spring clamps that are used to secure many of the hoses appear to be slackening, they should be updated with worm-drive clips to prevent the possibility of leaks.

6 Some other hoses are secured to their fittings with clamps. Where clamps are used, check to be sure they haven't lost their tension, allowing the hose to leak. If clamps aren't used, make sure the hose has not expanded and/or hardened where it slips over the fitting, allowing it to leak.

7 Check all fluid reservoirs, filler caps, drain plugs and fittings, etc, looking for any signs of leakage of oil, transmission and/or brake hydraulic fluid, coolant and power steering fluid. Also check the clutch hydraulic fluid lines which lead from the fluid reservoir and slave cylinder (on the transmission).

8 If the vehicle is regularly parked in the same place, close inspection of the ground underneath it will soon show any leaks; ignore the puddle of water which will be left if the air conditioning system is in use. Place a clean piece of cardboard below the engine, and examine it for signs of contamination after the vehicle has been parked over it overnight.

9 Remember that some leaks will only occur with the engine running, or when the engine is hot or cold. With the handbrake firmly applied, start the engine from cold, and let the engine idle while you examine the underside of the engine compartment for signs of leakage.

10 If an unusual smell is noticed inside or around the car, especially when the engine is thoroughly hot, this may point to the presence of a leak.

11 As soon as a leak is detected, its source must be traced and rectified. Where oil has been leaking for some time, it is usually necessary to use a steam cleaner, pressure washer or similar to clean away the accumulated dirt, so that the exact source of the leak can be identified.

Vacuum hoses

12 It's quite common for vacuum hoses, especially those in the emissions system, to be colour-coded, or to be identified by coloured stripes moulded into them. Various systems require hoses with different wall thicknesses, collapse resistance and temperature resistance. When renewing hoses, be sure the new ones are made of the same material.

13 Often the only effective way to check a hose is to remove it completely from the vehicle. If more than one hose is removed, be sure to label the hoses and fittings to ensure correct installation.

14 When checking vacuum hoses, be sure to include any plastic T-fittings in the check. Inspect the fittings for cracks, and check the hose where it fits over the fitting for distortion, which could cause leakage.

15 A small piece of vacuum hose (quarter-inch inside diameter) can be used as a stethoscope to detect vacuum leaks. Hold one end of the hose to your ear, and probe around vacuum hoses and fittings, listening for the 'hissing' sound characteristic of a vacuum leak.

⚠ *Warning: When probing with the vacuum hose stethoscope, be very careful not to come into contact with moving engine components such as the auxiliary drivebelt, radiator electric cooling fan, etc.*

Fuel hoses

⚠ *Warning: There are certain precautions which must be taken when inspecting or servicing fuel system components. Work in a well-ventilated area, and do not allow open flames (cigarettes, appliance pilot lights, etc) or bare light bulbs near the work area. Mop-up any spills immediately, and do not store fuel-soaked rags where they could ignite.*

16 Check all fuel hoses for deterioration and chafing. Check especially for cracks in areas where the hose bends, and also just before fittings, such as where a hose attaches to the fuel filter.

17 It is not unusual for a high-mileage diesel engine to exhibit a 'film' of diesel fuel around the injectors, resulting in an oily appearance. Unless there is clear evidence of a significant fuel leak, this is not normally a matter for concern. The best course of action would be to first clean the engine thoroughly; then, after several more miles have been covered, the source of the leak can be identified and its severity assessed.

18 High-quality fuel line, usually identified by the word 'Fluoroelastomer' printed on the hose, should be used for fuel line renewal. Never, under any circumstances, use non-reinforced vacuum line, clear plastic tubing or water hose as a substitute for fuel lines.

19 Spring-type clamps are commonly used on fuel lines. These clamps often lose their tension over a period of time, and can be 'sprung' during removal. Renew all spring-type clamps with proper petrol pipe clips whenever a hose is renewed.

Metal lines

20 Sections of metal piping are often used for fuel line between the fuel filter and the engine. Check carefully to be sure the piping has not been bent or crimped, and that cracks have not started in the line.

21 If a section of metal fuel line must be renewed, only seamless steel piping should be used, since copper and aluminium piping don't have the strength necessary to withstand normal engine vibration.

22 Check the metal lines where they enter the brake master cylinder, ABS hydraulic unit or clutch master/slave cylinders (as applicable) for cracks in the lines or loose fittings. Any sign of brake fluid leakage calls for an immediate and thorough inspection.

7 Engine compartment wiring check

1 With the vehicle parked on level ground, apply the handbrake firmly and open the bonnet. Using an inspection light or a small electric torch, check all visible wiring within and beneath the engine compartment. Make sure that the ignition is switched off – take out the key.

2 What you are looking for is wiring that is obviously damaged by chafing against sharp edges, or against moving suspension/transmission components and/or the auxiliary drivebelt, by being trapped or crushed between carelessly-refitted components, or melted by being forced into contact with the hot engine castings, coolant pipes, etc. In almost all cases, damage of this sort is caused in the first instance by incorrect routing on reassembly after previous work has been carried out.

3 Depending on the extent of the problem, damaged wiring may be repaired by rejoining the break or splicing-in a new length of wire, using solder to ensure a good connection, and remaking the insulation with adhesive insulating tape or heat-shrink tubing, as appropriate. If the damage is extensive, given the implications for the vehicle's future reliability, the best long-term answer may well be to renew that entire section of the loom, however expensive this may appear.

4 When the actual damage has been repaired, ensure that the wiring loom is re-routed correctly, so that it is clear of other components, and not stretched or kinked, and is secured out of harm's way using the plastic clips, guides and ties provided.

5 Check all electrical connectors, ensuring that they are clean, securely fastened, and that each is locked by its plastic tabs or wire clip, as appropriate. If any connector shows external signs of corrosion (accumulations of white or green deposits, or streaks of 'rust'), or if any is thought to be dirty, it must be unplugged and cleaned using electrical contact cleaner. If the connector pins are severely corroded, the connector must be renewed; note that this may mean the renewal of that entire section of the loom – see your local Ford dealer for details.

6 If the cleaner completely removes the corrosion to leave the connector in a satisfactory condition, it would be wise to pack the connector with a suitable material which will exclude dirt and moisture, preventing the corrosion from occurring again; a Ford dealer may be able to recommend a suitable product.

7 Check the condition of the battery connections – remake the connections or renew the leads if a fault is found (see Chapter 5). Use the same techniques to ensure that all earth points in the engine compartment provide good electrical contact through clean, metal-to-metal joints, and that all are securely fastened.

8 Check the wiring to the glow plugs, referring to Chapter 5 if necessary.

8 Seat belt check

1 Check the seat belts for satisfactory operation and condition. Inspect the webbing for fraying and cuts. Check that they retract smoothly and without binding into their reels.

2 Check the seat belt mountings, ensuring that all the bolts are securely tightened.

9 Brake pads, shoes and discs check

1 The work described in this Section should be carried out at the specified intervals, or whenever a defect is suspected in the braking system. Any of the following symptoms could indicate a potential brake system defect:
a) *The vehicle pulls to one side when the brake pedal is depressed.*

9.4 Check the brake pad friction material thickness

9.12 Bend the flexible hoses and check for cracks

b) *The brakes make squealing, scraping or dragging noises when applied.*

c) *Brake pedal travel is excessive, or pedal feel is poor.*

d) *The brake fluid requires repeated topping-up. Note that, because the hydraulic clutch shares the same fluid as the braking system (see Chapter 6), this problem could be due to a leak in the clutch system.*

Front disc brakes

2 Apply the handbrake, then loosen the front wheel nuts. Jack up the front of the vehicle, and support it on axle stands (see *Jacking and vehicle support*).

3 For better access to the brake calipers, remove the wheels.

4 Look through the inspection window in the caliper, and check that the thickness of the friction lining material on each of the pads is not less than the recommended minimum thickness given in the Specifications **(see illustration)**.

HAYNES HINT *Bear in mind that the lining material is normally bonded to a metal backing plate. To differentiate between the metal and the lining material, it is helpful to turn the disc slowly at first – the edge of the disc can then be identified, with the lining material on each pad either side of it, and the backing plates behind.*

5 If it is difficult to determine the exact thickness of the pad linings, or if you are at all concerned about the condition of the pads, then remove them from the calipers for further inspection (refer to Chapter 9 Section 2).

6 Check the other caliper in the same way.

7 If any one of the brake pads has worn down to, or below, the specified limit, all four pads at that end of the car must be renewed as a set. If the pads on one side are significantly more worn than the other, this may indicate that the caliper pistons have partially seized – refer to the brake pad renewal procedure in Chapter 9 Section 2, and push the pistons back into the caliper to free them.

8 Measure the thickness of the discs with

a micrometer, if available, to make sure that they still have service life remaining. Do not be fooled by the lip of rust which often forms on the outer edge of the disc, which may make the disc appear thicker than it really is – scrape off the loose rust if necessary, without scoring the disc friction (shiny) surface.

9 If any disc is thinner than the specified minimum thickness, renew it (refer to Chapter 9 Section 4).

10 Check the general condition of the discs. Look for excessive scoring and discolouration caused by overheating. If these conditions exist, remove the relevant disc and have it resurfaced or renewed (refer to Chapter 9 Section 4).

11 Make sure that the handbrake is firmly applied, then check that the transmission is in neutral. Spin the wheel, and check that the brake is not binding. Some drag is normal with a disc brake, but it should not require any great effort to turn the wheel – also, do not confuse brake drag with resistance from transmission.

12 Before refitting the wheels, check all brake lines and hoses (refer to Chapter 9). In particular, check the flexible hoses in the vicinity of the calipers, where they are subjected to most movement **(see illustration)**. Bend them between the fingers (but do not actually bend them double, or the casing may be damaged) and check that this does not reveal previously-hidden cracks, cuts or splits.

13 On completion, refit the wheels and lower the car to the ground. Tighten the wheel nuts to the specified torque.

10.5 Check the condition of the rubber mountings

Rear disc brakes

14 Loosen the rear wheel nuts, then chock the front wheels. Jack up the rear of the car, and support it on axle stands. Release the handbrake and remove the rear wheels.

15 The procedure for checking the rear brakes is much the same as described in paragraphs 2 to 13 above. Check that the rear brakes are not binding, noting that transmission resistance is not a factor on the rear wheels. Abnormal effort may indicate that the handbrake needs adjusting – see Chapter 9.

10 Exhaust system check

1 With the engine cold (at least three hours after the vehicle has been driven), check the complete exhaust system, from its starting point at the engine to the end of the tailpipe. Ideally, this should be done on a hoist, where unrestricted access is available; if a hoist is not available, raise and support the vehicle on axle stands.

2 Make sure that all brackets and rubber mountings are in good condition, and tight; if any of the mountings are to be renewed, ensure that the new ones are of the correct type – in the case of the rubber mountings, their colour is a good guide. Those nearest to the catalytic converter are more heat-resistant than the others.

3 Check the pipes and connections for evidence of leaks, severe corrosion, or damage. Leakage at any of the joints or in other parts of the system will usually show up as a black sooty stain in the vicinity of the leak. **Note:** *Exhaust sealants should not be used on any part of the exhaust system upstream of the catalytic converter (between the engine and the converter) – even if the sealant does not contain additives harmful to the converter, pieces of it may break off and foul the element, causing local overheating.*

4 At the same time, inspect the underside of the body for holes, corrosion, open seams, etc, which may allow exhaust gases to enter the passenger compartment. Seal all body openings with silicone or body putty.

5 Rattles and other noises can often be traced to the exhaust system, especially the rubber mountings **(see illustration)**. Try to move the system, silencer(s) and catalytic converter. If any components can touch the body or suspension parts, secure the exhaust system with new mountings.

11 Steering, suspension and roadwheel check

Front suspension and steering

1 Apply the handbrake, then raise the front of the vehicle and support it on axle stands.

11.2 Check the condition of the steering rack gaiters

11.4 Grasp the roadwheel at the 12 o'clock and 6 o'clock positions, and try to rock it

12.2 Check the condition of the driveshaft gaiters

2 Visually inspect the balljoint dust covers and the steering gear gaiters for splits, chafing or deterioration **(see illustration)**. Any wear of these components will cause loss of lubricant, together with dirt and water entry, resulting in rapid deterioration of the balljoints or steering gear.

3 Check the power-assisted steering fluid hoses for chafing or deterioration, and the pipe and hose unions for fluid leaks. Also check for signs of fluid leakage under pressure from the steering gear rubber gaiters, which would indicate failed fluid seals within the steering gear.

4 Grasp the roadwheel at the 12 o'clock and 6 o'clock positions, and try to rock it **(see illustration)**. Very slight free play may be felt, but if the movement is appreciable, further investigation is necessary to determine the source. Continue rocking the wheel while an assistant depresses the footbrake. If the movement is now eliminated or significantly reduced, it is likely that the hub bearings are at fault. If the free play is still evident with the footbrake depressed, then there is wear in the suspension joints or mountings.

5 Now grasp the wheel at the 9 o'clock and 3 o'clock positions, and try to rock it as before. Any movement felt now may again be caused by wear in the hub bearings or the steering track rod balljoints. If the outer track rod balljoint is worn, the visual movement will be obvious. If the inner joint is suspect, it can be felt by placing a hand over the rack-and-pinion rubber gaiter, and gripping the track rod. If the wheel is now rocked, movement will be felt at the inner joint if wear has taken place.

6 Using a large screwdriver or flat bar, check for wear in the suspension mounting and subframe bushes by levering between the relevant suspension component and its attachment point. Some movement is to be expected as the mountings are made of rubber, but excessive wear should be obvious. Also check the condition of any visible rubber bushes, looking for splits, cracks or contamination of the rubber.

7 With the vehicle standing on its wheels, have an assistant turn the steering wheel back-and-forth, about an eighth of a turn

each way. There should be very little, if any, lost movement between the steering wheel and roadwheels. If this is not the case, closely observe the joints and mountings previously described, but in addition, check the steering column joints for wear, and also check the rack-and-pinion steering gear itself.

Rear suspension

8 Chock the front wheels, then raise the rear of the vehicle and support it on axle stands.
9 Check the rear hub bearings for wear, using the method described for the front hub bearings (paragraph 4).
10 Using a large screwdriver or flat bar, check for wear in the suspension mounting bushes by levering between the relevant suspension component and its attachment point. Some movement is to be expected as the mountings are made of rubber, but excessive wear should be obvious.

Roadwheel check and balancing

11 Periodically remove the roadwheels, and clean any dirt or mud from the inside and outside surfaces. Examine the wheel rims for signs of rusting, corrosion or other damage. Light alloy wheels are easily damaged by 'kerbing' whilst parking, and similarly, steel wheels may become dented or buckled. Renewal of the wheel is very often the only course of remedial action possible.
12 The balance of each wheel and tyre assembly should be maintained, not only to avoid excessive tyre wear, but also to avoid wear in the steering and suspension components. Wheel imbalance is normally signified by vibration through the vehicle's bodyshell, although in many cases it is particularly noticeable through the steering wheel. Conversely, it should be noted that wear or damage in suspension or steering components may cause excessive tyre wear. Out-of-round or out-of-true tyres, damaged wheels and wheel bearing wear/maladjustment also fall into this category. Balancing will not usually cure vibration caused by such wear.
13 Wheel balancing may be carried out with the wheel either on or off the vehicle. If balanced on the vehicle, ensure that the

wheel-to-hub relationship is marked in some way prior to subsequent wheel removal, so that it may be refitted in its original position.

12 Driveshaft rubber gaiter and joint check

1 The driveshaft rubber gaiters are very important, because they prevent dirt, water and foreign material from entering and damaging the joints. External contamination can cause the gaiter material to deteriorate prematurely, so it's a good idea to wash the gaiters with soap and water occasionally.
2 With the vehicle raised and securely supported on axle stands, turn the steering onto full-lock, then slowly rotate each front wheel in turn. Inspect the condition of the outer constant velocity (CV) joint rubber gaiters, squeezing the gaiters to open out the folds. Check for signs of cracking, splits, or deterioration of the rubber, which may allow the escape of grease, and lead to the ingress of water and grit into the joint. Also check the security and condition of the retaining clips. Repeat these checks on the inner joints **(see illustration)**. If any damage or deterioration is found, the gaiters should be renewed as described in Chapter 8 Section 3.
3 At the same time, check the general condition of the outer CV joints themselves, by first holding the driveshaft and attempting to rotate the wheels. Repeat this check on the inner joints, by holding the inner joint yoke and attempting to rotate the driveshaft.
4 Any appreciable movement in the joint indicates wear in the joint, wear in the driveshaft splines, or a loose driveshaft retaining bolt.

13 Underbody and fuel/brake line check

1 With the vehicle raised and supported on axle stands or over an inspection pit, thoroughly inspect the underbody and wheel

13.5 Ensure the pipes are correctly supported in their clips

arches for signs of damage and corrosion. In particular, examine the bottom of the side sills, and any concealed areas where mud can collect.

2 Where corrosion and rust is evident, press and tap firmly on the panel with a screwdriver, and check for any serious corrosion which would necessitate repairs.

3 If the panel is not seriously corroded, clean away the rust, and apply a new coating of underseal. Refer to Chapter 11 for more details of body repairs.

4 At the same time, inspect the lower body panels for stone damage and general condition.

5 Inspect all of the fuel and brake lines on the underbody for damage, rust, corrosion and leakage. Also make sure that they are correctly supported in their clips **(see illustration)**. Where applicable, check the PVC coating on the lines for damage.

14 Hinge and lock lubrication

1 Work around the vehicle and lubricate the hinges of the bonnet, doors and tailgate with a light machine oil.

2 Check carefully the security and operation of all hinges, latches and locks, adjusting them where required. Check the operation of the central locking system (if fitted).

3 Where applicable, check the condition and operation of the tailgate struts, renewing them if either is leaking or no longer able to support the tailgate securely when raised.

15 Roadwheel nut tightness check

1 Checking the tightness of the wheel nuts is more relevant than you might think. Apart from the obvious safety aspect of ensuring they are sufficiently tight, this check will reveal whether they have been overtightened, as may have happened the last time new tyres were fitted, for example. If the car suffers a

puncture, you may find that the wheel nuts cannot be loosened with the wheel brace.

2 Apply the handbrake, chock the wheels, and engage 1st gear.

3 Remove the wheel cover (or wheel centre cover), using the flat end of the wheel brace supplied in the tool kit.

4 Loosen the first wheel nut, using the wheel brace if possible. If the nut proves stubborn, use a close-fitting socket and a long extension bar.

⚠️ **Warning: Do not use makeshift means to loosen the wheel nuts if the proper tools are not available. If extra force is required, make sure that the tools fit properly, and are of good quality. Even so, consider the consequences of the tool slipping or breaking, and take precautions – wearing stout gloves is advisable to protect your hands. Do not be tempted to stand on the tools used – they are not designed for this, and there is a high risk of personal injury if the tool slips or breaks. If the wheel nuts are simply too tight, take the car to a garage equipped with suitable power tools.**

5 Once the nut has been loosened, remove it and check that the wheel stud threads are clean. Use a small wire brush to clean any rust or dirt from the threads, if necessary.

6 Refit the nut, with the tapered side facing inwards. Tighten it fully, using the wheel brace alone – no other tools. This will ensure that the wheel nuts can be loosened using the wheel brace if a puncture occurs. However, if a torque wrench is available, tighten the nut to the specified torque wrench setting.

7 Repeat the procedure for the remaining nuts, then refit the wheel cover or centre cover, as applicable.

8 Work around the car, checking and retightening the nuts for all four wheels.

16 Road test

Braking system

1 Make sure that the vehicle does not pull to one side when braking, and that the wheels do not lock when braking hard.

2 Check that there is no vibration through the steering when braking. On models equipped with ABS brakes, if vibration is felt through the pedal under heavy braking, this is a normal characteristic of the system operation, and is not a cause for concern.

3 Check that the handbrake operates correctly, without excessive movement of the lever, and that it holds the vehicle stationary on a slope, in both directions (facing up and down a slope).

4 With the engine switched off, test the operation of the brake servo unit as follows.

Depress the footbrake four or five times to exhaust the vacuum, then start the engine. As the engine starts, there should be a noticeable 'give' in the brake pedal as vacuum builds-up. Allow the engine to run for at least two minutes, and then switch it off. If the brake pedal is now depressed again, it should be possible to detect a hiss from the servo as the pedal is depressed. After about four or five applications, no further hissing should be heard, and the pedal should feel considerably harder.

Steering and suspension

5 Check for any abnormalities in the steering, suspension, handling or road 'feel'.

6 Drive the vehicle, and check that there are no unusual vibrations or noises.

7 Check that the steering feels positive, with no excessive sloppiness or roughness, and check for any suspension noises when cornering and driving over bumps.

Drivetrain

8 Check the performance of the engine, transmission and driveshafts.

9 Check that the engine starts correctly, both when cold and when hot. Observe the glow plug warning light, and check that it comes on and goes off correctly.

10 Listen for any unusual noises from the engine and transmission.

11 Make sure that the engine runs smoothly when idling, and that there is no hesitation when accelerating.

12 Check that all gears can be engaged smoothly without noise, and that the gear lever action is smooth and not abnormally vague or 'notchy'.

13 Listen for a metallic clicking sound from the front of the vehicle as the vehicle is driven slowly in a circle with the steering on full-lock. Carry out this check in both directions. If a clicking noise is heard, this indicates wear in a driveshaft joint, in which case renew the joint if necessary.

Clutch

14 Check that the clutch pedal moves smoothly and easily through its full travel, and that the clutch itself functions correctly, with no trace of slip or drag.

15 If the clutch is slow to release, it is possible that the system requires bleeding (see Chapter 6 Section 5). Also check the fluid pipes under the bonnet for signs of leakage.

16 Check the clutch as described in Chapter 6, Section 6.

Instruments and electrical equipment

17 Check the operation of all instruments and electrical equipment.

18 Make sure that all instruments read correctly, and switch on all electrical equipment in turn, to check that it functions properly.

17.1 Remove the panel

17.2 Unhook and lower the fuse/junction box from the bracket

17.3a Remove the screws (shown with the heater assembly removed for clarity)...

17.3b ...and remove the cover

17.4 Pull the pollen filter from the housing

19.2 Disconnect the wiring plug

17 Pollen filter renewal

1 Release the 2 fasteners and remove the trim panel above the passenger's side footwell **(see illustration)**.
2 Rotate the locking catch and lower the fusebox (GEM) then unhook it from the mounting bracket on the bulkhead **(see illustration)**. Lower and move the fusebox to one side. There is no need to disconnect the wiring plugs.
3 Reach up and with difficulty remove the pollen filter cover. The cover is held in place by several screws possibly up to 4 **(see illustrations)**. Note that removing the glovebox as described in

Chapter 11 Section 27, will greatly improve access.
4 Remove the filter. It will be need to be distorted slightly to clear the housing and fusebox **(see illustration)**.
5 Fit the new filter using a reversal of the removal procedure, ensuring that the filter is fitted with the airflow arrows pointing straight back into the cabin.

18 Handbrake check and adjustment

1 In service, the handbrake should be fully applied within 3 to 5 clicks of the handbrake lever ratchet. Should adjustment be necessary, refer to Chapter 9 Section 19 for the full procedure description.

19 Fuel filter renewal

1.6 litre engine

1 Remove the engine cover and then remove the protection bracket from the top of the filter.
2 Disconnect the wiring plug from the water sensor on the top of the filter **(see illustration)**.
3 Disconnect the fuel supply and return pipes from the filter **(see illustration)**. Plug the openings to prevent contamination.
4 Disconnect the fuel heater wiring plug from the side of the filter (where fitted).
5 Remove the 2 outer mounting bolts and lift the filter assembly from the filter housing **(see illustrations)**.

19.3 Disconnect the fuel hoses

19.5a Remove the bolts (shown with the filter removed for clarity)

19.5b Lift out the filter

19.6 Release the sensor

19.7 Remove the filter

19.12 Undo the bolts and remove the metal shield

19.14a Depress the release button and disconnect the fuel supply pipe

19.14b Prise out the locking catch (1), push in or pull out the clip (2), and disconnect the fuel return pipe

19.16a Unscrew the collar…

6 Position the filter over a clean container and then drain the filter by rotating and lifting up the water sensor **(see illustration)**.

7 Remove the 3 filter mounting bolts and pull the filter free from the filter head **(see illustration)**.

8 Fit the new filter by reversing the removal procedure and then connect a length of hose and small funnel to the fuel inlet side of the filter.

9 With the filter assembly still positioned over a clean container, fill the new filter with clean diesel.

10 Refit the filter to the housing and then reconnect the fuel supply and return pipes.

11 The remainder of fitting is a reversal of removal. If necessary, bleed the fuel system as described in Chapter 4A Section 7.

1.8 litre engine

12 Undo the bolts and remove the metal shield over the top of the filter **(see illustration)**.

13 Disconnect the wiring plug from the side of the filter housing.

14 Disconnect the fuel supply and return pipes **(see illustrations)**. Plug the openings to prevent contamination.

15 Slide the filter housing upwards from the mounting bracket.

16 Unscrew the collar and lift the filter cover and element from the housing **(see illustrations)**.

17 Discard the seal **(see illustration)**.

18 Position the new seal on the filter housing, and fit the new filter element to the cover.

19 Fit the new element and cover to the housing, ensuring the alignment arrows are aligned correctly **(see illustration)**. Tighten the collar securely.

20 Refit the filter housing to the bracket, and reconnect the pipes/wiring plug.

21 The remainder of refitting is a reversal of removal. Bleed the fuel system as described in Chapter 4A Section 7.

19.16b …then lift the cover and element from the filter housing

19.17 Renew the seal

19.19 Ensure the arrows align

19.23 Remove the bracket

19.25 Depress the release buttons and disconnect the fuel hoses from the filter head

19.26 Unscrew the filter head

2.0 litre engine

Note: *There are two types of fuel filter fitted, however removal and refitting is similar for both versions.*

22 Remove the engine cover and then protect the alternator from any possibility of fuel spillage.

23 Release the wiring harnesses from the cable ties on the fuel filter bracket, then disconnect the filter wiring plug, release the fuel pipe from the clip, undo the bolts, then remove the bracket **(see illustration)**.

24 Drain the fuel filter as described in Section.

25 Depress the locking tabs and disconnect the fuel hoses from the filter head **(see illustration)**. Be prepared for fuel spillage. Use the plugs supplied in the filter kit to seal the hose openings.

26 On early models, unscrew the filter head using a 27 mm socket or spanner, and lift it from place **(see illustration)**. On later models remove the bolts.

27 Remove the filter element, and discard the O-ring seals.

28 Fit the new O-ring seals to the filter head **(see illustration)** and to the inner filter mounting. Refit the filter head (and filter) and tighten it by rotating it clockwise until the stop on the filter housing abuts the stop on the filter head. On later models tighten the mounting screws.

29 The remainder of refitting is a reversal of removal, but bleed the fuel system as described in Chapter 4A Section 7.

2.2 litre engine

30 Remove the engine cover.

31 Unbolt and then remove the protective cover and then thoroughly clean the top of the filter.

32 Place a suitable container below the drain pipe and drain the filter as described in Section.

33 Disconnect the wiring plug **(see illustration)**.

34 Anticipating some fuel spillage disconnect the fuel lines from the filter. Seal the fuel lines as soon as they are removed **(see illustrations)**. Genuine Ford filters are supplied with the seals.

35 Remove the mounting bolts and lift the filter from the housing **(see illustrations)**. Remove the bleed hose from the base of the filter.

36 The filter is a complete assembly. Dispose of the filter in a responsible manner.

19.28 Renew the filter element and the O-ring seal

19.33 Release the wiring plug

19.34a Disconnect the fuel lines ...

19.34b ... and seal the openings

19.35a Remove the mounting bolts and ...

19.35b ... lift out the filter

37 Fit the bleed hose to the new filter **(see illustration)** and then fit the filter. Bleed the filter and fuel lines as described in Chapter 4A Section 7.

38 Reconnect the fuel lines, start the engine and check for fuel leaks. Refit the protective cover and the engine cover.

20 Air filter element renewal

Caution: Never drive the vehicle with the air cleaner filter element removed. Excessive engine wear could result, and backfiring could even cause a fire under the bonnet.

1 The air filter element is located in the air cleaner assembly on the left-hand side of the engine compartment.

2 The 1.6, 1.8 and 2.0 litre models all share a common air filter. The 2.2 litre engine has a slightly different filter and housing.

3 Remove the screws from the air filter upper section. On the all but the 2.2 litre engine lift up the cover and slide out the filter. On the 2.2 litre engine, release the hose clip, disconnect the wiring plug and remove the

19.37 Fit the bleed hose to the new filter

top of the housing completely **(see illustrations)**.

4 Wipe clean (or vacuum out) the inner surfaces of the cover and main housing **(see illustration)**. If there is a considerable amount of debris inside the housing and if no vacuum is available, remove the complete housing as described in Chapter 4A Section 3.

5 Locate the new element in the housing, making sure that the sealing lip is correctly engaged with the edge of the housing **(see illustration)**. Refit the filter cover and tighten the bolts securely.

21 Timing belt renewal

1 The procedure is described in the relevant part of Chapter 2.

22 Auxiliary drivebelt check and renewal

Drivebelt check

1 A single auxiliary drivebelt is fitted at the right-hand side of the engine. An automatic adjuster is fitted, so checking the drivebelt tension is unnecessary.

2 Due to their function and material make-up, drivebelts are prone to failure after a long period of time, and should therefore be inspected regularly.

3 Since the drivebelt is located very close to the right-hand side of the engine compartment, it is possible to gain better access by raising the front of the vehicle, undoing the fasteners and removing the

20.3a Remove the screws on the 1.6, 1.8 and 2.0 litre engines...

20.3b ...and on the 2.2 litre engine

20.3c Slide out the filter

20.4 Clean out the interior of the housing

20.5 On 2.2 litre engines align the filter correctly

22.3a Remove the engine undershield

22.3b Remove the wing liner

engine undershield and right-hand wing liner **(see illustrations)**.

4 With the engine stopped, inspect the full length of the drivebelt for cracks and separation of the belt plies. It will be necessary to turn the engine (using a spanner or socket and bar on the crankshaft pulley bolt) in order to move the belt from the pulleys so that the belt can be inspected thoroughly. Twist the belt between the pulleys so that both sides can be viewed. Also check for fraying, and glazing which gives the belt a shiny appearance. Check the pulleys for nicks, cracks, distortion and corrosion.

5 Note that it is not unusual for a ribbed belt to exhibit small cracks in the edges of the belt ribs, and unless these are extensive or very deep, belt renewal is not essential.

Drivebelt renewal

6 To remove the drivebelt, first raise the front of the vehicle and support on axle stands (see *Jacking and vehicle support*). Undo the fasteners and remove the engine undershield, followed by the wheel arch liner **(see illustrations 29.3a and 29.3b)**.

7 Where fitted remove the crankshaft pulley protector from the chassis leg.

8 Remove the engine cover from the top of the engine.

1.6 litre engines

9 Use a spanner to rotate the tensioner, while an assistant lifts the belt from the pulleys **(see illustration)**.

10 Fit the spanner to the tensioner arm and rotate the tensioner clockwise until the tensioner arm passes the hole in the housing, and a 2.0 mm (or 5 mm) drill bit can be inserted, locking the tensioner in position **(see illustration)**.

11 Note how the belt is routed, then remove the belt from the pulleys **(see illustrations)**.

12 Fit the new drivebelt onto the crankshaft, air conditioning compressor, alternator and tensioner/idler pulleys. Fit the spanner to the tensioner arm, hold the tensioner stationary

22.9 Use a 15 mm open-ended spanner to rotate the tensioner clockwise

22.10 Insert a drill bit/rod into the hole in the tensioner housing

with the spanner and remove the locking drill bit. Slowly allow the tensioner arm to rotate and tension the belt. Remove the spanner.

1.8 litre engines

13 To remove the drivebelt, first raise the front of the vehicle and support on axle stands (see *Jacking and vehicle support*). Undo the fasteners and remove the engine undershield **(see illustration 3.12)**. Followed by the wheel arch liner.

22.11 Auxiliary belt routing – 1.6 litre

1 Alternator pulley
2 Air conditioning compressor
3 Crankshaft pulley
4 Tensioner

J46790

6299 01-29.16 HAYNES

22.16 Auxiliary drivebelt routing – 1.8 litre models

1 Power steering pump pulley
2 Coolant pump pulley
3 Alternator pulley
4 Tensioner pulley
5 Crankshaft pulley
6 Air conditioning
  compressor
7 Idler pulley

22.20 Rotate the tensioner bolt anti-clockwise, then insert a 4 mm drill bit/rod through the locking holes once they align

14 Unclip the fuel lines from the top of the timing belt cover and then disconnect the wiring plug from the intercooler to turbocharger intake hose. Slacken the hose clips and remove the hose.

15 Rotate the automatic tensioner until a 4 mm drill bit or dowel can be fitted into the slot at the base of the tensioner. Note that access is limited, but can be improved if the right-hand engine mounting is removed first, as described in Section 18.

16 Remove the drivebelt. noting the routing of the belt as it is removed **(see illustration)**.

17 Fit the new belt to the pulleys, ensuring they are correctly seated in the pulley grooves.

18 Rotate the tensioner and remove the drill bit (or dowel) and then slowly allow the tension to come onto the belt. Check that the belt is correctly aligned and then remove the spanner.

19 Refit the intercooler hose and clip the fuel lines back into the holders on the timing belt cover.

2.0 litre engines

20 Using a spanner on the tensioner centre bolt, turn the tensioner anti-clockwise to release the drivebelt tension, then insert a 4 mm drill bit or rod through the holes in the arm/body when they align to lock the tensioner in this position **(see illustration)**.

21 Note how the drivebelt is routed, then remove the belt from the pulleys **(see illustration)**.

22 Fit the new drivebelt onto the crankshaft, air conditioning compressor, alternator, and tensioner pulleys. Use a spanner to hold the tensioner arm, then remove the locking drill bit/rod, and allow the tensioner to rotate clockwise and gently tension the belt.

2.2 litre engines

23 Using a spanner on the tensioner centre

bolt, turn the tensioner anti-clockwise to release the drivebelt tension, then insert a 4 mm drill bit or rod through the holes in the arm/body. When they align to lock the tensioner in this position **(see illustration)**.

24 Remove the belt from below, noting the belt routing as it is removed **(see illustration)**.

25 Fit the new belt from above, passing it over the power steering and then hooking it over the idler pulley. Fit the belt over the compressor pulley and then finally fit the belt under the tensioner and over the crankshaft pulley.

26 Check that the belt is correctly aligned and then take the tension off the tensioner, remove the drill bit and slowly release the tensioner.

22.23 Lock the tensioner in position

H46400

22.21 Auxiliary drivebelt routing – 2.0 litre models

1 Crankshaft pulley
2 Air conditioning compressor
3 Alternator
4 Tensioner

6200 01-29.24 HAYNES

22.24 Auxiliary drivebelt routing – 2.2 litre models

1 Tensioner pulley
2 Alternator
3 Power steering
  pump
4 Air conditioning
  compressor
5 Idler pulley
6 Crankshaft pulley

All engines

27 Refit the engine top cover and undershield, then lower the car to the ground.

23 Brake fluid renewal

⚠️ *Warning: Brake hydraulic fluid can harm your eyes and damage painted surfaces, so use extreme caution when handling and pouring it. Do not use fluid that has been standing open for some time, as it absorbs moisture from the air. Excess moisture can cause a dangerous loss of braking effectiveness. Brake fluid is also highly flammable – treat it with the same respect as petrol.*

1 The procedure is similar to that for the bleeding of the hydraulic system as described in Chapter 4A Section 7.

2 Reduce the fluid level in the reservoir (by syphoning or using a poultry baster), but do not allow the fluid level to drop far enough to allow air into the system – if air enters the ABS hydraulic unit, the unit may need be bled using special Ford test equipment (see Chapter 9 Section 11).

Warning: Do not syphon the fluid by mouth; it is poisonous.

3 Working as described in Chapter 9 Section 11, open the first bleed screw in the sequence, and pump the brake pedal gently until nearly all the old fluid has been emptied from the master cylinder reservoir. Top-up to the MAX level with new fluid, and continue pumping until only the new fluid remains in the reservoir, and new fluid can be seen emerging from the bleed screw. Tighten the screw, and top the reservoir level up to the MAX level line. Old hydraulic fluid is invariably much darker in colour than the new, making it easy to distinguish the two.

4 Work through all the remaining bleed screws in the sequence until new fluid can be seen at all of them. Be careful to keep the master cylinder reservoir topped-up to above the MIN level at all times, or air may enter the system and greatly increase the length of the task.

5 When the operation is complete, check that all bleed screws are securely tightened, and that their dust caps are refitted. Wash off all traces of spilt fluid, and recheck the master cylinder reservoir fluid level.

6 Check the operation of the brakes before taking the car on the road.

7 Finally, check the operation of the clutch. Since the clutch shares the same fluid reservoir as the braking system, it may also be necessary to bleed the clutch as described in Chapter 6 Section 5.

24 Remote control battery renewal

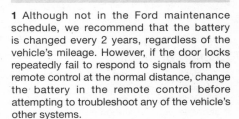

1 Although not in the Ford maintenance schedule, we recommend that the battery is changed every 2 years, regardless of the vehicle's mileage. However, if the door locks repeatedly fail to respond to signals from the remote control at the normal distance, change the battery in the remote control before attempting to troubleshoot any of the vehicle's other systems.

24.3a Insert a screwdriver into the slot

24.5 The battery fits positive side up

24.8 Release the upper half at the end first

24.9a Separate the 2 halves and ...

Models with a folding key blade

2 Press the button to release the key blade.

3 Use a small screwdriver and release the battery cover **(see illustrations)**.

4 Fully remove the battery cover and then remove the battery.

5 Fit a new battery – the '+' (positive) side of the battery must face up **(see illustration)**.

6 Refit the battery compartment cover and check the operation of the remote.

Models without a key blade

7 The emergency key blade is located under a cover. Press and hold the small buttons on the side of the remote to release the cover **(see illustration)**.

8 Remove the key blade and then use a small screwdriver, first at the end of the narrow end of the key blade compartment and then on the side of the remote **(see illustration)**.

9 Fully separate the two halves of the remote and then use the screwdriver to remove the battery **(see illustrations)**.

24.3b ... and prise off the cover

24.7 Release the key cover

24.9b ... remove the battery

24.10 The battery fits positive side down

25.4 Remove the intercooler hose

25.5 Undo the coolant drain plug at the left-hand lower corner of the radiator

10 Fit a new battery – the '+' (positive) side of the battery must face down **(see illustration)**.
11 Reassemble the two halves of the remote and refit the emergency key blade. Refit the blade compartment cover and check the operation of the remote.

25 Coolant strength check and renewal

> **Warning: Do not allow antifreeze to come in contact with your skin or painted surfaces of the vehicle.** *Flush contaminated areas immediately with plenty of water. Don't store new coolant, or leave old coolant lying around, where it's accessible to children or pets – they're attracted by its sweet smell. Ingestion of even a small amount of coolant can be fatal. Wipe up garage-floor and drip-pan spills immediately. Keep antifreeze containers covered, and repair cooling system leaks as soon as they're noticed.*

> **Warning: Never remove the expansion tank filler cap when the engine is running, or has just been switched off, as the cooling system will be hot, and the consequent escaping steam and scalding coolant could cause serious injury.**

> **Warning: Wait until the engine is cold before starting these procedures.**

Note: *If Ford pink/red antifreeze is used, the coolant can then be left indefinitely, providing the strength of the mixture is checked every year. If any antifreeze other than Ford's is to be used, the coolant must be renewed at regular intervals to provide an equivalent degree of protection; the conventional recommendation is to renew the coolant every two years.*

Strength check

1 Use a hydrometer to check the strength of the antifreeze. Follow the instructions provided with your hydrometer. The antifreeze strength should be approximately 50%. If it is significantly less than this, drain a little coolant from the radiator (see this Section), add

antifreeze to the coolant expansion tank, then recheck the strength.

Coolant draining

2 To drain the system, first remove the expansion tank filler cap.
3 Raise the front of the vehicle and support it securely on axle stands (see *Jacking and vehicle support*). Undo the fasteners and remove the engine undershield. Access can be further improved if the air deflector is removed from the base of the bumper cover.
4 Where the intercooler hose restricts access remove the hose **(see illustration)**.
5 Place a large drain tray underneath, and unscrew the radiator drain plug **(see illustration)**. Note that access is awkward. As soon as the coolant flows direct as much of the escaping coolant as possible into the tray.
6 Once the coolant has stopped draining from the radiator, close the drain plug.

System flushing

7 With time, the cooling system may gradually lose its efficiency, as the radiator core becomes choked with rust, scale deposits from the water, and other sediment. To minimise this, as well as using only good-quality antifreeze and clean soft water, the system should be flushed as follows whenever any part of it is disturbed, and/or when the coolant is renewed.
8 With the coolant drained, refit the drain plug and refill the system with fresh water. Refit the expansion tank filler cap, start the engine and warm it up to normal operating temperature, then stop it and (after allowing it to cool down completely) drain the system again. Repeat as necessary until only clean water can be seen to emerge, then refill finally with the specified coolant mixture.
9 If only clean, soft water and good-quality antifreeze (even if not to Ford's specification) has been used, and the coolant has been renewed at the suggested intervals, the above procedure will be sufficient to keep clean the system for a considerable length of time. If, however, the system has been neglected, a more thorough operation will be required, as follows.
10 First drain the coolant, then disconnect the radiator top and bottom hoses. Insert

a garden hose into the radiator top hose connection, and allow water to circulate through the radiator until it runs clean from the bottom outlet.
11 To flush the engine, insert the garden hose into the radiator bottom hose, wrap a piece of rag around the garden hose to seal the connection, and allow water to circulate until it runs clear.
12 Try the effect of repeating this procedure in the top hose, although this may not be effective, since the thermostat will probably close and prevent the flow of water.
13 In severe cases of contamination, reverse-flushing of the radiator may be necessary. This may be achieved by inserting the garden hose into the bottom outlet, wrapping a piece of rag around the hose to seal the connection, then flushing the radiator until clear water emerges from the top hose outlet.
14 If the radiator is suspected of being severely choked, remove the radiator (Chapter 3 Section 7), turn it upside-down, and repeat the procedure described in paragraph 12.
15 Flushing the heater matrix can be achieved using a similar procedure to that described in paragraph 12, once the heater inlet and outlet hoses have been identified. These two hoses will be of the same diameter, and pass through the engine compartment bulkhead (refer to the heater matrix removal procedure in Chapter 3 Section 9 for more details).
16 The use of chemical cleaners is not recommended, and should be necessary only as a last resort; the scouring action of some chemical cleaners may lead to other cooling system problems. Normally, regular renewal of the coolant will prevent excessive contamination of the system.

Coolant filling

17 With the cooling system drained and flushed, ensure that all disturbed hose unions are correctly secured, and that the radiator/engine drain plug(s) is securely tightened. Refit the engine undershield. If it was raised, lower the vehicle to the ground.
18 Prepare a sufficient quantity of the specified coolant mixture (see below); allow for a surplus, so as to have a reserve supply for topping-up.

19 Slowly fill the system through the expansion tank. Since the tank is the highest point in the system, all the air in the system should be displaced into the tank by the rising liquid. Slow pouring reduces the possibility of air being trapped and forming airlocks.

20 Continue filling until the coolant level reaches the expansion tank MAX level line (see *Weekly checks.*), then cover the filler opening to prevent coolant splashing out.

21 Start the engine and run it at idle speed, until it has warmed-up to normal operating temperature and the radiator electric cooling fan has cut in; watch the temperature gauge to check for signs of overheating. If the level in the expansion tank drops significantly, top-up to the MAX level line to minimise the amount of air circulating in the system.

22 Fit the expansion tank cap and then run the engine at 2,000 rpm for 10 minutes. Raise the engine speed to 3,000 rpm for 5 seconds. Check the system for leaks.

23 Stop the engine, wash off any spilt coolant from the engine compartment and bodywork, then leave the car to cool down completely (overnight, if possible).

24 With the system cool, remove the expansion tank cap and top-up the tank to the MAX level line. Refit the filler cap, tightening it securely, and clean up any further spillage.

25 After refilling, always check carefully all components of the system (but especially any unions disturbed during draining and flushing) for signs of coolant leaks. Fresh antifreeze has a searching action, which will rapidly expose any weak points in the system.

Antifreeze type and mixture

Note: *Do not use engine antifreeze in the windscreen/tailgate washer system, as it will damage the vehicle's paintwork. A screenwash additive should be added to the washer system in its maker's recommended quantities.*

26 If the vehicle's history (and therefore the quality of the antifreeze in it) is unknown, owners are advised to drain and thoroughly reverse-flush the system, before refilling with fresh coolant mixture.

27 If the antifreeze used is to Ford's specification, the levels of protection it affords are indicated in the coolant packaging.

28 To give the recommended standard mixture ratio for antifreeze, 50% (by volume) of antifreeze must be mixed with 50% of clean, soft water; if you are using any other type of antifreeze, follow its manufacturer's instructions to achieve the correct ratio.

29 You are unlikely to fully drain the system at any one time (unless the engine is being completely stripped), and the capacities quoted in Specifications are therefore slightly academic for routine coolant renewal. As a guide, only two-thirds of the system's total capacity is likely to be needed for coolant renewal.

30 As the drained system will be partially filled with flushing water, in order to establish the recommended mixture ratio, measure out 50% of the system capacity in antifreeze and pour it into the expansion tank as described above, then top-up with water. Any topping-up while refilling the system should be done with water – for *Weekly checks.* use a suitable mixture.

31 Before adding antifreeze, the cooling system should be drained, preferably flushed, and all hoses checked for condition and security. As noted earlier, fresh antifreeze will rapidly find any weaknesses in the system.

32 After filling with antifreeze, a label should be attached to the expansion tank, stating the type and concentration of antifreeze used, and the date installed. Any subsequent topping-up should be made with the same type and concentration of antifreeze.

General cooling system checks

33 The engine should be cold for the cooling system checks, so perform the following procedure before driving the vehicle, or after it has been shut off for at least three hours.

34 Remove the expansion tank filler cap, and clean it thoroughly inside and out with a rag. Also clean the filler neck on the expansion tank. The presence of rust or corrosion in the filler neck indicates that the coolant should be changed. The coolant inside the expansion tank should be relatively clean and transparent. If it is rust-coloured, drain and flush the system, and refill with a fresh coolant mixture.

35 Carefully check the radiator hoses and heater hoses along their entire length; renew any hose which is cracked, swollen or deteriorated (see Section 10).

36 Inspect all other cooling system components (joint faces, etc) for leaks. A leak in the cooling system will usually show up as white- or antifreeze-coloured deposits on the area adjoining the leak (see Haynes Hint). Where any problems of this nature are found on system components, renew the component or gasket with reference to Chapter 3.

A leak in the cooling system will usually show up as white- or antifreeze coloured deposits on the area adjoining the leak.

37 Clean the front of the radiator with a soft brush to remove all insects, leaves, etc, embedded in the radiator fins. Be careful not to damage the radiator fins, or cut your fingers on them. To do a more thorough job, remove the radiator grille as described in Chapter 11 Section 6.

Airlocks

38 If, after draining and refilling the system, symptoms of overheating are found which did not occur previously, then the fault is almost certainly due to trapped air at some point in the system, causing an airlock and restricting the flow of coolant; usually, the air is trapped because the system was refilled too quickly.

39 If an airlock is suspected, first try gently squeezing all visible coolant hoses. A coolant hose which is full of air feels quite different to one full of coolant when squeezed. After refilling the system, most airlocks will clear once the system has cooled, and been topped-up.

40 While the engine is running at operating temperature, switch on the heater and heater fan, and check for heat output. Provided there is sufficient coolant in the system, lack of heat output could be due to an airlock in the system.

41 Airlocks can have more serious effects than simply reducing heater output – a severe airlock could reduce coolant flow around the engine. Check that the radiator top hose is hot when the engine is at operating temperature – a top hose which stays cold could be the result of an airlock (or a non-opening thermostat).

42 If the problem persists, stop the engine and allow it to cool down completely before unscrewing the expansion tank filler cap or loosening the hose clips and squeezing the hoses to bleed out the trapped air. In the worst case, the system will have to be at least partially drained (this time, the coolant can be saved for re-use) and flushed to clear the problem. If all else fails, have the system evacuated and vacuum filled by a suitably-equipped garage.

Expansion tank pressure cap check

43 Wait until the engine is completely cold – perform this check before the engine is started for the first time in the day.

44 Place a wad of cloth over the expansion tank cap, then unscrew it slowly and remove it.

45 Examine the condition of the rubber seal on the underside of the cap. If the rubber appears to have hardened, or cracks are visible in the seal edges, a new cap should be fitted.

46 If the car is several years old, or has covered a large mileage, consider renewing the cap regardless of its apparent condition – they are not expensive. If the pressure relief valve built into the cap fails, excess pressure in the system will lead to puzzling failures of hoses and other cooling system components.

Chapter 2 Part A
1.6 litre engine in-car repair procedures

Contents

Degrees of difficulty

Easy, suitable for novice with little experience	**Fairly easy,** suitable for beginner with some experience	**Fairly difficult,** suitable for competent DIY mechanic	**Difficult,** suitable for experienced DIY mechanic	**Very difficult,** suitable for expert DIY or professional

Specifications

General

Designation	Duratorq-TDCi
Engine codes*	T1WB
Capacity	1560 cc
Bore	75.0 mm
Stroke	88.3 mm
Direction of crankshaft rotation	Clockwise (viewed from the right-hand side of vehicle)
No 1 cylinder location	At the transmission end of block
Maximum power output	85 kW (115 PS) @ 3600 rpm
Maximum torque output	270 Nm @ 2500 rpm
Compression ratio	16 : 1

Compression pressures (engine hot, at cranking speed)

Normal	20 ± 5 bar
Minimum	15 bar
Maximum difference between any two cylinders	5 bar

Cylinder head gasket selection

Piston protusion:	Gasket (mm)
0.53 to 0.63 mm	1.25 mm (2 hole)
0.63 to 0.68 mm	1.30 mm (3 holes)
0.68 to 0.73 mm	1.35 mm (1 holes)
0.73 to 0.78 mm	1.40 mm (4 holes)
0.78 to 0.88	1.45 mm (5 holes)
Maximum distortion	0.025 mm

Camshaft

Camshaft end float	0.195 – 0.3 mm

Lubrication system

Oil pump type	Gear-type, driven directly by the right-hand end of the crankshaft, by two flats machined along the crankshaft journal.
Minimum oil pressure at 80°C:	
Idle speed	1.0 to 2.0 bar
2000 rpm	2.3 to 3.7 bar

Torque wrench settings

	Nm	lbf ft
Ancillary drivebelt tensioner roller	20	15
Big-end bolts: *		
Stage 1	10	7
Stage 2	Slacken 180°	
Stage 3	10	7
Stage 4	Angle-tighten a further 130°	
Camshaft bearing caps	10	7
Camshaft cover/bearing ladder:		
Studs	10	7
Bolts	10	7
Camshaft position sensor bolt	5	4
Camshaft sprocket bolt		
Stage 1	20	15
Stage 2	Angle-tighten a further 50°	
Coolant outlet housing bolts	8	6
Crankshaft position/speed sensor bolt	10	7
Crankshaft pulley/sprocket bolt: *		
Stage 1	35	26
Stage 2	Angle-tighten a further 190°	
Cylinder head bolts: *		
Stage 1	20	15
Stage 2	40	30
Stage 3	Angle-tighten a further 260°	
Cylinder head cover/manifold	13	10
EGR valve	10	7
Engine-to-transmission fixing bolts	47	35
Flywheel bolts: *		
Stage 1	30	22
Stage 2	Angle-tighten a further 90°	
Fuel pump sprocket	50	37
Left-hand engine/transmission mounting:		
Mounting-to-bracket centre nut	148	109
Mounting-to-bracket outer nuts	48	35
Mounting bracket to transmission	80	59
Main bearing ladder outer seam bolts:		
Stage 1	5	4
Stage 2	10	7
Main bearing ladder to cylinder block:		
Stage 1	10	7
Stage 2	Slacken 180°	
Stage 3	30	22
Stage 4	Angle-tighten a further 140°	
Piston oil jet spray tube bolt	20	15
Oil cooler retaining bolts	10	7
Oil filter cover	25	18
Oil pick-up pipe	10	7
Oil pressure switch	30	22
Oil pump to cylinder block:		
Stage 1	5	4
Stage 2	9	7
Rear engine/transmission torque rod		
To subframe	70	52
To engine/transmission	63	47
Right-hand engine mounting:		
Mounting to Inner wing/engine	48	35
Mounting bracket to engine block	55	41
Sump drain plug	35	26
Sump bolts/nuts	10	7
Timing belt idler pulley	37	27
Timing belt tensioner pulley	30	22
Vacuum pump bolts	20	15

Note: * *Do not re-use*

1 General Information

How to use this Chapter

1 This Part of Chapter 2 describes the repair procedures that can reasonably be carried out on the engine while it remains in the vehicle. If the engine has been removed from the vehicle and is being dismantled as described in Part D, any preliminary dismantling procedures can be ignored.

Note: *While it may be possible physically to overhaul items such as the piston/connecting rod assemblies while the engine is in the car, such tasks are not usually carried out as separate operations. Usually, several additional procedures are required (not to mention the cleaning of components and oilways); for this reason, all such tasks are classed as major overhaul procedures, and are described in Part E of this Chapter.*

2 Part E describes the removal of the engine/transmission from the car, and the full overhaul procedures that can then be carried out.

DV series engines

3 The 1.6 litre DV series of engines are the result of development collaboration between Citroën/Peugeot and Ford. Originally specified as a double overhead camshaft (DOHC) 16-valve design, the latest version fitted to the Ford Galaxy and S-MAX is a single overhead cam (SOHC), 8 valve variant. The direct injection, turbocharged, four-cylinder engine is mounted transversely, with the transmission mounted on the left-hand side.

4 A toothed timing belt drives the camshaft, high-pressure fuel pump and coolant pump. The camshaft operates the inlet and exhaust valves via rocker arms which are supported at their pivot ends by hydraulic self-adjusting tappets. The camshaft Is supported by bearings machined directly in the cylinder head and camshaft bearing housing.

5 The high-pressure fuel pump supplies fuel to the fuel rail, and subsequently to the electronically-controlled injectors which inject the fuel direct into the combustion chambers. This design differs from the previous type where an injection pump supplies the fuel at high pressure to each injector. The earlier, conventional type injection pump required fine calibration and timing, and these functions are now completed by the high-pressure pump, electronic injectors and engine management ECM.

6 The crankshaft runs in five main bearings of the usual shell type. Endfloat is controlled by thrustwashers either side of No 2 main bearing.

7 The pistons are selected to be of matching weight, and incorporate fully-floating gudgeon pins retained by circlips.

Repair operations precaution

8 The engine is a complex unit with numerous accessories and ancillary components. The design of the engine compartment is such that every conceivable space has been utilised, and access to virtually all of the engine components is extremely limited. In many cases, ancillary components will have to be removed, or moved to one side, and wiring, pipes and hoses will have to be disconnected or removed from various cable clips and support brackets.

9 When working on this engine, read through the entire procedure first, look at the car and engine at the same time, and establish whether you have the necessary tools, equipment, skill and patience to proceed. Allow considerable time for any operation, and be prepared for the unexpected.

10 Because of the limited access, many of the engine photographs appearing in this Chapter were, by necessity, taken with the engine removed from the vehicle.

Warning: It is essential to observe strict precautions when working on the fuel system components of the engine, particularly the high-pressure side of the system. Before carrying out any engine operations that entail working on, or near, any part of the fuel system, refer to the special information given in Chapter 4A.

11 Operations with engine in vehicle
a) Compression pressure – testing.
b) Cylinder head cover – removal and refitting.
c) Crankshaft pulley – removal and refitting.
d) Timing belt covers – removal and refitting.
e) Timing belt – removal, refitting and adjustment.
f) Timing belt tensioner and sprockets – removal and refitting.
g) Camshaft oil seal – renewal.
h) Camshaft, rocker arms and hydraulic tappets – removal, inspection and refitting.
i) Sump – removal and refitting.
j) Oil pump – removal and refitting.
k) Crankshaft oil seals – renewal.
l) Engine/transmission mountings – inspection and renewal.
m) Flywheel – removal, inspection and refitting.

2 Compression and leakdown tests – description and interpretation

Compression test

Note: *A compression tester specifically designed for diesel engines must be used for this test.*

1 When engine performance is down, or if misfiring occurs which cannot be attributed to the fuel system, a compression test can provide diagnostic clues as to the engine's condition. If the test is performed regularly, it can give warning of trouble before any other symptoms become apparent.

2 A compression tester specifically intended for diesel engines must be used, because of the higher pressures involved. The tester is connected to an adapter which screws into the glow plug or injector hole. On this engine, an adapter suitable for use in the glow plug holes will be required, so as not to disturb the fuel system components. It is unlikely to be worthwhile buying such a tester for occasional use, but it may be possible to borrow or hire one – if not, have the test performed by a garage.

3 Unless specific instructions to the contrary are supplied with the tester, observe the following points:
a) *The battery must be in a good state of charge, the air filter must be clean, and the engine should be at normal operating temperature.*
b) *All the glow plugs should be removed as described in Chapter 5 Section 11 before starting the test.*
c) *Disconnect the fuel injector wiring plugs.*

4 The compression pressures measured are not so important as the balance between cylinders. Values are given in the Specifications.

5 The cause of poor compression is less easy to establish on a diesel engine than on a petrol one. The effect of introducing oil into the cylinders ('wet' testing) is not conclusive, because there is a risk that the oil will sit in the swirl chamber or in the recess on the piston crown instead of passing to the rings. However, the following can be used as a rough guide to diagnosis.

6 All cylinders should produce very similar pressures; any difference greater than that specified indicates the existence of a fault. Note that the compression should build-up quickly in a healthy engine; low compression on the first stroke, followed by gradually-increasing pressure on successive strokes, indicates worn piston rings. A low compression reading on the first stroke, which does not build-up during successive strokes, indicates leaking valves or a blown head gasket (a cracked head could also be the cause). Deposits on the undersides of the valve heads can also cause low compression.

7 A low reading from two adjacent cylinders is almost certainly due to the head gasket having blown between them; the presence of coolant in the engine oil will confirm this.

8 If the compression reading is unusually high, the cylinder head surfaces, valves and pistons are probably coated with carbon deposits. If this is the case, the cylinder head should be removed and decarbonised.

Note: *After performing this test, a fault code may be generated and stored in the PCM memory. Have the PCM self-diagnosis facility interrogated by a Ford dealer or suitably-equipped specialist, and the fault code erased.*

Leakdown test

9 A leakdown test measures the rate at which compressed air fed into the cylinder is lost. It is an alternative to a compression test, and in

many ways it is better, since the escaping air provides easy identification of where pressure loss is occurring (piston rings, valves or head gasket).

10 The equipment needed for leakdown testing is unlikely to be available to the home mechanic. If poor compression is suspected, have the test performed by a suitably-equipped garage.

3 Engine assembly/valve timing holes – general information and usage

Note: *Do not attempt to rotate the engine whilst the crankshaft and camshaft are locked in position. If the engine is to be left in this state for a long period of time, it is a good idea to place suitable warning notices inside the vehicle, and in the engine compartment. This will reduce the possibility of the engine being accidentally cranked on the starter motor, which is likely to cause damage with the locking pins in place.*

1 Timing holes or slots are located only in the crankshaft pulley flange and camshaft sprocket hub. The holes/slots are used to position the pistons halfway up the cylinder bores. This will ensure that the valve timing is maintained during operations that require removal and refitting of the timing belt. When the holes/slots are aligned with their corresponding holes in the cylinder block and cylinder head, suitable diameter bolts/pins can be inserted to lock the crankshaft and camshaft in position, preventing rotation.

2 Note that the fuel system used on these engines does not have a conventional diesel injection pump, but instead uses a high-pressure fuel pump. However, the fuel pump sprocket must be pegged in position in a similar fashion to the camshaft sprocket.

3 To align the engine assembly/valve timing holes, proceed as follows.

4 Apply the handbrake, then jack up the front of the vehicle and support it on axle stands (see *Jacking and vehicle support*). Remove the right-hand front roadwheel.

5 To gain access to the crankshaft pulley, to enable the engine to be turned, the wheel

3.9 Insert a 5.0 mm drill bit/bolt through the round hole in the sprocket flange into the hole in the oil pump housing (lower timing belt removed for clarity)

arch plastic liner must be removed. The liner is secured by several plastic expanding rivets/ nut/bolts. To remove the rivets, push in the centre pins a little, then prise the clips from place. Remove the liner from under the front wing.

6 Remove the starter motor and remove the crankshaft pulley as described in Section 5.

7 Remove the upper and lower timing belt covers as described in Section 6.

8 Temporarily refit the crankshaft pulley bolt (without the crankshaft pulley) and then remove the crankshaft locking tool.

9 Turn the crankshaft until the timing hole in the crankshaft sprocket aligns with the hole in the oil pump casing (this is at the 12 o'clock position). Fit the special tool 303-732, or a suitable alternative and lock the crankshaft in position **(see illustration)**.

10 With the crankshaft locked in position fit the camshaft locking tool (303-735 or similar). The hole in the camshaft sprocket should be at approximately the 1 o'clock position **(see illustration)**. If this is not the case remove the crankshaft locking pin and rotate the engine one revolution. Note that the crankshaft must always be turned in a clockwise direction (viewed from the right-hand side of vehicle).

11 When refitting the timing belt, insert Ford tool No 303-732 through the slot in the fuel pump sprocket and into the corresponding hole in the fuel pump mounting bracket. In the

3.10 Insert an 8.0 mm bolt through the hole in the camshaft sprocket into the corresponding hole in the cylinder head

absence of this tool use a 5 mm bolt or drill bit.

12 The crankshaft and camshaft are now locked in position, preventing unnecessary rotation.

4 Cylinder head cover – removal and refitting

Removal

1 Disconnect the battery negative lead as described in Chapter 5 Section 3 and then remove the air filter housing as described in Chapter 4A Section 3.

2 Remove the engine cover from the top of the engine and then remove the upper an lower windscreen cowl panels, as described in Chapter 12 Section 12.

3 Unbolt the fuel filter housing and move it to one side.

4 Release the hose clamp and remove the hose from the throttle body **(see illus- tration)**.

5 Unclip the fuel lines from the inlet manifold hose on top of the engine. Disconnect the wiring plug from the throttle body and then unbolt and remove the throttle body complete with the hose **(see illustrations)**. Plug the openings to prevent contamination.

4.4 Remove the hose from the throttle body

4.5a Disconnect the wiring plug and ...

4.5b ...remove the hose complete with the throttle body

4.6a Remove the hose clamps and mounting bolt ...

4.6b ... and then remove the hose

4.7 Remove the insulation

4.10 Remove the valve cover

4.11 Fit the seal correctly

5.5 Install the flywheel locking tool

6 Unbolt and then remove the turbocharger to intercooler hose **(see illustrations)**. Seal the opening to the turbocharger.

7 Remove the sound insulation from the top of the engine **(see illustration)**.

8 Disconnect the wiring plugs from the fuel injectors and camshaft position sensor and then remove the breather hose from the valve cover.

9 Unbolt and then remove the timing belt upper cover.

10 Remove the 9 bolts and then remove the cover **(see illustration)**. Recover the rubber seal.

Refitting

11 Refitting is a reversal of removal, but ensure that the valve cover seal is correctly located in the valve cover **(see illustration)**.

5 Crankshaft pulley – removal and refitting

Removal

1 Jack up and support the front of the vehicle (see *Jacking and vehicle support*).

2 Disconnect the battery and remove the engine undershield.

3 Remove the starter motor as described in Chapter 5 Section 8.

4 Remove wing liner and then remove the auxiliary drivebelt as described in Chapter 1 Section 22.

5 To lock the crankshaft, fit the Ford special tool 303-393 (or suitable equivalent) to the flywheel ring gear **(see illustration)**.

6 Using a suitable socket and extension

bar, unscrew the retaining bolt, remove the washer, then slide the pulley off the end of the crankshaft **(see illustrations)**. If the pulley is tight fit, it can be drawn off the crankshaft using a suitable puller. If a puller is being used, refit the pulley retaining bolt without the washer, to avoid damaging the crankshaft as the puller is tightened.

Caution: Do not touch the outer magnetic sensor ring of the sprocket with your fingers, or allow metallic particles to come into contact with it.

Refitting

7 Refit the pulley to the end of the crankshaft.

8 Refit the crankshaft pulley. Fit a new bolt and retaining washer. Tighten the bolt to the specified torque, then through the specified angle.

9 Remove the locking tool and refit the starter motor

5.6a Where fitted remove the cover

5.6b Remove the bolt and ...

5.6c ... then the pulley

6.2a Release the fuel lines and ...

6.2b ...remove the bracket

9 Undo the 4 bolts and remove the lower cover **(see illustration)**.

Refitting

10 Refitting of all the covers is a reversal of the relevant removal procedure, ensuring that each cover section is correctly located, and that the cover retaining bolts are securely tightened. Ensure that all disturbed hoses are reconnected and retained by their relevant clips.

7 Timing belt – removal, inspection, refitting and tensioning

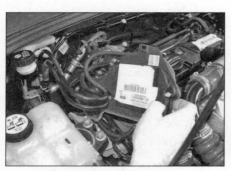

6.3 Remove the upper cover

6.9 Remove the lower timing belt cover from below

General

1 The timing belt drives the camshaft, high-pressure fuel pump, and coolant pump from a toothed sprocket on the end of the crankshaft. If the belt breaks or slips in service, the pistons are likely to hit the valve heads, resulting in expensive damage.
2 The timing belt should be renewed at the specified intervals, or earlier if it is contaminated with oil, or at all noisy in operation (a 'scraping' noise due to uneven wear).
3 If the timing belt is being removed, it is a wise precaution to renew the coolant pump at the same time. This may avoid the need to remove the timing belt again at a later stage, should the coolant pump fail. The timing belt tensioner should always be replaced when a new timing belt is fitted.

10 Refit and tension the auxiliary drivebelt as described in Chapter 1 Section 22.
11 Refit the remaining components in reverse order of removal.

the support bracket next to the cover and then work the bracket free **(see illustrations)**.
3 Undo the 4 bolts and remove the timing belt upper cover **(see illustration)**.

Removal

4 Apply the handbrake, then jack up the front of the vehicle and support it on axle stands (see *Jacking and vehicle support*). Remove the front right-hand roadwheel, wing liner **(see illustration)** and the engine undershield.
5 Remove the upper and lower timing belt covers, as described in Section 6.
6 Undo the bolt and remove the crankshaft position sensor adjacent to the crankshaft sprocket flange, and move it to one side **(see illustration)**.
7 Undo the retaining bolt and remove the timing belt protection bracket, again, adjacent to the crankshaft sprocket flange **(see illustration)**.

6 Timing belt covers – removal and refitting

Warning: Refer to the precautionary information contained in Section 1 before proceeding.

Lower cover

4 Remove the crankshaft pulley as described in Section 5.
5 Position a trolley/workshop jack under the engine. Place a block of wood on the jack head (to help spread the load on the sump), then take the weight of the engine.
6 Prise up the coolant expansion tank and move it to one side – there is no need to drain the coolant.
7 Undo the nuts/bolts, and remove the right-hand engine mounting.
8 Whilst not strictly necessary access is greatly improved if the mounting bracket is removed from the engine.

Removal

Upper cover

1 Remove the engine cover from the top of the engine.
2 Remove the fuel lines and wiring loom from

7.4 Remove the wing liner

7.6 Undo the bolt and remove the crankshaft position sensor

7.7 Remove the timing belt protection bracket

7.9 Slacken the bolt and allow the tensioner to rotate, relieving the tension on the belt

8 Lock the crankshaft and camshaft in the correct position as described in Section 3. If necessary, temporarily refit the crankshaft pulley bolt to enable the crankshaft to be rotated.

9 Insert a hexagon key into the belt tensioner pulley centre, slacken the pulley bolt, and allow the tensioner to rotate, relieving the belt tension **(see illustration)**. With belt slack, temporarily tighten the pulley bolt.

10 Note its routing, then remove the timing belt from the sprockets.

Inspection

11 Renew the belt as a matter of course, regardless of its apparent condition. The cost of a new belt is nothing compared with the cost of repairs should the belt break in service. If signs of oil contamination are found, trace the source of the oil leak and rectify it. Wash down the engine timing belt area and all related components, to remove all traces of oil. The tensioner must always be replaced. Check that the idler pulleys rotate freely without any sign of roughness, and also check that the coolant pump pulley rotates freely. It is highly recommended that both the coolant pump and the idler pulley are replaced at the same time as the timing belt and tensioner.

Refitting and tensioning

12 Commence refitting by ensuring that the crankshaft, camshaft and fuel pump sprocket timing pins are in position as described in Section 3.

13 Locate the timing belt on the crankshaft sprocket, then keeping it taut, locate it around the idler pulley, camshaft sprocket, high-pressure pump sprocket, coolant pump sprocket, and the tensioner roller **(see illustration)**.

14 Refit the timing belt protection bracket and tighten the retaining bolt securely.

15 Slacken the tensioner pulley bolt, and using a hexagonal key, rotate the tensioner anti-clockwise, which moves the index arm anti-clockwise, until the index arm is aligned as shown **(see illustration)**.

16 Remove the camshaft, crankshaft and

7.13 Timing belt routing

1 Crankshaft	4 Tensioner
2 Waterpump	5 Fuel pump
3 Idler	6 Camshaft

fuel pump sprocket (where applicable) timing pins and, using a socket on the crankshaft pulley bolt, rotate the crankshaft clockwise 10 complete revolutions. Refit the crankshaft and camshaft locking pins.

17 Check that the tensioner index arm is still aligned between the edges of the area shown **(see illustration 7.15)**. If it is not, remove and belt and begin the refitting process again, starting at Paragraph 12.

18 The remainder of refitting is a reversal of removal. Tighten all fasteners to the specified torque where given.

TOOL TiP 1

A sprocket holding tool can be made from two lengths of steel strip bolted together to form a forked end. Drill holes and insert bolts in the ends of the fork to engage with the sprocket spokes.

7.15 The index arm must align with the lug

8 Timing belt sprockets and tensioner – removal and refitting

Camshaft sprocket

Removal

1 Remove the timing belt as described in Section 7.

2 Remove the locking tool from the camshaft sprocket/hub. Slacken the sprocket hub retaining bolt. To prevent the camshaft rotating as the bolt is slackened, a sprocket holding tool will be required. In the absence of the special Ford tool, an acceptable substitute can be fabricated at home (see **Tool Tip 1**). Do not attempt to use the engine assembly/valve timing locking tool to prevent the sprocket from rotating whilst the bolt is slackened.

3 Remove the sprocket hub retaining bolt, and slide the sprocket and hub off the end of the camshaft.

4 Clean the camshaft sprocket thoroughly, and renew it if there are any signs of wear, damage or cracks.

Refitting

5 Refit the camshaft sprocket to the camshaft **(see illustration)**.

6 Refit the sprocket hub retaining bolt. Tighten the bolt to the specified torque, preventing the camshaft from turning as during removal.

7 Align the engine assembly/valve timing slot

8.5 Ensure the lug on the sprocket hub engages with the slot on the end of the camshaft

8.11a Slide the sprocket from the crankshaft ...

8.11b ...and recover the Woodruff key

Make a sprocket releasing tool from a short strip of steel. Drill two holes in the strip to correspond with the two holes in the sprocket. Drill a third hole just large enough to accept the flats of the sprocket retaining nut.

in the camshaft sprocket hub with the hole in the cylinder head and refit the timing pin to lock the camshaft in position.

8 Fit the timing belt around the pump sprocket and camshaft sprocket, and tension the timing belt as described in Section 7.

Crankshaft sprocket

Removal

9 Remove the timing belt as described in Section 7.

10 Check that the engine assembly/valve timing holes are still aligned as described in Section 3, and the camshaft sprocket and flywheel are locked in position.

11 Slide the sprocket off the end of the crankshaft and collect the Woodruff key **(see illustrations)**.

12 Examine the crankshaft oil seal for signs of oil leakage and, if necessary, renew it as described in Section 14.

13 Clean the crankshaft sprocket thoroughly, and renew it if there are any signs of wear, damage or cracks. Recover the crankshaft locating key.

Refitting

14 Refit the key to the end of the crankshaft, then refit the crankshaft sprocket (with the flange facing the crankshaft pulley).

15 Fit the timing belt around the crankshaft sprocket, and tension the timing belt as described in Section 7.

Fuel pump sprocket

Removal

16 Remove the timing belt as described in Section 7.

17 Using a suitable socket, undo the pump sprocket retaining nut. The sprocket can be held stationary by inserting a suitably-sized locking pin, drill or rod through the slot in the sprocket, and into the corresponding hole in the backplate, or by using a suitable forked tool engaged with the holes in the sprocket (see **Tool Tip 1**).

18 The pump sprocket is a taper fit on the pump shaft and it will be necessary to make up another tool to release it from the taper (see **Tool Tip 2**).

19 Partially unscrew the sprocket retaining

nut, fit the home-made tool, and secure it to the sprocket with two suitable bolts. Prevent the sprocket from rotating as before, and unscrew the sprocket retaining nut. The nut will bear against the tool as it is undone, forcing the sprocket off the shaft taper. Once the taper is released, remove the tool, unscrew the nut fully, and remove the sprocket from the pump shaft.

20 Clean the sprocket thoroughly, and renew it if there are any signs of wear, damage or cracks.

Refitting

21 Refit the pump sprocket and retaining nut, and tighten the nut to the specified torque. Prevent the sprocket rotating as the nut is tightened using the sprocket holding tool.

22 Refit the timing belt as described in Section 7.

Coolant pump sprocket

23 The coolant pump sprocket is integral with the pump, and cannot be removed. Coolant pump removal is described in Chapter 3 Section 8.

Tensioner pulley

Removal

24 Remove the timing belt as described in Section 7.

25 Remove the tensioner pulley retaining bolt, and then remove the tensioner.

26 Clean the tensioner pulley, but do not use any strong solvent which may enter the pulley bearings. Check that the pulley rotates freely, with no sign of stiffness or free play. The

8.31 Timing belt idler pulley retaining nut

pulley should always be replaced when the timing belt is replaced.

27 Examine the pulley mounting stud for signs of damage and if necessary, renew it.

Refitting

28 Refitting is a reversal of removal.

29 Refit the timing belt as described in Section 7.

Idler pulley

Removal

30 Remove the timing belt as described in Section 7.

31 Undo the retaining bolt/nut and withdraw the idler pulley from the engine **(see illustration)**.

32 Clean the idler pulley, but do not use any strong solvent which may enter the bearings. Check that the pulley rotates freely, with no sign of stiffness or free play. Renew the idler pulley if there is any doubt about its condition, or if there are any obvious signs of wear or damage.

Refitting

33 Locate the idler pulley on the engine, and fit the retaining bolt/nut. Tighten the bolt/nut to the specified torque.

34 Refit the timing belt as described in Section 7.

9 Camshafts, rocker arms and hydraulic tappets – removal, inspection and refitting

Removal

1 Remove the cylinder head cover/manifold as described in Section 4.

2 Remove the timing belt (Section 7) and the camshaft sprocket as described in Section 8.

3 Refit the right-hand engine mounting, but only tighten the bolts moderately; this will keep the engine supported during the camshaft removal.

4 Undo the bolts and remove the vacuum

9.4 Remove the vacuum pump

9.6 Remove the camshaft position sensor

9.7 Remove the bearing ladder

9.8 Remove the camshaft

9.10 Remove the rocker arms (cam followers)

pump (see Chapter 9 Section 20). Recover the pump O-ring seals **(see illustration)**.

5 Unbolt the fuel filter (see Chapter 1 Section 24) and move it to one side.

6 Disconnect the wiring plug from the camshaft position sensor **(see illustration)**. Unbolt and remove the sensor from the bearing ladder.

7 Working in reverse order to that shown **(see illustration 9.22)** remove the retaining bolts and then remove camshaft bearing cap ladder **(see illustration)**.

8 Lift out the camshaft **(see illustration)** and dispose of the oil seal. A new one will be required.

9 Obtain 8 small, clean plastic containers, and number them 1 to 4 inlet and 1 to 4 exhaust; alternatively, divide a larger container into 8 compartments.

10 Lift out each rocker arm. Place the rocker arms in their respective positions in the box or containers **(see illustration)**.

11 A compartmentalised container filled with engine oil is now required to retain the hydraulic tappets while they are removed from the cylinder head. Withdraw each hydraulic follower **(see illustration)** and place it in the container, keeping them each identified for correct refitting. The tappets must be totally submerged in the oil to prevent air entering them.

Inspection

12 Inspect the cam lobes and the camshaft bearing journals for scoring or other visible evidence of wear. Once the surface hardening of the cam lobes has been eroded, wear will occur at an accelerated rate. **Note:** *If*

these symptoms are visible on the tips of the camshaft lobes, check the corresponding rocker arm, as it will probably be worn as well.

13 Examine the condition of the bearing surfaces in the cylinder head and camshaft bearing housing. If wear is evident, the cylinder head and bearing housing will both have to be renewed, as they are a matched assembly.

14 Inspect the rocker arms and tappets for scuffing, cracking or other damage and renew any components as necessary. Also check the condition of the tappet bores in the cylinder head. As with the camshafts, any wear in this area will necessitate cylinder head renewal.

Refitting

15 Thoroughly clean the sealant from the mating surfaces of the cylinder head and camshaft bearing housing. Use a suitable liquid gasket dissolving agent (available from Ford dealers) together with a soft putty knife;

do not use a metal scraper or the faces will be damaged. As there is no conventional gasket used, the cleanliness of the mating faces is of the utmost importance.

16 Clean off any oil, dirt or grease from both components and dry with a clean lint-free cloth. Ensure that all the oilways are completely clean.

17 Liberally lubricate the hydraulic tappet bores in the cylinder head with clean engine oil.

18 Insert the hydraulic tappets into their original bores in the cylinder head unless they have been renewed.

19 Lubricate the rocker arms and place them over their respective tappets and valve stems. Lubricate the bearing surfaces **(see illustration)** and then refit the camshaft.

20 Apply a thin bead of silicone sealant (Ford part No WSE-M4G323-A4) to the mating surface of the camshaft cover/bearing ladder as shown **(see illustration)**.

9.11 Use long nose pliers to remove the hydraulic tappets

9.19 Lubricate the bearing surfaces

9.20 Apply sealant to the camshaft housing

9.21 Refit the bearing ladder

9.22 Tighten the bolts to the specified torque in the order shown

21 Assembly the bearing ladder within 10 minutes of applying the sealant **(see illustration)**. Ford technicians use a special tool (303-245) to align the bearing ladder, however 2 suitable bolts (with their heads and threads cut off) can be used if the tool is not available.
22 Tighten the bolts to the specified torque in sequence **(see illustration)**.
23 Fit a new camshaft oil seal as described in Section 14.
24 Refit the camshaft sprocket, and tighten the retaining bolt.
25 Refit the timing belt and temporarily refit the crankshaft pulley bolt – use the old bolt. Rotate the engine at least 20 revolutions to allow the oil pump to deliver oil to the

camshaft and associated components. Refit the timing belt cover.
26 Refit the remainder of the components in the reverse order of removal.

10 Cylinder head – removal and refitting

Removal

1 Apply the handbrake, then jack up the front of the vehicle and support it on axle stands (see *Jacking and vehicle support*). Remove the front right-hand roadwheel, the engine undershield, and the right-hand front wheel arch liner.

2 Remove the engine cover and then disconnect the battery negative lead as described in Chapter 5 Section 3. With reference to Chapter 12 Section 12 remove the wiper arms and screen cowl panel.
3 Drain the cooling system as described in Chapter 1 Section 25.
4 Remove the timing belt, camshaft, rocker arms and hydraulic tappets as described in Section 9.
5 Remove the turbocharger and exhaust manifold as described in Chapter 4A Section 14.
6 Unbolt the fuel filter assembly (and move it to one side) and the remove the glow plugs as described in Chapter 5 Section 11.
7 Undo the upper mounting bolts, and pivot the alternator away from the engine, undo the oil dipstick guide tube bolt, then undo the bolts securing the alternator mounting bracket to the cylinder head/block **(see illustration)**.
8 Undo the coolant outlet housing (left-hand end of the cylinder head) retaining bolts, slacken the two bolts securing the housing support bracket to the top of the transmission bellhousing, and move the outlet housing away from the cylinder head a little **(see illustration)**. There is no need to disconnect the hoses.
9 Remove the brake vacuum pump as described in Chapter 9 Section 20.
10 Disconnect the high-pressure fuel pipe from the common rail to the pump, and disconnect the fuel supply and return hoses. Where fitted, remove the bracket at the rear of the pump, then undo the bolt/nut and remove the pump and mounting bracket as an assembly **(see illustrations)**. Immediately seal all the openings in the fuel system. Note that a new high-pressure pipe must be fitted – see Chapter 4A.
11 Unbolt the EGR pipe and inlet duct from the rear of the cylinder head.
12 Check that no components or electrical connectors are still fitted to the cylinder head.
13 Working in the reverse of the sequence shown **(see illustration 10.32)** undo the cylinder head bolts. Discard the bolts – new ones must be fitted.
14 Release the cylinder head from the cylinder block and location dowels by rocking it. The Ford tool for doing this consists simply

10.7 The engine oil level dipstick guide tube is secured to the alternator bracket by a Torx bolt

10.8 Access to the coolant outlet housing will be improved if the vacuum pump is removed first

10.10a Remove the high-pressure pipe

10.10b Compress the collars and...

10.10c ...remove the fuel bleed hoses from the injectors

10.14 Free the cylinder head using angled rods

10.18a Pull the non-return valve from the cylinder head ...

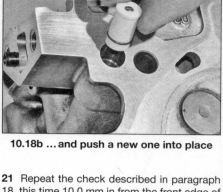

10.18b ... and push a new one into place

of two metal rods with 90-degree angled ends **(see illustration)**. Do not prise between the mating faces of the cylinder head and block, as this may damage the gasket faces.

15 Lift the cylinder head from the block, and recover the gasket.

Preparation for refitting

16 The mating faces of the cylinder head and cylinder block must be perfectly clean before refitting the head. Ford recommend the use of a scouring agent for this purpose, but acceptable results can be achieved by using a hard plastic or wood scraper to remove all traces of gasket and carbon. The same method can be used to clean the piston crowns. Take particular care to avoid scoring or gouging the cylinder head/cylinder block mating surfaces during the cleaning operations, as aluminium alloy is easily damaged. Make sure that the carbon is not allowed to enter the oil and water passages – this is particularly important for the lubrication system, as carbon could block the oil supply to the engine's components. Using adhesive tape and paper, seal the water, oil and bolt holes in the cylinder block. To prevent carbon entering the gap between the pistons and bores, smear a little grease in the gap. After cleaning each piston, use a small brush to remove all traces of grease and carbon from the gap, then wipe away the remainder with a clean rag.

17 Check the mating surfaces of the cylinder block and the cylinder head for nicks, deep scratches and other damage. If slight, they

may be removed carefully with a file, but if excessive, machining may be the only alternative to renewal. If warpage of the cylinder head gasket surface is suspected, use a straight-edge to check it for distortion. Refer to Part D of this Chapter if necessary.

18 Thoroughly clean the threads of the cylinder head bolt holes in the cylinder block. Ensure that the bolts run freely in their threads, and that all traces of oil and water are removed from each bolt hole. If required, pull the oil feed non-return valve from the cylinder head, and check the ball moves freely. Push a new valve into place if necessary **(see illustrations)**.

Gasket selection

19 The gasket thickness is indicated by notches/holes on the front edge of the gasket. If the crankshaft or pistons/connecting rods have not been disturbed, fit a new gasket with the same number of notches/holes as the previous one. If the crankshaft/piston or connecting rods have been disturbed, it's necessary to work out the piston protrusion as follows:

20 Remove the crankshaft timing pin, then turn the crankshaft until pistons 1 and 4 are at TDC (Top Dead Centre). Position a dial test indicator (dial gauge) on the cylinder block adjacent to the rear of No 1 piston, and zero it on the block face. Transfer the probe to the crown of No 1 piston (10.0 mm in from the rear edge), then slowly turn the crankshaft back-and-forth past TDC, noting the highest reading on the indicator. Record this reading as protrusion A.

21 Repeat the check described in paragraph 18, this time 10.0 mm in from the front edge of the No 1 piston crown. Record this reading as protrusion B.

22 Add protrusion A to protrusion B, then divide the result by 2 to obtain an average reading for piston No 1.

23 Repeat the procedure described in paragraphs 20 to 22 on piston 4, then turn the crankshaft through 180° and carry out the procedure on the piston Nos 2 and 3 **(see illustration)**. Check that there is a maximum difference of 0.07 mm protrusion between any two pistons.

24 If a dial test indicator is not available, piston protrusion may be measured using a straight-edge and feeler blades or Vernier calipers. However, this is much less accurate, and cannot therefore be recommended.

25 Note the greatest piston protrusion measurement, and use this to determine the correct cylinder head gasket from the table in the Specifications. The series of notches/holes on the side of the gasket are used for thickness identification **(see illustration)**.

Refitting

26 Turn the crankshaft and position Nos 1 and 4 pistons at TDC, then turn the crankshaft a quarter turn (90°) anti-clockwise.

27 Thoroughly clean the surfaces of the cylinder head and block.

28 Make sure that the locating dowels are in place, then fit the correct gasket the right way round on the cylinder block **(see illustration)**.

29 Carefully lower the cylinder head onto the

10.23 Measure the piston protrusion using a DTI gauge

10.25 Cylinder head gasket thickness identification notches

10.28 Ensure the gasket locates over the dowels

10.32 Cylinder head bolt tightening sequence

11.8 Apply a bead of sealant to the sump or crankcase mating surface. Ensure the sealant is applied to the inside of the retaining bolt holes

gasket and block, making sure that it locates correctly onto the dowels.

30 Apply a smear of grease to the threads, and to the underside of the heads of the new cylinder head bolts.

31 Carefully insert the cylinder head bolts into their holes (do not drop them in) and initially finger-tighten them.

32 Working progressively and in sequence, tighten the cylinder head bolts to their Stage 1 torque setting, using a torque wrench and suitable socket **(see illustration)**.

33 Once all the bolts have been tightened to their Stage 1 torque setting, working again in the specified sequence, tighten each bolt to the specified Stage 2 setting. Finally, angle-tighten the bolts through the specified Stage 3 angle. It is recommended that an angle-measuring gauge is used during this stage of tightening, to ensure accuracy. **Note:** *Retightening of the cylinder head bolts after running the engine is not required.*

34 Refit the hydraulic tappets, rocker arms, and camshaft housing (complete with camshafts) as described in Section 9.

35 Refit the timing belt as described in Section 7.

36 The remainder of refitting is a reversal of removal, noting the following points.

a) *Use a new seal when refitting the coolant outlet housing.*

b) *When refitting a cylinder head, it is good practice to renew the thermostat.*

c) *Refit the camshaft position sensor and set the air gap with reference to Chapter 4A Section 12.*

d) *Tighten all fasteners to the specified torque where given.*

e) *Refill the cooling system as described in Chapter 1 Section 25.*

f) *The engine may run erratically for the first few miles, until the engine management ECM relearns its stored values.*

11 Sum – removal and refitting

Removal

1 Drain the engine oil, then clean and refit the engine oil drain plug, tightening it securely. If the engine is nearing its service interval when the oil and filter are due for renewal, it is recommended that the filter is also removed, and a new one fitted. After reassembly, the engine can then be refilled with fresh oil. Refer to Chapter 1 Section 3 for further information.

2 Apply the handbrake, then jack up the front of the vehicle and support it on axle stands (see *Jacking and vehicle support*). Undo the bolts and remove the engine undershield.

3 Remove the exhaust front pipe as described in Chapter 4A Section 18.

4 Where necessary, disconnect the wiring connector from the oil temperature sender unit, which is screwed into the sump.

5 Progressively slacken and remove all the sump retaining bolts/nuts. Since the sump bolts vary in length, remove each bolt in turn, and store it in its correct fitted order by pushing it through a clearly-marked cardboard template. This will avoid the possibility of installing the bolts in the wrong locations on refitting.

6 Try to break the joint by striking the sump with the palm of your hand, then lower and withdraw the sump from under the car. If the sump is stuck (which is quite likely) use a putty knife or similar, carefully inserted between the sump and block. Ease the knife along the joint until the sump is released. While the sump is removed, take the opportunity to check the oil pump pick-up/strainer for signs of clogging or splitting. If necessary, remove the pump as

described in Section 12, and clean or renew the strainer.

Refitting

7 Clean all traces of sealant from the mating surfaces of the cylinder block/crankcase and sump, then use a clean rag to wipe out the sump and the engine's interior.

8 Ensure that the sump mating surfaces are clean and dry, then apply a 3mm diameter bead of sealant (Ford part No WSE-M4G323-A4) to the sump mating surface **(see illustration)**. The sealant must be applied to the inside of the bolt holes. Note that the sump must be installed within 10 minutes of applying the sealant, and the bolts tightened within a further 5 minutes.

9 Offer up the sump to the cylinder block/crankcase. Refit its retaining bolts/nuts, ensuring that each bolt is screwed into its original location. Tighten the bolts evenly and progressively to the specified torque setting **(see illustration)**.

10 Reconnect the wiring connector to the oil temperature sensor (where fitted).

11 Lower the vehicle to the ground, wait at least 30 minutes and then refill the engine with oil as described in Chapter 1 Section 3.

11.9 Refit the sump and tighten the bolts

12.4 Oil pick-up tube bolts

12.5 Oil pump retaining bolts

12 Oil pump – removal, inspection and refitting

Removal

1 Remove the sump as described in Section 11.

2 Remove the crankshaft sprocket as described in Section 8. Recover the locating key from the crankshaft.

3 Disconnect the wiring plug, undo the bolts and remove the crankshaft position sensor, located on the right-hand end of the cylinder block.

4 Undo the three bolts and remove the oil pump pick-up tube from the pump/block **(see illustration)**. Discard the oil seal, a new one must be fitted.

5 Undo the 8 bolts, and remove the oil pump **(see illustration)**.

Inspection

6 Undo and remove the Torx bolts securing the cover to the oil pump **(see illustration)**. Examine the pump rotors and body for signs of wear and damage. If worn, the complete pump must be renewed.

7 Remove the circlip, and extract the cap, valve piston and spring, noting which way around they are fitted **(see illustrations)**. The condition of the relief valve spring can only be measured by comparing it with a new one; if there is any doubt about its condition, it should also be renewed.

8 Refit the relief valve piston and spring, then secure them in place with the circlip.

9 Refit the cover to the oil pump, and tighten the Torx bolts securely.

Refitting

10 Remove all traces of sealant, and thoroughly clean the mating surfaces of the oil pump and cylinder block.

11 Apply a 4 mm diameter bead of silicone sealant to the mating face of the cylinder block **(see illustration)**. Ensure that no sealant enters any of the holes in the block.

12.6 Undo the Torx bolts and remove the pump cover

12.7a Remove the circlip …

12.7b …cap…

12.7c …spring…

12.7d …and piston

12.11 Apply a bead of sealant to the cylinder block mating surface

12.12a Fit a new seal …

12.12b …align the pump gear flats …

12.12c …with those of the crankshaft

12 With a new oil seal fitted, refit the oil pump over the end of the crankshaft, aligning the flats in the pump drive gear with the flats machined in the crankshaft **(see illustrations)**. Note that new oil pumps are supplied with the oil seal already fitted, and a seal protector sleeve. The sleeve fits over the end of the crankshaft to protect the seal as the pump is fitted.

13 Install the oil pump bolts and tighten them to the specified torque.

14 Refit the oil pick-up tube to the pump/cylinder block using a new O-ring seal. Ensure the oil dipstick guide tube is correctly refitted.

15 Refit the woodruff key to the crankshaft, and slide the crankshaft sprocket into place.

16 The remainder of refitting is a reversal of removal.

13 Oil cooler –
removal and refitting

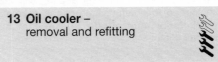

Removal

1 Apply the handbrake, then jack up the front of the vehicle and support it on axle stands (see *Jacking and vehicle support*). Undo the fasteners and remove the engine undershield.

2 The oil cooler is fitted to the front of the oil filter housing. Drain the coolant as described in Chapter 1 Section 25.

3 Drain the engine oil as described in Chapter 1 Section 6, or be prepared for fluid spillage.

4 Undo the bolts/stud and remove the oil cooler **(see illustration)**. Recover the gasket.

Refitting

5 Fit a new gasket into the recesses in the oil filter housing, and refit the cooler. Tighten the bolts securely.

6 Refill or top-up the cooling system and engine oil level as described in Chapter 1 or *Weekly checks* (as applicable). Start the engine, and check the oil cooler for signs of leakage.

14 Oil seals – renewal

Crankshaft

Right-hand oil seal

1 Remove the crankshaft sprocket and Woodruff key as described in Section 8.

2 Measure and note the fitted depth of the oil seal.

3 Pull the oil seal from the housing using a screwdriver. Alternatively, drill a small hole in the oil seal, and use a self-tapping screw and a pair of pliers to remove it **(see illustration)**.

4 Clean the oil seal housing and the crankshaft sealing surface.

5 The new seal should be supplied with a protective sleeve, which fits over the end of the crankshaft to prevent any damage to the seal lip. With the sleeve in place, press the seal (open end first) into the pump to the previously-noted depth, using a suitable tube or socket **(see illustrations)**.

13.4 Undo the oil cooler bolts/stud

6 Where applicable, remove the plastic sleeve from the end of the crankshaft.

7 Refit the crankshaft sprocket as described in Section 8.

Left-hand oil seal

8 Remove the flywheel, as described in Section 16.

9 Measure and note the fitted depth of the oil seal.

10 Pull the oil seal from the housing using a screwdriver. Alternatively, drill a small hole in the oil seal, and use a self-tapping screw and a pair of pliers to remove it **(see illustration 14.3)**.

11 Clean the oil seal housing and the crankshaft sealing surface.

12 The new seal should be supplied with a protective sleeve, which fits over the end of the crankshaft to prevent any damage to the

14.3 Take great care not to mark the crankshaft whilst levering out the oil seal

14.5a Slide the seal and protective sleeve over the end of the crankshaft …

14.5b …and press the seal into place

14.12 Slide the seal and protective sleeve over the left-hand end of the crankshaft

14.16 Drill a hole, insert a self-tapping screw, and pull the seal from place using pliers

14.18a Use the correct tool to fit the seal...

seal lip **(see illustration)**. With the sleeve in place, press the seal (open end first) into the housing to the previously-noted depth, using a suitable tube or socket.

13 Where applicable, remove the plastic sleeve from the end of the crankshaft.

14 Refit the flywheel, as described in Section 16.

Camshaft

15 Remove the camshaft sprocket as described in Section 8. In principle there is no need to remove the timing belt completely, but remember that if the belt has been contaminated with oil, it must be renewed.

16 Pull the oil seal from the housing using a hooked instrument. Alternatively, drill a small hole in the oil seal and use a self-tapping screw and a pair of pliers to remove it **(see illustration)**.

17 Clean the oil seal housing and the camshaft sealing surface.

18 Press the seal (open end first) into the housing to the previously-noted depth, using either the correct tool (303-684), a suitable tube or a socket which bears only of the outer edge of the seal **(see illustrations)**. If the seal was supplied with a protective sleeve, remove it.

19 Refit the camshaft sprocket as described in Section 8.

20 Where necessary, fit a new timing belt with reference to Section 7.

---

15 Oil pressure switch and level sensor – removal and refitting

---

Removal

Oil pressure switch

1 The oil pressure switch is located at the front of the cylinder block, adjacent to the oil dipstick guide tube. Note that on some models, access to the switch may be improved if the vehicle is jacked up and supported on axle stands, then undo the bolts and remove the engine undershield so that the switch can be reached from underneath (see *Jacking and vehicle support*).

2 Remove the protective sleeve from

the wiring plug (where applicable), then disconnect the wiring from the switch.

3 Unscrew the switch from the cylinder block, and recover the sealing washer **(see illustration)**. Be prepared for oil spillage, and if the switch is to be left removed from the engine for any length of time, plug the hole in the cylinder block.

Oil level sensor

4 The oil level sensor is located at the rear of the cylinder block. Jack up the front of the vehicle and support it securely on axle stands (see *Jacking and vehicle support*). Undo the bolts and remove the engine undershield.

5 Reach up between the driveshaft and the cylinder block, and disconnect the sensor wiring plug **(see illustration)**.

6 Using an open-ended spanner, unscrew the sensor and withdraw it from position.

Refitting

Oil pressure switch

7 Examine the sealing washer for any signs of damage or deterioration, and if necessary renew.

8 Refit the switch, complete with washer, and tighten it to the specified torque where given.

9 Refit the engine undershield, and lower the vehicle to the ground.

Oil level sensor

10 Smear a little silicone sealant on the threads and refit the sensor to the cylinder block, tightening it securely.

15.3 The oil pressure switch is located on the front face of the cylinder block (arrowed)

14.18b ...or a suitable socket

11 Reconnect the sensor wiring plug.

12 Refit the engine undershield, and lower the vehicle to the ground.

---

16 Flywheel – removal, inspection and refitting

Flywheel

Removal

Note: *New flywheel retaining bolts must be used on refitting.*

1 Remove the clutch assembly as described in Chapter 6 Section 6.

2 Prevent the flywheel from turning by locking the ring gear teeth with a similar arrangement

15.5 The oil level sensor is located on the rear face of the cylinder block (arrowed)

16.2 Homemade flywheel locking tool

16.5 On this example the flywheel bolts are off centre

16.6 Check the movement between the primary and secondary mass.

to that shown **(see illustration)**. Alternatively, bolt a strap between the flywheel and the cylinder block/crankcase.

3 Slacken and remove the retaining bolts and remove the flywheel, noting its locating dowel. Do not drop it, as it is very heavy. Discard the bolts, they must be renewed whenever they are disturbed.

Inspection

4 A dual mass flywheel is fitted to all engines. Detailed checking of the flywheel requires the use of specific tools, that are unlikely to be available to the home mechanic. However some basic checking can easily be performed.

5 Start by checking the alignment between the primary mass and the secondary mass. At rest the flywheel retaining bolts will be accessible through the holes in the secondary mass **(see illustration)**.

6 The maximum travel of the primary mass in relation to the secondary mass should not exceed 15 teeth (or 20 degrees). Note that this is a general guide and if in doubt remove the flywheel and have a suitably equipped specialist check the flywheel **(see illustration)**.

7 Inspect the flywheel for any grease or debris from the interface between the fixed part (the primary mass) and the movable part of the flywheel (the secondary mass). Replace any flywheel that has grease visible.

8 If the ring gear is badly worn or has missing teeth, then the entire dual mass flywheel must be replaced.

9 If any doubt to the condition of the flywheel exists, despite the expense we recommend replacing it.

16.12 Use an angle gauge to fully tighten the flywheel

Refitting

10 Clean the mating surfaces of the flywheel and crankshaft and remove all traces of locking compound from the crankshaft threaded holes.

11 Fit the flywheel to the crankshaft, engaging it with the crankshaft locating dowel, and fit the new retaining bolts. **Note:** *If the new bolts are not supplied pre-coated with locking compound, apply a few drops prior to fitting the bolts.*

12 Lock the flywheel using the method employed on dismantling then, working in a diagonal sequence, tighten all the retaining bolts to the specified torque setting **(see illustration)**.

13 Refit the clutch assembly as described in Chapter 6 Section 6.

| 17 | Engine/transmission mountings – inspection and renewal | |

General

1 The engine/transmission mountings seldom require attention, but broken or deteriorated mountings should be renewed immediately, or the added strain placed on the driveline components may cause damage or wear.

2 While separate mountings may be removed and refitted individually, if more than one is disturbed at a time – such as if the engine/transmission unit is removed from its mountings – they must be reassembled and their fasteners tightened in the position marked on removal.

17.10 Remove the mounting

3 On reassembly, the complete weight of the engine/transmission unit must not be taken by the mountings until all are correctly aligned with the marks made on removal. Tighten the engine/transmission mounting fasteners to their specified torque wrench settings.

Inspection

4 During the check, the engine/transmission unit must be raised slightly, to remove its weight from the mountings.

5 Raise the front of the vehicle, and support it securely on axle stands. Position a jack under the sump, with a large block of wood between the jack head and the sump, then carefully raise the engine/transmission just enough to take the weight off the mountings.

> ⚠️ *Warning: DO NOT place any part of your body under the engine when it is supported only by a jack.*

6 Check the mountings to see if the rubber is cracked, hardened or separated from the metal components. Sometimes the rubber will split right down the centre.

7 Check for relative movement between each mounting's brackets and the engine/transmission or body (use a large screwdriver or lever to attempt to move the mountings). If movement is noted, lower the engine and check-tighten the mounting fasteners.

Renewal

Note: *The following paragraphs assume the engine is supported beneath the sump as described earlier.*

Right-hand mounting

8 Lift up the coolant expansion tank and position it to one side. Note there is no need to disconnect the coolant pipes.

9 Mark the position of the mounting on the vehicle on the right-hand inner wing panel, and then undo the 2 bolts securing the mounting.

10 Undo the 2 retaining bolts from the engine side of the mounting and then remove the mounting **(see illustration)**.

11 Re-align the marks made on removal. Tighten all fasteners to the torque wrench settings specified.

Left-hand mounting

12 Remove the air filter housing as described in Chapter 4A Section 3.

17.14 Remove the battery tray

17.15a Remove the mounting bolts...

17.15b ...lift off the plate...

17.15c ...and remove the mounting

17.18 Remove the bolts

13 Remove the battery as described in Chapter 5 Section 3, then undo the 3 bolts and remove the battery tray. Disconnect any wiring as the tray is withdrawn.

14 Unclip the wiring loom from the battery tray support panel, remove the bolts and withdraw the support panel **(see illustration)**.

15 With the transmission supported, note the position of the mounting then unscrew the centre retaining bolt to release the upper half of the mounting from the transmission **(see illustrations)**. Note that there are several versions of the left-hand mounting, depending on the transmission fitted. Removal is similar in all cases.

16 Refitting is a reversal of removal. Re-align the mounting in the position noted on removal, then tighten all fasteners to the specified torque wrench settings.

Torque rod (roll restrictor)

17 Jack up and support the front of the vehicle (see *Jacking and vehicle support*) and then remove the engine undershield.

18 Remove the 3 mounting bolts from the transmission. Note, that the bolts are different lengths on five speed transmissions. Remove the single bolt from the subframe **(see illustration)**.

19 With the aid of an assistant pivot the engine (assuming the two main engine mountings are in position) and work the mounting free.

20 On refitting, ensure that the bolts are securely tightened to the specified torque wrench setting.

Notes

Chapter 2 Part B
1.8 litre engine in-car repair procedures

Contents

Degrees of difficulty

Easy, suitable for novice with little experience		**Fairly easy,** suitable for beginner with some experience		**Fairly difficult,** suitable for competent DIY mechanic		**Difficult,** suitable for experienced DIY mechanic		**Very difficult,** suitable for expert DIY or professional	

Specifications

General

Engine type.	Four-cylinder, in-line, single overhead camshaft, cast-iron cylinder head and engine block
Designation	DuraTorq-TDCi
Engine code	FFWA/QYWA
Power output:	
FFWA	74 kW @ 3850 rpm
QYWA 9	2 kW @ 3700 rpm
Torque output:	
FFWA	280 Nm
QYWA	320 Nm
Capacity	1753 cc
Bore	82.5 mm
Stroke	82.0 mm
Compression ratio	17.0: 1
Firing order	1-3-4-2 (No 1 cylinder at timing belt end)
Direction of crankshaft rotation	Clockwise (seen from right-hand side of vehicle)

Camshaft

Camshaft bearing journal diameter	27.96 to 27.98 mm
Camshaft endfloat	0.100 to 0.240 mm

Valves

Valve clearances (cold):	
Inlet	0.30 to 0.40 mm
Exhaust.	0.45 to 0.55 mm

Cylinder head gasket selection

	Gasket (mm)	
Piston protusion:		
0.55 to 0.60 mm	1.27 mm (2 notches)	
0.60 to 0.65 mm	1.32 mm (3 notches)	
0.65 to 0.70 mm	1.37 mm (4 notches)	
0.70 to 0.75 mm	1.42 mm (5 notches)	
0.75 to 0.80 mm	1.475 mm (6 notches)	
0.80 to 0.85 mm	1.52 (7 notches)	
Maximum distortion	0.600 mm	

Camshaft

Camshaft bearing diameter (nominal)	30.50 to 30.52 mm	
Camshaft endfloat	0.1 to 0.24 mm	

Lubrication

Oil pressure – minimum (engine at operating temperature):		
At idle	0.54 bars	
At 2000 rpm	1.39 bars	
Oil pump clearance (inner-to-outer rotors)	0.23 mm	

Torque wrench settings

	Nm	lbf ft
Air conditioning compressor	25	18
Alternator bracket to block:		
M10 bolts	23	17
M8 bolts	15	11
Nuts	15	11
Auxiliary drivebelt idler pulley bolt	48	35
Auxiliary drivebelt tensioner mounting bolts	23	17
Auxiliary shaft oil seal carrier	23	17
Big-end bearing cap bolts: *		
Stage 1	27	20
Stage 2	Angle-tighten a further 60°	
Stage 3	Angle-tighten a further 20°	
Camshaft bearing cap	20	15
Camshaft oil baffle	20	15
Camshaft sprocket bolt	50	37
Coolant pump pulley bolts	23	17
Crankcase ventilation oil separator	25	18
Crankshaft oil seal carrier	20	15
Crankshaft position sensor bracket	10	7
Crankshaft pulley bolt: *		
Stage 1	100	74
Stage 2	Angle-tighten a further 180°	
Cylinder head bolts: *		
Stage 1	20	15
Stage 2	54	40
Stage 3	Angle-tighten a further 90°	
Stage 4:		
Short bolts	Angle-tighten a further 70°	
Long bolts	Angle-tighten a further 90°	
Cylinder head cover bolts	5	4
Engine mountings:		
Right-hand mounting retaining bolts	90	66
Right-hand mounting bracket-to-engine bolts	56	41
Left-hand mounting nuts	48	35
Left-hand mounting bracket to transmission	80	59
Left-hand mounting centre bolt	148	109
Lower-rear torque rod bolts	80	59
Engine oil drain plug	36	27
Flywheel bolts: *		
Stage 1	35	26
Stage 2	Angle-tighten a further 45°	
Fuel injection pump sprocket	42	31
Lower crankcase to cylinder block	11	8
Main bearing cap bolts:		
Stage 1	45	33
Stage 2	70	52
Stage 2	Angle-tighten a further 60°	

Torque wrench settings (continued)

	Nm	lbf ft
Oil baffle plate nuts	20	15
Oil inlet pipe bracket to block	10	7
Oil pressure switch	20	15
Oil pump bolts/studs:		
Stage 1	10	7
Stage 2	23	17
Roadwheel nuts	Refer to Chapter 1	
Sump bolts	11	8
TDC setting plug cover	24	18
Timing belt inner cover bolts:		
M6	10	7
M8	24	18
Timing belt outer covers	7	5
Timing belt tensioner bolt	50	37
Timing belt tensioner to cylinder head	50	37
Timing chain guide retaining bolts	23	17
Timing chain housing:		
M6	10	7
M8	23	17
Timing chain tensioner	63	46
Transmission-to-engine bolts	48	35

Note: * Do not re-use

1 General Information

How to use this Chapter

1 This Part of Chapter 2 is devoted to repair procedures possible while the engine is still installed in the vehicle. Since these procedures are based on the assumption that the engine is installed in the vehicle, if the engine has been removed from the vehicle and mounted on a stand, some of the preliminary dismantling steps outlined will not apply.

2 Information concerning engine/transmission removal and refitting and engine overhaul, can be found in Part E of this Chapter.

Engine description

3 The DuraTorq-TDCi engine is a further development of the Endura-Di unit, and both units featured in previous Ford models. The engine is an eight-valve, single overhead camshaft (SOHC), four-cylinder, in-line type, mounted transversely at the front of the vehicle, with the transmission on its left-hand end. It is only available in 1.8 litre form.

4 All major engine castings are of cast-iron; the engine has a lower crankcase which is bolted to the underside of the cylinder block/crankcase, with a sump bolted under that. This arrangement offers greater rigidity than the normal sump arrangement, and helps to reduce engine vibration.

5 The crankshaft runs in five main bearings, the centre main bearing's upper half incorporating thrustwashers to control crankshaft endfloat. The connecting rods rotate on horizontally-split bearing shells at their big-ends. The pistons are attached to the connecting rods by gudgeon pins which are a floating fit in the connecting rod small-end eyes, secured by circlips. The aluminium alloy pistons are fitted with three piston rings: two compression rings and an oil control ring. After manufacture, the cylinder bores and piston skirts are measured and classified into two grades, which must be carefully matched together to ensure the correct piston/cylinder clearance; no oversizes are available to permit reboring.

6 The inlet and exhaust valves are each closed by coil springs; they operate in guides which are shrink-fitted into the cylinder head, as are the valve seat inserts.

7 These engines are unusual in that the fuel injection pump/high-pressure pump is driven by an offset double-row ('gemini') chain from a sprocket on the crankshaft, with the camshaft being driven from the injection pump sprocket by a conventional toothed timing belt.

8 The camshaft operates the eight valves via conventional cam followers with shims. The camshaft rotates in five bearings that are line-bored directly in the cylinder head and the (bolted-on) bearing caps; this means that the bearing caps are not available separately from the cylinder head, and must not be interchanged with caps from another engine.

9 The vacuum pump (used for the brake servo and other vacuum actuators) is driven by a pushrod operated directly by a special lobe on the camshaft.

10 The coolant pump is bolted to the right-hand end of the cylinder block, and is driven with the steering pump and alternator by a multi-ribbed auxiliary drivebelt from the crankshaft pulley.

11 When working on this engine, note that Torx-type (both male and female heads) and hexagon socket (Allen head) fasteners are widely used; a good selection of bits, with the necessary adapters, will be required so that these can be unscrewed without damage and, on reassembly, tightened to the torque wrench settings specified.

Lubrication system

12 Lubrication is by means of a G-rotor pump, which is mounted on the crankshaft right-hand end, and draws oil through a strainer located in the sump. The pump forces oil through an externally-mounted full-flow cartridge-type filter. From the filter, the oil is pumped into a main gallery in the cylinder block/crankcase, from where it is distributed to the crankshaft (main bearings) and cylinder head. An oil cooler is fitted next to the oil filter, at the rear of the block. The cooler is supplied with coolant from the engine cooling system.

13 While the crankshaft and camshaft bearings receive a pressurised supply, the camshaft lobes and valves are lubricated by splash, as are all other engine components. The undersides of the pistons are cooled by oil, sprayed from nozzles fitted above the upper main bearing shells. The turbocharger receives its own pressurised oil supply.

Operations with engine in car

14 The following major repair operations can be accomplished without removing the engine from the vehicle. However, owners should note that any operation involving the removal of the sump requires careful forethought, depending on the level of skill and the tools and facilities available; refer to the relevant text for details.

a) Compression pressure – testing.
b) Cylinder head cover – removal and refitting.
c) Timing belt cover – removal and refitting.
d) Timing belt – renewal.
e) Timing belt tensioner and sprockets – removal and refitting.
f) Camshaft oil seals – renewal.
g) Camshaft and cam followers – removal and refitting.

h) *Cylinder head – removal, overhaul and refitting.*
i) *Cylinder head and pistons – decarbonising.*
j) *Sump – removal and refitting.*
k) *Crankshaft oil seals – renewal.*
l) *Oil pump – removal and refitting.*
m) *Piston/connecting rod assemblies – removal and refitting (but see note below).*
n) *Flywheel – removal and refitting.*
o) *Engine/transmission mountings – removal and refitting.*

15 Note: It is possible to remove the pistons and connecting rods (after removing the cylinder head and sump) without removing the engine, however, this is not recommended. Work of this nature is more easily and thoroughly completed with the engine on the bench, as described in Chapter 2E.
16 Clean the engine compartment and the exterior of the engine with some type of degreaser before any work is done (and/or clean the engine using a steam cleaner). It will make the job easier and will help to keep dirt out of the internal areas of the engine.
17 Depending on the components involved, it may be helpful to remove the bonnet, to improve access to the engine as repairs are performed (refer to Chapter 11 Section 7 if necessary). Cover the wings to prevent damage to the paint; special covers are available, but an old bedspread or blanket will also work.

2 Compression and leakdown tests – description and interpretation

Compression test

Note: *A compression tester suitable for use with diesel engines will be required for this test.*
1 When engine performance is down, or if misfiring occurs which cannot be attributed to the fuel or emissions systems, a compression test can provide diagnostic clues as to the engine's condition. If the test is performed regularly, it can give warning of trouble before any other symptoms become apparent.
2 The engine must be fully warmed-up to normal operating temperature, the battery must be fully-charged and the glow plugs must be removed. The aid of an assistant will be required.
3 Make sure that the ignition is switched off (take out the key). Remove the cover from the top of the engine, then disconnect the wiring plugs from the injectors.
4 Remove the glow plugs as described in Chapter 5 Section 11.
5 Fit a compression tester to the No 1 cylinder glow plug hole.
6 Crank the engine for several seconds on the starter motor. After one or two revolutions, the compression pressure should build-up to a maximum figure and then stabilise. Record the highest reading obtained.

7 Repeat the test on the remaining cylinders, recording the pressure in each.
8 The cause of poor compression is less easy to establish on a diesel engine than on a petrol engine. The effect of introducing oil into the cylinders (wet testing) is not conclusive, because there is a risk that the oil will sit in the recess on the piston crown, instead of passing to the rings. However, the following can be used as a rough guide to diagnosis.
9 All cylinders should produce very similar pressures. Any great difference indicates the existence of a fault. Note that the compression should build-up quickly in a healthy engine. Low compression on the first stroke, followed by gradually increasing pressure on successive strokes, indicates worn piston rings. A low compression reading on the first stroke, which does not build-up during successive strokes, indicates leaking valves or a blown head gasket (a cracked head could also be the cause).
10 A low reading from two adjacent cylinders is almost certainly due to the head gasket having blown between them and the presence of coolant in the engine oil will confirm this.
11 On completion, remove the compression tester, and refit the glow plugs, with reference to Chapter 5 Section 11.
12 Take out the ignition key, then reconnect the injection pump wiring connector.

Leakdown test

13 A leakdown test measures the rate at which compressed air fed into the cylinder is lost. It is an alternative to a compression test, and in many ways it is better, since the escaping air provides easy identification of where pressure loss is occurring (piston rings, valves or head gasket).
14 The equipment required for leakdown testing is unlikely to be available to the home mechanic. If poor compression is suspected, have the test performed by a suitably-equipped garage.

3 Setting the engine to Top Dead Centre (TDC) on No 1 cylinder

General information

1 TDC is the highest point in the cylinder that each piston reaches as it travels up and down when the crankshaft turns. Each piston reaches TDC at the end of the compression stroke and again at the end of the exhaust stroke, but TDC generally refers to piston position on the compression stroke. No 1 piston is at the timing belt end of the engine.
2 Positioning No 1 piston at TDC is an essential part of many procedures, such as timing belt removal and camshaft removal.
3 The design of the engines covered in this Chapter is such that piston-to-valve contact may occur if the camshaft or crankshaft is turned with the timing belt removed. For this reason, it is important to ensure that the camshaft and crankshaft do not move in relation to each other once the timing belt has been removed from the engine.

Setting TDC on No 1 cylinder

Note: *Suitable tools will be required to lock the camshaft and the fuel injection pump sprocket in position during this procedure – see text.*
4 Disconnect the battery negative (earth) lead (refer to Chapter 5 Section 3).
5 Remove the cylinder head cover as described in Section 4.
6 Loosen the right-hand front wheel nuts, then firmly apply the handbrake. Jack up the front of the car, and support on axle stands (see *Jacking and vehicle support*, 5). Remove the right-hand front wheel.
7 Undo the fasteners and remove the engine undershield **(see illustration)**.

3.7 Undo the fasteners and remove the engine undershield

3.8a Offset slot in the camshaft aligned with the cylinder head

3.8b Flat bar engaged with the slot in the camshaft

3.10a Tool fabricated to locate the crankshaft at TDC...

3.10b ...screw the tool into the cylinder block to locate with the crankshaft

3.12a Unscrew the blanking plug...

3.12b ...and insert the timing pin

8 When No 1 cylinder is set to TDC on compression, an offset slot in the left-hand end of the camshaft (left as seen from the driver's seat) should align with the top surface of the cylinder head, to allow a special tool (Ford No 303-376) to be fitted. This tool can be substituted by a suitable piece of flat bar **(see illustrations)**. There is no need to fit this tool at this stage, but check that the slot comes into the required alignment while setting TDC – if the slot is above the level of the head, No 1 cylinder could be on the exhaust stroke.

9 If required, further confirmation that No 1 cylinder is on the compression stroke can be inferred from the positions of the camshaft lobes for No 1 cylinder. When the cylinder is on compression, the inlet and exhaust lobes should be pointing upwards (ie, not depressing the cam followers). The camshaft lobes are only visible once the oil baffle plate is removed, and the securing nuts also retain two of the camshaft bearing caps – for more information, refer to Section 9.

10 A TDC timing hole is provided on the front of the cylinder block, to permit the crankshaft to be located more accurately at TDC. A timing pin (Ford service tool 303-193, obtainable from Ford dealers or a tool supplier) screws into the hole, and the crankshaft is then turned so that it contacts the end of the tool. A tool can be fabricated to set the timing at TDC, using a piece of threaded rod **(see**

illustrations). The fabricated tool has the following dimensions:
a) *Thread diameter = 10 mm.*
b) *Length from 1st nut face to the point = 47 mm.*
c) *Point ground down to 8 mm.*

11 To gain access to the blanking plug fitted over the timing pin hole, remove the auxiliary drivebelt, then unbolt and remove the alternator coupling, as described in the alternator removal procedure in Chapter 5 Section 6.

12 Remove the camshaft setting tool from the slot, and turn the engine back slightly from the TDC position. Unscrew the timing pin blanking plug (which is located in a deeply-recessed hole), and screw in the timing pin **(see illustrations)**. Now carefully turn the crankshaft forwards until it contacts the timing pin (it should be possible to feel this point – the crankshaft cannot then be turned any further forward).

13 Once No 1 cylinder has been positioned at TDC on the compression stroke, TDC for any of the other cylinders can then be located by rotating the crankshaft clockwise 180° at a time and following the firing order (see *Specifications*).

14 Before rotating the crankshaft again, make sure that the timing pin and camshaft setting bar are removed. When operations are complete, do not forget to refit the timing pin blanking plug.

4 Cylinder head cover –
removal and refitting

Removal

1 Remove the cover from the top of the engine and then remove the upper and lower windscreen cowl panels as described in Chapter 12 Section 12.

2 Undo the 2 bolts and detach the Manifold Absolute Pressure (MAP) sensor from the cylinder head cover. Move the sensor to one side **(see illustration)**.

3 Noting their positions carefully for refitting, release the hose clips and detach the

4.2 Undo the bolts and move the MAP sensor to one side

4.3a Disconnect the ventilation hoses (1), and the camshaft position sensor (2)...

4.3b ...then disconnect the ventilation hose at the rear

4.5a Unscrew the securing bolts...

4.5b ...and lift away the cylinder head cover

crankcase ventilation hoses from the cylinder head cover **(see illustrations)**. There are two hoses at the front, and one at the rear. Move the hoses aside as far as possible.

4 Disconnect the camshaft position sensor wiring plug **(see illustration 4.3a)**.

5 Unscrew the three securing bolts, and lift the cylinder head cover off the engine **(see illustrations)**. Discard the gasket – a new one must be fitted.

6 If required, the baffle plate fitted below the cover can be removed by unscrewing the nuts and taking off the spacer plates and sleeves – note, however, that these nuts also secure Nos 2 and 4 camshaft bearing caps. Note the positions of all components carefully for refitting.

Refitting

7 Clean the sealing surfaces of the cover

and the head, and check the condition of the rubber seals fitted to the cover bolts.

8 Before refitting the cover, check that the crankcase ventilation holes are clear. The connection at the rear of the cover leads to the ventilation valve – if this appears to be blocked, use a suitable degreaser to wash out the valve (it is not advisable to use petrol, as this may damage the valve itself).

9 Lightly lubricate the surfaces of the gasket with fresh oil, then fit the gasket to the cover, making sure it is correctly located.

10 Lower the cover into position, ensuring that the gasket is not disturbed, then fit the three bolts and tighten them a little at a time, so that the cover is drawn down evenly to make a good seal.

11 Further refitting is a reversal of removal. Ensure that the pipes are routed as noted on removal, and that the ventilation hoses are

correctly and securely reconnected.

12 When the engine has been run for some time, check for signs of oil leakage from the gasket joint.

5 Valve clearances – checking and adjustment

Checking

1 Remove the cylinder head cover as described in Section 4.

2 Remove the baffle plate fitted below the cover by unscrewing the four nuts and taking off the spacer plates and sleeves. Note, however, that these nuts also secure Nos 2 and 4 camshaft bearing caps – refit the nuts temporarily, once the baffle plate has been removed **(see illustrations)**. Note the positions of all components carefully for refitting.

3 During the following procedure, the crankshaft must be turned in order to position the peaks of the camshaft lobes away from the valves. To do this, either turn the crankshaft on the pulley bolt or alternatively raise the front right-hand corner of the vehicle, engage 5th gear, and turn the front roadwheel. Access to the pulley bolt is gained by jacking up the front of the vehicle and supporting on axle stands, then removing the auxiliary drivebelt lower cover.

4 If desired, to enable the crankshaft to be turned more easily, remove the glow plugs as described in Chapter 5 Section 11.

5 Draw the valve positions on a piece of paper, numbering them 1 to 8 from the timing belt end of the engine. Identify them as inlet or exhaust (ie, 1I, 2E, 3I, 4E, 5I, 6E, 7I, 8E).

6 Turn the crankshaft until the valves of No 4 cylinder (flywheel end) are 'rocking' – the exhaust valve will be closing and the inlet valve will be opening. The piston of No 1 cylinder will be at the top of its compression stroke, with both valves fully closed. The clearances for both valves of No 1 cylinder may be checked at the same time.

7 Use feeler blade(s) to measure the exact clearance between the heel of the camshaft lobe and the shim on the cam follower; the

5.2a Unscrew the 4 nuts...

5.2b ...and lift off the baffle plate...

5.2c ...then refit the camshaft bearing cap nuts temporarily

5.7 Use feeler gauges to measure the exact clearance

6.6 Special tool used to stop the crankshaft from turning

6.7 Renew the crankshaft pulley bolt when reassembling

feeler blades should be a firm sliding fit **(see illustration)**. Record the measured clearance on the drawing. From this clearance it will be possible to calculate the thickness of the new shim to be fitted, where necessary. Note that the inlet and exhaust valve clearances are different, so it is important that you know which valve clearance you are checking.

8 With No 1 cylinder valve clearances checked, turn the engine through half a turn so that No 2 valves are 'rocking', then measure the valve clearances of No 3 cylinder in the same way. Similarly check the valve clearances of No 4 cylinder with No 1 valves 'rocking' and No 2 cylinder with No 3 valves 'rocking'. Compare the measured clearances with the values give in the Specifications – any which fall within the range do not require adjustment.

Adjustment

9 If adjustment is required, turn the engine in the normal direction of rotation through approximately 90°, to bring the pistons to mid-stroke. If this is not done, the pistons at TDC will prevent the cam followers being depressed, and valve damage may result. Depress the cam followers and then either shim can be withdrawn if the peak of the cam does not prevent access. The Ford tools for this operation are Nos 303-195 and 303-196, but with care and patience a C-spanner or screwdriver can be used to depress the cam follower and the shim can be flicked out with a small screwdriver.

10 If the valve clearance was too small, a thinner shim must be fitted. If the clearance was too large, a thicker shim must be fitted. The thickness of the shim (in mm) is engraved on the side facing away from the camshaft. If the marking is missing or illegible, a micrometer will be needed to establish shim thickness.

11 When the shim thickness and the valve clearance are known, the required thickness of the new shim can be calculated as follows (all measurements in mm):

Sample calculation

12 Desired clearance (A) = 0.50
13 Measured clearance (B) = 0.35
14 Shim thickness found (C) = 3.95
15 Shim thickness required (D) = C+B-A = 3.80

16 With the correct shim fitted, release the cam follower depressing tool. Turn the engine back so that the cam lobes are again pointing upwards and check that the clearance is now correct.

17 Repeat the process for the remaining valves, turning the engine each time to bring a pair of cam lobes upwards.

18 It will be helpful for future adjustment if a record is kept of the thickness of shim fitted at each position. The shims required can be purchased in advance once the clearances and the existing shim thicknesses are known.

19 It is permissible to interchange shims between cam followers to achieve the correct clearances but it is not advisable to turn the camshaft with any shims removed, since there is a risk that the cam lobe will jam in the empty cam follower.

20 When all the clearances are correct, refit the glow plugs (Chapter 5 Section 11), then refit the oil baffle plate and tighten the nuts to the specified torque. Refit the cylinder head cover as described in Section 4.

6 Crankshaft pulley – removal and refitting

Removal

1 Disconnect the battery negative lead as described in Chapter 5 Section 3.

2 Loosen the right-hand front roadwheel nuts, then raise the front of the vehicle, and support securely on axle stands (see *Jacking and vehicle support*). Remove the roadwheel.

3 Undo the fasteners and withdraw the engine undershield from under the car **(see illustration 3.8)**.

4 Remove the auxiliary drivebelt, as described in Chapter 1 Section 22.

5 The centre bolt which secures the crankshaft pulley must now be slackened. This bolt is tightened to a very high torque, and it is first of all essential to ensure that the car is adequately supported, as considerable effort will be needed.

6 Ford technicians use a special holding tool (205-072) which locates in the outer holes of the pulley and prevents it from turning **(see**

illustration). If this is not available, select a gear, and have an assistant firmly apply the handbrake and footbrake as the bolt is loosened. If this method is unsuccessful, remove the starter motor as described in Chapter 5 Section 8, and jam the flywheel ring gear, using a suitable tool, to prevent the crankshaft from rotating.

7 Unscrew the bolt securing the pulley to the crankshaft, and remove the pulley. It is essential to obtain a new bolt for reassembly **(see illustration)**.

8 With the pulley removed, it is advisable to check the crankshaft oil seal for signs of oil leakage. If necessary, fit a new seal as described in Section 16.

Refitting

9 Refit the pulley to the crankshaft sprocket, then fit the new pulley securing bolt and tighten it as far as possible before the crankshaft starts to rotate.

10 Holding the pulley against rotation as for removal, first tighten the bolt to the specified Stage 1 torque.

11 Stage 2 involves tightening the bolt though an angle, rather than to a torque. The bolt must be rotated through the specified angle – special angle gauges are available from tool outlets. As a guide, a 180° angle is equivalent to a half-turn, and this is easily judged by assessing the start and end positions of the socket handle or torque wrench.

12 Refit and tension the auxiliary drivebelt as described in Chapter 1 Section 22.

13 Refit the engine undershield.

14 Refit the roadwheel, lower the vehicle to the ground, and reconnect the battery negative lead as described in Chapter 5 Section 3. Tighten the wheel nuts to the specified torque.

7 Timing belt – removal and refitting

Removal

1 Disconnect the battery negative lead as described in Chapter 5 Section 3 and then remove the upper and lower windscreen cowl panels as described in Chapter 12 Section 12.

7.5a Unclip the fuel pipes from the timing belt cover

7.5b Intercooler hose-to-throttle body clamp

7.9 Engine mounting nuts and bolts

7.10a Using a suitable socket on the Torx end fitting …

7.10b …unscrew and remove the engine mounting front stud

2 Remove the cylinder head cover as described in Section 4.

3 Referring to the information in Section 3, set the engine to TDC on No 1 cylinder. The timing pin described must be used, to ensure accuracy.

4 Remove the coolant expansion tank by pulling it up from its mountings, and move it to one side without disconnecting the hoses.

5 Unclip the fuel pipes, then undo the nut, slacken the clamps and remove the intercooler outlet pipe from the right-hand end of the engine **(see illustrations)**.

6 Ford recommend that the engine is further prevented from turning by fitting another special tool, to lock the flywheel ring gear (this prevents the injection pump sprocket from moving). This tool (Ford No 303-393) is also available from Ford dealers, and is quite

simple. With the starter motor removed, as described in Chapter 5 Section 8, the tool bolts across the starter motor aperture in the bellhousing, and a peg on the back of the tool engages and locks the flywheel ring gear. A substitute for this tool could be made, or the ring gear jammed using another suitable tool.

7 Before unbolting the engine mounting, it is recommended that the right-hand wheel is refitted, and the car lowered to the ground (assuming the car has been raised as part of setting the engine to TDC).

8 The engine must now be supported before the right-hand mounting is removed. Ford technicians use an engine support bar, which locates in the channels at the top of each inner wing, and a further beam attached to this, which rests on the front crossmember. If such an arrangement is not available, use an

engine crane; either way, use a suitable length of chain and hooks to attach the lifting gear to the engine lifting eye. If the engine must be supported from below (and this is not recommended), use a large piece of wood on a trolley jack to spread the load and reduce the chance of damage to the sump.

9 With the weight of the engine supported, unscrew the two nuts and two bolts securing the top half of the engine right-hand mounting, and lift the mounting off the two studs **(see illustration)**.

10 Before the timing belt outer cover can be removed, the stud fitted to the front of the engine mounting must be unscrewed and removed. This can be achieved using a socket on the Torx end fitting provided **(see illustrations)**.

11 Unscrew the three bolts (and one stud/bolt at the top), and remove the timing belt outer cover **(see illustration)**.

12 If the timing belt is not being fitted straight away (or if the belt is being removed as part of another procedure, such as cylinder head removal), temporarily refit the engine right-hand mounting and tighten the bolts securely.

13 Before proceeding further, check once more that the engine is positioned at TDC on No 1 cylinder, as described in Section 3.

14 Slacken the timing belt tensioner bolt, and remove the tensioner completely. Slip the timing belt from the sprockets, and remove it **(see illustrations)**.

15 The camshaft sprocket must be removed

7.11 Remove the timing belt outer cover

7.14a Slacken the tensioner bolt …

7.14b …and slip the timing belt from its sprockets

7.16 Using a forked holding tool, unscrew the camshaft sprocket bolt

7.17a Fit Ford tool 303-651 to the camshaft sprocket

7.17b Using the special Ford pulley, free the sprocket from its taper …

– this is necessary as part of setting up the new timing belt, to ensure that the correct valve timing is preserved. Not only will a method for holding the sprocket stationary be required, but the sprocket itself is mounted on a taper, so a puller will be needed to free it from the camshaft. Due to its design, the sprocket cannot readily be removed using an ordinary puller, so either the Ford tool (303-651) must be obtained, or a suitable alternative fabricated.

16 Holding the camshaft sprocket using a suitable tool, loosen the sprocket bolt **(see illustration)**. **Note:** *Do not rely on the TDC setting bar engaged in the slot at the opposite end of the camshaft to hold it stationary – not only is this dangerous, it could well result in damage to the camshaft.*

17 Using a suitable puller, release the camshaft sprocket from the taper, and remove it **(see illustrations)**.

18 Do not be tempted to re-use the old timing belt under any circumstances – even if it is known to have covered less mileage than the renewal interval indicated in Chapter 1 Specifications. Ford state that, once a new timing belt has been run on the engine, it is considered worn, and should be discarded. In any case, given the potential expense involved should the belt fail in service, re-using an old belt would be a false economy.

7.17c … then remove the sprocket bolt and washer …

7.17d … and finally remove the camshaft sprocket

19 Before disposing of the old belt, however, examine it for evidence of contamination by coolant or lubricant. If there are any signs of contamination, find the source of the contamination before progressing any further. If an oil leak is evident, this will most likely be from the camshaft seal. Cure the problem, then wash down the whole area (including the sprockets) with degreaser and allow to dry before fitting the new belt.

20 Spin the tensioner pulley, and check for signs of sticking or roughness, indicating bearing wear. Many professional mechanics will fit a new tensioner as a matter of course when fitting a new timing belt. This should

be considered a good idea, especially if the engine has completed a large mileage.

Refitting

21 Ensure that the crankshaft and camshaft are still set to TDC on No 1 cylinder, as described in Section 3.

22 Refit the camshaft sprocket to the camshaft, tightening the bolt by hand only **(see illustration)**. The sprocket must be able to rotate independently of the camshaft.

23 Fit the timing belt tensioner into position, noting that the adjustment arm must be set pointing as shown **(see illustration)**. Fit the retaining bolt, tightening it finger-tight only at this stage.

7.22 Refit the camshaft sprocket bolt, hand-tight at first

7.23 Note that the adjustment arm must be approximately pointing as shown

7.25a Rotate the tensioner arm anti-clockwise ...

7.25b ... until the pointer is between the sides of the 'window'

24 Fit the new timing belt over the sprockets and above the tensioner pulley, ensuring that the injection pump sprocket does not move (the camshaft sprocket must be free to turn – remember that the camshaft itself is locked by the tool fitted to its slotted end). Where applicable, ensure the arrow on the back of the belt points in the direction of engine rotation.

25 Using an Allen key in the adjuster arm, maintain the tensioner's position whilst the retaining bolt is slackened, then rotate the adjuster arm anti-clockwise until the pointer is positioned between the sides of the adjustment 'window' **(see illustrations)**. Fully tighten the tensioner retaining bolt.

26 Hold the camshaft sprocket against rotation, and tighten the sprocket retaining bolt.

27 Remove the locking tools from the engine, so that it can be turned; these may include the timing pin, the plate fitted into the camshaft slot, and the tool used to lock the flywheel.

28 Mark the TDC position of the crankshaft pulley, using paint or typist's correction fluid, to give a rough indication of TDC, and so that the number of turns can be counted.

29 Using a spanner or socket on the crankshaft pulley centre bolt, turn the engine forwards (clockwise, viewed from the timing belt end) through six full turns, bringing the engine almost up to the TDC position on completion.

30 Using the information in Section 3, set the engine to TDC on No 1 cylinder. Make sure that the timing pin and camshaft locking tools are refitted – also lock the flywheel against rotation, using the same method used previously (see paragraph 6). If the special tools cannot be refitted, go back to paragraph 21 and repeat the setting procedure.

31 Check the position of the timing belt automatic tensioner pointer. If the pointer is still within the two sides of the 'window', proceed to next paragraph. If the pointer is outside the 'window', repeat the tensioning procedure.

32 Remove the locking tools from the engine; these may include the timing pin, the plate fitted into the camshaft slot, and the tool used to lock the flywheel.

33 If the engine right-hand mounting had been temporarily refitted as described in para-

graph 12, support the engine once more, and remove the mounting.

34 Refit the timing belt outer cover, and tighten the retaining bolts securely.

35 Refit the front stud to the engine mounting, and tighten it securely, using a similar method to that used for the stud's removal.

36 Refit the top half of the engine right-hand mounting, and tighten the nuts and bolts to the specified torque's.

37 With the engine securely supported by its mounting once more, the engine supporting tools can be carefully removed.

38 Refit the cylinder head cover as described in Section 4.

39 Refit the coolant expansion tank to the inner wing.

40 Refit the intercooler outlet pipe and reclip the fuel pipes.

41 Reconnect the battery negative lead as described in Chapter 5 Section 3.

8 Timing belt tensioner and sprockets – removal, inspection and refitting

Timing belt tensioner

1 The timing belt tensioner is removed as part of the timing belt renewal procedure, in Section 7.

Camshaft sprocket

2 The camshaft sprocket is removed as part of the timing belt renewal procedure, in Section 7.

9.6 Remove the camshaft bearing shells

Fuel injection pump sprocket

3 Removal of the injection pump sprocket is described as part of the injection pump removal procedure, in Chapter 4A Section 10. Note that the sprocket is sealed to the pump using two types of sealant/locking compound.

9 Camshaft and cam followers – removal, inspection and refitting

Note: *A new camshaft oil seal will be required on refitting.*

Removal

1 Remove the timing belt and camshaft sprocket as described in Section 7.

2 Remove the camshaft oil seal. The seal is quite deeply recessed – Ford dealers have a special seal extractor for this (tool No 303-293). In the absence of this tool, do not use any removal method which might damage the sealing surfaces, or a leak will result when the new seal is fitted.

> **HAYNES HINT** *One of the best ways to remove an oil seal is to carefully drill or punch two holes through the seal, opposite each other (taking care not to damage the surface behind the seal as this is done). Two self-tapping screws are then screwed into the holes; by pulling on the screw heads alternately with a pair of pliers, the seal can be extracted.*

3 Unscrew and remove the nuts securing the oil baffle plate to the top of the engine, noting that these nuts also secure Nos 2 and 4 camshaft bearing caps. Lift off the baffle plate, and recover the bearing caps – if no identification numbers are evident on the caps, mark them for position, as they must be refitted to the correct locations.

4 Progressively unscrew (by half a turn at a time) the nuts securing the remaining bearing caps (Nos 1, 3 and 5) until the camshaft is free.

5 Lift off each bearing cap and bearing shell in turn, and mark it for position if necessary – all the caps must be refitted in their original positions.

6 Carefully lift out the camshaft, and place it somewhere safe – the lobes must not be scratched. Remove the lower part of the bearing shells in turn, and mark them for position **(see illustration)**.

7 Before lifting out the cam followers and shims, give some thought to how they will be stored while they are removed. Unless new components are being fitted, the cam followers and shims must be identified for position. The best way to do this is to take a box, and divide it into eight compartments,

each with a clearly-marked number; taking No 1 cam follower and shim as being that nearest the timing belt end of the engine, lift out each cam follower and shim, and place it in the box. Alternatively, keep the cam follower/shim assemblies in line, in fitted order, as they are removed – mark No 1 to avoid confusion.

Inspection

8 With the camshaft removed, examine the bearing caps and the bearing locations in the cylinder head for signs of obvious wear or pitting. If evident, a new cylinder head will probably be required. Also check that the oil supply holes in the cylinder head are free from obstructions. (New bearing shells should be used on reassembly.)

9 Visually inspect the camshaft for evidence of wear on the surfaces of the lobes and journals. Normally their surfaces should be smooth and have a dull shine; look for scoring, erosion or pitting and areas that appear highly polished, indicating excessive wear. Accelerated wear will occur once the hardened exterior of the camshaft has been damaged, so always renew worn items. **Note:** *If these symptoms are visible on the tips of the camshaft lobes, check the corresponding cam follower/shim, as it will probably be worn as well.*

10 If suitable precision measuring equipment (such as a micrometer) is available, the camshaft bearing journals can be checked for wear, by comparing the values measured with those specified.

11 If the machined surfaces of the camshaft appear discoloured or blued, it is likely that it has been overheated at some point, probably due to inadequate lubrication. This may have distorted the shaft, in which case the runout should be checked; Ford do not quote a runout tolerance, so if this kind of damage is suspected, an engine reconditioning specialist should be consulted. In the case of

9.16 Lubricate the cam followers before refitting

inadequate lubrication, distortion is unlikely to be the only damage which has occurred, and a new camshaft will probably be needed.

12 To measure the camshaft endfloat, temporarily refit the camshaft to the cylinder head, then fit Nos 1 and 5 bearing caps and tighten the retaining nuts to the specified torque setting. Anchor a DTI gauge to the timing belt end of the cylinder head. Push the camshaft to one end of the cylinder head as far as it will travel, then rest the DTI gauge probe on the end face of the camshaft, and zero the gauge. Push the camshaft as far as it will go to the other end of the cylinder head, and record the gauge reading. Verify the reading by pushing the camshaft back to its original position and checking that the gauge indicates zero again. **Note:** *The cam followers must not be fitted whilst this measurement is being taken.*

13 Check that the camshaft endfloat measure- ment is within the limit listed in the Specifications. If the measurement is outside the specified limit, wear is unlikely to be confined to any one component, so renewal of the camshaft, cylinder head and bearing caps must be considered.

14 Inspect the cam followers and shims for

9.17 Refit the brake vacuum pump pushrod before refitting the camshaft

obvious signs of wear or damage, and renew if necessary.

Refitting

15 Make sure that the top surfaces of the cylinder head, and in particular the camshaft bearings and the mating surfaces for the camshaft bearing caps, are completely clean.

16 Smear some clean engine oil onto the sides of the cam followers, and offer each one into position in their original bores in the cylinder head, together with its respective shim **(see illustration)**. Push them down until they contact the valves, then lubricate the top surface of each shim.

17 Lubricate the camshaft and cylinder head bearing journals with clean engine oil. If the pushrod which operates the brake vacuum pump has been removed from the cylinder head **(see illustration)**, refit it now – once the camshaft is in position, the pushrod cannot be refitted.

18 Carefully lower the camshaft into position in the cylinder head, making sure that the cam lobes for No 1 cylinder are pointing upwards. Also use the position of the locking tool slot at the end of the camshaft as a guide to correct alignment when refitting – the slot should be flush to the top surface of the cylinder head (the larger 'semi-circle' created by the offset slot should be uppermost).

19 Prior to refitting the No 1 camshaft bearing cap, the front halves of the flat sealing surface must be coated with a smear of suitable sealant, as shown **(see illustration)**.

20 Lubricate Nos 1, 3 and 5 bearing caps and shells with clean oil (taking care not to get any on the sealant-coated surfaces of No 1 cap), then place them into their correct positions. Refit the bearing cap nuts, and tighten them progressively to the specified torque wrench setting.

21 The outer edges of No 1 bearing cap must now be sealed to the cylinder head surface with a thin bead of suitable sealant.

22 Clean out the oil seal housing and the sealing surface of the camshaft by wiping it with a lint-free cloth. Remove any swarf or burrs that may cause the seal to leak.

23 Apply a little oil to the new camshaft oil seal, and fit it over the end of the camshaft, lips facing inwards. To avoid damaging the

9.19 Camshaft refitting details

1 Bearing caps (1 to 5)
2 Camshaft
3 Cylinder head
4 Camshaft oil seal
5 Bearing shells
A Sealant application areas on No 1 bearing cap

H45136

seal lips, wrap a little tape over the end of the camshaft. Ford dealers have a special tool (No 303-199) for fitting the seal, but if this is not available, a deep socket of suitable size can be used. It is important that the seal is fitted square to the shaft, and is fully-seated.

24 Refit the camshaft sprocket and timing belt as described in Section 7.

25 Check the valve clearances as described in Section 5.

26 Oil the bearing surfaces of Nos 2 and 4 bearing caps, then refit them and the oil baffle plate to the engine. Tighten the bearing cap nuts to the specified torque.

27 Refit the cylinder head cover as described in Section 4.

28 Further refitting is a reversal of removal.

10 Camshaft oil seal – renewal

1 Remove the timing belt and camshaft sprocket as described in Section 7. Access to the seal is hampered by the presence of the timing belt backplate, but this can only be removed after taking off the injection pump sprocket; it should not prove necessary to remove the backplate in practice.

2 Remove the camshaft oil seal. The seal is quite deeply recessed – Ford dealers have a special seal extractor for this (tool No 303-293). In the absence of this tool, do not use any removal method which might damage the sealing surfaces, or a leak will result when the new seal is fitted (see **Haynes Hint**).

HAYNES HINT *One of the best ways to remove an oil seal is to carefully drill or punch two holes through the seal, opposite each other (taking care not to damage the surface behind the seal as this is done). Two self-tapping screws are then screwed into the holes; by pulling on the screw heads alternately with a pair of pliers, the seal can be extracted.*

3 Clean out the seal housing and the sealing surface of the camshaft by wiping it with a

10.4a Lubricate the oil seal before fitting over the camshaft…

lint-free cloth. Remove any swarf or burrs that may cause the seal to leak.

4 Apply a little oil to the new camshaft oil seal, and fit it over the end of the camshaft, lips facing inwards. To avoid damaging the seal lips, wrap a little tape over the end of the camshaft. Ford dealers have a special tool (No 303-199) for fitting the seal, but if this is not available, a deep socket of suitable size can be used. **Note:** *Select a socket that bears only on the hard outer surface of the seal, not the inner lip which can easily be damaged. It is important that the seal is fitted square to the shaft, and is fully-seated* (see illustrations).

5 Refit the camshaft sprocket and timing belt as described in Section 7.

11 Cylinder head – removal, inspection and refitting

Note: *Ford technicians remove the cylinder head complete with the inlet and exhaust manifolds. Whilst this may reduce the overall time spent, it makes the cylinder head assembly incredibly heavy and awkward to lift clear (the head is of cast iron, and is quite heavy enough on its own). We felt that, for the DIY mechanic at least, removing the manifolds would be the more sensible option.*

Removal

1 Remove the battery and battery tray as described in Chapter 5 Section 3 and then

10.4b …and use a suitable socket to tap the seal in squarely

remove the upper and lower windscreen cowl panels as described in Chapter 12 Section 12.

2 Remove the air cleaner housing, as described in Chapter 4A Section 3.

3 Remove the cylinder head cover as described in Section 4.

4 Using the information in Section 3, bring the engine round to just before the TDC position on No 1 cylinder. Do not insert any of the locking tools at this stage.

5 Apply the handbrake, then jack up the front of the car and support it on axle stands (see *Jacking and vehicle support*).

6 Drain the cooling system as described in Chapter 1 Section 25.

7 Remove the turbocharger/exhaust manifold and the inlet manifold as described in Chapter 4A Section 17

8 Remove the timing belt as described in Section 7.

9 Remove the bolt securing the timing belt backplate to the cylinder head, and the seven nuts around the injection pump sprocket (see illustrations). While this does not allow the backplate to be removed, it makes it possible to bend the plate enough for the camshaft's tapered end to pass as the head is lifted. If the backplate is to be removed completely, this requires that the injection pump sprocket and its oil seal housing are also removed, as described in Chapter 4A Section 10.

10 Disconnect the glow plug supply lead in front of the dipstick tube, and move the wiring harness to one side (see illustration).

11 Release the clips from the crankcase ventilation hoses as necessary, and

11.9a Remove the timing belt backplate bolt from the cylinder head…

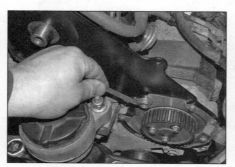

11.9b …and the 7 nuts around the injection pump sprocket

11.10 Unscrew the nut securing the glow plug supply lead

11.11a Disconnect the breather hoses…

11.11b …unscrew the mounting bolt…

11.11c …disconnect the oil pressure warning light switch…

disconnect the wiring plug from the oil pressure switch, then unbolt and remove the oil separator from the left-hand end of the cylinder head (see illustrations).

12 Unclip and disconnect the wiring plug for the cylinder head temperature sensor, next to the brake vacuum pump (see illustration).

13 Disconnect the vacuum hose and the oil return pipe from the vacuum pump at the left-hand end of the cylinder head (left as seen from the driver's seat). Unscrew the top mounting bolt, and loosen the lower bolt – the lower mounting is slotted, to make removal easier – and lift off the pump. Recover the large O-ring seal – a new one must be used on reassembly (see illustrations).

14 Remove the screw securing the glow plug supply lead to the thermostat housing. Remove the two bolts securing the thermostat

11.11d …and remove the oil separator from the end of the cylinder head

11.12 Disconnect the cylinder head temperature sensor wiring plug

housing to the front of the head, then pull the housing forwards and rest it clear of the head without disconnecting any further

pipework (see illustrations). Note that a new thermostat housing gasket will be needed for reassembly.

11.13a Unscrew the vacuum hose union…

11.13b …release the hose clip and disconnect the oil return pipe…

11.13c …then unbolt…

11.13d …and remove the vacuum pump – recover the O-ring

11.14a Remove the glow plug supply lead securing bolt

11.14b Unscrew the thermostat housing bolts

11.18 Note their positions, then remove the pipe clamps

11.19 Disconnect the pressure sensor wiring plug

11.20a Use a second spanner to counter-hold the adapters whilst undoing the union nuts at the injectors...

11.20b ...and at the fuel supply manifold (common rail)

11.21 Remove the pipe support bracket

15 Clean the area around the high-pressure fuel injection pipes from the pump to the supply manifold (common rail), and the from injectors to the supply manifold.

16 Disconnect the fuel return pipes from the injectors (see Chapter 4A Section 11). Cover, or plug the openings to prevent dirt ingress.

17 Disconnect the wiring plugs from each injector.

18 Make a note of their exact fitted positions, then remove the high-pressure pipe clamps **(see illustration)**.

19 Disconnect the wiring plug from the pressure sensor on the fuel supply manifold **(see illustration)**.

20 Unscrew the union nuts and remove the high-pressure fuel injection pipes from the fuel supply manifold to the injectors. When unscrewing the unions, counter-hold

the adapters with one spanner, and loosen the unions with another. Cover over the end fittings on the supply manifold and on the injectors, to keep the dirt out **(see illustrations)**. Ford insist that the fuel injection delivery pipes are not re-used – discard the pipes.

21 Undo the bolt/nut and remove the bracket supporting the high-pressure fuel pipe from the pump to the supply manifold **(see illustration)**.

22 Unscrew the union nuts and remove the high-pressure fuel pipe from the pump to the supply manifold – again, counter-hold the adapters with a second spanner. Note its fitted position, then remove the clamp from the pipe, Cover or plug the openings to prevent dirt ingress. Ford insist that the pipe is not re-used – discard it.

23 Remove the three bolts securing the fuel supply manifold bracket to the engine, and withdraw the supply manifold complete with the bracket.

24 If not already done, it is recommended before removing the cylinder head that the engine right-hand mounting is refitted, and the engine supporting tools removed. This will improve working room if a hoist or engine support bar was used, and avoids the risk of the engine slipping if it was supported from below.

25 Remove the four nuts securing the oil baffle plate, and carefully lift the plate off the engine. Note that these nuts are also used to secure Nos 2 and 4 camshaft bearing caps, which will then be loose. Once the plate is removed, refit the nuts by hand, to keep the caps in place.

26 Check around the head and the engine bay that there is nothing still attached to the cylinder head, nor anything which would prevent it from being lifted away.

27 Working in the reverse order of the tightening sequence **(see illustration 11.53)**, loosen the cylinder head bolts by half a turn at a time, until they are all loose. Remove the head bolts, and discard them – Ford state that they must not be re-used, even if they appear to be serviceable **(see illustrations)**. Note the fitted positions of the two shorter bolts, which should be the two nearest the timing belt end of the engine.

28 Bend the timing belt backplate gently away from the head sufficiently for the camshaft stub to clear it. Lift the cylinder head away; use assistance if possible, as it is a very heavy assembly.

29 If the head is stuck (as is possible), be careful how you choose to free it. Striking the head with tools carries the risk of damage, and the head is located on two dowels, so its movement will be limited. Do not, under any circumstances, lever the head between the mating surfaces, as this will certainly damage the sealing surfaces for the gasket, leading to leaks.

30 Once the head has been removed, recover the gasket from the two dowels. The gasket is manufactured from laminated steel, and cannot be re-used, but see paragraph 32.

11.27a Working in the reverse of the tightening sequence, unscrew...

11.27b ...and remove the cylinder head bolts

11.35 Measure piston projection with a dial test indicator (DTI)

11.49 Cylinder head bolt positions and gasket details

1 Cylinder head
2 Longer bolts (eight, 177 mm long)
3 Cylinder head gasket
4 Thickness markings (notches)
5 Position marking (cut-out)
6 Shorter bolts (two, 137 mm long)

H45137

Inspection

31 If required, dismantling and inspection of the cylinder head is covered in Part D of this Chapter.

Cylinder head gasket selection

32 Examine the old cylinder head gasket for manufacturer's identification markings. These will be in the form of notches (two to seven) on the front edge of the gasket, which indicate the gasket's thickness (see illustration 11.49).

33 Unless new components have been fitted, or the cylinder head has been machined (skimmed), the new cylinder head gasket must be of the same type as the old one. Purchase the required gasket, and proceed to paragraph 40.

34 If the head has been machined, or if new pistons have been fitted, it is likely that a head gasket of different thickness to the original will be needed. Gasket selection is made on the basis of the measured piston protrusion above the cylinder head gasket surface. If the head has not been machined, and the pistons, connecting rods, and crankshaft have not been disturbed, use a new head gasket with the same number of notches as the old one.

35 To measure the piston protrusion, anchor a dial test indicator (DTI) to the top face (cylinder head gasket mating face) of the cylinder block, and zero the gauge on the gasket mating face (see illustration).

36 Rest the gauge probe above No 1 piston crown, and turn the crankshaft slowly by hand until the piston reaches TDC (its maximum height). Measure and record the maximum piston projection at TDC.

37 Repeat the measurement for the remaining pistons, and record the results.

38 If the measurements differ from piston to piston, take the highest figure, and use this to determine the thickness of the head gasket required.

39 Note the greatest piston protrusion measurement, and use this to determine the correct cylinder head gasket with reference to the Specifications at the beginning of this Chapter. The series of notches/holes on the side of the gasket are used for thickness identification (see illustration 11.49).

Preparation for refitting

40 The mating faces of the cylinder head and cylinder block must be perfectly clean before refitting the head. Use a hard plastic or wooden scraper to remove all traces of gasket and carbon; also clean the piston crowns. **Note:** *The new head gasket has rubber-coated surfaces, which could be damaged from sharp edges or debris left by a metal scraper.*

41 Take particular care when cleaning the piston crowns, as the soft aluminium alloy is easily damaged.

42 Make sure that the carbon is not allowed to enter the oil and water passages – this is particularly important for the lubrication system, as carbon could block the oil supply to the engine's components. Using adhesive tape and paper, seal the water, oil and bolt holes in the cylinder block.

43 To prevent carbon entering the gap between the pistons and bores, smear a little grease in the gap. After cleaning each piston, use a small brush to remove all traces of grease and carbon from the gap, then wipe away the remainder with a clean rag. Clean all the pistons in the same way.

44 Check the mating surfaces of the cylinder block and the cylinder head for nicks, deep scratches and other damage (refer to the Note in paragraph 40). If slight, they may be removed carefully with a file, but if excessive, machining may be the only alternative to renewal.

45 If warpage of the cylinder head gasket surface is suspected, use a straight-edge to check it for distortion. Refer to Part E of this Chapter if necessary.

46 Ensure that the cylinder head bolt holes in the crankcase are clean and free of oil. Syringe or soak up any oil left in the bolt holes. This is most important in order that the correct bolt tightening torque can be applied, and to prevent the possibility of the block being cracked by hydraulic pressure when the bolts are tightened.

Refitting

47 Turn the crankshaft anti-clockwise all the pistons at an equal height, approximately halfway down their bores from the TDC position. This will eliminate any risk of piston-to-valve contact as the cylinder head is refitted.

48 To guide the cylinder head into position, screw two long studs (or old cylinder head bolts with the heads cut off, and slots cut in the ends to enable the bolts to be unscrewed) into the end cylinder head bolt locations on the manifold side of the cylinder block.

49 Ensure that the cylinder head locating dowels are in place at the front corners of the cylinder block, then fit the new cylinder head gasket over the dowels, ensuring that the OBEN/TOP marking is uppermost, and the notches are at the front (there is a further cut-out at the timing belt end of the gasket) (see illustration). Take care to avoid damaging the gasket's rubber coating.

50 Lower the cylinder head into position on the gasket, ensuring that it engages correctly over the guide studs and dowels.

51 Fit the new cylinder head bolts to the eight remaining bolt locations, (remember that the two shorter bolts are fitted at the timing belt end of the engine) and screw them in as far as possible by hand. Do not apply oil to the bolts.

52 Unscrew the two guide studs from the exhaust side of the cylinder block, then screw in the two remaining new cylinder head bolts as far as possible by hand.

11.53 Cylinder head bolt tightening sequence

53 Working in sequence **(see illustration)**, tighten all the cylinder head bolts to the specified Stage 1 torque.
54 Again working in sequence, tighten all the cylinder head bolts to the specified Stage 2 torque.
55 Stages 3 and 4 involve tightening the bolts though an angle, rather than to a torque **(see illustration)**. Each bolt in sequence must be rotated through the specified angle – special angle gauges are available from tool outlets. As a guide, a 90° angle is equivalent to a quarter-turn, and this is easily judged by assessing the start and end positions of the socket handle or torque wrench. **Note:** The two shorter bolts at the timing belt end of the engine are tightened through a smaller angle than the remaining eight bolts – do not get confused when following the tightening sequence.
56 After finally tightening the cylinder head bolts, turn the crankshaft forwards to bring No 1 piston up to TDC, so that the crankshaft contacts the timing pin (see Section 3).
57 The remainder of the refitting procedure is a reversal of the removal procedure, bearing in mind the following points:
a) Refit the timing belt with reference to Section 7.
b) Reconnect the exhaust front section to the exhaust manifold with reference to Chapter 4A Section 18.
c) Refit the common rail and new high-pressure fuel delivery pipes as described in Chapter 4A Section 11.
d) Refit the cylinder head cover with reference to Section 4.

11.55 The 2 shorter bolts are tightened through less of an angle than the longer bolts

e) Refit the air cleaner and intercooler as described in Chapter 4A.
f) Refill the cooling system as described in Chapter 1 Section 25.
g) Check and if necessary top up the engine oil level and power steering fluid level as described in Weekly checks.
h) Before starting the engine, read through the section on engine restarting after overhaul, at the end of Chapter 2E Section 20.

12 Sump – removal and refitting

Note: The full procedure outlined below must be followed so that the mating surfaces can be cleaned and prepared to achieve an oil-tight joint on reassembly.

Removal

1 Apply the handbrake, then jack up the front of the vehicle and support it on axle stands (see Jacking and vehicle support). Remove the engine undershield.
2 Referring to Chapter 1 Section 3 if necessary, drain the engine oil, then clean and refit the engine oil drain plug, tightening it to the specified torque wrench setting. Although not strictly necessary as part of the dismantling procedure, owners are advised to remove and discard the oil filter, so that it can be renewed with the oil.
3 A conventional sump gasket is not used, and sealant is used instead.
4 Progressively unscrew the sump retaining bolts, and the two retaining nuts (the bolts are of different lengths, but it will be obvious where they fit on reassembly). Break the joint by striking the sump with the palm of the hand, then lower the sump away, turning it as necessary.
5 Unfortunately, the use of sealant can make removal of the sump more difficult. If care is taken not to damage the surfaces, the sealant can be cut around using a sharp knife. On no account lever between the mating faces, as this will almost certainly damage them, resulting in leaks when finished. Ford technicians have a tool comprising a metal rod which is inserted through the sump drain hole, and a handle to pull the sump downwards.

Refitting

6 On reassembly, thoroughly clean and degrease the mating surfaces of the cylinder block/crankcase and sump, removing all traces of sealant, then use a clean rag to wipe out the sump and the engine's interior.
7 If the two studs have been removed, they must be refitted before the sump is offered up, to ensure that it is aligned correctly. If this is not done, some of the sealant may enter the blind holes for the sump bolts, preventing the bolts from being fully fitted.
8 Referring to the accompanying illus- tration, apply silicone sealant (Ford part No WSE-M4G323-A4) to the sump flange. Do not allow sealant to enter the bolts holes. Ford specify that the sealant must be applied in a bead of 2.5 mm diameter **(see illustration)**. **Note:** The sump must be refitted within 10 minutes of applying the sealant.
9 Fit the sump over the studs, and insert the sump bolts and two nuts, tightening them by hand only at this stage.
10 Tighten all the bolts and nuts in the sequence shown **(see illustration 12.8)**.
11 Lower the car to the ground. Wait at least 1 hour for the sealant to cure (or whatever time is indicated by the sealant manufacturer) before refilling the engine with oil. If removed, fit a new oil filter with reference to Chapter 1 Section 3.

12.8 Sump bolt tightening sequence and sealant application details

Dotted line – 2.5 mm diameter bead of sealant

13.8 Undo the retaining bolts and remove the rotor cover

13.9 Check the condition of the pressure relief valve and clean out the oilways

13.10 Check the clearance between the inner and outer rotor

13 Oil pump – removal, inspection and refitting

Removal

1 Remove the crankshaft pulley as described in Section 6.

2 Unbolt the auxiliary drivebelt idler pulley in front of the crank pulley location.

3 Remove the timing belt and camshaft sprocket as described in Section 7.

4 Remove the injection pump sprocket and oil seal housing as described in Chapter 4A Section 10.

5 Unbolt and remove the timing belt backplate from the engine.

6 The oil pump is secured by 7 studs and 12 bolts – note their positions carefully for refitting. The studs can be unscrewed using a spanner on the hex provided.

7 Once all the fasteners have been removed, carefully lift the pump from its location. Recover the main gasket, and the smaller spacer ring from below the injection pump. Neither gasket may be re-used – obtain new ones for reassembly.

Inspection

8 Undo the retaining screws and remove the cover from the oil pump **(see illustration)**. Note the location of the identification marks on the inner and outer rotors for refitting.

9 Unscrew the plug and remove the pressure relief valve, spring and plunger, clean out and check condition of components **(see illustration)**.

10 The clearance between the inner and outer rotors can be checked using feeler blades, and compared with the value given in the Specifications **(see illustration)**.

11 Check the general condition of the oil pump, and in particular, its mating face to the cylinder block. If the mating face is damaged significantly, this may lead to oil loss (and a resulting drop in oil pressure).

12 Inspect the rotors for obvious signs of wear or damage; it is not clear at the time of writing whether individual components are available separately. Lubricate the rotors with

13.12 Align the dots on the 2 rotors

fresh engine oil and refit them into the body, making sure that the identification marks are positioned as noted on removal **(see illustration)**.

13 If the oil pump has been removed as part of a major engine overhaul, it is assumed that the engine will have completed a substantial mileage. In this case, it is often considered good practice to fit a new (or reconditioned) pump as a matter of course. In other words, if the rest of the engine is being rebuilt, the engine has completed a large mileage, or there is any question as to the old pump's condition, it is preferable to fit a new oil pump.

13.15 Fit a new metal gasket and spacer ring in position

Refitting

14 Before fitting the oil pump, ensure that the mating faces on the pump and the engine block are completely clean.

15 Lay the main metal gasket and a new spacer ring in position on the engine – in the case of the spacer ring, 'stick' it in position with a little oil or grease if required **(see illustration)**.

16 Offer the pump into position, and secure it with the studs and bolts, tightened only loosely at this stage **(see illustration)**.

17 Ford technicians use a special tool

13.16 Oil pump nut/bolt tightening sequence – note special tool 303-652 used to align the pump

13.17 Tool used to align the oil pump before tightening the bolts fully

14.4 Disconnect the wiring from the oil pressure warning switch

(303-652) to align the oil pump as it is being fitted and tightened **(see illustration)**. The tool is basically a circular socket, which fits over the end of the crankshaft, and ensures that the corresponding hole in the oil pump is centrally located over the end of the crankshaft. In the absence of the tool, this alignment could be confirmed visually, or a large socket/piece of tubing (perhaps wrapped with tape) could be used instead.

18 Ensuring that the correct alignment of the pump is maintained, tighten the pump securing studs and bolts to the specified Stage 1 torque, in sequence **(see illustration 13.16)**.

19 When all the fasteners have been tightened to the Stage 1 torque, go around again in the sequence, and tighten them all to the specified Stage 2 torque.

20 Refit the timing belt backplate to the engine.

21 Refit the injection pump sprocket and oil seal housing as described in Chapter 4A Section 10.

22 Refit the timing belt and camshaft sprocket as described in Section 7.

23 Refit the auxiliary drivebelt idler pulley, and tighten the bolt to the specified torque.

24 Refit the crankshaft pulley as described in Section 6.

25 When the engine is next started, check for correct oil pump operation (at least, as indicated by the oil pressure warning light going out).

14 Oil pressure warning light switch – removal and refitting

Removal

1 The switch is screwed into the left-hand (flywheel) end of the cylinder head, behind the vacuum pump.

2 Open the bonnet and disconnect the battery negative (earth) lead as described in Chapter 5 Section 3.

3 To improve access to the switch, it will be necessary to remove (or partially remove) the air cleaner inlet duct and the intercooler right-hand air duct, using the information in Chapter 4A Section 16. It will also be

helpful to release the hoses and remove the crankcase ventilation system oil separator from the left-hand end of the cylinder head.

4 Unplug the wiring from the switch and unscrew it; be prepared for some oil loss **(see illustration)**.

Refitting

5 Refitting is the reverse of the removal procedure; apply a thin smear of suitable sealant to the switch threads, and tighten it to the specified torque wrench setting.

6 Refit all components removed for access to the switch.

7 Check the engine oil level and top-up as necessary (see *Weekly checks.*).

8 Check for correct warning light operation, and for signs of oil leaks, once the engine has been restarted and warmed-up to normal operating temperature.

15 Oil cooler – removal and refitting

Note: *New sealing rings will be required on refitting.*

Removal

1 The oil cooler is mounted next to the oil filter on the rear of the cylinder block.

2 Access to the oil cooler is best obtained from below – apply the handbrake, then jack up the front of the car and support it on axle stands. Undo the screws and remove the engine undershield.

15.5 Disconnect the turbocharger oil supply union bolt

3 Position a container beneath the oil filter to catch escaping oil and coolant. To improve access to the coolant hoses, unscrew and remove the oil filter, making sure that the filter sealing ring is removed with the filter cartridge – anticipate a small loss of engine oil as the filter is removed. Provided the filter is not due for renewal, it can be refitted on completion.

4 Clamp the oil cooler coolant hoses to minimise spillage, then remove the clips, and disconnect the hoses from the oil cooler. Be prepared for coolant spillage.

5 Loosen the turbocharger oil supply union bolt at the top of the cooler **(see illustration)**, and separate the pipe (be prepared for oil spillage). Recover the copper washers from the union – new ones must be used on reassembly.

6 Unscrew the four bolts securing the oil cooler, noting their positions, as they are of different lengths. Remove the oil cooler from the engine, and recover the gasket (a new gasket must be used on refitting).

Refitting

7 Refitting is a reversal of removal, bearing in mind the following points:

a) Use a new gasket **(see illustration)**.

b) Fit the oil cooler mounting bolts to the positions noted on removal, and tighten them securely. Refit the oil filter if removed – apply a little oil to the filter sealing ring, and tighten the filter securely by hand (do not use any tools).

c) Use new copper washers when reconnecting the oil supply union at the top of the cooler, and tighten the union bolt securely.

d) On completion, lower the car to the ground. Check and if necessary top-up the oil and coolant levels, then start the engine and check for signs of oil or coolant leakage.

16 Crankshaft oil seals – renewal

Timing belt end seal

1 Remove the crankshaft pulley (see Section 6).

2 Note the fitted depth of the oil seal as a guide for fitting the new one.

15.7 Renew the oil cooler gasket

16.7 Use a locating tool to press the seal in squarely (locating sleeve not required when using this tool)

16.11 The oil seal is renewed complete with the carrier

3 Using a screwdriver or similar tool, carefully prise the oil seal from its location. Take care not to damage the oil seal contact surfaces or the oil seal seating. An alternative method of removing the seals is to drill a small hole in the seal (taking care not to drill any deeper than necessary), then insert a self-tapping screw and use pliers to pull out the seal.

4 Wipe clean the oil seal contact surfaces and seating, and clean up any sharp edges or burrs which might damage the new seal as it is fitted, or which might cause the seal to leak once in place.

5 The new oil seal should be supplied fitted with a locating sleeve, which must not be removed prior to fitting. No oil should be applied to the oil seal, which is made of PTFE.

6 Ford technicians use a special seal-fitting tool (303-652), but an adequate substitute can be achieved using a large socket or piece of tubing of sufficient size to bear on the outer edge of the new seal.

7 Locate the new seal (lips facing inwards) over the end of the crankshaft, using the tool **(see illustration)**, socket, or tubing to press the seal squarely and fully into position, to the previously-noted depth. Once the seal is fully fitted, remove the locating sleeve, if necessary.

8 The remainder of reassembly is the reverse of the removal procedure, referring to the relevant text for details where required. Check for signs of oil leakage when the engine is restarted.

Flywheel end seal

9 Remove the transmission as described in Chapter 7 Section 7, and the clutch assembly as described in Chapter 6 Section 6.

10 Unbolt the flywheel (see Section 17).

11 Unbolt and remove the oil seal carrier; the seal is renewed complete with the carrier, and is not available separately. A complete set of new carrier retaining bolts should also be obtained for reassembly **(see illustration)**.

12 Clean the end of the crankshaft, polishing off any burrs or raised edges, which may have caused the seal to fail in the first place. Clean also the seal carrier mating face on the engine block, using a suitable solvent for degreasing if necessary.

13 The new oil seal is supplied fitted with a locating sleeve, which must not be removed prior to fitting (it will drop out on its own when the carrier is bolted into position). No oil should be applied to the oil seal, which is made of PTFE.

14 Offer up the carrier into position, feeding the locating sleeve over the end of the crankshaft. Insert the new seal carrier retaining bolts, and tighten them all by hand **(see illustrations)**.

15 Ford technicians use a special tool (308-204) to centre the oil seal carrier around the end of the crankshaft. In the absence of the tool, this alignment could be confirmed visually, or a large socket/piece of tubing (perhaps wrapped with tape) could be used instead.

16 Ensuring that the correct alignment of the carrier is maintained, tighten the retaining bolts to the specified torque. If the seal locating sleeve is still in position, remove it now.

17 The remainder of the reassembly procedure is the reverse of dismantling, referring to the relevant text for details where required. Check for signs of oil leakage when the engine is restarted.

17 Flywheel – removal, inspection and refitting

Removal

1 Remove the transmission as described in Chapter 7 Section 7. Now is a good time to check components such as oil seals and renew them if necessary.

2 Remove the clutch as described in Chapter 6 Section 6. Now is a good time to check or renew the clutch components and release bearing.

3 Use a centre-punch or paint to make alignment marks on the flywheel and crankshaft, to ensure correct alignment during refitting.

4 Prevent the flywheel from turning by locking the ring gear teeth, or by bolting a strap between the flywheel and the cylinder block/crankcase **(see illustration)**. Slacken the bolts evenly until all are free.

5 Remove each bolt in turn and ensure that new ones are obtained for reassembly; these bolts are subjected to severe stresses and so must be renewed, regardless of their apparent condition, whenever they are disturbed.

6 Withdraw the flywheel, remembering that it is very heavy – do not drop it.

Inspection

7 Clean the flywheel to remove grease and oil. Inspect the surface for cracks, rivet grooves, burned areas and score marks. Light scoring can be removed with emery cloth. Check for cracked and broken ring gear teeth. Lay the flywheel on a flat surface and use a straight-edge to check for warpage.

8 Clean and inspect the mating surfaces

16.14a Fit the new seal assembly, complete with guide sleeve over the end of the crankshaft...

16.14b ...then remove the guide sleeve

17.4 Home made flywheel locking tool

17.11 On this example the flywheel bolts are off centre

17.12 Check the movement between the primary and secondary mass.

of the flywheel and the crankshaft. If the crankshaft seal is leaking, renew it (see Section 16) before refitting the flywheel. If the engine has covered a high mileage, it may be worth fitting a new seal as a matter if course, given the amount of work needed to access it.

9 While the flywheel is removed, clean carefully its inboard (right-hand) face, particularly the recesses which serve as the reference points for the crankshaft speed/position sensor. Clean the sensor's tip and check that the sensor is securely fastened.

10 A dual mass flywheel is fitted to all engines. Detailed checking of the flywheel requires the use of specific tools, that are unlikely to be available to the home mechanic. However some basic checking can easily be performed.

11 Start by checking the alignment between the primary mass and the secondary mass. At rest the flywheel retaining bolts will be accessible through the holes in the secondary mass (see illustration).

12 The maximum travel of the primary mass in relation to the secondary mass should not exceed 15 teeth (or 20 degrees). Note that this is a general guide and if in doubt remove the flywheel and have a suitably equipped specialist check the flywheel.

13 Inspect the flywheel for any grease or debris from the interface between the fixed part (the primary mass) and the movable part of the flywheel (the secondary mass). Replace any flywheel that has grease visible.

14 If the ring gear is badly worn or has missing teeth, then the entire dual mass flywheel must be replaced.

15 If any doubt to the condition of the flywheel exists, despite the expense we recommend replacing it.

Refitting

16 Fit the flywheel to the crankshaft so that all bolt holes align – it will fit only one way – check this using the marks made on removal (see illustration). Apply suitable locking compound to the threads of the new bolts, then insert them.

17 Lock the flywheel by the method used on dismantling (see illustration). Working in a diagonal sequence, tighten the bolts to the specified Stage 1 torque wrench setting.

18 Stage 2 involves tightening the bolts though an angle, rather than to a torque. Each bolt must be rotated through the specified angle – special angle gauges are available from tool outlets.

19 The remainder of reassembly is the reverse of the removal procedure, referring to the relevant text for details where required.

18 Engine/transmission mountings – inspection and renewal

Inspection

1 If improved access is required, firmly apply the handbrake, raise the front of the vehicle and support it securely on axle stands (see *Jacking and vehicle support*). Undo the retaining screws and fasteners and remove the undershield from beneath the engine/transmission unit.

17.16 Align the bolts holes in the crankshaft – they will only line up in one position

17.17 Tighten the bolts to the specified torque

18.8a Remove the cover plate bolts (A), the outer bolts (B) and
then the central bolt (C)

18.8b Lift off the cover plate ...

2 Check the mounting rubber to see if it is cracked, hardened or separated from the metal at any point. Renew the mounting if any such damage or deterioration is evident.

3 Check that all mounting fasteners are securely tightened. Use a torque wrench to check, if possible.

4 Using a large screwdriver or a pry bar, check for wear in the mountings by carefully levering against it to check for free play. Where this is not possible, enlist the aid of an assistant to move the engine/gearbox unit back and forth or from side to side while you watch the mountings. While some free play is to be expected even from new components, excessive wear should be obvious. If excessive free play is found, check first that the fasteners are correctly secured, then renew any worn components as described below.Add

Renewal

Left-hand mounting

5 Firmly apply the handbrake, raise the front of the vehicle and support it securely on axle stands (see *Jacking and vehicle support*).

Undo the retaining screws and fasteners and remove the undershield from beneath the engine/transmission unit.

6 Remove the air filter housing as described in Chapter 4A Section 3, and then remove the battery and battery tray as described in Chapter 5 Section 3.

7 Position a jack under the transmission with a block of wood between the jack head and casing, and take the weight of the engine and transmission.

8 Remove the cover plate bolts and then remove the four main bolts followed by the central bolt **(see illustrations)**

9 Remove the left-hand wing liner and lower the transmission on the jack to expose the mounting bracket. Remove the bolts and lift out the bracket **(see illustration)**.

10 Refitting is a reversal of removal, but the centre nut must be replaced. If the bracket has been removed from the transmission the mounting bolts must also be replaced. Tighten all fixings to the specified torque and angle where given.

Right-hand mounting

11 Firmly apply the handbrake, raise the front

18.8c ...followed by the main mounting

of the vehicle and support it securely on axle stands (see *Jacking and vehicle support*). Undo the retaining screws and fasteners and remove the undershield from beneath the engine/transmission unit.

12 Position a jack under the engine sump with a block of wood between the jack head and the sump. Raise the jack and take the weight of the engine on the jack.

13 Remove the bolts and remove the mounting **(see illustrations)**.

18.9 Remove the transmission support bracket

18.13a Unbolt and then ...

18.13b ...remove the mounting

18.16a The torque rod mounting bolts

18.16b Unbolt and then...

18.16c ...remove the torque rod

14 Refitting is a reversal of removal. When the vehicle is back on the ground, start the engine and bleed the power steering by turning the steering from lock to lock several times.

Torque rod

15 Firmly apply the handbrake, raise the front of the vehicle and support it securely on axle stands (see *Jacking and vehicle support*). Undo the retaining screws and fasteners and remove the undershield from beneath the engine/transmission unit.

16 Remove the bolts and manovre the the torque rod out from underneath **(see illustrations)**. A pry bar should be used to swing the engine away from the subframe – this will allow the mounting to be removed easily.

17 Refitting is a reversal of removal.

Chapter 2 Part C
2.0 litre engine in-car repair procedures

Contents

Degrees of difficulty

Easy, suitable for novice with little experience	Fairly easy, suitable for beginner with some experience	Fairly difficult, suitable for competent DIY mechanic	Difficult, suitable for experienced DIY mechanic	Very difficult, suitable for expert DIY or professional

Specifications

General

Engine type.	Four-cylinder, in-line, double overhead camshaft, aluminium cylinder head and cast iron engine block with turbocharger
Designation	2.0 litre Duratorq-TDCi.
Engine code	AZWA, UKWA, UFWA, TXWA and QXWA
Power output:	
AZWA	96 kW @ 4000 rpm
QXWA	105 kW @ 4000 rpm
UKWA	100 kW @ 3750 rpm
UFWA	103 kW @ 3750 rpm
TXWA	120 kW @ 3750 rpm
Torque output (average)	320 Nm @ 1750 rpm
Capacity	1998 cc
Bore	85.0 mm
Stroke	88.0 mm
Compression ratio	18: 1
Firing order	1-3-4-2 (No 1 cylinder at transmission end)
Direction of crankshaft rotation	Clockwise (seen from right-hand side of vehicle)

Cylinder head gasket selection

Piston protusion:	Gasket (mm)
0.55 to 0.60 mm	1.21 to 1.29 mm (1 hole)
0.61 to 0.65 mm	1.26 to 1.34 mm (2 holes)
0.66 to 0.70 mm	1.31 to 1.39 mm (3 holes)
0.71 to 0.75 mm	1.36 to 1.44 mm (2 holes with space)
Maximum distortion	0.030 mm

Camshaft

Camshaft endfloat . . . . 0.07 to 0.16 mm

Valves

Valve clearances. . . . . Hydraulic adjusters – no adjustment necessary

Lubrication

Oil pressure – minimum (engine at operating temperature):

    At 2000 rpm . . . . 2.0 bar

    At 4000 rpm . . . . 4.0 bar

Torque wrench settings

	Nm	lbf ft
Air conditioning compressor	28	21
Big-end bearing cap bolts: *		
Stage 1	20	15
Stage 2	Angle-tighten a further 70°	
Camshaft bearing housing:		
Stage 1	5	4
Stage 2	10	7
Camshaft sprocket bolt:		
Stage 1	20	15
Stage 2	Angle-tighten a further 60°	
Camshaft position sensor	10	7
Crankshaft oil seal carrier	14	10
Crankshaft pulley bolt: *		
Stage 1	70	52
Stage 2	Angle-tighten a further 60°	
Cylinder head lower section-to-block bolts: *		
Stage 1	60	44
Stage 2	Angle-tighten a further 220°	
Cylinder head upper section-to-lower section bolts:		
Stage 1	5	4
Stage 2	10	7
Cylinder head cover/inlet manifold:		
Stage 1	5	4
Stage 2	10	7
Engine mountings:		
Right-hand mounting bracket to body bolts	90	66
Right-hand mounting bracket-to-engine bolts	133	98
Left-hand mounting nuts	48	35
Left-hand mounting bracket to transmission	80	59
Left-hand mounting centre bolt	133	98
Lower-rear torque rod bolts	80	59
Engine oil drain plug	34	25
Engine-to-transmission bolts	48	35
Flywheel bolts*	48	35
Fuel high-pressure pump mounting bolts	20	15
Fuel high-pressure pipe unions	30	22
Fuel injector mounting studs	10	7
Main bearing bolts:		
Stage 1	25	18
Stage 2	Angle-tighten a further 60°	
Oil pressure switch	35	26
Oil pump bolts	16	12
Oil pump pick-up tube bolts	12	9
Piston cooling jet	10	7
Roadwheel nuts	Refer to Chapter 1	
Subframe mounting bolts: *		
Front	120	89
Rear	280	207
Subframe rear mounting brackets to body	25	18
Sump bolts	16	12
Thermostat housing to cylinder head	18	13
Timing belt tensioner	21	15
Timing chain tensioner	6	4

Note: * *Do not re-use*

1 General Information

How to use this Chapter

1 This Part of Chapter 2 is devoted to repair procedures possible while the engine is still installed in the vehicle. Since these procedures are based on the assumption that the engine is installed in the vehicle, if the engine has been removed from the vehicle and mounted on a stand, some of the preliminary dismantling steps outlined will not apply.

2 Information concerning engine/transmission removal and refitting and engine overhaul, can be found in Part E of this Chapter.

Engine description

3 The engine is a result of a joint venture between Ford and Peugeot. This DOHC (Double Overhead Camshaft) 16-valve engine features common rail direct injection, and a VNT (Variable Nozzle Turbine) turbocharger.

4 All major components are made from aluminium, apart from the cast-iron cylinder block – no liners are fitted, the cylinders are bored directly into the block. An aluminium main bearing ladder is fitted. This arrangement offers greater rigidity than the normal sump arrangement, and helps to reduce engine vibration.

5 The crankshaft runs in five main bearings, thrustwashers are fitting either side of the No 1 cylinder main bearings to control crankshaft endfloat. The connecting rods rotate on horizontally-split bearing shells at their big-ends. The pistons are attached to the connecting rods by gudgeon pins which are a floating fit in the connecting rod small-end eyes, secured by circlips. The aluminium alloy pistons are fitted with three piston rings: two compression rings and an oil control ring. After manufacture, the cylinder bores and piston skirts are measured and classified into four weight grades, which must be carefully matched together to ensure the correct piston/cylinder clearance; no oversizes are available to permit reboring.

6 The inlet and exhaust valves are each closed by coil springs; they operate in guides which are shrink-fitted into the cylinder head, as are the valve seat inserts.

7 A rubber toothed-belt driven by the crankshaft sprocket rotates the coolant pump and the exhaust camshaft sprocket. The inlet camshaft is driven by a short timing chain from the exhaust sprocket.

8 The camshafts operate the 16 valves via roller-rocker arms with hydraulic clearance adjusters. The camshafts rotate in five bearings that are line-bored directly into the two sections of the cylinder head.

9 The vacuum pump (used for the brake servo and other vacuum actuators) is driven from the end of the inlet camshaft, whilst the fuel pump is driven from the end of the exhaust camshaft.

10 When working on this engine, note that Torx-type (both male and female heads) and hexagon socket (Allen head) fasteners are widely used; a good selection of bits, with the necessary adapters, will be required so that these can be unscrewed without damage and, on reassembly, tightened to the torque wrench settings specified.

Lubrication system

11 The oil pump is mounted under the cylinder block, and is chain driven from a crankshaft sprocket. The pump forces oil through an externally-mounted full-flow cartridge-type filter. From the filter, the oil is pumped into a main gallery in the cylinder block/crankcase, from where it is distributed to the crankshaft (main bearings) and cylinder head. An oil cooler is fitted next to the oil filter, at the rear of the block. The cooler is supplied with coolant from the engine cooling system.

12 While the crankshaft and camshaft bearings receive a pressurised supply, the camshaft lobes and valves are lubricated by splash, as are all other engine components. The undersides of the pistons are cooled by oil, sprayed from nozzles fitted above the upper main bearing shells. The turbocharger receives its own pressurised oil supply.

Operations with engine in car

13 The following major repair operations can be accomplished without removing the engine from the vehicle. However, owners should note that any operation involving the removal of the sump requires careful forethought, depending on the level of skill and the tools and facilities available; refer to the relevant text for details.

a) Compression pressure – testing.
b) Cylinder head cover – removal and refitting.
c) Timing belt cover – removal and refitting.
d) Timing belt/chain – renewal.
e) Timing belt tensioner and sprockets – removal and refitting.
f) Camshaft oil seal – renewal.
g) Camshaft and cam followers – removal and refitting.
h) Cylinder head – removal, overhaul and refitting.
i) Cylinder head and pistons – decarbonising.
j) Sump – removal and refitting.
k) Crankshaft oil seals – renewal.
l) Oil pump – removal and refitting.
m) Piston/connecting rod assemblies – removal and refitting (but see note below).
n) Flywheel – removal and refitting.
o) Engine/transmission mountings – removal and refitting.

Note: It is possible to remove the pistons and connecting rods (after removing the cylinder head and sump) without removing the engine, however, this is not recommended. Work of this nature is more easily and thoroughly completed with the engine on the bench, as described in Chapter 2E.

14 Clean the engine compartment and the exterior of the engine with some type of degreaser before any work is done (and/or clean the engine using a steam cleaner). It will make the job easier and will help to keep dirt out of the internal areas of the engine.

15 Depending on the components involved, it may be helpful to remove the bonnet, to improve access to the engine as repairs are performed (refer to Chapter 11 Section 7 if necessary). Cover the wings to prevent damage to the paint; special covers are available, but an old bedspread or blanket will also work.

2 Compression and leakdown tests – description and interpretation

Compression test

Note: A compression tester suitable for use with diesel engines will be required for this test.

1 When engine performance is down, or if misfiring occurs which cannot be attributed to the fuel or emissions systems, a compression test can provide diagnostic clues as to the engine's condition. If the test is performed regularly, it can give warning of trouble before any other symptoms become apparent.

2 The engine must be fully warmed-up to normal operating temperature, the battery must be fully-charged and the glow plugs must be removed. The aid of an assistant will be required.

3 Pull the plastic cover on the top of the engine upwards to release it from its mountings.

4 Disconnect the wiring plugs from the injectors.

5 Remove the glow plugs as described in Chapter 5 Section 11.

6 Raise the front of the vehicle and support it securely on axle stands (see Jacking and vehicle support).

7 Undo the fasteners and remove the engine undershield.

8 Fit a compression tester to the No 1 cylinder glow plug hole.

9 Crank the engine for several seconds on the starter motor. After one or two revolutions, the compression pressure should build-up to a maximum figure and then stabilise. Record the highest reading obtained.

10 Repeat the test on the remaining cylinders, recording the pressure in each.

11 The cause of poor compression is less easy to establish on a diesel engine than on a petrol engine. The effect of introducing oil into the cylinders (wet testing) is not conclusive, because there is a risk that the oil will sit in the recess on the piston crown, instead of passing to the rings. However, the following can be used as a rough guide to diagnosis.

12 All cylinders should produce very similar pressures. Any great difference indicates the existence of a fault. Note that the compression should build-up quickly in a healthy engine. Low compression on the first stroke, followed by gradually increasing pressure on successive strokes, indicates worn piston rings. A low compression reading on the first stroke, which does not build-up during successive strokes, indicates leaking valves or a blown head gasket (a cracked head could also be the cause).

13 A low reading from two adjacent cylinders is almost certainly due to the head gasket having blown between them and the presence of coolant in the engine oil will confirm this.

14 On completion, remove the compression tester, and refit the glow plugs.

15 Reconnect the injector wiring plugs, refit the glow plug relay and the engine/radiator undershields.

3.1 Remove the engine cover

Leakdown test

16 A leakdown test measures the rate at which compressed air fed into the cylinder is lost. It is an alternative to a compression test, and in many ways it is better, since the escaping air provides easy identification of where pressure loss is occurring (piston rings, valves or head gasket).

17 The equipment required for leakdown testing is unlikely to be available to the home mechanic. If poor compression is suspected, have the test performed by a suitably-equipped garage.

3 Cylinder head cover – removal and refitting

Removal

1 The cylinder head cover is integral with the inlet manifold. Begin by removing the plastic cover from the top of the engine by pulling it straight up from its mountings at the right-hand rear corner, right-hand front corner and left-hand front corner, then sliding it forwards **(see illustration)**.

2 Undo the 2 bolts securing the brake fluid remote reservoir (where fitted) to the engine compartment bulkhead.

3 Remove the wiper arms as described in Chapter 12 Section 12.

4 Remove the upper and lower windscreen

cowl panels as described in Chapter 12 Section 12.

5 Disconnect the battery negative lead as described in Chapter 5 Section 3.

6 Disconnect the crankcase ventilation hoses from the inlet manifold/cover, then release the clamp and disconnect the EGR pipe from the inlet manifold **(see illustrations)**.

7 Undo the bolts and remove the throttle body/anti-shudder valve and retaining bracket **(see illustration)**.

8 Undo the remaining bolts and remove the EGR pipe.

9 Release the clips and detach the wiring harness and fuel pipes from the timing belt upper cover.

10 Undo the bolt and remove the wiring bracket from the right-hand rear corner of the cylinder head.

11 Disconnect the wiring plug, undo the retaining bolt and remove the camshaft position sensor **(see illustration)**.

12 Undo the bolts, slacken the nut, then remove the timing belt upper cover.

13 Disconnect the injector wiring plugs, then detach the harness duct from the inlet manifold/cover and position it to one side **(see illustration)**.

14 Release the glow plugs wiring harness from the 2 clips on the manifold.

15 Unclip the fuel temperature sensor (located on underside the inlet manifold).

16 Undo the manifold/cover retaining bolts in the reverse of the sequence shown **(see**

3.6a Release the clamps and disconnect the breather hose from the cylinder head cover…

3.6b …the EGR pipe from the inlet manifold…

3.6c… then depress the clip and disconnect the breather hose from the rear of the cylinder head cover

3.7 Anti-shudder valve/throttle body bolts

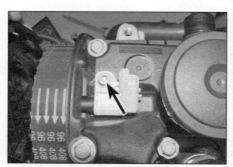

3.11 Undo the bolt and remove the camshaft position sensor

3.13 Release the clips and detach the injector wiring harness duct

3.18 Inlet manifold/cylinder head cover bolt tightening sequence

Note that the 55 mm bolt is fitted to position 14, and 70 mm bolts are fitted to positions 16 and 17

4.2 Undo the fasteners and remove the engine undershield

illustration 3.18). Discard the gaskets, new ones must be fitted.

Refitting

17 Clean the sealing surfaces of the manifold/cover and the head.

18 Fit the new seals to the inlet manifold/cover, then fit it to the cylinder head. Use a little petroleum jelly on the manifold O-rings to ease assembly. Tighten the bolts to the specified torque in sequence **(see illustration)**.

19 The remainder of refitting is a reversal of removal, noting the following points:

a) *Tighten all fasteners to their specified torque where given.*

b) *The camshaft position sensor must be refitted in accordance with the instructions given in Chapter 4A Section 12, otherwise it will not function correctly.*

4 Crankshaft pulley – removal and refitting

Removal

1 Loosen the right-hand front roadwheel nuts, then raise the front of the vehicle, and support securely on axle stands (see *Jacking and vehicle support*). Remove the roadwheel. Access is greatly improved once the wheel arch liner has been removed.

2 Release the fasteners and withdraw the engine undershield from under the car **(see illustration)** and then remove the wing liner.

3 Remove the auxiliary drivebelt as described in Chapter 1 Section 22.

4 The centre bolt which secures the crank-shaft pulley must now be slackened. This bolt is tightened to a very high torque, and it is first of all essential to ensure that the car is adequately supported, as considerable effort will be needed.

5 Ford technicians use a special holding tool (303-393/303-393-01) which bolts to the transmission housing and engages with the starter ring gear teeth once the starter motor has been removed. The tool is widely available in the aftermarket. Where this tool is not available it may be possible to jamb the ring gear with a pry bar or large screwdriver.

6 Unscrew the bolt securing the pulley to the crankshaft, and remove the pulley. It is essential to obtain a new bolt for reassembly **(see illustrations)**. If required, remove the sensor ring/spacer. **Note:** *Do not touch the outer sensor ring.*

7 With the pulley removed, it is advisable to check the crankshaft oil seal for signs of oil leakage. If necessary, fit a new seal as described in Section 14.

Refitting

8 Refit the pulley to the crankshaft sprocket, then fit the new pulley securing bolt and tighten it as far as possible before the crankshaft starts to rotate.

9 Holding the pulley against rotation as for removal, first tighten the bolt to the specified Stage 1 torque.

10 Stage 2 involves tightening the bolt though an angle, rather than to a torque. The bolt must be rotated through the specified angle – special angle gauges are available from tool outlets.

11 The remainder of refitting is a reversal of removal.

5 Timing belt and tensioner – removal and refitting

Removal

1 Disconnect the battery negative lead as described in Chapter 5 Section 3.

2 Undo the 2 bolts securing the brake fluid remote reservoir (where fitted) to the engine compartment bulkhead.

3 Remove the wiper arms and then remove the upper and lower windscreen cowl panels as described in Chapter 12 Section 12.

4 Remove the cover from top of the engine.

5 Remove the auxiliary drivebelt as described in Chapter 1 Section 22.

6 Release the wiring harness from the timing belt cover, then unclip the fuel pipes.

7 Undo the 2 bolts, slacken the nut, and

4.6a Undo the bolt and remove the crankshaft pulley ...

4.6b ...followed by the TDC sensor ring/spacer

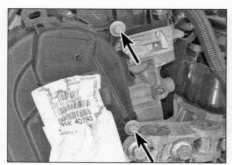

5.7a Undo the 2 bolts ...

5.7b ...and slacken the nut

5.11 Undo the bolts and remove the right-hand engine mounting

5.16a The tool fits through the hole in the cylinder block flange

5.16b ...and into a hole in the rear of the flywheel

5.17 The tool fits through the hole in the exhaust camshaft sprocket, into the timing hole in the cylinder head

remove the upper timing belt cover **(see illustrations)**.

8 Slacken the front right-hand roadwheel bolts, then jack up the front of the vehicle and support it securely on axle stands (see *Jacking and vehicle support*). Remove the roadwheel.

9 Release the fasteners and remove the engine undershield **(see illustration 4.2)**.

10 The engine must now be supported before the right-hand mounting is removed. Ford technicians use an engine support bar, which locates in the channels at the top of each inner wing, and a further beam attached to this, which rests on the front crossmember. If such an arrangement is not available, use an engine crane; either way, use a suitable length of chain and hooks to attach the lifting gear to the engine lifting eye. If the engine must be supported from below (and this is not recommended), use a large piece of wood on a trolley jack to spread the load and reduce the chance of damage to the sump.

11 With the weight of the engine supported, unscrew the bolts/nuts, and remove the right-hand engine mounting **(see illustration)**.

12 Slacken the crankshaft pulley bolt as described in Section 4. Do not discard the old bolt yet – it is used during reassembly.

13 Two special tools are now required to set the engine at TDC (Top Dead Centre) for No1 cylinder (at the transmission end). Ford tool No 303-105 locates through a hole in the rear flange of the cylinder block into a corresponding hole in the rear of the flywheel, whilst tool No 303-735 locates through a hole in the exhaust camshaft sprocket into a hole in the cylinder head casting. In the absence of these tools, use an 8 mm drill bit to lock the camshaft sprocket, and an 8 mm rod to lock the flywheel. **Note:** *The flywheel locking bolt must be flat (not tapered at all) at the end.*

14 Undo the starter motor bolts and position the motor to one side, to expose the

crankshaft setting tool hole in the cylinder block flange. Refer to if necessary.

15 Using a spanner or socket on the crankshaft pulley bolt, rotate the engine in a clockwise direction (viewed from the timing belt end of the engine) until the hole in the camshaft sprocket begins to align with the corresponding hole in the cylinder head.

16 Insert the crankshaft setting tool though the hole in the cylinder block flange and press it against the back of the flywheel. Have an assistant very slowly rotate the crankshaft clockwise, and the tool should slide into the flywheel as the holes align **(see illustrations)**.

17 It should now be possible to insert the camshaft locking tool (303-735) or equivalent through the hole in the camshaft sprocket into the hole in the cylinder head **(see illustration)**. Note that it may be necessary to rotate the camshaft sprocket backwards or forwards very slightly to be able to insert the tool.

18 At this point, Ford technicians use the tool described in paragraph 5 of Section 4 to lock the crankshaft in this position. The use of this tool, or an equivalent is strongly recommended.

19 Disconnect the crankshaft position sensor wiring plug, then undo the bolt and remove the sensor **(see illustration)**.

20 Remove the crankshaft pulley, followed by the sensor ring/spacer **(see illustration 4.6a and 4.6b)**. **Note:** *Do not touch the outer sensor ring.*

21 Undo the bolts/nut and remove the lower timing belt cover **(see illustration)**.

5.19 Crankshaft position sensor bolt

5.21 Timing belt lower cover bolts

5.22 Slacken the tensioner pulley bolt

5.24 Slacken the engine mounting bracket bolts and remove the idler pulley

5.27 Fit the new idler pulley

22 Raise the engine slightly, then relieve the timing belt tension by slackening the bolt in the centre of the tensioning pulley **(see illustration)**.
23 Remove the timing belt from the sprockets. Note that the belt must not be re-used.
24 Slacken the bolts a few turns, remove the engine mounting bracket and the idler pulley, then undo the tensioner bolt **(see illustration)**. Discard both the tensioner and idler pulleys – new ones must be fitted.
25 If a new timing belt is not being fitted straight away (or if the belt is being removed as part of another procedure, such as cylinder head removal), temporarily refit the engine right-hand mounting and tighten the bolts securely.

Refitting

26 Ensure that the crankshaft and camshaft are still set to TDC on No 1 cylinder.
27 Position the new idler pulley and insert the retaining bolt **(see illustration)**.
28 Refit the engine mounting bracket, then tighten the retaining bolts (including the idler pulley bolt) to the specified torque, where given.
29 Fit the new timing belt tensioner into position, but tighten the retaining finger-tight only at this stage.
30 Fit the new timing belt over the various sprockets in the following order: crankshaft,

5.30a Timing belt routing

5.30b The arrows on the belt must point in the direction of rotation

idler pulley, camshaft, tensioner and coolant pump **(see illustrations)**. Pay attention to any arrows on the belt indicating direction of rotation.
31 Using an Allen key in the tensioner arm, rotate the arm anti-clockwise until the pointer is positioned between the sides of the adjustment 'window' **(see illustrations)**. Fully tighten the tensioner retaining bolt.
32 Refit the timing belt lower cover and tighten the bolts securely.
33 Refit the sensor ring/spacer and the crankshaft pulley, then tighten the old pulley bolt to 50 Nm (37 lbf ft).
34 Remove the crankshaft and camshaft setting/locking tools, then rotate the crankshaft 2 complete revolutions clockwise, until the crankshaft setting tool can be

re-inserted. Check that the camshaft locking tool can be inserted.
35 Check position of the tensioner pointer, and if necessary slacken the retaining bolt and use the Allen key to align the pointer in the centre of the adjustment 'window'. Tighten the retaining bolt securely.
36 Remove the old crankshaft pulley bolt, and fit the new one. Tighten the bolt to the specified torque, using the method employed during removal to prevent the crankshaft from rotating.
37 Remove the crankshaft and camshaft locking tools.
38 The remainder of refitting is a reversal of removal, remembering to tighten all fasteners to their specified torque where given.

5.31a Use an Allen key in the tensioner arm hole

5.31b Rotate the arm anti-clockwise until the pointer is between the sides of the adjustment 'window'

6 Timing chain and tensioner – removal and refitting

Timing chain

1 Removal of the timing chain is included in the camshaft removal and refitment procedure, as described in Section 7.

Tensioner

2 Remove the cylinder head cover as described in Section 3.
3 Press the tensioner upper guide rail upwards into the housing, then insert a 2.0

6.3 Lift up the chain upper guide rail and insert a 2.0 mm diameter rod/drill bit into the hole in the tensioner housing

6.4 Undo the tensioner retaining bolts

7.4a Depress the release tab and disconnect the servo hose from the pump

7.4b Undo the nut securing the EGR pipe and fuel hose

7.4c Vacuum pump securing bolts

7.5 Undo the unions and remove the high-pressure fuel pipe between the fuel rail and pump

7.6a Depress the release tab and disconnect the fuel return hose ...

7.6b ... and the fuel supply hose

mm locking pin/drill bit to secure the rail in position **(see illustration)**.

4 Undo the 2 retaining bolts and withdrawn the tensioner **(see illustration)**.

5 Begin refitting by ensuring the tensioner and cylinder head mating faces are clean and free of debris.

6 Install the tensioner and tighten the retaining bolts to the specified torque.

7 Press the tensioner upper guide rail into the housing, pull out the locking pin/drill bit, then slowly release the guide rail.

8 Refit the cylinder head cover as described in Section 3.

7 Camshaft, rocker arms and hydraulic adjusters – removal, inspection and refitting

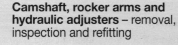

Note: *A new camshaft oil seal will be required on refitting.*

Removal

1 Remove the timing belt as described in Section 5.

2 Remove the timing chain tensioner as described in Section 6.

3 Remove the air cleaner assembly as described in Chapter 4A Section 3.

4 Working at the left-hand end of the cylinder head, depress the release tab and disconnect the hose from the vacuum pump, undo the nut securing the EGR pipe and fuel supply hose, then undo the 3 Allen bolts and remove the pump from the cylinder head **(see illustrations)**. Check the condition of the pump O-ring seals and renew if necessary.

5 Undo the unions and remove the high-pressure fuel pipe between the fuel rail and the high-pressure pump located at the left-hand end of the cylinder head **(see illustration)**. Discard the pipe, a new one must be fitted. Plug or seal the openings to prevent contamination.

6 Slide off the retaining clip/depress the release tab and disconnect the fuel supply and return hoses from the high-pressure pump **(see illustrations)**. Plug or seal the openings to prevent contamination.

7.8 High-pressure fuel pump retaining bolts

To make a camshaft sprocket holding tool, obtain two lengths of steel strip about 6 mm thick by 30 mm wide or similar, one 600 mm long, the other 200 mm long (all dimensions are approximate). Bolt the two strips together to form a forked end, leaving the bolt slack so that the shorter strip can pivot freely. Drill holes and insert bolts of a suitable size in the ends of the fork to engage in the sprocket spokes. Hold the bolts at the ends firmly in place by using a nut on the other side of the steel strip.

7.12 Remove the bolts securing the belt inner cover

7 Note their fitted positions, and disconnect the wiring plug(s) from the high-pressure fuel pump.

8 Undo the 3 retaining bolts and pull the high-pressure fuel pump out from the cylinder head **(see illustration)**. Be prepared for fuel spillage.

9 Remove the injectors as described in Chapter 4A Section 11.

10 Undo the retaining bolt and pull the sprocket from the exhaust camshaft. Use a tool to prevent the camshaft and sprocket from rotating whilst the nut is released (see Tool Tip).

TOOL TIP:

11 Undo the bolts and remove the engine mounting bracket from the right-hand end of the cylinder head/block.

12 Undo the bolts securing the timing belt inner cover to the cylinder head **(see illustration)**.

13 Undo the 2 bolts and remove the EGR pipe from over the left-hand end of the cylinder head.

14 Unscrew the injector mounting studs using a Torx socket, in sequence **(see illustration)**.

15 Working in the reverse of the sequence given **(see illustration 7.28)**, gradually and evenly remove the bolts securing the upper section of the cylinder head.

16 Carefully tap around the edge of the cylinder head upper section and lift it from position. Note that the cover will probably be reluctant to lift due to the sealant used, and possible corrosion around the two locating dowels at the front edge.

17 Lift the camshafts from position, disengage the timing chain from the sprockets, and remove the exhaust camshaft seal.

18 Have ready a box divided into 16 segments, or some containers or other means of storing and identifying the rockers arms and hydraulic adjusters after removal. It's essential that if they are to be refitted, they return to their original positions. Mark the segments in the box or the containers with the cylinder number for each rocker arm/adjuster, and left or right, for the particular cylinder.

19 Lift out the rockers arms and hydraulic adjusters, Keep them identified for position, and place them in their respective positions in the box or container **(see illustration)**.

Inspection

20 With the camshaft removed, examine the bearing surfaces in the upper and lower sections of the cylinder head for signs of obvious wear or pitting. If evident, a new cylinder head will probably be required. Also check that the oil supply holes in the cylinder head are free from obstructions.

21 Visually inspect the camshaft for evidence of wear on the surfaces of the lobes and journals. Normally their surfaces should be smooth and have a dull shine; look for scoring, erosion or pitting and areas that appear highly polished, indicating excessive wear. Accelerated wear will occur once the hardened exterior of the camshaft has been damaged, so always renew worn items. **Note:** *If these symptoms are visible on the tips of the camshaft lobes, check the rocker arm, as it will probably be worn as well.*

22 If any doubt exists as to the condition of the camshafts or cylinder head, have them examined at a Ford dealer workshop or suitably-equipped automotive repair facility.

23 Inspect the rocker arms and hydraulic adjusters for obvious signs of wear or damage, and renew if necessary.

7.14 Injector mounting stud removal sequence

7.19 Lift out the rocker arms and hydraulic adjusters

7.24 Fit the secondary timing chain lower guide rail

7.25a Apply clean oil to the hydraulic adjusters...

7.25b ...and refit them to their original positions

7.26a Align the coloured links on the chain with the marks on the camshaft sprockets...

7.26b ...the mark on the sprockets is a dot, and a line...

7.26c ...then fit the camshafts with the mark on the inlet camshaft in the 12 o'clock position

Refitting

24 Make sure that the top surfaces of the cylinder head, and in particular the camshaft bearings and the mating surfaces are completely clean. Ensure the secondary timing chain lower guide rail is in place **(see illustration)**.

25 Smear some clean engine oil onto the sides of the hydraulic adjusters, and offer each one into position in their original bores in the cylinder head, together with its rocker arm **(see illustrations)**.

26 Locate the timing chain on the camshaft sprockets, aligning the two coloured chain links with the marks on the camshaft sprockets, then lubricate the camshaft and cylinder head bearing journals with clean engine oil, and lower the camshafts into position **(see illustrations)**. The mark on the inlet camshaft must be in the 12 o'clock position.

27 Apply a thin bead of silicone sealant (Ford part No WSE-M4G323-A4) to the mating surface of the cylinder head. Take great care to ensure the chain tensioner oil supply hole is free from sealant **(see illustrations)**.

28 Lower the upper section of the cylinder head into place, and tighten the retaining

7.27a Apply a thin bead of sealant as indicated by the heavy black line

7.27b We inserted a tapered rod into the tensioner oil supply hole to prevent any sealant from entering

7.28 Cylinder head upper section bolt tightening sequence

bolts to the specified torque in sequence **(see illustration)**.

29 Refit the fuel injector mounting studs and tighten them to the specified torque.

30 Refit the camshaft timing chain tensioner assembly, and tighten the retaining bolts to the specified torque. Press the tensioner guide rail up into the housing and pull out the locking pin/drill bit. Slowly release the guide rail to tension the chain.

31 Fit a new exhaust camshaft oil seal as described in Section 8.

32 Refit the 2 bolts securing the timing belt inner cover to the cylinder head, and the single bolt to the cylinder block, then tighten the bolts securely.

33 Slide the exhaust camshaft sprocket into place, aligning the integral key with the camshaft and fit the camshaft sprocket locking tool **(see illustration 5.19)**.

34 Fit the sprocket retaining bolt and tighten it to the specified torque, preventing the sprocket from turning using the tool used during removal.

35 Refit the engine mounting bracket to the right-hand end of the cylinder head/block, and tighten the bolts to the specified torque.

36 The remainder of refitting is a reversal of removal, noting the following points:
a) Refit the injectors as described in Chapter 4A.
b) Fit the new timing belt, tensioner and idler pulley as described in Section 5.
c) Tighten all fasteners to their specified torque, where given.
d) Check the engine oil and coolant levels as described in 'Weekly checks.'.

8 Camshaft oil seal – renewal

1 Remove the timing belt as described in Section 5, and the camshaft sprocket as described in the previous Section 7. Recover the sprocket locating key from the end of the camshaft.

2 Carefully prise or pull the seal from position.

3 Clean out the seal housing and the sealing surface of the camshaft by wiping it with a lint-free cloth. Remove any swarf or burrs that may cause the seal to leak.

4 Apply a little oil to the new camshaft oil

HAYNES HINT *One of the best ways to remove an oil seal is to carefully drill or punch two holes through the seal, opposite each other (taking care not to damage the surface behind the seal as this is done). Two self-tapping screws are then screwed into the holes; by pulling on the screw heads alternately with a pair of pliers, the seal can be extracted.*

seal, and fit it over the end of the camshaft, lips facing inwards. To avoid damaging the seal lips, wrap a little tape over the end of the camshaft. Ford dealers have a special tool (No 303-684/1) for fitting the seal, but if this is not available, a deep socket of suitable size can be used. **Note:** *Select a socket that bears only on the hard outer surface of the seal, not the inner lip which can easily be damaged. It is important that the seal is fitted square to the shaft, and is fully-seated* **(see illustrations)**.

5 Refit the camshaft sprocket (and key – Section 7) and timing belt as described in Section 5.

9 Cylinder head – removal, inspection and refitting

Removal

1 Remove the battery as described in Chapter 5 Section 3, then unscrew the three bolts securing the battery tray, and remove the tray from the engine compartment.

2 Remove the wiper arms, the upper and then the lower windscreen cowl panels as described in Chapter 12 Section 12. Drain the coolant as described in Chapter 1 Section 25.

3 Remove the camshafts, rocker arms and hydraulic adjusters as described in Section 7.

4 Undo the bolts, and remove the bracket over the fuel filter.

5 Undo the Torx bolt, lift out the filter housing, then undo the bolts and remove

8.4a Apply a little clean oil to the oil seal inner lip...

8.4b ...then use a socket (or similar) to drive the seal into place...

8.4c ...until the seal is flush with the casing surface

9.5a Undo the Torx bolt on the side and lift out the filter housing ...

9.5b ... then undo the bolts and remove the filter bracket

9.7 Thermostat housing studs

the fuel filter bracket. Refit the bolt securing the lifting bracket to the cylinder head (see illustrations).

6 Remove the turbocharger/exhaust manifold as described in Chapter 4A Section 14.

7 Disconnect the wiring plugs, then undo the 4 nuts, unscrew the 4 mounting studs and detach the thermostat housing from the left-hand of the cylinder head. Be prepared for coolant spillage (see illustration).

8 Disconnect the wiring plug from the pressure sensor on the underside of the common fuel rail at the front of the cylinder head.

9 Undo the retaining bolt, and remove the oil filler pipe support bracket.

10 Working in the reverse of the sequence shown in paragraph 34, gradually and evenly slacken and remove the cylinder head bolts. Discard the bolts, new ones must be fitted.

11 Lift the cylinder head away; use assistance if possible, as it is a very heavy assembly. Do not place the cylinder head flat on its sealing surface, as the ends of the glow plugs may be damaged – support the ends of the cylinder head on wooden blocks.

12 If the head is stuck (as is possible), be careful how you choose to free it. Striking the head with tools carries the risk of damage, and the head is located on two dowels, so its movement will be limited. Do not, under any circumstances, lever the head between the mating surfaces, as this will certainly damage the sealing surfaces for the gasket, leading to leaks.

9.20 Zero the DTI on the gasket face

13 Once the head has been removed, recover the gasket from the two dowels.

14 Do not discard the gasket at this stage – it will be needed for correct identification of the new gasket.

Inspection

15 If required, dismantling and inspection of the cylinder head is covered in Part E of this Chapter.

Cylinder head gasket selection

16 Examine the old cylinder head gasket for manufacturer's identification markings. These will be in the form of holes on the front edge of the gasket, which indicate the gasket's thickness.

17 Unless new components have been fitted, or the cylinder head has been machined (skimmed), the new cylinder head gasket must be of the same type as the old one. Purchase the required gasket, and proceed to paragraph 24.

18 If the head has been machined, or if new pistons have been fitted, it is likely that a head gasket of different thickness to the original will be needed.

19 Gasket selection is made on the basis of the measured piston protrusion above the cylinder head gasket surface.

20 To measure the piston protrusion, anchor a dial test indicator (DTI) to the top face (cylinder head gasket mating face) of the cylinder block, and zero the gauge on the gasket mating face (see illustration).

21 Rest the gauge probe above No 1 piston crown, and turn the crankshaft slowly by hand until the piston reaches TDC (its maximum height). Measure and record the maximum piston projection at TDC.

22 Repeat the measurement for the remaining pistons, and record the results.

23 If the measurements differ from piston to piston, take the highest figure, and use this to determine the thickness of the head gasket required (see Specifications).

Preparation for refitting

24 The mating faces of the cylinder head

and cylinder block must be perfectly clean before refitting the head. Use a hard plastic or wooden scraper to remove all traces of gasket and carbon; also clean the piston crowns. Note: The new head gasket has rubber-coated surfaces, which could be damaged from sharp edges or debris left by a metal scraper. Take particular care when cleaning the piston crowns, as the soft aluminium alloy is easily damaged.

25 Make sure that the carbon is not allowed to enter the oil and water passages – this is particularly important for the lubrication system, as carbon could block the oil supply to the engine's components. Using adhesive tape and paper, seal the water, oil and bolt holes in the cylinder block.

26 To prevent carbon entering the gap between the pistons and bores, smear a little grease in the gap.

27 After cleaning each piston, use a small brush to remove all traces of grease and carbon from the gap, then wipe away the remainder with a clean rag. Clean all the pistons in the same way.

28 Check the mating surfaces of the cylinder block and the cylinder head for nicks, deep scratches and other damage (refer to the Note in paragraph 24). If slight, they may be removed carefully with a file, but if excessive, machining may be the only alternative to renewal.

29 If warpage of the cylinder head gasket surface is suspected, use a straight-edge to check it for distortion. Refer to Part D of this Chapter if necessary.

30 Ensure that the cylinder head bolt holes in the crankcase are clean and free of oil. Syringe or soak up any oil left in the bolt holes. This is most important in order that the correct bolt tightening torque can be applied, and to prevent the possibility of the block being cracked by hydraulic pressure when the bolts are tightened.

Refitting

31 Ensure that the cylinder head locating dowels are in place at the corners of the cylinder block, then fit the new cylinder head gasket over the dowels, ensuring that the identification holes are at the front (see

9.31 Fit the new gasket over the dowels, with the thickness identification holes at the front

9.34 Cylinder head lower section bolt tightening sequence

illustration). Take care to avoid damaging the gasket's rubber coating.

32 Lower the cylinder head into position on the gasket, ensuring that it engages correctly over the dowels.

33 Fit the new cylinder head bolts and screw them in as far as possible by hand.

34 Working in sequence **(see illustration)**, tighten all the cylinder head bolts to the specified Stage 1 torque using an E14 Torx socket.

35 Stage 2 involves tightening the bolts though an angle, rather than to a torque **(see illustration)**. Each bolt in sequence must be rotated through the specified angle – special angle gauges are available from tool outlets.

36 The remainder of the refitting procedure is a reversal of the removal procedure, bearing in mind the following points:

a) *Refit the camshafts, rocker arms and hydraulic adjusters as described in Section 7.*

b) *Reconnect the exhaust front section to the exhaust manifold with reference to Chapter 4A Section 18.*

c) *Fit new high-pressure fuel delivery pipes as described in Chapter 4A Section 11.*

d) *Refit the inlet manifold/cylinder head cover with reference to Section 3.*

e) *Refit the air cleaner as described in Chapter 4A Section 3.*

f) *Refill the cooling system as described in Chapter 1 Section 25.*

g) *Check and if necessary top-up the engine*

oil level and power steering fluid level as described in 'Weekly checks.'.

h) *Before starting the engine, read through the section on engine restarting after overhaul, at the end of Chapter 2E Section 20.*

10 Sump – removal and refitting

Note: *The full procedure outlined below must be followed so that the mating surfaces can be cleaned and prepared to achieve an oil-tight joint on reassembly.*

Removal

1 Apply the handbrake, then jack up the front of the vehicle and support it on axle stands (see *Jacking and vehicle support*). Undo the fasteners and remove the engine undershield **(see illustration 4.2)**.

2 Referring to Chapter 1 Section 3 if necessary, drain the engine oil, then clean and refit the engine oil drain plug, tightening it to the specified torque wrench setting. We strongly advise renewing the oil filter element, also described in Chapter 1 Section 3.

3 Remove the cover from the top of the engine.

4 Slacken the hose clamps, undo the bracket bolt and remove the charge air pipe from the underside of the engine **(see illustration)**.

5 Remove the air conditioning compressor

9.35 Use an angle gauge for the Stage 2 torque setting

drivebelt as described in Chapter 1 Section 22, then undo the mounting bolts and move the compressor to one side without disconnecting the refrigerant pipes. Suspend the compressor from the radiator crossmember using wires or straps.

6 Progressively unscrew the sump retaining bolts, including the 2 bolts securing the sump to the transmission housing. Don't forget the 4 bolts at the left-hand end accessed through the holes. Break the joint by carefully inserting a putty knife (or similar) between the sump and cylinder block **(see illustrations)**. Take care not to damage the sealing surfaces.

Refitting

7 On reassembly, thoroughly clean and degrease the mating surfaces of the cylinder

10.4 Undo the charge air pipe bracket bolt

10.6a Undo the 2 bolts securing the sump to the transmission ...

10.6b ...access to the sump end bolts is through the holes

10.8 Apply sealant around the inside of the bolt holes

11.1a Slide off the crankshaft sprocket ...

11.1b ... and recover the crankshaft key

block/crankcase and sump, removing all traces of sealant, then use a clean rag to wipe out the sump and the engine's interior.

8 Apply a 3 mm thick bead of sealant (Ford part No WSE-M4G323-A4) to the sump flange, making sure the bead is around the inside edge of the bolt holes. Do not allow the sealant to enter the bolt holes **(see illustration)**. **Note:** *The sump must be refitted within 4 minutes of applying the sealant.*

9 Refit the sump and fit the retaining bolts, tightening them by hand only at this stage.

10 Tighten the 2 bolts securing the sump to the transmission casing to the specified torque, then tighten the remaining bolts, gradually and evenly to the specified torque.

11 Lower the car to the ground. Wait at least 1 hour for the sealant to cure (or whatever time is indicated by the sealant manufacturer) before refilling the engine with oil. If removed,

fit a new oil filter with reference to Chapter 1 Section 3.

11 Oil pump – removal, inspection and refitting

Removal

1 Remove the timing belt as described in Section 5, then slide off the crankshaft sprocket **(see illustrations)**.

2 Remove the sump as described in Section 10.

3 Undo the retaining bolts and remove the cover and crankshaft seal. Note the original locations of the cover bolts – they are of different lengths.

4 Undo the bolt securing the oil level pipe **(see illustration)**.

5 Pull out the key from the crankshaft sprocket, then undo the pump mounting bolts, slide the pump, chain, and crankshaft sprocket from the end of the engine **(see illustrations)**. Recover the O-ring between the sprocket and crankshaft.

Inspection

6 Undo the retaining bolts and remove the cover from the oil pump **(see illustration)**. Note the location of any identification marks on the inner and outer rotors for refitting.

7 Unscrew the plug and remove the pressure relief valve, spring and plunger, clean out and check condition of components **(see illustration)**.

8 No specifications for the pump internal components are given by Ford.

11.4 Oil level pipe bracket bolt

11.5a Remove the sprocket key ...

11.5b ... undo the oil pump mounting bolts, slide the assembly from the crankshaft ...

11.5c ... and recover the O-ring between the sprocket and crankshaft

11.6 Oil pump cover bolts

11.7 Oil pressure relief valve plug

11.13 Fit the O-ring to the end of the crankshaft

9 Check the general condition of the oil pump, and in particular, its mating face to the cylinder block. If the mating face is damaged significantly, this may lead to oil loss (and a resulting drop in available oil pressure).
10 Inspect the rotors for obvious signs of wear or damage; at the time of writing, no new parts are available. If the pump is faulty, it must be renewed as a complete unit. Lubricate the rotors with fresh engine oil and refit them into the body, making sure that the identification marks are positioned as noted on removal.
11 If the oil pump has been removed as part of a major engine overhaul, it is assumed that the engine will have completed a substantial mileage. In this case, it is often considered good practice to fit a new (or reconditioned) pump as a matter of course. In other words, if the rest of the engine is being rebuilt, the engine has completed a large mileage, or there is any question as to the old pump's condition, it is preferable to fit a new oil pump.

Refitting

12 Before fitting the oil pump, ensure that the mating faces on the pump and the engine block are completely clean.
13 Fit the O-ring to the end of the crankshaft **(see illustration)**.

14 Engage the drive chain with the oil pump and crankshaft sprockets, then slide the crankshaft sprocket into place (aligning the slot in the sprocket with the keyway in the crankshaft) as the pump is refitted. Refit the crankshaft key.
15 Refit the mounting bolts and tighten them to the specified torque. Note that the front, left-hand bolt is slightly longer than the others.
16 Apply a 3 mm wide bead of silicone sealant (Ford part No WSE-M4G323-A4) to the oil seal carrier flange. Refit the cover and tighten the bolts to the specified torque. Note that the bolts must be tightened within 4 minutes of the sealant being applied.
17 Fit a new oil seal to the cover as described in Section 14.
18 Refit the bolt securing the oil level pipe.
19 The remainder of refitting is a reversal of removal, remembering to fit a new oil filter element, and replenish the engine oil.

12 Oil pressure warning light switch – removal and refitting

Removal

1 The switch is screwed into the oil filter housing **(see illustration)**. Access is from under the vehicle. Undo the fasteners and remove the engine undershield. To further improve access, undo the mounting bolts and move the air conditioning compressor to one side. Suspend the compressor from the radiator crossmember using wire or straps. There is no need to disconnect the refrigerant pipes.
2 Disconnect the switch wiring plug.
3 Unscrew the switch from the housing; be prepared for some oil loss.

Refitting

4 Refitting is the reverse of the removal procedure; fit a new pressure switch sealing washer, and tighten the switch to the specified torque wrench setting.
5 Reconnect the switch wiring plug.
6 Refit all components removed for access to the switch.
7 Check the engine oil level and top-up as necessary (see *Weekly checks*.).
8 Check for correct warning light operation, and for signs of oil leaks, once the engine has been restarted and warmed-up to normal operating temperature.

13 Oil cooler – removal and refitting

Note: *New sealing rings will be required on refitting – check for availability prior to commencing work.*

Removal

1 The cooler is fitted to the oil filter housing on the front of the cylinder block. Access is from under the vehicle. Undo the fasteners and remove the engine undershield. To further improve access, undo the mounting bolts and move the air conditioning compressor to one side. Suspend the compressor from the radiator crossmember using wire or straps. There is no need to disconnect the refrigerant pipes.
2 Undo the 4 retaining bolts and detach the cooler from the housing **(see illustration)**. Recover the sealing rings and be prepared for oil/coolant spillage.

Refitting

3 Refitting is a reversal of removal, bearing in mind the following points:
a) *Use new sealing rings.*
b) *Tighten the cooler mounting bolts securely.*
c) *On completion, lower the car to the ground. Check and if necessary top-up the oil and coolant levels, then start the engine and check for signs of oil or coolant leakage.*

12.1 Oil pressure warning switch

13.2 Oil cooler retaining bolts

14.4a Drill a small hole in the seal…

14.4b …insert a self-tapping screw and pull out the seal

14.7a Locate the new seal and guide over the end of the crankshaft…

14.7b …then drive the seal home until it's flush with the cover

14.11a Drill a hole in the seal…

14.11b …then insert a self-tapping screw and pull out the seal

14 Crankshaft oil seals – renewal

Timing belt end seal

1 Remove the timing belt as described in Section 5.

2 Slide the belt sprocket from the crankshaft, and recover the locating key from the groove on the crankshaft (see illustrations 11.1a and 11.1b).

3 Note the fitted depth of the oil seal as a guide for fitting the new one.

4 Using a screwdriver or similar tool, carefully prise the oil seal from its location. Take care not to damage the oil seal contact surfaces or crankshaft. Alternatively, drill a small hole in the seal (taking care not to drill any deeper than necessary), then insert a self-tapping screw and use pliers to pull out the seal (see illustrations).

5 Wipe clean the oil seal contact surfaces and seating, and clean up any sharp edges or burrs which might damage the new seal as it is fitted, or which might cause the seal to leak once in place.

6 No oil should be applied to the oil seal, which is made of PTFE. Ford technicians use a special seal-fitting tool (303-255/303-395), but an adequate substitute can be achieved using a large socket or piece of tubing of sufficient size to bear on the outer edge of the new seal. Note that the new seal is supplied with a guide which fits over the end of the crankshaft.

7 Locate the new seal (with guide still fitted) over the end of the crankshaft, using the tool (see illustrations), socket, or tubing to press the seal squarely and fully into position, to the previously-noted depth. Remove the guide from the end of the crankshaft.

8 The remainder of reassembly is the reverse of the removal procedure, referring to the relevant text for details where required. Check for signs of oil leakage when the engine is restarted.

Flywheel end seal

9 Remove the transmission as described in Chapter 7 Section 7, and the clutch assembly as described in Chapter 6 Section 6.

10 Unbolt the flywheel (see Section 15).

11 Using a screwdriver or similar, carefully prise the oil seal from place. Take great care not to damage the seal seating area or the crankshaft sealing surface. Alternatively, punch or drill two small holes opposite each other in the oil seal, then screw a self-tapping

screw into each hole, and pull the screws with pliers to extract the seal (see illustrations).

12 Clean the end of the crankshaft, polishing off any burrs or raised edges, which may have caused the seal to fail in the first place. Clean also the seal mating face on the engine block, using a suitable solvent for degreasing if necessary.

13 The new oil seal is supplied fitted with a locating sleeve, which must not be removed prior to fitting (it will drop out on its own when the seal is fitted). Do not lubricate the seal.

14 Offer the new seal into position, feeding the locating sleeve over the end of the crankshaft (see illustration).

15 Ford technicians use a special tool (205-307) to pull the seal into position. In the absence of the tool, use a large socket/piece of tubing which bears only on the hard outer edge of the seal, and carefully tap the seal into position (see illustration).

14.14 Locate the seal and locating sleeve over the end of the crankshaft

14.15 Press the seal in until it's flush with the surface

16 If the seal locating sleeve is still in position, remove it now.

17 The remainder of the reassembly procedure is the reverse of dismantling, referring to the relevant text for details where required. Check for signs of oil leakage when the engine is restarted.

---

15 Flywheel – removal, inspection and refitting

15.2 Homemade flywheel locking tool

15.5 On this example the flywheel bolts are off centre

Flywheel

Removal

Note: *New flywheel retaining bolts must be used on refitting.*

1 Remove the clutch assembly as described in Chapter 6 Section 6.

2 Prevent the flywheel from turning by locking the ring gear teeth with a similar arrangement to that shown **(see illustration)**. Alternatively, bolt a strap between the flywheel and the cylinder block/crankcase.

3 Slacken and remove the retaining bolts and remove the flywheel, noting its locating dowel. Do not drop it, as it is very heavy. Discard the bolts, they must be renewed whenever they are disturbed.

Inspection

4 A dual mass flywheel is fitted to all engines. Detailed checking of the flywheel requires the use of specific tools, that are unlikely to be available to the home mechanic. However some basic checking can easily be performed.

5 Start by checking the alignment between the primary mass and the secondary mass. At rest the flywheel retaining bolts will be accessible through the holes in the secondary mass **(see illustration)**.

6 The maximum travel of the primary mass in relation to the secondary mass should not

exceed 15 teeth (or 20 degrees). Note that this is a general guide and if in doubt remove the flywheel and have a suitably equipped specialist check the flywheel **(see illustration)**.

7 Inspect the flywheel for any grease or debris from the interface between the fixed part (the primary mass) and the movable part of the flywheel (the secondary mass). Replace any flywheel that has grease visible.

8 If the ring gear is badly worn or has missing teeth, then the entire dual mass flywheel must be replaced.

9 If any doubt to the condition of the flywheel exists, despite the expense we recommend replacing it.

Refitting

10 Clean the mating surfaces of the flywheel and crankshaft and remove all traces of locking compound from the crankshaft threaded holes.

11 Fit the flywheel to the crankshaft, engaging it with the crankshaft locating dowel, and fit the new retaining bolts. **Note:** *If the new bolts are not supplied pre-coated with locking compound, apply a few drops prior to fitting the bolts.*

12 Lock the flywheel using the method employed on dismantling then, working in a

diagonal sequence, tighten all the retaining bolts to the specified torque setting **(see illustration)**.

13 Refit the clutch assembly as described in Chapter 6 Section 6.

---

16 Engine/transmission mountings – inspection and renewal

Inspection

1 If improved access is required, firmly apply the handbrake, raise the front of the vehicle and support it securely on axle stands (see *Jacking and vehicle support*). Undo the retaining screws and fasteners and remove the undershield from beneath the engine/ transmission unit.

2 Check the mounting rubber to see if it is cracked, hardened or separated from the metal at any point. Renew the mounting if any such damage or deterioration is evident.

3 AddCheck that all mounting fasteners are securely tightened. Use a torque wrench to check, if possible.

4 Using a large screwdriver or a pry bar, check for wear in the mountings by carefully levering against it to check for free play.

15.6 Check the movement between the primary and secondary mass.

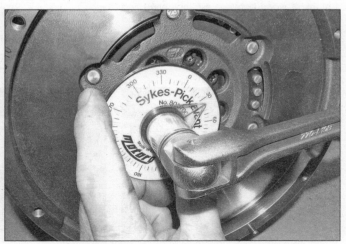

15.12 Use an angle gauge to fully tighten the flywheel

16.8a Remove the cover plate bolts (A), the outer bolts (B) and then the central bolt (C)

16.8b Lift off the cover plate ...

Where this is not possible, enlist the aid of an assistant to move the engine/gearbox unit back and forth or from side to side while you watch the mountings. While some free play is to be expected even from new components, excessive wear should be obvious. If excessive free play is found, check first that the fasteners are correctly secured, then renew any worn components as described below.

Renewal

Left-hand mounting

5 Firmly apply the handbrake, raise the front of the vehicle and support it securely on axle stands (see *Jacking and vehicle support*). Undo the retaining screws and fasteners and remove the undershield from beneath the engine/transmission unit.

6 Remove the air filter housing as described in Chapter 4A Section 3, and then remove the battery and battery tray as described in Chapter 5 Section 3.

7 Position a jack under the transmission with a block of wood between the jack head and casing, and take the weight of the engine and transmission.

8 Remove the cover plate bolts and then remove the four main bolts followed by the central bolt **(see illustrations)**

16.8c ... followed by the main mounting

9 Remove the left-hand wing liner and lower the transmission on the jack to expose the mounting bracket. Remove the bolts and lift out the bracket **(see illustration)**.

10 Refitting is a reversal of removal, but the centre nut must be replaced. If the bracket has been removed from the transmission the mounting bolts must also be replaced. Tighten all fixings to the specified torque and angle where given.

Right-hand mounting

11 Firmly apply the handbrake, raise the front of the vehicle and support it securely on axle

16.9 Remove the transmission support bracket

stands (see *Jacking and vehicle support*). Undo the retaining screws and fasteners and remove the undershield from beneath the engine/transmission unit.

12 Position a jack under the engine sump with a block of wood between the jack head and the sump. Raise the jack and take the weight of the engine on the jack.

13 Where fitted, unclip the glow plug control relay from the suspension strut tower **(see illustration)**.

14 Unclip the fuel lines from the timing belt cover and then unbolt the mounting **(see illustrations)**.

16.13 Unclip the glow plug relay

16.14a Unbolt and then ...

16.14b ... remove the mounting

16.15 The engine mounting support bracket. The lower bolt (A) holds the idler pulley

16.18a The torque rod mounting bolts

16.18b Unbolt and then...

15 If required the engine side of the mounting can be removed after the timing belt has been removed – see Section 5. Note that the lower bolt is the timing belt idler pulley bolt **(see illustration)**.

16 Refitting is a reversal of removal. When the vehicle is back on the ground, start the engine and bleed the power steering by turning the steering from lock to lock several times.

Torque rod

17 Firmly apply the handbrake, raise the front of the vehicle and support it securely on axle stands (see *Jacking and vehicle support*). Undo the retaining screws and fasteners and remove the undershield from beneath the engine/transmission unit.

18 Remove the bolts and manovre the the torque rod out from underneath **(see illustrations)**. A pry bar should be used to swing the engine away from the subframe – this will allow the mounting to be removed easily.

19 Refitting is a reversal of removal.

16.18c ...remove the torque rod

Notes

Chapter 2 Part D
2.2 litre engine in-car repair procedures

Contents

Degrees of difficulty

Easy, suitable for novice with little experience	**Fairly easy,** suitable for beginner with some experience	**Fairly difficult,** suitable for competent DIY mechanic	**Difficult,** suitable for experienced DIY mechanic	**Very difficult,** suitable for expert DIY or professional

Specifications

General

Engine type...	Four cylinder in-line double overhead camshaft, 16 valve, common rail, turbocharged diesel
Designation	Duratorq-TDCi (DW)
Engine code	Q4WA, KNWA and KNWB
Power output (@ 3,500 rpm):	
Q4WA	129 kW
KNWA	147 kW
KNWB	146 kW
Torque output at 1750 to 3000 rpm	420 Nm (nominal)
Idle speed...	750 rpm
Capacity	2197 cc
Bore	85.0 mm
Stroke	96.0 mm
Compression ratio	15.8 : 1
Firing order...	1-3-4-2 (No 1 cylinder at transmission end)
Direction of crankshaft rotation	Clockwise (seen from right-hand side of vehicle)

Valves

Valve clearances.......................................	Hydraulic adjusters – no adjustment necessary

Lubrication

Oil pressure – minimum (engine at operating temperature):	
At 2000 rpm	2.0 bar
At 4000 rpm	4.0 bar

Cylinder head gasket selection

Piston protusion:	
0.55 to 0.60 mm...................................	1.25 mm (1 hole)
0.61 to 0.65 mm...................................	1.30 mm (2 holes)
0.66 to 0.70 mm...................................	1.35 mm (3 holes)
0.71 to 0.75 mm...................................	1.40 mm (4 holes)
Maximum distortion	0.03 mm

Balancer shaft

Measurement shim thickness. . . . .   1.57 mm (marked 57)

Shaft clearance

	Shim thickness	Shim marking
0.01 to 0.05 mm	1.57	57
0.05	1.51	51
0.06 mm	1.49	49
0.07	1.47	47
0.09	1.45	45
0.1	1.43	43
0.11	1.41	41
0.12	1.41	41
0.13	1.39	39
0.14	1.37	37
0.15	1.35	35
0.16	1.35	35
0.17	1.33	33
0.18	1.31	31
0.19	1.29	29
0.2	1.29	29
0.21	1.27	27
0.22	1.25	25
0.23	1.23	23
0.24	1.23	23
0.25	1.21	21
0.26	1.19	19
>0.26	1.19	19

Torque wrench settings

	Nm	lbf ft
Accessory mounting bracket	28	21
Air conditioning compressor	24	18
Balancer shaft housing bolts:		
Stage 1	5	4
Stage 2	22	16
Big-end bearing cap bolts: *		
Stage 1	20	15
Stage 2	Angle-tighten a further 70°	
Camshaft bearing housing:		
Stage 1	8	6
Stage 2	11	8
Camshaft chain tensioner bolts	6	4
Camshaft sprocket bolt: *		
Stage 1	20	15
Stage 2	Angle-tighten a further 60°	
Camshaft position sensor	4	3
Crankshaft oil seal carrier.	14	10
Crankshaft pulley bolt: *		
Stage 1	70	52
Stage 2	Angle-tighten a further 82°	
Cylinder head bolts: *		
Stage 1	20	15
Stage 2	60	44
Stage 3	Angle-tighten a further 220°	
Cylinder head cover	9	7
Engine mountings:		
Right-hand mounting to engine bracket.	133	98
Right-hand mounting to body	90	66
Right-hand mounting bracket to engine bolt (upper bolt)	80	59
Right-hand mounting bracket to engine bolts (front bolts).	60	44
Left-hand mounting centre nut*	148	109
Left-hand mounting to body nuts	80	59
Left-hand mounting bracket to transmission: *		
Stage 1	35	26
Stage 2	Angle-tighten a further 60°	
Rear torque rod:		
Centre bolt	80	59
Subframe bolts	110	81
Engine/transmission bolts	48	35
Engine oil drain plug.	20	15

Torque wrench settings (continued)

	Nm	lbf ft
Engine to transmission bolts	48	36
Exhaust manifold: *		
Stage 1	12	9
Stage 2	20	15
Flywheel bolts*		
Stage 1	33	24
Stage 2	Angle-tighten a further 34°	
Fuel high-pressure pump mounting bolts	22	16
Fuel high-pressure pipe unions*		
Stage 1	22	16
Stage 2	25	18
Fuel injector mounting bolts: *		
Stage 1	5	3
Stage 2	Angle-tighten a further 130°	
Inlet manifold:		
Stage 1	5	3
Stage 2	2	
Main bearing bolts: *		
Stage 1	30	22
Stage 2	Angle-tighten a further 82°	
Oil filter housing/cooler:		
Lower bolts	20	15
Upper bolt	9	7
Oil pressure sensor	32	24
Oil pump bolts:		
Stage 1	7	5
Stage 2	9	7
Oil temperature sensor	27	20
Piston cooling jet	10	7
Roadwheel nuts	Refer to Chapter 1	
Subframe mounting bolts: *		
Front and rear bolts:		
Stage 1	150	110
Stage 2	Angle-tighten a further 90°	
Intermediate bolts:		
Stage 1	140	103
Stage 2	Angle-tighten a further 45°	
Subframe rear support brackets to body	30	22
Sump bolts (upper):		
Stage 1	10	7
Stage 2	16	12
Sump bolts (lower)	9	7
Thermostat housing	8	6
Timing belt idler bolt	60	44
Timing belt tensioner*	25	18

Note: * *Do not re-use*

---

1 General information

How to use this Chapter

1 This Part of the Chapter describes those repair procedures that can reasonably be carried out on the engine whilst it remains in the vehicle. If the engine has been removed from the vehicle and is being dismantled as described in Part E of this Chapter, any preliminary dismantling procedures can be ignored.

2 Note that whilst it may be possible physically to overhaul items such as the piston/connecting rod assemblies with the engine in the vehicle, such tasks are not usually carried out as separate operations and usually require the execution of several additional procedures (not to mention the cleaning of components and of oilways). For this reason, all such tasks are classed as major overhaul procedures and are described in Chapter 2E.

Engine description

3 The 2.2 litre diesel engine is the result of a joint development between Ford and PSA (Peugeot/Citroen), and is a four-cylinder, double overhead camshaft, 16-valve, in-line unit, mounted transversely at the front of the vehicle with the clutch and transmission on the left-hand end.

4 The crankshaft is supported within the cylinder block on five shell-type main bearings. Thrustwashers are integral with the No.2 main bearing shells to control crankshaft endfloat.

5 The cylinder head is of the double overhead camshaft, 16-valve design – two intake and two exhaust valves per cylinder. The valves are operated by one intake camshaft and one exhaust camshaft, via rocker fingers. One end of each finger acts upon the valve stem, whilst the other end pivots on a support pillar. Valve clearances are maintained automatically by hydraulic compensation elements incorporated within the support pillars.

6 The connecting rods rotate on horizontally-split bearing shells at their big-ends. The pistons are attached to the connecting rods by gudgeon pins which are secured in position with circlips. The aluminium alloy pistons are fitted with three piston rings, comprising two compression rings and an oil control ring.

7 The intake and exhaust valves are each closed by coil springs and operate in guides pressed into the cylinder head. Valve guides cannot be replaced.

8 A timing belt, driven by the crankshaft, drives the coolant pump and exhaust camshaft. A Simplex chain from the exhaust camshaft then drives the intake camshaft. The high-pressure fuel pump is fitted to the left-hand end of the cylinder head, and is driven by the exhaust camshaft, whilst a vacuum pump is driven from the left-hand end of the intake camshaft.

9 Lubrication is by means of an eccentric-rotor type pump driven by the crankshaft via a Simplex chain. The pump draws oil through a strainer located in the sump, and then forces it through an externally-mounted full-flow paper element type oil filter into galleries in the cylinder block/crankcase, from where it is distributed to the crankshaft (main bearings), timing chain (sprayed by a jet), and camshaft. The big-end bearings are supplied with oil via internal drillings in the crankshaft, while the camshaft bearings and the followers receive a pressurised supply via drillings in the cylinder head. The camshaft lobes and valves are lubricated by oil splash, as are all other engine components. An oil cooler (integral with the oil filter housing) is fitted to keep the oil temperature stable under arduous operating conditions.

10 A pair of balancer shafts are fitted in the sump to even out crankshaft imbalance. The shafts are driven by a crankshaft mounted gear and rotate in the opposite direction to the crankshaft.

Repair operations possible with the engine in the car

11 The following work can be carried out with the engine in the vehicle:

a) Compression pressure – testing.
b) Camshaft cover – removal and refitting.
c) Crankshaft pulley – removal and refitting.
d) Camshaft oil seals – renewal.
e) Camshaft and rocker arms – removal, inspection and refitting.
f) Cylinder head – removal and refitting.
g) Cylinder head and pistons* – decarbonising.
h) Sump – removal and refitting.
i) Oil pump – removal and refitting.
j) Balancer shafts – removal and refitting.
k) Oil filter housing/cooler – removal and refitting.
l) Crankshaft oil seals – renewal.
m) Engine/transmission mountings – inspection and renewal.

n) Flywheel/driveplate – removal, inspection and refitting.
o) Timing belt – removal and refitting.

Note: *Although in theory it is possible to remove these components with the engine in place, for reasons of access and cleanliness, it is recommended that the engine is removed.*

---

2 Compression test – description and interpretation

Compression test

Note: *A compression tester specifically designed for diesel engines must be used for this test.*

1 When engine performance is down, or if misfiring occurs which cannot be attributed to the fuel system, a compression test can provide diagnostic clues as to the engine's condition. If the test is performed regularly, it can give warning of trouble before any other symptoms become apparent.

2 A compression tester specifically intended for diesel engines must be used, because of the higher pressures involved. The tester is connected to an adaptor which screws into the glow plug hole or into the injector hole. It is unlikely to be worthwhile buying such a tester for occasional use, but it may be possible to borrow or hire one – if not, have the test performed by a garage.

3 Unless specific instructions to the contrary are supplied with the tester, observe the following points:

a) The battery must be in a good state of charge, the air filter must be clean, and the engine should be at normal operating temperature.
b) All the glow plugs (or injectors) should be removed before starting the test, as described in Chapter 5 Section 11 or Chapter 4A Section 11.

4 There is no need to hold the accelerator pedal down during the test, because the diesel engine air intake is not throttled.

5 Crank the engine on the starter motor; after one or two revolutions, the compression pressure should build up to a maximum figure, and then stabilise. Record the highest reading obtained.

6 Repeat the test on the remaining cylinders, recording the pressure in each.

7 All cylinders should produce very similar pressures; a difference of more than 10% between any two cylinders indicates a fault. Note that the compression should build up quickly in a healthy engine; low compression on the first stroke, followed by gradually-increasing pressure on successive strokes, indicates worn piston rings. A low compression reading on the first stroke, which does not build up during successive strokes, indicates leaking valves or a blown head gasket (a cracked head could also be

the cause). Deposits on the undersides of the valve heads can also cause low compression.

Note: *The cause of poor compression is less easy to establish on a diesel engine than on a petrol one. The effect of introducing oil into the cylinders ("wet" testing) is not conclusive, because there is a risk that the oil will sit in the swirl chamber or in the recess on the piston crown instead of passing to the rings.*

8 Although Ford do not specify exact compression pressures, as a guide, any cylinder pressure of below 20 bar can be considered as less than healthy. Refer to a Ford dealer or other specialist if in doubt as to whether a particular pressure reading is acceptable.

9 On completion of the test, refit the glow plugs (or injectors) as described in Chapter 5 or Chapter 4A.

Leakdown test

10 A leakdown test measures the rate at which compressed air fed into the cylinder is lost. It is an alternative to a compression test, and in many ways it is better, since the escaping air provides easy identification of where pressure loss is occurring (piston rings, valves or head gasket).

11 The equipment needed for leakdown testing is unlikely to be available to the home mechanic. If poor compression is suspected, have the test performed by a suitably-equipped garage.

---

3 Engine assembly/valve timing settings – general information and usage

Note: *Ford tools No. 303-1059 and No. 303-735 (or suitable home-made equivalents) will be required to lock the crankshaft and camshafts in position (see illustration). Equivalent tools are widely available in the aftermarket from suppliers such as AST tools or Draper tools amongst others.*

1 The flywheel is equipped with a hole, which aligns with a hole in the engine block when Nos.1 and 4 pistons are at TDC (top dead centre). In this position, if No.1 piston

3.0a The special tools can be replaced with suitable drill bits

3.4 Undo the fasteners and remove the wing liner

3.6 Starter motor aperture cover bolt

3.7a Prise the blanking plug from the timing cover

3.7b Fit the special tool or drill bit into the cylinder block

3.7c Insert the special tool through the slot in the sprocket and into the hole in the cylinder head, or....

3.7d ....use an 8.0 mm drill bit

is at TDC on its compression stroke (and the crankshaft pin is in place) then it will be possible to fit the special tool (No. 303-735) or home-made equivalent, through a hole in the timing belt cover, into corresponding holes in the exhaust camshaft sprocket and cylinder head.

2 Disconnect the battery negative lead as described in Chapter 5 Section 3.

3 Slacken the right-hand front road wheel nuts, firmly apply the handbrake then jack up the front of the vehicle and support it securely on axle stands (see *Jacking and vehicle support*). Remove the front right-hand road wheel.

4 Undo the retaining screws/clips and remove the engine undertray, and right-hand wing liner **(see illustration)**.

5 Remove the starter motor as described in Chapter 5 Section 8.

6 Undo the retaining bolt and remove the plastic cover from the lower part of the starter motor aperture **(see illustration)**.

7 Pull out the blanking plug from the timing belt cover, then using a socket and extension bar on the crankshaft pulley centre bolt, turn the crankshaft clockwise (viewed from the right-hand end of the engine) until the special tool can be inserted into the flywheel. Fit the camshaft locking tool through the cambelt cover. It should pass through the exhaust camshaft sprocket and into the corresponding hole in the cylinder head **(see illustrations)**. If the tool will not fit into the camshaft sprocket

slot then the engine is more than likely to be on the compression stroke on number four cylinder. Remove the tool and rotate the engine one complete revolution and refit the tools. **Note:** *Do not turn the engine anti-clockwise.*

8 Refitting is a reversal of removal

4 Camshaft cover – removal and refitting

1 The camshaft cover is in two sections:
● An upper plastic cover that also contains the PCV valve and oil separator
● A lower main aluminium cover that also incorporates the camshaft upper bearings

Note: *The main camshaft cover and cylinder head are matched. If there is fault with either the cover or the cylinder head upper surface, then the cylinder head and camshaft cover must be replaced as a matched pair. This may also involve the replacement of the camshafts and ancillary components. Consult a Ford dealer or an automotive machine shop.*

Removal

2 Disconnect the battery negative lead (refer to Chapter 5 Section 3).

3 Remove the wiper arms, upper windscreen cowl and the lower cowl panel as described in Chapter 12 Section 12.

4 Remove the air cleaner assembly as described in Chapter 4A Section 3.

5 Raise the front of the vehicle and support it securely on axle stands (see *Jacking and vehicle support*).

6 Remove the timing belt (Section 6) and then remove the exhaust camshaft seal as described in Section 13. Alternatively the exhaust camshaft oil seal can be removed after the camshaft cover has been removed.

7 Unbolt the oil filler neck **(see illustration)** and then remove the vacuum pump as described in Chapter 9 Section 20.

8 With reference to Chapter 4A, remove the fuel rail, fuel injectors, high pressure fuel pump and inlet manifold.

4.7 Remove the bolts

4.9a Depress the release button and disconnect the breather hose at the left-hand end of the camshaft cover...

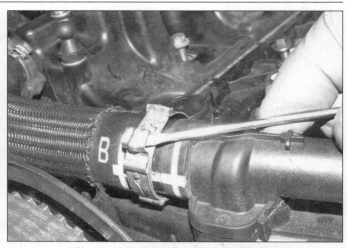

4.9b ...and the hoses at the right-hand end

9 Note their fitted positions, then disconnect the various hoses from the camshaft cover **(see illustrations)**.

10 Remove the camshaft position sensor **(see illustrations)**.

11 Undo the retaining bolts and remove the oil separator from the camshaft cover **(see illustrations)**. Discard the seals – new ones must be fitted.

12 Remove the crankshaft timing tool, and rotate the crankshaft backwards (anti-clockwise) through 90°. This positions all the pistons half way down their bores, to prevent accidental valve-to-piston contact.

13 Slowly pull the timing chain tensioner service pin upwards (retracting the tensioner piston), then rotate it clockwise to lock it in place **(see illustration)**.

4.10a Disconnect and then...

4.10b ...remove the camshaft position sensor

4.11a Oil separator retaining bolts

4.11b Renew the oil separator seals

4.13 Pull the service pin upwards, and rotate it clockwise to lock it

4.14 Undo the retaining bolts and remove the camshaft cover

4.16 Apply a continuous bead of sealant to the areas shown

4.18a Position the new gasket between the camshafts

4.18b Lower the camshaft cover into position

14 Working in a diagonal pattern, evenly slacken and remove the 27 bolts securing the camshaft cover to the cylinder head (see illustration).
15 Remove the cover and discard its gasket.

Refitting

16 Ensure the mating surfaces are clean, then apply a continuous bead of sealant (Loctite No. 518) to the mating surface of the cylinder head (see illustration).
17 Temporarily refit the exhaust camshaft sprocket, then rotate the camshaft clockwise and re-insert the camshaft timing pin.
18 Lubricate the camshaft bearing surfaces with clean engine oil, then refit the camshaft cover, with a new gasket, and tighten the retaining bolts gradually and evenly in sequence to the specified torque (see illustrations).
Caution: If the camshaft cover bolts are carelessly tightened, the bearing caps might break. If the caps are broken then

4.18c Camshaft cover bolt tightening sequence

*the complete cylinder head assembly must
be renewed; the cover/caps are matched to
the head and are not available separately*

19 Rotate the chain tensioner service pin
anti-clockwise and release it.

20 Carefully rotate the crankshaft 90°
clockwise and re-insert the crankshaft timing
pin.

21 Remove the camshaft sprocket and timing
pin.

22 The remainder of refitting is a reversal of
removal, noting the following points:
a) Renew all gaskets/seals.
b) Tighten all fasteners to their specified
   torque where given.
c) Check for fuel/oil leaks before venturing
   out onto the road.

5 Crankshaft pulley –
removal and refitting

Removal

1 Remove the engine cover and then
disconnect the battery negative lead as
described in Chapter 5 Section 3.

2 Firmly apply the handbrake then slacken
the right-hand front road wheel nuts. Jack up
the front of the vehicle and support it securely
on axle stands as described in *Jacking and
vehicle support*. Unscrew the bolts and
remove the right-hand front road wheel.

3 Remove the starter motor as described in
Chapter 5 Section 8.

4 Remove the wing liner and then remove the
auxiliary drivebelt as described in Chapter 1
Section 22.

5 The crankshaft pulley can be removed with
the engine in any position, however if the
pulley is to be removed for the the replacement
of the timing belt it is recommended that the
timing is checked first, with the special tools
as described in Section 3.

6 To prevent the crankshaft from rotating
whist the retaining bolt is slackened, use
Ford tool No. 303-393A or equivalent. This
tool bolts to the starter motor aperture, and
engages with the teeth on the outer edge of
the flywheel **(see illustration)**. **Note:** *Do not
be tempted to use just the crankshaft timing
tool to prevent rotation – damage may result.*

7 With the crankshaft firmly locked, undo the
crankshaft pulley retaining bolt, and recover
the washer **(see illustration)**. Note that a new
bolt must be fitted upon reassembly.

8 Withdrawn the pulley from the end of
the crankshaft. Recover the timing disk,
regardless of the task as it is fragile. Store the
disk safely **(see illustrations)**.

Refitting

9 Refit the timing disk and then locate the
pulley on the nose of the crankshaft. Screw in
the new retaining bolt with the washer fitted.

10 Lock the crankshaft by the method
used on removal, and tighten the pulley
retaining bolt to the specified Stage 1 torque
setting then angle-tighten the bolt through
the specified Stage 2, using a socket and
extension bar **(see illustrations)**. It is

recommended that an angle-measuring
gauge is used during the final stages of the
tightening, to ensure accuracy. If a gauge is
not available, use paint to make alignment
marks between the bolt head and pulley prior
to tightening; the marks can then be used to
check that the bolt has been rotated through
the correct angle.

11 The remainder of refitting is a reversal of
removal.

6 Timing belt, tensioner and
idler pulley – removal and
refitting

Note: *If the timing belt is removed it should
always be replaced. Ford insist that the
tensioner, mounting stud, nut, idler and idler
mounting bolt are are also replaced at the
same time. Ford (and aftermarket suppliers)
will not offer any warranty on the belt unless
both tensioner and idler are replaced.
Consideration should also be given to
replacing the coolant pump at the same time.*

Removal

1 Remove the engine cover and then
disconnect the battery negative lead as
described in Chapter 5 Section 3.

2 Remove the wiper arms and then remove
the upper and lower windscreen cowl panels
(as described in Chapter 12 Section 12).

3 Clamp the power steering pump fluid
supply hose and then unhook the reservoir
from the bonnet slam panel. Unbolt the power

5.6 Install the flywheel locking tool

5.7 Remove the retaining bolt and washer

5.8a Remove the pulley…

5.8b …and recover the timing disk

5.10a Use a torque wrench and…

5.10b …an angle gauge to correctly
tighten the new bolt

6.3a Unbolt the power steering pump from the engine

6.3b Clamp the supply hose, remove it ...

6.3c ... and seal the inlet on the power steering pump

steering pump and place it on the top of the engine. Disconnect the supply hose from the pump and then seal the pump – anticipate some fluid loss **(see illustrations)**.

4 Remove the crankshaft pulley as described in Section 5, then extract the crankshaft position sensor ring from the end of the crankshaft **(see illustration)**.

5 Use a trolley jack and with a block of wood placed on the head of the jack (to spread the load) support the right-hand end of the engine on the edge of the sump **(see illustration)**.

6 With the engine supported from below, remove the right-hand engine mount as described in Section 15.

7 Remove the auxiliary drivebelt as described in Chapter 1 Section 22.

8 Release the fuel lines from the upper timing belt cover **(see illustrations)** and secure them to the inner wing with cable ties.

6.4 Carefully extract the sensor ring from the end of the crankshaft

6.5 Support the engine

9 Unclip the wiring harness from the crankshaft position sensor and then release the loom from the rear of the timing belt cover.

10 Undo the retaining bolts and remove the upper timing belt cover **(see illustration)**.

11 Working underneath the vehicle undo the retaining bolt and remove the crankshaft position sensor **(see illustration)**.

12 Undo the 3 retaining bolts and remove the lower timing belt cover **(see illustrations)**.

6.8a Unclip the fuel lines and ...

6.8b ... secure them to the side

6.10 Remove the upper timing belt cover

6.11 Crankshaft position sensor retaining bolt

6.12a Remove the bolts and ...

6.12b ... lower the cover

6.13 Insert an Allen key into the hole

6.14 Remove the belt

6.15 Timing belt tensioner nut and idler
pulley bolt

13 Insert an Allen key into the hole, then slacken the tensioner retaining nut, and slowly release the tension **(see illustration)**.
14 Slide the belt from the pulleys **(see illustration)**. Note that the belt must not be re-used.
15 Undo the retaining nut and remove the tensioner. Remove the idler pulley bolt (it may be necessary to slacken the engine mounting bracket bolts) and lower the idler from the bracket **(see illustration)**. Lock two nuts together and remove the tensioner mounting stud. **Note:** *The crankshaft and camshafts must not be rotated with the belt removed.*

Refitting

16 Fit the new tensioner mounting stud, the new tensioner and new idler pulley.
17 Rotate the coolant pump sprocket, checking for any roughness/play. Check for any signs of leaking from the pump. It is not uncommon from the increased tension from the new belt to cause failure of the coolant pump shortly after the vehicle is returned to service. If in any doubt as to its condition, renew it.
18 Ensure that the camshaft sprocket and crankshaft timing tools are still in place (see Section 3), and that the crankshaft key is centred within the key way **(see illustration)**.

19 Ensure the belt sprockets are clean, then fit the new belt, starting with the camshaft sprocket, followed by the idler pulley, crankshaft sprocket, coolant pump sprocket, then the tensioner pulley. Keep the belt taut between the camshaft and crankshaft sprockets, so all the belt slack is at the tensioner pulley.
20 Slacken the tensioner retaining nut, insert an Allen key into the hole in the tensioner hub, and rotate the hub anti-clockwise until the pointer arm is in the position shown **(see illustration)**. Tighten the tensioner nut to the specified torque.
21 Refit the crankshaft position sensor signal ring, and the crankshaft pulley, then insert the old pulley bolt and tighten it to 70 Nm.
22 Remove the crankshaft locking tool (Section 5) and the camshaft/crankshaft timing tools (Section 3), then rotate the crankshaft 10 complete revolutions and refit the camshaft/crankshaft timing tools.
23 Refit the crankshaft locking tool (Section 5), and slacken the crankshaft pulley bolt.
24 Insert the Allen key into the hole in the tensioner hub, then slacken the tensioner retaining nut, and rotate the hub clockwise until the pointer aligns with the notch in the pointer arm backplate **(see illustration)**. **Note:** *If the pointer arm is to the right-hand side of the backplate (ie. the belt is too slack), repeat the tensioning procedure from Paragraph 17 onwards.*

25 With the pointer aligned correctly, tighten the tensioner nut to the specified torque.
26 Tighten the crankshaft pulley bolt to 70 Nm (still using the old bolt).
27 Remove the camshaft/crankshaft timing/locking tools, and rotate the crankshaft 2 complete revolutions, and check that the tensioner pointer arm is still aligned with the notch on the backplate. If not, repeat the tensioning procedure.
28 Refit the camshaft/crankshaft timing/locking tools, undo the retaining bolt, and remove the crankshaft pulley and position sensor signal ring (using the two 6 mm bolts).
29 The remainder of refitting is a reversal of removal, noting the following points:
a) Renew the crankshaft pulley bolt.
b) Tighten all fasteners to their specified torque where given.
c) Reconnect the battery negative lead as described in Chapter 5 Section 3.

---

7 Camshafts, rocker arms and hydraulic tappets – removal, inspection and refitting

Removal

1 Remove the camshaft cover as described in Section 4.
2 Undo the 3 bolts securing the timing

6.18 Ensure the key is centred within the key way

6.20 Rotate the hub anti-clockwise until the pointer arm is almost at the 6 o'clock position

6.24 The pointer arm must align with the notch in the backplate

7.2 Timing chain tensioner retaining bolts

7.4 Lift each rocker arm and tappet assembly from the cylinder head

7.8a Each camshaft sprocket has a mark which must align with the marked/coloured link in the chain

7.8b With the camshafts correctly located in the chain, there must be 5 links between the sprocket arrows/coloured links

7.9a Lubricate the bearing surfaces

7.9b Lower the camshaft/chain and tensioner assembly into place

chain tensioner to the cylinder head (**see illustration**).

3 Carefully lift the camshafts, timing chain and tensioner from place.

4 Lift the rocker arms and hydraulic tappets from the cylinder head and place them in sixteen small, clean plastic containers – label them for identification. Alternatively, divide a larger container into compartments. Withdraw each hydraulic tappet in turn, invert it to prevent oil loss and place it in its respective container, which should then be filled with clean engine oil (**see illustration**).
Caution: Do not interchange the tappets, and do not allow the tappets to lose oil, as they will take a long time to refill with oil on restarting the engine, which could result in incorrect valve clearances. Absolute cleanliness is essential at all times when handling the tappets.

Inspection

5 Examine the camshaft bearing surfaces and cam lobes for signs of wear ridges and scoring. Renew the camshaft if any of these conditions are apparent. Examine the condition of the bearing surfaces both on the camshaft journals and in the cylinder head. If the head bearing surfaces are worn excessively, the cylinder head will need to be renewed.

6 Examine the rocker bearing surfaces which contact the camshaft lobes for wear ridges and scoring. If the engine's valve clearances have sounded noisy, particularly if the noise

persists after initial start-up from cold, then there is reason to suspect a faulty tappet. If any tappet is thought to be faulty or is visibly worn it should be renewed.

Refitting

7 Where removed, lubricate the tappets and rocker arms with clean engine oil and carefully insert each one into its original location in the cylinder head.

8 To facilitate correct camshaft timing, the timing chain has 2 links marked/coloured which must align with the arrows, mark or number on the front face of each camshaft sprocket (the mark must be uppermost) (**see illustrations**). Position the chain around the sprockets with the marks/links aligned and fit the tensioner between the chain runs.

9 Lubricate the lower bearing surfaces in the cylinder head with clean engine oil, and carefully lower the camshafts/chain/tensioner assembly into place (**see illustrations**).

10 Insert the tensioner retaining bolts and tighten them to the specified torque.

11 The remainder of refitting is a reversal of removal.

8 Cylinder head – removal and refitting

Removal

1 Jack up and support the front of the vehicle

as described in Chapter 13 Section 5. Remove the engine undershield.

2 Remove the engine cover and then disconnect the battery as described in Chapter 5 Section 3.

3 Drain the cooling system, as described in Chapter 1 Section 25.

4 With reference to Chapter 12 Section 12, remove the upper and lower windscreen cowl panels.

5 Remove the timing belt as described in Section 6.

6 Remove the camshaft cover as described in Section 4 and then remove the EGR valve from the rear of the cylinder head (Chapter 4B).

7 Remove the camshafts, rocker arms and tappets as described in Section 7.

8 Remove the turbocharger as described in Chapter 4A Section 14.

9 Disconnect the coolant hoses from the thermostat housing and then remove the housing as described in Chapter 3 Section 4.

10 If not already done so, position a workshop jack under the sump to support the engine. Use a block of wood to spread the load and prevent damage to the sump.

11 Remove the right-hand engine mounting as described in Section 15.

12 Unbolt the power steering pump and secure it to one side (as described at the start of Section 6).

13 Undo the bolts securing the engine mounting support bracket to the cylinder head

8.13 The support bracket bolts

8.14 Inner timing belt cover retaining bolts

8.15 Remove the bolt

8.17 Remove the cylinder head bolts

8.18 Remove the cylinder head

(see illustration). Note that this mounting also holds the timing belt idler pulley.

14 Undo the 3 retaining bolts and remove the timing belt inner cover **(see illustration)**. Alternatively remove the upper bolts and leave the inner cover in place.

15 Remove the upper bolt from the power steering pump/alternator mounting bracket **(see illustration)**.

16 Unclip the wiring harness, and disconnect the wiring plugs from the glow plugs.

17 Working in the reverse of the tightening sequence **(see illustration 8.36)**, progressively slacken the cylinder head bolts by a third of a turn at a time until all bolts can be unscrewed by hand **(see illustration)**. Withdraw and discard the bolts, new ones must be fitted.

18 With the help of an assistant, lift the cylinder head from the cylinder block **(see illustration)**. If necessary, tap the cylinder head gently with a soft-faced mallet to free it from the block, but do not lever at the mating faces.

19 When the joint is broken, lift the cylinder head away then remove the gasket. Note the fitted positions of the two locating dowels, and remove them for safe-keeping if they are loose. Keep the gasket for identification purposes (see paragraph 25).

Caution: Do not lay the head on its lower mating surface; support the head on wooden blocks, ensuring each block only contacts the head mating surface not the glow plugs. The glow plugs protrude out the bottom of the head and they will be damaged if the head is placed directly onto a bench.

20 If the cylinder head is to be dismantled, refer to the relevant Sections of Chapter 2E.

Preparation for refitting

21 The mating faces of the cylinder head and block must be perfectly clean before refitting the head. Use a scraper to remove all traces of gasket and carbon, and also clean the

tops of the pistons. Take particular care with the aluminium surfaces, as the soft metal is damaged easily. Also, make sure that debris is not allowed to enter the oil and water channels – this is particularly important for the oil circuit, as carbon could block the oil supply to the camshaft or crankshaft bearings. Using adhesive tape and paper, seal the water, oil and bolt holes in the cylinder block. To prevent carbon entering the gap between the pistons and bores, smear a little grease in the gap. After cleaning the piston, rotate the crankshaft so that the piston moves down the bore, then wipe out the grease and carbon with a cloth rag. Clean the piston crowns in the same way.

22 Check the block and head for nicks, deep scratches and other damage. If slight, they may be removed carefully with a file. More serious damage may require a new cylinder head. Consult a Ford dealer or specialist.

23 If warpage of the cylinder head gasket surface is suspected, use a straight-edge to check it for distortion. Refer to Chapter 2E Section 7.

24 Ensure that the cylinder head bolt holes in the crankcase are clean and free of oil. Syringe or soak up any oil left in the bolt holes. This is most important in order that the correct bolt tightening torque can be applied and to prevent the possibility of the block being cracked by hydraulic pressure when the bolts are tightened.

25 On this engine, the cylinder head to piston clearance is controlled by fitting different thickness head gaskets. The piston protrusion is represented by the number of holes in the gasket at the front edge **(see illustrations)**.

8.25a The holes representing the piston protrusion may be at each end of the gasket...

8.25b ...the forwardmost holes at the flywheel end (3 holes in this instance)...

8.25c ...and/or all the holes at the timing chain end (3 holes in this instance)

8.28 Measure the piston protrusion with a DTI gauge

8.31a Remove the check valve and...

8.31b ...fit a new one

26 Select the replacement gasket which has the same thickness/number of holes as the original, unless new piston and connecting rod assemblies have been fitted. In that case, the correct thickness of gasket required is selected by measuring the piston protrusions as follows.

27 Remove the timing pin from the flywheel and mount a dial test indicator securely on the block so that its pointer can be easily pivoted between the piston crown and block mating surface.

28 Ensure the piston is at exactly TDC then zero the dial test indicator on the gasket surface of the cylinder block. Carefully move the indicator over No.1 piston, taking measurements in line with the gudgeon pin axis, measure the protrusion on both the left-hand and right-hand side of the piston **(see illustration)**. Repeat this procedure on No.4 piston.

29 Rotate the crankshaft half-a-turn to bring Nos.2 and 3 pistons to TDC. Ensure the crankshaft is accurately positioned then measure the protrusions of Nos.2 and 3 pistons, taking two measurements for each piston. Once both pistons have been measured, rotate the crankshaft through half-a-turn to bring Nos.1 and 4 pistons back to TDC and lock the crankshaft in position again.

30 Refer to the Specifcations at the beginning of this Chapter to select the appropriate gasket.

Refitting

31 Using a hook type tool, remove the check valve from the cylinder head and fit a new one **(see illustrations)**.

32 Wipe clean the mating faces of the head and block and ensure that the two locating dowels are in position at each end of the cylinder block/crankcase surface **(see illustration)**.

33 Fit the new gasket to the cylinder block, ensuring that it fits correctly over the locating dowels.

34 With the help of an assistant, carefully refit the cylinder head, locating it on the dowels.

35 Carefully enter the new bolts into the cylinder head screw them in, by hand only, until finger-tight **(see illustration)**.

Caution: Do not drop the bolts into their holes.

36 Working progressively and in the sequence shown, first tighten all the cylinder head bolts to the Stage 1 torque setting **(see illustration)**.

37 Again, in sequence, tighten the bolts to the Stage 2 torque setting.

38 Now angle-tighten the bolts in sequence to the stage 3 setting, using an angle-measuring gauge **(see illustration)**.

39 The remainder of refitting is a reversal of removal, noting the following points:
a) Tighten all fasteners to their specified torque where given.
b) Fill the cooling system as described in Chapter 1 Section 25.
c) Reconnect the battery negative lead as described in Chapter 5 Section 3.

8.32 Ensure the locating dowels are in position

8.33 Fit the new gasket to the engine block

8.35 Fit the new bolts

8.36 Cylinder head bolt tightening sequence

8.38 Using an angle-measuring gauge

9.3 The intercooler air duct rear bracket

9.4a Remove the sump and ...

9.4b ...recover the nylon washers from the bolt holes

9 Sump – removal and refitting

Note: *The sump is in two sections: a lower pressed steel main sump and a cast aluminium upper extension. Removal of the lower sump allows access to the oil pump, but access to the balancer shafts and crankshaft requires removal of the upper section.*

Sump pan

Removal

1 Apply the handbrake, then jack up the front of the vehicle and support it securely on axle stands (see *Jacking and vehicle support*). Remove the retaining screws and fasteners and remove the undershield from beneath the engine and transmission.

2 Drain the engine oil and remove the oil filter as described in Chapter 1 Section 3. Refit the sump plug with a new washer and tighten the plug to the specified torque.

3 Undo the bolts securing the intercooler air duct beneath the sump **(see illustration)**.

4 Unscrew the sump pan retaining bolts and remove the sump **(see illustrations)**. The sump does not use a traditional gasket and the 'instant' gasket used effectively bonds

the main sump to the upper sump. We used a sharp knife to slice through the seal. After cautiously cutting through the sealant the sump broke free from the upper sump.

Refitting

5 Ensure the pan and extension mating surfaces are clean and dry. Check that all the nylon washers are in place and then apply a 3mm diameter bead of sealant (Ford 2U7J-M4G323-AB or equivalent) to the sump pan mating surface. The sealant should pass inside all the bolt holes and the sump must be fitted within 5 minutes of applying the sealant **(see illustration)**.

6 Refit the sump and evenly tighten the bolts to the specified torque.

7 The remainder of refitting is a reversal of removal.

Sump extension

Removal

8 Apply the handbrake, then jack up the front of the vehicle and support it securely on axle stands (see *Jacking and vehicle support*). Remove the retaining screws and fasteners and remove the undershield from beneath the engine and transmission.

9 Remove the accessory drivebelt as described in Chapter 1 Section 22.

10 With the drivebelt removed, unbolt and

9.5 Apply sealant to the to sump extension. Note the nylon washers

move to the side the power steering pump (Chapter 10 Section 19).

11 Undo the retaining bolt and remove the auxiliary drivebelt tensioner **(see illustration)**.

12 Remove the alternator as described in Chapter 5 Section 6, and then unbolt the air conditioning compressor. DO NOT disconnect the refrigerant hoses from the compressor, simply remove the bolts and using cable ties or similar secure the compressor to the front radiator support panel.

13 Unbolt and then remove the accessory mounting bracket **(see illustration)**.

14 If not already done so, drain the engine

9.11 Auxiliary drivebelt tensioner Torx bolt

9.13 Remove the bracket (shown with oil cooler removed for clarity)

9.15 Dipstick guide tube upper bolt...

9.16 ...lower bolt, and breather hose clamp

9.21a Apply sealant....

oil and remove the sump pan as described previously in this Section.

15 Undo the 2 retaining bolts, release the wiring loom and then pull the engine oil level dipstick guide tube from the sump **(see illustration)**. Discard and renew the O-ring seal.

16 Disconnect the engine oil temperature sensor wiring plug, then release the clamp and disconnect the breather hose from the sump **(see illustration)**.

17 Remove the 4 bolts securing the sump extension to the transmission bellhousing.

18 Progressively slacken and remove the 20 bolts securing the sump extension to the base of the cylinder block.

19 Break the joint by striking the sump extension with the palm of the hand, then lower it away from the engine.

Refitting

20 Clean all traces of sealant from the mating surfaces of the cylinder block and sump extension, then use a clean rag to wipe out the sump and the engine interior.

21 Apply a 3 mm bead of suitable sealant (Ford 2U7J-M4G323-AB or equivalent) to the sump extension mating surface in the areas shown **(see illustrations)**.

22 Refit the sump extension retaining bolts, and tighten the bolts finger-tight only.

23 Fit the bolts securing the sump extension to the transmission bellhousing. In order to align the rear sump flange with the gearbox, lightly tighten the bolts, then slacken them. If the sump extension is being refitted to the engine with the gearbox removed, use a straight edge to ensure that the sump extension casting is flush with the end of the engine block.

24 Tighten the sump extension to engine block bolts **(see illustration)**, and then the sump extension to transmission bolts to the specified torque.

25 The remainder of refitting is a reversal of removal.

10 Balance shafts and housing
– general information, removal and refitting

General information

1 On these engines, a housing with twin-counter rotating balance shafts is fitted to the base of the cylinder block. The function of the assembly is to counteract the vibration caused by the crankshaft rotating, and the pistons etc. The shafts are linked by helical gears integral with the shafts, and the front shaft is driven by a matched helical gear

9.21b ...to the areas shown...

integral with the crankshaft. Backlash between the gears is controlled by shims located between the housing and the engine block.

Removal

2 Remove the sump and sump extension as described in Section 9.

9.21c ...and lower the extension into position

9.24 Tighten the bolts to the specified torque

10.5a Check the position of the shafts at the timing belt end and...

10.5b ...and then install the locking tool at the transmission end

10.5c Alternatively, lock the shafts with a hose clip

10.7a Remove the shaft assembly ...

10.7b ...and (noting their positions) recover the shims

Refitting

8 Refitting is a reversal of removal, unless the balancer shafts have been replaced. If the balancer shaft assembly is replaced then the gear backlash must be checked and adjusted as described below. Note that Ford special tool 303-1330, a dial gauge (complete with a magnetic stand) and a pair of measuring shims will be required – see the table in the Specifications at the beginning of this Chapter.
9 Install the measuring shims and tighten the balancer shaft bolts in the correct order to the specified torque.
10 Install the special tool to the rear balancer shaft, push the shaft into the housing and tighten the thumbscrew on the special tool.
11 Install the dial gauge and then zero the dial gauge. Rotate the special tool and record the movement on the dial gauge. Remove the special tool and dial gauge and then rotate the crankshaft 45 degrees. Install special tool and dial gauge and measure the backlash again. Repeat this procedure for one complete crankshaft revolution – taking eight readings.
12 Using the minimum clearance values, select the correct shim from the table listed in the specifications.
13 Install the special tool (303-1329) and lock the shafts into position. Remove the balancer shaft assembly and recover the measuring shims.
14 Fit the selected shims and install the balancer shaft assembly. Tighten the bolts to the specified torque in the order show (in two stages) **(see illustration)** and then remove the balancer shaft locking tool.

3 Unbolt and remove the oil pump as described in Section 11.
4 Remove the starter motor and insert the special timing tool into the engine block. Rotate the engine in the normal direction of rotation (clockwise when viewed from the timing belt end of the engine) and then lock the crankshaft in position as described in Section 3.
5 Check the position of the balancer shafts and then lock them in position using Ford special tool 303-1329. Alternatively the

shafts can be locked using worm drive hose clip and a pair of locking pliers **(see illustrations)**.
6 Slacken the bolts a turn at a time in the reverse order to that shown **(see illustration 10.14)**.
7 Remove the bolts, lift out the balancer shaft assembly and recover the metal gaskets **(see illustration)**. No further dismantling is recommended – replacement shafts are supplied as a matched pair complete with the housing.

10.14 The balancer shaft bolt tightening sequence. The arrow indicates the front of the engine

6299 02d-10.14 HAYNES

11 Oil pump – removal and refitting

Removal

1 Remove the sump pan as described in Section 9.
2 Undo the retaining bolts and remove the pump, noting the fitted position of the bolts. Disengage the sprocket from the chain as the

11.2 Disengage the sprocket from the chain as the pump is withdrawn

11.4 Note the location of the shouldered bolt

pump is withdrawn **(see illustration). Note:** *No information concerning the inspection or dismantling of the pump is available from Ford. If faulty, the pump should be renewed.*

Refitting

3 Ensure the mating surfaces of the oil pump and cylinder block are clean and dry.
4 Position the oil pump, engaging the sprocket with the chain, and tighten the retaining bolts to the specified torque. Note that the shouldered-bolt is fitted at the front, upper location on the pump **(see illustration)**.
5 Refit the sump as described in Section 9.

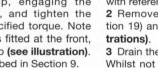

12 Oil cooler –
removal and refitting

Removal

1 Remove the air conditioning compressor with reference to Chapter 3 Section 12.
2 Remove the fuel filter (Chapter 1 Section 19) and the fuel filter housing **(see illustrations)**.
3 Drain the engine coolant and the engine oil. Whilst not strictly necessary the oil filter can

be removed to improve access. (As described in Chapter 1 Section 3).
4 With reference to Chapter 4A Section 17, remove the throttle body.
5 Disconnect the engine oil pressure sensor wiring plug.
6 Disconnect the hoses from the cooler, and unclip the wiring harness **(see illustration)**. Note that removal of the hoses is slightly easier, if the cooler mounting bolts are removed and the cooler slid part way off the mounting studs.
7 Undo the 4 retaining nuts and remove the oil cooler and filter housing **(see illustrations)**.

12.2a Remove the plastic front cover and…

12.2b …then remove the housing

12.6 Remove the coolant hoses

12.7a Oil filter housing retaining nuts

12.7b Remove the housing and…

12.7c …and recover the seal

Discard and renew the seal. Be prepared for fluid spillage.

8 If required, undo the bolts and detach the oil cooler from the oil filter housing. Note however that the oil filter housing and cooler are only supplied as a complete assembly.

Refitting

9 Refit the oil filter housing with a new seal and tighten the bolts to the specified torque.

10 The remainder of refitting is a reversal of removal.

13 Oil seals – renewal

Crankshaft right-hand (timing belt end) seal

1 Remove the timing belt as described in Section 6.

2 Slide the crankshaft sprocket from place and recover the key **(see illustrations)**.

3 Very carefully punch or drill two small holes opposite each other in the oil seal. Screw a self-tapping screw into each and pull on the screws with pliers to extract the seal **(see illustrations)**.

Caution: Great care must be taken to avoid damage to the crankshaft

4 Clean the seal housing and polish off any burrs or raised edges which may have caused the seal to fail in the first place.

5 Drive the new seal into position on the end of the shaft, pressing squarely into position until it is flush with the housing, using a suitable tubular drift, such as a socket, which bears only on the hard outer edge of the seal. Take great care not to damage the seal lips during fitting and ensure that the seal lips face inwards. Do not apply any lubricant to the seal.

6 Refit the keys to the crankshaft, followed by the sprocket.

7 Refit the timing belt as described in Section 6.

Crankshaft left-hand (flywheel end) oil seal

8 Remove the flywheel as described in Section 14.

9 Very carefully punch or drill two small holes opposite each other in the oil seal. Screw a self-tapping screw into each and pull on the screws with pliers to extract the seal **(see illustration 13.3a and 13.3b)**.

10 Clean the seal housing and polish off any burrs or raised edges which may have caused the seal to fail.

11 Ford use a special tool (No 303-1176) to fit the new seal into the housing. One part of the tool fits over the end of the crankshaft to guide the seal, whilst the other part is used to push the seal into position. Genuine Ford seals are supplied with the replacement seal mounted on a plastic sleeve. This can be used to guide the replacement seal into position.

Caution: Where a PTFE ('Teflon') seal is supplied as a replacement, the seal must not be lubricate to aid installation. It must be installed dry.

12 Press the seal evenly into the housing, until its outer flange is flush with the housing lip **(see illustrations)**. If necessary a small block of wood can be used to tap the seal into position. Work around the seal (taping the outer edge of the seal only) until it is in position.

13 Refit the flywheel/driveplate as described in Section 14.

Camshaft oil seal

14 Remove the timing belt as described in Section 6.

15 Slacken the camshaft sprocket retaining bolt and remove it, along with its washer. To prevent the camshaft rotating as the bolt is slackened, a sprocket-holding tool will be required. In the absence of the special Ford tool, an acceptable substitute can be fabricated as follows. Use two lengths of steel strip (one long, the other short), and three nuts and bolts; one nut and bolt forms the pivot of a forked tool, with the remaining two nuts and bolts at the tips of the 'forks' to engage with the sprocket spokes (see **Tool Tip**). Discard the bolt – a new one must be fitted.

Caution: Do not attempt to use just the sprocket locking pin to prevent the sprocket from rotating whilst the bolt is slackened.

16 Very carefully punch or drill two small holes opposite each other in the oil seal.

13.2a Slide the sprocket from the crankshaft...

13.2b ...and recover the key

13.3a Drill a hole in the hard, outer shell of the oil seal...

13.3b ...insert a self-tapping screw, and pull the seal out

13.12a Fit the guide sleeve and seal to the crankshaft

13.12b Slide the seal off the guide and push it home

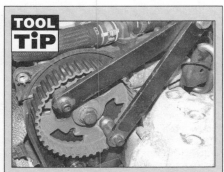

TOOL TiP

Fabricate a holding tool from 2 lengths of steel strip bolted together, with a bolt/nut at each end.

Screw a self-tapping screw into each and pull on the screws with pliers to extract the seal **(see illustration 13.3a and 13.3b)**.
Caution: Great care must be taken to avoid damage to the camshaft.
17 Clean the seal housing and polish off any burrs or raised edges which may have caused the seal to fail in the first place.
18 Drive the new seal into position on the end of the shaft, pressing squarely into position until it is flush with the housing, using a suitable tubular drift, such as a socket, which bears only on the hard outer edge of the seal **(see illustrations)**. Take great care not to damage the seal lips during fitting and ensure that the seal lips face inwards. Do not apply any lubricant to the seal.
19 Refit the sprocket, and tighten the new bolt and washer to the specified torque. Hold the sprocket using the same method employed on removal.
20 Refit the timing belt as described in Section 6.

14 Flywheel – removal, inspection and refitting

Flywheel
Removal

Note: *New flywheel retaining bolts must be used on refitting.*

14.2 Homemade flywheel locking tool

13.18a New seals may be supplied with a guide sleeve

13.18c ...better still use a length of threaded bar, washer and nut to draw the seal into position

1 Remove the transmission (Chapter 7 Section 7) and the clutch assembly as described in Chapter 6 Section 6.
2 Prevent the flywheel from turning by locking the ring gear teeth with a similar arrangement to that shown **(see illustration)**. Alternatively, bolt a strap between the flywheel and the cylinder block/crankcase.
3 Slacken and remove the retaining bolts and remove the flywheel, noting its locating dowel. Do not drop it, as it is very heavy. Discard the bolts, they must be renewed whenever they are disturbed.

Inspection

4 A dual mass flywheel is fitted to all engines. Detailed checking of the flywheel requires the use of specific tools, that are unlikely to be available to the home mechanic. However some basic checking can easily be performed.

14.5 On this example the flywheel bolts are off centre

13.18b Use a suitable tubular drift to install the new seal, or ...

13.18d The replacement seal correctly fitted

5 Start by checking the alignment between the primary mass and the secondary mass. At rest the flywheel retaining bolts will be accessible through the holes in the secondary mass **(see illustration)**.
6 The maximum travel of the primary mass in relation to the secondary mass should not exceed 15 teeth (or 20 degrees). Note that this is a general guide and if in doubt remove the flywheel and have a suitably equipped specialist check the flywheel **(see illustration)**.
7 Inspect the flywheel for any grease or debris from the interface between the fixed part (the primary mass) and the movable part of the flywheel (the secondary mass). Replace any flywheel that has grease visible.
8 If the ring gear is badly worn or has missing teeth, then the entire dual mass flywheel must be replaced.

14.6 Check the movement between the primary and secondary mass.

14.12 Use an angle gauge to fully tighten the flywheel

9 If any doubt to the condition of the flywheel exists, despite the expense we recommend replacing it.

Refitting

10 Clean the mating surfaces of the flywheel and crankshaft and remove all traces of locking compound from the crankshaft threaded holes.

11 Fit the flywheel to the crankshaft, engaging it with the crankshaft locating dowel, and fit the new retaining bolts. **Note:** *If the new bolts are not supplied pre-coated with locking compound, apply a few drops prior to fitting the bolts.*

12 Lock the flywheel using the method employed on dismantling then, working in a diagonal sequence, tighten all the retaining bolts to the specified torque setting **(see illustration)**.

13 Refit the clutch assembly as described

in Chapter 6 Section 6 and then refit the transmission as described in Chapter 7 Section 7.

15 Engine/transmission mountings – inspection and renewal

Inspection

1 If improved access is required, firmly apply the handbrake, raise the front of the vehicle and support it securely on axle stands (see *Jacking and vehicle support*). Undo the retaining screws and fasteners and remove the undershield from beneath the engine/transmission unit.

2 Check the mounting rubber to see if it is cracked, hardened or separated from the metal at any point. Renew the mounting if any such damage or deterioration is evident.

3 Check that all mounting fasteners are securely tightened. Use a torque wrench to check, if possible.

4 Using a large screwdriver or a pry bar, check for wear in the mountings by carefully levering against it to check for free play. Where this is not possible, enlist the aid of an assistant to move the engine/gearbox unit back and forth or from side to side while you watch the mountings. While some free play is to be expected even from new components, excessive wear should be obvious. If excessive free play is found, check first that

the fasteners are correctly secured, then renew any worn components as described below.

Renewal

Left-hand mounting

5 Firmly apply the handbrake, raise the front of the vehicle and support it securely on axle stands (see *Jacking and vehicle support*). Undo the retaining screws and fasteners and remove the undershield from beneath the engine/transmission unit.

6 Remove the air filter housing as described in Chapter 4A Section 3, and then remove the battery and battery tray as described in Chapter 5 Section 3.

7 Position a jack under the transmission with a block of wood between the jack head and casing, and take the weight of the engine and transmission.

8 Remove the cover plate bolts and then remove the four main bolts followed by the central bolt **(see illustrations)**

9 Remove the left-hand wing liner and lower the transmission on the jack to expose the mounting bracket. Remove the bolts and lift out the bracket **(see illustration)**.

10 Refitting is a reversal of removal, but the centre nut must be replaced. If the bracket has been removed from the transmission the mounting bolts must also be replaced. Tighten all fixings to the specified torque and angle where given.

Right-hand mounting

11 Firmly apply the handbrake, raise the front of the vehicle and support it securely on axle stands (see *Jacking and vehicle support*). Undo the retaining screws and fasteners and remove the undershield from beneath the engine/transmission unit.

12 Position a jack under the engine sump with a block of wood between the jack head and the sump. Raise the jack and take the weight of the engine on the jack.

13 Unclip the glow plug control relay from the suspension strut tower **(see illustration)**.

14 Unclip the power steering pump reservoir from the bonnet slam panel and then unbolt the power steering pump. Clamp the outlet

15.8a Remove the cover plate bolts (A), the outer bolts (B) and then the central bolt (C)

15.8b Lift off the cover plate …

15.9 Remove the transmission support bracket

15.13 Unclip the glow plug relay

15.8c …followed by the main mounting

15.14a Lift out the power steering pump

15.14b Clamp the supply hose (note the tray). Remove the hose ...

15.14c ... and seal it

hose from the reservoir and then disconnect it from the power steering pump. Plug the power steering pump inlet and then place the pump on the top of the engine (see illustrations).

15 Unclip the fuel lines from the timing belt cover and then unbolt the mounting (see illustrations).

16 If required the engine side of the mounting can be removed after the timing belt has been removed – see Section 6. Note that the lower bolt is the timing belt idler pulley bolt (see illustration).

17 Refitting is a reversal of removal. When the vehicle is back on the ground, start the engine and bleed the power steering by turning the steering from lock to lock several times.

Torque rod

18 Firmly apply the handbrake, raise the front of the vehicle and support it securely on axle stands (see Jacking and vehicle support). Undo the retaining screws and fasteners and remove the undershield from beneath the engine/transmission unit.

19 Remove the bolts and manovre the the torque rod out from underneath (see illustrations). A pry bar should be used to swing the engine away from the subframe – this will allow the mounting to be removed easily.

20 Refitting is a reversal of removal.

15.15a Unclip the fuel lines

15.15b Unbolt and then ...

15.15c ... remove the mounting

15.16 The engine mounting support bracket. The lower bolt (A) holds the idler pulley

15.19a The torque rod mounting bolts

15.19b Unbolt and then ...

15.19c ... remove the torque rod

16.2 The oil pressure sensor is hidden between the oil cooler and oil filter

16.5 Remove the oil temperature sensor

16 Engine oil pressure and temperature sensors – renewal

Oil pressure sensor

1 Raise the front of the vehicle and support it securely on axle stands (see *Jacking and vehicle support*). Undo the retaining screws and fasteners and remove the undershield from beneath the engine/transmission unit.

2 Disconnect the wiring plug, then unscrew the sensor from the filter housing **(see illustration)**. Renew the sealing washer. Be prepared for fluid spillage.

3 Refitting is a reversal of removal, noting the following points:

a) *Renew the sensor sealing washer.*
b) *Tighten the sensor to the specified torque.*
c) *Check the engine oil level as described in Weekly checks.*

Oil temperature sensor

4 Remove the starter motor as described in Chapter 5 Section 8.

5 Disconnect the wiring plug, and unscrew the sensor from the housing **(see illustration)**. Renew the sealing washer. Be prepared for fluid spillage.

6 Refitting is a reversal of removal, noting the following points:

a) *Renew the sensor sealing washer.*
b) *Tighten the sensor to the specified torque.*
c) *Check the engine oil level as described in Weekly checks.*

Chapter 2 Part E
Engine removal and overhaul procedures

Contents

Degrees of difficulty

Easy, suitable for novice with little experience	**Fairly easy,** suitable for beginner with some experience	**Fairly difficult,** suitable for competent DIY mechanic	**Difficult,** suitable for experienced DIY mechanic	**Very difficult,** suitable for expert DIY or professional

Specifications

Note: *At the time of writing, some specifications for certain engines were not available. Where the relevant specifications are not given here, refer to your Ford dealer for further information.*

Cylinder head
Maximum gasket face distortion:

1.6 litre engines	0.05 mm
1.8 litre engines	0.06 mm
2.0 litre engines	0.03 mm
2.2 litre engines	0.03 mm

Valves

Valve stem diameter:	Inlet	Exhaust
1.6 litre engines	5.485 +0.0, -0.015 mm	5.475 +0.0, -0.015 mm
1.8 litre engines	Not available	
2.0 litre engines	5.978 ± 0.009 mm	5.968 ± 0.009 mm
2.2 litre engines	5.978 ± 0.009 mm	5.968 ± 0.009 mm

Cylinder block
Cylinder bore diameter (nominal):

1.6 litre engines	75.00 mm
1.8 litre engines	82.50 mm
2.0 litre engines	85.00 mm
2.2 litre engines	85.00mm

Piston rings

End gaps:

1.6 litre engines:	
Top compression ring	0.20 to 0.35 mm
Second compression ring	0.20 to 0.40 mm
Oil control ring	0.80 to 1.00 mm
1.8 litre engines:	
Top compression ring	0.31 to 0.50 mm
Second compression ring	0.31 to 0.50 mm
Oil control ring	0.25 to 0.58 mm
2.0 litre engines:	
Top compression ring	0.20 to 0.35 mm
Second compression ring	0.80 to 1.00 mm
Oil control ring	0.25 to 0.50 mm
2.2 litre engines:	
Top compression ring	0.20 to 0.35 mm
Second compression ring	0.80 to 1.00 mm
Oil control ring	0.25 to 0.50 mm

Crankshaft

Endfloat:

1.6 litre engines thrustwasher thickness	2.4 ± 0.05 mm
1.8 litre engines	0.11 to 0.37 mm
2.0 litre engines	0.07 to 0.32 mm
2.2 litre engines	0.07 to 0.32 mm
Maximum bearing journal out-of-round (all engines)	0.007 mm

1 General Information

1 Included in this Part of Chapter 2 are details of removing the engine/transmission from the car and general overhaul procedures for the cylinder head, cylinder block/crankcase and all other engine internal components.

2 The information given ranges from advice concerning preparation for an overhaul and the purchase of parts, to detailed step-by-step procedures covering removal, inspection, renovation and refitting of engine internal components.

3 After Section 8, all instructions are based on the assumption that the engine has been removed from the car. For information concerning in-car engine repair, as well as the removal and refitting of those external components necessary for full overhaul, refer to Part A, B or C of this Chapter (as applicable) and to Section 5. Ignore any preliminary dismantling operations described in Part A, B, C or D that are no longer relevant once the engine has been removed from the car.

2 Engine overhaul – general information

1 It is not always easy to determine when, or if, an engine should be completely overhauled, as a number of factors must be considered.

2 High mileage is not necessarily an indication that an overhaul is needed, while low mileage does not preclude the need for an overhaul. Frequency of servicing is probably the most important consideration. An engine which has had regular and frequent oil and filter changes, as well as other required maintenance, should give many thousands of miles of reliable service. Conversely, a neglected engine may require an overhaul very early in its life.

3 Excessive oil consumption is an indication that piston rings, valve seals and/or valve guides are in need of attention. Make sure that oil leaks are not responsible before deciding that the rings and/or guides are worn. Perform a compression test, as described in Part A, B, C or D of this Chapter, to determine the likely cause of the problem.

4 Check the oil pressure with a gauge fitted in place of the oil pressure switch, and compare it with that specified. If it is extremely low, the main and big-end bearings, and/or the oil pump, are probably worn out.

5 Loss of power, rough running, knocking or metallic engine noises, excessive valve gear noise, and high fuel consumption may also point to the need for an overhaul, especially if they are all present at the same time. If a complete service does not cure the situation, major mechanical work is the only solution.

6 An engine overhaul involves restoring all internal parts to the specification of a new engine. During an overhaul, the pistons and the piston rings are renewed. New main and big-end bearings are generally fitted; if necessary, the crankshaft may be renewed to restore the journals. The valves are also serviced as well, since they are usually in less-than-perfect condition at this point. While the engine is being overhauled, other components, such as the distributor, starter and alternator, can be overhauled as well. The end result should be an as-new engine that will give many trouble-free miles.

Note: *Critical cooling system components such as the hoses, thermostat and coolant pump should be renewed when an engine is overhauled. The radiator should be checked carefully, to ensure that it is not clogged or leaking. Also, it is a good idea to renew the oil pump whenever the engine is overhauled.*

7 Before beginning the engine overhaul, read through the entire procedure, to familiarise yourself with the scope and requirements of the job. Overhauling an engine is not difficult if you follow carefully all of the instructions, have the necessary tools and equipment, and pay close attention to all specifications. It can, however, be time-consuming. Plan on the car being off the road for a minimum of two weeks, especially if parts must be taken to an engineering works for repair or reconditioning. Check on the availability of parts and make sure that any necessary special tools and equipment are obtained in advance. Most work can be done with typical hand tools, although a number of precision measuring tools are required for inspecting parts to determine if they must be renewed. Often the engineering works will handle the inspection of parts and offer advice concerning reconditioning and renewal.

8 Always wait until the engine has been completely dismantled, and until all components (especially the cylinder block/crankcase and the crankshaft) have been inspected, before deciding what service and repair operations must be performed

by an engineering works. The condition of these components will be the major factor to consider when determining whether to overhaul the original engine, or to buy a reconditioned unit. Do not, therefore, purchase parts or have overhaul work done on other components until they have been thoroughly inspected. As a general rule, time is the primary cost of an overhaul, so it does not pay to fit worn or sub-standard parts.

9 As a final note, to ensure maximum life and minimum trouble from a reconditioned engine, everything must be assembled with care, in a spotlessly-clean environment.

3 Engine/transmission removal – methods and precautions

1 If you have decided that the engine must be removed for overhaul or major repair work, several preliminary steps should be taken.

2 Engine/transmission removal whilst not complicated, is time consuming. It must be stated, that unless the vehicle can be raised (to a reasonable height) and supported on axle stands it will be very difficult to carry out the work involved, as the engine is removed by lowering it from the engine bay. It will certainly be worth checking (with a tape measure) that with the equipment available the vehicle can be safely raised sufficiently to carry out the work.

3 Cleaning the engine compartment and engine/transmission before beginning the removal procedure will help keep tools clean and organised.

4 An engine hoist will also be necessary. Make sure the equipment is rated in excess of the combined weight of the engine and transmission. Safety is of primary importance, considering the potential hazards involved in removing the engine/transmission from the car.

5 The help of an assistant is essential. Apart from the safety aspects involved, there are many instances when one person cannot simultaneously perform all of the operations required during engine/transmission removal.

6 Plan the operation ahead of time. Before starting work, arrange for the hire of or obtain all of the tools and equipment you will need.

Some of the equipment necessary to perform engine/transmission removal and installation safely (in addition to an engine hoist) is as follows: a heavy duty trolley jack, complete sets of spanners and sockets as described in the rear of this manual, wooden blocks, and plenty of rags and cleaning solvent for mopping-up spilled oil, coolant and fuel. If the hoist must be hired, make sure that you arrange for it in advance, and perform all of the operations possible without it beforehand. This will save you money and time.

7 Plan for the car to be out of use for quite a while. An engineering machine shop or engine reconditioning specialist will be required to perform some of the work which cannot be accomplished without special equipment. These places often have a busy schedule, so it would be a good idea to consult them before removing the engine, in order to accurately estimate the amount of time required to rebuild or repair components that may need work.

8 During the engine/transmission removal procedure, it is advisable to make notes of the locations of all brackets, cable ties, earthing points, etc, as well as how the wiring harnesses, hoses and electrical connections are attached and routed around the engine and engine compartment. An effective way of doing this is to take a series of photographs of the various components before they are disconnected or removed; the resulting photographs will prove invaluable when the engine/transmission is refitted.

9 Always be extremely careful when removing and refitting the engine/transmission. Serious injury can result from careless actions. Plan ahead and take your time, and a job of this nature, although major, can be accomplished successfully.

10 On all models, the engine must be removed complete with the transmission as an assembly. There is insufficient clearance in the engine compartment to remove the engine leaving the transmission in the vehicle. The assembly is removed by raising the front of the vehicle, and lowering the assembly from the engine compartment.

Note: *Such is the complexity of the power unit arrangement on these vehicles, and the variations that may be encountered*

according to model and optional equipment fitted, that the following should be regarded as a guide to the work involved, rather than a step-by-step procedure. Where differences are encountered, or additional component disconnection or removal is necessary, make notes of the work involved as an aid to refitting.

4 Engine and transmission – removal, separation and refitting

Removal

1 Remove the engine cover and then remove the air filter housing assembly as described in Chapter 4A Section 3.

2 Disconnect and then remove the battery (see Chapter 5 Section 3). Undo the bolts and then remove the battery tray.

3 Undo the 2 bolts securing the brake fluid remote reservoir to the engine compartment bulkhead **(see illustration)**.

4 Remove the wiper arms as described in Chapter 12 Section 12.

5 Release the clips and remove the windscreen cowl panel, then undo the bolt at each end, release the 2 clips and remove the bulkhead extension panel **(see illustrations)**.

6 With the upper panel removed, unbolt and remove the lower windscreen cowl panel.

7 Remove the earth connection from the transmission and then with reference to Chapter 7 Section 3, remove the gear selector cables.

8 Remove the accessory drivebelt (Chapter 1 Section 22) on all engines apart from 2.0 litre models and then unbolt the power steering pump (Chapter 10 Section 19). Unclip the power steering pump reservoir, unbolt the pipe from the bracket and then move the pump and reservoir to the side. Alternatively, leave the drivebelt in position and disconnect the power steering pump supply and outlet lines – anticipate the loss of power steering fluid.

9 Apply the handbrake, then jack up the front of the vehicle and support it on axle stands (see *Jacking and vehicle support*). Remove both front roadwheels and wheel arch liners.

4.3 Remove the remote reservoir

4.5a Prise off the clips …

4.5b … and remove the windscreen cowl panel

4.16 Unclip the fuel lines

4.18 Remove the subframe.

4.19 Disconnect the wiring plugs

4.23 Disconnect the vacuum pipe

10 Remove the engine undershield and then remove the air deflector from the base of the front bumper cover.

11 Drain the cooling system with reference to Chapter 1 Section 25.

12 Drain the transmission oil as described in Chapter 7 Section 6. Refit the drain plug, and tighten it to the specified torque setting.

13 If the engine is to be dismantled, drain the engine oil and remove the oil filter as described in Chapter 1 Section 3. Clean and refit the drain plug, tightening it to the specified torque.

14 Refer to Chapter 8 Section 2 and remove both front driveshafts.

15 Work around the engine bay and disconnect the radiator hoses. Release the degas hoses and then (with difficulty) remove the heater matrix supply and return hoses.

16 Disconnect the fuel supply pipe(s) at the right-hand side of the engine compartment **(see illustration)**. Plug/cover the openings to prevent contamination.

17 Undo the bolts and remove the engine rear lower torque rod/movement limiter.

18 Remove the front subframe as described in Chapter 10 Section 16 **(see illustration)**.

19 Remove the cover from the PCM (Power Control Module) and disconnect the wiring plugs **(see illustration)**. Unclip the loom from the inner wing.

20 Remove the cover from the fusebox and disconnect/unplug the front section of the wiring block. Unbolt the earth connections from the inner wing. Note that the engine will be removed with most of the wiring loom still on the engine.

21 With reference to Chapter 4A Section 18, unbolt the front section of the exhaust pipe/particulate filter from the catalytic converter.

22 Disconnect the wiring plug, undo the retaining bolts and move the air conditioning compressor to one side. There is no need to disconnect the refrigerant pipes. Secure the compressor to the radiator support panel using cable ties/straps to prevent any strain on the pipes.

23 Depress the release button and disconnect the vacuum pipe from the brake vacuum pump **(see illustration)**. Disconnect the vacuum feed pipe from the servo hose.

24 Disconnect the fluid supply pipe from the clutch slave cylinder as described in Chapter 6 Section 4. Remove the clip and detach the pipe/hose from the retaining bracket. Plug the opening to prevent contamination **(see illustration)**.

25 Check that when lowered the engine/transmission assembly will pass out from the engine bay – raise the vehicle if necessary. Attach an engine lifting hoist and take the weight of the engine.

26 Refer to the relevant Chapter and unbolt the right- hand engine mounting **(see illustration)**.

27 Make a final check that any components which would prevent the removal of the engine/transmission from the car have been removed or disconnected. Ensure that components such as the gearchange selector

4.24 Seal the clutch hydraulic hose

4.26 Remove the left-hand mounting

4.28a Lower the engine/transmission assembly to the ground

4.28b We removed the assembly out through the wheel arch on a dolly

cables are secured so that they cannot be damaged on removal.
28 Carefully lower the assembly to the ground, making sure it clears the surrounding engine compartment components **(see illustrations)**.

Separation
29 Remove the starter motor.
30 Remove the bolts securing the transmission to the engine.
31 With the aid of an assistant, draw the transmission off the engine. Once it is clear of the dowels, do not allow it to hang on the input shaft.

Refitting
32 Make sure that the clutch is correctly centred and that the clutch release components are fitted to the bellhousing. Do not apply any grease to the transmission input shaft, the guide sleeve, or the release bearing itself, as these components have a friction-reducing coating which does not require lubrication.
33 Manoeuvre the transmission squarely into position, and engage it with the engine dowels. Refit the bolts securing the transmission to the engine, and tighten them to the specified torque. Refit the starter motor.
34 The remainder of refitting is essentially a reversal of removal, noting the following points:
a) Tighten all fastenings to the specified torque and, where applicable, torque angle. Refer to the relevant Chapters of this manual for torque wrench settings not directly related to the engine.
b) Reconnect and if necessary, adjust the manual transmission selector cables as described in Chapter 7 Section 3.
c) Refit the air cleaner assembly as described in Chapter 4A Section 3.
d) Refit the auxiliary drivebelt(s), then refill the engine with coolant and oil as described in Chapter 1.

e) Refill the transmission with lubricant if necessary as described in Chapter 7 Section 6.
f) Refer to Section 20 before starting the engine.

5 Engine overhaul – dismantling sequence

1 It is much easier to dismantle and work on the engine if it is mounted on a portable engine stand. These stands can often be hired from a tool hire shop. Before the engine is mounted on a stand, the flywheel/driveplate should be removed, so that the stand bolts can be tightened into the end of the cylinder block/crankcase.
2 If a stand is not available, it is possible to dismantle the engine with it blocked up on a sturdy workbench, or on the floor. Be extra careful not to tip or drop the engine when working without a stand.
3 If you are going to obtain a reconditioned engine, all the external components must be removed first, to be transferred to the new engine (just as they will if you are doing a complete engine overhaul yourself). These components include the following:
a) Engine wiring harness and support brackets.
b) Alternator, power steering pump and air conditioning compressor mounting brackets (as applicable).
c) Coolant inlet and outlet housings.
d) Dipstick tube.
e) Fuel system components.
f) All electrical switches and sensors.
g) Inlet and exhaust manifolds and, where fitted, the turbocharger.
h) Oil filter and oil cooler.
i) Flywheel.
Note: When removing the external components from the engine, pay close attention to details that may be helpful or

important during refitting. Note the fitted position of gaskets, seals, spacers, pins, washers, bolts, and other small items.
4 If you are obtaining a 'short' engine (which consists of the engine cylinder block/crankcase, crankshaft, pistons and connecting rods all assembled), then the cylinder head, sump, oil pump, and timing belt will have to be removed also.
5 If you are planning a complete overhaul, the engine can be dismantled, and the internal components removed, in the order given below, referring to Part A, B, C or D of this Chapter unless otherwise stated.
a) Inlet and exhaust manifolds (Chapter 4A Section 17).
b) Timing belt, sprockets and tensioner.
c) Coolant pump (Chapter 3 Section 8).
d) Cylinder head.
e) Flywheel.
f) Sump.
g) Oil pump.
h) Pistons/connecting rods (Section 10 of this Chapter).
i) Crankshaft (Section 11 of this Chapter).
6 Before beginning the dismantling and overhaul procedures, make sure that you have all of the correct tools necessary. See Tools and working facilities for further information.

6 Cylinder head – dismantling

Note: New and reconditioned cylinder heads are available from the manufacturer, and from engine overhaul specialists. Be aware that some specialist tools are required for the dismantling and inspection procedures, and new components may not be readily available. It may therefore be more practical and economical for the home mechanic to purchase a reconditioned head, rather than dismantle, inspect and recondition the original head.

6.3 Remove the camshaft drive chain guide – DOHC engines

6.5a Compress the valve spring using a spring compressor ...

6.5b ... then extract the collets and release the spring compressor

6.5c Remove the spring retainer ...

6.5d ... followed by the valve spring ...

6.5e ... and the spring seat (not all models)

1 Remove the cylinder head as described in Part A, B, C or D of this Chapter (as applicable).
2 If not already done, remove the inlet and exhaust manifolds with reference to Chapter 4A Section 17. Remove any remaining brackets or housings as required.
3 Remove the camshaft(s), tappets and rockers (as applicable) as described in Part A, B, C or D of this Chapter. On the DOHC engines, remove the camshaft drive chain guide from the cylinder head **(see illustration)**.
4 If not already done so, remove the glow plugs as described in Chapter 5 Section 11.
5 On all models, using a valve spring compressor, compress each valve spring in turn until the split collets can be removed.

Release the compressor, and lift off the spring retainer, spring and, where fitted, the spring seat. Using a pair of pliers, carefully extract the valve stem oil seal from the top of the guide. On 16-valve engines, the valve stem oil seal also forms the spring seat and is deeply recessed in the cylinder head. It is also a tight fit on the valve guide making it difficult to remove with pliers or a conventional valve stem oil seal removal tool. It can be easily removed, however, using a self-locking nut of suitable diameter screwed onto the end of a bolt and locked with a second nut. Push the nut down onto the top of the seal; the locking portion of the nut will grip the seal allowing it to be withdrawn from the top of the valve guide. Access to the valves is limited, and it may be necessary to make up an adapter

out of metal tube – cut out a 'window' so that the valve collets can be removed **(see illustrations)**.
6 If, when the valve spring compressor is screwed down, the spring retainer refuses to free and expose the split collets, gently tap the top of the tool, directly over the retainer, with a light hammer. This will free the retainer.
7 Withdraw the valve from the combustion chamber. Remove the valve stem oil seal from the top of the guide, then lift out the spring seat where fitted.
8 It is essential that each valve is stored together with its collets, retainer, spring, and spring seat. The valves should also be kept in their correct sequence, unless they are so badly worn that they are to be renewed. If they are going to be kept and used again,

6.5f Remove the valve stem oil seal using a pair of pliers

6.5g Metal tube adapter for access to the valve collets

6.5h Secure a self-locking nut of suitable diameter to a long bolt, then use the tool to remove the valve stem oil seal place each valve assembly in a labelled polythene bag or similar small container (see illustration). Note that No 1 valve is nearest to the transmission (flywheel) end on the 1.6. 2.0 and 2.2 litre engines.

6.8 Place each valve and its associated components in a labelled bag

7.5 Check the cylinder head gasket surface for distortion

7 Cylinder head and valves – cleaning and inspection

1 Thorough cleaning of the cylinder head and valve components, followed by a detailed inspection, will enable you to decide how much valve service work must be carried out during the engine overhaul. **Note:** *If the engine has been severely overheated, it is best to assume that the cylinder head is warped – check carefully for signs of this.*

Cleaning

2 Scrape away all traces of old gasket material from the cylinder head.
3 Scrape away the carbon from the combustion chambers and ports, then wash the cylinder head thoroughly with paraffin or a suitable solvent.
4 Scrape off any heavy carbon deposits that may have formed on the valves, then use a power-operated wire brush to remove deposits from the valve heads and stems.

Inspection

Note: *Be sure to perform all the following inspection procedures before concluding that the services of a machine shop or engine overhaul specialist are required. Make a list of all items that require attention.*

Cylinder head

5 Inspect the head very carefully for cracks, evidence of coolant leakage, and other damage. If cracks are found, a new cylinder head should be obtained. Use a straight-edge and feeler blade to check that the cylinder head gasket surface is not distorted (see illustration). If it is, it may be possible to have it machined, provided that the cylinder head height is not significantly reduced.
6 Examine the valve seats in each of the combustion chambers. If they are severely pitted, cracked, or burned, they will need to

be renewed or recut by an engine overhaul specialist. If they are only slightly pitted, this can be removed by grinding-in the valve heads and seats with fine valve-grinding compound, as described below. If in any doubt, have the cylinder head inspected by an engine overhaul specialist.
7 Check the valve guides for wear by inserting the relevant valve, and checking for side-to-side motion of the valve. A very small amount of movement is acceptable. If the movement seems excessive, remove the valve. Measure the valve stem diameter (see below), and renew the valve if it is worn. If the valve stem is not worn, the wear must be in the valve guide, and the guide must be renewed. The renewal of valve guides is best carried out by a Ford dealer or engine overhaul specialist, who will have the necessary tools available. Where no valve stem diameter is specified, seek the advice of a Ford dealer on the best course of action.
8 If renewing the valve guides, the valve seats should be recut or reground only after the guides have been fitted.
9 Examine the camshaft oil supply non-return valve (where fitted) in the oil feed bore at the timing belt end of the cylinder head. Check that the valve is not loose in the cylinder head and that the ball is free to move within the valve body. If the valve is a loose fit in its bore, or if there is any doubt about its condition, it should be renewed. The non-return valve can be removed (assuming it is not loose), using compressed air, such as that generated by a

tyre foot pump. Place the pump nozzle over the oil feed bore of the camshaft bearing journal and seal the corresponding oil feed bore with a rag. Apply the compressed air and the valve will be forced out of its location in the underside of the cylinder head (see illustrations). Fit the new non-return valve to its bore on the underside of the head ensuring it is fitted the correct way. Oil should be able to pass upwards through the valve to the camshafts, but the ball in the valve should prevent the oil from returning back to the cylinder block. Use a thin socket or similar to push the valve fully into position.

Valves

10 Examine the head of each valve for pitting, burning, cracks, and general wear. Check the valve stem for scoring and wear ridges. Rotate the valve, and check for any obvious indication that it is bent. Look for pits or excessive wear on the tip of each valve stem. Renew any valve that shows any such signs of wear or damage.
11 If the valve appears satisfactory at this stage, measure the valve stem diameter at several points using a micrometer (see illustration). Any significant difference in the readings obtained indicates wear of the valve stem. Should any of these conditions be apparent, the valve must be renewed.
12 If the valves are in satisfactory condition, they should be ground (lapped) into their respective seats, to ensure a smooth, gas-tight seal. If the seat is only lightly pitted, or if it has been recut, fine grinding compound

7.9a Apply compressed air to the oil feed bore of the inlet camshaft; seal the bore in the exhaust camshaft with a rag ...

7.9b ... and the camshaft oil supply non-return valve will be ejected from the underside of the cylinder head

7.11 Measure the valve stem diameter with a micrometer

only should be used to produce the required finish. Coarse valve-grinding compound should not be used, unless a seat is badly burned or deeply pitted. If this is the case, the cylinder head and valves should be inspected by an expert, to decide whether seat recutting, or even the renewal of the valve or seat insert (where possible) is required.

13 Valve grinding is carried out as follows. Place the cylinder head upside-down on a bench.

14 Smear a trace of (the appropriate grade of) valve-grinding compound on the seat face, and press a suction grinding tool onto the valve head **(see illustration)**. With a semi-rotary action, grind the valve head to its seat, lifting the valve occasionally to redistribute the grinding compound. A light spring placed under the valve head will greatly ease this operation.

15 If coarse grinding compound is being used, work only until a dull, matt even surface is produced on both the valve seat and the valve, then wipe off the used compound, and repeat the process with fine compound. When a smooth unbroken ring of light grey matt finish is produced on both the valve and seat, the grinding operation is complete. Do not grind-in the valves any further than absolutely necessary, or the seat will be prematurely sunk into the cylinder head.

16 When all the valves have been ground-in, carefully wash off all traces of grinding compound using paraffin or a suitable solvent, before reassembling the cylinder head.

Valve components

17 Examine the valve springs for signs of damage and discoloration. No minimum free length is specified by Ford, so the only way of judging valve spring wear is by comparison with a new component.

18 Stand each spring on a flat surface, and check it for squareness. If any of the springs are damaged, distorted or have lost their tension, obtain a complete new set of springs. It is normal to renew the valve springs as a matter of course if a major overhaul is being carried out.

19 Renew the valve stem oil seals regardless of their apparent condition.

8 Cylinder head – reassembly

1 Working on the first valve assembly, refit the spring seat then dip the new valve stem oil seal in fresh engine oil. Locate the seal on the valve guide and press the seal firmly onto the guide using a suitable socket **(see illustrations)**.

2 Lubricate the stem of the first valve, and insert it in the guide **(see illustration)**.

3 Locate the valve spring on top of its seat, then refit the spring retainer.

4 Compress the valve spring, and locate the split collets in the recess in the valve stem. Release the compressor, then repeat the procedure on the remaining valves. Ensure that each valve is inserted into its original location. If new valves are being fitted, insert them into the locations to which they have been ground.

5 With all the valves installed, support the cylinder head and, using a hammer and interposed block of wood, tap the end of each valve stem to settle the components.

6 Refit the camshafts, tappets and rocker arms (as applicable) as described in Part A, B, C or D of this Chapter.

7 Refit any remaining components using the reverse of the removal sequence and with new seals or gaskets as necessary.

8 The cylinder head can then be refitted as described in Part A, B, C or D of this Chapter.

9 Fuel pump drive (1.8 litre models) – removal, inspection and refitting

Note: *The high-pressure fuel pump will be driven either by a double-row chain or a toothed belt, depending on the year of manufacture. The following procedures are applicable to both types.*

Removal

1 With the engine removed from the vehicle, proceed as follows.

2 Remove the oil pump as described in Chapter 2B Section 13.

3 At the rear of the engine block, locate the drive chain hydraulic tensioner (below and behind the coolant pump). Using the hex in the top of the tensioner body, unscrew and extract the tensioner from the block **(see illustration)**. Be prepared for a small amount of oil spillage as this is done.

4 Unscrew the two bolts securing the chain/belt guides, then carefully slide the two sprockets simultaneously from their locations

7.14 Grinding-in a valve

8.1a Locate the valve stem oil seal (arrowed) on the valve guide …

8.1b …and press the seal firmly onto the guide using a suitable socket

8.1c On some engines, the valve stem oil seal is integral with the spring seat

8.2 Lubricate the stem of the valve and insert it into the guide

9.3 Unscrew the tensioner from the housing

9.5 Examine the guides for wear

9.6 Two chains ('gemini') which run next to one another, offset by half a link

9.8 Tighten the chain guide retaining bolts

and remove the complete chain/belt, guide and sprocket assembly from the engine.

Inspection

5 Examine the guides for scoring or wear ridges, and for chipping or wear of the sprocket teeth **(see illustration)**.

6 On engines with a chain driven fuel pump, check the chains for wear, which will be evident in the form of excess play between the links **(see illustration)**. If the chains can be lifted at either 'end' of their run so that the sprocket teeth are visible, they have stretched excessively. If the chains have covered more than 150 000 miles, they must be renewed regardless of condition. On engines with a belt driven fuel pump, do not be tempted to re-use the old belt under any circumstances – even if it is known to have covered less than the 150 000 mile recommended renewal interval. Ford state that, once a drive belt has been run on an engine, it is considered worn, and should be discarded. In any case, given the potential expense involved should the belt fail in service, re-using an old belt would be a false economy.

7 Check the chain tensioner for signs of wear, and renew if required.

Refitting

8 Refitting is a reversal of removal, noting the following points:
a) Tighten the chain guide retaining bolts securely **(see illustration)**.
b) Especially if a new chain and sprocket assembly has been fitted, lubricate it thoroughly with fresh engine oil.

c) Refit the chain tensioner, and tighten it securely.
d) Refit the oil pump as described in Chapter 2B, Section 13.

10 Piston/connecting rod assembly – removal

1 Remove the cylinder head, sump and oil pump as described in Part A, B, C or D.
2 If there is a pronounced wear ridge at the top of any bore, it may be necessary to remove it with a scraper or ridge reamer, to avoid piston damage during removal. Such a ridge indicates excessive wear of the cylinder bore.
3 If working on the 2.2 litre engine remove the balancer shaft assembly as described in Chapter 2D Section 10.
4 Using quick-drying paint, mark each connecting rod and big-end bearing cap with its respective cylinder number on the flat machined surface provided; if the engine has been dismantled before, note carefully any identifying marks made previously **(see illustration)**.
5 Turn the crankshaft to bring pistons 1 and 4 to BDC (bottom dead centre).
6 Unscrew the nuts or bolts, as applicable from No 1 piston big-end bearing cap. Take off the cap, and recover the bottom half bearing shell **(see illustration)**. If the bearing shells are to be re-used, tape the cap and the shell together.

7 Where applicable, to prevent the possibility of damage to the crankshaft bearing journals, tape over the connecting rod stud threads **(see illustration)**.
8 Using a hammer handle, push the piston up through the bore, and remove it from the top of the cylinder block. Recover the bearing shell, and tape it to the connecting rod for safe-keeping.
9 Loosely refit the big-end cap to the connecting rod, and secure with the nuts/bolts – this will help to keep the components in their correct order.
10 Remove No 4 piston assembly in the same way.
11 Turn the crankshaft through 180° to bring pistons 2 and 3 to BDC (bottom dead centre), and remove them in the same way.

11 Crankshaft – removal

1 Remove the crankshaft sprocket and the oil pump as described in Part A, B, C or D of this Chapter (as applicable).
2 Remove the pistons and connecting rods, as described in Section 10. If no work is to be done on the pistons and connecting rods, there is no need to remove the cylinder head, or to push the pistons out of the cylinder bores. The pistons should just be pushed far enough up the bores so that they are positioned clear of the crankshaft journals.
3 Check the crankshaft endfloat as described in Section 14, then proceed as follows.

10.4 Connecting rod and big-end bearing cap identification marks (No 3 shown)

10.6 Remove the big-end bearing shell and cap

10.7 To protect the crankshaft journals, tape over the connecting rod stud threads

11.5 Prise up the two caps to expose the main bearing bolts at the flywheel end

11.6 Remove the crankshaft bearing cap housing

11.9 Main bearing caps are marked with cylinder number and arrowhead

1.6 litre engines

4 Working around the inner periphery of the crankcase, unscrew the small bolts securing the crankshaft bearing cap housing to the base of the cylinder block. Note the correct fitted depth of the left-hand crankshaft oil seal in the cylinder block/bearing cap housing.

5 Working in the reverse of the tightening sequence, evenly and progressively slacken the ten large bearing cap housing retaining bolts by a turn at a time. Once all the bolts are loose, remove them from the housing. **Note:** *Prise up the two caps at the flywheel end of the housing to expose the two end main bearing bolts* (see illustration).

6 With all the retaining bolts removed, tap around the outer periphery of the bearing cap housing using a soft-faced mallet to break the seal between the housing and cylinder block. Once the seal is released and the housing is clear of the locating dowels, lift it up and off the crankshaft and cylinder block (see illustration). Recover the lower main bearing shells, and tape them to their respective locations in the housing. If the two locating dowels are a loose fit, remove them and store them with the housing for safe-keeping.

7 Lift out the crankshaft, and collect the left-hand oil seal.

8 Recover the upper main bearing shells, and store them along with the relevant lower bearing shell. Also recover the two thrustwashers (one fitted either side of No 2 main bearing) from the cylinder block.

1.8 litre engines

9 Check the main bearing caps, to see if they are marked to indicate their locations. They should be numbered consecutively from the timing belt end of the engine – if not, mark them with number-stamping dies or a centre-punch. The caps will also have an embossed arrow pointing to the timing belt end of the engine (see illustration). Noting, where applicable, the different fasteners (for the oil baffle nuts) used on caps 2 and 4, slacken the cap bolts a quarter-turn at a time each, starting with the left- and right-hand end caps and working toward the centre, until they can be removed by hand.

10 Gently tap the caps with a soft-faced hammer, then separate them from the cylinder block/crankcase. If necessary, use the bolts as levers to remove the caps. Try not to drop the bearing shells if they come out with the caps.

11 Carefully lift the crankshaft out of the engine. It may be a good idea to have an assistant available, since the crankshaft is quite heavy. With the bearing shells in place in the cylinder block/crankcase and main bearing caps, return the caps to their respective locations on the block, or refit the lower crankcase, and tighten the bolts finger-tight. Leaving the old shells in place until reassembly will help prevent the bearing recesses from being accidentally nicked or gouged. New shells should be used on reassembly.

2.0 litre engines

12 Slacken and remove the retaining bolts, and remove the oil seal carrier from the timing belt end of the cylinder block, along with its gasket (where fitted) (see illustration).

13 Remove the oil pump drive chain, and slide the drive sprocket and spacer (where fitted) off the end of the crankshaft. Remove the Woodruff key, and store it with the sprocket for safe-keeping (see illustrations).

14 The main bearing caps should be numbered 1 to 5, starting from the transmission (flywheel) end of the engine (see

11.12 Remove the oil seal housing from the right-hand end of the cylinder block

11.13a Remove the oil pump drive chain ...

11.13b ...then slide off the drive sprocket...

11.13c ...and remove the Woodruff key from the crankshaft

illustration). If not, mark them accordingly using quick-drying paint. Also note the correct fitted depth of the crankshaft oil seal in the bearing cap.

15 Slacken and remove the main bearing cap retaining bolts/nuts, and lift off each bearing cap. Recover the lower bearing shells, and tape them to their respective caps for safe-keeping. Also recover the lower thrust -washer halves from the side of No 2 main bearing cap (see illustration). Remove the rubber sealing strips from the sides of No 1 main bearing cap, and discard them.

16 Lift out the crankshaft, and discard the oil seal (see illustration).

17 Recover the upper bearing shells from the cylinder block, and tape them to their respective caps for safe-keeping (see illustration). Remove the upper thrustwasher halves from the side of No 2 main bearing, and store them with the lower halves.

2.2 litre engines

18 The crankshaft on 2.2 litre engines is removed in the same manner as the 2.0 litre engine. Follow the procedure outlined above.

12 Cylinder block/crankcase –
cleaning and inspection

Cleaning

1 Remove all external components and electrical switches/sensors from the block. For complete cleaning, the core plugs should ideally be removed (see illustrations). Drill a small hole in the plugs, then insert a self-tapping screw into the hole. Pull out the plugs by pulling on the screw with a pair of grips, or by using a slide hammer.

2 Where applicable, undo the retaining bolts and remove the piston oil jet spray tubes from inside the cylinder block (see illustration).

3 Scrape all traces of gasket from the cylinder block/crankcase, and from the main bearing ladder (where fitted), taking care not to damage the gasket/sealing surfaces.

4 Remove all oil gallery plugs (where fitted). The plugs are usually very tight – they may have to be drilled out, and the holes retapped. Use new plugs when reassembling.

5 If any of the castings are extremely dirty, all should be steam-cleaned.

6 After the castings are returned, clean all oil holes and oil galleries one more time. Flush all internal passages with warm water until the water runs clear. Dry thoroughly, and apply a light film of oil to all mating surfaces, to prevent rusting. On cast-iron block engines, also oil the cylinder bores. If you have access to compressed air, use it to speed up the drying process, and to blow out all the oil holes and galleries.

 Warning: Wear eye protection when using compressed air.

11.14 Main bearing cap identification markings

11.16 Lift out the crankshaft

7 If the castings are not very dirty, you can do an adequate cleaning job with hot (as hot as you can stand), soapy water and a stiff brush. Take plenty of time, and do a thorough job. Regardless of the cleaning method used, be

12.1a Cylinder block core plugs

12.1c Remove the cylinder block ventilation/oil separator box

11.15 Note the thrustwasher fitted to the No 2 main bearing cap

11.17 Remove the upper main bearing shells

sure to clean all oil holes and galleries very thoroughly, and to dry all components well. On cast-iron block engines, protect the cylinder bores as described above, to prevent rusting.

8 All threaded holes must be clean, to ensure

12.1b Remove the air conditioning compressor bracket

12.2 Piston cooling jets may be fitted to the base of each cylinder bore

accurate torque readings during reassembly. To clean the threads, run the correct-size tap into each of the holes to remove rust, corrosion, thread sealant or sludge, and to restore damaged threads. If possible, use compressed air to clear the holes of debris produced by this operation.

9 Apply suitable sealant to the new oil gallery plugs, and insert them into the holes in the block. Tighten them securely. Apply suitable sealant to the new core plugs, and insert them into the holes in the block. Tap them into place with a close-fitting tube or socket.

10 Where applicable, clean the threads of the piston oil jet retaining bolt, and apply a drop of thread-locking compound to the bolt threads. Refit the piston oil jet spray tube to the cylinder block, and tighten its retaining bolt to the specified torque setting.

11 If the engine is not going to be reassembled right away, cover it with a large plastic bag to keep it clean; protect all mating surfaces and the cylinder bores as described above, to prevent rusting.

Inspection

12 Visually check the castings for cracks and corrosion. Look for stripped threads in the threaded holes. If there has been any history of internal water leakage, it may be worthwhile having an engine overhaul specialist check the cylinder block/crankcase with special equipment. If defects are found, have them repaired if possible, or renew the assembly.

13 Check each cylinder bore for scuffing and scoring. Check for signs of a wear ridge at the top of the cylinder, indicating that the bore is excessively worn.

14 If wear is suspected, have the cylinder bores measured by an automotive engineering workshop, who will be able to carry out the reboring, and supply suitable pistons/rings, etc, as applicable.

15 At the time of writing, it was not clear whether oversize pistons were available for all models. Consult your Ford dealer for the latest information on piston availability. If oversize pistons are available, then it may be possible to have the cylinder bores rebored and oversize pistons fitted. If oversize pistons are not available, and the bores are worn, renewal of the block is the only option.

13 Piston/connecting rod assembly – inspection

1 Before the inspection process can begin, the piston/connecting rod assemblies must be cleaned, and the original piston rings removed from the pistons.

2 Carefully expand the old rings over the top of the pistons. The use of two or three old feeler blades will be helpful in preventing the rings dropping into empty grooves **(see illustration)**. Be careful not to scratch the piston with the ends of the ring. The rings are brittle, and will snap if they are spread too far. They are also very sharp – protect your hands and fingers. Note that the third ring incorporates an expander. Always remove the rings from the top of the piston.

3 Scrape away all traces of carbon from the top of the piston. A hand-held wire brush (or a piece of fine emery cloth) can be used, once the majority of the deposits have been scraped away.

4 Remove the carbon from the ring grooves in the piston, using an old ring. Break the ring in half to do this. Be careful to remove only the carbon deposits – do not remove any metal, and do not nick or scratch the sides of the ring grooves.

5 Once the deposits have been removed, clean the piston/connecting rod assembly with paraffin or a suitable solvent, and dry thoroughly. Make sure that the oil return holes in the ring grooves are clear.

6 If the pistons and cylinder bores are not damaged or worn excessively, and if the cylinder block does not need to be rebored, the original pistons can be refitted. Normal piston wear shows up as even vertical wear on the piston thrust surfaces, and slight looseness of the top ring in its groove. New piston rings should always be used when the engine is reassembled.

7 Carefully inspect each piston for cracks around the skirt, around the gudgeon pin holes, and at the piston ring 'lands' (between the ring grooves).

8 Look for scoring and scuffing on the piston skirt, holes in the piston crown, and burned areas at the edge of the crown. If the skirt is scored or scuffed, the engine may have been suffering from overheating, and/or abnormal combustion which caused excessively high operating temperatures. The cooling and lubrication systems should be checked thoroughly. Scorch marks on the sides of the pistons show that blow-by has occurred. A hole in the piston crown, or burned areas at the edge of the piston crown, indicates that abnormal combustion (pre-ignition, knocking, or detonation) has been occurring. If any of the above problems exist, the causes must be investigated and corrected, or the damage will occur again.

9 Corrosion of the piston, in the form of pitting, indicates that coolant has been leaking into the combustion chamber and/or the crankcase. Again, the cause must be corrected, or the problem may persist in the rebuilt engine.

10 On aluminium-block engines with wet liners, it is not possible to renew the pistons separately; pistons are only supplied with piston rings and a liner, as a part of a matched assembly. On iron-block engines, pistons can be purchased from a Ford dealer.

11 Examine each connecting rod carefully for signs of damage, such as cracks around the big-end and small-end bearings. Check that the rod is not bent or distorted. Damage is highly unlikely, unless the engine has been seized or badly overheated. Detailed checking of the connecting rod assembly can only be carried out by a Ford dealer or engine repair specialist with the necessary equipment.

12 The big-end cap bolts/nuts must be renewed as a complete set prior to refitting. This should be done after the big-end bearing running clearance check has been carried out.

13 The gudgeon pins are of the floating type, secured in position by two circlips. The pistons and connecting rods can be separated as described in the following paragraphs.

14 Before separating the piston and connecting rod, check the position of the valve recesses or markings on the piston crown in relation to the connecting rod big-end bearing shell cut-outs and make a note of the orientation.

15 Using a small flat-bladed screwdriver, prise out the circlips, and push out the gudgeon pin **(see illustrations)**. Hand

13.2 Remove the piston rings with the aid of feeler gauges

13.15a Prise out the circlip ...

13.15b ... and withdraw the gudgeon pin

pressure should be sufficient to remove the pin. Identify the piston and rod to ensure correct reassembly. Discard the circlips – new ones must be used on refitting.

16 Examine the gudgeon pin and connecting rod small-end bearing for signs of wear or damage. Wear can be cured by renewing both the pin and bush. Bush renewal, however, is a specialist job – press facilities are required, and the new bush must be reamed accurately.

17 The connecting rods themselves should not be in need of renewal, unless seizure or some other major mechanical failure has occurred. Check the alignment of the connecting rods visually, and if the rods are not straight, take them to an engine overhaul specialist for a more detailed check.

18 Examine all components, and obtain any new parts from your Ford dealer. If new pistons are purchased, they will be supplied complete with gudgeon pins and circlips. Circlips can also be purchased individually.

19 Position the piston in relation to the connecting rod big-end bearing shell cut-outs as noted during separation.

20 Apply a smear of clean engine oil to the gudgeon pin and slide it into the piston and through the connecting rod small-end. Check that the piston pivots freely on the rod, then secure the gudgeon pin in position with two new circlips. Ensure that each circlip is correctly located in its groove in the piston.

14 Crankshaft – inspection

Checking endfloat

1 If the crankshaft endfloat is to be checked, this must be done when the crankshaft is installed in the cylinder block/crankcase, but is free to move.

2 Check the endfloat using a dial gauge in contact with the end of the crankshaft. Push the crankshaft fully one way, and then zero the gauge. Push the crankshaft fully the other way, and check the endfloat. The result can be compared with the specified amount, and will give an indication as to whether new thrustwashers are required (see illustration).

14.2 Check the crankshaft endfloat using a DTI gauge…

3 If a dial gauge is not available, feeler gauges can be used. First push the crankshaft fully towards the flywheel end of the engine, then use feeler gauges to measure the gap between the web and the thrustwasher (see illustration).

Inspection

4 Clean the crankshaft using paraffin or a suitable solvent, and dry it, preferably with compressed air if available. Be sure to clean the oil holes with a pipe cleaner or similar probe, to ensure that they are not obstructed.

 Warning: Wear eye protection when using compressed air.

5 Check the main and big-end bearing journals for uneven wear, scoring, pitting and cracking.

6 Big-end bearing wear is accompanied by distinct metallic knocking when the engine is running (particularly noticeable when the engine is pulling from low speed) and by some loss of oil pressure.

7 Main bearing wear is accompanied by severe engine vibration and rumble – getting progressively worse as engine speed increases – and again by loss of oil pressure.

8 Check the bearing journal for roughness by running a finger lightly over the bearing surface. Any roughness (which will be accompanied by obvious bearing wear) indicates that the crankshaft requires regrinding (where possible) or renewal.

9 If the crankshaft has been reground, check for burrs around the crankshaft oil holes (the holes are usually chamfered, so burrs should not be a problem unless regrinding has been carried out carelessly). Remove any burrs with a fine file or scraper, and thoroughly clean the oil holes as described previously.

10 Have the crankshaft inspected and measured by an automotive engineering workshop, who will be able to carry out any necessary repairs, and supply relevant parts.

11 Check the oil seal contact surfaces at each end of the crankshaft for wear and damage. If the seal has worn a deep groove in the surface of the crankshaft, consult an engine overhaul specialist; repair may be possible, but otherwise a new crankshaft will be required.

14.3 …or with feeler gauges

12 Ford produce a set of undersize bearing shells for both the main and big-end bearings on most engines. Where the crankshaft journals have not already been reground, it may be possible to have the crankshaft reconditioned, and to fit undersize shells. If no undersize shells are available and the crankshaft has worn beyond the specified limits, the crankshaft will have to be renewed. Consult your Ford dealer or engine specialist for further information on parts availability.

15 Main and big-end bearings – inspection

1 Even though the main and big-end bearings should be renewed during the engine overhaul, the old bearings should be retained for close examination, as they may reveal valuable information about the condition of the engine. The bearing shells are graded by thickness, the grade of each shell being indicated by the colour code marked on it.

2 Bearing failure can occur due to lack of lubrication, the presence of dirt or other foreign particles, overloading the engine, or corrosion (see illustration). Regardless of the cause of bearing failure, the cause must be corrected (where applicable) before the engine is reassembled, to prevent it from happening again.

3 When examining the bearing shells, remove them from the cylinder block/crankcase, the main bearing ladder/caps (as appropriate), the connecting rods and the connecting rod big-end bearing caps. Lay them out on a clean surface in the same general position as their location in the engine. This will enable you to match any bearing problems with the corresponding crankshaft journal. Do not

15.2 Typical bearing failures

touch any shell's bearing surface with your fingers while checking it, or the delicate surface may be scratched.

4 Dirt and other foreign matter gets into the engine in a variety of ways. It may be left in the engine during assembly, or it may pass through filters or the crankcase ventilation system. It may get into the oil, and from there into the bearings. Metal chips from machining operations and normal engine wear are often present. Abrasives are sometimes left in engine components after reconditioning, especially when parts are not thoroughly cleaned using the proper cleaning methods. Whatever the source, these foreign objects often end up embedded in the soft bearing material, and are easily recognised. Large particles will not embed in the bearing, and will score or gouge the bearing and journal. The best prevention for this cause of bearing failure is to clean all parts thoroughly, and keep everything spotlessly-clean during engine assembly. Frequent and regular engine oil and filter changes are also recommended.

5 Lack of lubrication (or lubrication breakdown) has a number of interrelated causes. Excessive heat (which thins the oil), overloading (which squeezes the oil from the bearing face) and oil leakage (from excessive bearing clearances, worn oil pump or high engine speeds) all contribute to lubrication breakdown. Blocked oil passages, which usually are the result of misaligned oil holes in a bearing shell, will also oil-starve a bearing, and destroy it. When lack of lubrication is the cause of bearing failure, the bearing material is wiped or extruded from the steel backing of the bearing. Temperatures may increase to the point where the steel backing turns blue from overheating.

6 Driving habits can have a definite effect on bearing life. Full-throttle, low-speed operation (labouring the engine) puts very high loads on bearings, tending to squeeze out the oil film. These loads cause the bearings to flex, which produces fine cracks in the bearing face (fatigue failure). Eventually, the bearing material will loosen in pieces, and tear away from the steel backing.

7 Short-distance driving leads to corrosion of bearings, because insufficient engine heat is produced to drive off the condensed water and corrosive gases. These products collect in the engine oil, forming acid and sludge. As the oil is carried to the engine bearings, the acid attacks and corrodes the bearing material.

8 Incorrect bearing installation during engine assembly will lead to bearing failure as well. Tight-fitting bearings leave insufficient bearing running clearance, and will result in oil starvation. Dirt or foreign particles trapped behind a bearing shell result in high spots on the bearing, which lead to failure.

9 Do not touch any shell's bearing surface with your fingers during reassembly; there is a risk of scratching the delicate surface, or of depositing particles of dirt on it.

10 As mentioned at the beginning of this Section, the bearing shells should be renewed as a matter of course during engine overhaul; to do otherwise is false economy.

16 Engine overhaul – reassembly sequence

1 Before reassembly begins, ensure that all new parts have been obtained, and that all necessary tools are available. Read through the entire procedure to familiarise yourself with the work involved, and to ensure that all items necessary for reassembly of the engine are at hand. In addition to all normal tools and materials, thread-locking compound will be needed. A suitable tube of liquid sealant will also be required for the joint faces that are fitted without gaskets. It is recommended that Ford's own products are used, which are specially formulated for this purpose; the relevant product names are quoted in the text of each Section where they are required.

2 In order to save time and avoid problems, engine reassembly can be carried out in the following order:
a) Crankshaft (Section 18).
b) Piston/connecting rod assemblies (Section 19).
c) Oil pump (see Part A, B, C or D – as applicable).
d) Sump (see Part A, B, C or D – as applicable).
e) Flywheel (see Part A, B, C or D – as applicable).
f) Cylinder head (see Part A, B, C or D – as applicable).
g) Timing belt tensioner and sprockets, and timing belt (see Part A, B, C or D – as applicable).
h) Engine external components.

3 At this stage, all engine components should be absolutely clean and dry, with all faults repaired. The components should be laid out (or in individual containers) on a completely clean work surface.

17 Piston rings – refitting

1 Before fitting new piston rings, the ring end gaps must be checked as follows.
2 Lay out the piston/connecting rod assemblies and the new piston ring sets, so that the ring sets will be matched with the same piston and cylinder during the end gap measurement and subsequent engine reassembly.
3 Insert the top ring into the first cylinder, and push it down the bore using the top of the piston. This will ensure that the ring remains square with the cylinder walls. Position the

17.5 Measure the piston ring end gap with feeler gauges

ring near the bottom of the cylinder bore, at the lower limit of ring travel. Note that the top and second compression rings are different. The second ring is easily identified by the step on its lower surface, and by the fact that its outer face is tapered.
4 Measure the end gap using feeler gauges.
5 Repeat the procedure with the ring at the top of the cylinder bore, at the upper limit of its travel, and compare the measurements with the figures given in the Specifications **(see illustration)**. Where no figures are given, seek the advice of a Ford dealer or engine reconditioning specialist.
6 If the gap is too small (unlikely if genuine Ford parts are used), it must be enlarged, or the ring ends may contact each other during engine operation, causing serious damage. Ideally, new piston rings providing the correct end gap should be fitted. As a last resort, the end gap can be increased by filing the ring ends very carefully with a fine file. Mount the file in a vice equipped with soft jaws, slip the ring over the file with the ends contacting the file face, and slowly move the ring to remove material from the ends. Take care, as piston rings are sharp, and are easily broken.
7 With new piston rings, it is unlikely that the end gap will be too large. If the gaps are too large, check that you have the correct rings for your engine and for the particular cylinder bore size.
8 Repeat the checking procedure for each ring in the first cylinder, and then for the rings in the remaining cylinders. Remember to keep rings, pistons and cylinders matched up.
9 Once the ring end gaps have been checked and if necessary corrected, the rings can be fitted to the pistons.
10 Fit the piston rings using the same technique as for removal. Fit the bottom (oil control) ring first, and work up. When fitting the oil control ring, first insert the expander (where fitted), then fit the ring with its gap positioned 180° from the expander gap. Ensure that the second compression ring is fitted the correct way up, with its identification mark (either a dot of paint or the word TOP stamped on the ring surface) at the top, and the stepped surface at the bottom **(see**

illustration). Arrange the gaps of the top and second compression rings 120° either side of the oil control ring gap. **Note:** *Always follow any instructions supplied with the new piston ring sets – different manufacturers may specify different procedures. Do not mix up the top and second compression rings, as they have different cross-sections.*

18 Crankshaft – refitting

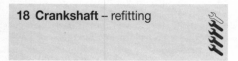

New main bearing shells

1 To ensure that the main bearing running clearance is correct, the bearing shells are supplied in various thicknesses or grades. The grades are indicated by a colour-coding marked on the edge of each shell. The grade of the new bearing shells required (either standard size or undersize) is selected using the reference marks on the cylinder block and on the crankshaft. The cylinder block marks identify the diameter of the bearing bores in the block, and the crankshaft marks identify the diameter of the crankshaft journals.

2 Note that on the engines described in this Manual, the upper shells are all of the same size, and the running clearance is controlled by fitting a lower bearing shell of the required thickness.

3 Numerous grades of standard and oversize bearing shells are available, depending on the engine type, year of manufacture, and country of export. Using the cylinder block and crankshaft reference marks together with the crankshaft journal diameter, a Ford dealer or engine overhaul specialist will be able to supply the correct bearing shells to give the required bearing running clearance for each journal.

Final crankshaft refitting

4 Crankshaft refitting is the first major step in engine reassembly. It is assumed at this point that the cylinder block/crankcase and crankshaft have been cleaned, inspected and repaired or reconditioned as necessary. Position the engine upside-down.

17.10 Piston ring details (typical)

1 Top compression ring
2 2nd compression ring
3 Oil scraper ring assembly

1.6 litre engines

5 Place the bearing shells in their locations. If new shells are being fitted, ensure that all traces of protective grease are cleaned off using paraffin. Wipe dry the shells with a lint-free cloth. The upper bearing shells all have a grooved surface, whereas the lower shells have a plain surface. It's essential that the lower bearing shells are centrally located in the bearing cap housing/ladder. To ensure this use a Ford tool (No 303-245) positioned over the housing/ladder, and insert the bearing shells through the slots in the tool **(see illustration)**.

6 Liberally lubricate each bearing shell in the cylinder block with clean engine oil then lower the crankshaft into position.

7 Insert the thrustwashers to either side of No 2 main bearing upper location and push them around the bearing journal until their edges are horizontal **(see illustration)**. Ensure that the oilway grooves on each thrustwasher face outwards (away from the bearing journal).

8 Thoroughly degrease the mating surfaces of the cylinder block and the crankshaft bearing cap housing. Apply a thin bead of silicone sealant (Ford part No WSE-M4G323-A4) to the bearing cap housing mating surface **(see illustration)**.

18.5 Main bearing shell fitment – 1.6 litre engine

1 Bearing shell
2 Main bearing ladder
3 Ford tool No 303-245
4 Aligning pins

9 Lubricate the lower bearing shells with clean engine oil, then refit the bearing cap housing, ensuring that the shells are not displaced, and that the locating dowels engage correctly.

10 Install the ten large diameter, and sixteen smaller diameter crankshaft bearing cap housing retaining bolts, and screw them in until they are just making contact with the housing.

11 Working in sequence, tighten the bolts to the torque settings given in the Specifications **(see illustration)**.

12 With the bearing cap housing in place, check that the crankshaft rotates freely.

13 Refit the piston/connecting rod assemblies to the crankshaft as described in Section 19.

14 Refit the oil pump and sump.

15 Fit a new crankshaft left-hand oil seal, then refit the flywheel.

16 Where removed, refit the cylinder head, crankshaft sprocket and timing belt.

1.8 litre engines

17 If they're still in place, remove the old bearing shells from the block and the main bearing caps. Wipe the bearing recesses with a clean, lint-free cloth. They must be kept spotlessly clean.

18.7 Place the thrustwashers each side of the No 2 bearing upper location

18.8 Apply a thin bead of RTV sealant to the bearing cap housing mating surface

18.11 Main bearing cap housing/ladder retaining bolt tightening sequence

18.18a Ensure the tab (A) and oil hole (B) are correctly aligned when refitting the shells

18.18b Note the thrustwashers fitted to the No 3 main bearing shell

18.18c Make sure the tab on the cap bearing shell engages correctly

18.19 Oil the bearing shells before fitting the crankshaft

18 Clean the backs of the new main bearing shells. Fit the shells with an oil groove in each main bearing location in the block. Note the thrustwashers integral with the No 3 (centre) upper main bearing shell, or the thrustwasher halves fitted either side of No 3 upper main bearing location. Fit the other shell from each bearing set in the corresponding main bearing cap. Make sure the tab on each bearing shell fits into the notch in the block or cap/lower crankcase. Also, the oil holes in the block must line up with the oil holes in the bearing shell **(see illustrations)**. Don't hammer the shells into place, and don't nick or gouge the bearing faces.

19 Clean the bearing surfaces of the shells in the block, then apply a thin, uniform layer of clean molybdenum disulphide-based grease, engine assembly lubricant, or clean engine oil to each surface **(see illustration)**. Coat the thrustwasher surfaces as well.

20 Lubricate the crankshaft oil seal journals with molybdenum disulphide-based grease, engine assembly lubricant, or clean engine oil.

21 Make sure the crankshaft journals are clean, then lay the crankshaft back in place in the block **(see illustration)**.

22 Refit and tighten the main bearing caps as follows:

a) Clean the bearing surfaces of the shells in the caps, then lubricate them. Refit the caps in their respective positions, with the arrows pointing to the timing belt end of the engine.

b) Working on one cap at a time, from the centre main bearing outwards (and ensuring that each cap is tightened down squarely and evenly onto the block), tighten the main bearing cap bolts to the specified torque wrench setting **(see illustration)**.

23 Rotate the crankshaft a number of times by hand, to check for any obvious binding.

24 Check the crankshaft endfloat (see Section 14). It should be correct if the crankshaft thrustwashers/thrust control bearing(s) aren't worn or damaged, or have been renewed.

25 Refit the crankshaft left-hand oil seal carrier and install a new seal (Chapter 2B Section 16).

2.0 litre and 2.2 litre engines

26 Using a little grease, stick the upper thrustwashers to each side of the No 2 main bearing upper location. Ensure that the oilway grooves on each thrustwasher face outwards (away from the cylinder block) **(see illustration)**.

27 Place the bearing shells in their locations. If new shells are being fitted, ensure that all traces of protective grease are cleaned off using paraffin. Wipe dry the shells and connecting rods with a lint-free cloth. Liberally lubricate each bearing shell in the cylinder block/crankcase and cap with clean engine oil.

28 Lower the crankshaft into position so that Nos 2 and 3 cylinder crankpins are at TDC; Nos 1 and 4 cylinder crankpins will be at BDC, ready for fitting No 1 piston. Check the crankshaft endfloat, referring to Section 14.

29 Lubricate the lower bearing shells in the main bearing caps with clean engine oil. Make sure that the locating lugs on the shells engage with the corresponding recesses in the caps.

30 Fit main bearing caps Nos 2 to 5 to their correct locations, ensuring that they are fitted the correct way round (the bearing shell tab recesses in the block and caps must be on the same side). Insert the bolts/nuts, tightening them only loosely at this stage.

31 Apply a small amount of sealant to the No 1 main bearing cap mating face on the

18.21 Lower the crankshaft gently into place

18.22 Tighten the main bearing cap bolts

18.26 Ensure the oil grooves on each thrustwasher are facing outwards from the No 2 main bearing location

18.31 Apply sealant to the No 1 main bearing cap mating face on the cylinder block, around the sealing strip holes inthe corners

18.32 Fit the sealing strips to the No 1 main bearing cap

cylinder block, around the sealing strip holes **(see illustration)**.

32 Locate the tab of each sealing strip over the pins on the base of No 1 bearing cap, and press the strips into the bearing cap grooves. It is now necessary to obtain two thin metal strips, of 0.25 mm thickness or less, in order to prevent the strips moving when the cap is being fitted. Ford garages use the tool shown, which acts as a clamp. Metal strips (such as old feeler blades) can be used, provided all burrs which may damage the sealing strips are first removed **(see illustration)**.

33 Where applicable, oil both sides of the metal strips, and hold them on the sealing strips. Fit the No 1 main bearing cap, insert the bolts loosely, then carefully pull out the metal strips in a horizontal direction, using a pair of pliers **(see illustration)**.

34 Tighten all the main bearing cap bolts/nuts

evenly to the specified torque. Using a sharp knife, trim off the ends of the No 1 bearing cap sealing strips, so that they protrude above the cylinder block/crankcase mating surface by approximately 1.0 mm **(see illustration)**.

35 Fit a new crankshaft left-hand oil seal as described in Part C or Part D of this Chapter.

36 Refit the piston/connecting rod assemblies to the crankshaft as described in Section 19.

37 Refit the Woodruff key, then slide on the oil pump drive sprocket and spacer (where fitted), and locate the drive chain on the sprocket.

38 Ensure that the mating surfaces of the right-hand oil seal carrier and cylinder block are clean and dry. Note the correct fitted depth of the oil seal then, lever or drive out the old seal from the housing. If preferred, a new

oil seal can be pressed into the housing at this stage **(see illustrations)**.

39 Apply a smear of suitable silicone sealant (Ford part No WSE-M4G323-A4) to the oil seal carrier mating surface. Ensure that the locating dowels are in position, then slide the carrier over the end of the crankshaft and into position on the cylinder block **(see illustrations)**. Tighten the carrier retaining bolts to the specified torque.

40 If not already done, fit a new crankshaft right-hand oil seal as described in Part C or Part D of this Chapter.

41 Ensuring that the drive chain is correctly located on the sprocket, refit the oil pump and sump as described in Part C or Part D of this Chapter.

42 Where removed, refit the cylinder head as described in Part C or D of this Chapter.

18.33 Use 2 metal strips (arrowed) to hold the sealing strips in place as the bearing cap is fitted

18.34 Trim off the ends of the bearing cap sealing strips, so that they protrude by approximately 1.0 mm

18.38a Drive out the old oil seal ...

18.38b ... then press in the new one to the previously-noted depth

18.39a Apply the sealant ...

18.39b ... and refit the oil seal housing

19 Pistons/connecting rods – refitting

Note: *New big-end cap nuts/bolts must be used on refitting.*

1 Note that the following procedure assumes that the crankshaft and main bearing ladder/caps are in place.

2 Clean the backs of the bearing shells, and the bearing locations in both the connecting rod and bearing cap.

All engines except 1.6 litre

3 Press the bearing shells into their locations, ensuring that the tab on each shell engages in the notch in the connecting rod and cap. Take care not to touch any shell's bearing surface with your fingers **(see illustration)**.

All engines

4 Lubricate the cylinder bores, the pistons, and piston rings, then lay out each piston/connecting rod assembly in its respective position.

5 Start with assembly No 1. Make sure that the piston rings are still spaced as described in Section 17, then clamp them in position with a piston ring compressor.

6 Insert the piston/connecting rod assembly into the top of cylinder/liner No 1, ensuring the piston is correctly positioned as follows.

a) On 1.6 and 1.8 litre engines, ensure that the DIST mark or arrow on the piston crown is towards the timing belt end of the engine.

b) On 2.0 and 2.2 litre diesel engines, ensure that the valve recesses on the piston crown are towards the rear of the cylinder block.

7 Once the piston is correctly positioned, using a block of wood or hammer handle against the piston crown, tap the assembly into the cylinder/liner until the piston crown is flush with the top of the cylinder/liner **(see illustration)**.

All engines except 1.6 litre

8 Ensure that the bearing shell is still correctly installed. Liberally lubricate the crankpin and both bearing shells. Taking care not to mark the cylinder/liner bores, pull the piston/connecting rod assembly down the bore and onto the crankpin. Refit the big-end bearing

19.8 Fit the big-end bearing cap, ensuring it is fitted the right-way around, and fit the new nuts

19.3 Ensure the bearing shell tab locates correctly in the cut-out

cap and fit the new nuts, tightening them finger-tight at first **(see illustration)**. Note that the faces with the identification marks must match (which means that the bearing shell locating tabs abut each other).

9 Tighten the bearing cap retaining nuts evenly and progressively to the specified torque setting.

1.6 litre engines

10 On these engines, then connecting rod is made in one piece, then the big-end bearing cap is 'cracked' off. This ensures that the cap fits onto the connecting rod only in one position, and with maximum rigidity. Consequently, there are no locating notches for the bearing shells to fit into.

11 To ensure that the big-end bearing shells are centrally located in the connecting rod and cap, two special tools are available from Ford (part No 303-736). These half-moon shaped tools are pressed in from either side of the rod/cap and locate the shell exactly in the centre **(see illustration)**. Fit the shells into the connecting rods and big-end caps and lubricate them with plenty of clean engine oil.

12 Pull the connecting rods and pistons down the bores and onto the crankshaft journals. Fit the big-end caps – they will only fit properly one way round (see paragraph 10), and insert the new bolts.

13 Tighten the bolts to the specified torque settings.

19.11 Big-end bearing shell positioning – 1.6 litre engine

1 Ford tool No 303-736
2 Bearing shell in the cap

19.7 Tap the piston into the bore using a hammer handle

All engines

14 Once the bearing cap retaining nuts have been correctly tightened, rotate the crankshaft. Check that it turns freely; some stiffness is to be expected if new components have been fitted, but there should be no signs of binding or tight spots.

15 Refit the cylinder head and oil pump as described in Part A, B, C or D of this Chapter (as applicable).

20 Engine – initial start-up after overhaul

1 With the engine refitted in the vehicle, double-check the engine oil and coolant levels. Make a final check that everything has been reconnected, and that there are no tools or rags left in the engine compartment.

2 Prime the fuel system (refer to Chapter 4A Section 7). Although the system is self-priming, it will help if the ignition is switched on and off several times before attempting to start the engine in order to purge air from the system.

3 Turn the engine on the starter until the oil pressure warning light goes out.

4 Fully depress the accelerator pedal, turn the ignition key to position M, and wait for the preheating warning light to go out.

5 Start the engine, noting that this may take a little longer than usual, due to the fuel system components having been disturbed.

6 While the engine is idling, check for fuel, water and oil leaks. Don't be alarmed if there are some odd smells and smoke from parts getting hot and burning off oil deposits.

7 Assuming all is well, keep the engine idling until hot water is felt circulating through the top hose, then switch off the engine.

8 After a few minutes, recheck the oil and coolant levels as described in *Weekly checks.*, and top-up as necessary.

9 Note that there is no need to retighten the cylinder head bolts once the engine has first run after reassembly.

10 If new pistons, rings or crankshaft bearings have been fitted, the engine must be treated as new, and run-in for the first 500 miles. Do not operate the engine at full-throttle, or allow it to labour at low engine speeds in any gear. It is recommended that the oil and filter be changed at the end of this period.

Chapter 3
Cooling, heating and air conditioning systems

Contents

Degrees of difficulty

Easy, suitable for novice with little experience	**Fairly easy,** suitable for beginner with some experience	**Fairly difficult,** suitable for competent DIY mechanic	**Difficult,** suitable for experienced DIY mechanic	**Very difficult,** suitable for expert DIY or professional

Specifications

System pressure
Pressure test . . . . 1.3 to 1.5 bars approximately – see cap for actual value

Expansion tank filler cap
Pressure rating . . . . 1.3 to 1.5 bars approximately – see cap for actual value

Thermostat
1.6 litre engine . . . . 88°C
1.8 litre and 2.0 litre:
   Starts to open. . . . . 92°C
   Fully open. . . . . 99°C
2.2 litre engine
   Starts to open. . . . . 88°C
   Fully open. . . . . 102°C

Air conditioning system
Refrigerant R134a
Refrigerant quantity:
   Front AC models. 600
   Front and rear AC models 850
Refrigerant oil. . . . . Ford WSH-M17B19-A
Refrigerant oil capacity:
   When refilling . . . . 200 ml
   When renewing the condenser. . . . . 30 ml
   When renewing the evaporator . . . . 30 ml
   When renewing the accumulator/dehydrator. . . . . 90 ml
   When renewing the compressor:
      If the oil drained from the faulty compressor is less than 150 ml. . 150 ml
      If the oil drained from the faulty compressor is more than 150 ml . 200 ml
   When renewing the refrigerant pipes . . . . 200 ml

Torque wrench settings

	Nm	lbf ft
Air conditioning compressor mounting bolts	25	18
Air conditioning high pressure cut-off switch	8	6
Coolant by-pass pipe retaining bolts:		
1.8 litre engine	48	35
2.0 litre engine	18	13
Coolant pump bolts:		
1.6 litre engine	25	18
1.8 litre engine:		
Lower front bolt	23	17
Upper bolts	10	7
2.0 litre engine	16	12
2,2 litre engine		
Stage 1	5	4
Stage 2	16	12
Coolant pump pulley bolts 1.8 litre engines only	23	17
Cylinder head temperature sensor (1.8 litre engine only)	20	15
Radiator mounting panel	25	18
Refrigerant line connection	8	6
Refrigerant line to compressor	24	18
Thermostat housing bolts/nuts:		
1.6 litre engine	7	5
1.8 litre engine	9	7
2.0 litre engine	10	7
2.2 litre engine	8	6

1 General Information

Warning: DO NOT attempt to remove the expansion tank filler cap, or to disturb any part of the cooling system, while it or the engine is hot, as there is a very great risk of scalding. If the expansion tank filler cap must be removed before the engine and radiator have fully cooled down (even though this is not recommended) the pressure in the cooling system must first be released. Cover the cap with a thick layer of cloth, to avoid scalding, and slowly unscrew the filler cap until a hissing sound can be heard. When the hissing has stopped, showing that pressure is released, slowly unscrew the filler cap further until it can be removed; if more hissing sounds are heard, wait until they have stopped before unscrewing the cap completely. At all times, keep well away from the filler opening.

Warning: Do not allow coolant to come in contact with your skin, or with the painted surfaces of the vehicle. Rinse off spills immediately with plenty of water. Never leave coolant lying around in an open container, or in a puddle in the driveway or on the garage floor. Children and pets are attracted by its sweet smell, but coolant is fatal if ingested.

Warning: If the engine is hot, the electric cooling fan may start rotating even if the engine is not running, so be careful to keep hands, hair and loose clothing well clear when working in the engine compartment.

1 The cooling system is of pressurised semi-sealed type with the inclusion of an expansion tank to accept coolant displaced from the system when hot and to return it when the system cools.

2 Water-based coolant is circulated around the cylinder block and head by the coolant pump which is driven by the engine timing belt. As the coolant circulates around the engine it absorbs heat as it flows then, when hot, it travels out into the radiator to pass across the matrix. As the coolant flows across the radiator matrix, air flow created by the forward motion of the vehicle cools it, and it returns to the cylinder block. Airflow through the radiator matrix is assisted by a two-speed electric fan, which is controlled by the engine management system ECM.

3 A thermostat is fitted to control coolant flow through the radiator. When the engine is cold, the thermostat valve remains closed so that the coolant flow which occurs at normal operating temperatures through the radiator matrix is interrupted.

4 As the coolant warms up, the thermostat valve starts to open and allows the coolant flow through the radiator to resume.

5 The engine temperature will always be maintained at a constant level (according to the thermostat rating) whatever the ambient air temperature.

6 Most models have an oil cooler mounted on the sump/cylinder block – this is basically a heat exchanger with a coolant supply, to take heat away from the oil in the sump.

7 The vehicle interior heater operates by means of coolant from the engine cooling system. Coolant flow through the heater matrix is constant; temperature control being achieved by blending cool air from outside the vehicle with the warm air from the heater matrix, in the desired ratio.

8 Air entering the passenger compartment is filtered by a pleated paper filter element, sometimes known as a pollen filter. Also available instead of a pollen filer is a multifilter, which is a carbon impregnated filter which absorbs incoming smells, etc. With this system a pollution sensor monitors the quality of the incoming air, and opens and closes the recirculation flaps accordingly.

9 The standard climate control (air conditioning) systems are described in detail in Section 11.

10 Available as options are additional electric and fuel-fired cabin and engine block heaters. These can be remotely operated, or programmed to operate for a suitable period before the vehicle is required.

2 Engine coolant (antifreeze) – general information

Warning: Engine coolant (anti-freeze) contains monoethylene glycol and other constituents, which are toxic if taken internally. They can also be absorbed into the skin after prolonged contact.

Note: *Refer to Chapter 1 Section 25 for further information on coolant renewal.*

1 The cooling system should be filled with a water/monoethylene glycol-based coolant solution, of a strength which will prevent freezing down to at least –25°C, or lower if the local climate requires it. Coolant also provides protection against corrosion, and increases the boiling point.

2 The cooling system should be maintained according to the schedule described in Chapter 1 Section 25. If the engine coolant used is old or contaminated it is likely to cause damage, and encourage the formation of corrosion and scale in the system. Use coolant which is to Ford's specification and to the correct concentration.

3 Before adding the coolant, check all hoses and hose connections, because coolant tends to leak through very small openings. Engines don't normally consume coolant, so if the level goes down, find the cause and correct it.

4 The engine coolant concentration should be between 40% and 55%. If the concentration drops below 40% there will be insufficient protection, this must then be brought back to specification. Hydrometers are available at most automotive accessory shops to test the coolant concentration.

3 Cooling system hoses – disconnection and renewal

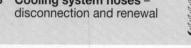

Note: *Refer to the warnings given in Section 1 of this Chapter before starting work.*

1 If the checks described in Chapter 1 reveal a faulty hose, it must be renewed as follows.

2 First drain the cooling system (see Chapter 1 Section 25); if the coolant is not due for renewal, the drained coolant may be re-used, if it is collected in a clean container.

3 To disconnect any hose, use a pair of pliers, or special release type tools to release the spring clamps **(see illustrations)**. A screwdriver (or flexible driver to fit the hex head of the clamp) will be required to slacken screw-type clamps. Slacken or release the hose clamp and then move the clamp along the hose clear of the union. Carefully work the hose off its stubs. The hoses can be removed with relative ease when new – on an older car, they may have stuck.

4 If a hose proves stubborn, try to release it by rotating it on its unions before attempting to work it off. Gently prise the end of the hose with a blunt instrument (such as a flat-bladed screwdriver), but do not apply too much force, and take care not to damage the pipe stubs or hoses. Note in particular that the radiator hose

3.3a A comprehensive range of hose clamp and fuel line tools are included in this set

unions are fragile; do not use excessive force when attempting to remove the hoses. If all else fails, cut the hose with a sharp knife, then slit it so that it can be peeled off in two pieces. While expensive, this is preferable to buying a new radiator. Check first, however, that a new hose is readily available.

5 When refitting a hose, first slide the clamps onto the hose, then work the hose onto its unions. If the hose is stiff, use soap (or washing-up liquid) as a lubricant, or soften it by soaking it in boiling water, but take care to prevent scalding.

6 Work each hose end fully onto its union, then check that the hose is settled correctly and is properly routed. Slide each clip along the hose until it is behind the union flared end, before tightening it securely.

7 Refill the system with coolant (see Chapter 1 Section 25).

8 Check carefully for leaks as soon as possible after disturbing any part of the cooling system.

4 Thermostat – removal, testing and refitting

Note: *Refer to the warnings given in Section 1 of this Chapter before starting work.*

Removal

1 Drain the cooling system (see Chapter 1 Section 25). If the coolant is relatively new

3.3b Releasing a hose clamp with specialist pliers

or in good condition, drain it into a clean container and re-use it.

1.6 litre engines

2 Remove the air cleaner assembly as described in Chapter 4A Section 3.

3 The thermostat housing is located at the left-hand end of the cylinder head. Release the clips and disconnect the coolant hoses from the thermostat housing **(see illustration)**.

4 Disconnect the wiring plug from the engine coolant temperature sensor.

5 Undo the coolant bypass pipe retaining bolt.

6 Undo the 4 retaining bolts and remove the thermostat housing **(see illustration)**. Note that the thermostat is integral with the housing. If the thermostat is faulty, the housing must be renewed.

1.8 litre engines

7 Remove the cover from the top of the engine.

8 The thermostat cover is located at the front of the engine cylinder block. Undo the 3 retaining bolts and move the cover to one side **(see illustration)**.

9 Note the position of the air bleed valve (where fitted), and how the thermostat is installed (ie, which end is facing outwards), then pull the thermostat and rubber seal from place. Discard the rubber seal if it is damaged.

2.0 litre engines

Note: *The thermostat is part of the thermostat housing. If the thermostat is faulty the complete housing must be replaced.*

4.3 Release the clips and disconnect the coolant hoses from the housing

4.6 Undo the bolts and detach the thermostat housing

4.8 Undo the thermostat cover bolts

4.10 Pull the plastic cover upwards to release it

4.12a Remove the solenoids

4.12b Undo the nuts and move the bracket to one side

4.15a Thermostat housing retaining nuts

4.15b Renew the thermostat housing sealing ring

4.18 Release the spring type hose clips

10   Remove the cover from the top of the engine **(see illustration)**. The thermostat housing is located at the left-hand end of the cylinder head.
11   Remove the complete air filter housing as described in Chapter 4A Section 3.
12   Disconnect the wiring plug and remove the control solenoids and then remove the protective bracket **(see illustrations)**.
13   Release the clamps and disconnect the hoses from the thermostat housing.
14   Disconnect the wiring plug(s) from the thermostat housing.

15   Undo the 4 retaining nuts and remove the housing **(see illustrations)**. Examine the rubber seal and renew if necessary.

2.2 litre engines

Note: *The thermostat is part of the thermostat housing. If the thermostat is faulty the complete housing must be replaced.*

16   Drain the cooling system as described in Chapter 1 Section 25.
17   Remove the air filter housing as described in Chapter 4A Section 3.
18   Release the spring clips and remove the radiator flow and return hoses **(see illustration)**.
19   Depress the locking tabs and release the de-gas hose **(see illustration)**.
20   Lever up the spring clip and pull free the front hose **(see illustrations)**.
21   At the rear of the housing unbolt and remove the crescent shaped washer **(see illustration)** (this holds the rear coolant hose

4.19 Release the degas/vent hose

4.20a Prise up the spring clip and …

4.20b …remove the hose

4.21a Remove the crescent shaped retaining washer

4.21b Disconnect the coolant temperature sensor

4.23 Remove the thermostat housing

in place) and then disconnect the coolant temperature sensor.

22 Remove the mounting bolts, slacken the nuts on the studs and then using a Torx socket remove the studs.

23 Remove the thermostat housing by pulling it forward and off the rear hose seal **(see illustration)**.

Testing

General

24 Before assuming the thermostat is to blame for a cooling system problem, check the coolant level (see *Weekly checks.*), the auxiliary drivebelt tension and condition (see Chapter 1 Section 22) and the temperature gauge operation.

25 If the engine seems to be taking a long time to warm up (based on heater output or temperature gauge operation), the thermostat may be stuck open.

26 If the engine runs hot, use your hand to check the temperature of the radiator top hose. If the hose isn't hot, but the engine is, the thermostat is probably stuck closed, preventing the coolant inside the engine from escaping to the radiator.

27 If the radiator top hose is hot, it means that the coolant is flowing and the thermostat is open. Consult the Fault Finding Section at the end of this manual to assist in tracing possible cooling system faults.

Thermostat test

Note: *The following only applies to the 1.8 litre engine with a traditional thermostat.*

Note: *Frankly, if there is any question about the operation of the thermostat, it's best to renew it – they are not usually expensive items. Testing involves heating in, or over, an open pan of boiling water, which carries with it the risk of scalding. A thermostat which has seen more than five years' service may well be past its best already.*

28 If the thermostat remains in the open position at room temperature, it is faulty, and must be renewed as a matter of course.

29 To test it fully, suspend the (closed) thermostat on a length of string in a container of cold water, with a thermometer beside it; ensure that neither touches the side of the container.

30 Heat the water, and check the temperature at which the thermostat begins to open; compare this value with that specified. Checking the fully-open temperature may not be possible in an open container, if it is higher than the boiling point of water at atmospheric pressure. Remove the thermostat and allow it to cool down; check that it closes fully.

31 If the thermostat does not open and close as described, if it sticks in either position, or if it does not open at the specified temperature, it must be renewed.

Refitting

32 Refitting is the reverse of the removal procedure, noting the following points:

a) *Clean the mating surfaces carefully, and renew the thermostat's sealing ring/gasket.*

b) *Fit the thermostat in the same position as noted on removal.*

c) *Tighten the thermostat cover/housing bolts/nuts to the specified torque wrench setting.*

d) *Remake all the coolant hose connections, then refill the cooling system as described in Chapter 1 Section 25.*

e) *Start the engine and allow it to reach normal operating temperature, then check for leaks and proper thermostat operation.*

---

5 Radiator cooling fan – testing, removal and refitting

Note: *Refer to the warnings given in Section 1 of this Chapter before starting work.*

5.6a Remove the locating pegs ...

5.7a Remove the panel and ...

Testing

1 The radiator cooling fan is controlled by the engine management system's ECM, acting on the information received from the cylinder head temperature sensor and engine coolant temperature sensor.

2 First, check the relevant fuses and relays (see Chapter 12 Section 3).

3 To test the fan motor, unplug the electrical connector, and use fused jumper wires to connect the fan directly to the battery. If the fan still does not work, renew the motor.

4 If the motor proved sound, the fault lies in the engine coolant temperature sensor/cylinder head temperature sensor (see Section 4), in the wiring loom (see Chapter 12 Section 2 for testing details) or in the engine management system (see Chapter 4A Section 12).

Removal

Note: *The cooling fan is removed in a similar manner on all engines, but with minor differences in the layout of the coolant hoses and wiring loom.*

5 Disconnect the battery negative (earth) lead (see Chapter 5 Section 3).

6 Remove the radiator assembly locating pegs and then secure the radiator to the slam panel with strong cable ties – the radiator, fan and condenser will be held in place by the cable ties. **(see illustrations)**.

7 Remove the bonnet slam panel cover and then unclip the degas hose (where fitted) from the top of the fan shroud **(see illustrations)**.

8 Jack up the front of the vehicle (see *Jacking and vehicle support*) and then remove the

5.6b ... and secure the radiator with cable ties or similar

5.7b ... unclip the coolant (degas) hose

5.9 Remove the support panel bolts (at both sides)

5.10 Disconnect the wiring plug

5.11a The fan shroud retaining clips

engine undershield. Unbolt and then remove the air deflector from the base of the bumper cover.

9 Remove the bolts and lower the radiator support panel from the vehicle **(see illustration)**.

10 Disconnect the wiring plug **(see illustration)** and unclip the coolant hoses from the cooling fan shroud.

11 At each side of the fan shroud release the retaining clips whilst pushing up the fan from below. Unhook the fan and shroud and lower it from the vehicle **(see illustrations)**.

12 If required the fan can now be removed from the shroud. Note, however that the fan and shroud are supplied only as a single assembly.

Refitting

13 Refitting is the reverse of the removal procedure.

6   Coolant system electronic components – removal and refitting

Cylinder head temperature sensor

Note: *Only the 1.8 litre engine is fitted with this sensor.*

1 Remove the cover from the top of the engine.

2 Disconnect the hoses, then undo the retaining bolt and remove the crankcase vent

5.11b The fan and shroud removed from the vehicle

oil separator from the end of the cylinder head **(see illustration)**.

3 Undo the 2 retaining bolts and remove the crash shield above the fuel filter **(see illustration)**.

4 Disconnect the fuel filter wiring plug, then release the clips securing the fuel hoses and move the fuel filter to one side.

5 Disconnect the wiring plug, unclip the plug from the bracket, then unscrew the cylinder head temperature sensor from place **(see illustration)**.

6 Refitting is a reversal of removal. Tighten the sensor to the specified torque.

Coolant temperature sensor

Note: *Refer to the warnings given in Section 1 of this Chapter before starting work.*

7 Drain the cooling system (see Chapter 1 Section 25). If the coolant is relatively new

6.2 Unbolt and remove the crankcase vent

or in good condition, drain it into a clean container and re-use it. There is no need to completely drain the system, just drain the coolant to below the level of the sensor.

1.6 litre engines

8 Remove the air cleaner assembly as described in Chapter 4A Section 3.

9 The sensor is fitted to the thermostat housing at the left-hand end of the cylinder head. Disconnect the sensor wiring plug, pull out the retaining clip, and remove the sensor **(see illustration)**. Renew the sensor seal if necessary.

10 Refitting is a reversal of removal.

2.0 and 2.2 litre engines

11 Remove the air cleaner assembly as described in Chapter 4A Section 3.

12 Disconnect the sensor wiring plug, pull out the retaining clip, and remove the

6.3 Undo the 2 bolts and remove the crash shield

6.5 Disconnect the wiring plug and remove the sensor

6.9 Slide out the clip and remove the coolant temperature sensor – 1.6 litre engines

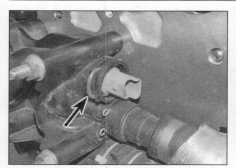

6.12a Slide out the clip and remove the coolant temperature sensor on the 2.0 litre engine ...

6.12b ... and on the 2.2 litre engine

6.12c Remove the seal and check it's condition

engine coolant temperature sensor **(see illustrations)**. Renew the sensor seal if necessary.

13 Refitting is a reversal of removal.

Coolant shut-off valve

Note: *This valve is only fitted to 2.0 litre engines*

14 The coolant shut-off valve is controlled by the engine management ECM, and limits coolant flow to the coolant expansion tank during the engine warm-up phase. It's located in the feed pipe from the thermostat housing to the tank.

15 To remove the valve, begin by draining the cooling system as described in Chapter 1 Section 25, or be prepared for coolant spillage as the hoses are disconnected.

16 Disconnect the valve wiring plug, then release the clips and disconnect the hoses from the valve.

17 Undo the retaining bolts and remove the valve.

18 Refitting is the reversal of removal.

Coolant by-pass valve

Note: *This valve is only fitted to 2.0 litre engines*

19 The coolant by-pass valve is controlled by the engine management ECM, and limits coolant flow to the coolant pump during the engine warm-up phase. It's located on the top of the thermostat housing.

20 To remove the valve, begin by draining the cooling system as described in Chapter 1 Section 25.

21 Remove the brake vacuum pump as described in Chapter 9 Section 20.

22 Disconnect the wiring plug, then undo the 2 retaining bolts and remove the by-pass valve. Renew the valve O-ring seals if necessary.

23 Refitting is a reversal of removal.

7 Radiator and expansion tank – removal, inspection and refitting

Note: *Refer to the warnings given in Section 1 of this Chapter before starting work.*

Radiator

Note: *If leakage is the reason for removing the radiator, bear in mind that minor leaks can often be cured using a radiator sealant added to the coolant with the radiator in situ.*

Removal

1 Drain the coolant system as described in Chapter 1 Section 25.

2 Remove the radiator assembly locating pegs and then secure the condenser to the slam panel with strong cable ties. Seperately secure the radiator to the slam panel **(see illustrations)**.

3 Remove the bonnet slam panel cover and then unclip the degas hose (where fitted) from the top of the fan shroud **(see illustrations)**.

4 To provide greater clearance for the radiator to be lowered and removed, ensure that the handbrake is firmly applied, then raise and support the front of the car on axle stands (see *Jacking and vehicle support*). Remove the engine undershield and the air deflector.

5 Unbolt and remove the radiator support panel **(see illustration)** and then remove the intercooler as described in Chapter 4A Section 16.

7.2a Remove the locating pegs and ...

7.2b ... and secure with cable ties

7.3a Remove the panel and ...

7.3b ... release the coolant hose

7.5 Remove the bolts (one side shown)

7.6a The radiator lower hose...

7.6b ...and the upper hose

7.6c Release the clip

6 Slacken the clamps and disconnect the radiator upper and lower coolant hoses. Unclip the hoses from the cooling fan shroud **(see illustrations)**.

7 Remove the radiator cooling fan as described in Section 5.

8 Release the degas hose from the top right-hand corner of the radiator **(see illustration)**.

9 Support the radiator and cut the cable ties (an assistant is useful at this point) and carefully lower the radiator from place. Take care not to damage the condenser or radiator cooling fins.

Inspection

10 With the radiator removed, it can be inspected for leaks and damage. If it needs repair, have a radiator specialist or dealer service department perform the work, as special techniques are required.

11 Insects and dirt can be removed from the radiator with a garden hose or a soft brush. Take care not to damage the cooling fins as this is being done.

Refitting

12 Refitting is the reverse of the removal procedure, noting the following points:

a) *Be sure the mounting rubbers are seated properly at the base of the radiator.*

b) *After refitting, refill the cooling system with the recommended coolant (see Chapter 1 Section 25).*

c) *Start the engine, and check for leaks. Allow the engine to reach normal operating temperature, indicated by the radiator top hose becoming hot. Once*

the engine has cooled (ideally, leave overnight), recheck the coolant level, and add more if required.

Expansion tank

13 With the engine completely cool, remove the expansion tank filler cap to release any pressure, then refit the cap.

14 Disconnect the degas hoses from the tank **(see illustration)**.

15 Remove the bolt and pull the tank upwards from the mountings on the inner wing. Clamp the main hose **(see illustration)**.

16 Using a cable type spring clamp removal tool, release the spring clamp and remove the hose **(see illustration)**. Anticipate some coolant spillage.

17 Wash out the tank, and inspect it for cracks and chafing – renew it if damaged.

18 Refitting is the reverse of the removal procedure. Refill the cooling system with the recommended coolant (see Chapter 1 Section 25), then start the engine and allow it to reach normal operating temperature, indicated by the radiator top hose becoming hot. Recheck the coolant level and add more if required, then check for leaks.

7.8 Remove the hose

7.14 Remove the degas hoses

7.15 Clamp the main hose

7.16 Remove the main hose

| 8 | Coolant pump – checking, removal and refitting | |

Note: *Refer to the warnings given in Section 1 of this Chapter before starting work.*

Checking

1 A failure in the coolant pump can cause serious engine damage due to overheating.

2 There are three ways to check the operation of the coolant pump while it's installed on the engine. If the pump is defective, fit a new unit.

3 With the engine running at normal operating temperature, squeeze the radiator top hose. If the coolant pump is working properly, a pressure surge should be felt as the hose is released.

 Warning: Keep your hands away from the radiator electric cooling fan blades.

4 Coolant pumps are equipped with weep or vent holes. If a failure occurs in the pump seal,

8.10a Undo the bolts and remove the coolant pump

8.10b Renew the coolant pump gasket

8.16 Remove the coolant pump from the cylinder block

coolant will leak from the hole. In most cases you'll need an electric torch to find the hole on the coolant pump from underneath to check for leaks.

5 If the coolant pump shaft bearings fail, there may be a howling sound at the drivebelt end of the engine while it's running. Shaft wear can be felt if the coolant pump pulley is rocked up and down (only possible on the 1.8 litre engine).

6 Don't mistake drivebelt slippage, which causes a squealing sound, for coolant pump bearing failure. Note only the 1.8 litre engine has a drivebelt driven coolant pump.

7 On engines that have a timing belt driven coolant pump and it is suspected that the pump is worn or leaking do not drive the vehicle. Remove the timing belt cover and inspect the belt – uneven wear may indicate a worn coolant pump bearing (or other bearing failure). If the timing belt is due for replacement careful consideration should be given to replacing the coolant pump at the same time, regardless of its apparent condition.

Removal

8 Drain the cooling system (see Chapter 1 Section 25).

1.6 litre engines

9 Remove the timing belt as described in Chapter 2A Section 7.
10 Undo the bolts and remove the coolant pump **(see illustrations)**.

1.8 litre engines

11 Disconnect the battery negative lead with reference to Chapter 5 Section 3.
12 Slacken the coolant pump pulley bolts, then remove the auxiliary drivebelt as described in Chapter 1 Section 22.
13 Unbolt the coolant pump pulley and remove it.
14 Remove the timing belt cover and engine mounting as described in Chapter 2B Section 7. The engine must be supported as the engine front mounting is disconnected; support the engine from above with a hoist or engine support bar, if available. If the engine is supported from below with a trolley jack, use a wide block of wood between the jack head and the sump, to spread the load.
15 Remove the four bolts securing the engine front mounting bracket to the block, then lift the engine up by approximately 20 mm.
16 Unscrew the seven coolant pump securing bolts and withdraw the pump **(see illustration)**. Recover the gasket. **Note:** *Take care not to damage or contaminate the timing belt as the pump is removed. Place some stiff cardboard around the belt in the pump area.*

2.0 and 2.2 litre engines

17 Remove the timing belt as described in Chapter 2C Section 5 or Chapter 2D Section 6.
18 Undo the retaining bolts and remove the coolant pump **(see illustrations)**. Recover the gasket.

Refitting

All models

19 Clean the pump mating surfaces carefully. The gasket/O-ring must be renewed whenever it is disturbed. Refit the pump and tighten the bolts evenly in a diagonal pattern, to the specified torque wrench setting.
20 The remainder of the refitting procedure is the reverse of dismantling, noting the following points:
a) *Tighten all fixings to the specified torque wrench settings (where given).*
b) *Where applicable always replace the timing belt.*
c) *On completion, refill the cooling system as described in Chapter 1 Section 25.*

9	**Heater/ventilation components** – removal and refitting

Heater blower motor

Note: *In theory it is possible to remove the blower motor with the facia in place. We found this impossible and removed the facia and crossmember as described in Chapter 11 Section 28.*

1 Disconnect the battery negative lead as described in Chapter 5 Section 3 and then remove the facia and crossmember as described in Chapter 11 Section 28.

8.18a Coolant pump retaining bolts (2.0 litre engine)

8.18b Coolant pump retaining bolts (2.2 litre engine)

8.18c Renew the coolant pump gasket

9.2a Disconnect the wiring plug

9.2b Remove the retaining screws…

9.2c …and remove the housing

9.3a Disconnect the wiring plug and release the wiring loom clip

9.3b Depress the clip and rotate the housing

9.3c Pass the motor through the housing and remove it

2 Disconnect the wiring plug from the recirculation control motor, then undo the 3 bolts and remove the air recirculation flap housing **(see illustrations)**.

3 Disconnect the blower motor wiring plug, then depress the release clip, and rotate the blower motor clockwise (RHD) or anti-clockwise (LHD) and pull the motor from the housing **(see illustrations)**. Take great care not to damage the motor fan – it's extremely delicate. Do not pull on the fan, or allow the motor to rest on the fan.

4 Refitting is the reverse of the removal procedure.

Blower motor resistor

5 Remove the glovebox as described in Chapter 11 Section 27.

6 To avoid damaging the GEM, unclip and then lower it **(see illustration)**.

7 Reach up (and behind) the intake air housing and disconnect the wiring plugs, undo the screw and pull the resistor from the housing **(see illustrations)**.

8 Refitting is a reversal of removal.

Heater matrix removal

Note: *Removal of the heater matrix requires removal of the facia and most of the crossmember components. On first inspection it seem as if the matrix cover can be removed and the matrix pulled out of the heater housing. Unfortunately the matrix cover extends up and over the front section of the housing.*

9 Disconnect the battery negative (earth) lead (see Chapter 5 Section 3).

10 Remove the engine cover and then remove the upper and lower windscreen cowl panels as described in Chapter 12 Section 12.

11 Clamp off the heater hoses at the bulkhead and disconnect the heater hoses. Early models have quick release clamps and later models have spring type hose clamps. In both case access in very limited. Access can be improved if the battery, air filter housing and the inlet ducting are removed. With these components removed access from the side is now possible – but still not easy.

12 Remove the facia and crossmember as described in Chapter 11 Section 28.

Note: *There will be coolant in the matrix, so seal the flow and return pipes as soon as*

9.6 Lower the GEM (Generic Electronic Module)

9.7a The location of the heater blower motor resistor pack

9.7b Shown here with the heater/air distribution housing removed from the vehicle

9.13a Remove the matrix cover screws

9.13b Remove the lower cover rear screws…

9.13c …the front screws and then…

9.13d …lift off the panel

the crossmember is pulled away from the bulkhead.

13 On the bench invert the heater housing – we supported the housing upside down with the crossmember on axle stands. Disconnect the wiring plugs and then remove the screws from the lower housing **(see illustrations)**.

14 Remove the support housing and then peel off the rubber seal **(see illustrations)**.

Heater matrix refitting

15 Refill the cooling system with the recommended coolant (see Chapter 1 Section 25). Start the engine and allow it to reach normal operating temperature, indicated by the radiator top hose becoming hot. Recheck the coolant level and add more if required, then check for leaks. Check the operation of the heater.

Pollen filter

16 Refer to Chapter 1 Section 17.

9.14a Remove the support bracket…

9.14b …and remove the seal

9.14c Finally remove the matrix from the housing

10.2a Prise up the panel and ...

10.2b ...disconnect the wiring plugs

10.5a Remove the screws ...

10.5b ...lift out the panel ...

10.5c ...and disconnect the wiring plugs

10.5d Remove the screws

10 Heater/air conditioning controls – removal and refitting

Heater control panel

Note: *On vehicles fitted with a navigation system (Satnav) the heater/AC controls are built into the audio/satnav unit. Removal is described in Chapter 12 Section 17.*

1 Disconnect the battery negative (earth) lead (see Chapter 5 Section 3).

2 Working from the outer edge (and using a plastic trim tool) prise up the facia embellisher panel/switch panel. Disconnect the wiring plugs and remove the panel **(see illustrations)**.

3 On some models (depending on the year and type of audio unit fitted) remove the facia-mounted audio unit as described in Chapter 12 Section 17.

4 Prise up and remove the gear shift/handbrake trim panel as described in Chapter 11 Section 25.

5 Remove the screws and remove the audio trim panel. Where the control panel is part of the trim panel disconnect the wiring plugs and remove the panel. Unscrew the controls from the panel **(see illustrations)**.

6 On models where the control panel is mounted on the support panel, remove the screws, pull the switch panel forward and disconnect the wiring plugs.

7 Refitting is a reversal of removal.

11 Air conditioning system – general information and precautions

General information

1 The Air Conditioning (AC) system consists of a condenser mounted in front of the radiator, an evaporator mounted adjacent to the heater matrix, a compressor driven by an auxiliary drivebelt, an accumulator/dehydrator, and the plumbing connecting all of the above components – this contains a choke (or 'venturi') mounted in the inlet to the evaporator, which creates the drop in pressure required to produce the cooling effect.

2 Some models have dual zone AC fitted. On these models the the passenger and drivers side temperature can be controlled independently. Triple zone AC may be fitted as well. On triple zone AC models a secondary evaporator, blower motor and expansion valve are fitted in a compartment beneath the third row of seats.

3 A blower fan forces the warmer air of the passenger compartment through the evaporator core (rather like a radiator in reverse), transferring the heat from the air to the refrigerant. The liquid refrigerant boils off into low-pressure vapour, taking the heat with it when it leaves the evaporator.

4 The refrigerant circuit high and low pressure service ports are located in the engine compartment **(see illustrations)**. Access to the bulkhead low pressure connector is limited. On some models removal of the windscreen cowl panels will be required to access the service port.

11.4a Evacuating the refrigerant from the high pressure service port

11.4b The low pressure service port

Precautions

Warning: It is a criminal offence to knowingly discharge refrigerant to the atmosphere.

Caution: The air conditioning system is under high pressure. Do not loosen any fittings or remove any components until after the system has been discharged. Air conditioning refrigerant should be properly discharged at a dealer service department or an automotive air conditioning repair facility capable of handling R134a refrigerant. Always wear eye protection when disconnecting air conditioning system fittings.

5 Where an air conditioning system is fitted, it is necessary to observe the following special precautions whenever dealing with any part of the system, its associated components, and any items which necessitate disconnection of the system:

a) *While the refrigerant used is less damaging to the environment than the previously-used R12, it is still a very dangerous substance. It must not be allowed into contact with the skin or eyes, or there is a risk of frostbite. It must also not be discharged in an enclosed space – while it is not toxic, there is a risk of suffocation. The refrigerant is heavier than air, and so must never be discharged over a pit.*

b) *The refrigerant must not be allowed to come in contact with a naked flame, otherwise a poisonous gas will be created – under certain circumstances, this can form an explosive mixture with air. For similar reasons, smoking in the presence of refrigerant is highly dangerous, particularly if the vapour is inhaled through a lighted cigarette.*

c) *Never discharge the system to the atmosphere – R134a is not an ozone-depleting ChloroFluoroCarbon (CFC) like*
R12, but is instead a hydrofluorocarbon, which causes environmental damage by contributing to the 'greenhouse effect' if released into the atmosphere.

d) *R134a refrigerant must not be mixed with R12; the system uses different seals (now green-coloured, previously black) and has different fittings requiring different tools, so that there is no chance of the two types of refrigerant becoming mixed accidentally.*

e) *If for any reason the system must be discharged, entrust this task to your Ford dealer or an air conditioning specialist.*

f) *It is essential that the system be professionally discharged prior to using any form of heat – welding, soldering, brazing, etc – in the vicinity of the system, before having the vehicle oven-dried at a temperature exceeding 70°C after repainting, and before disconnecting any part of the system.*

12 Air conditioning system components – removal and refitting

Note: *The air conditioning system is under high pressure. Do not loosen any fittings or remove any components until after the system has been discharged. Air conditioning refrigerant should be properly discharged into an approved type of container at a dealer service department or an automotive air conditioning repair facility capable of handling R134a refrigerant. Cap or plug the pipe lines as soon as they are disconnected to prevent the entry of moisture. Always wear eye protection when disconnecting air conditioning system fittings.*

Note: *This Section refers to the components of the air conditioning system itself – refer to Sections 9 and 10 for details of components*
common to the heating/ventilation system.

Condenser

1 Have the refrigerant discharged at a dealer service department or an automotive air conditioning repair facility.

2 Disconnect the battery negative (earth) lead (see Chapter 5 Section 3) and remove both front headlights as described in Chapter 12 Section 9.

3 Remove the bonnet slam panel cover.

4 Working through the headlight aperture disconnect the condenser pipe work **(see illustrations)**. Recover the seals and plug the openings in the condenser and the pipework.

5 Apply the handbrake, then raise the front of the vehicle and support on axle stands.

6 Remove the engine undershield and then remove the air deflector from the rear of the front bumper cover.

7 Remove the intercooler as described in Chapter 4A Section 16.

8 Unclip the lower mountings, then lift the condenser upwards to disengage the condenser upper mountings, and lower it from under the vehicle **(see illustration)**. Store it upright, to prevent fluid loss. Take care not to damage the condenser fins.

12.4a Remove the bolt…

12.4b …and disconnect the pipework

12.8 Depress the clips (one shown) on each side and lift the condenser upwards

12.17a Remove the end cover and …

12.17b … lift out the evaporator

12.23 Compressor refrigerant lines clamp bolts

9 Refitting is the reverse of removal. Renew the O-rings and lubricate with refrigerant oil.

10 Have the system evacuated, charged and leak-tested by the specialist who discharged it.

Evaporator

11 The evaporator is mounted inside the heater housing with the heater matrix. In order to remove the evaporator, the complete heater housing must be removed.

12 Have the refrigerant discharged at a dealer service department or an automotive air conditioning repair facility.

13 Disconnect the battery negative (earth) lead (see Chapter 5 Section 3).

14 Drain the cooling system as described in Chapter 1 Section 25.

15 Remove the facia and crossmember as described in Chapter 11 Section 28.

16 Proceed as described in Section 9, and remove the heater matrix.

17 Remove the evaporator cover and lift out the evaporator **(see illustrations)**.

Compressor

18 Have the refrigerant discharged at a dealer service department or at a garage with an AC recovery machine.

19 Disconnect the battery negative (earth) lead (see Chapter 5 Section 3).

20 Apply the handbrake, then raise the front

of the vehicle and support on axle stands (see *Jacking and vehicle support*). Remove the right-hand front roadwheel.

21 Remove the right-hand front wheel arch liner, and engine undershield. Access can be improved if the right-hand headlight is also removed, although this is not strictly required.

22 Remove the auxiliary drivebelt as described in Chapter 1 Section 22.

23 Unscrew the clamping bolt to disconnect the refrigerant lines from the compressor. Plug the line connections to prevent entry of any dirt or moisture **(see illustration)**. Discard the O-ring seals, new ones must be fitted.

24 Unbolt the compressor from the cylinder block/crankcase, unplug its electrical connector, then withdraw the compressor from the vehicle **(see illustration)**. **Note:** *Keep the compressor level during handling and storage. If the compressor has seized, or if you find metal particles in the refrigerant lines, the system must be flushed out by an air conditioning technician, and the accumulator/ dehydrator must be renewed.*

25 Prior to installation, turn the compressor clutch centre six times, to disperse any oil that has collected in the head.

26 Refit the compressor in the reverse order of removal. Renew the seal, lubricating them with compressor oil before refitting.

27 If you are installing a new compressor, refer to the compressor manufacturer's instructions for adding refrigerant oil to the system.

28 Have the system evacuated, charged and leak-tested by the specialist that discharged it.

Receiver/drier

29 Have the refrigerant discharged at a dealer service department or an automotive air conditioning repair facility.

30 Apply the handbrake, then raise the front of the vehicle and support on axle stands (see *Jacking and vehicle support*).

31 Remove the bonnet slam panel cover.

32 Remove the engine undershield and the air deflector from beneath the front bumper cover.

33 Remove the intercooler as described in Chapter 4A Section 16.

34 Remove the plug from the base of the receiver/drier (a large torx type socket will be required) lift up the condenser so that it is clear of the locating points on the radiator, pull it slightly towards the rear of the vehicle and pull out the receiver drier **(see illustration)**. Manoeuvre it past the radiator support panel and out of the vehicle.

35 Refit the accumulator/dehydrator in the reverse order of removal. Coat the new seal in compressor oil before fitting the new receiver/ drier.

36 Have the system evacuated, charged and leak-tested by the specialist that discharged it.

Pressure switch

Caution: The refrigerant line has a schrader type valve fitted below the pressure switch. When the pressure switch is removed the valve seals and stops the release of the AC refrigerant. If the valve is faulty the refrigerant will escape, so always unscrew the switch slowly and if there is any hissing (a sure sign that the valve has not sealed) then tighten the switch back up and have the system evacuated with specialist equipment.

37 The switch is located close to the low-pressure service port.

38 Remove the wiper arms and windscreen cowl panels as described in Chapter 12 Section 12

12.24 The compressor mounting bolts (2.2 litre engine, other engines similar)

12.34 The receiver/drier

12.39 Disconnect the wiring plug and unscrew the switch

12.45a Open the cover ...

12.45b ... disconnect the wiring plug ...

12.45c ... and remove the speed controller

12.47 Remove the cover

39 Unplug the electrical connector and then unscrew the switch **(see illustration)**.
40 Refitting is the reverse of the removal procedure. Renew the O-ring and lubricate with refrigerant oil.

Auxiliary air conditioning

41 Available on Galaxy models with automatic temperature control the auxiliary AC provides cooling to passengers in the third row of seats. The system comprises a blower motor, fan speed control, an evaporator, temperature sensors and associated pipe work. All the components are fitted into a compartment below the third seat row.
42 The operation of the auxiliary AC is controlled from the facia AC control panel switch. A control module is mounted behind the right-hand load area side panel.
43 Before starting work on the refrigerant circuit have the refrigerant discharged at a

dealer service department or at a garage with an AC recovery machine.
44 Slide the rear seats forward and then open the load space cover.

Fan speed control

45 Disconnect the wiring plug, rotate the control anti-clockwise and remove the control unit **(see illustrations)**.

Evaporator

46 Disconnect the wiring plugs from the temperature sensors.
47 Remove the screws from the top cover **(see illustration)** and then unbolt the evaporator from the expansion valve.
48 Lift out the evaporator and remove it **(see illustration)**.

Blower motor

49 Remove the evaporator and speed controller as described above.
50 Lift out the complete housing, invert it and

remove the blower mounting screws. Remove the motor.

Temperature sensors

51 Two sensor are fitted. One monitors the evaporator temperature (to prevent icing) and one monitors the output temperature.
52 Disconnect the wiring plugs and remove the housing top cover.
53 Depress the locking tabs and remove the sensor **(see illustrations)**.

---

13 Electric booster heater –
general information, removal and refitting

General information

1 Because diesel engines give off low residual heat, an electric booster heating element is fitted into the heater housing. At

12.48 The evaporator and expansion valve

12.53a The output temperature sensor

12.53b The evaporator temperature sensor

13.3a Remove the lower panel ...

13.3b ...unscrew and...

13.3c ...remove the quarter panel

13.4 The electric heater wiring plugs

13.5a Remove the bolts (shown with the facia removed) ...

13.5b ...and remove the panel

engine coolant temperatures of less than 60°C and ambient temperatures of less then 10°C, when the high temperature setting is selected, the GEM (see Chapter 12 Section 23), provides power to the heating element. Power is cut to the element when the engine coolant temperature exceeds 70°C or the ambient temperature exceeds 20°C.

Removal

2 Disconnect the battery as described in Chapter 5 Section 3.
3 Remove the lower right-hand side trim panel and then remove the quarter panel (see illustrations).
4 Fold back the carpet and disconnect the wiring plugs (see illustration).
5 Unclip the footwell lamp and then undo the upper bolts (hidden behind the facia). Remove the lower bolts and remove the support bracket (see illustrations).
6 Release the wiring loom, disconnect the

sensor wiring plug and remove the fixing screws. Remove the heater (see illustrations).

Refitting

7 Refitting is a reversal of removal.

14 Fuel fired heater

General information

1 Some models feature a fuel fired heater instead of an electric auxiliary heater, mounted inside the right-hand front wing. An additional (electric) coolant pump is fitted to models with a fuel fired heater. The heater is supplied with fuel via a separate fuel line from the fuel tank. A fuel pump is mounted close to the fuel tank.
2 The heater will only operate when:
● The fuel tank must be a quarter full.

● The ambient temperature must be below 5 °C.
● The engine must be running above 500 rpm

Removal

3 Using hose clamps, clamp the flow and return coolant hoses at the bulkhead. If clamps are not available, drain the coolant as described in Chapter 1 Section 25.
4 Jack up and support the front of the vehicle (see Jacking and vehicle support).
5 Remove the right-hand wheel and wheel arch liner.
6 Disconnect the fuel supply line and seal it – anticipate some fuel spillage.
7 Disconnect the coolant hoses and then unplug the wiring connector.
8 Unbolt the heater and remove it from the vehicle.

Refitting

9 Refitting is a reversal of removal.

13.6a Disconnect the sensor wiring plug

13.6b Remove the screws and ...

13.6c ...and slide out the heater

Chapter 4 Part A
Fuel and exhaust systems

Contents

Degrees of difficulty

Easy, suitable for novice with little experience | **Fairly easy,** suitable for beginner with some experience | **Fairly difficult,** suitable for competent DIY mechanic | **Difficult,** suitable for experienced DIY mechanic | **Very difficult,** suitable for expert DIY or professional

Specifications

General

System type:

1.6 litre engines . . . . Siemens direct injection common rail, with timing belt driven high-pressure delivery pump, variable nozzle turbocharger, and intercooler

1.8 litre engines . . . . Siemens direct injection common rail with a chain- or belt-driven high-pressure delivery pump, variable nozzle turbocharger and intercooler

2.0 litre engines . . . . Siemens direct injection common rail with a camshaft-driven high-pressure delivery pump, variable nozzle turbocharger, and intercooler

2.2 litre engines . . . . Bosch direct injection common rail with a camshaft-driven high-pressure delivery pump, variable nozzle turbocharger, and intercooler

Torque wrench settings

	Nm	lbf ft
Catalytic converter to turbocharger:		
1.6 litre engine	15	11
1.8 litre engine	24	18
2.0 litre engine	24	18
2.2 litre engine	24	18
Catalytic converter to exhaust system		
1.6 litre engine	25	18
1.8 litre engine	48	35
2.0 litre engine	48	35
2.2 litre engine	48	35
Camshaft position sensor:		
1.6 litre engines	8	6
1.8 litre engines	10	7
2.2 litre engines	4	3
Common rail mounting bolts:		
1.6 litre engines	22	16
1.8 litre engines	24	18
2.0 litre engines	22	16
2.2 litre engines	18	13
Crankshaft position sensor:		
1.6 litre engines	10	7
1.8 litre engines	6	4
2.0 litre engines	10	7
2.2 litre engines	8	6

Torque wrench settings (continued)

	Nm	lbf ft
Exhaust manifold to cylinder head:		
1.6 litre engines	25	18
1.8 litre engines	20	15
2.0 litre engines	30	22
2.2 litre engines*		
Stage 1	12	9
Stage 2	20	15
Fuel high-pressure pipe union nuts: *		
To fuel rail:		
1.6 litre engines		
Stage 1	20	15
Stage 2	25	18
1.8 litre engines	38	28
2.0 litre engines		
Stage 1	18	13
Stage 2	27	20
2.2 litre engines		
Stage 1	22	16
Stage 2	25	18
To fuel pump:		
1.6 litre engines		
Stage 1	20	15
Stage 2	25	18
1.8 litre engines	38	28
2.0 litre engines		
Stage 1	18	13
Stage 2	27	20
2.2 litre engines:		
Stage 1	22	16
Stage 2	25	18
To fuel injectors:		
1.6 litre engines	25	18
1.8 litre engines	25	18
2.0 litre engines (Euro IV)		
Stage 1	19	14
Stage 2	30	22
2.0 litre engines (Euro V)		
Stage 1	18	13
Stage 2	27	20
2.2 litre engines		
Stage 1	22	16
Stage 2	25	18
Fuel injector clamp nuts/bolts: *		
1.6 litre engines:		
Stage 1	7	5
Stage 2	Angle-tighten a further 85°	
1.8 litre engines:		
Stage 1	5	4
Stage 2	Angle-tighten a further 90°	
2.0 litre engine (Euro IV):		
Stage 1	4	3
Stage 2	Angle-tighten a further 45°	
2.0 litre engines (Euro V):		
Stage 1	7	5
Stage 2	Angle-tighten a further 55°	
2.2 litre engines		
Stage 1	5	4
Stage 2	Angle-tighten a further 130°	
Fuel injection pump mounting bolts:		
1.6 litre engines	22	16
1.8 litre engines	20	15
2.0 litre engines	20	15
2.2 litre engines	22	16
Fuel injection pump sprocket (1.8 litre engines)	42	31
Fuel tank sender unit collar	85	63
Fuel tank straps	24	18
Throttle body bolts:		
1.6 litre engines	8	6
2.2 litre engines	10	7

Torque wrench settings (continued)

	Nm	lbf ft
Turbocharger oil supply banjo bolt:		
1.6 litre engines	30	22
1.8 litre engines	18	13
2.0 litre engines:		
To engine block	40	30
To turbocharger	28	21
2.2 litre engines	38	28
Turbocharger oil return pipe:		
2.2 litre engines	10	7
Turbocharger support bracket bolt:		
1.6 litre engines	25	18
1.8 litre engines	45	33
2.0 litre engines	15	11
Turbocharger to exhaust manifold:		
1.6 litre engines	25	18
1.8 litre engines	10	7
2.0 litre engines	25	18
2.2 litre engines	25	18
Turbocharger support bracket (to turbocharger):		
1.8 litre engines	25	18
2.0 litre engines	30	22
2.2 litre engines	25	18

Note: * Do not re-use

1 General information and precautions

General information

1 The operation of the fuel injection system is described in more detail in Section 6.

2 Fuel is drawn from a tank under the rear of the vehicle by a tank-immersed electric pump, and then forced through a filter to the injection pump.

3 The camshaft-driven injection pump is a tandem pump – a low pressure vane-type pump which supplies the high-pressure pump with fuel at a constant pressure, and a high-pressure piston-type pump which supplies fuel to the common fuel rail at variable pressure.

4 Fuel is supplied from the common fuel rail to the injectors. Also inside the injection pump assembly is a pressure control valve which regulates the pressure of fuel from the high-pressure pump, and a fuel volume control valve which regulates the fuel flow to the high-pressure side of the pump. The injectors are operated by solenoids controlled by the PCM, based on information supplied by various sensors. The engine PCM also controls the preheating side of the system – refer to Chapter 5 for more details.

5 The engine management system fitted, incorporates a 'drive-by-wire' system, where the traditional accelerator cable is replaced by an accelerator pedal position sensor. The position and rate-of-change of the accelerator pedal is reported by the position sensor to the PCM, which then adjusts the fuel injectors and fuel pressure to deliver the required amount of fuel and optimum combustion efficiency.

6 The exhaust system incorporates a turbocharger and an EGR system. Further detail of the emission control systems can be found in Chapter 4B.

Precautions

• *When working on diesel fuel system components, scrupulous cleanliness must be observed, and care must be taken not to introduce any foreign matter into fuel lines or components.*

• *After carrying out any work involving disconnection of fuel lines, it is advisable to check the connections for leaks; pressurise the system by cranking the engine several times.*

• *Electronic control units are very sensitive components, and certain precautions must be taken to avoid damage to these units.*

• *When carrying out welding operations on the vehicle using electric welding equipment, the battery and alternator should be disconnected.*

• *Although the underbonnet-mounted modules will tolerate normal underbonnet conditions, they can be adversely affected by excess heat or moisture. If using welding equipment or pressure-washing equipment in the vicinity of an electronic module, take care not to direct heat, or jets of water or steam, at the module. If this cannot be avoided, remove the module from the vehicle, and protect its wiring plug with a plastic bag.*

• *Before disconnecting any wiring, or removing components, always ensure that the ignition is switched off.*

• *Do not attempt to improvise PCM fault diagnosis procedures using a test lamp or multimeter, as irreparable damage could be caused to the module.*

• *After working on fuel injection/engine management system components, ensure that all wiring is correctly reconnected before reconnecting the battery or switching on the ignition.*

2 Fuel pipe and connectors

1 Disconnect the cable from the negative battery terminal as described in Chapter 5 Section 3 before proceeding.

2 The fuel supply pipe connects the fuel pump in the fuel tank to the fuel filter on the engine.

3 Whenever you're working under the vehicle, be sure to inspect all fuel and evaporative emission pipes for leaks, kinks, dents and other damage. Always replace a damaged fuel pipe immediately.

4 If you find signs of dirt in the pipes during disassembly, disconnect all pipes and blow them out with compressed air. Inspect the fuel strainer on the fuel pump pick-up unit for damage and deterioration.

Steel tubing

5 It is critical that the fuel pipes be replaced with pipes of equivalent type and specification.

6 Some steel fuel pipes have threaded fittings. When loosening these fittings, hold the stationary fitting with a spanner while turning the union nut.

Plastic tubing

 Warning: When removing or installing plastic fuel tubing, be careful not to bend or twist it too much, which can damage it. Also, plastic fuel tubing is NOT heat resistant, so keep it away from excessive heat.

7 When replacing fuel system plastic tubing, use only original equipment replacement plastic tubing.

Flexible hoses

8 When replacing fuel system flexible hoses, use original equipment replacements, or hose to the same specification.

9 Don't route fuel hoses (or metal pipes) within 100 mm of the exhaust system or within 280 mm of the catalytic converter. Make sure that no rubber hoses are installed directly against the vehicle, particularly in places where there is any vibration. If allowed to touch some vibrating part of the vehicle, a hose can easily become chafed and it might start leaking. A good rule of thumb is to maintain a minimum of 8.0 mm clearance around a hose (or metal pipe) to prevent contact with the vehicle underbody.

Disconnecting Fuel pipe Fittings

10 Typical fuel pipe fittings:

2.10a Two-tab type fitting; depress both tabs with your fingers, then pull the fuel pipe and the fitting apart

2.10b On this type of fitting, depress the two buttons on opposite sides of the fitting, then pull it off the fuel pipe

2.10c Threaded fuel pipe fitting; hold the stationary portion of the pipe or component (A) while loosening the union nut (B) with a flare-nut spanner

2.10d Plastic collar-type fitting; rotate the outer part of the fitting

2.10e Metal collar quick-connect fitting; pull the end of the retainer off the fuel pipe and disengage the other end from the female side of the fitting ...

2.10f ...insert a fuel pipe separator tool into the female side of the fitting, push it into the fitting and pull the fuel pipe off the pipe

2.10g Some fittings are secured by lock tabs. Release the lock tab (A) and rotate it to the fully-opened position, squeeze the two smaller lock tabs (B) ...

2.10h ...then push the retainer out and pull the fuel pipe off the pipe

2.10i Spring-lock coupling; remove the safety cover, install a coupling release tool and close the tool around the coupling ...

2.10j ...push the tool into the fitting, then pull the two pipes apart

2.10k Hairpin clip type fitting: push the legs of the retainer clip together, then push the clip down all the way until it stops and pull the fuel pipe off the pipe

3.1 Remove the cover (2.0 litre model shown)

3.2 Disconnect the wiring plug

3.3a The location of the mountings (two hidden)

3.3b Remove the air filter housing

3.5 Remove the outlet ducting

3.6a Slide back the locking tab ...

3.6b ...release the wiring plug...

3.6c ...and unclip the loom

3.7 Remove the housing

3 Air filter assembly – removal and refitting

Removal

Note: *All engines except the 2.2 litre engine share a common air filter assembly.*

1.6, 1.8 and 2.0 litre engines

1 Open the bonnet and remove the engine cover **(see illustration)**.
2 Slide back the locking tab and disconnect the wiring plug from the MAF (Mass Airflow Sensor) **(see illustration)**.
3 Slacken the hose clamp and pull off the outlet ducting. Pull the complete filter housing from the vehicle with a slight rocking motion – there are three mounting points **(see illustrations)**. Recover any of the mounting rubbers that have come away with the housing and refit them.
4 If required the ducting to the turbocharger can now be removed.

2.2 litre engines

5 Slacken off the outlet duct hose clip and remove the ducting **(see illustration)**.
6 Disconnect the mass airflow sensor wiring plug and then unclip the wiring loom from the bracket on the air filter housing **(see illustrations)**.
7 With a slight rocking motion, pull up the housing from the mountings and remove it **(see illustration)**.
8 If the complete housing and inlet ducting requires removal, disconnect the engine breather hose at the rear of the cylinder head and then slacken the main hose clip that secures the ducting to the turbocharger. Depending on the position of the hose clip it can be released from either above or from below.

Refitting

9 To aid refitting lubricate the mounting pegs with silicon grease (or similar). The inlet duct can be fitted easily if the left-hand headlight is removed (as described in Chapter 12 Section 9) and the filter housing guided onto the duct. The remainder of refitting is a reversal of removal.

4.7a Remove the metal threaded fasteners…

4.7b …the plastic retainers…

4.7c …and the bolt(s)

4 Fuel tank –
removal and refitting

Note: *Observe the precautions in Section 1 before working on any component in the fuel system.*

Removal

1 Run the fuel level as low as possible prior to removing the tank. There is no drain plug fitted (and syphoning may prove difficult). It is preferable to keep as much fuel in the pipes as possible, to reduce the need for bleeding the system when restarting the engine.
2 Equalise tank pressure by removing the fuel filler cap.
3 Disconnect the battery negative (earth) lead (see Chapter 5 Section 3).
4 Chock the front wheels, then jack up the rear of the car and support it on axle stands (see *Jacking and vehicle support*).
5 Where fitted remove the air deflectors from either side of the fuel tank.
6 Unhook the exhaust system mounting rubbers from the centre and rear hangers, and allow the exhaust system to rest on the rear suspension crossmember.
7 Undo the fasteners and remove the exhaust centre and rear section heat shields from the vehicle underside **(see illustrations)**.
8 Disconnect the fuel supply and return hoses at the front of the tank **(see illustrations)**. Where a fuel fired heater is fitted, disconnect the fuel lines.
9 At the rear of the fuel tank disconnect the wiring plug.
10 Clamp the fuel filler neck with a suitable clamp (we fabricated one from short lengths of tube) and then release the hose clamps. Dispose of the hose clips – they should be replaced **(see illustrations)**.

4.7d Manoeuvre the heatshield past the exhaust system and out of the vehicle

11 Slacken – but DO NOT remove the fuel tank straps at this point.
12 Support the tank using a trolley jack and a large sheet of wood to spread the load **(see illustration)**.

4.8a Prise open the locking collars and release the fuel lines

4.8b Seal the fuel lines on the body and…

4.8c …at the the tank

4.10a Clamp the flexible section of the filler pipe

4.10b Remove the hose clips

4.12 Support the fuel tank

4.14 Fuel tank strap bolt

5.3a Disconnect the wiring plug ...

5.3b ... and unbolt the pedal

13 Note exactly how the fuel tank retaining straps are arranged, to make refitting easier. In particular, note their fitted order under the retaining bolt heads, where applicable.
14 Unbolt and remove the fuel tank retaining straps **(see illustration)**.
15 Partially lower the tank on the jack, taking care that no strain is placed on any fuel lines or wiring.
16 Lower the fuel tank to the ground and then remove the tank from under the vehicle.

Inspection

17 Whilst removed, the fuel tank can be inspected for damage or deterioration. Removal of the fuel pump/fuel gauge sender unit (see Section 8) will allow a partial inspection of the interior. If the tank is contaminated with sediment or water, swill it out with clean fuel. Do not under any circumstances undertake any repairs on a leaking or damaged fuel tank.

Refitting

18 Refitting is a reversal of the removal procedure, noting the following points:
a) *Ensure that all pipe and wiring connections are securely fitted.*
b) *When refitting the quick-release couplings, press them together and fit the locking collars*
c) *Tighten the tank strap retaining bolts securely.*
d) *If evidence of contamination was found, do not return any previously-drained fuel to the tank.*

5 Accelerator pedal – removal and refitting

Removal

1 Disconnect the battery negative lead as described in Chapter 5 Section 3. Wait a minimum of 5 minutes before proceeding.
2 Remove the driver's side facia lower panel and knee airbag as described in Chapter 11 Section 24.
3 Disconnect the wiring plug from the throttle position sensor, then unscrew the 3 mounting nuts and remove the pedal/sensor assembly from the bulkhead studs **(see illustrations)**.

Note that the sensor is not available separately from the pedal assembly.

Refitting

4 Refit in the reverse order of removal. On completion, check the action of the pedal to ensure that the throttle has full unrestricted movement, and fully returns when released.
5 Reconnect the battery as described in Chapter 5 Section 3.

6 Fuel Injection system – general information

1 The system is under the overall control of the engine management PCM (Powertrain Control Module), which also controls the preheating system (see Chapter 5 Section 9).
2 Fuel is supplied from the rear-mounted fuel tank, via an electrically-powered lift pump and the fuel filter, to the fuel injection pump. The fuel injection pump supplies fuel under high pressure to the common fuel rail. The fuel rail provides a reservoir of fuel under pressure ready for the injectors to deliver direct to the combustion chamber. The individual fuel injectors incorporate piezoelectrical/electromagnetic elements, which when operated, allow the high-pressure fuel to be injected. The elements are controlled by the PCM. The fuel injection pump purely provides high-pressure fuel. The timing and duration of the injection is controlled by the PCM based, on the information received from the various sensors. In order to increase combustion efficiency and reduce combustion noise (diesel 'knock'), a small amount of fuel is injected before the main injection takes place – this is known as Pre- or Pilot-injection.
3 Additionally, the engine management PCM activates the preheating system (Chapter 5 Section 9), and the exhaust gas recirculation (EGR) system (see Chapter 4B Section 4).
4 The system uses the following sensors.
a) *Crankshaft sensor – informs the PCM of the crankshaft speed and position.*
b) *Coolant/cylinder head temperature sensor – informs the PCM of engine temperature.*
c) *Mass airflow sensor – informs the PCM of the mass air entering the inlet tract.*

d) *Wheel speed sensor – informs the PCM of the vehicle speed.*
e) *Accelerator pedal position sensor – informs the PCM of throttle position, and the rate of throttle opening/closing.*
f) *Fuel high-pressure sensor – informs the PCM of the pressure of the fuel in the common rail.*
g) *Camshaft position sensor – informs the PCM of the camshaft position so that the engine firing sequence can be established.*
h) *Stop-light switch – informs the PCM when the brakes are being applied*
i) *Boost pressure sensor – informs the PCM of the boost pressure generated by the turbocharger.*
j) *Air conditioning pressure sensor – informs the PCM of the high-pressure side of the air conditioning circuit, in case a raised idle speed is required to compensate for compressor load.*
k) *Inlet air temperature sensor – informs the PCM of the inlet air temperature.*
l) *Clutch pedal switch – informs the PCM of the clutch pedal position.*
m) *Turbocharger position sensor – informs the PCM of the position of the variable in take nozzle guide rails.*

5 On all models, a 'drive-by-wire' throttle control system is used. The accelerator pedal is not physically connected to the fuel injection pump with a traditional cable, but instead is monitored by a dual potentiometer mounted on the pedal assembly, which provides the powertrain control module (PCM) with a signal relating to accelerator pedal movement.
6 The signals from the various sensors are processed by the PCM, and the optimum fuel quantity and injection timing settings are selected for the prevailing engine operating conditions.
7 Catalytic converters and an exhaust gas recirculation (EGR) system are fitted, to reduce harmful exhaust gas emissions. Later models also have a Diesel Particulate Filter (DPF) fitted. Details of this and other emissions control system equipment are given in Chapter 4B.
8 If there is an abnormality in any of the readings obtained from any sensor, the PCM enters its back-up mode (often called 'limp home'). In this event, the PCM ignores

6.9 The diagnostic connector socket

6.10a The diagnostic socket uses a standard 16 pin connector

6.10b A cost effective code reader connected to the diagnostic socket

the abnormal sensor signal, and assumes a preprogrammed value which will allow the engine to continue running (albeit at reduced efficiency). If the PCM enters this back-up mode, the warning light on the instrument panel will come on, and the relevant fault code will be stored in the PCM memory.

9 If the warning light comes on, the vehicle should be taken to a Ford dealer or specialist at the earliest opportunity. A complete test of the system can then be carried out, using a special electronic test unit which is simply plugged into the system's diagnostic connector. The connector is located in the storage compartment on the driver's side of the facia **(see illustration)**.

10 Increasingly basic diagnostic testers are becoming available to the home mechanic **(see illustrations)**. These will provide access to the mandatory emissions related

fault codes. Some will also allow access to 'pending codes'. These are faults seen by the engine management that are being monitored, but have not passed the threshold required to illuminate the check engine warning light.

11 The amount of information displayed will vary from code reader to code reader. Very basic fault code readers will only display the fault codes as a number – a 'P' code that can be checked against a list. More advanced models will display the code and a description of the fault code.

7 Fuel system – priming and bleeding

1 After disturbing the fuel system before the system must be bled. To do this, Ford technicians use a hand pump (No 310-110A)

that connects to the fuel filter and draws fuel up from the tank, or through the leak-off pipe return. In the absence of this tool, use a hand-held vacuum pump or an inline 'bulb' type syphon/pump.

2 A selection of various diameter hoses and adapters will be required to connect the pump to the filter head.

3 Remove the cover on the top of the engine.

4 Depress the release tab(s) and disconnect the fuel outlet hose from the fuel filter **(see illustrations)**.

5 Connect the vacuum pump pipe to the outlet on the filter, and continue to pull a vacuum until bubble-free fuel emerges from the hose **(see illustration)**.

6 Reconnect the fuel hose.

7 Operate the starter motor and run the engine until it reaches normal operating temperature.

7.4a Depress the button and disconnect the fuel outlet hose – 1.6 litre models …

7.4b … prise out the clip on 1.8 litre models …

7.4c … depress the clip on 2.0 litre models …

7.4d … and depress the clip on 2.2 litre models

7.5a Attach the hand-held vacuum pump hose to the filter outlet …

7.5b … or connect an inline pump, and pump until bubble-free fuel emerges

8.2a Depress the locking pegs and disconnect the supply and return hoses from the tank sender unit

8.2b Disconnect the wiring plug

8.3a Use a home fabricated tool to unscrew the sender unit plastic collar...

8.3b ...or a factory made one

8.4a Lift the sender unit from the tank...

8.4b ...discard the seal, a new one should be fitted

Caution: Do not operate the starter motor for more than 10 seconds, then wait 30 seconds before trying again.

8 Stop the engine. Wipe up any fuel spillage, and refit the engine cover.

8 Fuel gauge sender unit – removal and refitting

Note: *Observe the precautions in Section 1 before working on any component in the fuel system.*

Removal

1 Remove the fuel tank as described in Section 4.

2 Depress the release buttons, and disconnect the fuel supply and return hoses from the sender unit **(see illustration)**. Where a fuel fired heater is fitted, disconnect the fuel supply line.

3 Unscrew the sender unit plastic retaining collar using a commercially available tool, or fabricate a tool **(see illustrations)**.

4 Lift the sender unit from the tank **(see illustrations)**. Discard the O-ring seal, a new one should be fitted. If the sender unit is to be removed for any length of time, then refit the locking collar to the tank – this will avoid any chance of the course threads on the tank distorting.

5 If required, attach the leads from a multimeter to the sender unit wires, and measure the resistance at full float deflection

and zero deflection. No actual figures are provided, but as long as the resistance changes smoothly from one end of the resistance track to the other, the sender should be considered in good working order **(see illustration)**.

Refitting

6 Refitting is a reversal of removal, bearing in mind the following points:
a) Use a new O-ring seal smeared with petroleum jelly.
b) Position the sender unit so the arrow on the cover aligns with the marks on the fuel tank **(see illustration)**.
c) Tighten the sender unit retaining collar to the specified torque **(see illustration)**.

8.5 Use a multimeter to measure the sender unit resistance at full and zero float arm deflection

8.6a The arrow on the sender cover must align with the marks on the fuel tank

8.6b Tighten the collar to the specified torque (where possible)

10.3a Undo the 2 bolts securing the EGR pipe to the manifold/cover…

10.3b …then the bolt securing the pipe to the head…

10.3c …then release the clamp and remove the EGR pipe

9 Fuel injection system – testing and adjustment

Testing

1 If a fault appears in the fuel injection system, first ensure that all the system wiring connectors are securely connected and free from corrosion. Ensure that the fault is not due to poor maintenance; ie, check that the air cleaner filter element is clean, that the cylinder compression pressures are correct and that the engine breather hoses are clear and undamaged.

2 Most faults will be indicated by the 'check engine' light being illuminated. A serious fault may force the engine management to implement a Limited Operating Strategy (LOS). This will reduce power and economy to prevent engine damage, but allow the vehicle to be driven home, or to a suitable garage – hence this mode is often referred to as 'limp home'.

3 If these checks fail to reveal the cause of the problem and a basic code reader is not available (see Section 6) then the vehicle should be taken to a Ford dealer or garage equipped with suitable diagnostic equipment. Many independent garages will have

sophisticated diagnostic equipment, some will even have the factory approved tool (IDS).
4 With the right equipment in the hands of a trained technician, then the fault should be isolated fairly quickly. However it is important to remember, that no matter how sophisticated the diagnostic equipment the tool will only report the error code, but this may be a symptom and not the cause of the fault. A skilled operative will be able to distinguish between cause and symptom and take the appropriate action.

10 Fuel injection pump – removal and refitting

Caution: Cleanliness is essential. Be careful not to allow dirt into the injection pump or injector pipes during this procedure.
Note: *Any rigid high-pressure fuel pipes disturbed must be renewed.*

1.6 litre engines

Removal

1 Disconnect the battery (see Chapter 5 Section 3) and remove the timing belt as described in Chapter 2A Section 7. After removal of the timing belt, temporarily refit the

right-hand engine mounting but do not fully tighten the bolts.
2 Remove the air filter assembly as described in Section 3.
3 Remove the EGR cooler as described in Chapter 4B Section 4, **(see illustrations)**.
4 Undo the bolts/nuts and remove the support brackets above the fuel common rail and the high-pressure pump.
5 Undo the union nuts and remove the high-pressure fuel pipe between the fuel common rail and the high-pressure pump. Plug the openings to prevent contamination.
6 Disconnect the wiring plug from the high-pressure fuel pump.
7 Depress the release buttons and disconnect the fuel supply and return hoses from the pump. Note that the hoses may have a release button on each side of the fitting. Plug the openings to prevent contamination.
8 Hold the pump sprocket stationary, and loosen the centre nut securing it to the pump shaft (see **Tool Tip 1**).
9 The fuel pump sprocket is a taper fit on the pump shaft and it will be necessary to make up a tool to release it from the taper (see **Tool Tip 2**). Partially unscrew the sprocket retaining nut, fit the home-made tool, and secure it to the sprocket with two 7.0 mm bolts and nuts. Prevent the sprocket from rotating as before, and screw down the nuts, forcing the sprocket off the shaft taper.
10 Once the taper is released, remove the tool, unscrew the nut fully, and remove the sprocket from the pump shaft.
11 Undo the three bolts, and remove the pump from the mounting bracket.
12 Caution: The high-pressure fuel pump is manufactured to extremely close tolerances and must not be dismantled in any way. Do not unscrew the fuel pipe male union on the rear of the pump, or attempt to remove the sensor, piston de-activator switch, or the seal on the pump shaft. No parts for the pump are available separately and if the unit is in any way suspect, it must be renewed.

Refitting

13 Refitting is a reversal of removal, noting the following points:
a) *Always renew the pump-to-common rail high-pressure pipe.*

A sprocket holding tool can be made from two lengths of steel strip bolted together to form a forked end. Bend the ends of the strip through 90° to form the 'prongs'.

Make a sprocket releasing tool from a short strip of steel. Drill two holes in the strip to correspond with the two holes in the sprocket. Drill a third hole just large enough to accept the flats of the sprocket retaining nut.

b) With everything reassembled and reconnected, and observing the precautions listed in Section 1, start the engine and allow it to idle. Check for leaks at the high-pressure fuel pipe unions with the engine idling. If satisfactory, increase the engine speed to 3000 rpm and check again for leaks.

c) Take the car for a short road test and check for leaks once again on return. If any leaks are detected, obtain and fit another new high-pressure fuel pipe. Do not attempt to cure even the slightest leak by further tightening of the pipe unions.

1.8 litre engines

Removal

14 Disconnect the battery negative lead as described in Chapter 5 Section 3.

15 Remove the timing belt as described in Chapter 2B Section 7.

16 Slacken the three bolts securing the injection pump timing belt sprocket, and remove the sprocket from the pump. The sprocket may need to be prevented from turning as this is done – it should prove sufficient to select a gear and apply the handbrake, but it may be necessary to jam the flywheel ring gear as described in Chapter 2B Section 6. The sprocket is sealed to the inner pulley using RTV sealant, and may need to be prised free; recover the metal gasket.

17 Remove the 7 nuts which secure the injection pump oil seal housing, and withdraw the seal housing from around the pump inner pulley **(see illustration)**. Withdraw the timing belt backplate from the oil pump housing studs, noting which way round it fits.

18 Undo the bolt/nut and remove the high-pressure fuel supply pipe support bracket from the pump **(see illustration)**. **Note:** *Place rags over the alternator to prevent fuel damaging the unit.*

19 Ensure the area around fuel pipes connections on the pump and supply manifold are absolutely clean, place rags over the top of the alternator to protect it from fuel spillage. Slacken the unions and the clamp bolt, clean the pipes once the unions nuts have been moved along the pipe, then remove the

10.17 Remove the seal housing retaining nuts

10.18 Undo the support bracket bolts

10.19 Place the spanner on the thickest section of the union nut

10.21 Remove the support bracket bolts at the rear of the pump

pump-to-supply manifold rigid metal fuel pipe **(see illustration)**. Plug or cap the openings to prevent dirt ingress. Make a note of the exact position of the pipe clamp, to enable it to be fitted in exactly the same place on the new pipe.

20 Note their fitted positions, then disconnect all wiring plugs from the pump.

21 Undo the 2 bolts (or 4 bolts on some models) securing the support bracket to the rear of the pump **(see illustration)**.

22 Depress the locking tabs and disconnect the fuel return pipe from the pump **(see illustration)**. Plug or cap the opening to prevent dirt ingress.

23 Prise out the locking catch, then using a small screwdriver, prise out the clip and disconnect the fuel supply pipe from the pump

(see illustration). Plug or cap the opening to prevent dirt ingress.

24 Unscrew and remove the 4 bolts securing the drive chain/belt sprocket to the injection pump. As with removal of its timing belt sprocket, it may be necessary to prevent the pulley from turning as the bolts are loosened.

25 Undo the 3 bolts securing the pump to the engine casing. It may not be possible to remove the bolts completely.

26 Manoeuvre the pump from the engine.

Refitting

27 Align the hole in the fuel pump drive flange with the etched mark on the pump body **(see illustration)**.

28 With a new gasket and seal, refit the pump to the front engine casing, and tighten the bolts to the specified torque.

10.22 Depress the clip and disconnect the fuel return pipe

10.23 Prise out the locking catch, then prise out the clip and disconnect the fuel supply pipe

10.27 Align the hole in the drive flange with the mark on the pump body

10.44 Remove the pipe between the high-pressure pump and the fuel rail

10.45a Depress the release tabs and disconnect the fuel supply ...

10.45b ... and return hoses from the pump

29 Refit the 4 chain/belt sprocket bolts and tighten them to the specified torque.

30 Before reconnecting the return and supply pipes, the injection pump should be primed with fuel, to reduce the length of time spent cranking the engine at start-up. If a new pump has been fitted (or the old pump has been off the engine for some time), priming with fuel is essential, as the fuel lubricates the pump internals, which may otherwise be dry. Follow the procedures in Section 7. If a vacuum pump is not available, a new pump can be partially primed by pouring in clean fuel via the fuel supply and return connections – take precautions against fuel spillage on delicate components by covering the surrounding area with clean rags, and be very careful not to introduce dirt into the pump.

31 Remove the blanking plugs/cap (if not already done so), and reconnect the fuel return and supply pipes to the pump.

32 If removed, refit the fuel pump rear support bracket to the pump, and tighten the bolts securely.

33 Reconnect the wiring plugs to the pump.

34 Fit the clamp to the new rigid pump-to-supply manifold metal pipe in exactly the same position as it was fitted to the original.

35 Spray the threads of the pump and supply manifold unions with a lubricant (eg, WD40, etc), then remove the blanking plugs and fit the pipe in place, but only finger-tighten the unions at this stage.

36 Refit the pump rear support bracket, and tighten the bolts securely.

37 Using a crow's-foot spanner, tighten the rigid metal pipe unions to the specified torque, starting at the supply manifold first. Ensure the spanner acts upon the part of the union where there is the most metal, to avoid damage to the union (see illustration 9.18).

38 Refit the support bracket to the ridged metal pipe at the pump, and tighten the bolt/nut securely.

39 Fit a new metal gasket to the pump drive chain sprocket. Apply a coating of Loctite RTV 5910 sealant to the sprocket (avoiding the three sprocket bolt holes). The three bolts should be cleaned, then lightly coated with Loctite 518 locking fluid. Offer up the timing belt sprocket, aligning the bolt holes carefully, then fit the three bolts and tighten to the specified torque.

40 Refit the timing belt as described in Chapter 2B Section 7.

41 Start the engine, and let it idle, noting that it may take a while before a stable idle speed is achieved, as the engine management module (PCM) may have to relearn some of the 'adaptive' values. As the engine warms-up, check for signs of leakage from the fuel unions. If no leakage is evident, take the car for a short journey (of at least 5 miles) to allow the PCM to complete its 'learning' process.

2.0 litre engines

Removal

42 Remove the cover from the top of the engine, by pulling it straight up from its mountings at the front and right-hand edges, then pull it forwards.

43 Remove the air cleaner assembly as described in Section 3 and then remove the EGR pipe from the top of the engine (see Chapter 4B).

44 Undo the unions and remove the high-pressure fuel pipe between the pump and the fuel rail (see illustration). Discard the pipe, a new one must be fitted.

45 Note their fitted positions, depress the release tabs, and disconnect the fuel supply and return pipes from the pump (see illustrations). Be prepared for fuel spillage. Plug the openings to prevent contamination.

46 Note their fitted positions, and disconnect the wiring plugs from the pump.

47 Undo the 3 retaining bolts and pull the pump from the cylinder head (see illustration). Discard the gasket.

Refitting

48 Ensure that the mating surfaces of the pump and cylinder head are clean and dry, and fit the new gasket.

49 Ensure the slot in the end of the camshaft and the pump drive dog are aligned, then refit the pump, tightening the mounting bolts to the specified torque (see illustration).

50 Reconnect the fuel supply and return pipes to the pump, and the wiring plugs.

51 Fit the new high-pressure fuel pipe between the pump and common rail, then tighten to the specified torque, using a crow's-foot adapter.

52 The remainder of refitting is a reversal of removal, bearing in mind the following points:
a) Bleed the fuel system as described in Section 7.
b) Once the engine has started, thoroughly check for fuel leaks from the disturbed pipes/hoses.

2.2 litre engines

Removal

53 Remove the engine cover and then remove the air filter housing as described in Section 3.

10.47 Undo the 3 bolts and remove the pump

10.49 Ensure the pump drive dog is aligned with the slot in the end of the camshaft

10.54 Remove the EGR pipe

10.55 Remove the protective cover

10.56a Remove the fuel lines and ...

10.56b ... seal the pump

10.57 The high pressure pipe at the base of the pump

10.58a Remove the bolts

54 Unbolt and remove the EGR pipe from the top left-hand end of the engine **(see illustration).**
55 Unbolt and remove the crash protector/ engine cover support bracket **(see illustration).**
56 Disconnect the fuel supply and return lines. Seal the openings on both the pipes and the pump as soon as the pipes are removed **(see illustrations).**
57 Unbolt the high pressure pipe from the pump and the fuel rail **(see illustration).** Dispose of the pipe – a new one must be used.
58 Remove the retaining bolts and pull the pump from end of the cylinder head. Recover the drive dog and the gasket **(see illustrations).**

59 As the pump is removed disconnect the wiring plug **(see illustration).**

Refitting

60 Ensure that the mating surfaces of the pump and cylinder head are clean and dry, and fit the new gasket.
61 Ensure the slot in the end of the camshaft and the pump drive dog are aligned, then refit the pump, tightening the mounting bolts to the specified torque **(see illustration 10.49).**
62 Reconnect the fuel supply and return pipes to the pump, and the wiring plugs.
63 Fit the new high-pressure fuel pipe between the pump and common rail, then tighten to the specified torque, using a crow's-foot adapter.

64 The remainder of refitting is a reversal of removal, bearing in mind the following points:
a) Bleed the fuel system as described in Section 7.
b) Once the engine has started, thoroughly check for fuel leaks from the disturbed pipes/hoses.

11 Fuel injectors – removal and refitting

Note: Be careful not to allow dirt into the injection pump or injector pipes during this procedure.

Removal

All engines

1 Disconnect the battery as described in Chapter 5 Section 3.
2 Remove the engine cover.
3 Unbolt the brake fluid reservoir and then remove the upper and lower windscreen cowl panels – as described in Chapter 12 Section 12.

1.6 litre engines

4 Remove the air filter housing.
5 Remove the protective cover/heatshield from the turbocharger and then disconnect the wiring from the throttle body. Unbolt and remove the throttle body and pipework.

10.58b Remove the pump, noting the position of the drive dog

10.59 Disconnect the wiring plug

11.6 Remove the throttle body to inlet manifold pipe

11.7a Remove the sound insulation panel …

11.7b …and then disconnect the wiring plugs from the injectors

11.8a Compress the locking collar and …

11.8b …remove the bleed off hoses

11.9 Use a second spanner to counter-hold the high-pressure pipe union nuts

6 Remove the pipe from the throttle body to the the inlet manifold **(see illustration)**.

7 Remove the sound insulation and then disconnect the wiring plugs from the fuel injectors **(see illustrations)**.

8 Compress the wings of the locking collars and remove the bleed off hoses from the 4 fuel injectors **(see illustrations)**. Disconnect the hose assembly at the junction with the fuel return pipe and remove it from the vehicle. Seal the now exposed bleed off ports on the injectors

9 Clean the area around the high-pressure fuel pipes between the injectors and the common rail, then unscrew the pipe unions. Use a second spanner to counter-hold the union screwed into the injector body**(see illustration)**. The injectors screwed-in unions must not be allowed to move. Plug the openings in the common rail and injectors to prevent dirt ingress. Dispose of the high pressure pipes, they must be replaced.

10 Unscrew the injector retaining bolt **(see illustration)** and carefully pull or lever the injector from place. If necessary, use an open-ended spanner and twist the injector to free it from position. Do not lever against or pull on the solenoid housing at the top of the injector. Note that special tools (consisting of a slide hammer and collar that locks onto the injector) are available to help with the removal of the injectors. In extreme cases a hydraulic puller tool may be required. A specialist or well equipped garage should have these tools.

11 Note down the injector's position – if the injectors are to be refitted, they must be refitted to their original locations. Where possible keep the injectors vertical at all times and store them in a suitable place **(see illustration)**.

12 Remove the copper washer and the upper seal from each injector, or from the cylinder head if they remained in place during injector

removal. New copper washers and upper seals will be required for refitting. Cover the injector hole in the cylinder head to prevent dirt ingress.

13 Examine each injector visually for any signs of obvious damage or deterioration. If any defects are apparent, renew the injector(s).

Caution: The injectors are manufactured to extremely close tolerances and must not be dismantled in any way. Do not unscrew the fuel pipe union on the side of the injector, or separate any parts of the injector body. Do not attempt to clean carbon deposits from the injector nozzle or carry out any form of ultrasonic or pressure testing.

1.8 litre engines

14 Release the clamps and disconnect the breather hoses from the cylinder head cover **(see illustration)**.

11.10 Remove the injector retaining bolts

11.11 Store the injectors upright at all times

11.14 Disconnect the breather hoses from the cylinder head cover

11.16a Disconnect the fuel temperature sensor wiring plug

11.16b Depress the clip and disconnect the injector wiring plugs

11.21a Slacken the injector clamp bolts ...

11.21b ... and pull the injectors from place

11.25a Prise down the lower edge of the retaining clip (shown with the return hose disconnected for clarity) ...

11.25b ... then pull the return hoses from the injectors

15 Disconnect the wiring plugs from the high pressure fuel pump and the common rail.
16 Disconnect the wiring plug from the fuel temperature sensor, then disconnect the wiring plug from each injector **(see illustrations)**. Move the wiring harness to one side.
17 Ensure the areas around the injection pipes and unions is absolutely clean. If possible, use a vacuum cleaner to remove all debris from the vicinity.
18 Slacken and unscrew the pipe unions at the injectors and the fuel supply manifold (common rail), but keep the metal pipes in contact with the injectors and manifold until the unions have been moved along the pipe and the areas at the ends of the pipes cleaned. Use a second spanner to counter-hold the unions at the injectors. Be prepared for fuel spillage.
19 With any dirt/debris removed, detach the pipes from the injectors and manifold, then plug the openings to prevent dirt ingress. Discard the pipes – Ford insist that new ones must be fitted.
20 Ensure the area around the injectors is absolutely clean and free from debris. If possible, use a vacuum cleaner to remove any dirt.
21 Slacken the injector clamps retaining bolts, and pull the injectors from place **(see illustrations)**. Discard the clamp bolts – new ones must be fitted. If the original injectors are to be refitted, it is absolutely essential that they are refitted in to their original positions.

22 Discard the injectors sealing washers – new ones must be fitted.

2.0 litre engines

23 Remove the cylinder head cover/inlet manifold as described in Chapter 2C Section 3.
24 Make sure the areas around the high pressure fuel pipe unions from the fuel rail to the injectors are scrupulously clean and free from debris, etc. If possible, use a vacuum cleaner and a degreaser to clean the area.
25 Where fitted remove the protective covers from the injectors and disconnect the wiring plugs. Carefully prise down the lower edge of the retaining clips, then disconnect the fuel return hoses from the injectors **(see illustrations)**. Take care not to drop the retaining clips as they are removed, and check

the condition of the O-ring seals – renew if necessary.
26 Undo the unions, then remove the high-pressure fuel pipes from the fuel rail to the injectors. Discard the fuel pipes, new ones must be fitted. Use a second open-ended spanner on the injector port to counter-hold when slackening the pipe union **(see illustration)**. Be prepared for fuel spillage and plug/cover the ports in the injectors and fuel rail to prevent dirt ingress.
27 Unscrew the two bolts securing each injector clamp, and carefully remove the injectors. Slide the copper sealing washer from the end of each injector. Discard the sealing washers – new ones must be fitted **(see illustration)**.

11.26 Use a second spanner to counter-hold the injector port when slackening the union nut

11.27 Injector clamp bolts

11.29a Release the bleed off hoses

11.29b Note the O-rings

11.30a Remove the fuel lines

11.30b Blanking plugs can be fabricated from old high pressure pipes

11.31a Remove the bolts ...

11.31b ... slide out the yoke ...

2.2 litre engines

28 Make sure the areas around the high-pressure fuel pipe unions from the fuel rail to the injectors is scrupulously clean and free from debris, etc. If possible, use a vacuum cleaner and a degreaser to clean the area.

29 Depress the wings of the clips and remove the bleed off hoses from the fuel injectors (**see illustrations**). Disconnect the wiring plugs

30 Seal the bleed off connections on each injector and then remove the high pressure fuel lines (**see illustrations**). Dispose of the pipes – they must be replaced.

31 Remove the mounting bolts, recover the yokes and remove the injectors (**see illustrations**). Always keep the injectors in cylinder order and store them upright.

Refitting

32 Locate a new upper seal (1.6 and 2.0 and 2.2 litre) on the body of each injector, and

11.31c ... and remove the injector

place a new copper washer on the injector nozzle (**see illustration**).

33 If not already done so, make a note of the number on the side (or top) of each injector and then fit each injector to to the correct cylinder (**see illustrations**).

34 Refit the injector clamp locating dowels (where fitted) to the cylinder head.

11.32 Upper seal (A) and copper washer (B)

35 Ensure the injector clamps are in place over their respective circlips on the injector bodies and then fit the injectors into place in the cylinder head. On 2.2 litre engines slide the retaining yoke into position as the injectors are refitted. If the original injectors are being refitted, ensure they are fitted into their original positions (**see illustration**).

11.33a Note the classification number on 1.6 litre engines ...

11.33b ... and on 1.8 litre engines (2.0 and 2.2 litre engines are similar)

11.35 Fit the injectors into their original locations (1.6 litre shown)

11.36 Fit new bolts to the injector clamps

11.40 Tighten the high-pressure pipe union nuts using a 'crow's-foot' adapter

12.1 Remove the wing liner

36 Fit the injector retaining bolts/nuts **(see illustration)** but only finger-tighten them at this stage. When tightening the nuts/bolts, ensure the clamps stay horizontal.
37 Slacken the fuel rail mounting bolts (where possible).
38 Working on one fuel injector at a time, remove the blanking plugs from the fuel pipe unions on the common rail and the relevant injector. Locate a new high-pressure fuel pipe over the unions and screw on the union nuts. Take care not to cross-thread the nuts or strain the fuel pipes as they are fitted. Once the union nut threads have started, finger-tighten the nuts only at this stage, to the ends of the threads.
39 When all the fuel pipes are in place, tighten the injector clamp retaining nuts/bolts to the specified torque and angle and then tighten the fuel rail mounting bolts.
40 Using an open-ended spanner, hold each fuel pipe union in turn and tighten the union nut to the specified torque using a torque wrench and crow's-foot adapter **(see illustration)**. Tighten all the disturbed union nuts in the same way.
41 If new injectors have been fitted, their classification numbers must be programmed into the engine management PCM (Power Control Module) using Ford's IDS diagnostic tool. A Ford dealer will have this tool, but increasingly the genuine Ford tool will be found in the independent trade. A large number of third party tools are capable of performing this task. Note that it should be possible to drive the vehicle, albeit with

reduced performance/increased emissions, to a repairer for the numbers to be programmed.
42 The remainder of refitting is a reversal of removal, noting the following points:
a) *Ensure all wiring connectors and harnesses are correctly refitting and secured.*
b) *Reconnect the battery as described in Chapter 5 Section 3.*
c) *Observing the precautions listed in Section 1, start the engine and allow it to idle. Check for leaks at the high-pressure fuel pipe unions with the engine idling. If satisfactory, increase the engine speed to 3000 rpm and check again for leaks. Take the car for a short road test and check for leaks once again on return. If any leaks are detected, obtain and fit additional new high-pressure fuel pipes as required. Do not attempt to cure even the slightest leak by further tightening of the pipe unions.*

12 Engine management system components – removal and refitting

Crankshaft position/speed sensor

Note: *On all models, except the 1.8 litre engine the sensor is located at the crankshaft pulley end of the engine. On 1.8 litre engines the sensor is located at the flywheel – low down and to the rear of the engine.*
1 On all engines jack up and support the

front of the vehicle (see *Jacking and vehicle support*). Remove the engine undershield. On all but the 1.8 litre engine remove the right-hand road wheel and then remove the wing liner **(see illustration)**.

1.6 litre engines
2 The crankshaft position sensor is located adjacent to the crankshaft pulley on the right-hand end of the engine. Slacken the right-hand front roadwheel bolts, then jack the front of the vehicle up and support it on axle stands (see *Jacking and vehicle support*). Remove the right-hand front roadwheel.
3 Release the fasteners and remove the right-hand front wheel arch liner.
4 Disconnect the sensor wiring plug **(see illustration)**.
5 Undo the bolt and remove the sensor.
6 Refitting is a reversal of removal, tightening the sensor retaining bolt to the specified torque.

1.8 litre engines
7 Before removing the sensor, set the crankshaft at TDC on No 1 cylinder, as described in Chapter 2B Section 3.
8 The sensor is located at the flywheel end of the engine, low down at the rear **(see illustration)**.
9 Disconnect the wiring plug from the sensor.
10 Unscrew the mounting bolt, then slide the sensor towards the timing belt end of the engine and withdraw it **(see illustration)**.
11 Ford recommend that the sensor is replaced if removed. One of two types of repleacement sensor maybe supplied: A flat

12.4 Crankshaft position sensor (1.6 litre)

12.8 Crankshaft position sensor – 1.8 litre

12.10 Undo the bolt and then slide the sensor from place

12.16 The crankshaft position sensor

12.22a Camshaft position sensor bolt (1.6 litre)

12.22b Camshaft position sensor (2.0 litre)

12.22c Camshaft position sensor (2.2 litre)

faced sensor or a sensor with a raised lip. The replacement procedure is different for each type.

12 If a sensor with a raised lip is supplied, fit the sensor and push it against the flywheel. Tighten the bolt to the specified torque and reconnect the wiring plug.

13 If a sensor with a flat face is supplied, push the sensor against the flywheel and measure the gap between the sensor face (using feeler gauges) and the sensor mounting. Add 1.2 mm to this figure and set the sensor accordingly. Tighten the mounting bolt to the specified torque and reconnect the wiring plug.

14 The remainder of refitting is a reversal of removal.

2.0 and 2.2 litre engines

Note: *On some models it is possible to remove the sensor with the crankshaft pulley in place.*

15 Remove the crankshaft pulley as described in Chapter 2C Section 4 or Chapter 2D Section 5.

16 The sensor is located adjacent to the crankshaft pulley **(see illustration)**. Disconnect the sensor wiring plug.

17 On 2.0 litre models remove the timing belt cover lower bolts, unbolt the sensor and manoeuvre the sensor out of the engine. On 2.2 litre models remove the timing belt lower cover, unbolt and remove the sensor.

18 Refitting is the reverse of removal, tightening the retaining bolt to the specified torque.

Camshaft position sensor

1.6 and 2.0 and 2.2 litre engines

19 The camshaft position sensor is mounted on the right-hand end of the cylinder head cover, directly behind the camshaft sprocket.

20 Remove the upper timing belt cover, as described in Chapter 2A Section 6, Chapter 2C Section 5 or Chapter 2D Section 6 as applicable.

21 Unplug the sensor wiring connector.

22 Undo the bolt and pull the sensor from position **(see illustrations)**.

23 Upon refitting, position the sensor so that the nipple of the sensor is just in contact with the camshaft signal wheel. On 2.2 litre engines when refitting the old sensor, use a 7.5 mm diameter drill to position the sensor **(see illustration)** Tighten the sensor retaining bolt to the specified torque.

24 The remainder of refitting is a reversal of removal.

1.8 litre engines

25 Carefully pull the plastic cover on the top of the engine upwards from place.

26 The sensor is located on the cylinder head cover. Disconnect the sensor wiring plug **(see illustration)**.

27 Undo the bolt and pull the sensor from position.

28 Refitting is a reversal of removal.

Mass airflow sensor

All engines

29 The Mass AirFlow (MAF) sensor also incorporates an Inlet Air Temperature (IAT) sensor. On all models the sensor is fitted to the air filter housing outlet **(see illustration)**.

30 Undo the bolts then remove the airflow sensor from the air cleaner housing, along with its sealing ring.

31 Refitting is the reverse of removal, lubricating the sealing ring.

Charge air temperature sensor

32 All models have a charge air temperature sensor fitted. It monitors the air temperature after the air has passed through the inter cooler. The location varies from engine to engine: On the 1.6 litre engine it is fitted to the cylinder head inlet pipe at the rear of the engine. On the 1.8 litre engine it is fitted to the pipework just before the inlet manifold/EGR valve. On the 2.0 litre engines the sensor is fitted to the throttle housing/anti-rattle shut

12.23 Use a 7.5 mm drill bit to position the sensor (2.2 litre engines only)

12.26 Camshaft position sensor (1.8 litre)

12.29 Slide up the red locking clip and disconnect the MAF sensor (2.0 litre shown)

474744444

12.32 The charge air temperature sensor on the 2.2 litre engine

12.35a The MAP sensor on the 1.6 litre …

12.35b … the 2.0 litre …

12.35c …and the 2.2 litre engine

12.44 Remove the cover

down valve. On the 2.2 litre engine the sensor is fitted to the throttle body **(see illustration)**.

Coolant temperature sensor

33 Refer to Chapter 3 Section 6 for removal and refitting details.

Accelerator pedal position sensor

34 The sensor is part of the accelerator pedal. Refer to Section 5 of this Chapter for pedal removal.

Manifold absolute pressure (MAP) sensor

Note: *No MAP sensor is fitted to the 1.8 litre engine*

35 The sensor is mounted on the inlet manifold/throttle body **(see illustrations)**.
36 Remove the engine cover.
37 Ensure the ignition is switched off then disconnect the wiring connector from the sensor.
38 Slacken and remove the retaining bolt and remove the sensor from the vehicle.
39 Refitting is the reverse of removal, tightening the sensor retaining securely.

Stop-light switch

40 The powertrain control module receives a signal from the stop-light switch which indicates when the brakes are being applied. Stop-light switch removal and refitting details can be found in Chapter 9 Section 17.

Powertrain control module (PCM)

Note: *The PCM (Power Control Module) is the engine management control module. It handles all the running of the engine. Whilst Ford call it a PCM, it is more commonly referred to as an ECU (Electronic Control Unit).*
Note: *If a new control module is fitted, it must be programmed using dedicated Ford test equipment. Entrust this task to a Ford dealer or suitably-equipped specialist.*
41 Disconnect the battery negative lead (see Chapter 5 Section 3), then wait at least 2 minutes before commencing work, to allow any stored electrical energy to dissipate.
42 Slacken the left-hand front roadwheel

nuts, then raise the front of the vehicle and support it securely on axle stands (see *Jacking and vehicle support*). Remove the roadwheel.
43 Remove the fixings and remove the left-front wing liner.
44 Remove the screws and then unclip the lower section of the protective cover **(see illustration)**.
45 Where fitted remove the security cover/crash protector. Some model have a 'shear' bolt holding the cover in place **(see illustrations)**. It may be possible to get a pair of locking pliers on the remains of the bolt, but if this fails the bolt will require drilling out (a 3.5mm is ideal).
46 Remove the mounting bolts and lower the control unit. Disconnect the wiring plugs **(see**

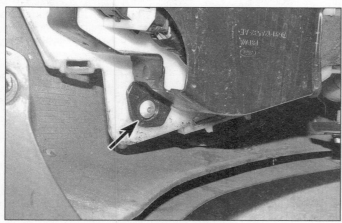

12.45a Remove the 'shear' bolt

12.45b Remove the cover

12.46a Remove the bolts and ...

12.46b ...lower the control unit

12.46c Open the latch and disconnect the wiring plug(s)

12.56 Undo the bolts and move aside the coolant outlet assembly

12.58 The pressure sensor is located at the end of the common rail

Note: *Ford insist that the fuel pressure sensor on the common rail must not be removed.*

Caution: Do not attempt to remove the four high-pressure fuel pipe male unions from the common rail. These parts are not available separately and if disturbed are likely to result in fuel leakage on reassembly.

Removal – 1.8 litre engines

60 Disconnect the high-pressure fuel pipes from the common rail as described in Section 11. Discard the pipes, new ones must be fitted.

61 Ensure the area around the pump-to-fuel supply manifold pipe is absolutely clean. If possible, use a vacuum cleaner to remove any debris.

62 Slacken the nut/bolt securing the pipe support bracket to the pump. Make a note of the fitted position of the clamp on the pipe – it will need to be transferred to the new pipe.

63 Slacken and undo the pump-to-supply manifold pipe unions, then clean the area at the ends of the pipe before removing and discarding it. Plug or cover the openings in the pump and manifold to prevent dirt ingress.

64 Disconnect the wiring plug from the fuel pressure sensor on the supply manifold.

65 Undo the two bolts and remove the fuel supply manifold **(see illustration)**.

66 No further dismantling of the manifold is advised, no parts are available separately.

Removal – 2.0 litre engines

67 Remove the inlet manifold/cylinder head cover as described in Chapter 2C Section 3.

68 Remove the fuel filter as described in Chapter 1 Section 19, then undo the bolts and remove the fuel filter bracket **(see illustration)**.

illustrations). The plugs can be removed with the PCM in place, but access is slightly easier if the PCM is lowered first.

47 Refitting is a reversal of removal, but fit a new shear bolt.

Fuel pressure sensor

48 It is not possible to replace the sensor separately from the fuel rail. Ford advise that no attempt should be made to remove it. If the sensor is faulty, renew the fuel rail as described in this Section.

Fuel (common) rail

Removal – 1.6 litre engines

49 Remove the upper and lower windscreen cowl panels as described in Chapter 12 Section 12.

50 Remove the engine cover by pulling it upwards.

51 Drain the cooling system as described in Chapter 1 Section 25.

52 Slacken the hose clamp and remove the hose from the throttle body. Disconnect the wiring plug from the throttle body.

53 Remove the bolts, slacken the hose clamp and remove the throttle body and inlet hose as a single part.

54 Unclip and remove the insulation panels.

55 At the rear of the engine disconnect the vacuum lines from the EGR vacuum control.

56 Undo the mounting bolts, slacken the clamps, and move aside the coolant pump outlet assembly **(see illustration)**.

57 Clean around the pipe, then undo the unions and remove the high-pressure pipe from the common rail to the high-pressure pump. Seal the openings to prevent contamination.

58 Disconnect the pressure sensor wiring plug from the common rail **(see illustration)**.

59 Unscrew the two rail mounting bolts and manoeuvre it from place **(see illustration)**.

12.59 Common rail mounting bolt/stud

12.65 Undo the two bolts and remove the supply manifold

12.68 Undo the 3 bolts and remove the fuel filter bracket

12.71 The fuel pressure sensor is located on the underside of the common fuel rail

12.74 Remove the EGR pipe

12.76 Disconnect the wiring plug and fuel return hose

69 Make sure the areas around the high-pressure fuel pipe unions from the fuel rail to the injectors, and the high-pressure pump is scrupulously clean and free from debris, etc. If possible, use a vacuum cleaner and a degreaser to clean the area.

70 Undo the unions, then remove the high-pressure fuel pipes from the fuel rail to the injectors, and from the fuel rail to the high-pressure pump. Discard the fuel pipes, new ones must be fitted. Use a second open-ended spanner on the ports to counter-hold when slackening the pipe union **(see illustration 11.9)**. Be prepared for fuel spillage and plug/cover the ports in the injectors, high-pressure pump and fuel rail to prevent dirt ingress.

71 Disconnect the fuel pressure sensor wiring plug **(see illustration)**.

72 Undo the nuts and remove the fuel rail.

Removal 2.2 litre engines

73 Remove the engine cover and then remove the air filter housing as described in Section 3.

74 Unbolt and remove the EGR pipe from the top of the engine **(see illustration)**.

75 Thoroughly clean the area around the fuel rail, fuel injectors, fuel pipe and fuel pump.

76 Disconnect the fuel return hose (anticipate some fuel spillage) and then unplug the fuel pressure sensor connector **(see illustration)**.

77 Remove the crash protector from the fuel pump to gain access to the fuel pump to common rail high pressure pipe. Unbolt the pipe. Seal the opening in the pump and common rail.

78 Remove the high pressure fuel lines and dispose of them – they must be replaced **(see illustration)**. Seal the openings in fuel rail and the fuel injectors.

79 Disconnect the wiring plug from the sensor and then unbolt and remove the fuel rail **(see illustrations)**.

Refitting – all engines

80 Locate the common rail in position, refit and finger-tighten the mounting bolts/nuts.

81 Reconnect the common rail wiring plug(s).

82 Fit the new pump-to-rail high-pressure pipe, and only finger-tighten the unions at first, then tighten the unions to the Stage 1 torque setting, followed by the Stage 2 torque setting. Use a second spanner to counter-hold the union screwed into the pump body.

83 Fit the new set high pressure pipes, and finger-tighten the unions. If it's not possible to fit the new pipes to the injector unions, remove and refit the injectors as described in Section 11, and try again.

84 Tighten the common rail mounting bolts/nuts to the specified torque.

85 Tighten the pipe unions to the Stage 1 torque setting, followed by the Stage 2 setting. Use a second spanner to counter-hold the injector unions. Use a crow's-foot adapter to tighten the union nuts **(see illustration)**.

86 The remainder of refitting is a reversal of removal, noting the following points:

a) Ensure all wiring connectors and harnesses are correctly refitting and secured.

b) Reconnect the battery as described in Chapter 5 Section 3.

c) Observing the precautions listed in Section 1, start the engine and allow it to idle. Check for leaks at the high-pressure

12.78 Remove the high pressure fuel pipes

12.79a Disconnect the wiring plug

12.79b Unbolt and then…

12.79c …remove the fuel rail

12.85 Use a 'crow's-foot' adapter to tighten the union nuts

fuel pipe unions with the engine idling. If satisfactory, increase the engine speed to 3000 rpm and check again for leaks. Take the car for a short road test and check for leaks once again on return. If any leaks are detected, obtain and fit additional new high-pressure fuel pipes as required.

Turbocharger boost pressure regulator valve

1.6 and 2.0 litre engines only

87 Remove the cover from the top of the engine.
88 Disconnect the wiring plug, then undo the 2 regulator retaining nuts **(see illustrations)**.
89 Note their fitted locations and disconnect the vacuum hoses as the regulator is withdrawn.
90 Refitting is a reversal of removal.

Fuel pressure control valve, fuel volume control and fuel metering valve

91 These valves are fitted to the high-pressure injection pump. Apart from the 1.6 litre engine (where the fuel metering valve is listed) they are part of the pump assembly and not available from Ford as a separate part. Third party suppliers may list the valves as an available part.
92 Whilst the fuel metering valve can be removed from the 1.6 litre engine, diagnostic equipment will be required to programme the replacement valve to the pump. This task is best left to a Ford dealer or garage with suitable diagnostic equipment.

Anti-shudder control valve

93 All engines except the 1.8 litre engine have an anti-shudder valve (confusingly called a 'throttle body' by Ford) fitted to the inlet manifold to reduce vibration when the engine is turned off. It achieves this by closing the inlet port, preventing any air from being drawn into the cylinders. The valve body is fitted between the inlet manifold and the intercooler.
94 Remove the engine cover.
95 To remove the valve body, note their fitted positions, and disconnect wiring plugs from the various sensors/motors fitted to the valve body **(see illustration)**.

12.88a Turbocharger boost pressure control valve on the 1.6 litre engine ...

96 Slacken the clamps, and disconnect the air inlet hoses from the valve body.
97 Undo the mounting bolts and remove the valve body **(see illustrations)**.
98 Refitting is a reversal of removal.

13 Turbocharger – description and precautions

Description

1 A turbocharger increases engine efficiency by raising the pressure in the inlet manifold above atmospheric pressure. Instead of the air simply being sucked into the cylinders, it is forced in. Additional fuel is supplied by the injection pump in proportion to the increased air inlet.
2 Energy for the operation of the turbocharger comes from the exhaust gas. The gas flows through a specially-shaped housing (the turbine housing) and in so doing, spins the turbine wheel. The turbine wheel is attached to a shaft, at the end of which is another vaned wheel known as the compressor wheel. The compressor wheel spins in its own housing and compresses the inducted air on the way to the inlet manifold.
3 The compressed air passes through an intercooler. This is an air-to-air heat exchanger, mounted with the radiator at the front of the vehicle. The purpose of the intercooler is to remove from the inducted air some of the heat gained in being compressed. Because cooler

12.88b ... and at the left-hand end of the cylinder head on the 2.2 litre

air is denser, removal of this heat further increases engine efficiency.
4 The turbocharger has adjustable guide vanes controlling the flow of exhaust gas into the turbine. On 1.6 and 2.0 litre engines, the vanes are swivelled by a vacuum unit on the turbocharger, controlled by the boost pressure regulator valve, controlled in turn by the engine management PCM. On 1.8 and 2.2 litre engines, the position of the vanes is controlled by an electric motor attached to the turbocharger, again, controlled by the PCM. At lower engine speeds, the vanes close together, giving a smaller exhaust gas entry port, and therefore higher gas speed, which increases boost pressure at low engine speed. At high engine speed, the vanes are turned to give a larger exhaust gas entry port, and therefore lower gas speed, effectively maintaining a reasonably constant boost pressure over the engine rev range. This is known as a Variable Nozzle Turbocharger (VNT).
5 The turbo shaft is pressure-lubricated by an oil feed pipe from the main oil gallery. The shaft 'floats' on a cushion of oil. A drain pipe returns the oil to the sump.

Precautions

• *The turbocharger operates at extremely high speeds and temperatures. Certain precautions must be observed to avoid premature failure of the turbo or injury to the operator.*
• *Do not operate the turbo with any parts exposed. Foreign objects falling onto the*

12.95 Anti-shudder valve (1.6 litre)

12.97a Anti-shudder valve bolts (2.0 litre)

12.97b Removing the valve on the 2.2 litre engine

14.4a Slacken the clamp and disconnect the turbocharger inlet hose

14.4b Slacken the clamp and disconnect the outlet hose

14.4c Undo the outlet pipe bolt ...

rotating vanes could cause excessive damage and (if ejected) personal injury.
• *Do not race the engine immediately after start-up, especially if it is cold. Give the oil a few seconds to circulate.*
• *Always allow the engine to return to idle speed before switching it off – do not blip the throttle and switch off, as this will leave the turbo spinning without lubrication.*
• *Allow the engine to idle for several minutes before switching off after a high-speed run.*
• *Observe the recommended intervals for oil and filter changing, and use a reputable oil of the specified quality (see Lubricants and fluids). Neglect of oil changing, or use of inferior oil, can cause carbon formation on the turbo shaft and subsequent failure.*

14.4d ... pull the pipe up from the mounting stud ...

14.4e ... and rotate it to remove it

14 Turbocharger – removal and refitting

Note: *On all engines apart from the 1.6 litre, access to the turbocharger is limited. A certain amount of dexterity will be required. Some of the fixings will be accessed from below, whilst others can be reached from the engine bay. Removal of the right-hand driveshaft will improve the access.*
1 On all engines disconnect the battery (Chapter 5 Section 3). On 1.8, 2.0 and 2.2 litre engines remove the upper and lower windscreen cowl panels (Chapter 12 Section 12).
2 Apply the handbrake, then jack up the front of the vehicle and support it on axle stands (see *Jacking and vehicle support*). Undo the bolts and remove the engine undershield.

1.6 litre engines

Removal

3 Place a sheet of thick cardboard over the rear of the radiator to protect it from accidental damage.
4 Slacken the clamps, undo the bolts, and remove the air ducts to and from the turbocharger and air filter assembly **(see illustrations)**. Note their fitted positions and disconnect the various wiring plugs as the assembly is withdrawn.
5 Slacken the clamps, undo the bolts

14.5a Intercooler inlet pipe bolt on the transmission housing ...

14.5b ... and above the oil filter

and remove the intercooler inlet pipe **(see illustrations)**.
6 Undo the mounting bolts **(see illustration)** and remove the heat shield from above turbocharger/catalytic converter.

14.6 Undo the bolts and remove the heat shield above the turbocharger

7 Undo the 2 bolts and remove the heat shield above the exhaust manifold.
8 Disconnect the vacuum hose from the turbocharger wastegate control assembly **(see illustration)**.

14.8 Disconnect the vacuum hose

14.9 Turbocharger oil supply and return pipes

14.11 Slacken the clamp securing the catalytic converter to the turbocharger

14.12 Turbocharger upper retaining nuts

9 Undo the oil supply pipe banjo bolts and recover the sealing washers **(see illustration)**. The filter fitted to the banjo bolt at the lower end of the oil supply pipe must be removed, using pliers, and discarded.

10 Slacken the retaining clip and disconnect the oil return pipe from the turbocharger and cylinder block.

11 Make a note of its fitted position, then slacken the clamp securing the catalytic converter to the turbocharger **(see illustration)**. Slacken the catalytic converter mounting bolts.

12 Unscrew the four nuts, and the nut securing the support bracket, then remove the turbocharger from the exhaust manifold **(see illustration)**.

Inspection

13 With the turbocharger removed, inspect the housing for cracks or other visible damage.

14 Spin the turbine or the compressor wheel, to verify that the shaft is intact and to feel for excessive shake or roughness. Some play is normal, since in use, the shaft is 'floating' on a film of oil. Check that the wheel vanes are undamaged.

15 If oil contamination of the exhaust or induction passages is apparent, it is likely that turbo shaft oil seals have failed.

16 No DIY repair of the turbo is possible and none of the internal or external parts are available separately. If the turbocharger is suspect in any way a complete new unit must be obtained.

14.24 Turbocharger wastegate actuator wiring plug

Refitting

17 Refitting is a reverse of the removal procedure, bearing in mind the following points:

a) *Renew the turbocharger retaining nuts and gaskets.*

b) *When refitting the oil supply pipe, it's absolutely essential that the banjo bolts are tightened without placing the pipe under stress.*

c) *If a new turbocharger is being fitted, change the engine oil and filter.*

d) *Prime the turbocharger by injecting clean engine oil through the oil feed pipe union before reconnecting the union.*

e) *Disable the ignition and crank the engine to ensure oil is delivered to the turbocharger before restarting.*

1.8 litre engines

Removal

18 The turbocharger should only be removed with the engine completely cool.

19 Remove the catalytic converter as described in Section 18.

20 Remove the air cleaner and inlet duct as described in Section 3.

21 Remove the EGR tube or cooler, as described in Chapter 4B.

22 Using the information in Section 16 if necessary, disconnect the intercooler air ducts from the turbocharger and inlet manifold, and remove them from the top of the engine – there is no need to remove the intercooler itself.

23 Undo the nuts and remove the turbocharger to exhaust manifold retaining clamp.

24 Disconnect the turbocharger wastegate actuator wiring plug **(see illustration)**.

25 Undo the nut securing the turbocharger oil supply pipe support bracket, then undo the banjo bolt and disconnect the oil supply pipe from the cylinder block. Note that the banjo bolt cannot be removed from the pipe. Dispose of the pipe – it must be replaced.

26 Slacken the 3 nuts securing the turbocharger support bracket to the cylinder block.

27 Undo the bolts and remove the oil return pipe from the underside of the turbocharger. Discard the gaskets.

28 Undo the 2 bolts securing the turbocharger to the support bracket, and manoeuvre it from position.

29 No further dismantling of the turbocharger is recommended. Interfering with the wastegate setting may lead to a reduction in performance, or could result in engine damage. No parts appear to be available separately for the turbocharger.

30 If on inspection there are any signs of internal oil contamination on the turbine or compressor wheels, this indicates failure of the turbocharger oil seals. Renewing these seals is a job best left to a turbocharger specialist. In the event of any problem with the turbocharger, one of these specialists will usually be able to rebuild a defective unit, or offer a rebuilt unit on an exchange basis, either of which will prove cheaper than a new unit.

Refitting

31 Refitting is a reversal of removal, noting the following points:

a) *Clean the mating surfaces, use a new exhaust manifold gasket, and tighten the manifold bolts to the specified torque.*

b) *Refit and tighten the engine rear mounting bolt to the specified torque.*

c) *Fit a new turbocharger oil supply pipe*

d) *Use new gaskets for the turbocharger oil return connections.*

e) *When refitting the EGR tube/cooler, offer it into position, and hand-tighten the bolts. Position the new clamp as noted on removal, tighten the clamp nut/bolt to the specified torque, then tighten the remaining bolts.*

f) *Refer to Section 18 when refitting the catalytic converter. (A new clamp should be fitted).*

g) *On models with the EGR cooler, top-up the cooling system as necessary (see 'Weekly checks.').*

h) *If a new turbocharger is being fitted, change the engine oil and filter.*

i) *Prime the turbocharger by injecting clean engine oil through the oil feed pipe union before reconnecting the union.*

j) *Disable the ignition and crank the engine to ensure oil is delivered to the turbocharger before restarting.*

14.36 Turbocharger inlet hose support bracket bolt

14.40 Undo the bolts/nuts and remove the bracket under the turbocharger

14.41 Turbocharger vane position sensor/ actuator wiring plug and vacuum hose

2.0 litre engines

Note: *Models from built from March 2010 have a water cooled turbocharger fitted.*

Removal

32 Drain the cooling system as described in Chapter 1 Section 25.

33 Remove the cover from the top of the engine.

34 Depress the release button and disconnect the engine breather hose from the inlet manifold.

35 Remove the right-hand driveshaft as described in Chapter 8 Section 2.

36 Undo the bolt securing the turbocharger inlet hose support bracket **(see illustration)**.

37 Slacken the clamp and disconnect the outlet pipe from the turbocharger.

38 Remove the catalytic converter as described in Section 18.

39 Remove the catalytic converter support bracket.

40 Undo the nuts/bolts and remove the support bracket from the underside of the turbocharger **(see illustration)**.

41 Note their fitted positions, then disconnect the vacuum hose and wiring plug from the wastegate control assembly **(see illustration)**.

42 Undo the bolts and detach the inlet hose from the turbocharger **(see illustration)**. Depress the release clip and detach the pipe from the cylinder head cover.

43 Release the clamp and disconnect the heater core-to-bypass coolant hose.

44 Slacken the clamp, remove the support bracket bolt, undo the connection bolts and

14.42 Undo the two bolts securing the inlet hose

remove the bypass hose **(see illustration)**. Recover the O-ring seal, and renew if necessary.

45 Undo the banjo bolts and securing the oil supply pipe to the cylinder block. Renew the sealing washers. Note that a small filter is fitted into the banjo bolt – renew it **(see illustration)**.

46 Undo the 2 bolts securing the oil return hose to the underside of the turbocharger **(see illustration)**. Renew the gasket.

47 Undo the nuts and separate the turbocharger from the manifold **(see illustration)**.

48 If required, undo the banjo bolt and detach the oil supply pipe from the turbocharger. Renew the seals.

Refitting

49 Refitting is a reversal of removal, noting the following points:

14.44 Coolant bypass pipe bolt

a) *Ensure all mating surfaces are clean and dry.*

b) *Renew all O-rings, seals and gaskets.*

c) *Always fit a new filter to the oil supply banjo bolt*

d) *Tighten all fasteners to the specified torque where available.*

e) *If a new turbocharger is being fitted, change the engine oil and filter.*

f) *Prime the turbocharger by injecting clean engine oil through the oil feed pipe union before reconnecting the union.*

g) *Disable the ignition and crank the engine to ensure oil is delivered to the turbocharger before restarting.*

2.2 litre engine

Removal

50 Drain the engine coolant as described in Chapter 1 Section 25.

14.45 The oil feed banjo bolt incorporates a filter

14.46 Turbocharger oil return hose retaining bolts

14.47 Undo the nuts securing the turbocharger to the manifold

14.54a Remove the coolant hose from the pipe …

14.54b … and from the engine block (where fitted)

14.54c Disconnect the temperature sensor

14.54d Remove the bolts and …

14.54e … manoeuvre the heatshield out from the rear of the engine

54 Remove the heatshield **(see illustrations)** and then disconnect the coolant supply and return hoses.

55 Unbolt the oil supply pipe and the oil drain pipe **(see illustration)**. Anticipate some oil spillage as the pipes are removed. Dispose of the oil feed pipe – a new one must be fitted.

56 Remove the mounting bolts from the exhaust manifold and then from the support bracket. Remove the turbocharger. The turbocharger is heavy and the help of an assistant will be required to manoeuvre the turbocharger out of the engine bay **(see illustrations)**. Removal is awkward, we found the best method was up and out from the left-hand side of the engine.

51 Remove the EGR valve (and cooler) as described in Chapter 4B Section 4 and then remove the catalytic converter as described in Section 18.

52 Remove the air filter housing and then remove the turbocharger air inlet hose.

53 Remove the intercooler hose and disconnect the wiring plug from the control unit.

14.55a Unbolt the oil supply pipe …

14.55b … recover the seals …

14.55c … and remove the filter

14.55d Remove the oil return pipe

14.56a Remove the bolts and …

14.56b … remove the turbocharger

14.57a Fit a new gasket

14.57b Always fit a new filter

Refitting

57 Refitting is a reversal of removal, noting the following points:

a) *Ensure all mating surfaces are clean and dry.*

b) *Renew all O-rings, seals and gaskets* **(see illustration).**

c) *Always fit a new filter to the oil supply banjo bolt* **(see illustration).**

d) *Tighten all fasteners to the specified torque where available.*

e) *If a new turbocharger is being fitted, change the engine oil and filter.*

f) *Prime the turbocharger by injecting clean engine oil through the oil feed pipe union before reconnecting the union.*

g) *Disable the ignition and crank the engine to ensure oil is delivered to the turbocharger before restarting.*

15 Turbocharger –
examination and overhaul

1 With the turbocharger removed, inspect the housing for cracks or other visible damage.

2 Spin the turbine or the compressor wheel to verify that the shaft is intact and to feel for excessive shake or roughness. Some play is normal since in use the shaft is 'floating' on a film of oil. Check that the wheel vanes are undamaged.

3 The wastegate and actuator are integral with the turbocharger, and cannot be checked or renewed separately. Consult a Ford dealer or other specialist if it is thought that the wastegate may be faulty.

4 If the exhaust or induction passages are oil-contaminated, the turbo shaft oil seals have probably failed. (On the induction side, this will also have contaminated the intercooler, where applicable, which if necessary should be flushed with a suitable solvent.)

5 No DIY repair of the turbo is possible. A new unit may be available on an exchange basis.

16 Intercooler –
removal and refitting

Removal

1 Raise the front of the vehicle and support it securely on axle stands (see *Jacking and vehicle support*).

2 Undo the fasteners and remove the engine undershield, followed by the air deflector at the base of the bumper cover **(see illustrations).**

16.2a Remove the undershield and then...

16.2b ...remove the air deflector

16.5a Undo the left-hand and then…

16.5b …the right-hand mounting bolt

16.5c Lower down the intercooler

3 On most models the intercooler can be removed after the supply and return hose clips have been released (and the hoses disconnected). However access to the hose clips is limited, but can be improved if the radiator support panel is removed first. The radiator, cooling fan and condenser must now be supported from above as described in Chapter 3 Section 7, if this approach is adopted.
4 Remove the intercooler hoses.
5 Undo the 2 retaining bolts, lift the intercooler upwards to disengage the upper mounting lugs, and lower the intercooler from position **(see illustrations)**.

Refitting
6 Refitting is a reversal of removal.

17 Manifolds –
removal and refitting

Inlet manifold

1.6 litre engines
1 The inlet manifold is integral with the cylinder head cover and EGR valve – refer to Chapter 2A and Chapter 4B.

1.8 litre engines
2 The manifold is integral with the EGR valve – refer to Chapter 4B.

2.0 litre engines
3 The manifold is integral with the cylinder head cover – refer to Chapter 2C Section 3.

2.2 litre engines
4 Disconnect the battery, as described in Chapter 5 Section 3.
5 Remove the fuel filter as described in Chapter 1 Section 19.
6 Remove the main fuel filter mounting and then lower section of the fuel filter mounting **(see illustrations)** – note that one bolt is hidden behind the oil cooler supply pipe.
7 Remove the EGR pipe from the inlet manifold **(see illustration)**. Note that access to the pipe at the EGR valve is difficult and

17.6a Remove the filter mounting bracket…

17.6b …to access the lower bracket

17.6c The hidden bolt

17.6d Remove the bracket

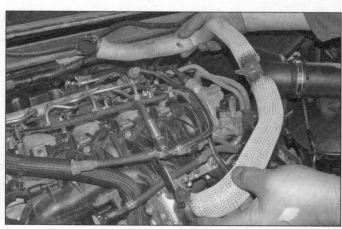

17.7 Remove the EGR pipe

17.9a Unclip and then...

17.9b ...remove the wiring loom

17.13a Remove the bolts. Note the hidden bolt (A)

17.13b Lift off the manifold and...

requires the release of the wiring loom from the top of the valve cover.

8 Unplug the wiring loom from the throttle body, boost pressure sensor and the temperature sensor. Remove the throttle body as described in Section 12.

9 Disconnect the wiring plugs from the fuel injectors and then release the wiring loom from the retaining clips **(see illustrations)**. Move the loom to the side.

10 Release the fuel injector bleed hose from each fuel injector – seal the fuel line and the injector as soon as the fuel return line is removed.

11 Disconnect the fuel return and supply pipes from the fuel pump. Seal the openings on the pump and then unbolt the oil filler pipe from the cylinder head. Remove the fuel lines from the engine.

12 Disconnect the vacuum line from the control solenoid at the left-hand end of the inlet manifold.

13 Note the position of the lower hidden manifold bolt. Remove the inlet manifold bolts and remove the inlet manifold. Recover the seals from the cylinder head and the manifold – if they are in good condition they can be reused **(see illustrations)**.

14 Refitting is a reversal of removal. If the gaskets are in good condition, they can be reused.

Exhaust manifold

Removal

15 On all engines, remove the turbocharger as described in Section 14.

16 On 1.6 litre engines, remove the small heat

17.13c ...recover the lower...

17.13d ...and the upper gaskets

17.18 Undo the nuts and recover the manifold spacers – 2.0 litre

17.19a Remove the heat shields

17.19b Remove the nuts …

17.19c …recover the studs …

shield and then unbolt the manifold. Recover the gasket.

17 On the 1.8 litre engine remove the EGR cooler (Chapter 4B) and then remove the manifold.

18 On 2.0 litre engines, undo the nuts securing the exhaust manifold to the cylinder head, and recover the spacers **(see illustration)**. Pull the manifold from the mounting studs. Recover the gasket.

19 On 2.2 litre engines remove the heat shields. Remove the nut/studs and spacers. Slide of the manifold and recover the gasket **(see illustrations)**.

Refitting

20 Examine the studs for signs of damage and corrosion; remove traces of corrosion, and repair or renew any damaged studs.

21 Ensure the mating surfaces of the exhaust manifold and cylinder head are clean and dry.

Position the new gasket **(see illustration)** and refit the exhaust manifold to the cylinder head. Tighten the nuts to the specified torque.

22 The remainder of refitting is a reversal of removal, noting the following points:

a) Tighten all fasteners to their specified torque where available.

b) Apply a little high-temperature anti-seize grease (Copperslip) to the manifold studs.

c) Top-up the coolant system as described in 'Weekly checks.'.

d) Check and, if necessary, top-up the oil level as described in Weekly checks.

18 Exhaust system – general information and component renewal

1 The exhaust system consists of several sections: the front pipe with the catalytic converter and the rear section with either, an intermediate silencer or particulate filter. Single or twin rear silencers complete the

17.19d …and slide off the manifold

17.21 Fit a new gasket

18.11a Unscrew the pressure take-off union from the side of the catalyst/filter ...

18.11b ... and the one at the base

18.20 Catalytic converter nuts

system. If required, the rear silencer can be renewed independently of the remainder of the system. Depending on the engine size and exhaust system Ford supply an adapter sleeve (and clamps) that enables the factory fitted system to be cut away and the rear silencer replaced without the need to replace the complete system.

2 The exhaust system is joined together by a mixture of flanged, or sliding joints. Apply plenty of penetrating fluid to the fasteners prior to removal, undo the fasteners, unhook the rubber mountings, and manoeuvre the system from under the vehicle.

3 On all models (except for models fitted with the 1.6 litre engine) then removal of the catalytic converter is considerably easier if the right-hand driveshaft is removed first.

4 Each section is refitted by reversing the removal sequence, noting the following points:
a) *Ensure that all traces of corrosion have been removed from the flanges and renew all gaskets.*
b) *Inspect the rubber mountings for signs of damage or deterioration, and renew as necessary.*
c) *Prior to tightening the exhaust system fasteners to the specified torque, ensure that all rubber mountings are correctly located, and that there is adequate clearance between the exhaust system and vehicle underbody.*

Catalytic converter – 1.6 litre engines

Note: *On 1.6 litre engines the particulate filter is combined with the catalytic converter into a single unit.*

5 Remove the plastic cover from the top of the engine.

6 Raise the front of the vehicle and support it securely on axle stands (see *Jacking and vehicle support*).

7 Remove the cooling fan and shroud as described in Chapter 3 Section 5.

8 Undo the bolt securing the intercooler inlet pipe bracket to the cylinder block.

9 Slacken the clamps and remove the intercooler inlet pipe assembly.

10 Disconnect the wiring plug, and unscrew the temperature sensor from the catalytic converter/particulate filter.

11 Note their fitted positions, and disconnect the pressure take-off hoses from the catalytic converter/particulate filter **(see illustrations)**.

12 Undo the bolts and remove the heat shield over the catalytic converter.

13 Slacken the clamp securing the catalytic converter to the turbocharger. Note its fitted position to aid refitment.

14 Remove the heat shield bracket.

15 Manoeuvre the catalytic converter/filter from place.

Catalytic converter – 1.8 litre engines

16 Raise the front of the vehicle and support it securely on axle stands (see *Jacking and vehicle support*).

17 Undo the fasteners and remove the engine undershield.

18 Unless the converter (or flexible joint) is to be replaced, support the flexible joint with wooden splints and cable ties.

19 Undo the bolts and remove the subframe mounting bracket.

20 Undo the nuts securing the catalytic converter to the turbocharger **(see illustration)**.

21 Undo the catalytic converter support bracket nuts, release the mounting rubbers, and manoeuvre the catalytic converter from position.

Catalytic converter – 2.0 litre engines

22 Remove the engine cover and then remove the upper and lower windscreen cowl

18.27 Catalytic converter to turbocharger clamp

panels as described in Chapter 12 Section 12.

23 Raise the front of the vehicle and support it securely on axle stands (see *Jacking and vehicle support*).

24 Undo the fasteners and remove the engine undershield.

25 Attach wooden 'splints' each side of the exhaust flexible section using cable ties. This is to prevent excessive bending of the section as it's disconnected. Undo the nuts securing the flexible section to the intermediate section. Pull the intermediate section rearwards, and allow the exhaust to hang down.

26 Disconnect the wiring plug, then unscrew the temperature sensor (where fitted) from the front section of the catalytic converter.

27 Slacken the clamp securing the catalytic converter to the turbocharger **(see illustration)**.

28 Undo the catalytic converter support bracket nuts, release the mounting rubbers, and manoeuvre the catalytic converter from position.

Catalytic converter 2.2 litre engines

29 Remove the engine cover and then remove the upper and lower windscreen cowl panels as described in Chapter 12 Section 12.

30 Raise the front of the vehicle and support it securely on axle stands (see *Jacking and vehicle support*).

31 Undo the fasteners and remove the engine undershield.

32 Disconnect the wiring plug from the temperature sensor and then remove the turbocharger to intercooler pipe **(see illustration)**.

18.32 Remove the intercooler pipes

18.34 Disconnect the fuel line

33 Attach wooden 'splints' each side of the exhaust flexible section using cable ties. This is to prevent excessive bending of the section as it's disconnected. Undo the nuts securing the flexible section to the intermediate section.

Pull the intermediate section rearwards, and allow the exhaust to hang down.
34 On models fitted with a fuel vapouriser disconnect the fuel supply and the unplug the electrical connector **(see illustration)**.
35 Remove the rear subframe support panel and then remove the exhaust support bracket from the subframe **(see illustration)**.
36 Unbolt and remove the converter support bracket and then (where fitted) disconnect the wiring plug from the second temperature sensor.
37 Remove the main turbocharger to catalytic converter clamp and then manoeuvre the converter from the vehicle.

Particulate filter

1.6 litre engines

38 The filter is part of the catalytic converter. Removal of the catalytic converter is described earlier in this section.

2.0 and 2.2 litre engines

39 Raise the front of the vehicle and support it securely on axle stands (see *Jacking and vehicle support*).
40 Attach wooden 'splints' each side of the exhaust flexible section using cable ties. This is to prevent excessive bending of the section as it's disconnected. Undo the nuts securing the flexible section to the particulate filter.
41 Note their fitted positions, and disconnect the pressure pipes and sensors from the particulate filter **(see illustration)**.
42 Undo the nuts securing the rear exhaust section to the particulate filter, and manoeuvre the filter from position.

Rear silencer

43 Slacken the various clamps securing the exhaust pipe/silencer, then release it from the rubber mountings.

18.35 Remove the mounting

18.41 Disconnect the pressure sensor hoses (A) and the sensors (B) from the particulate filter

Chapter 4 Part B
Emission control systems

Contents

Degrees of difficulty

Easy, suitable for novice with little experience	Fairly easy, suitable for beginner with some experience	Fairly difficult, suitable for competent DIY mechanic	Difficult, suitable for experienced DIY mechanic	Very difficult, suitable for expert DIY or professional

Specifications

Torque wrench settings	Nm	lb ft
EGR cooler/valve to cylinder head		
1.6 litre engine		
Mounting bolts	20	15
EGR pipe	8	5
1.8 litre engine		
Cooler lower pipe bolts	23	17
Cooler upper pipe bolts	10	7
Manifold bolts	24	18
Mounting bolts	10	7
2.0 litre engine	10	7
2.2 litre engine	10	7

1 General Information

1 All models covered by this manual have various features built into the fuel and exhaust systems to help minimise harmful emissions. These features fall broadly into two categories; crankcase emission control and exhaust emission control. The main features of these systems are as follows.

Crankcase emission control

2 To reduce the emission of unburned hydrocarbons from the crankcase into the atmosphere, the engine is sealed and the blow-by gases and oil vapour are drawn from inside the crankcase, through a wire mesh oil separator, into the inlet tract to be burned by the engine during normal combustion.
3 Under all conditions, the gases are forced out of the crankcase by the (relatively) higher crankcase pressure. All diesel engines have a ventilation valve in the camshaft cover, to control the flow of gases from the crankcase.

Exhaust emission control
EGR system

4 An Exhaust Gas Recirculation (EGR) system is fitted to all diesel-engined models. This reduces the level of nitrogen oxides produced during combustion by introducing a proportion of the exhaust gas back into the inlet manifold, under certain engine operating conditions, via a plunger valve. The system is controlled electronically by the engine management system. On some models, a cooler is fitted to the EGR, through which engine coolant is passed. This lowers the temperature of the recirculated gas, thus reducing the formation of NOx (oxides of nitrogen) in the exhaust gases.

Particulate filter

5 A Diesel Particulate Filter (DPF) is fitted as standard to all models apart from those fitted with the 1.8 litre engines. On 1.6 litre models the particulate filter is incorporated into the catalytic convertor. On all other engines the particulate filter is a separate component mounted after the catalytic convertor.
6 The DPF has front and rear pressure transducers fitted and when the pressure differential reaches a pre-set point the PCM will initiate a regeneration phase. By initiating a post TDC fuel injection strategy the temperature in the particulate filter can be raised and the accumulated soot particles burnt off.
7 Some later models have a fuel vapouriser system fitted to regenerate the particulate filter. On these models an additional glow plug and fuel injector are fitted in the exhaust system. When the PCM detects that the DPF is full (via the pressure differential between the sensors) vapourised fuel is injected in the exhaust system, where it ignites and burns off the accumulated soot particles.

Catalytic converters

8 An oxidation catalyst is fitted in the exhaust system of all diesel-engined models. This has the effect of removing a large proportion of the gaseous hydrocarbons, carbon monoxide and particulates present in the exhaust gas.

2 Catalytic converter – general information and precautions

1 An oxidation catalytic converter is fitted downstream from the turbocharger.

2 The catalytic converter is a reliable and simple device, which needs no maintenance in itself, but there are some facts of which an owner should be aware if the converter is to function properly for its full service life.

a) *DO NOT use fuel or engine oil additives – these may contain substances harmful to the catalytic converter.*

b) *DO NOT continue to use the vehicle if the engine burns oil to the extent of leaving a visible trail of blue smoke.*

c) *Remember that the catalytic converter operates at very high temperatures. DO NOT, therefore, park the vehicle in dry undergrowth, over long grass or piles of dead leaves, after a long run.*

d) *Remember that the catalytic converter is FRAGILE. Do not strike it with tools during servicing work.*

e) *The catalytic converter used on a well-maintained and well-driven vehicle should last for between 50 000 and 100 000 miles. If the converter is no longer effective, it must be renewed*

3 Crankcase emission control system – checking and component renewal

Checking

1 The components of this system require no attention other than to check that the hoses are clear and undamaged.

Oil separator

1.6 litre engines

2 The oil separator is integral with the cylinder head cover/inlet manifold – refer to Chapter 2A Section 4.

1.8 litre engines

3 The oil separator is located at the left-hand end of the cylinder head. Pull the plastic cover

3.5a Unscrew the mounting bolts...

3.5b ...and remove the separator from the engine

on the top of the engine upwards from its mountings at the front and right-hand edges, then pull it forwards.

4 Release the clamps and disconnect the breather hoses from the separator.

5 Undo the retaining bolts and remove the oil separator **(see illustrations)**.

6 Refitting is a reversal of removal.

2.0 litre engines

7 The oil separator is integral with the cylinder head cover/inlet manifold – refer to Chapter 2C Section 3.

2.2 litre engines

8 The oil separator is integral with the cylinder head cover/inlet manifold – refer to Chapter 2D Section 4.

4 Exhaust emission control systems – checking and component renewal

Checking

1 Checking of the system as a whole entails a close visual inspection of all hoses, pipes and connections for condition and security. Apart from this, any known or suspected faults should be attended to by a Ford dealer or suitably-equipped specialist.

Catalytic converter

2 Removal of the catalytic converter is described in Chapter 4A, Section 18.

EGR solenoid/valve

1.6 litre engines

3 Disconnect the battery negative lead as described in Chapter 5 Section 3.

4 Remove the engine cover from the top of the engine.

5 Remove the wiper arms and then remove the upper and lower windscreen cowl panels as described Chapter 12 Section 12.

6 Remove the crash protector and then remove the fuel filter (as described in Chapter 1 Section 19).

7 Disconnect the EGR valve wiring plug.

8 Make a note of its fitted position, then remove the clamp securing the pipe to the EGR valve **(see illustration)**.

9 Undo and then remove the valve. Note that if a new valve is fitted, the base setting must be programmed using Ford specialist diagnostic equipment (IDS).

10 Refitting is a reversal of removal.

1.8 litre engines

11 Proceed as described in Paragraphs 3 to 7 in this Section.

12 Remove the exhaust manifold as described in Chapter 4A Section 17.

13 Disconnect the vacuum hose from the MAP sensor on the inlet manifold.

14 Note their fitted positions, then disconnect the various wiring plugs from the EGR valve/inlet manifold **(see illustration)**.

15 Unclip the EGR cooler coolant hose from the support bracket.

16 Slacken the clamp and disconnect the air hose from the inlet manifold **(see illustration)**.

4.8 Release the EGR pipe clamp

4.14 Disconnect the wiring plug from the EGR valve

4.16 Air inlet hose clamp (1) and MAP sensor vacuum hose (2)

4.20 Undo the nut and remove the stud securing the EGR pipe support bracket

4.21a Release the EGR pipe clamp ...

4.21b ... and undo the 2 bolts securing the pipe to the valve

17 Undo the retaining nuts/bolts and remove the inlet manifold. Note that the EGR valve is integral with the manifold.
18 Refitting is a reversal of removal.

2.0 litre engines

19 Proceed as described in Paragraphs 3 to 7 in this Section.
20 Undo the EGR pipe support bracket retaining nut **(see illustration)**.
21 Release the clamp securing the EGR pipe to the inlet manifold, and the 2 bolts securing the pipe to the EGR valve **(see illustrations)**.
22 Disconnect the wiring plug from the EGR valve.
23 Undo the bolts securing the EGR cooler to the valve **(see illustration)**.
24 Slacken the EGR valve lower retaining bolt
25 Undo the 2 remaining retaining bolts and remove the valve. Note that if a new valve is fitted, the base setting must be programmed using Ford specialist diagnostic equipment (IDS).
26 Refitting is a reversal of removal.

2.2 litre engine

27 On the 2.2 litre engine the valve is removed with the EGR cooler as described below.

EGR cooler

28 Drain the cooling system as described in Chapter 1 Section 25.

1.6 litre engines

29 Proceed as described in Paragraphs 3 to 7 in this Section.

4.23 EGR cooler to valve bolts

4.30 Injector wiring harness bolts

30 Disconnect the injector wiring plugs, then undo the bolts and move the injector wiring harness guide to one side **(see illustration)**.
31 Release the clamps and disconnect the coolant hoses from the EGR cooler **(see illustration)**.
32 Release the clamp securing the EGR pipe to the cooler, then undo the 2 bolts securing the pipe to the inlet manifold **(see illustration)**. Remove the pipe.
33 Release the clamp securing the EGR cooler to the EGR valve, then undo the nut/bolt and remove the cooler **(see illustration)**.
34 Refitting is a reversal of removal.

1.8 litre engines

35 Proceed as described in Paragraphs 3 to 7 in this Section.
36 Release the clamps and disconnect the coolant hoses from the EGR cooler.

37 Undo the bolts securing the cooler to the exhaust manifold and inlet manifold, then manoeuvre it from position.
38 Refitting is a reversal of removal.

2.0 litre engines

39 Proceed as described in Paragraphs 3 to 7 in this Section.
40 Pull the coolant expansion tank upwards to release its mountings. Move it to one side.
41 Raise the front of the vehicle and support it securely on axle stands (see *Jacking and vehicle support*). Remove the engine undershield.
42 Position a trolley jack under the engine, with a block of wood between the jack head and take the weight of the engine.
43 Undo the bolts securing the right-hand engine mounting to the inner wing, then carefully pull the engine forwards a little.

4.31 Release the EGR cooler hose clamps

4.32 EGR pipe-to-manifold bolts

4.33 Release the clamp securing the EGR cooler to the valve

4.45 EGR cooler pipe clamp and coolant hose clamps

4.47 EGR 'elbow'-to-manifold nuts

4.50 Remove the pipe from the top of the engine

4.51 Remove the pipe (one bolt hidden)

4.52a Remove the special bolts ...

4.52b ...and then remove the cooler/EGR valve assembly

44 Release the clamp and disconnect the turbocharger inlet pipe breather hose.

45 Prise out the wire clip and disconnect the heater-to-EGR cooler hose, then release the clamp and disconnect the coolant bypass-to-EGR cooler hose **(see illustration)**.

46 Undo the nuts and remove the EGR tube heat shield.

47 Release the clamp, undo the 2 retaining nuts, and remove the EGR cooler 'elbow'

connecting pipe **(see illustration)**. Renew the gasket.

48 Undo the 2 retaining bolts, and remove the EGR cooler.

2.2 litre engine

49 Proceed as described in paragraphs 3 to 7 of this section.

50 Disconnect the coolant hoses and then remove the EGR to inlet manifold pipe **(see illustration)**.

51 Disconnect the wiring plug and then unbolt the transfer pipe **(see illustration)**.

52 Remove the special bolts and remove the complete cooler and EGR valve **(see illustrations)**.

53 With the assembly on the bench separate the cooler from the EGR valve.

Particulate filter

54 Particulate filter renewal is described in Chapter 4A Section 18, Exhaust system.

Chapter 5
Starting and charging systems

Contents

Degrees of difficulty

Easy, suitable for novice with little experience	Fairly easy, suitable for beginner with some experience	Fairly difficult, suitable for competent DIY mechanic	Difficult, suitable for experienced DIY mechanic	Very difficult, suitable for expert DIY or professional

Specifications

System type . . . . 12 volt, negative earth, with Smart Regenerative Charging (SRG)

Battery
Type . . . . Silver-calcium (marked Ca) enhanced flooded battery.
Capacity . . . . 50, 60, 70 or 80 Ah (depending on model)
Charge condition:
  Minimum. . . . . 12.2 volts
  Normal . . . . 14.5 to 14.9 volts
  Refresh phase. . . . . 15.2 volts

Alternator
Output . . . . 120 or 150 A

Torque wrench settings

	Nm	lbf ft
Alternator mounting bolts:		
1.6 litre models		
Front upper and lower bolts	45	33
Rear upper bolt	39	29
1.8 litre models	24	18
1.8 litre model coupler bolts	24	18
2.0 litre models		
Front upper and lower bolts	41	30
Rear upper bolt	49	36
2.2 litre models	48	38
Auxiliary belt tensioner bolt	45	33
Auxiliary belt idler pulley bolt	48	35
Battery disconnection post	24	18
Glow plugs:		
1.6 litre models	8	6
1.8 litre models	15	11
2.0 litre models	10	7
2.2 litre models	8	6
Starter motor mounting bolts:		
1.6 litre models	25	18
1.8 litre models	40	30
2.0 litre models	40	30
2.2 litre models	40	30

1 General information and precautions

General information

1 The engine electrical system consists mainly of the charging, starting, and diesel preheating systems. Because of their engine-related functions, these components are covered separately from the body electrical devices such as the lights, instruments, etc (which are covered in Chapter 12).

2 The electrical system is of the 12 volt negative earth type.

3 The battery is of the low-maintenance or maintenance-free (sealed for life) type, and is charged by the alternator, which is belt-driven from the crankshaft pulley.

4 The starter motor is of the pre-engaged type, incorporating an integral solenoid. On starting, the solenoid moves the drive pinion into engagement with the flywheel ring gear before the starter motor is energised. Once the engine has started, a one-way clutch prevents the motor armature being driven by the engine until the pinion disengages from the flywheel.

5 Further details of the various systems are given in the relevant Sections of this Chapter. While some repair procedures are given, the usual course of action is to renew the component concerned.

Precautions

⚠️ *Warning: It is necessary to take extra care when working on the electrical system to avoid damage to semi-conductor devices (diodes and transistors), and to avoid the risk of personal injury. In addition to the precautions given in Safety first!, observe the following when working on the system:*

• *Always remove rings, watches, etc before working on the electrical system. Even with the battery disconnected, capacitive discharge could occur if a component's live terminal is earthed through a metal object. This could cause a shock or nasty burn.*

• *Do not reverse the battery connections. Components such as the alternator, electronic control units, or any other components having semi-conductor circuitry could be irreparably damaged.*

• *Never disconnect the battery terminals, the alternator, any electrical wiring or any test instruments when the engine is running.*

• *Do not allow the engine to turn the alternator when the alternator is not connected.*

• *Never test for alternator output by 'flashing' the output lead to earth.*

• *Always ensure that the battery negative lead is disconnected when working on the electrical system.*

• *If the engine is being started using jump leads and a slave battery, connect the batteries positive-to-positive and negative-*

to-negative (see Jump starting). This also applies when connecting a battery charger.

• *Never use an ohmmeter of the type incorporating a hand-cranked generator for circuit or continuity testing.*

• *Before using electric-arc welding equipment on the car, disconnect the battery, alternator and components such as the electronic control units (where applicable) to protect them from the risk of damage.*

2 Battery – testing and charging

Testing

1 All models are fitted with a maintenance-free battery and may have a built-in charge condition indicator. The indicator is located in the top of the battery casing, and indicates the condition of the battery from its colour. The charge conditions denoted by the colour of the indicator should be printed on a label attached to the battery – if not, consult a Ford dealer or automotive electrician for advice.

2 The only way to test the battery is by using a voltmeter or specialist battery tester (see illustration). Connect the voltmeter across the battery and note the voltage. The test is only accurate if the battery has not been subjected to any kind of charge for the previous six hours. If this is not the case, switch on the headlights for 30 seconds, then wait four to five minutes before testing the battery after switching off the headlights. All other electrical circuits must be switched off, so check that the doors and tailgate are fully shut when making the test.

3 If the voltage reading is less than 12.2 volts, then the battery is discharged, whilst a reading of 12.2 to 12.4 volts indicates a partially-discharged condition.

4 If the battery is to be charged, remove it from the vehicle and charge it as described later in this Section.

Charging

Note: *The following is intended as a guide only. Always refer to the manufacturer's recommendations (often printed on a label attached to the battery) before charging a battery.*

2.2 An electronic battery tester in use

5 An automatic charger, designed for silver calcium batteries should be used. An automatic charger will detect the state of charge and adjust the charging rate to suit. When the battery is fully charged the charger will switch to stand-by and only charge the battery if the voltage drops. This avoids over gassing of the battery cells.

6 Some automatic chargers have a 'recovery mode' where a heavily sulfated (discharged) battery can be recovered and recharged.

7 When an automatic charger is not available, in an emergency it is possible to use a standard charger, but this must only be used on the lowest setting and must be disconnected as soon as the battery is charged.

3 Battery – disconnection, removal and refitting

Caution: Wait at least 5 minutes after turning off the ignition switch before disconnecting the battery. This is to allow sufficient time for the various control modules to store information and shut down in a controlled manner.

Caution: If a Ford 'Keycode' audio unit is fitted, the unit will not function again on reconnection until the correct security code is entered. Details of this procedure, which varies according to the unit and model year, are given in the 'Ford Audio Systems Operating Guide' supplied with the car when new, with the code itself being given in a 'Radio Passport' and/or a 'Keycode label' at the same time. Ensure you have the correct code before you disconnect the battery.

Disconnection

⚠️ *Warning: Only disconnect the battery at the chassis mounted disconnection point. Disconnecting the battery at the battery terminals will affect the operation of the battery monitoring sensor.*

1 The battery is located on the left-hand rear side of the engine compartment. Between the battery cover and the fusebox is a battery disconnection point. Disconnect the battery at this point (see illustration).

3.1 The battery disconnection point

3.4 Remove the front cover

3.5 Isolate the terminal post after removing the cable

3.6a Remove the battery clamp

3.6b Slide the battery forward and disconnect the negative cable

3.8a Remove the mounting bolts …

3.8b … and lift out the battery support tray

Removal

2 Disconnect the battery as described in this Section.

3 To remove the battery, begin by removing the air cleaner as described in Chapter 4A, Section 3.

4 Unclip and remove the plastic cover from the front of the battery **(see illustration)**.

5 Slacken the clamp nut and disconnect the battery positive lead terminal **(see illustration)**.

6 Remove the battery holding clamp and then slide the battery forward to access the battery negative table **(see illustrations)**.

7 Fold out the lifting handles and remove the battery.

8 If required the battery support tray can now be removed. Release the battery positive cable from the battery tray, remove the 3 bolts and remove the battery support tray **(see illustrations)**. Unclip the rear section of the battery cover from the tray if required.

Refitting

9 If removed, refit the battery support tray.

10 Position the battery on the battery support tray, so that the battery negative post is still accessible.

11 Refit the negative cable retaining clamp and tighten the retaining nut securely.

12 Slide the battery fully home and then reconnect the battery positive terminal. Refit the front section of the battery box.

13 Ensure no-one is inside the vehicle as the battery is reconnected. Reconnect the battery negative lead at the chassi mounted terminal post. Tighten the nut securely.

14 Refit the air cleaner assembly.

15 After reconnecting the battery, the engine may run erratically until it's been driven for a few minutes to allow the PCM to relearn. Also the electric windows will need to be re-initialised as follows:

a) *Start the engine*

b) *Press and hold the window control close button until the window is fully closed.*

c) *Release the button and then press the button 3 times for 1 second each time.*

d) *Briefly press the open button to the second detent, then release it. The window should open automatically.*

e) *Briefly press the close button to the second detent, then release it. If the window does not close automatically, repeat the complete procedure.*

f) *Repeat this procedure on each window.*

g) *Turn off the engine*

4   Charging system – general information

1 The charging system features Ford's latest version of their 'Smart' charging system, called 'Smart Regenerative Charging' (SRG). The main aim of the system is to closely match the alternator output to all the electrical demands of the system and to maintain the battery in an optimum state of charge.

2 A battery monitoring sensor is fitted to the negative terminal of the battery. The sensor monitors the battery to maintain a calibrated charge of approximately 80% of the batteries capacity. If the charge exceeds 80% the alternator output is reduced, if the battery charge falls below 80% then the alternator output is increased. Note however that the alternator output may increase to 15.2 volts during a refresh phase. The refresh phase is required to minimise sulfation of the battery cells

3 To maintain the accuracy of the SRG system the battery monitor sensor must be recalibrated. This is an automatic process that takes place during a rest period.

5   Charging system – testing

Note: *Refer to the warnings given in Safety first0,2 ! and in Section 1 of this Chapter before starting work.*

1 If the ignition/no-charge warning light fails to illuminate when the ignition is switched on, first check the alternator wiring connections for security.

2 If all is satisfactory, the alternator maybe at fault and should be renewed or taken to an auto-electrician for testing and repair.

3 If the ignition warning light illuminates when the engine is running, stop the engine and check that the drivebelt is correctly tensioned (see Chapter 1 Section 22) and that the alternator connections are secure. If all is so far satisfactory, have the alternator checked by an auto-electrician for testing and repair.

6.4 Remove the bolts

6.5 Disconnect the alternator wiring connections

6.8 Prise up the plastic cover then disconnect the alternator wiring

6.10a Undo the two pulley bolts ...

6.10b ... slacken the three coupling bolts ...

6.10c ... and remove the coupling from the alternator

4 If the alternator output is suspect even though the warning light functions correctly, the regulated voltage may be checked as follows.

5 Connect a voltmeter across the battery terminals and start the engine.

6 Increase the engine speed until the voltmeter reading remains steady; the reading should be between 13.5 and 14.8 volts.

7 Switch on as many electrical accessories (eg, the headlights, heated rear window and heater blower) as possible, and check that the alternator maintains the regulated voltage between 13.5 and 14.8 volts.

8 If the regulated voltage is not as stated, the fault may be due to worn brushes, weak brush springs, a faulty voltage regulator, a faulty diode, a severed phase winding, or worn or damaged slip-rings. The brushes and slip-rings may be checked (see Section), but if the fault persists the alternator should be renewed or taken to an auto-electrician for testing and repair.

6 Alternator –
removal and refitting

Removal

1 Remove the engine cover

2 Disconnect the battery negative lead (see Section 3).

3 Remove the auxiliary drivebelt as described in Chapter 1 Section 22.

1.6 litre engines

4 Unbolt and then remove the automatic belt tensioner **(see illustration)**.

5 Disconnect the wiring plug from the alternator, then prise up the rubber cap, undo the nut and disconnect the battery cable from the alternator **(see illustration)**.

6 Remove the alternator upper rear and front retaining bolts.

7 Remove the lower retaining bolt and lower the alternator from position.

1.8 litre engines

8 Remove the plastic cover, unscrew the nut and disconnect the wiring from the alternator **(see illustration)**.

9 Unclip the wiring loom and then undo the bolts from the air conditioning compressor.

6.11 Slacken the air pipe clamp

Secure the compressor to the radiator support panel.

Caution: Do not disconnect the refrigerant pipes.

10 Undo the pulley bracket bolts, then slacken the three generator coupling bolts and remove the coupling **(see illustrations)**. Unscrew the alternator mounting bolts and carefully lift the alternator from the engine

2.0 litre models

11 Slacken the clamp and disconnect the intercooler outlet pipe from the anti-shudder valve **(see illustration)**.

12 Undo the bolts and remove the crash shield from the top of the fuel filter **(see illustration)**.

13 Note their fitted positions, then disconnect

6.12 Remove the crash shield

6.14 Unscrew the bolt on the right-hand side of the filter

6.15 Fuel filter bracket bolts

6.17 Undo the upper bolts, and slacken the lower bolt

6.19 Remove the accessory drive idler pulley

6.23a Remove the mounting bolts

6.23b Lever the alternator free from the bracket if necessary

the various wiring plugs from the fuel filter assembly.

14 Undo the retaining bolt, then lift the fuel filter upwards from the bracket and position it to one side **(see illustration)**. There's no need to disconnect the fuel pipes, but release them from the various retaining clips.

15 Undo the 3 retaining bolts and remove the fuel filter bracket **(see illustration)**.

16 Disconnect the wiring plug, then undo the nut and disconnect the cable from the alternator.

17 Slacken the alternator lower mounting clamp bolt, then undo the upper mounting bolts, slide the alternator to the right, and manoeuvre it from place **(see illustration)**.

6.24 Remove the alternator

2.2 litre models

18 Remove the right-hand headlight.

19 Remove the cover from the accessory belt idler pulley and then remove the pulley **(see illustration)**.

20 With reference to Chapter 10 Section 19, remove the power steering pump. There is no need to remove the high pressure outlet pipe from the pump, but the supply pipe from the reservoir must be removed (and immediately sealed). Seal the pump fluid inlet and place the power steering pump on top of the engine.

21 On models fitted with air conditioning remove the bolts from the engine mounting on the inner wing. Using a block of wood to spread the load, raise the engine slightly on a trolley jack.

22 Disconnect the wiring plug from the top of the alternator, remove the cover and the unbolt the main output cable from the front of the alternator.

23 Remove the lower bolt and then remove the upper bolt **(see illustrations)**.

24 On AC models push the engine back sufficiently to allow the alternator to be removed from the space between the engine mounting and the bonnet slam panel **(see illustration)**. On non-AC models simply remove the alternator upwards and out of the engine bay.

Refitting

25 Refitting is a reversal of removal. Remembering to tighten the various fasteners to their specified torque where given.

7 Starting system – testing

Note: *Refer to the precautions given in* Safety first! *and in Section 1 of this Chapter before starting work.*

1 If the starter motor fails to operate when the ignition key is turned to the appropriate position, the following possible causes may be to blame:

a) *The battery is faulty.*

b) *The electrical connections between the switch, solenoid, battery and starter motor are somewhere failing to pass the necessary current from the battery through the starter to earth.*

c) *The solenoid is faulty.*

d) *The starter motor is mechanically or electrically defective.*

2 To check the battery, switch on the headlights. If they dim after a few seconds, this indicates that the battery is discharged – recharge (see Section 2) or renew the battery. If the headlights glow brightly, operate the ignition switch and observe the lights. If they dim, then this indicates that current is reaching the starter motor, therefore the fault must lie in the starter motor. If the lights continue to glow brightly (and no clicking sound can be heard from the starter motor solenoid), this indicates that there is a fault in the circuit or solenoid – see following paragraphs. If the starter motor

8.9 Undo the fasteners and remove the engine undershield

8.10 Remove the wiring connectors from the starter motor

turns slowly when operated, but the battery is in good condition, then this indicates that either the starter motor is faulty, or there is considerable resistance somewhere in the circuit.

3 If a fault in the circuit is suspected, disconnect the battery leads (including the earth connection to the body), the starter/solenoid wiring and the engine/transmission earth strap. Thoroughly clean the connections, and reconnect the leads and wiring, then use a voltmeter or test light to check that full battery voltage is available at the battery positive lead connection to the solenoid, and that the earth is sound. Smear petroleum jelly around the battery terminals to prevent corrosion – corroded connections are amongst the most frequent causes of electrical system faults.

4 If the battery and all connections are in good condition, check the circuit by disconnecting the wire from the solenoid blade terminal. Connect a voltmeter or test light between the wire end and a good earth (such as the battery negative terminal), and check that the wire is live when the ignition switch is turned to the start position. If it is, then the circuit is sound – if not, the circuit wiring can be checked as described in Chapter 12 Section 2.

5 The solenoid contacts can be checked by connecting a voltmeter or test light between the battery positive feed connection on the starter side of the solenoid, and earth. When the ignition switch is turned to the start position, there should be a reading or lighted bulb, as applicable. If there is no reading or lighted bulb, the solenoid is faulty and should be renewed.

6 If the circuit and solenoid are proved sound, the fault must lie in the starter motor. In this event, it may be possible to have the starter motor overhauled by a specialist, but check on the cost of spares before proceeding, as it may prove more economical to obtain a new or exchange motor.

8 Starter motor – removal and refitting

Removal

1.6 litre engines

1 The starter motor is located at the rear left-hand end of the engine. Jack up and support the engine (see *Jacking and vehicle support*) and then remove the engine undershield.

2 Access can be improved if the battery and battery tray are removed (as described in Section 3) but this is not strictly necessary.

3 Note their fitted positions, then disconnect the wiring connections from the starter motor, which is located on the rear of the cylinder block.

4 Undo the starter motor lower mounting bolt from underneath.

5 Remove the upper mounting bolts, and remove the starter motor.

1.8 litre engines

6 Disconnect the battery negative lead as described in Section 3.

8.14 Undo the nuts and disconnect the wiring

7 Remove the engine cover and then remove the air filter outlet pipe or remove the complete air filter assembly (as described in Chapter 4A Section 3).

8 Undo the upper starter motor retaining bolts.

9 Raise the front of the vehicle and support it securely on axle stands (see *Jacking and vehicle support*). Undo the fasteners and remove the engine undershield (see illustration).

10 Undo the nuts, and disconnect the wiring connections from the starter motor (see illustration).

11 Undo the mounting bolt and remove the starter downwards.

2.0 litre engines

12 Disconnect the battery negative lead as described in Section 3.

13 Pull the cover from the top of the engine upwards to release its mountings.

14 Undo the nuts and disconnect the wiring from the starter motor solenoid (see illustration).

15 Undo the 3 mounting bolts, and remove the starter motor (see illustration). Check the locating dowel is still in place in the starter motor mounting face.

8.15 Starter motor bolts

2.2 litre engines

16 Disconnect the wiring plugs from the throttle body, the boost pressure sensor and the temperature sensor. Move the wiring loom and secure it to the side.

17 Slacken the inlet hose clip and then remove the inlet hose from the throttle body **(see illustration)**.

18 Release the wiring loom from the engine oil dipstick tube and then unbolt and remove the dipstick **(see illustration)**. Ensure the O-ring seals are removed with the dipstick.

19 At the rear of the throttle body slacken, but do not remove the 2 bolts. Remove the front bolt and then slide the throttle body off the upper section of the housing. Remove the throttle body.

20 At the rear of the starter motor unbolt the main battery cable bolt and the solenoid cable. Lift the wiring plug off and move it to the side **(see illustration)**.

21 Remove the 3 starter motor mounting bolts and then remove the starter motor **(see illustration)**. Note the location of the dowel as the motor is removed

Refitting

22 Refitting is a reversal of removal. Tighten all fasteners to their specified torque where given.

8.17 Remove the hose

8.18 Unbolt the dipstick tube

8.20 Remove the wiring loom

8.21 Remove the starter motor

9 Preheating system – general information

1 To assist cold starting, diesel engine models are fitted with a preheating system, which comprises a relay, and four glow plugs. The system is controlled by the engine management PCM (Powertrain Control Module), using information provided by the coolant temperature sensor (see Chapter 3 Section 6).

2 On modern diesel engines the glow plugs also play an important part in emissions control. The PCM will operate the glow plugs at post start and during a 'regeneration' phase of the DPF (Diesel Particulate Filter). See Chapter 4B for coverage of the emission control systems

3 The glow plugs are miniature electric heating elements, encapsulated in a metal case with a probe at one end, and an electrical connection at the other. The combustion chambers have a glow plug threaded into it. When the glow plug is energised, it heats up rapidly causing the temperature of the air charge drawn into each of the combustion chambers to rise. Each glow plug probe is positioned directly in line with the incoming spray of fuel from the injector. Hence the fuel passing over the glow plug probe is also heated, allowing its optimum combustion temperature to be achieved more readily.

4 The duration of the preheating period is governed by the engine management Powertrain control module (PCM), using information provided by the coolant temperature sensor (see Chapter 3 Section 6). The PCM alters the preheating time (the length for which the glow plugs are supplied with current) to suit the prevailing conditions.

5 A warning light informs the driver that preheating is taking place. The lamp extinguishes when sufficient preheating has taken place to allow the engine to be started, but power will still be supplied to the glow plugs for a further period, known as post-heating, to reduce exhaust emissions. If no attempt is made to start the engine, the power supply to the glow plugs is switched off to prevent battery drain and glow plug burn-out.

10 Preheating system – testing

1 Full testing of the system can only be carried out using specialist diagnostic equipment which is connected to the engine management system diagnostic wiring connector (see Chapter 4A Section 6). If the preheating system is thought to be faulty, some preliminary checks of the glow plug operation may be made as described in the following paragraphs.

2 Connect a voltmeter or 12 volt test lamp between the glow plug supply cable, and a good earth point on the engine.

Caution: Make sure that the live connection is kept well clear of the engine and bodywork.

3 Have an assistant activate the preheating system by turning the ignition key to the second position, and check that battery voltage is applied to the glow plug electrical connection. **Note:** *The supply voltage will be less than battery voltage initially, but will rise and settle as the glow plug heats up. It will then drop to zero when the preheating period ends and the safety cut-out operates.*

4 If no supply voltage can be detected at the glow plug, then the glow plug relay or the supply cable may be faulty.

5 To locate a faulty glow plug, measure the electrical resistance between the glow plug terminal and the engine earth, and compare it with the resistance of the other glow plugs, or known working example. If the reading is significantly different, the glow plug is probably defective.

6 If no problems are found, take the vehicle to a Ford dealer or specialist for testing using the appropriate diagnostic equipment.

11 Glow plugs – removal, inspection and refitting

Note: *Glow plugs can be notoriously difficult to remove. Always apply penetrating fluid. If care is taken then removing them with a warm engine is often the easiest method.*

Removal

1 Disconnect the battery negative lead as described in Section 3.

1.6 litre engines

2 Remove the engine cover from the top of the engine.

11.4 Pull the electrical connector from each glow plug

11.9 Undo the nuts (right-hand side glow plugs) and disconnect the supply cable

11.12 Undo the nuts (arrowed) securing the electrical connections to the glow plugs

11.13 Unscrew the glow plugs from the cylinder head

3 Remove both upper and lower windscreen cowl panels as described in Chapter 12 Section 12.

4 Reach down the back of the engine, pull the electrical connector from each glow plug, and move the supply cable to one side **(see illustration)**. Access to No 1 glow plug is extremely limited – if improved access is required, remove the EGR cooler as described in Chapter 4B Section 4.

5 Using a deep socket, carefully unscrew each glow plug from the cylinder head.

1.8 litre engines

6 Pull the plastic cover on the top of the engine upwards to release it from the mountings.

7 Release the clamps and disconnect the 2 engine breather hoses from the front of the cylinder head cover.

8 Undo the bolt securing the engine oil level dipstick guide tube.

9 Undo the nuts and disconnect the electrical supply cable from the top of each glow plug **(see illustration)**.

10 Using a deep socket, carefully unscrew each glow plug from the cylinder head.

2.0 litre engines

11 Remove the EGR valve and cooler as described in Chapter 4B Section 5.

12 Undo the nuts (1 per plug) and disconnect the wiring harness from the glow plugs **(see illustration)**.

13 Unscrew each glow plug from the cylinder head using a deep socket **(see illustration)**.

2.2 litre engines

14 Remove the engine cover and then remove the inlet manifold as described in Chapter 4A Section 17.

15 Disconnect the wiring plugs and then remove the glow plugs **(see illustrations)**.

Inspection

16 Inspect the glow plugs for signs of damage. Burnt or eroded glow plug tips can be caused by a bad injector spray pattern. Have the injectors checked if this sort of damage is found.

17 If the glow plugs are in good condition,

check them electrically, as described in Section 10.

18 The glow plugs can be energised by applying 12 volts to them to verify that they heat up evenly and in the required time. Observe the following precautions:

a) *Support the glow plug by clamping it carefully in a vice or self-locking pliers. Remember it will be red hot.*

b) *Make sure that the power supply or test lead incorporates a fuse or overload trip to protect against damage from a short-circuit.*

c) *After testing, allow the glow plug to cool for several minutes before attempting to handle it.*

19 A glow plug in good condition will start to glow red at the tip after drawing current for 5 seconds or so. Any plug which takes much longer to start glowing, or which starts glowing in the middle instead of at the tip, is probably defective.

Refitting

20 Thoroughly clean the glow plugs, and the glow plug seating areas in the cylinder head.

21 Apply a smear of anti-seize compound to the glow plug threads, then refit the glow plug and tighten it to the specified torque.

22 Reconnect the wiring to the glow plug and tighten the nut securely.

23 The remainder of refitting is a reversal of removal.

11.15a Unclip the loom and …

11.15b … disconnect the wiring plug

11.15c Remove the glow plugs

Chapter 6
Clutch

Contents

Chapter 6
Clutch

Contents

Degrees of difficulty

Easy, suitable for novice with little experience	Fairly easy, suitable for beginner with some experience	Fairly difficult, suitable for competent DIY mechanic	Difficult, suitable for experienced DIY mechanic	Very difficult, suitable for expert DIY or professional

Specifications

Torque wrench settings

	Nm	lbf ft
Clutch cover/pressure plate to flywheel: *		
MTX75 and MMT6 transmissions	29	21
MM6 transmission	23	17
Clutch pedal bracket nuts	28	21
Clutch slave cylinder mounting	11	8

Note: * Do not re-use

1 General Information

1 All manual transmission models are equipped with a single dry plate diaphragm spring clutch assembly. The pressure plate assembly consists of a steel cover (doweled and bolted to the flywheel face), the pressure plate, and a diaphragm spring.

2 The driven plate is free to slide along the splines of the transmission input shaft, and is held in position between the flywheel and the pressure plate by the pressure of the diaphragm spring. Friction lining material is riveted to the driven plate (friction disc), which on some models, has a spring-cushioned hub, to absorb transmission shocks and help ensure a smooth take-up of the drive. On other models, a dual-mass flywheel is fitted, where the flywheel is split into to masses – a primary mass (incorporating the starter ring gear) secured to the engine crankshaft, and secondary mass which is the driving surface mated to the clutch driven plate. Between these two masses are rubber/spring elements which absorb the power pulses from the engine as well as the transmission shocks.

3 The clutch release bearing contacts the fingers of the diaphragm spring. Depressing the clutch pedal pushes the release bearing against the diaphragm fingers, so moving the centre of the diaphragm spring inwards. As the centre of the spring is pushed inwards, the outside of the spring pivots outwards, so moving the pressure plate backwards and disengaging its grip on the driven plate.

4 When the pedal is released, the diaphragm spring forces the pressure plate back into contact with the friction linings on the driven plate. The plate is now firmly held between the pressure plate and the flywheel, thus transmitting engine power to the transmission. On some models, a self-adjusting clutch (SAC) is fitted, where an adjustment ring rotates in the pressure plate assembly, adjusting the diaphragm spring fingers pivot points as the driven plate wears. This maintains the clutch pedal 'bite point'.

5 All models have a hydraulically-operated clutch. A master cylinder is mounted below the clutch pedal, and takes its hydraulic fluid supply from a separate chamber in the brake fluid reservoir. Depressing the clutch pedal operates the master cylinder pushrod, and the fluid pressure is transferred along the fluid lines to a slave cylinder mounted inside the bellhousing. The slave cylinder is incorporated into the release bearing – when the slave cylinder operates, the release bearing moves against the diaphragm spring fingers and disengages the clutch.

6 The hydraulic clutch offers several advantages over a cable-operated clutch – it is completely self-adjusting, requires less pedal effort, and is less subject to wear problems.

7 Since many of the procedures covered in this Chapter involve working under the vehicle, make sure that it is securely supported on axle stands placed on a firm, level floor (see *Jacking and vehicle support*).

8 Warning: The hydraulic fluid used in the system is brake fluid, which is poisonous. Take care to keep it off bare skin, and in particular out of your eyes. The fluid also attacks paintwork, and may discolour carpets, etc – keep spillages to a minimum, and wash any off immediately with cold water. Finally, brake fluid is highly inflammable, and should be handled with the same care as petrol.

2 Clutch pedal – removal and refitting

⚠️ *Warning: Hydraulic fluid is poisonous; wash off immediately and thoroughly in the case of skin contact, and seek immediate medical advice if any fluid is swallowed or gets into the eyes. Certain types of hydraulic fluid are inflammable, and may ignite when allowed into contact with hot components; when servicing any hydraulic system, it is safest to assume that the fluid IS inflammable, and to take precautions against the risk of fire as though it is petrol that is being handled. Hydraulic fluid is also an effective paint stripper, and will attack plastics; if any is spilt, it should be washed off immediately, using copious quantities of clean water. Finally, it is hygroscopic (it absorbs moisture from the air) – old fluid may be contaminated and unfit for further use. When topping-up or renewing the fluid, always use the recommended type, and ensure that it comes from a freshly-opened sealed container.*

Removal

1 Disconnect the battery and then remove the driver's knee airbag panel as described in Chapter 11 Section 24.
2 Remove the steering column lower inch bolt (as described in Chapter 10 Section 15) slide up the universal joint and secure it to the side.

2.5 Remove the mounting nuts

3 Disconnect the wiring plugs from the pedal switch or switches (depending on the model).
4 Prise out the peg (or remove the locking washer) from the clutch master cylinder piston rod. Dispose of the peg (or washer) – a new one must be fitted.
5 Unbolt the pedal from the bulkhead **(see illustration)**. Pull the pedal backwards and rotate it slightly to remove it and disengage it from the clutch master cylinder.

Refitting

6 Refit by reversing the removal operations. Note the following points:
a) *Tighten all fasteners securely.*
b) *Replace the clutch cylinder clevis pin*
c) *Bleed the clutch hydraulic system as described in Section 5.*
d) *Check the operation of the clutch before refitting the lower facia panel.*

3 Clutch master cylinder – removal and refitting

Note: *No internal components are available and therefore no repair or overhaul of the cylinder is possible. In the event of a hydraulic system fault, or any sign of visible fluid leakage on or around the master cylinder or clutch pedal, the unit should be renewed.*

Removal

1 Remove the upper and lower windscreen cowl panels as described in Chapter 12 Section 12.
2 Drin down the remote fluid reservoir until it is just below the minimum mark – that is to say just below the takeoff point for the clutch master cylinder. Anticipate some fluid spillage and then disconnect the master cylinder supply hose from the master cylinder. Repeat the procedure for the outlet hose.
3 Remove the clutch pedal assembly as described in this Section.
4 Rotate the locking collar on the master cylinder (Ford list a special tool for this – 308-554) using waterpump/sliding joint pliers, or the correct tool.
5 Remove the master cylinder and the seal.

Refitting

6 Refit by reversing the removal operations and then bleed the clutch as described in Section 5.

4 Clutch slave cylinder and release bearing – removal and refitting

Note: *Refer to the warning at the beginning of Section 2 before proceeding.*

Removal

1 Remove the transmission as described in Chapter 7 Section 7. The internal slave cylinder cannot be removed with the transmission in place.
2 Release the rubber seal from the transmission.
3 Remove the mounting bolt (or bolts depending on the transmission fitted) securing the cylinder and release bearing assembly to the transmission. On some transmissions the feed pipe must be split before the slave cylinder can be removed. Remove the assembly, feeding the fluid pipe in through the transmission aperture **(see illustrations)**.

Refitting

4 Ensure the release bearing/slave cylinder and transmission casing mating surfaces are clean. On MTX75 transmissions apply a bead of sealant (Ford No WSK-M2G348-A5) to the bearing/cylinder as shown **(see illustration)**.
5 Refit the release bearing/slave cylinder on the input shaft, and tighten the bolt(s) to the specified torque. Take care not to damage the seal lips with the input shaft splines – wrap adhesive tape around the splines prior to fitting the cylinder.
6 Refit the rubber seal around the pipes, ensuring it is correctly positioned.
7 The remainder of refitting is a reversal of removal, noting the following points:
a) *Remove the adhesive tape from the input shaft splines.*
b) *Refit the transmission as described in Chapter 7 Section 7.*
c) *Bleed the clutch hydraulic system on completion (Section 5).*

4.3a Remove the 3 bolts on the MTX75 and on the MMT6 transmissions

4.3b Remove the bolt and the circlip on the 6 speed transmission

4.4 Apply a bead of sealant to the slave cylinder around the edge

5 Clutch hydraulic system – bleeding

Note: *Refer to the warning at the beginning of Section 2 before proceeding.*

1 Top-up the hydraulic fluid reservoir on the brake master cylinder with fresh clean fluid of the specified type (see *Weekly checks.*).

2 Remove the air cleaner assembly as described in Chapter 4A Section 3.

3 Remove the dust cover, and fit a length of clear hose over the bleed nipple on the slave cylinder **(see illustration)**. Place the other end of the hose in a jar containing a small amount of hydraulic fluid.

4 Slacken the bleed nipple half a turn, then have an assistant depress the clutch pedal. Tighten the bleed screw when the pedal is depressed. Have the assistant release the pedal, then slacken the bleed screw again.

5 Repeat the process until clean fluid, free of air bubbles, emerges from the bleed nipple. Tighten the nipple at the end of a pedal downstroke, and remove the hose and jar. Refit the dust cover.

6 Top-up the hydraulic fluid reservoir.

7 Pressure bleeding equipment may be used if preferred – refer to the information in Chapter 9, Section 11.

6 Clutch components – removal, inspection and refitting

Warning: Dust created by clutch wear and deposited on the clutch components may contain asbestos, which is a health hazard. DO NOT blow it out with compressed air, and do not inhale any of it. DO NOT use petrol or petroleum-based solvents to clean off the dust. Brake system cleaner or methylated spirit should be used to flush the dust into a suitable receptacle. After the clutch components are wiped clean with rags, dispose of the contaminated rags and cleaner in a sealed, marked container.

Removal

1 Access to the clutch may be gained in one of two ways. The engine/transmission unit can be removed, as described in Chapter 2E Section 3, and the transmission separated from the engine on the bench. Alternatively, the engine may be left in the vehicle and the transmission removed independently, as described in Chapter 7 Section 7.

2 Having separated the transmission from the engine, check if there are any marks identifying the relation of the clutch pressure plate to the flywheel. If not, make your own marks using a dab of paint or a scriber. These marks will be used if the original pressure plate is refitted, and will help to maintain the balance of the unit. A new pressure plate

5.3 Connect the hose to the bleed nipple on the transmission housing

may be fitted in any position allowed by the locating dowels.

3 Unscrew the six clutch pressure plate retaining bolts, working in a diagonal sequence, and slackening the bolts only a turn at a time **(see illustration)**. If necessary, the flywheel may be held stationary using a wide-bladed screwdriver, inserted in the teeth of the starter ring gear and resting against part of the cylinder block. Ford state that new pressure plate bolts must be used when refitting.

4 Ease the clutch pressure plate off its locating dowels. Be prepared to catch the clutch driven plate, which will drop out as the pressure plate is removed. Note which way round the driven plate is fitted.

Inspection

Note: *On models equipped with a self-adjusting clutch, Ford insist that if a new driven plate is fitted, the pressure plate must also be renewed.*

5 The most common problem which occurs in the clutch is wear of the clutch driven plate (friction disc). However, all the clutch components should be inspected at this time, particularly if the engine has covered a high mileage. Unless the clutch components are known to be virtually new, it is worth renewing them all as a set (driven plate, pressure plate and release bearing). Renewing a worn driven plate by itself is not always satisfactory, especially if the old one was slipping and causing the pressure plate to overheat.

6 Examine the linings of the driven plate for wear and loose rivets, and the plate hub and rim for distortion, cracks, broken torsion springs, and worn splines (where applicable). The surface of the friction linings may be highly glazed, but as long as the friction material pattern can be clearly seen, and the rivet heads are at least 1 mm below the lining surface, this is satisfactory. The plate must be renewed if the lining thickness has worn down to, or just above, the level of the rivet heads.

7 If there is any sign of oil contamination, indicated by shiny black discoloration, the driven plate must be renewed, and the source of the contamination traced and rectified. This will be a leaking crankshaft oil seal or transmission input shaft oil seal. The renewal

6.3 Undo the pressure plate retaining bolts

procedure for the former is given in the relevant Part of. Renewal of the transmission input shaft oil seal should be entrusted to a Ford dealer, as it involves dismantling the transmission, and (where applicable) the renewal of the clutch release bearing guide tube, using a press.

8 Check the machined faces of the flywheel and pressure plate. If either is grooved, or heavily scored, renewal is necessary. The pressure plate must also be renewed if any cracks are apparent, or if the diaphragm spring is damaged or its pressure suspect. Pay particular attention to the tips of the spring fingers, where the release bearing acts upon them.

9 With the transmission removed, it is also advisable to check the condition of the release bearing, although having got this far, it is almost certainly worth renewing it. Note that the release bearing is integral with the slave cylinder – the two must be renewed together; however, given that access to the slave cylinder is only possible with the transmission removed, not to renew it at this time is probably a false economy.

Refitting

10 On reassembly, ensure that the friction surfaces of the flywheel and pressure plate are completely clean, smooth, and free from oil or grease. Use solvent to remove any protective grease from new components.

11 New pressure plates are supplied with the self-adjusting mechanism preset, however, if the original pressure plate is to be refitted, the self-adjustment mechanism must be reset as follows.

12 A large diameter bolt (M14 at least) long enough to pass through the pressure plate, a matching nut, and several large diameter washers, will be needed for this procedure. Mount the bolt head in the jaws of a sturdy vice, with one large washer fitted.

13 Offer the plate over the bolts, friction plate surface facing down, and locate it centrally over the bolt and washer – the washer should bear on the centre hub.

14 Fit several further large washers over the bolt, so that they bear on the ends of the spring fingers, then add the nut and tighten by hand to locate the washers.

6.15a Tighten the nut until the adjuster nut is free to turn

6.15b Rotate the adjuster disc anti-clockwise until the springs are fully compressed

6.17 The friction plate should be marked to indicate which side faces the transmission or flywheel

15 The purpose of the procedure is to turn the plate's internal adjuster disc so that the 3 small coil springs visible on the plate's outer surface are fully compressed. Tighten the nut just fitted until the adjuster disc is free to turn. Using a pair of thin-nosed or circlip pliers in one of the 3 windows on the top surface, open the jaws of the pliers to turn the adjuster disc anti-clockwise, so that the springs are fully compressed (see illustrations).

16 Hold the pliers in this position, and then unscrew the centre nut. Once the nut is released, the adjuster disc will be gripped in position, and the pliers can be removed. Take the pressure plate from the vice, and it's ready to fit.

17 Fit the friction plate so that its spring hub assembly faces away from the flywheel; there may also be a marking showing which way round the plate is to be refitted. On genuine Ford clutches the friction plate should be fitted with the "Transmission side" or "Flywheel side" marking facing away from the flywheel (see illustration).

18 Refit the pressure plate assembly, aligning the marks made on dismantling (if the original pressure plate is re-used), and locating the pressure plate on its locating dowels. Fit the new pressure plate bolts, but tighten them only finger-tight, so that the friction plate can still be moved.

19 The friction plate must now be centralised, so that when the transmission is refitted, its input shaft will pass through the splines at the centre of the friction plate.

20 Centralisation can be achieved by passing a screwdriver or other long bar through the friction plate and into the hole in the crankshaft; the friction plate can then be moved around until it is centred on the crankshaft hole. Alternatively, a clutch-aligning tool can be used to eliminate the guesswork; these can be obtained from most accessory shops (see illustration).

21 An alternative method is to use a universal clutch tool. This tool clamps the friction disc to the clutch cover. The cover and the friction disc are aligned off the vehicle and then offered up to the engine as a complete assembly (see illustration).

22 When the friction plate is centralised, tighten the pressure plate bolts evenly and in a diagonal sequence to the specified torque setting. Ensure the pressure plate is drawn squarely onto the flywheel, to prevent the pressure plate being distorted.

23 Refit the transmission as described in Chapter 7 Section 7.

6.20 Position the drive plate with a clutch aligning tool

6.21 An alternative tool clamps the friction plate to the cover plate

Chapter 7
Manual transmission

Contents

Degrees of difficulty

Easy, suitable for novice with little experience	Fairly easy, suitable for beginner with some experience	Fairly difficult, suitable for competent DIY mechanic	Difficult, suitable for experienced DIY mechanic	Very difficult, suitable for expert DIY or professional

Specifications

General

Transmission type. . . . . Five or six forward gears and one reverse. Synchromesh on all gears
Designation:
   1.6 and 1.8 litre models (5-speed) MTX75
   2.0 litre models (6-speed). MMT6
   2.2 litre models (6 speed) M66

Lubricant capacity

MTX75 . . . . 1.9 litres
MMT6 . . . . 1.75 litres
M66 . . . . 2.0 litres

Torque wrench settings

	Nm	lbf ft
Engine/transmission mountings	See Chapter 2A, 2B, 2C or 2D Specifications	
Oil filler/drain plugs	35	26
Reversing light switch	25	18
Roadwheel nuts:		
M12 standard nuts	140	103
M12 locking nut with conical washer	110	81
M12 locking nut with one-piece nut	140	103
M14 nuts	170	125
Transmission to engine bolts	48	35

2.2a Remove the nuts (uppers shown) and …

2.2b …lower the gear lever housing

2.3a Depress the button ….

2.3b …and release the inner cable

2.4 Slide up the collar to release the outer cable

1 General Information

1 The transmission and final drive are housed in an aluminium casing, bolted directly to the left-hand side of the engine. Gear selection is by a remotely-sited lever assembly, operating the transmission selector mechanism via cables.

2 Because of the complexity, possible unavailability of parts and special tools necessary, internal repair procedures for the manual transmission are not included for the home mechanic. For readers who wish to tackle a transmission rebuild, brief notes on overhaul are provided in Section 8. The bulk of the information in this Chapter is devoted to the removal and refitting procedures.

2 Gear lever housing – removal and refitting

Removal

1 Remove the centre console as described in Chapter 11 Section 25.

2 Undo the bolts and remove the housing from the facia central support bracket (see illustrations).

3 Depress the release button on the inner cable and release the cable from the balljoints on the levers (see illustrations).

4 Slide up the locking collars and release the outer cables (see illustration).

5 Lift up the complete housing and manoeuvre it from the vehicle.

Refitting

6 Refit by reversing the removal operations. Tighten the 4 bolts securely and adjust the cables as described in the next Section 3 (if necessary).

3 Selector cables – removal, refitting and adjustment

Removal

1 Remove the air cleaner assembly as described in Chapter 4A Section 3.

5-speed transmission

2 Depress the release button and pull the end of the selector cable from the transmission lever balljoint (see illustration). Repeat this procedure with the shift cable.

3 Rotate the collars anti-clockwise and detach the selector and shift outer cables from the bracket on the transmission (see illustration).

3.2 Depress the release button and pull the cable from the balljoint

3.3 Rotate the collar anti-clockwise

3.4a Depress the release button and detach the selector cable

3.4b Prise the gearchange cable from the balljoint

3.5 Slide open the locking collar

6-speed transmissions

4 Depress the release button and pull the end of the selector cable from the transmission lever balljoint, then carefully prise the end of the gearchange cable from the balljoint on the transmission lever **(see illustrations)**. MM6 transmission shown, but MMT6 transmission is very similar.
5 Slide back the locking collar and lift the outer cable end fittings from the bracket on the transmission **(see illustration)**.

All models

6 Jack up the front of the vehicle and support it securely on axle stands (see *Jacking and vehicle support*).
7 Undo the 4 fasteners, and slide the heat shield above the intermediate section of the exhaust pipe rearwards.
8 Release the cables from the retaining clips on the underside of the floor.
9 Remove the centre console as described in Chapter 11 Section 25 and then disconnect the selector cables from the gear lever as described in Section 2.
10 On the left-hand side of the facia remove the support panels **(see illustration)**.
11 Make a cut in the carpet where the gear cables exit the cabin. Fold back the carpet and carefully cut away the sound insulation around the cable grommet.
12 Undo the 2 nuts securing the cable grommet to the floor, and lift the grommet from the mounting studs **(see illustration)**.
13 Manoeuvre the cable assembly into the passenger cabin, then out of the vehicle.

Refitting

14 Manoeuvre the cable assembly into position, through the hole in the floor, up to the transmission, then fit the grommet over the mounting studs and tighten the retaining nuts securely.
15 Reposition the sound insulation around the grommet, and tape over the cuts.
16 Reconnect the selector cables to the gear lever as described in Section 2.
17 Reclip the cables to the underside of the floor.
18 Refit the heat shield above the exhaust system.

3.10 Remove the side panels

19 Adjust the selector cable as described in this Section.

Adjustment

20 All transmissions require the use of Ford special tool 308-640. This tool fits into the gear lever housing and correctly positions the gear lever. Where the tool is not available it is possible to position the gear lever correctly by either measuring the gap (13 mm on the left-hand side and 14 mm on the right-hand side) between the gear lever and the side of the housing and having an assistant hold the gear lever in this position. Alternatively a simple 'U' shaped tool can be fabricated **(see illustrations)**.
21 If not already done so, remove the centre air cleaner assembly as described in Chapter 4A Section 3.

3.20a The special gear shift alignment tool

3.12 Undo the 2 nuts securing the cable grommet to the floor

22 If the centre console is still in place, carefully prise up the gear lever gaiter from the console.

5-speed transmission

23 Check that the selector lever on the transmission is in the 4th gear position.
24 Push out the lock button/clip on the side of the inner cable at the selector lever on the transmission and install the special tool **(see illustration 3.20b)** at the gear lever.
25 With the special tool still in position push in the cable locking clip.
26 Refit the air cleaner assembly, and centre console/gaiter using a reversal of the removal procedure.

6-speed transmission – MMT6

27 On early models (built up to 10/2007) disconnect both gearchange cables from the

3.20b The tool correctly installed

3.27 Prise out the locking catch on the side of the selector cable

3.34 The lever must be vertical

4.3 Prise the driveshaft oil seal from place

levers on the transmission as described earlier in this Section, then prise up the locking catch on the end fitting of the selector cable (see illustration).

28 On later models remove the selector cable only.

29 On early models (up to 10/2007) insert a 2.5 mm drill bit into the centre of the roll-pin securing the selector mechanism preload sleeve, set the vertical distance to 44 mm (measured from the base of the reverse light switch) and turn the selector arm to engage 4th gear as shown.

30 If the centre console is still in place, carefully prise up the gear lever gaiter from the console.

31 Fit the special tool (308-640) or fabricated tool (see illustration 3.20b) and then re-attach the selector lever cable to the balljoint, and press down the locking catch. Re-attach the shift cable end fitting.

32 Remove the drill bit and special tools (where applicable) and check the operation of the gearchange mechanism. If all appears satisfactory, refit the air cleaner assembly, and centre console/gaiter.

6-speed transmission – M66

33 At the transmission, remove the selector cables (as described in this Section) and then prise out the locking catch.

34 Engage fourth gear and ensure the selector lever is vertical (see illustration).

35 If the centre console is still in place, carefully prise up the gear lever gaiter from the console.

36 Fit the special tool (038-640) or fabricated tool (see illustration 3.20b) and then re-attach the selector lever cable to the balljoint, and press down the locking catch. Re-attach the shift cable end fitting.

37 Check the operation of the gearchange mechanism. If all appears satisfactory, refit the air cleaner assembly, and centre console/ gaiter.

4   Oil seals – renewal

Driveshaft seals

1 Remove the left or right-hand driveshaft (as appropriate) with reference to Chapter 8 Section 2.

2 Drain the transmission oil as described in Section 6.

3 Using a large screwdriver or suitable lever, carefully prise the oil seal out of the transmission casing, taking care not to damage the casing (see illustration).

4 Wipe clean the oil seal seating in the transmission casing.

5 Apply a small amount of general purpose grease to the new seal lips, then press it a

little way into the casing by hand, making sure that it is square to its seating.

6 Using suitable tubing or a large socket, carefully drive the oil seal fully into position until it is flush with the casing edge (see illustration).

7 Refit the driveshaft(s) as described in Chapter 8 Section 2.

8 Replenish the transmission oil as described in Section 6.

Input shaft oil seal

5-speed transmission

9 The input shaft seal is integral with the clutch slave cylinder/release bearing. Renew the cylinder/bearing as described in Chapter 6 Section 4.

6-speed transmission

10 Remove the clutch release bearing/slave cylinder as described in Chapter 6 Section 4.

11 Note its fitted depth, then drill a small hole in the hard outer surface of the seal, insert a self-tapping screw, and use pliers to extract the seal (see illustration).

12 Lubricate the new seal with grease and fit it to the bellhousing, lips pointing to the gearbox side. Use a deep socket or suitable tubing to seat it (see illustration).

13 Refit the release bearing/slave cylinder using a reversal of removal.

4.6 Drive the new oil seal into place using a socket which bears only on the hard, outer edge of the seal

4.11 Insert a self-tapping screw and pull the seal from place

4.12 Drive the new seal squarely into place to its original depth

5.2 Reversing light switch (5-speed transmission)

5.4a Reversing light switch (MMT6, 6 speed transmission)

5.4b Reversing light switch (M66, 6 speed transmission)

5 Reversing light switch – removal and refitting

Removal

5-speed transmission

1 Remove the air cleaner assembly as described in Chapter 4A Section 3.
2 Disconnect the wiring plug, then unscrew the switch from the top of the transmission casing (see illustration).

6-speed transmission

3 The reversing light switch is located on the upper face of the transmission close to the two gear selector levers. Remove the air cleaner assembly as described in Chapter 4A Section 3.
4 Clean around the switch, disconnect the wiring connector (see illustrations) and unscrew the switch.

Refitting

5 Refit by reversing the removal operations.

6 Manual transmission oil – draining and refilling

Note: Renewal of the transmission oil is not a service requirement and will normally only be necessary if the unit is removed for overhaul or renewal. However, if the car has completed a high mileage, or is used under arduous conditions (eg, extensive towing or taxi work), it would be advisable to change the oil as a precaution, especially if the gearchange quality has deteriorated.

Draining

1 Slacken the left-hand front roadwheel bolts, then jack up the front of the vehicle and support it securely on axle stands (see Jacking and vehicle support 5). Remove the roadwheel.
2 Release the fasteners and remove the engine undershield (where fitted), then position a suitable container beneath the transmission.

5-speed transmission

3 On the right-hand side of the transmission

casing, you will see the drain plug. Unscrew and remove the drain plug and allow the oil to drain into the container (see illustration). Check the condition of the drain plug sealing washer, and renew if necessary.

6-speed transmission

4 The drain plug is located on the left-hand side of the transmission. Unscrew and remove the drain plug and allow the oil to drain into the container (see illustration). Check the condition of the drain plug sealing washer (where fitted), and renew if necessary.

All models

5 When all the oil has drained, refit the drain plug and tighten it to the specified torque.

Refilling

Note: For the level check to be accurate, the car must be completely level. If the front of the

car has been jacked up, the rear should be jacked up also.

5-speed transmission

6 Unscrew the level/filler plug located on the front of the transmission casing (see illustration).
7 Discard the sealing washer, a new one must be fitted.
8 Add oil of the correct specification (see Lubricants and fluids) until oil begins to trickle out of the filler/level plug.
9 Fit a new sealing washer to the filler plug and tighten it to the specified torque.

6-speed transmission

10 Wipe clean the area around the filler/level plug, and unscrew the plug from the casing (see illustration).
11 Fill the transmission through the filler plug orifice with the correct type of oil (see

6.3 Transmission drain plug – 5-speed transmission

6.4 Transmission drain plug – 6-speed transmission

6.6 Oil filler/level plug – 5-speed transmission

6.10 Oil filler/level plug – 6-speed transmission

Lubricants and fluids) until the oil begins to run out of the orifice.

12 Refit the filler/level plug with a new seal (where fitted), and tighten it to the specified torque.

All models

13 Dispose of the old oil safely in accordance with environmental regulations. Refit the undershield (where applicable) and the roadwheel, then lower the vehicle to the ground.

7 Manual transmission – removal and refitting

Note: *Removal of the transmission, requires the engine to be supported, whilst the transmission is removed. Ford list a special tool for this that uses the subframe mountings to support (and lower) the engine. We supported the engine on a trolley jack (with a block of wood on the head of the jack to spread the load) and then used an engine* crane to lower the transmission. The help of an assistant is essential, regardless of the method used.

Removal

1 Remove the cover from the top of the engine and then to improve access remove the windscreen upper and lower cowl panels, as described in Chapter 12 Section 12.

2 Remove the air filter housing as described in Chapter 4A Section 3 and then remove the inlet ducting from the turbocharger. Access to the hose clamp on the ducting is difficult.

3 Remove the battery as described in Chapter 5 Section 3. Undo the 3 bolts and remove the battery tray **(see illustration)**.

4 Disconnect the gearchange cables as described in Section 3 and then remove the cable support bracket **(see illustration)**.

5 Remove the bolts and lift out the lower battery support **(see illustration)**. DO NOT remove the centre bolt.

6 Prise out the retaining clip and disconnect the clutch hydraulic fluid pipe from the

7.3 Remove the battery tray

junction at the transmission bellhousing **(see illustration)**. Plug or seal the openings to prevent fluid leaks and contamination.

7 Remove the earth lead from the front of the transmission and then disconnect the reversing light switch wiring plug **(see illustration)**. Unclip the wiring loom from the transmission and the top of the bell housing.

7.4 Remove the cable bracket

7.5 Remove the tray

7.6 Disconnect the clutch pipe

7.7 Remove the earth strap

7.18a The transmission supported

7.18b Remove the engine mounting ...

7.18c ... followed by the transmission mounting bracket

7.21a Remove the lower bolts ...

8 Slacken the bolts on the starter motor and pull back the starter motor from the bell housing – there is no need to remove the starter motor completely.

9 Jack up and support the front of the vehicle – see *Jacking and vehicle support*.

10 Undo the fasteners and remove the engine under shield followed by the air deflector from beneath the bumper.

11 Remove the left-hand wing liner.

12 Remove both driveshafts as described in Chapter 8 Section 2.

13 At the rear of the engine disconnect the temperature sensor from the catalytic convertor.

14 Undo the bolts and remove the engine lower torque rod/movement limiter link.

15 Slacken the bolt, undo the clamp and remove the intercooler intake pipe/hose.

16 Remove the subframe as described in Chapter 10 Section 16.

17 Unbolt and disconnect the exhaust from the catalytic converter. Support the exhaust system on an axle stand.

18 Support the engine (see the note at the start of this Section), then undo the nuts/bolts and remove the left-hand engine/transmission mounting and bracket **(see illustrations)**.

19 On 2.0 litre models, remove the clutch housing cover at the rear of the engine adjacent to the right-hand driveshaft aperture.

20 Undo the upper bolts securing the transmission to the engine.

21 Undo the remaining bolts securing the transmission to the engine **(see illustrations)**. Withdraw the transmission squarely off the engine dowels, taking care not to allow the weight of the transmission to hang on the input shaft. Lower the engine slightly as the transmission is withdrawn to clear the chassis sidemember.

22 Lower the jack/engine crane and remove the unit from under the car.

Refitting

23 Ensure the transmission input shaft is clean and free of rust or grease, then apply a little grease (Ford part No SA-M1C9107-A) to the splines of the input shaft – wipe off

7.21b ... and separate the transmission from the engine

any excess grease. Check to make sure all locating dowels are in good condition and fitted correctly.

24 Manoeuvre the transmission squarely into position, and engage it with the engine dowels. Refit the lower bolts securing the transmission to the engine, and tighten them to the specified torque.

25 Raise the engine to its approximate fitted position. Refit the left-hand engine mounting bracket and torque rod, and secure with the bolts tightened to the specified torque.

26 The remainder of refitting is a reversal of removal, noting the following points:

a) *Tighten all fasteners to their specified torque where given.*

b) *Top-up the gearbox oil as described in Section 6 of this Chapter.*

c) *Adjust the selector lever cables as described in Section 3.*

d) *Bleed the clutch hydraulic system as described in Chapter 6 Section 5.*

e) *Reconnect the battery negative lead as described in Chapter 5 Section 3.*

8 Manual transmission overhaul – general information

1 Overhauling a manual transmission is a difficult job for the do-it-yourselfer. It involves the dismantling and reassembly of many small parts. Numerous clearances must be precisely measured and, if necessary, changed with selected spacers and circlips. As a result, if transmission problems arise, while the unit can be removed and refitted by a competent do-it-yourselfer, overhaul should be left to a transmission specialist. Rebuilt transmissions may be available – check with your dealer parts department, motor factors, or transmission specialists. At any rate, the time and money involved in an overhaul is almost sure to exceed the cost of a rebuilt unit.

2 Nevertheless, it's not impossible for an experienced mechanic to rebuild a transmission, providing the special tools are available, and the job is done in a deliberate step-by-step manner, so nothing is overlooked.

3 The tools necessary for an overhaul include: internal and external circlip pliers, a bearing puller, a slide hammer, a set of pin punches, a dial test indicator, and possibly a hydraulic press. In addition, a large, sturdy workbench and a vice or transmission stand will be required.

4 During dismantling of the transmission, make careful notes of how each part comes off, where it fits in relation to other parts, and what holds it in place.

5 Before taking the transmission apart for repair, it will help if you have some idea what area of the transmission is malfunctioning. Certain problems can be closely tied to specific areas in the transmission, which can make component examination and renewal easier. Refer to the Fault finding section at the rear of this manual for information regarding possible sources of trouble.

Chapter 8
Driveshafts

Contents

Degrees of difficulty

Easy, suitable for novice with little experience	**Fairly easy,** suitable for beginner with some experience	**Fairly difficult,** suitable for competent DIY mechanic	**Difficult,** suitable for experienced DIY mechanic	**Very difficult,** suitable for expert DIY or professional

Specifications

General

Driveshaft type	Equal-length solid-steel shafts, splined to inner and outer constant velocity joints. Intermediate shaft incorporated in right-hand driveshaft assembly
Outer constant velocity joint type	Ball-and-cage
Inner constant velocity joint type	Tripod

Lubrication

Lubricant type	Special grease supplied in repair kit, or suitable molybdenum disulphide grease – consult a Ford dealer or partsspecialist
CV joint grease capacity (approximate):	
Outboard joint	100 g
Inboard joint	100 g

Torque wrench settings

	Nm	lbf ft
Brake flexible hose (to suspension strut)	10	7
Driveshaft bolt: *		
Stage 1	45	33
Stage 2	Angle-tighten a further 80°	
Headlight levelling sensor bracket to lower arm	11	8
Lower arm balljoint to hub carrier*	83	61
Right-hand driveshaft support bearing cap nuts*		
Stage 1	6	4
Stage 2	25	18
Roadwheel nuts:		
M12 standard nuts	140	103
M12 locking nut with conical washer	110	81
M12 locking nut with one-piece nut	140	103
M14 nuts	170	125

Note: * *Do not re-use*

1 General Information

1 Drive is transmitted from the differential to the front wheels by means of two solid-steel, equal-length driveshafts equipped with constant velocity (CV) joints at their inner and outer ends. Due to the position of the transmission, an intermediate shaft and support bearing are incorporated into the right-hand driveshaft assembly.

2 A ball-and-cage type CV joint is fitted to the outer end of each driveshaft. The joint has an outer member, which is splined at its outer end to accept the wheel hub, and is threaded so that it can be fastened to the hub by a large bolt. The joint contains six balls within a cage, which engage with the inner member. The complete assembly is protected by a flexible gaiter secured to the driveshaft and joint outer member.

3 At the inner end, the driveshaft is splined to engage a tripod type CV joint, containing

2.3a Unbolt and then …

2.3b …unhook the level sensor

2.4 Counter hold the drop link nut with a hex key

needle roller bearings and cups. On the left-hand side, the driveshaft inner CV joint engages directly with the differential sun wheel. On the right-hand side, the inner joint is integral with the intermediate shaft, the inner end of which engages with the differential sun wheel. As on the outer joints, a flexible gaiter secured to the driveshaft and CV joint outer member protects the complete assembly.

2 Driveshafts – removal and refitting

Caution: When removing the driveshafts, the inner CV joint must not be bent by more than 18°, and the outer CV joint must not be bent by more than 45° – in other words, keep the shaft as straight as possible. The outer CV joint must not be dismantled from the driveshaft, as it is a press-fit.

Front driveshafts

Removal

1 Remove the wheel trim (or centre cap on models with alloy wheels) and then slacken the driveshaft hub bolt.

2 Loosen the front wheel retaining nuts. Jack up the front of the car and support it on axle stands (see *Jacking and vehicle support*). Remove both front wheels. Remove the engine undershield.

2.6 Free the shaft from the hub

2.7 Undo the driveshaft hub bolt

3 On models fitted with Zenon headlights, detach the level sensor from the control arm **(see illustrations)**. The sensor is only fitted to the left-hand control arm.

4 Undo the nut and detach the lower (or upper) end of the anti roll bar drop link **(see illustration)**. Note that a new nut will be required. If the drop link is detached at the strut, recover the ABS sensor wiring bracket.

5 Undo the nut and detach the steering trackrod end from the hub carrier using a joint-separator tool (see Chapter 10 Section 20).

6 At this point it is worth checking that the driveshaft is free to move in the swivel hub. Unscrew the driveshaft hub bolt several turns and then (using a soft faced hammer)

drive the bolt (and shaft) back into the hub **(see illustration)**. Apply penetrating fluid if necessary.

7 Remove and discard the driveshaft hub bolt **(see illustration)**. A new one must be fitted.

8 Undo the nut and detach the lower balljoint from the hub carrier using either Ford's special tool or a joint-separator tool (see Chapter 10 Section 2).

9 Hold the driveshaft in position and pull the hub from the driveshaft.

Left-hand driveshaft

10 Insert a lever between the inner driveshaft joint and the transmission case, with a thin piece of wood against the case. Prise free the inner joint from the differential **(see illustration)**. If it proves reluctant to move, strike the lever firmly with the palm of the hand. Be careful not to damage adjacent components, and in particular, make sure that the driveshaft oil seal in the differential is not damaged. Be prepared for some oil spillage from the transmission.

11 Withdraw the driveshaft from under the car.

12 Extract the circlip from the groove on the inner end of the driveshaft, and obtain a new one **(see illustration)**.

Right-hand driveshaft

13 Undo the nuts and remove the intermediate bearing support bracket **(see**

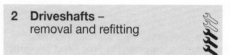

2.10 Gently lever the driveshaft from the differential

2.12 Renew the circlip on the end of the driveshaft

illustration). Dispose of the nuts and bracket, as both must be replaced.

14 Prise free the inner shaft from the differential **(see illustration)**. There is no circlip fitted, so the shaft should just pull out.

Refitting

15 Refitting is a reversal of removal, noting the following points:

a) *Renew the circlip at the inner end of the*
a) *driveshaft (where fitted).*
b) *Renew the anti-roll bar link rod nut.*
c) *Renew the driveshaft hub bolt.*
d) *Tighten all fasteners to their specified torque where given.*
e) *Replenish the transmission fluid where necessary (see Chapter 7 Section 6).*

3 CV joint gaiters – renewal

1 Remove the driveshaft as described in Section 2, and mount it in a bench vice.
2 Mark the driveshaft in relation to the joint housing, to ensure correct refitting.
3 Note the fitted location of both of the inner joint gaiter retaining clips, then release the clips from the gaiter, and slide the gaiter back along the driveshaft a little way **(see illustrations)**. Note that new clips will be required – normally supplied in the driveshaft gaiter kit.
4 Withdraw the inner joint housing from the tripod. As the housing is being removed, be prepared for some of the bearing rollers to fall out – identify them for position with a dab of paint and tape **(see illustration)**. Scoop out the grease from the joint and gaiter. Note that on some driveshafts, it may be necessary to remove the lip on the inside of the inner joint housing using a small file. If this is the case, it's absolutely essential that all swarf/filings are washed out of the housing and tripod joint **(see illustration)**.
5 Check that the inner end of the driveshaft is marked in relation to the splined tripod hub. If not, carefully centre-punch the two items, to ensure correct refitting. Alternatively, use dabs of paint on the driveshaft and one end of the tripod.
6 Extract the circlip retaining the tripod on the driveshaft **(see illustration)**.

7 Using a puller, remove the tripod from the end of the driveshaft, and slide off the gaiter **(see illustration)**.
8 Clean the driveshaft and housing.
9 Slide the new gaiters on the driveshaft,

together with new clips. Make sure that the gaiter is located at its previously-noted position on the driveshaft, then tighten the small diameter clip **(see illustration)**.
10 Refit the tripod on the driveshaft splines,

2.13 Intermediate bearing support bracket nuts

2.14 Remove the right-hand driveshaft

3.3a Cut away the large clip …

3.3b … and release the small clip

3.4a If necessary, remove the lip from the inner joint housing with a small file

3.4b Withdraw the joint housing from the driveshaft tripod

3.6 Remove the circlip from the driveshaft

3.7 Use a puller to extract the tripod

3.9 Slide the new outer gaiter into place

3.10a Engage the chamfered edge of the tripod with the driveshaft first

3.10b Align the previously made marks, and fit a new circlip

3.12a Pack the outer joint housing with the grease supplied in the kit…

3.12b …as well as the inner joint housing and tripod rollers

3.13 Located the gaiter in the grooves

3.14 The 'open' end of the clip must point away from the normal direction of rotation

if necessary using a soft-faced mallet and a suitable metal tube to drive it fully onto the splines. It must be fitted with the chamfered edge leading (towards the driveshaft), and with the previously-made marks aligned. Secure it in position using a new circlip. Ensure that the circlip is fully engaged in its groove **(see illustrations)**.

11 Locate the bearing rollers on the tripod (if removed) in their previously-noted positions, using grease to hold them in place.

12 Pack sufficient CV joint grease into the tripod and joint housings **(see illustrations)**.

13 Guide the joint housing onto the tripod fully, and locate the gaiter in the special groove, ensuring it is not twisted or distorted **(see illustration)**.

14 Insert a small screwdriver under the lip of the gaiter at the housing end, to allow trapped air to escape, then slide the retaining clips into place, ensuring the 'open' end of the clips point away from the normal direction of rotation **(see illustration)**.

15 Tighten the retaining clips. If possible, use the special tool to tighten the clips, otherwise, use pincers **(see illustrations)**.

16 Refit the driveshaft with reference to Section 2.

4 Driveshaft inspection and joint renewal

Note: *Read the Caution in Section 2 before proceeding.*

1 If any of the checks described in the appropriate part of Chapter 1 reveal apparent excessive wear or play in any driveshaft joint, check that the hub nut (driveshaft outer nut) is tightened to the specified torque. Repeat this check on the hub nut on the other side.

2 Road test the car, and listen for a metallic clicking from the front as the car is driven slowly in a circle on full-lock. If a clicking noise is heard, this indicates wear in the outer constant velocity joint, which means that the driveshaft and outer joint must be renewed; it is not possible to renew the joint separately.

3 If vibration, consistent with roadspeed, is felt through the car when accelerating, there is a possibility of wear in the inner tripod joints. To renew an inner joint, remove the driveshaft as described in Section 2, then separate the joint from the driveshaft with reference to Section 3.

4 Continual noise from the right-hand driveshaft, increasing with roadspeed, may indicate wear in the support bearing. The bearing is not available separately from the intermediate shaft, which prises from the transmission once the driveshaft has been removed.

5 With the exception of the rubber gaiters and circlips, no replacement parts for the shafts are available. If faulty, the complete shaft must be renewed. Consult a Ford dealer or parts specialist.

3.15a Use a special tool to secure the large diameter…

3.15b …and small diameter clips on both gaiters

Chapter 9
Braking system

Contents

Degrees of difficulty

Easy, suitable for novice with little experience	Fairly easy, suitable for beginner with some experience	Fairly difficult, suitable for competent DIY mechanic	Difficult, suitable for experienced DIY mechanic	Very difficult, suitable for expert DIY or professional

Specifications

Front brakes

Type	Ventilated disc, with single sliding piston caliper
Disc diameter:	
1.6, 1.8 and 2.2 litre models	300 mm
2.2 litre models	316 mm
Disc thickness:	
New	28.0 mm
Minimum	26.0 mm
Maximum disc thickness variation	0.018 mm
Maximum disc/hub run-out (installed)	0.1 mm
Brake pad friction material minimum thickness	2.0 mm

Rear brakes

Type	Solid disc, with single-piston floating caliper
Disc diameter:	
All models	302 mm
Disc thickness:	
New	11.0 mm
Minimum	9.0 mm
Maximum disc thickness variation	0.020 mm
Maximum disc/hub runout (installed)	0.1 mm
Brake pad friction material minimum thickness	1.5 mm

Torque wrench settings

	Nm	lbf ft
ABS wheel sensor securing bolts.	5	4
Brake pipe to hydraulic control unit:		
6 mm pipes.	14	10
8 mm pipes.	18	13
Brake pipe to master cylinder	18	13
Brake pipe unions	15	11
Front caliper guide bolts.	28	21
Front caliper mounting bracket bolts *	200	148
Handbrake lever mountings	25	18
Master cylinder to servo mountings.	25	18
Pedal bracket to servo mountings	24	18
Rear caliper bracket	110	81
Rear caliper guide bolts	35	26
Roadwheel nuts:		
M12 standard nuts	140	103
M12 locking nut with conical washer	110	81
M12 locking nut with one-piece nut	140	103
M14 nuts.	170	125
Vacuum pump:		
1.6 litre models		
Stage 1	5	4
Stage 2	20	15
1.8 litre models	22	16
2.0 litre models	9	7
2.2 litre models	9	7

Use new bolts

1 General Information

1 The braking system is of diagonally-split, dual-circuit design, with ventilated discs at the front, and disc brakes at the rear. The front calipers are of single sliding piston design, and the rear calipers are of a single-piston floating design.

2 The servo unit uses vacuum generated from the camshaft-driven vacuum pump to boost the effort applied by the driver at the brake pedal and transmits this increased effort to the master cylinder pistons.

3 On most models the handbrake is cable-operated, and acts on the rear brakes. Some models have an electronic handbrake fitted where the operation of the brake is controlled by a caliper mounted electric motor.

4 The anti-lock braking system (ABS) uses the basic conventional brake system, together with an ABS hydraulic unit fitted between the master cylinder and the four brake units at each wheel. The hydraulic unit consists of a hydraulic actuator, an ABS brake pressure pump, and an ABS module. Braking at each of the four wheels is controlled by separate solenoid valves in the hydraulic actuator. If wheel lock-up is detected by one of the wheel sensors, when the vehicle speed is above 3 mph, the valve opens releasing pressure to the relevant brake until the wheel regains a rotational speed corresponding to the speed of the vehicle. The cycle can be repeated many times a second. In the event of a fault in the ABS system, the conventional braking system is not affected. Diagnosis of a fault in the ABS system requires the use of special equipment, and this work should therefore be left to a Ford dealer or suitably-equipped specialist. The wheel speed sensor signal rings are built-into the oil seals of the wheel bearings.

5 Where fitted, the traction control systems are integrated with the ABS, and use the same wheel sensors. The hydraulic control unit has additional solenoid valves incorporated to enable control of the wheel brake pressure. The system is only active at speeds up to 53 mph – when the system is active the warning light on the instrument panel illuminates to warn the driver. This uses controlled braking of the spinning driving wheel when the grip at the driven wheels are different. The spinning wheel is braked by the ABS system, transferring a greater proportion of the engine torque through the differential to the other wheel, which increases the use of the available traction control.

6 On several models in the range, there is an Electronic Stability Program (ESP) available. This system supports the vehicle's stability and steering through a combination of ABS and traction control operations. There is a switch on the centre console, so that if required the system can be switched off. This will then illuminate the warning light on the instrument panel, to inform the driver that the ESP is not in operation. The stability of the vehicle is measured by Yaw rate and Accelerometer sensors, which sense the movement of the vehicle about its vertical axis, and also lateral acceleration.

Note: *When servicing any part of the system, work carefully and methodically; also observe scrupulous cleanliness when overhauling any part of the hydraulic system. Always renew components (in axle sets, where applicable) if in doubt about their condition, and use only genuine Ford parts, or at least those of known good quality. Note the warnings given in 'Safety first!' and at relevant points in this Chapter concerning the dangers of asbestos dust and hydraulic fluid.*

2 Front brake pads – renewal

Warning: Renew both sets of front brake pads at the same time – never renew the pads on only one wheel, as uneven braking may result. Note that the dust created by wear of the pads may contain asbestos, which is a health hazard. Never blow it out with compressed air, and don't inhale any of it. An approved filtering mask should be worn when working on the brakes. DO NOT use petrol or petroleum-based solvents to clean brake parts; use brake cleaner or methylated spirit only.

1 Apply the handbrake, then slacken the front roadwheel nuts. Jack up the front of the vehicle and support it on axle stands. Remove both front roadwheels.

2 Follow the accompanying photos (illustrations 2.2a to 2.2p) for the actual pad renewal procedure. Be sure to stay in order and read the caption under each illustration, and note the following points:

a) *New pads may have an adhesive foil on the backplates. Remove this foil prior to installation.*

b) *Thoroughly clean the caliper guide surfaces, and apply a little brake assembly (polycarbamide) grease.*

c) *When pushing the caliper piston back to accommodate new pads, keep a close eye on the fluid lever in the reservoir.*

d) *If there is any doubt as to the condition of the brake pads, always replace them.*

2.2a Use pliers to carefully prise off the caliper retaining spring

2.2b Prise out the rubber caps...

2.2c ...and use a hex key to undo the caliper guide bolts

2.2d Slide the caliper and inner pad from the disc

2.2e Pull the inner brake pad from the caliper piston...

2.2f ...and lift the outer pad from the caliper bracket

2.2g Push the piston back into the caliper using a piston retraction tool or G-clamp...

2.2h ...however, best practise is to clamp the hose, release the nipple and push the fluid into a brake bleeding bottle

2.2i Clean the pad mounting surfaces with a wire brush

2.2j Measure the thickness of the pad's friction material. If it's 1.5 mm or less, renew all the front pads

2.2k Apply a little copper grease to the pad and then fit the outer pad to the caliper mounting bracket...

2.2l …and then fit the inner pad to the caliper piston

2.2m Slide the caliper with the inner pad fitted over the disc and outer pad

2.2n Refit the caliper guide bolts and tighten them to the specified torque and then refit the rubber caps

3 Depress the brake pedal repeatedly, until the pads are pressed into firm contact with the brake disc, and normal (non-assisted) pedal pressure is restored.

4 Repeat the above procedure on the remaining front brake caliper.

5 Refit the roadwheels, then lower the vehicle to the ground and tighten the roadwheel nuts to the specified torque.

6 Check the hydraulic fluid level as described in *Weekly checks*.

Caution: New pads will not give full braking efficiency until they have bedded-in. Be prepared for this, and avoid hard braking as far as possible for the first hundred miles or so after pad renewal.

2.2o Press in and then …

2.2p …refit the caliper retaining spring

3 Front brake caliper – removal and refitting

Note: *Refer to the warning at the beginning of the previous Section before proceeding.*

Removal

1 Apply the handbrake. Loosen the front wheel nuts, then jack up the front of the vehicle and support it on axle stands. Remove the appropriate front wheel.

2 Fit a brake hose clamp to the flexible hose leading to the caliper **(see illustration)**. This will minimise brake fluid loss during subsequent operations.

3 Loosen the union on the caliper end of the flexible brake hose. Once loosened, do not try to unscrew the hose at this stage.

4 Remove the brake pads as described in Section 2.

5 Support the caliper in one hand, and prevent the hydraulic hose from turning with the other hand. Unscrew the caliper from the hose, making sure that the hose is not

twisted unduly or strained. Once the caliper is detached, plug the open hydraulic unions in the caliper and hose, to keep out dust and dirt.

6 If required, the caliper bracket can be unbolted from the hub carrier **(see illustration)**.

7 No parts are available to overhaul or repair the caliper. If it is faulty, it must be replaced.

Refitting

8 Refit the caliper by reversing the removal operations. Make sure that the flexible brake

3.2 Use a hose clamp on the flexible hoses

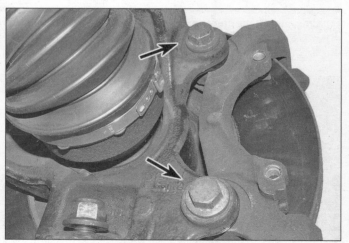

3.6 Caliper bracket bolts

hose is not twisted. Tighten the mounting bolts and wheel nuts to the specified torque.
9 Bleed the brake circuit according to the procedure given in Section 11, remembering to remove the brake hose clamp from the flexible hose. Make sure there are no leaks from the hose connections. Test the brakes carefully before returning the vehicle to normal service.

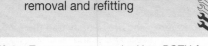

4 Front brake disc – inspection, removal and refitting

Note: *To prevent uneven braking, BOTH front brake discs should be renewed at the same time.*

Inspection

1 Apply the handbrake. Loosen the relevant wheel nuts, jack up the front of the vehicle and support it on axle stands. Remove the appropriate front wheel.
2 Remove the front brake caliper from the disc with reference to Section 3, and undo the two caliper bracket securing bolts. Do not disconnect the flexible hose. Support the caliper on an axle stand, or suspend it out of the way with a piece of wire, taking care to avoid straining the flexible hose **(see illustration)**.
3 Temporarily refit two of the wheel nuts to diagonally opposite studs, with the flat sides of the nuts against the disc. Tighten the nuts progressively, to hold the disc firmly.
4 Scrape any corrosion from the disc. Rotate the disc, and examine it for deep scoring, grooving or cracks. Using a micrometer, measure the thickness of the disc in several places **(see illustration)**. The minimum thickness is stamped on the disc hub. Light wear and scoring is normal, but if excessive, the disc should be removed and replaced. If the disc is cracked, it must be renewed. If there is any doubt as to the condition the

4.2 Suspend the caliper from the spring using wire or string

4.4 Measure the thickness of the disc using a micrometer

discs replace them. Always replace the brake pads when the brake discs are replaced.
5 Using a dial gauge or a flat metal block and feeler gauges, check that the disc run-out 10 mm from the outer edge does not exceed the limit given in the Specifications. To do this, fix the measuring equipment, and rotate the disc, noting the variation in measurement as the disc is rotated. The difference between the minimum and maximum measurements recorded is the disc run-out.
6 If the run-out is greater than the specified amount, check for variations of the disc thickness as follows. Mark the disc at eight positions 45° apart then, using a micrometer, measure the disc thickness at the eight positions, 15 mm in from the outer edge. If the variation between the minimum and maximum readings is greater than the specified amount, the disc should be renewed.
7 The hub face run-out can also be checked in a similar way. First remove the disc as described later in this Section, fix the measuring equipment, then slowly rotate the hub, and check that the run-out does not exceed the amount given in the Specifications. If the hub face run-out is excessive, this should be corrected (by renewing the hub

bearings – see Chapter 10 Section 2) before rechecking the disc run-out.

Removal

8 With the wheel, caliper and bracket removed **(see illustration)** remove the wheel nuts which were temporarily refitted in paragraph 3.
9 Mark the disc in relation to the hub, if it is to be refitted.
10 Remove the washer/retaining clip(s) (where fitted), and withdraw the disc over the wheel studs **(see illustration)**.

Refitting

11 Make sure that the disc and hub mating surfaces are clean, then locate the disc on the wheel studs. Align the previously-made marks if the original disc is being refitted.
12 Refit the washer/retaining clip(s), where fitted.
13 Refit the brake caliper and bracket with reference to Section 3.
14 Refit the wheel, and lower the vehicle to the ground. Tighten wheel nuts to their specified torque.
15 Test the brakes carefully before returning the vehicle to normal service.

4.8 Remove the caliper mounting bracket

4.10 Lift the brake disc from the studs

5.3a Remove the caliper guide bolts ...

5.3b ...and lift off the caliper

5.3c Remove the brake pads and then the recover the shims

5.3d Retract the piston using a piston wind back tool

5.3e Use a wire brush and ...

5.3f ...brake cleaner to clean the caliper mounting

5.3g Fit the new shims and then ...

5.3h ...apply a little copper based grease to the pads. DO NOT contaminate the friction material

5.3i Fit the new inner brake pad ...

5.3j ...followed by the outer brake pad

5.3k Refit the caliper and then fit the new caliper guide bolts

5.3l Tighten the bolts to the specified torque

5 Rear brake pads – renewal

⚠️ **Warning: Renew both sets of rear brake pads at the same time – never renew the pads on only one wheel, as uneven braking may result. Note that the dust created by wear of the pads may contain asbestos, which is a health hazard. Never blow it out with compressed air, and don't inhale any of it. An approved filtering mask should be worn when working on the brakes. DO NOT use petrol or petroleum-based solvents to clean brake parts; use brake cleaner or methylated spirit only.**

1 On models fitted with an Electronic Parking Brake (EPB) a suitable service tool will be required to place the rear brakes in service mode. The tool communicates with the EPB via the diagnostic socket. Where the tool is not available then the disconnect the wiring plug and remove the motor from the brake caliper. Using a hex or torx key wind back the piston – note that this is also the procedure to follow in the event of a total failure of the vehicle electrics, when the vehicle needs to be moved and there is no alternative power source.

2 Chock the front wheels, slacken the rear road wheel nuts, then jack up the rear of the vehicle and support it on axle stands (see *Jacking and vehicle support*). Remove the rear wheels.

3 With the handbrake lever fully released, follow the accompanying photos **(see illustrations 5.3a to 5.3l)** for the actual pad renewal procedure. Be sure to stay in order and read the caption under each illustration, and note the following points:

a) *If re-installing the original pads, ensure they are fitted to their original position.*

b) *Thoroughly clean the caliper guide surfaces and guide bolts.*

c) *If new pads are to be fitted, use a piston retraction tool to push the piston back and twist it clockwise at the same time – keep an eye on the fluid level in the reservoir whilst retracting the piston.*

Caution: Pushing back the piston causes a reverse-flow of brake fluid, which has been known to 'flip' the master cylinder rubber seals, resulting in a total loss of braking. To avoid this, clamp the caliper flexible hose and open the bleed screw – as the piston is pushed back, the fluid can be directed into a suitable container using a hose attached to the bleed screw. Close the screw just before the piston is pushed fully back, to ensure no air enters the system.

4 Depress the brake pedal repeatedly, until the pads are pressed into firm contact with the brake disc, and normal (non-assisted) pedal pressure is restored.

5 Repeat the above procedure on the remaining brake caliper.

6 If necessary, adjust the handbrake as described in Section 18.

7 Refit the roadwheels, then lower the vehicle to the ground and tighten the roadwheel nuts to the specified torque.

8 Check the hydraulic fluid level as described in *Weekly checks.*.

Caution: New pads will not give full braking efficiency until they have bedded-in. Be prepared for this, and avoid hard braking as far as possible for the first hundred miles or so after pad renewal.

6 Rear brake caliper – removal and refitting

Removal

Note: *Where an Electronic Parking Brake (EPB) is fitted, the caliper must be placed in the service mode using a diagnostic tool. Alternatively, follow the procedure detailed in the previous Section 6.*

1 Chock the front wheels, and engage 1st gear. Loosen the rear wheel nuts, jack up the rear of the vehicle and support it on axle stands. Remove the appropriate rear wheel.

2 Fit a brake hose clamp to the flexible hose leading to the caliper. This will minimise brake fluid loss during subsequent operations.

3 Slacken (but do not completely unscrew) the union on the caliper end of the flexible hose.

4 Unclip the handbrake inner cable fitting from the lever on the caliper (it may be necessary to slacken the handbrake cable) then detach the outer cable from the bracket **(see illustrations)**.

5 Unscrew the caliper from the hydraulic brake hose, making sure that the hose is not twisted or strained unduly. Plug the open hydraulic unions to keep dust and dirt out.

6 If necessary, unbolt the caliper bracket from the hub carrier **(see illustration)**.

7 No overhaul procedures, or parts, were available at the time of writing. Check the availability of spares before dismantling the caliper. Do not attempt to dismantle the handbrake mechanism inside the caliper; if the mechanism is faulty, the complete caliper assembly must be renewed.

Refitting

8 Refit the caliper, and where applicable the bracket, by reversing the removal operations. Refer to the points made in Section 18 when reconnecting the handbrake cable. Tighten the mounting bolts and wheel nuts to the specified torque, and do not forget to remove the brake hose clamp from the flexible brake hose.

9 Bleed the brake circuit according to the procedure given in Section 11. Make sure there are no leaks from the hose connections. Test the brakes carefully before returning the vehicle to normal service.

7 Rear brake disc – inspection, removal and refitting

Removal

1 Remove the rear caliper and pads as described in Section 5.

2 Unbolt the caliper bracket from the hub **(see illustration 6.6)**, then mark the disc in relation to the hub, if it is to be refitted.

3 Remove the retaining clip from the wheel

6.4a Unclip the cable end fitting from the caliper lever...

6.4b ...and pull out the cable

6.6 Undo the caliper mounting bracket bolts

stud (where fitted), and withdraw the disc over the wheel studs **(see illustration)**.

4 Procedures for inspection of the rear brake discs are the same as the front brake discs as described in Section 4.

Refitting

5 Refitting is a reversal of removal, as described in the relevant Sections. Apply a little thread locking compound to the caliper bracket-to-hub carrier bolts.

8   Master cylinder –
removal and refitting

7.3 Pull the rear brake disc over the wheel studs

> ⚠️ **Warning: Brake fluid is poisonous. Take care to keep it off bare skin, and in particular not to get splashes in your eyes. The fluid also attacks paintwork and plastics – wash off spillages immediately with cold water. Finally, brake fluid is highly inflammable, and should be handled with the same care as petrol.**

Removal

1 Exhaust the vacuum in the servo by pressing the brake pedal a few times, with the engine switched off.

2 Disconnect the battery negative lead as described in Chapter 5 Section 3.

3 Unbolt the brake fluid reservoir from the lower windscreen cowl panel **(see illustration)** and then remove the upper and lower windscreen cowl panels as described in Chapter 11.

4 Fit a hose clamp to the remote reservoir feed pipe and then disconnect the feed pipe – anticipate some fluid spillage as the pipe is disconnected.

5 Raise the vehicle and remove the wheels. Slacken the front bleed nipples, attach a rubber hose to the nipple, and place the other end of the hose in a suitable container. Operate the brake pedal until the fluid level is down to the base of the reservoir.

6 Depress the release button and detach the clutch master cylinder fluid supply hose from

the base of the brake fluid reservoir. Plug the openings to prevent contamination.

7 Disconnect the wiring plug from the fluid level sensor on the side of the reservoir.

8 Identify the locations of each brake pipe on the master cylinder, then place rags beneath the master cylinder to catch spilt hydraulic fluid.

9 Clean around the hydraulic union nuts. Unscrew the nuts, and disconnect the hydraulic lines from the master cylinder. If the nuts are tight, a split ring spanner should be used in preference to an open-ended spanner. Cap the end of the pipes and the master cylinder to prevent any dirt contamination.

10 Undo the master cylinder securing nuts, and withdraw the master cylinder from the studs on the servo unit.

11 Recover the gasket/seal from the master cylinder.

12 Prise out the locking peg and free the reservoir from the master cylinder.

13 If the master cylinder is faulty, it must be renewed.

Refitting

14 Refitting is a reversal of the removal procedure, noting the following points:

a) *Clean the contact surfaces of the master cylinder and servo, and locate a new gasket on the master cylinder.*

b) *Refit and tighten the nuts to the specified torque.*

8.3 Unbolt the reservoir

c) *Carefully insert the brake pipes in the apertures in the master cylinder, then tighten the union nuts. Make sure that the nuts enter their threads correctly.*

d) *Fill the reservoir with fresh brake fluid.*

e) *Bleed the brake hydraulic system as described in Section 11.*

f) *Test the brakes carefully before returning the vehicle to normal service.*

9   Brake pedal –
removal and refitting

Removal

1 Working inside the vehicle, move the driver's seat fully to the rear, to allow maximum working area.

2 Remove the driver's side lower facia panel as described in Chapter 11 Section 24.

3 Remove the accelerator pedal as described in Chapter 4A Section 5.

4 Disconnect the electrical connectors to the brake pedal switches. Remove the switches by turning them, then pulling them out of the pedal bracket **(see illustration)**.

5 Prise out the pin securing the servo pushrod to the pedal **(see illustration)**. Discard the pin – a new one must be fitted.

9.4 Disconnect the wiring plugs from the brake pedal switches

9.5 Prise out and discard the servo pushrod pin

9.6 Brake pedal bracket assembly retaining nuts

10.7 Use a brake pipe spanner to slacken the union nuts

6 Remove the brake pedal to brake servo nuts and then ten remove the bulkhead nuts **(see illustration)**.

7 Manoeuvre the pedal assembly rearwards, and down from under the facia. No further dismantling of the assembly is recommended – it would appear that only the complete assembly is available.

Refitting

8 Refitting is a reversal of the removal procedure.

9 Refit the brake pedal switches as described in Section 17.

---

10 Hydraulic pipes and hoses – inspection, removal and refitting

Note: *Refer to the warning at the start of Section 11 concerning the dangers of brake fluid.*

Inspection

1 Jack up the front and rear of the vehicle, and support on axle stands (see *Jacking and vehicle support*). Making sure the vehicle is safely supported on a level surface.

2 Check for signs of leakage at the pipe unions, then examine the flexible hoses for signs of cracking, chafing and fraying.

3 The brake pipes should be examined carefully for signs of dents, corrosion or other damage. Corrosion should be scraped off, and if the depth of pitting is significant, the pipes renewed. This is particularly likely in those areas underneath the vehicle body where the pipes are exposed and unprotected.

4 Renew any defective brake pipes and/or hoses.

Removal

5 If a section of pipe or hose is to be removed, loss of brake fluid can be reduced by unscrewing the filler cap, and completely sealing the top of the reservoir with cling film or adhesive tape. Alternatively, the reservoir can be emptied (see Section 8).

6 To remove a section of pipe, hold the adjoining hose union nut with a spanner to prevent it from turning, then unscrew the union nut at the end of the pipe, and release it. Repeat the procedure at the other end of the pipe, then release the pipe by pulling out the clips attaching it to the body.

7 Where the union nuts are exposed to the full force of the weather, they can sometimes be quite tight. If an open-ended spanner is used, burring of the flats on the nuts is not uncommon, and for this reason, it is preferable to use a split ring (brake) spanner **(see illustration)** which will engage all the flats. If such a spanner is not available, self-locking grips may be used as a last resort. These may well damage the nuts, but if the pipe is to be renewed, this does not matter.

8 To further minimise the loss of fluid when disconnecting a flexible brake line from a rigid pipe, clamp the hose as near as possible to the pipe to be detached, using a brake hose clamp or a pair of self-locking grips with protected jaws.

9 To remove a flexible hose, first clean the ends of the hose and the surrounding area, then unscrew the union nuts from the hose ends. Remove the spring clip, and withdraw the hose from the serrated mounting in the support bracket. Where applicable, unscrew the hose from the caliper.

10 Brake pipes supplied with flared ends and union nuts can be obtained individually or in sets from Ford dealers or accessory shops. The pipe is then bent to shape, using the old pipe as a guide, and is ready for fitting. Be careful not to kink or crimp the pipe when bending it. Ideally, a proper pipe-bending tool should be used.

Refitting

11 Refitting of the pipes and hoses is a reversal of removal. Make sure that all brake pipes are securely supported in their clips, and ensure that the hoses are not kinked. Check also that the hoses are clear of all suspension components and underbody fittings, and will remain clear during movement of the suspension and steering.

12 On completion, bleed the hydraulic system as described in Section 11.

---

11 Hydraulic system – bleeding

> **Warning: Brake fluid contains polyglycol ethers and polyglycols which are poisonous. Take care to keep it off bare skin, and in particular not to get splashes in your eyes. Wash hands thoroughly after handling and if fluid contacts the eyes, flush out with cold running water. If irritation persists get medical attention immediately. The fluid also attacks paintwork and plastics – wash off spillages immediately with cold water. Finally, brake fluid is highly inflammable, and should be handled with the same care as petrol.**

1 If the master cylinder has been disconnected and reconnected, then the complete system (all circuits) must be bled of air. If a component of one circuit has been disturbed, then only that particular circuit need be bled.

2 Bleeding should commence on the furthest bleed nipple from the master cylinder, followed by the next one until the bleed nipple remaining nearest to the master cylinder is bled last.

3 There are a variety of do-it-yourself 'one-man' brake bleeding kits available from motor accessory shops, and it is recommended that one of these kits be used wherever possible, as they greatly simplify the brake bleeding operation. Follow the kit manufacturer's instructions in conjunction with the following procedure. If a pressure-

11.7a Prise off the dust cap from the bleed screw

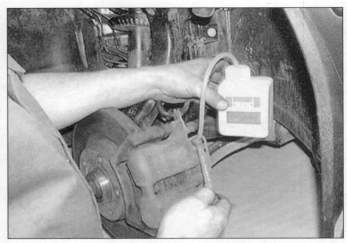

11.7b Connect the kit and open the bleed screw

bleeding kit is obtained, then it will not be necessary to depress the brake pedal in the following procedure.

4 During the bleeding operation, do not allow the brake fluid level in the reservoir to drop below the minimum mark. If the level is allowed to fall so far that air is drawn in, the whole procedure will have to be started again from scratch. Only use new fluid for topping-up, preferably from a freshly-opened container. Never re-use fluid bled from the system.

5 Before starting, check that all rigid pipes and flexible hoses are in good condition, and that all hydraulic unions are tight. Take great care not to allow hydraulic fluid to come into contact with the vehicle paintwork, otherwise the finish will be seriously damaged. Wash off any spilt fluid immediately with cold water.

6 If a brake bleeding kit is not being used, gather together a clean jar, a length of plastic or rubber tubing which is a tight fit over the bleed screw, and a new container of the specified brake fluid (see *Lubricants and fluids*). The help of an assistant will also be required.

7 Clean the area around the bleed screw on the rear brake unit to be bled (it is important that no dirt be allowed to enter the hydraulic system), and remove the dust cap. Connect one end of the tubing to the bleed screw, and immerse the other end in the jar **(see illustrations)**. The jar should be filled with sufficient brake fluid to keep the end of the tube submerged.

8 Open the bleed screw by half a turn, and have the assistant depress the brake pedal to the floor. Tighten the bleed screw at the end of the downstroke, then have the assistant release the pedal. Continue this procedure until clean brake fluid, free from air bubbles, can be seen flowing into the jar. Finally tighten the bleed screw with the pedal in the fully-depressed position.

9 Remove the tube, and refit the dust cap. Top-up the master cylinder reservoir if

necessary, then repeat the procedure on the opposite rear brake.

10 Repeat the procedure on the front brake furthest from the master cylinder, followed by the brake nearest to the master cylinder.

11 Check the feel of the brake pedal – it should be firm. If it is spongy, there is still some air in the system, and the bleeding procedure should be repeated.

12 When bleeding is complete, top-up the master cylinder reservoir and refit the cap.

13 Check the clutch operation on completion; it may be necessary to bleed the clutch hydraulic system as described in Chapter 6 Section 5.

12 Vacuum servo unit – testing, removal and refitting

Testing

1 To test the operation of the servo unit, depress the footbrake four or five times to dissipate the vacuum, then start the engine while keeping the footbrake depressed. As the engine starts, there should be a noticeable give in the brake pedal as vacuum builds-up. Allow the engine to run for at least two minutes, and then switch it off. If the brake pedal is now depressed again, it should be possible to hear a hiss from the servo when the pedal is depressed. After four or five applications, no further hissing should be heard, and the pedal should feel harder.

2 Before assuming that a problem exists in the servo unit itself, inspect the non-return valve. This can be done by pulling the servo hose from the brake servo and blowing through the valve – air should only pass in one direction.

Removal

Caution: On all models the air conditioning system must be degassed before proceeding – see Chapter 3.

1.6 and 1.8 litre models

3 Disconnect the battery (Chapter 5 Section 3) and then remove the upper and lower windscreen cowl panels as described in Chapter 12 Section 12.

4 Drain the brake fluid and then remove the brake master cylinder as described in Section 8.

5 Disconnect the AC pipes at the expansion valve and remove the wiring plug from the AC pressure switch.

6 If not already done so disconnect the brake pipes at the connection above the expansion valve.

7 Remove the driver's side lower facia panel/knee airbag as described in Chapter 11 Section 24.

8 Remove the brake light switches and then remove the brake pedal assembly as described in Section 9.

9 Prise out the servo vacuum pipe and check valve.

10 Lift out the brake servo unit.

11 Note that the servo unit cannot be dismantled for repair or overhaul and, if faulty, must be renewed.

2.0 and 2.2 litre models

12 On 2.0 litre and 2.2 litre models the engine must be lowered and moved slightly forward to create sufficient room to remove the brake servo.

13 Jack up and support the front of the vehicle – see *Jacking and vehicle support* and then remove the engine undershield.

14 Remove the accessory (Chapter 1 Section 22) drivebelt and then unbolt the compressor from the front of the engine (Chapter 3 Section 12). Secure the compressor with cable ties to the radiator support panel.

15 Disconnect the exhaust and then support the flexible section with wooden splints. Remove the exhaust/catalytic converter support bracket from the subframe.

16 Remove the engine torque rod as

described in Chapter 2C Section 16 (2.0 litre) or Chapter 2D Section 15 (2.2 litre).

17 Support the timing belt end of the engine with a trolley jack on the sump. Use a block of wood on the head of the jack to spread the load and then just take the weight of the engine on the jack.

18 Unclip the fuel lines from the timing belt cover and then unhook the power steering fluid reservoir from the slam panel.

19 Remove the right-hand engine mounting as described in Section 2C Section 16 (2.0 litre engine) or Chapter 2D Section 15 (2.2 litre engine).

20 Lower the engine on the jack and pull it slightly forward. Lowering the engine approximately 100mm should be sufficient to allow the sero to be removed.

21 Drain the brake fluid and then remove the brake master cylinder as described in Section 8.

22 Disconnect the AC pipes at the expansion valve and remove the wiring plug from the AC pressure switch.

23 If not already done so disconnect the brake pipes at the connection above the expansion valve.

24 Prise out the servo vacuum pipe and check valve.

25 Remove the driver's side lower facia/knee airbag panel as described in Chapter 11 Section 24.

26 Remove the brake light switches and then remove the brake pedal assembly as described in Section 9.

27 Lift out the brake servo unit.

28 Note that the servo unit cannot be dismantled for repair or overhaul and, if faulty, must be renewed.

Refitting

29 Refitting is a reversal of the removal procedure, noting the following points:

a) *Refer to the relevant Sections/Chapters for details of refitting the other components removed.*

b) *Compress the actuator rod into the brake servo, before refitting.*

c) *Fit a new clevis pin to the actuating rod*

d) *Make sure the gasket is correctly positioned on the servo.*

e) *Test the brakes carefully before returning the vehicle to normal service.*

13 ABS hydraulic unit – removal and refitting

Note: *No individual parts are available for the ABS hydraulic unit. It must be renewed as complete assembly. Refer to the warning at the start of Section 11 concerning the dangers of brake fluid.*

Removal

1 Remove the upper and lower windscreen cowl panels as described in Chapter 12 Section 12.

2 Remove the battery and battery tray as described in Chapter 5 Section 3.

3 Raise the vehicle and remove the wheels. Slacken the front bleed nipples, attach a rubber hose to the nipple, and place the other end of the hose in a suitable container. Operate the brake pedal until the fluid level is down to the base of the reservoir.

 Warning: Do not syphon the fluid by mouth; it is poisonous. Any brake fluid spilt on paintwork should be washed off with clean water, without delay – brake fluid is also a highly-effective paint-stripper.

4 Depress the retaining clips, release the retainer and disconnect the wring plug from the ABS control unit **(see illustration)**. Cover the disconnected plug and socket to prevent contamination.

5 Undo the brake pipes from the hydraulic control unit. Cap the end of the pipes and the hydraulic unit to prevent any dirt contamination. Unclip the brake lines from the retaining clips.

6 Undo the securing bolts from the brake hydraulic unit, and withdraw from the bulkhead. Remove it from the engine compartment, taking care not to damage any other components.

Refitting

7 Refitting is a reversal of removal. Ensure that the multiplug is securely connected, and that the brake pipe unions are tightened to the specified torque. On completion, bleed the hydraulic system as described in Section 11.

14 ABS wheel sensor – testing, removal and refitting

Testing

1 Checking of the sensors is done either by substitution with a known good unit, or by interrogating the ABS ECU for stored fault codes, using dedicated test equipment found at Ford dealers or suitably-equipped specialists.

Removal

Front wheel sensor

2 Apply the handbrake and loosen the relevant front wheel nuts. Jack up the front of the vehicle and support it on axle stands. Remove the wheel.

3 Disconnect the sensor wiring plug.

4 Unscrew the sensor mounting bolt from the hub carrier and withdraw the sensor **(see illustration)**. Withdraw the O-ring seal.

Rear wheel sensor

5 Chock the front wheels, and engage 1st gear. Jack up the rear of the vehicle and support it on axle stands. Remove the relevant wheel.

6 Disconnect the sensor wiring plug.

7 Unscrew the sensor mounting bolt, and withdraw the sensor **(see illustration)**. Withdraw the O-ring seal.

Refitting

8 Refitting is a reversal of the removal procedure. Fit a new O-ring seal to the hub carrier – not the sensor.

15 Electronic stability control components – removal and refitting

Note: *This system uses the same components as the ABS and Traction control system. The only additional components are the 'yaw rate' sensor and 'accelerometer sensor', which are mounted on the same bracket on the floor crossmember, and the steering wheel rotation sensor.*

13.4 Release the latch and disconnect the ABS unit wiring plug

14.4 Front ABS sensor mounting bolt

14.7 Remove the ABS sensor (shown with the hub removed)

Yaw rate and accelerometer sensor

Removal

1 Remove the driver's side front seat as described in Chapter 11 Section 22.
2 Open the relevant door, then pull the trim upwards from along the sill.
3 Remove the driver's side B-pillar trim panel as described in Chapter 11 Section 24.
4 Pull the carpet back to gain access to the sensors.
5 Disconnect the sensor wiring plug.
6 Undo the two retaining bolts and remove the sensor and bracket.

Refitting

7 Refitting is a reversal of the removal procedure. Ensure the sensor and bracket is correctly positioned.

Steering wheel rotation sensor

8 The steering wheel rotation sensor is integral with the driver's airbag contact unit, beneath the steering wheel. Removal of the unit is described in Chapter 12 Section 21.

16 Traction control system – general information

1 The Traction control system is an expanded version of the ABS system. It is integrated with the ABS, and uses the same wheel sensors. It also uses the hydraulic control unit, which incorporates additional internal solenoid valves.

18.5 Unhook the exhaust system

17 Brake switches – removal, refitting and adjustment

Removal

Brake pedal position switch

1 Disconnect the battery negative (earth) lead (see Chapter 5 Section 3).
2 Remove the driver's side lower facia/knee airbag panel as described in Chapter 11 Section 24.
3 Disconnect the wiring connector from the brake pedal position switch. This is the left-hand switch and is coloured blue (see illustration 17.6).
4 Rotate the switch anti-clockwise by a quarter-turn, and withdraw it from the pedal bracket. Do not depress the brake pedal during the removal or refitting procedure – the pedal must be 'at rest'.

Brake light switch

5 Proceed as described in Paragraphs 1 and 2 in this Section.
6 Disconnect the wiring connector from the brake light switch. This is the right-hand switch and is coloured black (see illustration).
7 Rotate the switch clockwise by a quarter-turn, and withdraw it from the pedal bracket. Do not depress the brake pedal during the removal or refitting procedure – the pedal must be 'at rest'.

17.6 Disconnect the wiring plug

18.6 Remove the heatshield fixings

Refitting and adjustment

8 Refitting is a reversal of the removal procedure. Note: If both switches have been removed, the brake pedal position switch must be installed before the light switch.
9 Both switches are automatically adjusted/calibrated by the vehicle system.

18 Handbrake lever – removal and refitting

Removal

1 Chock the front wheels and engage 1st gear.
2 Remove the upper section of the centre console as described in Chapter 11 Section 25.
3 Disconnect the electrical connector from the handbrake switch (see illustration).
4 Jack up and support the rear of the vehicle – see Jacking and vehicle support.
5 Unhook the exhaust system from the rubber mountings and move it to the side (see illustration). On models with twin rear exhaust silencers it may be necessary to disconnect the exhaust system.
6 Remove the fixings and manoeuvre the exhaust heat shield out from the transmission tunnel and over the exhaust pipe (see illustration).
7 Note the position of the handbrake travel adjustment nut and then slacken the nut (see illustration). Disconnect the handbrake cable.
8 Remove the handbrake mounting nuts and then lift out the handbrake lever from the lower section of the centre console.
9 Withdraw the handbrake from inside the vehicle.

Refitting

10 Refitting is a reversal of removal, ensuring the cable retaining tab is positioned away from the cable.
11 When refitting the lever, it will be necessary to adjust the mechanism, as follows. Note: The handbrake should only be adjusted when the brakes are cool.
12 Working on one rear calipers, insert a 1.2 mm feeler gauge between the handbrake

18.3 Disconnect the handbrake warning light switch

18.7 Slacken the adjuster nut

18.12 Insert a 1.2 mm feeler gauge

19.5 Release the handbrake cable from the operating arm

19.6 Free the cable from the guide

lever and the caliper abutment on both sides **(see illustration)**.

13 Tighten the cable adjustment nut until one of the operating levers (at the calipers) just starts to move.

14 Remove the feeler gauges from both sides, then check the wheels rotate freely with no excess friction or drag caused by the brake.

15 Pull on the handbrake lever and check the operation of the brake. No figures are given for the number of 'clicks' on the handbrake lever travel, but there should be plenty of travel in reserve when the wheels are locked. An MOT test centre will be able to test the brakes if necessary.

19 Handbrake cables – removal and refitting

Removal

1 Slacken the handbrake adjustment nut to the end of the threads.

2 Chock the front wheels and engage 1st gear. Loosen the wheel nuts on the relevant rear wheel, then jack up the rear of the vehicle and support it on axle stands – see *Jacking and vehicle support*. Fully release the handbrake lever.

3 Unhook the exhaust system from the rubber mounting and then remove the heatshield from the transmission tunnel – see the previous Section 18.

4 Fully slacken off the handbrake adjusting nut and unhook the cables.

5 Remove the relevant rear wheel and unclip the handbrake outer cable from its retaining clips **(see illustration)**.

6 Unbolt the cable on both sides **(see illustration)**.

7 Work along the cable and unclip and unbolt the cable as required **(see illustrations)**.

Refitting

8 Refitting is a reversal of the removal procedure, noting the following points:

a) *Adjust the cable as described in Section 18.*

b) *Make sure that the cable end fittings are correctly located*

19.7a Unclip and ...

19.7b ... unbolt the cable

c) *Check the operation of the handbrake. Make sure that both wheels are locked, then free to turn, as the handbrake is operated.*

20 Vacuum pump – removal and refitting

Removal

1.6 litre models

1 Remove the cover from the top of the engine.

2 Disconnect the hoses from the vacuum pump **(see illustration)**. The second hose is a push fit.

20.2 Depress the button and pull the hose from the vacuum pump

3 Undo the 2 retaining bolts and remove the vacuum pump Discard the O-ring seals, new ones must be fitted.

1.8 litre models

4 Remove the plastic cover from the top of the engine.

5 Unscrew the union nut and disconnect the vacuum line from the top of the pump **(see illustration)**.

6 Release the retaining clips and disconnect the oil separator/return hose(s) from the cylinder head cover.

7 Unbolt the air inlet hoses from the top of the cylinder head cover, and detach the breather hoses.

8 Unbolt and remove the cylinder head cover.

9 Using a suitable socket or spanner on the crankshaft pulley bolt, turn the crankshaft until the vacuum pump pushrod (operated

20.5 Undo the vacuum line from the top of the pump

20.12 Slacken the bolts evenly, then remove the top bolt

20.13 Renew the sealing ring when refitting the brake vacuum pump

20.16 Remove the solenoids

by the eccentric on the camshaft end) is fully retracted into the cylinder head.

10 Disconnect the electrical connectors from the heater/glow plug, the engine temperature sensor and the oil pressure switch.

11 Release the retaining clips and disconnect the oil separator/return hose(s) from the pump. Be prepared for some oil spillage as the hose is disconnected and mop-up any spilt oil.

12 Evenly and progressively slacken the bolts securing the pump to the front of the cylinder head **(see illustration)**. Note that there is no need to remove the lower bolt completely, as the lower end of the pump is slotted.

13 Remove the pump from the engine compartment, along with its sealing ring **(see illustration)**. Discard the sealing ring, a new one should be used on refitting.

2.0 litre models

14 Remove the cover from the top of the engine.

15 Remove the air filter housing outlet duct. Note that on some models the duct is held by a cable tie – cut the cable tie to remove the duct.

16 Remove the nuts and (noting the position of the vacuum pipes and electrical connectors) remove the vacuum solenoids **(see illustration)**.

17 Remove the crash protector (where fitted) and then disconnect the vacuum lines from the pump.

18 Undo the bolts and remove the vacuum pump **(see illustration)**. Discard the O-ring seals, new ones must be fitted.

2.2 litre models

19 Remove the cover from the top of the engine.

20 Unbolt the oil filler neck and move it to the side **(see illustration)** securing it out of the way if needs be.

20.18a Vacuum pump retaining bolts

20.18b Renew the pump O-ring seals

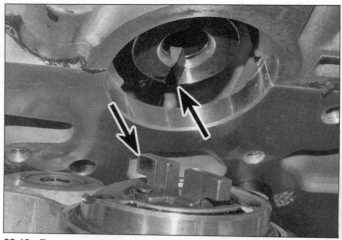

20.18c Ensure the drive lugs engage with the slot in the end of the camshaft

20.20 Unbolt the filler neck

20.21a Unclip the fuel lines...

20.21b ...and disconnect the vacuum lines

20.22a Remove the bolts and...

20.22b ...withdraw the vacuum pump

21 Unclip the fuel lines and vacuum lines **(see illustrations)**.

22 Undo the bolts and remove the vacuum pump **(see illustrations)**. Discard the O-ring seals, new ones must be fitted.

Refitting

23 Refitting is a reversal of removal, noting the following points:

a) *Ensure the pump and cylinder head mating surfaces are clean and dry. Fit the new sealing ring to the pump recess.*

b) *On 1.6 and 2.0 and 2.2 litre models, ensure the drive coupling is aligned with the slot in the camshaft (see illustrations).*

c) *Start the engine and check for correct operation of the pump (check brakes have servo action) as described in Section 12.*

d) *Make sure all the hose connections are secure, and check for leaks.*

21 Vacuum pump –
  testing and overhaul

Note: *A vacuum gauge will be required for this check.*

1 The operation of the braking system vacuum pump can be checked using a vacuum gauge.

2 Disconnect the vacuum pipe from the pump, and connect the gauge to the pump union using a suitable length of hose.

3 Start the engine and allow it to idle, then measure the vacuum created by the pump. As a guide, after one minute, a minimum of approximately 500 mm Hg should be recorded. If the vacuum registered is significantly less than this, it is likely that the pump is faulty. However, seek the advice of a Ford dealer before condemning the pump.

4 Overhaul of the vacuum pump is not possible, since no components are available separately. If faulty, the complete pump assembly must be renewed.

Chapter 10
Suspension and steering

Contents

Degrees of difficulty

Easy, suitable for novice with little experience	**Fairly easy,** suitable for beginner with some experience	**Fairly difficult,** suitable for competent DIY mechanic	**Difficult,** suitable for experienced DIY mechanic	**Very difficult,** suitable for expert DIY or professional

Specifications

Front suspension
Type . . . . Independent, with MacPherson struts incorporating coil springs and telescopic shock absorbers. Anti-roll bar fitted to all models

Rear suspension
Type . . . . Fully-independent, multilink with separate coil springs and hydraulic telescopic shock absorbers. Anti-roll bar fitted to all models

Steering
Type . . . . Electro-hydraulic or accessory belt driven hydraulic power-assisted rack and pinion

Wheel alignment and steering angles
Front wheel: *
  Camber angle:
    Standard chassis . . . . -1.85° to 0.69°
    Sports chassis . . . . -2.10° to 0.44°
  Castor angle:
    Standard chassis . . . . 1.91 to 3.97°
    Sports chassis . . . . 2.04° to 4.10°
  Toe setting . . . . 0.20° ± 0.14° (toe-in)
Rear wheel:
  Camber angle:
    Standard chassis . . . . -2.57° to -0.07°
    Sports chassis . . . . -2.81° to -0.31°
  Toe setting . . . . 0.40° ± 0.14° (toe-in)
*All figures are decimal degrees

Tyres
Tyre pressures . . . . See *Weekly checks*

Torque wrench settings

	Nm	lbf ft
Front suspension		
ABS sensor	5	4
Anti-roll bar clamp bolts*		
Stage 1	140	103
Stage 2	Angle tighten a further 45°	
Anti-roll bar drop link nuts*	70	52
Control arm ball joint nut	100	74
Control arm to subframe: *		
Front bolt		
Stage 1	80	59
Stage 2	Angle tighten a further 120°	
Rear bolts		
Stage 1	140	103
Stage 2	Angle tighten a further 45°	
Driveshaft bolt: *		
Stage 1	45	33
Stage 2	Angle tighten a further 80°	
Subframe front and rear mounting bolts: *		
Stage 1	150	111
Stage 2	Angle tighten a further 90°	
Subframe rear support panel	30	22
Suspension strut piston nut*	58	43
Suspension strut to hub carrier	110	81
Suspension strut to body	35	26
Rear suspension		
Anti-roll bar drop link to trailing arm	60	44
Anti-roll bar drop link to anti-roll bar	15	11
Anti-roll bar to subframe bolts	48	35
Front lower arm	130	96
Lower control arm	120	88
Rear hub assembly	110	81
Shock absorber lower mounting bolt:		
with standard suspension	175	129
with load-levelling suspension	280	206
Shock absorber upper mounting bolt	30	22
Subframe mounting bolts	110	81
Trailing arm (to body)	180	133
Upper control arm	130	96
Steering		
Power steering pump bolts (1.8)	25	18
Steering column mounting bolts	24	18
Steering rack mounting bolts	120	88
Steering wheel bolt	48	35
Steering shaft universal joint pinch-bolt*	32	24
Track rod end balljoint nuts*	80	59
Track rod locknuts	90	66
Wheels		
Roadwheel nuts:		
M12 standard nuts	140	103
M12 locking nut with conical washer	110	81
M12 locking nut with one-piece nut	140	103
M14 nuts	170	125

*Use new nuts/bolts

1 General Information

1 The independent front suspension is of the MacPherson strut type, incorporating coil springs and integral telescopic shock absorbers. The struts are located by transverse control arms, which are attached to the front subframe via rubber bushes at their inner ends, and incorporate a balljoint at their outer ends. The hub carriers, which carry the hub bearings, brake calipers and the hub/disc assemblies, are bolted to the MacPherson struts, and connected to the control arms through the balljoints. A front anti-roll bar is fitted to all models, and is attached to the subframe and to the MacPherson struts via link arms **(see illustration)**.

2 The rear suspension is of the fully independent, multilink type, consisting of an upper and lower control arm mounted via rubber bushes, to the lateral link/hub carrier and rear subframe. The lateral link is attached to the vehicle body at the front end and incorporate the hub carrier at the rear. The assembly is located by a tie rod each side. Coil springs are fitted between the lower control arm and the subframe. Separate hydraulic telescopic shock absorbers are fitted between the hub carrier between the lower control arm and the vehicle body **(see illustration)**.

3 Power assistance for the steering is derived from a belt driven hydraulic pump, except on 1.6 and 2.0 litre models where an electrically driven hydraulic pump is used.

1.1 The front suspension
A Subframe
B Hub
C Swivel hub
D Shock absorber and spring
E Control Arm
F Anti-roll bar
G Anti-roll bar drop link

6299 10-01.01 HAYNES

1.2 The rear suspension
A Hub
B Shock absorber
C Spring
D Lower control arm
E Subframe
F Trailing arm
G Anti-roll bar
H Anti-roll bar drop link
I Front lower arm
J Upper control arm

6299 10-01.02 HAYNES

2.5 Slacken the driveshaft bolt

2.6 Ensure the driveshaft is free to move in the swivel hub

2.9 Disconnect the ABS sensor wiring plug

2 Front swivel hub carrier and bearing – removal and refitting

Removal

1 Slacken, but do not remove the driveshaft hub nut.

2 Loosen the appropriate front wheel nuts, then jack up the front of the car and support it on axle stands (see *Jacking and vehicle support*). Remove the appropriate front roadwheel.

3 Undo the bolt securing the headlight levelling sensor bracket to the front lower arm (where applicable). On models fitted with dynamic suspension disconnect the wiring plug from the suspension strut.

4 Release the brake flexible hose from the mounting bracket and then remove the track rod end ball joint nut from the hub – see Section 20. Use a ball joint taper splitting tool and remove the ball joint from the hub assembly.

5 Remove the bolt securing the driveshaft to the hub **(see illustration)**. Have an assistant depress the brake pedal to prevent the hub from rotating. Discard the bolt, a new one must be used.

6 Check that the driveshaft is free to move in the hub. Apply penetrating oil as required. Refit the driveshaft nut and drive the driveshaft back into the hub **(see illustration)**. Do not attempt to driveshaft completely from the hub, just aim to have the driveshaft moving freely in the hub.

7 Remove the brake caliper as described in Chapter 9 Section 3. Secure the caliper to the suspension strut with a length of stout cord or wire.

8 Remove the front brake disc as described in Chapter 9 Section 4.

9 Disconnect the wiring plug **(see illustration)** undo the bolt and remove the ABS wheel sensor from the hub carrier – refer to Chapter 9 Section 14 if necessary.

10 Slacken the control arm balljoint nut until it is level with the end of the balljoint shank, then install Ford special tool 204-607 (joint separator tool) and detach the suspension control arm balljoint **(see illustrations)**. If the Ford special tool is not available the taper can be broken with yoke type ball joint seperator, but this will destroy the dust seal, leading to premature failure of the ball joint. A scissor type ball joint separator will not fit (we tried several) due to the restricted clearance. Note that Ford do not list the ball joint or dust seal as individual parts. If the seal is damaged or the ball joint worn the complete control arm must be replaced.

2.10a The special balljoint separator tool

2.10b Remove the brake caliper mounting bracket upper bolt...

2.10c ...and install the tool, using the bolt from the kit

2.10d Fully unwind the ball joint nut to break the taper

2.12a Lever the control arm down and ...

2.12b ...free the arm from the swivel hub

2.13 Free the driveshaft from the hub

2.14a Remove the bolt

2.14b With the bolt removed, spread the hub carrier slightly ...

2.14c ...and drive the hub off the suspension strut using a soft faced hammer

11 Remove the nut (dispose of it as a new one must be fitted) and then remove the special tool.

12 Use a stout bar to lever the control arm downwards and move the hub carrier over the end of the balljoint shank **(see illustrations)**. Take care not to damage the balljoint dust cover during and after disconnection.

13 Swivel the hub carrier assembly outwards, and withdraw the driveshaft CV joint from the hub flange **(see illustration)**.

14 Remove the bolt securing the hub carrier to the shock absorber. Insert a flat-bladed tool into the gap and very slightly spread the hub carrier where it clamps onto the lower end of the shock absorber. Tap the hub carrier downwards from the shock absorber at the same time. Note which way the bolt is inserted – from the front **(see illustrations)**.

15 The hub and bearing must now be removed from the hub carrier as an assembly. Due to the design of the assembly, we found it impossible to press the new hub/bearing

2.15a Using the Ford special tool to support the hub carrier, press the hub flange and bearing out ...

into the carrier without using Ford special tool 204-348 **(see illustrations)**. The bearing will be rendered unserviceable by removal and cannot be re-used.

2.15b ...then assembly the special tool around the new bearing/flange assembly ...

2.15c ...position the hub carrier over the new bearing, and the special tool in place on the hub carrier ...

2.15d ...then press the hub carrier ...

2.15e ...fully onto the bearing

3.4 Use an Allen key to counter-hold the anti-roll bar link balljoint nut

3.7 Remove the bolts

4.2 Checking the alignment of the strut to the top mount

Refitting

16 Prior to refitting, remove all traces of metal adhesive, rust, oil and dirt from the splines and threads of the driveshaft outer CV joint and the bearing housing mating surface on the hub carrier.

17 The remainder of refitting is a reversal of removal, but observe the following points:

a) Ensure that the hub and brake disc mating faces are spotlessly clean, and refit the disc with the orientation marks aligned

b) A new driveshaft retaining bolt should be used.

c) Ensure that the ABS sensor, and the sensor location in the hub carrier, are perfectly clean before refitting.

d) Tighten all nuts and bolts to the specified torque (see Chapter 9 for brake component torque settings).

3 Front suspension strut – removal and refitting

Removal

1 Open the bonnet and with reference to Chapter 11 Section 7, remove the windscreen cowl panel and windscreen wiper motor.

2 Loosen the appropriate front wheel nuts,

then jack up the front of the car and support it on axle stands (see *Jacking and vehicle support*). Remove the appropriate front roadwheel.

3 On vehicles fitted with dynamic suspension disconnect the wiring plug from the strut.

4 Undo the nut securing the anti-roll bar link balljoint to the suspension strut. Use an Allen key to counter-hold the balljoint shank **(see illustration)**. A new nut will be required.

5 Unclip the brake hose from the bracket on the suspension strut.

6 Remove the bolt securing the swivel hub to the shock absorber. Insert a flat-bladed tool into the gap and very slightly spread the hub carrier where it clamps onto the lower end of the shock absorber. Tap the hub carrier downwards from the shock absorber at the same time. Note which way the bolt is inserted – from the front **(see illustrations 2.14a and 2.14b)**. A new bolt will be required.

7 Have an assistant support the strut and then remove the upper mounting bolts **(see illustration)**. DO NOT remove the centre nut. Manoeuvre the strut out from underneath the wheel arch.

Refitting

8 Refitting is a reversal of removal, but observe the following point:

a) Tighten all nuts and bolts to the specified torque, using new nuts/bolts where necessary.

4 Front suspension strut – dismantling, inspection and reassembly

Warning: Before attempting to dismantle the suspension strut, a suitable tool to hold the coil spring in compression must be obtained. Adjustable coil spring compressors which can be positively secured to the spring coils are readily available, and are recommended for this operation. Any attempt to dismantle the strut without such a tool is likely to result in damage or personal injury.

Dismantling

1 Remove the strut from the car as described in Section 3.

2 Before dismantling the spring and strut assembly, note the relationship between the centre of the brake flexible hose bracket and the fixed mark on the upper spring seat **(see illustration)**.

3 Slacken the strut mounting nut 1/2 a turn, while holding the protruding portion of the piston rod with an Allen key **(see illustration)**. Do not remove the nut at this stage.

4 Fit the spring compressors to the coil springs, and tighten the compressors until the load is taken off the spring seats **(see illustration)**.

5 Remove the piston nut **(see illustration)**. Discard the nut – a new one should be fitted.

4.3 Hold the strut piston rod with an Allen key, and slacken the retaining nut

4.4 Fit the compressors to the springs

4.5 Remove the piston nut

6 Remove the upper mounting/spring seat, bump stop and gaiter followed by the spring **(see illustration)**.

Inspection

7 With the strut assembly now completely dismantled, examine all the components for wear, damage or deformation. Renew any of the components as necessary.

8 Examine the shock absorber for signs of fluid leakage, and check the strut piston for signs of pitting along its entire length. Test the operation of the shock absorber, while holding it in an upright position, by moving the piston through a full stroke and then through short strokes of 50 to 100 mm. In both cases, the resistance felt should be smooth and continuous. If the resistance is jerky, or uneven, or if there is any visible sign of wear or damage, renewal is necessary.

Caution: Always renew shock absorbers and coil spring as matched pairs across the axle. Never fit a single shock absorber or spring to a vehicle.

9 If any doubt exists about the condition of the coil spring, gradually release the spring compressor, and check the spring for distortion and signs of cracking. Since no minimum free length is specified by Ford, the only way to check the tension of the spring is to compare it to a new component. Renew the spring if it is damaged or distorted, or if there is any doubt as to its condition.

10 Inspect all other components for signs of damage or deterioration, and renew any that are suspect.

11 If a new shock absorbers are being fitted, hold it vertically and pump the piston a few times to prime it.

Reassembly

12 Reassembly is a reversal of dismantling, but ensure that the spring is fully compressed before fitting. Make sure that the spring end is correctly located in the lower seat. Fit the upper seat/swivel and ensure the fixed mark is aligned with the centre of the brake hose bracket (as noted on removal) The movable mark must be 6 degrees to the left of the fixed mark, when the fixed pointer is correctly aligned. Tighten the new shock absorber piston retaining nut and strut mounting bolts to the specified torque **(see illustrations)**.

5 Front suspension control arm – removal and refitting

Note: The ball joint is only supplied by Ford complete with the control arm.

Control arm

Removal

1 The ball joint must be separated from the swivel hub. This procedure is covered in Section 2. If the only the control arm is to be removed, there is no requirement to remove the brake caliper or brake disc – although access to the ball joint is improved if both are removed.

2 Undo the two bolts securing the control arm rear mounting and the single bolt securing the front mounting and manoeuvre the control arm from under the vehicle **(see illustration)**. Discard the bolts, new ones must be fitted.

3 Press the rear compliance bush off the control arm. (Replacement bushes are available).

Refitting

4 Where removed refit the rear compliance bush. Locate the arm in its mountings and fit the new mounting bolts. Note that because the rear mounting bolts also secure the anti-roll bar it may ne necessary to unbolt the drop links to allow the anti-roll bar fee movement. This will aid alignment of the arm, bolts and anti-roll bar clamps. Once all the bolts are in place, tighten the bolts to their specified torque. Do not allow the control arm to move during the tightening procedure.

5 Engage the balljoint shank in the control arm, then tighten the new nut to the specified torque.

6 The remainder of refitting is a reversal of removal. Have the front wheel alignment checked at the earliest opportunity.

4.6 With the springs fully compressed, remove the upper spring seat, bump stop and gaiter

4.12a Ensure the spring end is correctly located in the lower seat

4.12b The fixed pointer (A) must be in line with the brake hose bracket centre

5.2 Remove the bolts

6.1 Undo the fasteners and remove the engine undershield

6.4 The anti-roll bar bushes are split to facilitate renewal, and are shaped to fit the bar profile

6 Front anti-roll bar – removal and refitting

Removal

Note: *The anti-roll bar can only be removed with the front subframe.*

1 Loosen the appropriate front wheel nuts. Chock the rear wheels and apply the handbrake, then jack up the front of the vehicle and support it on axle stands (see *Jacking and vehicle support*). Remove the appropriate front roadwheel, then release the fasteners and remove the engine undershield **(see illustration)**

2 The subframe must now be removed as described in Section 22.

3 With the subframe out of the vehicle, note the orientation of the anti-roll bar clamps (the curved edges must be inboard) and then remove the anti-roll bar clamp nuts (dispose of both the nuts and bolts – new ones must be used).

4 Examine the anti-roll bar for signs of damage or distortion, and the connecting links and mounting bushes for signs of deterioration of the rubber. The bushes are split along their length and must be fitted in their original positions **(see illustration)**.

Refitting

5 Refitting is a reversal of removal. Given the amount of work required to remove the anti-roll bar, new bushes should be fitted. Note that the bushes must only be lubricated with water to aid fitting.

7 Anti-roll bar drop link – removal and refitting

Removal

1 Jack up and support the front of the vehicle – see *Jacking and vehicle support*.

2 Remove the appropriate road wheel.

3 Use a hex key to counterhold the ball joint shank and then unbolt the top drop link ball joint **(see illustrations)**. Repeat the procedure for the lower ball joint and then remove the drop link.

Refitting

4 Refitting is a reversal of removal.

8 Rear hub bearings – renewal

1 The rear hub bearings cannot be renewed separately, and are supplied with the rear hub as a complete assembly.

2 Remove the brake disc as described in Chapter 9 Section 7.

3 Disconnect the wiring plug, undo the bolt and remove the ABS wheel speed sensor from the hub carrier.

4 Undo the four Torx bolts and withdrawn the bearing assembly from the hub carrier/trailing arm **(see illustration)**.

5 Fit the new assembly to the hub carrier/trailing arm then insert and tighten the bolts to the specified torque.

6 Refit the ABS wheel speed sensor and brake disc as described in Chapter 9.

9 Rear trailing arm – removal and refitting

Removal

1 Jack up and support the rear of the vehicle

7.3a Remove the the top fixing and …

7.3b … recover the bracket

8.4 Remove the hub

9.4 Release the handbrake cable

9.6 Unclip the wiring loom

9.8 Remove the lower mounting bolt

9.9 Remove the fixings

A Lower (main) control arm
B Anti-roll bar drop link
C Front lower control arm

– see *Jacking and vehicle support*. Remove the appropriate rear wheel.

2 Remove the rear hub as described in the previous Section 8 and then remove then unbolt and remove the disc shield.

3 Where fitted, remove the air deflector from the rear floor.

4 Work along the arm and unclip (or unbolt) the handbrake cable **(see illustration)**. On models fitted with an electronic parking brake disconnect and unclip the wiring loom.

5 Unclip and unbolt the brake hose from the hub carrier. On models fitted with Zenon headlights (and if working on the left-hand arm) disconnect the ride height sensor.

6 Release the ABS wheel speed sensor wiring harness from the clips on the trailing arm **(see illustration)**.

9.10 Remove the bolts

7 Remove the relevant rear coil spring as described in Section 11.

8 Unbolt the shock absorber at the lower mounting **(see illustration)**.

9 Remove the rear lower control arm, the front lower control arm, the anti-roll bar drop link **(see illustration)** and then unbolt the upper control arm.

10 Unbolt the front trailing arm bolts **(see illustration)** and then lower the arm from the vehicle.

Refitting

11 Refit the trailing arm, lower control arms and upper control arm. Insert all the fixings, but only tighten them finger tight at this stage.

12 Fabricate a spacer, 40 mm in diameter, and 226 mm long. Insert the spacer between the lower control arm and the coil spring upper seat, then raise the lower control arm

with a trolley jack until the spacer is lightly trapped. Ensure the spacer is vertical.

13 With the spacer in position tighten the all the fixings to the specified torque.

14 Refit the remaining components in reverse order to removal.

15 Have the rear tracking checked (it is adjustable) as soon as possible. On models with Zenon headlights the headlight aim should be checked (and if necessary) adjusted using diagnostic equipment.

10 Rear shock absorber –
removal and refitting

Note: *Always replace shock absorbers as matched pairs. Never replace a single shock absorber.*

Removal

1 Slacken the rear roadwheel nuts, then chock the front wheels then jack up the rear of the vehicle and support it on axle stands (see *Jacking and vehicle support*). Remove the rear wheels.

2 Place a trolley jack under the hub carrier and raise the suspension a little to take the load off the shock absorber.

3 Undo the shock absorber upper mountings **(see illustration)**.

4 Undo and remove the shock absorber lower mounting bolt **(see illustration)**. Manoeuvre the shock absorber from under the vehicle.

5 With the shock absorber on the bench remove the flexible upper mounting **(see illustration)**.

10.3 Shock absorber upper mountings

10.4 Rear shock absorber lower mounting bolt

10.5 Remove the mounting

11.5a Mark the position of the snail cam washer (on both sides)...

11.5b ...remove the lower arm bolt...

11.5c ... and then lower the jack

Refitting

6 Refitting is a reversal of removal, tightening all nuts and bolts to the specified torques.

11 Rear coil spring –
removal and refitting

Note: *Always replace road springs in matched pairs across the axle.*
Note: *Removal of the rear spring requires the use of a professional spring compressor. Ford specify the use of special tool 204-167 and adapter 204-167-01. Equivalent tools are available in the aftermarket. However this is an expensive tool and is unlikely to be available to the home mechanic. An alternative method of removal is described below.*

Removal

1 Slacken the roadwheel nuts, then chock the front wheels and raise the rear of the vehicle. Support it securely on axle stands (see *Jacking and vehicle support*). Remove the roadwheels.
2 Position a trolley jack under the control arm and take the weight.
3 Remove the shock absorber lower mounting bolt (see Section 10).
4 Where available, attach spring compressors to the spring and compress the spring.

11.6 Remove the spring

Remove the trolley jack, and remove the spring.
5 Where the correct spring compressors are not available, mark the position of the snail cam bolt on on the control arm and then slacken the bolt. Remove the outer bolt from the control arm and then lower the arm on the trolley jack **(see illustrations)**. Continue lowering the jack until the spring is fully uncompressed.
6 Remove the trolley jack, press down on the control arm and remove the spring **(see illustration)**.
7 Recover the lower spring seat rubber mountings **(see illustration)**. The upper seat and bump stop will more than likely have come away with the spring – if not recover these as well.

11.7 Recover the spring seat

8 Where spring compressors have been used, release the tension on the spring (assuming the spring is to be replaced).
9 Examine all the components for wear or damage, and renew as necessary.

Refitting

10 Refit the rubbers seats to the control arm and spring, ensuring the ends of the spring locate correctly **(see illustrations)**.
11 Where spring compressors have been used, refit the compressed spring onto the seat in the lower control arm. Engage the spring correctly in the control arm and on the chassis.
12 Reposition the trolley jack and raise the control arm (where spring compressors have not been used). Align the control arm bush

11.10a Rotate the spring into position

11.10b Align the spring, rubber and upper mounting correctly

11.10c Locate the spring on the chassis

with the trailing arm and refit the bolt **(see illustration)**.

13 If the snail cam bolt has been slackened, rotate the cam until the snail cam is aligned with the previously made marks. Fully raise the arm and tighten the bolt. Check that the cam is still aligned after final tightening.

14 Refit the shock absorber lower mounting bolt, securing it in place before removing the jack. Tighten all nuts and bolts to the specified torque.

15 Where a spring compressor was used, release and remove the spring compressor.

16 Remainder of refitting is a reversal of removal. Have the rear tracking checked on completion of the work.

12 Rear suspension link arms
– removal and refitting

Removal

1 Loosen the rear wheel bolts. Chock the front wheels, then jack up the rear of the vehicle and support it on axle stands (see *Jacking and vehicle support*). Remove the appropriate rear roadwheel(s).

Upper control arm

2 Remove the rear spring as described in Section 11.

3 Fabricate a spacer, 40 mm in diameter, and 226 mm long. Insert the spacer between the lower control arm and the coil spring upper seat, then raise the lower control arm with a trolley jack until the spacer is lightly trapped. Ensure the spacer is vertical.

4 Undo the outer and inner bolts, then remove the control arm **(see illustration)**.

5 Examine the condition of the metal-elastic bushes in the control arm. Ford do not list the bushes as a separate part. If the bushes are damaged or worn the complete arm must be replaced.

Lower control arm

6 Remove the coil spring as described in Section 11.

7 Mark the position of the inner bolt snail cam washer/bolt – mark both sides. If not already done so, remove the outer bolt (to the trailing arm) and then remove the special snail cam bolt, snail cam washer and nut. Lower the arm and remove it.

8 Examine the condition of the metal-elastic bushes in the control arm. Ford do not list the bushes as a separate part. If the bushes are damaged or worn the complete arm must be replaced.

Front lower control arm

9 Remove the coil spring as described in Section 11.

10 Fabricate a spacer, 40 mm in diameter, and 226 mm long. Insert the spacer between the lower control arm and the coil spring upper seat, then raise the lower control arm

11.12 Raise the control arm on the jack

with a trolley jack until the spacer is lightly trapped. Ensure the spacer is vertical.

11 Remove the inner and outer bolts and then remove the arm.

12 Examine the condition of the metal-elastic bushes in the control arm. Ford do not list the bushes as a separate part. If the bushes are damaged or worn the complete arm must be replaced.

Refitting

13 Refitting any of the control arms/tie rods is essentially a reversal of removal, noting the following points:
a) *Tighten all fasteners to their specified torque where given, using a little thread-locking compound.*
b) *Before tightening any control arm/tie rod mounting bolts, ensure the suspension is in the 'normal' position using the fabricated spacers as described in the removal procedures.*

13 Rear anti-roll bar –
removal and refitting

Removal

1 Chock the front wheels, then jack up the rear of the vehicle and support it on axle stands (see *Jacking and vehicle support*).

2 Undo the nuts securing the outer ends of the anti-roll bar to the drop links **(see illustration)**. Take care not to damage the

13.2 Rear anti-roll bar drop link

12.4 Upper control arm bolt

rubber boots and check the condition of the upper rubber spacers as the drop link is removed.

3 Undo the bolts securing the anti-roll bar clamps to the subframe, manoeuvre the anti-roll bar from under the vehicle **(see illustration)**.

4 Examine the anti-roll bar for signs of damage or distortion, and the connecting links and mounting bushes for signs of deterioration of the rubber. The bushes are split along their length and must be fitted in their original positions.

Refitting

5 Position the anti-roll bar, then fit and tighten the bolts securing the anti-roll bar clamps to the subframe.

6 Refit the anti-roll bar links and tighten the nuts to the specified torque.

7 The remainder of refitting is a reversal of removal.

14 Steering wheel –
removal and refitting

⚠️ *Warning: Handle the airbag unit with extreme care as a precaution against personal injury, and always hold it with the cover facing away from the body.*

Removal

1 Drive the car forwards, and park it with the front wheels in the straight-ahead position.

13.3 Undo the bolts securing the anti-roll bar clamps

14.4 Steering wheel retaining bolt

14.5 Feed the wiring through the steering wheel

15 Steering column –
removal and refitting

Removal

2 Remove the driver's airbag as described in Chapter 12 Section 21.

3 Disconnect the wiring plug at the top of the steering wheel aperture.

4 Undo the steering wheel centre retaining bolt **(see illustration)**.

5 Make alignment marks between the steering wheel centre and the column shaft, then lift the steering wheel off the column shaft, and feed the wiring and plastic strip through the hole in the wheel **(see illustration)**.

Refitting

6 Ensure that the front wheels are still in the straight-ahead position.

7 Check the airbag rotary contact unit is still aligned. If necessary refer to Chapter 12. Remove the securing tape.

8 Feed the wiring through the hole in the steering wheel, then engage the wheel with the steering column shaft. Ensure that the marks made on removal are aligned, and that the pegs on the contact reel engage with the recesses on the steering wheel hub.

9 Refit the steering wheel retaining bolt, and tighten it to the specified torque.

10 Refit the airbag unit to the steering wheel as described in Chapter 12 Section 21.

1 Disconnect the battery negative lead (Chapter) 5 Section 3.

2 Set the steering in the straight ahead position and then remove the steering wheel as described in Section 14.

3 Fully extend the steering column and then remove the upper and lower steering column shrouds as described in Chapter 11 Section 24

4 Remove the airbag clockspring as described in Chapter 12 Section 21.

5 Undo the fasteners and remove the knee airbag panel – see Chapter 11 Section 24.

6 Note their fitted positions and routing, then disconnect the various column wiring plugs and release the loom retaining clips **(see illustration)**.

7 Undo the steering column lower pinch-bolt and pull the joint upwards from the pinion **(see illustration)**. Ensure the column adjustment lever is released before detaching the joint from the pinion. Discard the pinch-bolt, a new one must be fitted.

8 Undo the 4 retaining bolts and manoeuvre the column from the vehicle **(see illustrations)**.

Refitting

9 Refitting is a reversal of removal, bearing in mind the following points:

a) Lubricate universal joint splines with grease before engaging the steering column.

b) Use a new universal joint pinch-bolt.

c) If the steering column has been rotated, or the front wheels turned from straight-ahead, reset the airbag contact reel as described in Chapter 12 Section 21.

15.6 Release the wiring loom

15.7 Steering column lower pinch-bolt

15.8a Steering column upper mounting bolts

15.8b Remove the column

16.2 Remove the bolt

16.8 Unbolt the level sensor

16.10 Remove the bracket

16 Steering rack –
removal and refitting

Removal

1 Drive the car forwards and park it with the steering wheels in the straight-ahead position. Remove the ignition key to lock the steering in this position.
2 Working in the driver's footwell, mark the position of the steering column in relation to the steering rack pinion shaft and then undo the pinch-bolt **(see illustration)**. Pull the joint upwards from the pinion.
3 Loosen the front wheel nuts. Chock the rear wheels then jack up the front of the vehicle and support it on axle stands (see *Jacking and vehicle support*). Remove both front roadwheels.
4 Remove the engine undershield and then remove the air deflector from below the front bumper cover.
5 Anticipate some fluid spillage and disconnect the power steering fluid supply and return lines. Ford list two special tools for this purpose (307-242 and 308-440), however it is possible to release these pipes without the use of these tools. As access is awkward it is also possible to release the pipes at a later stage in the removal procedure. Should it prove necessary the pipes can also be removed with the steering pump and separated on the bench.

16.11 Work along the rear of the subframe and release the wiring loom

6 Disconnect the track rod ends from the swivel hub as described in Section 20.
7 Separate the swivel hubs from the control arms as described in Section 2.
8 Where fitted disconnect the headlight level sensor from the left-hand control arm **(see illustration)**.
9 Remove both anti-roll bar drop links (at the anti-roll bar) – see Section 7.
10 Support the flexible section of the exhaust system with wooden splits and then remove the mounting bracket from the subframe **(see illustration)**.
11 Where fitted unclip (and disconnect) the wiring loom **(see illustration)**. On some models unclip the fuel line from the emissions control fuel vapouriser.
12 Remove the engine rear torque rod **(see illustration)**.

16.12 Remove the torque rod

13 Unbolt the support clips from the power steering fluid pipes and then unbolt the pipes from the steering rack pinion.
14 On 1.6 and 2.0 litre models unbolt the power steering reservoir and pump **(see illustration)** from the right-hand front of the subframe. Secure the pump and reservoir assembly to the chassis with cable ties (or similar).
15 Slacken the steering rack mounting bolts and then remove the support panel from the rear of the subframe **(see illustration)**. At this point the steering rack can be secured to the bulkhead and the bolts removed. This will be the easier option if the subframe is being removed as part of the transmission removal procedure.
16 Support the subframe – we used a large plank of wood on a trolley jack **(see illustration)**.

16.14 Unbolt the power steering reservoir and pump

16.15 Remove the support panel bolts (one side shown)

16.16 Support the subframe

16.17 Remove the subframe bolts

16.18 Lower and then remove the subframe

17 With the subframe supported, remove the front and rear subframe bolts **(see illustration)**. Note that new subframe mounting bolts will be required for refitting.
18 With the aid of an assistant carefully lower the jack and subframe **(see illustration)**. Take care not to damage the power steering hoses.
19 Undo the retaining bolts, and lift the steering rack from the subframe.

Refitting

20 Manipulate the steering rack into position and tighten the bolts to the specified torque.
21 Ensure the steering rack pinion bulkhead seal is in place, then raise the subframe into position. If a new replacement steering rack is being fitted, ensure that the bulkhead seal is swapped to the new steering rack – alignment marks are provided on the rack and seal
22 Position the subframe and steering rack assembly on the jack and length of wood used to lower it from the vehicle.
23 With the aid of an assistant raise the subframe into position and fit the new front

subframe bolts. Fit the rear stiffener plate and the new rear bolts.
24 The alignment of the subframe must be checked by inserting round tools' though the holes provided in the subframe and body shell **(see illustration)**. Ford list a special tool (part No 205-316A) for this. Aftermarket equivalents are widely available. Alternatively, using two lengths of wooden dowel, 20 mm in diameter, and approximately 150 mm in length.
25 With the subframe correctly aligned, tighten all the subframe bolts to the specified torque.
26 Engage the steering shaft universal joint with the pinion shaft, and push it fully home.
27 Fit the new universal joint pinch-bolt and tighten it to the specified torque.
28 Refit the fluid pipes to the steering rack using new O-ring seals, and tighten the retaining bolt securely.
29 The remainder of refitting is a reversal of removal, noting the following points:
a) *Tighten all fasteners to their specified torque where given.*

b) *Bleed the power steering system as described in Section 18.*
c) *Have the front wheel alignment checked at the earliest opportunity.*

17 Steering rack gaiters – renewal

1 Remove the track rod end on the side concerned as described in Section 20. Unscrew the locknut from the track rod.
2 Release the two clips and peel off the gaiter. Disconnect the breather hose as the gaiter is withdrawn **(see illustration)**.
3 Clean out any dirt and grit from the inner end of the track rod and (when accessible) the rack.
4 Wrap insulating tape around the track rod threads to protect the new gaiter whilst installing.
5 Refit the track rod end locknut.
6 Refit the track rod end as described in Section 20.

16.24 Fit the alignment pins to the subframe

17.2 Release the rack gaiter clips

19.9 Remove the bolts (2 shown, 1 hidden)

19.10 Clamp the hose

18 Steering system – bleeding

1 Wipe clean the area around the reservoir filler neck, and unscrew the filler cap/dipstick from the reservoir.
2 If topping-up is necessary, use clean fluid of the specified type (see *Weekly checks.*). Check for leaks if frequent topping-up is required. Do not run the engine without fluid in the reservoir.
3 After component renewal, or if the fluid level has been allowed to fall so low that air has entered the hydraulic system, bleeding must be carried out as follows.
4 Fill the reservoir to the MAX mark as described in *Weekly checks.*. Note that the power steering fluid should be cold, and poured slowly into the reservoir to minimise aeration.
5 Start the engine, slowly turn the steering wheel from lock to lock, and add power steering fluid until the fluid level ceases to drop.
6 Switch off the engine and check the fluid level. Top-up if necessary.
7 Start the engine and turn the steering from lock to lock. If excessive noise is still apparent

19.11 Seal the pump inlet

(indicating air in the system), leave the vehicle overnight, then try again.
8 If the steering is still noisy, it may be that the pump is faulty. Consult a Ford dealer or specialist.
9 On completion, stop the engine, lower the vehicle to the ground, and recheck the fluid level.

19 Power steering pump – removal and refitting

Note: *1.8 litre and 2.2 litre engines have a belt driven power steering pump fitted. 1.6 litre and 2.0 litre models have an Electro Hydraulic Power Steering (EHPS) pump fitted. The EHPS pump is fitted to the front right-hand side of the subframe.*

Removal

Mechanical power steering pump

1.8 litre engines

1 Jack up and support the front of the vehicle – see *Jacking and vehicle support*.
2 Remove the engine undershield and then remove the accessory drivebelt as described in Chapter 1 Section 22.

19.15 Remove the supply hose

3 Clamp the fluid supply hose using a hose clamp. Anticpate some fluid spillage and then remove the hose clip from the supply pipe. Remove the pipe.
4 Unbolt the outlet pipe – again anticipate some fluid spillage (place absorbent cloths or workshop paper towels below the pipe). Remove the pipe and recover the O-ring seal.
5 Remove the mounting bolts and lift out the pump.

2.2 litre engines

6 To improve access, remove the right-hand side headlight as described in Chapter 12 Section 9.
7 Remove the accessory drivebelt as described in Chapter 1 Section 22 and then slacken slightly the high pressure outlet pipe retaining bolt.
8 Unclip the reservoir from the bonnet slam panel.
9 Remove the mounting bolts and lift out the pump **(see illustration)**.
10 Place the pump on the engine with a tray or numerous rags beneath it and then clamp the fluid supply hose using a hose clamp **(see illustration)**.
11 Remove the supply hose and then seal the pump opening **(see illustration)**.
12 Remove the outlet hose – again seal the pipe and the pump outlet. Remove the pump and tray from the engine bay.

Electro hydraulic power steering pump (EHPS)

13 Jack up the front of the vehicle and support it securely on axle stands (see *Jacking and vehicle support*). Remove the right-hand road wheel.
14 Undo the fasteners and remove engine undershield. Remove the air deflector from the base of the bumper cover and then remove the wing liner.
15 Clamp the fluid supply hose with a hose clamp. Anticipate some the fluid spillage and remove the hose **(see illustration)**.

19.16 Unbolt the pressure pipe

19.17a Remove the bolts at the rear ...

19.17b ...and at the front

19.17c Disconnect the wiring plugs

20.2a Measure the number of exposed threads

20.2b Slacken the track rod end locknut

16 Undo the union nut and disconnect the pump pressure pipe **(see illustration)**. Be prepared for fluid spillage. Plug the openings to prevent contamination.

17 Remove the mounting bolts and pull the pump out from the crash protection bracket to access the wiring plugs. Disconnect the wiring plugs and release the wiring loom **(see illustrations)**.

18 No individual parts are available. If faulty, exchange units are available from Ford.

Refitting

19 Refitting is a reversal of removal, bearing in mind the following points:
a) *Use a new O-ring on pressure pipe union.*
b) *Tighten the mounting bolts to the specified torque.*

c) *Refill/top-up the fluid reservoir, and bleed the system as described in Section 18.*

20 Track rod end – removal and refitting

Removal

1 Loosen the appropriate front wheel nuts. Chock the rear wheels, then jack up the front of the vehicle and support it on axle stands (see *Jacking and vehicle support*). Remove the appropriate front roadwheel.

2 Counter-hold the track rod, and slacken the track rod end locknut by half a turn. If the locknut is now left in this position, it will act as

a further guide for refitting. Alternatively (and if the steering rack gaiter is to be removed) measure the number of expose threads **(see illustrations)**.

3 Unscrew the track rod end balljoint nut, using and Allen key to counter-hold the balljoint shank. Separate the balljoint from the steering arm with a proprietary balljoint separator, then remove the nut and disengage the balljoint from the arm **(see illustrations)**.

4 Unscrew the track rod end from the track rod, counting the number of turns needed to remove it. Make a note of the number of turns, so that the tracking can be reset (or at least approximated) on refitting.

Refitting

5 Screw the track rod end onto the track rod

20.3a Clean the exposed threads and apply penetrating oil

20.3b Use an Allen key to counter-hold the track rod end balljoint shank

20.3c Use a separator tool to detach the track rod end from the hub carrier

by the same number of turns noted during removal.

6 Engage the balljoint in the steering arm. Fit a new nut and tighten it to the specified torque.

7 Counter-hold the track rod and tighten the locknut.

8 Refit the front wheel, lower the car and tighten the wheel bolts in a diagonal sequence to the specified torque.

9 Have the front wheel toe-in (tracking) checked and adjusted by a Ford dealer or suitably-equipped repairer.

21 Wheel alignment and steering angles – general information

1 A car's steering and suspension geometry is defined in four basic settings – all angles are expressed in degrees (toe settings are also expressed as a measurement); the relevant settings are camber, castor, steering axis inclination, and toe setting **(see illustration)**. On the models covered by this manual, only the front and rear wheel toe settings are adjustable.

2 Camber is the angle at which the front wheels are set from the vertical when viewed from the front or rear of the car. Negative camber is the amount (in degrees) that the wheels are tilted inward at the top from the vertical.

3 The front camber angle is adjusted by slackening the steering knuckle-to-suspension strut mounting bolts and repositioning the hub carrier assemblies as necessary.

4 Castor is the angle between the steering axis and a vertical line when viewed from each side of the car. Positive castor is when the steering axis is inclined rearward at the top.

5 Steering axis inclination is the angle (when viewed from the front of the vehicle) between the vertical and an imaginary line drawn through the front suspension strut upper mounting and the control arm balljoint.

6 Toe setting is the amount by which the distance between the front inside edges of the roadwheels (measured at hub height) differs from the diametrically opposite distance measured between the rear inside edges of the roadwheels. Toe-in is when the roadwheels point inwards, towards each other at the front, while toe-out is when they splay outwards from each other at the front.

7 The front wheel toe setting is adjusted by altering the length of the steering track rods on both sides. This adjustment is normally referred to as the tracking.

8 The rear wheel toe setting is adjusted by rotating the lateral link front mounting bolt in the chassis. The bolt incorporates an eccentric washer, and the pivot point for the link varies as the bolt is rotated.

9 All other suspension and steering angles are set during manufacture, and no adjustment is possible. It can be assumed, therefore, that unless the vehicle has suffered accident damage, all the preset angles will be correct.

10 Special optical measuring equipment is necessary to accurately check and adjust the front and rear toe settings and front camber angles, and this work should be carried out by a Ford dealer or similar expert. Most tyre-fitting centres have the expertise and equipment to carry out at least a front wheel toe setting (tracking) check for a nominal charge.

22 Front subframe – removal and refitting

1 The front subframe removal and refitting is described within the steering rack removal and refitting procedure, as described in Section 16.

2 If the subframe is to be removed as part of another procedure (eg, transmission removal), the steering rack can be unbolted from the subframe and secure to the bodywork. This avoids the need to remove the power steering fluid hoses from the steering rack.

21.1 Front wheel geometry

Chapter 11
Bodywork and fittings

Contents

Degrees of difficulty

Easy, suitable for novice with little experience	**Fairly easy,** suitable for beginner with some experience	**Fairly difficult,** suitable for competent DIY mechanic	**Difficult,** suitable for experienced DIY mechanic	**Very difficult,** suitable for expert DIY or professional

Specifications

Torque wrench settings	Nm	lbf ft
Cross member (facia):		
A-pillar through bolts	80	59
A-pillar rear facing bolts	25	18
Bulkhead bolts	25	18
Bonnet hinge bolts:		
To bonnet	11	8
To body	24	18
Door hinge bolts:		
Upper hinge bolts	35	26
Lower hinge bolt	47	35
Front bumper bolts:		
Main bolts (to chassis leg)	30	22
Upper panel bolts	24	18
Front seat mounting bolts	40	30
Passenger's airbag:		
To crossmember	10	7
To airbag	8	6
To facia	8	6
Rear bumper bolts	30	22
Rear seat bolts	48	35
Seat belt mounting bolts	35	26
Front seat belt buckle	38	28
Tailgate hinge bolts	22	16

1 General Information

1 The bodyshell and underframe on all models feature variable thickness steel. Achieved by laser-welded technology, used to join steel panels of different gauges. This gives a stiffer structure, with mounting points being more rigid, which gives an improved crash performance.

2 An additional safety crossmember is incorporated between the A-pillars in the upper area of the bulkhead, and the facia and steering column are secured to it. The lower bulkhead area is reinforced by additional systems of members connected to the front of the vehicle. The body side rocker panels (sills) have been divided along the length of the vehicle by internal reinforcement, this functions like a double tube which increases its strength. All doors are reinforced and incorporate side impact protection, which is secured in the door structure. There are additional impact absorbers to the front and rear of the vehicle, behind the bumper assemblies.

3 All sheet metal surfaces which are prone to corrosion are galvanised. The painting process includes a base colour which closely matches the final topcoat, so that any stone damage is not as noticeable. The front wings are of a bolt-on type to ease their renewal if required.

4 Automatic seat belts are fitted to all models, and the front seat safety belts are equipped with a pyrotechnic pretension seat belt buckle, which is attached to the seat frame of each front seat. In the event of a serious front impact, the system is triggered and pulls the stalk buckle downwards to tension the seat belt. It is not possible to reset the tensioner once fired, and it must therefore be renewed. The tensioners are fired by an explosive charge similar to that used in the airbag, and are triggered via the airbag control module. The safety belt retractor, which is fitted in the base of the B-pillar, has a device to control the seat belt, if the deceleration force is enough to activate the airbags.

5 Central locking is standard on all models. Where double-locking is fitted, the lock mechanism is disconnected (when the system is in use) from the interior door handles, making it impossible to open any of the doors or the tailgate/boot lid from inside the vehicle. This means that, even if a thief should break a side window, they will not be able to open the door using the interior handle. In the event of a serious accident, a crash sensor unlocks all doors if they were previously locked.

6 Many of the procedures in this Chapter require the battery to be disconnected, refer to Chapter 5 Section 3.

2 Maintenance – bodywork and underframe

1 The general condition of a vehicle's bodywork is the one thing that significantly affects its value. Maintenance is easy, but needs to be regular. Neglect, particularly after minor damage, can lead quickly to further deterioration and costly repair bills. It is important also to keep watch on those parts of the vehicle not immediately visible, for instance the underside, inside all the wheel arches, and the lower part of the engine compartment.

2 The basic maintenance routine for the bodywork is washing – preferably with a lot of water, from a hose. This will remove all the loose solids which may have stuck to the vehicle. It is important to flush these off in such a way as to prevent grit from scratching the finish. The wheel arches and underframe need washing in the same way, to remove any accumulated mud, which will retain moisture and tend to encourage rust. Paradoxically enough, the best time to clean the underframe and wheel arches is in wet weather, when the mud is thoroughly wet and soft. In very wet weather, the underframe is usually cleaned of large accumulations automatically, and this is a good time for inspection.

3 Periodically, except on vehicles with a wax-based underbody protective coating, it is a good idea to have the whole of the underframe of the vehicle steam-cleaned, engine compartment included, so that a thorough inspection can be carried out to see what minor repairs and renovations are necessary. Steam-cleaning is available at many garages, and is necessary for the removal of the accumulation of oily grime, which sometimes is allowed to become thick in certain areas. If steam-cleaning facilities are not available, there are some excellent grease solvents available which can be brush-applied; the dirt can then be simply hosed off. Note that these methods should not be used on vehicles with wax-based underbody protective coating, or the coating will be removed. Such vehicles should be inspected annually, preferably just prior to Winter, when the underbody should be washed down, and any damage to the wax coating repaired. Ideally, a completely fresh coat should be applied. It would also be worth considering the use of such wax-based protection for injection into door panels, sills, box sections, etc, as an additional safeguard against rust damage, where such protection is not provided by the vehicle manufacturer.

4 After washing paintwork, wipe off with a chamois leather to give an unspotted clear finish. A coat of clear protective wax polish will give added protection against chemical pollutants in the air. If the paintwork sheen has dulled or oxidised, use a cleaner/polisher combination to restore the brilliance of the shine. This requires a little effort, but such dulling is usually caused because regular washing has been neglected. Care needs to be taken with metallic paintwork, as special non-abrasive cleaner/polisher is required to avoid damage to the finish. Always check that the door and ventilator opening drain holes and pipes are completely clear, so that water can be drained out. Brightwork should be treated in the same way as paintwork. Windscreens and windows can be kept clear of the smeary film which often appears, by the use of proprietary glass cleaner. Never use any form of wax or other body or chromium polish on glass.

3 Maintenance – upholstery and carpets

1 Mats and carpets should be brushed or vacuum-cleaned regularly, to keep them free of grit. If they are badly stained, remove them from the vehicle for scrubbing or sponging, and make quite sure they are dry before refitting. Seats and interior trim panels can be kept clean by wiping with a damp cloth. If they do become stained (which can be more apparent on light-coloured upholstery), use a little liquid detergent and a soft nail brush to scour the grime out of the grain of the material. Do not forget to keep the headlining clean in the same way as the upholstery. When using liquid cleaners inside the vehicle, do not over-wet the surfaces being cleaned. Excessive damp could get into the seams and padded interior, causing stains, offensive odours or even rot.

Caution: If the inside of the vehicle gets wet accidentally, it is worthwhile taking some trouble to dry it out properly, particularly where carpets are involved. Do not leave oil or electric heaters inside the vehicle for this purpose.

4 Minor body damage – repair

Minor scratches in bodywork

1 If the scratch is very superficial, and does not penetrate to the metal of the bodywork, repair is very simple. Lightly rub the area of the scratch with a paintwork renovator, or a very fine cutting paste, to remove loose paint from the scratch, and to clear the surrounding bodywork of wax polish. Rinse the area with clean water.

2 Apply touch-up paint to the scratch using a fine paint brush; continue to apply fine layers of paint until the surface of the paint in the scratch is level with the surrounding paintwork. Allow the new paint at least two weeks to harden, then blend it into the surrounding paintwork by rubbing the scratch

area with a paintwork renovator or a very fine cutting paste. Finally, apply wax polish.

3 Where the scratch has penetrated right through to the metal of the bodywork, causing the metal to rust, a different repair technique is required. Remove any loose rust from the bottom of the scratch with a penknife, then apply rust-inhibiting paint to prevent the formation of rust in the future. Using a rubber or nylon applicator, fill the scratch with bodystopper paste. If required, this paste can be mixed with cellulose thinners to provide a very thin paste which is ideal for filling narrow scratches. Before the stopper-paste in the scratch hardens, wrap a piece of smooth cotton rag around the top of a finger. Dip the finger in cellulose thinners, and quickly sweep it across the surface of the stopper-paste in the scratch; this will ensure that the surface of the stopper-paste is slightly hollowed. The scratch can now be painted over as described earlier in this Section.

Dents in bodywork

4 When deep denting of the vehicle's bodywork has taken place, the first task is to pull the dent out, until the affected bodywork almost attains its original shape. There is little point in trying to restore the original shape completely, as the metal in the damaged area will have stretched on impact, and cannot be reshaped fully to its original contour. It is better to bring the level of the dent up to a point which is about 3 mm below the level of the surrounding bodywork. In cases where the dent is very shallow anyway, it is not worth trying to pull it out at all. If the underside of the dent is accessible, it can be hammered out gently from behind, using a mallet with a wooden or plastic head. Whilst doing this, hold a suitable block of wood firmly against the outside of the panel, to absorb the impact from the hammer blows and thus prevent a large area of the bodywork from being 'belled-out'.

5 Should the dent be in a section of the bodywork which has a double skin, or some other factor making it inaccessible behind, a different technique is called for. Drill several small holes through the metal inside the area – particularly in the deeper section. Then screw long self-tapping screws into the holes, just sufficiently for them to gain a good purchase in the metal. Now the dent can be pulled out by pulling on the protruding heads of the screws with a pair of pliers.

6 The next stage of the repair is the removal of the paint from the damaged area, and from an inch or so of the surrounding 'sound' bodywork. This is accomplished most easily by using a wire brush or abrasive pad on a power drill, although it can be done just as effectively by hand, using sheets of abrasive paper. To complete the preparation for filling, score the surface of the bare metal with a screwdriver or the tang of a file, or alternatively, drill small holes in the affected area. This will provide a really good 'key' for the filler paste.

7 To complete the repair, see the Section on filling and respraying.

Rust holes or gashes in bodywork

8 Remove all paint from the affected area, and from an inch or so of the surrounding 'sound' bodywork, using an abrasive pad or a wire brush on a power drill. If these are not available, a few sheets of abrasive paper will do the job most effectively. With the paint removed, you will be able to judge the severity of the corrosion, and therefore decide whether to renew the whole panel (if this is possible) or to repair the affected area. New body panels are not as expensive as most people think, and it is often quicker and more satisfactory to fit a new panel than to attempt to repair large areas of corrosion.

9 Remove all fittings from the affected area, except those which will act as a guide to the original shape of the damaged bodywork (e.g. headlight shells etc). Then, using tin snips or a hacksaw blade, remove all loose metal and any other metal badly affected by corrosion. Hammer the edges of the hole inwards, in order to create a slight depression for the filler paste.

10 Wire-brush the affected area to remove the powdery rust from the surface of the remaining metal. Paint the affected area with rust-inhibiting paint, if the back of the rusted area is accessible, treat this also.

11 Before filling can take place, it will be necessary to block the hole in some way. This can be achieved by the use of aluminium or plastic mesh, or aluminium tape.

12 Aluminium or plastic mesh, or glass-fibre matting, is probably the best material to use for a large hole. Cut a piece to the approximate size and shape of the hole to be filled, then position it in the hole so that its edges are below the level of the surrounding bodywork. It can be retained in position by several blobs of filler paste around its periphery.

13 Aluminium tape should be used for small or very narrow holes. Pull a piece off the roll, trim it to the approximate size and shape required, then pull off the backing paper (if used) and stick the tape over the hole; it can be overlapped if the thickness of one piece is insufficient. Burnish down the edges of the tape with the handle of a screwdriver or similar, to ensure that the tape is securely attached to the metal underneath.

Filling and respraying

14 Before using this Section, see the Sections on dent, deep scratch, rust holes and gash repairs.

15 Many types of bodyfiller are available, but generally speaking, those proprietary kits which contain a tin of filler paste and a tube of resin hardener are best for this type of repair. A wide, flexible plastic or nylon applicator will be found invaluable for imparting a smooth and well-contoured finish to the surface of the filler.

16 Mix up a little filler on a clean piece of card or board – measure the hardener carefully (follow the maker's instructions on the pack), otherwise the filler will set too rapidly or too slowly. Using the applicator, apply the filler paste to the prepared area; draw the applicator across the surface of the filler to achieve the correct contour and to level the surface. As soon as a contour that approximates to the correct one is achieved, stop working the paste – if you carry on too long, the paste will become sticky and begin to 'pick-up' on the applicator. Continue to add thin layers of filler paste at 20-minute intervals, until the level of the filler is just proud of the surrounding bodywork.

17 Once the filler has hardened, the excess can be removed using a metal plane or file. From then on, progressively-finer grades of abrasive paper should be used, starting with a 40-grade production paper, and finishing with a 400-grade wet-and-dry paper. Always wrap the abrasive paper around a flat rubber, cork, or wooden block – otherwise the surface of the filler will not be completely flat. During the smoothing of the filler surface, the wet-and-dry paper should be periodically rinsed in water. This will ensure that a very smooth finish is imparted to the filler at the final stage.

18 At this stage, the 'dent' should be surrounded by a ring of bare metal, which in turn should be encircled by the finely 'feathered' edge of the good paintwork. Rinse the repair area with clean water, until all of the dust produced by the rubbing-down operation has gone.

19 Spray the whole area with a light coat of primer – this will show up any imperfections in the surface of the filler. Repair these imperfections with fresh filler paste or bodystopper, and once more smooth the surface with abrasive paper. Repeat this spray-and-repair procedure until you are satisfied that the surface of the filler, and the feathered edge of the paintwork, are perfect. Clean the repair area with clean water, and allow to dry fully.

20 The repair area is now ready for final spraying. Paint spraying must be carried out in a warm, dry, windless and dust-free atmosphere. This condition can be created artificially if you have access to a large indoor working area, but if you are forced to work in the open, you will have to pick your day very carefully. If you are working indoors, dousing the floor in the work area with water will help to settle the dust which would otherwise be in the atmosphere. If the repair area is confined to one body panel, mask off the surrounding panels; this will help to minimise the effects of a slight mis-match in paint colours. Bodywork fittings (e.g. chrome strips, door handles etc) will also need to be masked off. Use genuine masking tape, and several thicknesses of newspaper, for the masking operations.

21 Before commencing to spray, agitate the aerosol can thoroughly, then spray a test area (an old tin, or similar) until the technique is mastered. Cover the repair area with a thick coat of primer; the thickness should be built up using several thin layers of paint, rather than one thick one. Using 400-grade wet-and-dry paper, rub down the surface of the primer until it is really smooth. While doing this, the work area should be thoroughly doused with water, and the wet-and-dry paper periodically rinsed in water. Allow to dry before spraying on more paint.

22 Spray on the top coat, again building up the thickness by using several thin layers of paint. Start spraying at one edge of the repair area, and then, using a side-to-side motion, work until the whole repair area and about 2 inches of the surrounding original paintwork is covered. Remove all masking material 10 to 15 minutes after spraying on the final coat of paint.

23 Allow the new paint at least two weeks to harden, then, using a paintwork renovator, or a very fine cutting paste, blend the edges of the paint into the existing paintwork. Finally, apply wax polish.

Plastic components

24 With the use of more and more plastic body components by the vehicle manufacturers (e.g. bumpers. spoilers, and in some cases major body panels), rectification of more serious damage to such items has become a matter of either entrusting repair work to a specialist in this field, or renewing complete components. Repair of such damage by the DIY owner is not really feasible, owing to the cost of the equipment and materials required for effecting such repairs. The basic technique involves making a groove along the line of the crack in the plastic, using a rotary burr in a power drill. The damaged part is then welded back together, using a hot-air gun to heat up and fuse a plastic filler rod into the groove. Any excess plastic is then removed, and the area rubbed down to a smooth finish. It is important that a filler rod of the correct plastic is used, as body components can be made of a variety of different types (e.g. polycarbonate, ABS, polypropylene).

25 Damage of a less serious nature (abrasions, minor cracks etc) can be repaired by the DIY owner using a two-part epoxy filler repair material. Once mixed in equal proportions, this is used in similar fashion to the bodywork filler used on metal panels. The filler is usually cured in twenty to thirty minutes, ready for sanding and painting.

26 If the owner is renewing a complete component himself, or if he has repaired it with epoxy filler, he will be left with the problem of finding a suitable paint for finishing which is compatible with the type of plastic used. At one time, the use of a universal paint was not possible, owing to the complex range of plastics encountered in body component applications. Standard paints, generally speaking, will not bond to plastic or rubber satisfactorily. However, it is now possible to obtain a plastic body parts finishing kit which consists of a pre-primer treatment, a primer and coloured top coat. Full instructions are normally supplied with a kit, but basically, the method of use is to first apply the pre-primer to the component concerned, and allow it to dry for up to 30 minutes. Then the primer is applied, and left to dry for about an hour before finally applying the special-coloured top coat. The result is a correctly-coloured component, where the paint will flex with the plastic or rubber, a property that standard paint does not normally posses.

5 Major body damage – repair

1 Where serious damage has occurred, or large areas need renewal due to neglect, it means that complete new panels will need welding-in; this is best left to professionals. If the damage is due to impact, it will also be necessary to check completely the alignment of the bodyshell; this can only be carried out accurately by a Ford dealer, using special jigs. If the body is left misaligned, it is primarily dangerous, as the car will not handle properly, and secondly, uneven stresses will be imposed on the steering, suspension and possibly transmission, causing abnormal wear or complete failure, particularly to items such as the tyres.

6 Bumper covers – removal and refitting

Front bumper cover removal

1 Remove both front headlights as described in Chapter 12 Section 9.
2 Apply the handbrake, jack up the front of the vehicle and support it on axle stands (see *Jacking and vehicle support*). Undo the fasteners and remove the engine undershield.
3 Unscrew and unclip the air deflector from the base of the bumper **(see illustration)** and the front edge of both wing liners.
4 Where fitted disconnect the wiring plugs from the front fog lights and parking sensors. On some later models a single wiring connector is fitted to the right-hand side chassis leg close to the headlight mounting point **(see illustration)**.
5 Fold back the wing liner (or remove it completely) and then remove the bolts from the bracket that holds the bumper to the front wing (two per side). Note that the nuts for the bolts are captive in the plastic bracket that clips into the front bumper **(see illustration)**.

6.3 Remove the air deflector

6.4 A single multi-plug is fitted to some versions

6.5 Remove the bolts

6.6a Prise up and…

6.6b …and remove the two part trim clip

6.6c Remove the panel

6.7a Remove the retaining trim clip

6.7b Remove the bumper cover

6.10 Remove the wing liner fixings

6 Remove the plastic trim clips from the bonnet slam panel cover and then unclip the cover from the slam panel **(see illustrations)**.

7 Prise up the trim clips and release the locking tabs from the headlight apertures. With the aid of an assistant remove the bumper cover **(see illustrations)**. Recover the polystyrene backing panel and (where fitted) disconnect the washer hose from the headlight washers.

8 If required the bumper can now be removed by unclipping the wiring loom, removing the horns and unbolting the bumper.

Rear bumper cover removal

9 Chock the front wheels, jack up the rear of the vehicle and support it on axle stands (see *Jacking and vehicle support*). Remove both road wheels and then open up the tailgate.

10 Release the screws or bolts (on both sides) and then fold back the wing liner to

6.11 Remove the cross head screws

6.12 Remove the plastic nuts

gain access to the bumper cover bolts **(see illustration)**.

11 Where fitted, remove the mud flap bolts and then remove the bumper cover bolts **(see illustration)**.

12 On some models, remove the air deflector from the base of the bumper (below the load

area floor) and then remove the lower bumper cover mountings **(see illustration)**.

13 Where fitted disconnect the wiring plug for the rear parking sensors **(see illustration)**.

14 Release the bumper from the rear wing **(see illustrations)**.

6.13 Disconnect the wiring plug

6.14a Release the upper edge. Note the locking tabs

6.14b Release the lower edge. Again note the locking tabs

6.15 Remove the upper fixings (corner one shown)

6.16 The bumper mounting bolts

7.1 Remove the retaining clips

7.2 Disconnect the washer hose

7.3 Disconnect the wiring plug

7.4 Mark the position of the hinges in relation to the bonnet

15 Have an assistant support the bumper cover and then remove the upper fixings **(see illustration)**.

16 If required the bumper can now be removed by unclipping the wiring loom (where fitted) and unbolting the bumper **(see illustration)**.

Refitting

17 Refitting is a reversal of the removal procedure. Check all electrical components that have been disconnected.

---

7 Bonnet – removal, refitting and adjustment

Removal

1 Open the bonnet, and support it in the open position using the stay. Release the clips and remove the bonnet insulation panel **(see illustration)**.

2 Disconnect the windscreen washer hose. We released it at the left-hand washer jet **(see illustration)**.

3 Disconnect the windscreen washer jet heater wiring connector at the right-hand side **(see illustration)**.

4 To assist in correctly aligning the bonnet when refitting it, make alignment marks **(see illustration)**. Loosen the two hinge retaining nuts on each side.

5 With the help of an assistant, unscrew the

four nuts, release the stay, and lift the bonnet from the vehicle.

Refitting and adjustment

6 Refitting is a reversal of the removal procedure, noting the following points:

a) *Position the bonnet hinges within the outline marks made during removal, but if necessary, alter its position to provide a uniform gap all round.*

b) *Adjust the front height by repositioning the lock (see Section 8) and turning the rubber buffers on the engine compartment front cross panel up or down to support the bonnet.*

---

8 Bonnet lock – removal, refitting and adjustment

Removal

1 Release the 2 trim clips and unclip the bonnet slam panel cover as described in Section 6.

2 Make alignment marks between the lock and panel and then undo the 2 bolts securing the lock assembly to the bonnet slam panel **(see illustrations)**.

3 Partially remove the lock and then rotate it.

8.2a Undo the bonnet lock bolts from the rear and ...

8.2b ... remove the security plate

8.3a Release and then ...

8.3b ... remove the cable

8.3c Disconnect the wiring plug

Disconnect the wiring plug and then detach the release cable **(see illustrations)**.

Refitting and adjustment

4 Refitting is a reversal of the removal procedure, starting by positioning the lock as noted before removal.

5 If the front of the bonnet is not level with the front wings, the lock may be moved up or down within the mounting holes. After making an adjustment, raise or lower the rubber buffers to support the bonnet correctly.

---

9   Door inner trim panel –
removal and refitting

Removal

1 Disconnect the battery negative (earth) lead (Chapter 5 Section 3).

Front door

2 Remove the door mirror trim panel by prising it free **(see illustration)**.
3 Prise up the combined power window and door mirror control switch **(see illustration)**. Remove the switch panel and disconnect the wiring plug.
4 Remove the screw cover from the door release handle. Remove the screw and release the handle surround **(see illustrations)**.
5 Carefully prise the cover from the door grab handle **(see illustration)**. Undo the two bolts from behind the cover inside the door pull handle.

6 Working around the outer edge of the door panel remove the six screws.**(see illustration)**. Lift the door panel up to remove it.
7 If working on the door fittings the door

membrane can now be removed. Disconnect the wiring plug and then unbolt the door control module. Disconnect the wiring plug from the loudspeaker and then unscrew the

9.2 Remove the door mirror inner trim

9.3 Remove the switch panel

9.4c Remove the surround

9.5 Remove the cover

9.6 Work around the panel and remove the screws

9.4a Remove the cover and ...

9.4b ... then remove the screw

9.7 The door panel with the membrane removed

9.8a Remove the screw

9.8b Disconnect the wiring plug

speaker, followed by the speaker support panel.. Using a sharp knife carefully cut through the mastic sealant.that secures the membrane. Remove the membrane from the door **(see illustration)**. If the membrane is to be removed for any length of time, then take measures to ensure that the mastic does not become contaminated with dust. Covering the seal with kitchen film will protect the mastic.

Rear door

8 Remove the screw cover from the door release handle. Remove the screw and release the surround complete with the power window switch (where fitted). Disconnect the wiring plug from the power window switch **(see illustrations)**.

9 On models fitted with manual rear windows, fully shut the window, and note the position of the regulator handle. Release the spring clip by inserting a clean cloth between the handle and the door trim. Using a 'sawing' action, pull the cloth against the open ends of the clip to release it, at the same time pulling the handle from the regulator shaft splines. Withdraw the handle and the spacer.

10 Carefully prise the cover from the door grab handle. Undo the two bolts from behind the cover inside the door pull handle **(see illustrations)**.

11 Working around the outer edge of the door panel remove the six screws. **(see illustrations)**. Lift the door panel up to remove it and where fitted disconnect the tweeter speaker wiring plug as the panel is withdrawn.

12 If working on the door fittings the door membrane can now be removed. Release the wiring loom retaining clips and unbolt the door control module. Using a sharp knife carefully cut through the mastic sealant.that secures the membrane **(see illustrations)**. Remove the membrane from the door. If the membrane is to be removed for any length of time, then take measures to ensure that the mastic does not become contaminated with dust. Covering the seal with kitchen film will protect the mastic.

Refitting

13 Refitting is a reversal of the removal procedure. On the rear manual windows,

9.10a Remove the cover and …

9.10b … then remove the screws

9.11a Lift off the door panel and …

9.11b … disconnect the tweeter wiring plug

9.12a Release the wiring loom

9.12b Cut through the sealant

10.2 Remove the inner weather seal

10.3a Remove the screws…

10.3b …then the single trim clip…

ensure the retaining clip is fitted to the winder handle before refitting the handle to the regulator shaft.

14 Initialise the power windows as described in Chapter 5 Section 3.

10 Door window glass –
removal and refitting

Removal

Front door

1 Fully lower the door glass and then remove the door inner trim panel and membrane as described in Section 9.

2 Prise up and remove the door inner weatherstrip **(see illustration)** and then partially free the upper rear door trim (from the trailing edge of the door).

3 Pull out (or work around) the rear upper section of the window channel guide rubber and then remove the 3 screws and single trim clip from the outer door rear trim panel **(see illustrations)**.

4 Reconnect the power window switch and raise the door glass so that the retaining clips are visible.

5 Carefully release the locking pegs from the holes in the glass. An assistant pulling the glass up will stop the glass falling back into

10.3c …and then remove the panel

10.5 A detailed view of the glass locking peg

the retaining clips **(see illustration)**. As soon as the glass is released place cloths over the the clips to stop the glass falling back into the clip.

6 Lift the glass up and out of the door frame.

Rear door

7 Remove the door inner trim panel and membrane as described in Section 9.

8 On models with power windows, reconnect the window switch. On models with manual windows refit the winder handle.

9 Disconnect the wiring plug and remove the door speaker.

10 Lower the window until the glass retaining brackets are visible **(see illustration)**.

Carefully release the locking pegs from the holes in the glass **(see illustration 10.5)**. An assistant pulling the glass up will stop the glass falling back into the brackets. As soon as the glass is released place cloths over the the brackets to stop the glass falling back into the bracket.

11 Remove the door inner weatherstrip and then lower the glass (guiding it past the regulator and retaining brackets) to the bottom of the door.

12 At the rear inner edge of the door partially free the upper trim panel – there is no need to remove it completely – and then pull out the rubber seal from the glass guide channel **(see illustrations)**.

13 Remove the 3 screws and single trim clip

10.10 The glass retaining brackets

10.12a Partially release the inner door frame trim

10.12b Pull out the glass guide channel rubber

10.13a Remove the trim clip and…

10.13b …then unhook and remove the panel

and then remove the door outer trim panel **(see illustrations)**.

14 Lift the window glass from the door while tilting it up slightly at the rear, and withdraw it from the outside of the door frame **(see illustration)**.

Refitting

15 Refitting is a reversal of the removal procedure, making sure that the glass is correctly located in the clamps. Initialise the power windows as described in Chapter 5 Section 3.

11 Door window regulator –
removal and refitting

Removal
Front door

1 Remove the door panel and membrane as described in Section 9.

2 Refit the power window switch and lower the door glass, so that the glass retaining brackets are visible. Release the glass from the regulator as described in Section 10.

3 Slide up the glass and secure it in the fully closed position with adhesive ('gaffer') tape.

4 Disconnect the wiring plug and then slacken the regulator mounting screws. Slide the regulator up from the keyhole slots and then lower it down and out from the door frame **(see illustrations)**.

5 If required the motor can now be unscrewed from the regulator **(see illustration)**.

Rear door

6 Remove the rear door inner trim panel and membrane as described in Section 9.

7 On models with manual windows, refit the window winder handle. On models with power windows, reconnect the window switch. Lower the window until the retaining brackets are visible.

8 Release the glass from the retaining clips (as described Section 10) and then push the glass up to the fully closed position. Secure the glass in the closed position with adhesive ('gaffer') tape **(see illustration 11.3)**.

9 Slacken, but do not fully remove the regulator mounting screws. On models with power window, slacken the additional motor screw. Lift the regulator and (where fitted) the motor from the keyhole slots. Lower the assembly,disconnecting the wiring plug as the regulator is withdrawn **(see illustrations)**.

10.14 Remove the door glass

11.4a Disconnect the wiring plug

11.4b Slacken the screws

11.4c Lower the regulator from the door frame

11.5 The motor mounting screws

11.9a Slacken the screws. Release the cable clip (A)

11.9b Disconnect the wiring plug and then...

10 If required the motor can now be unscrewed from the regulator **(see illustration 11.5)**.

Refitting

11 Refitting is a reversal of the removal procedure.

12 Door handle and lock components – removal and refitting

⚠️ *Warning: Before working on any electrical components, disconnect the battery negative (earth) lead (Chapter 5, Section 1).*

Removal

Exterior handle – front door

1 Prise out the rubber grommet from the end of the door adjacent to the exterior handle **(see illustration)**.

2 Working through the aperture, slacken the handle retaining bolt **(see illustration)**.

3 Carefully pull the trim and lock cylinder from the door (if working on the right-hand door) **(see illustration)**.

4 Pull the exterior handle rearwards, and manoeuvre it from the door. Recover the seals between the handle and the door skin **(see illustrations)**.

11.9c ...manoeuvre the regulator from the door frame

12.1 Prise out the grommet at the end of the door

12.2 Slacken the handle retaining bolt...

12.3 ...until the lock cylinder and trim can be pulled from the door

12.4a Unhook the main section of the handle

12.4b Recover the front and...

12.4c ...rear handle gaskets

Exterior handle – rear door

5 The rear door handle is removed in a similar manner to the front door handle. Prise out the rubber grommet from the end of the door adjacent to the exterior handle.

6 Working through the aperture, slacken the handle retaining bolt until the smaller section of the handle can be removed **(see illustration)**.

7 Pull the exterior handle rearwards, and manoeuvre it from the door. Recover the gaskets from between the handle and the door skin **(see illustration)**.

Interior door release handle

Note: *The simple way to remove the inner section of the exterior handle, door latch and inner release handle is to remove them as a complete assembly, however the components can be removed individually if required.*

8 Remove the door inner trim panel as described in Section 9.

9 Remove the single screw and unhook the release handle **(see illustrations)**.

10 Unclip the release cable cover and unhook the cable from the release handle **(see illustration)**.

Latch assembly – front

Note: *The door latch, operating cables and the interior section of the exterior door handle are best removed as single assembly.*

11 Remove the exterior door handle as described in this Section.

12 Remove the door panel and membrane as described in Section 9 and then disconnect the wiring plug from the door latch.

12.6 Remove the smaller section

12.7 Recover the gasket

12.9a Remove the screw ...

12.9b ...and unhook the handle.

13 At the end of the door, remove the 3 screws that hold the lock in place and then remove the single upper screw **(see illustrations)**.

14 Remove the single screw from the outer door panel. If not already removed, recover the outer handle gaskets **(see illustration)**.

15 Remove the inner release handle as described in this section. Unclip the cable from the retaining clip and then manoeuvre the complete assembly from the door frame **(see illustrations)**.

16 If required the latch, inner section of the

12.10 Unhook the cable

12.13a Remove the latch screws and ...

12.13b ...the single upper screw

12.14 Remove the screw

12.15a Unclip the cable

12.15b Manoeuvre the complete assembly from the door

outer handle and the inner release handle can now be separated on the bench **(see illustrations)**.

Latch assembly – rear door

Note: *The door latch, operating cables and the interior section of the exterior door handle are best removed as single assembly.*

17 Remove the exterior door handle as described in this Section.

18 Remove the door panel and membrane as described in Section 9.

19 Disconnect the door latch wiring plug **(see illustration)**.

20 At the end of the door, remove the 3 screws that hold the latch in place **(see illustration)**.

21 Remove the single screw from the outer door panel **(see illustration 12.12)**. If not already removed, recover the outer handle gaskets.

22 Remove the inner release handle as described in this section. Unclip the cable from the retaining clip and then manoeuvre the complete assembly from the door frame **(see illustrations)**.

23 If required the the latch, inner section of the outer handle and the inner release handle can now be separated on the bench **(see illustrations)**.

Lock cylinder

24 Only the drivers door has a traditional lock

12.16a Unhook the cable from the inner section of the handle…

12.16b …and from the latch

12.19 Release the latch wiring plug

12.20 Remove the screws

cylinder fitted. Remove the exterior handle as described this Section.

25 With the lock cylinder on the bench

remove the decorative cover **(see illustration)**.

26 Remove the circlip from the end of the

12.22a Release the bowden cable clip

12.22b Manoeuvre the assembly from the door

12.23a Unclip the cover

12.23b Separate the sections and…

12.23c …disconnect the cables

12.25 Remove the cover

12.26a Remove the circlip and then…

12.26b …the operating link

13.2 Disconnect the wiring plug

13.3 Support the door

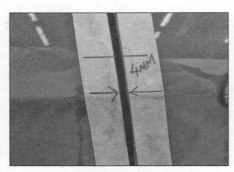

13.4 Use masking tape and mark the gap and alighment

13.5a Remove the upper …

13.5b …and lower hinge bolts

14.1 Remove the trim

cylinder and then (noting their positions) remove the operating link and washer **(see illustrations)**.
27 Insert the key blade into the cylinder and then (using a small drift) push out the locking pin. Remove the barrel complete with the key blade from the cylinder. Replacement key barrels can be matched to the existing key by a Ford dealer.

Refitting

28 Refitting is a reversal of removal, but check the operation of the locks and handles before fitting the door inner trim panel.

13 Door – removal and refitting

Removal

1 Disconnect the battery negative (earth) lead (Chapter 5 Section 3).
2 Fully open the door and disconnect the wiring plug **(see illustration)**.
3 Cover the head of a jack with protective cloth or card and have an assistant support the door. The jack should just support the door, not lift it **(see illustration)**.
4 Measure the door gaps and make alignment marks between the door and the body to aid refitting **(see illustration)**.
5 With an assistant supporting the door remove the upper and lower hinge bolts **(see illustrations)**. Remove the door and store it safely.

Refitting

6 Refitting is a reversal of the removal procedure.

14 Exterior mirror and glass – removal and refitting

Removal

Mirror

1 Unclip the trim panel from the front of the door **(see illustration)**.

14.3a Disconnect the wiring plug

14.3b Peel back the cover to access the mounting bolt

14.4 Prise the mirror from the housing

2 Remove the door panel as described in Section 9.

3 Disconnect the wiring plug and then undo the mirror retaining bolt whilst keeping one hand on the mirror **(see illustrations)**. Remove the mirror.

Mirror glass

4 Tip the upper edge of the glass rearwards, insert a broad lever in between the frame and the glass and gently prise the glass from place **(see illustration)**. Protect your self from glass shards by covering the glass with a cloth, or by wearing gloves.

5 Withdraw the mirror glass and disconnect the wiring connectors for the heated mirrors **(see illustration)**.

Refitting

6 Refitting is a reversal of the removal procedure.

14.5 Disconnect the wiring plugs

15.1 Squeeze together the sides and slide up the upper cover

15 Interior mirror – removal and refitting

1 Squeeze together the sides, and slide up the mirror base upper cover **(see illustration)**.

2 Pull apart the top edges and slide down the mirror base lower cover **(see illustration)**.

3 Disconnect the mirror wiring plug (where applicable).

4 Rotate the mirror 60° anti-clockwise to release it **(see illustration)**.

5 Refitting is the reversal of the removal procedure.

16 Tailgate – removal and refitting

Removal

1 Disconnect the battery as described in Chapter 5 Section 3.

2 Open the tailgate and remove the the trim panels as described in Section 24.

3 Disconnect the wiring plugs from the:
 Tailgate mounted lamps
 High level brake light
 Number plate lamp
 Tailgate release handle/switch

15.2 Pull apart the top edges and slide down the lower cover

15.4 Remove the mirror

 Heated rear screen
 Wiper motor
 Tailgate latch

4 Work around the tailgate and unclip the wiring loom from the various loom retaining clips **(see illustration)**.

5 Disconnect the rear screen washer jet hose.

6 Attach a strong fine cord to the end of the wiring loom, to act as an aid to guiding the wiring through the tailgate when it is refitted.

7 Prise the rubber grommet from the tailgate aperture **(see illustration)** and pull out the

16.4 Release the wiring loom

16.7 Peel back the grommet

16.9 Prise off the clip

16.10 Remove the bolts

wiring loom. Untie the cord, leaving it in position in the tailgate for guiding the wire through on refitting.

 Warning: The tailgate is heavy. At least one assistant will be required to remove it.

8 Have an assistant support the tailgate in its open position.

9 Using a small screwdriver, prise off the clip securing the struts to the tailgate. Pull the sockets from the ball-studs, and move the struts downwards **(see illustration)**.

10 Unscrew and remove the hinge bolts (two each side) from the tailgate **(see illustration)**. Withdraw the tailgate from the body aperture, taking care not to damage the paintwork.

Refitting

11 Refitting is a reversal of the removal procedure, but check that the tailgate is located centrally in the body aperture, and that the striker enters the lock centrally. If necessary, loosen the mounting nuts and reposition the tailgate as required.

17 Tailgate lock components – removal and refitting

Note: *The lock assembly includes the electrically operated release switch and the lock and latch assembly. The latch and lock are a single item incorporating all the central locking components.*

Removal

1 Remove the tailgate trim panel as described in Section 24.

Latch/lock assembly

2 Disconnect the wiring plug from the lock assembly.

3 Using a Torx key, unscrew the lock mounting bolts, and withdraw the lock **(see illustration)**.

Tailgate release switch

Caution: Attempting to remove the tailgate release switch from the outside will damage it.

4 The release button can only be removed if the number plate lamp panel is removed first. Remove the mounting bolts from the inside of the tailgate.

5 The lamp panel is also held in place by a self-adhesive tape. Pivot the panel away from the tailgate and cut through the adhesive tape with a sharp knife or blade **(see illustration)**.

6 Protect the bodywork if necessary and prise free the lamp panel. The panel has a series of trim clips as well as the nuts holding it in place **(see illustration)**.

7 Release the switch/release handle from the inside of the panel **(see illustrations)**.

Refitting

8 Refitting is a reversal of the removal procedure, but always check the operation of the lock and release switch before refitting the tailgate trim panel.

18 Central locking system – testing, reprogramming, removal and refitting

General information

1 All models have remote central locking. Higher specification models may have 'keyless' entry fitted. All locks have integrated locking motors and separate control modules mounted in each door (except for the tailgate). The coded lock/unlock command is received by the antenna (located in the headlining) and

17.3 Remove the bolts

17.5 Slice through the adhesive tape

17.6 Tailgate lamp panel retaining clip

17.7a Release the switch and...

17.7b ...disconnect the wiring plug

18.13 Keyless entry module retaining bolts

sent to the Central Junction Box (CJB). If the signal is valid, a lock (or unlock) signal is sent via the 'CAN' (Controller Area Network) bus to the door lock/unlock modules and the tailgate lock.

2 Two versions of the keyless entry systems are available: Full keyless entry with keyless start/stop and keyless stop/start with standard remote remote locking/unlocking. The keyless system is controlled by a keyless entry control module located behind the right-hand load area trim panel. If the keyless entry system develops a fault then the remote key fob contains a hidden key blade that will allow entry to the vehicle via the drivers door handle key barrel. The blanking plug fitted in place of the conventional ignition key/steering wheel lock must be removed and the remote inserted.

3 Testing of the central locking/alarm system can only be carried out using Ford's IDS (Integrated Diagnostic System) diagnostic tester.

Programming the remote control

Note: *This is only applicable to models where a standard mechanical key starts the engine.*

4 Before attempting to programme the remote, the battery must be fully charged, all lights must be off, the seat belts must be fastened and the anti-theft system must be off. Close all doors.

5 Turn the ignition switch from position 0 to position II four times within 6 seconds, then turn it to position 0 (off).

6 Press any button on the remote (within 10 seconds). A chime will be heard (or an LED will flash) to indicate that programming was successful.

7 Within 10 seconds of the previous step insert additional remotes and press any button on the remote transmitter. A chime or LED flash indicates the programming was successful.

8 Remove the key/remote and after 10 seconds the system will exit the learning mode.

Removal

Generic electronic module (GEM)

9 If the GEM is to be renewed it must be programmed to the vehicle. The GEM is the

key 'gateway' module for all other modules fitted to the vehicle. The configuration data programmed into the GEM module is replicated in the instrument cluster, so (and unlike previous models) a replacement GEM is programmed by retrieving the data held in the instrument cluster. Ford's IDS diagnostic tool will be required for this task.

10 Removal and refitting of the GEM is described in Chapter 12 Section 15.

Keyless entry system module

Note: *If the module is to be renewed, the unit settings must be saved prior to removal, then initialised using the FORD IDS diagnostic tester.*

11 Disconnect the battery negative lead as described in Chapter 5 Section 3.

12 On Galaxy models, remove the right-hand load area side panel as described in Section 24. On S-Max models open the access panel in the right-hand side load area trim panel.

13 Undo the 2 retaining bolts, and remove the module **(see illustration)**. Disconnect the wiring plugs as the module is withdrawn.

Door motors

14 The door lock motors are integral with the locks. Refer to Section 12.

Tailgate motor

15 The tailgate motors are integral with the locks. Refer to Section 17.

Refitting

16 In all cases, refitting is a reversal of the removal procedure.

19 Windscreen and fixed windows – removal and refitting

1 The windscreen and rear window on all models are bonded in place with special mastic, as are the rear side windows and front quarter lights. Special tools are required to cut free the old units and fit new ones; special cleaning solutions and primer are also required. It is therefore recommended that this work is entrusted to a Ford dealer or windscreen specialist.

20 Body side-trim mouldings and adhesive emblems – removal and refitting

Removal

1 Body side trims and mouldings are attached either by retaining clips or adhesive bonding. On bonded mouldings, insert a length of strong cord (fishing line is ideal) behind the moulding or emblem concerned. With a sawing action, break the adhesive bond between the moulding or emblem and the panel.

2 Thoroughly clean all traces of adhesive from the panel using methylated spirit, and allow the location to dry.

3 On mouldings with retaining clips, unclip the mouldings from the panel, taking care not to damage the paintwork.

Refitting

4 Peel back the protective paper from the rear face of the new moulding or emblem. Carefully fit it into position on the panel concerned, but take care not to touch the adhesive. When in position, apply hand pressure to the moulding/emblem for a short period, to ensure maximum adhesion to the panel.

5 Renew any broken retaining clips before refitting trims or mouldings.

21 Sunroof – general information

Glass panel

1 Some models feature a fixed glass sunroof. The sunroof is bonded in place with special mastic. Special tools are required to cut free the old glass and fit a new one. Special cleaning solutions and primer are also required. It is therefore recommended that this work is entrusted to a Ford dealer or windscreen specialist.

Sun blind

2 All models fitted with a fixed sunroof have a motorised blind fitted. Removal and replacement of the motor and sun blind requires the removal of the headlining. Whilst this is not a particularly difficult task it is very time consuming, as removal of all the upper interior fittings is required. Note also that the wiring loom is bonded to the headlining – Ford recommend the use of a hot melt glue gun to fix the loom to the headlining should it prove necessary.

22 Seats – removal and refitting

Removal

Front seat

1 Disconnect the battery as described in Chapter 5 Section 3. Position the lead away from the battery.

⚠ *Warning: Before proceeding, wait a minimum of 5 minutes, as a precaution against accidental firing of the airbag unit or seat belt pretensioner. This period ensures that any residual electrical energy is dissipated.*

2 Undo the security bolt and disconnect the

22.2a Undo the bolt ...

22.2b ... and disconnect the seat wiring plug

22.3a Remove the front bolts, slide the seat forward ...

22.3b ... and remove the rear bolts

22.5a Remove the front bolts and ...

22.5b ... then remove the rear bolts

22.7a The rear bolts

22.7b The front bolts

23.4 Remove the cover

wiring plug under the front of the seat (**see illustrations**).

3 Undo the 4 seat retaining bolts and with the help of an assistant, manoeuvre the seat from the vehicle (**see illustrations**). Note that the seat is extremely heavy.

Rear seats

4 The rear seats are removed in the same manner as the front seats.

5 Slide the seat forward to access the rear bolts and then slide the seat backwards to access the front bolts (**see illustrations**).

Third row seats

6 The third row seats are removed in a similar manner to the other seats, except that the seat cushion must be lifted to access the front mounting bolts.

7 Remove the rear bolts and then lift up the seat cushion to access the front bolts (**see illustrations**).

Refitting

8 Refitting is a reversal of the removal procedure. Tighten the mounting bolts to the specified torque.

23 Seat belts – removal and refitting

Removal

Front seat belt

1 Disconnect the battery negative lead, and position the lead away from the battery (see Chapter 5 Section 3).

⚠️ *Warning: Before proceeding, wait a minimum of 5 minutes, as a precaution against accidental firing of the seat belt tensioner.* *This period ensures that any residual electrical energy is dissipated.*

2 Remove the front seat as described in Section 22.

3 Remove both door step panels and then remove the lower B-pillar trim as described in Section 24.

4 Release the cover from the adjustable shoulder mounting (**see illustration**).

23.5 Remove the bolt

23.6 Disconnect the wiring plug and remove the bolt

23.8 Remove the cover

5 Unbolt the upper mounting **(see illustration)**.

6 At the base of the B-pillar disconnect the wiring plug from the pretensioner. If working on the right-hand belt open the storage compartment and remove the emergency tyre sealant and compressor and then unbolt both lower belt mountings **(see illustrations)**.

Removal – rear side seat belt

7 Disconnect the battery negative lead, and position the lead away from the battery (see Chapter 5 Section 3).

8 Remove the upper anchor cover and then remove the bolt **(see illustration)**.

9 Remove the C-pillar trim and load area area side panel as described in Section 24.

10 Remove the bolts from the inertia reel **(see illustration)** and the lower anchor.

Removal – rear centre seat belt

11 A three point seat belt is provide for the centre, second row seat. This uses a roof mounted main anchor and the belt has two different buckle clips fitted. This ensures that the belt can only be fitted correctly.

12 Remove the cover and then unbolt the centre roof anchor bolt. Note that this does not give access to the inertia reel. To remove the reel the complete headlining must be removed.

Removal – third row seat belt

13 Disconnect the battery negative lead, and position the lead away from the battery (see Chapter 5 Section 3).

14 Remove the upper anchor cover and then remove the bolt **(see illustration)**.

15 Remove the D-pillar trim and load area area side panel as described in Section 24.

16 Unhook (or remove) the seatbelt guide and then remove the inertia reel bolt and the lower anchor bolt **(see illustrations)**.

Removal – seat belt stalks

17 The seat belt stalks are bolted to the seat frames **(see illustration)** and can be removed after removing the appropriate seat as described in Section 22. Where necessary remove the seat trim panel and disconnect the stalk wiring plug (if fitted).

23.10 Remove the bolt

23.14 Remove the bolt

23.16a Remove the seat belt guide

23.16b Unbolt the reel and then ...

23.16c ... the lower anchor

23.17 Typical seat belt stalk mounting

24.1 Sunvisor outer mounting bolts

24.2 Prise up the cover to expose the sunvisor inner mounting bolt

24.3 Prise up the covers to expose the grab handle bolts

Refitting

18 Refitting is a reversal of the removal procedure, noting the following points:
a) *Tighten the mounting nuts and bolts to the specified torque.*
b) *Make sure the seat belt reel locating dowel is correctly positioned.*
c) *Refit spacers in their correct position.*

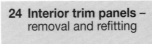

24 Interior trim panels –
removal and refitting

Note: *This section covers the removal and installation of the interior trim panels. It may be necessary to remove an overlapping trim before you can remove the one required. For more information on trim removal, look at relevant Chapters and Sections, where the trims may need to be removed to carry out any other procedures (eg, to remove the steering column you will need to remove the shrouds).*

Sun visor removal

1 Unscrew the mounting bolts and remove the visor **(see illustration)**.
2 Prise up the cover, unscrew the inner bracket mounting bolts, and remove the bracket **(see illustration)**.

Passenger grab handle removal

3 Prise up the covers, then unscrew the mounting bolts and remove the grab handle **(see illustration)**.

Door step trim panels removal

4 Partially release the door weatherseal at the appropriate door step.
5 On the rear door steps remove the single trim retaining clip **(see illustration)**.
6 Prise up the trim panel and remove it. Recover any of the trim clips that remain in the bodywork and replace them where necessary **(see illustration)**.

A-pillar trim removal

7 Work the top of the panel free. Note the special upper retaining clip – if this is damaged it must be replaced **(see illustration)**.
8 Work the lower section of the panel free and then slide it backwards to release it completely **(see illustration)**.

24.5 Remove the clip

24.6 Note the retaining clips

24.7 Note the special retaining clip

24.8 Remove the panel

B-pillar trim removal

Note: *It is possible to remove the B-pillar trim with the seats in position, however the task is considerably easier if the appropriate front seat is removed first.*

9 The B-pillar trim is in 2 sections – an upper and a lower section. They can be removed

24.10a Partially remove the door seal

together or separately, but the lower section must always be removed first.
10 Remove both door step trim panels and then (if removing only the lower section) prise the panel free from the door pillar **(see illustrations)**. Release the panel from the upper section and remove it. Recover any of

24.10b Work around the panel and prise it from the pillar

24.11a Remove the blanking plug, followed ...

24.11b ... by the retaining screw

24.13 Remove the upper panel

24.14 Remove the main upper panel

24.15 Remove the cover and screw

the pillar. Reform the trim clips and refit them to the panel.

C-pillar trim removal

14 Pull down the centre panel cover from above the load area window. Remove the 3 screws (or 4 screws on Galaxy models) and release the main section of the panel **(see illustration)**. Note that it is slightly easier to remove this panel if both the C-pillar and the D-pillar panels are partially removed first.

15 Remove the blanking cover (marked 'Airbag') from the panel and then remove the single screw **(see illustration)**.

16 Prise the cover from the seatbelt upper anchor and then remove the bolt, noting the order of the washers and spacers.

17 Peel back the door weatherstrip and then (using a plastic trim tool) prise the panel free from the pillar **(see illustration)**. Recover any of the metal trim clips that have been left in the pillar. Reform the trim clips and refit them to the panel.

D-pillar trim removal

18 Pull down the centre panel cover from above the load area window. Remove the 3 screws (or 4 screws on Galaxy models) and release the main section of the panel **(see illustration 24.14)**.Note that it is slightly easier to remove this panel if both the C-pillar and the D-pillar panels are partially removed first.

19 Prise the cover from the seatbelt upper anchor and then remove the bolt, noting the order of the washers and spacers.

20 Peel back the door weatherstrip and then (using a plastic trim tool) prise the panel free from the pillar **(see illustration)**. Recover any of the metal trim clips that have been left in the pillar. Reform the trim clips and refit them to the panel.

Steering column shrouds removal

21 To release the upper shroud from the lower shroud, turn the steering wheel 90°, insert a thin screwdriver into a hole at each side of the column **(see illustrations)**. Lift the upper shroud from the column and unclip it from the bottom of the instrument panel.

22 Remove the screws from the lower shroud and (where fitted) disconnect the wiring plug

24.17 Remove the panel

24.20 Remove the D-pillar panel

the metal trim clips that have been left in the pillar. Reform the trim clips and refit them to the panel.

11 On the upper section, remove the blanking cover (marked 'Airbag') from the panel and then remove the single screw **(see illustration)**.

12 Prise the cover from the seatbelt upper anchor and then remove the bolt, noting the order of the washers and spacers.

13 Peel back the door weatherstrip and then (using a plastic trim tool) prise the panel free from the pillar **(see illustration)**. Recover any of the metal trim clips that have been left in

24.21a Release the upper shroud clips and ...

24.21b ... and then unhook the shroud from the instrument panel

24.22a Release the lower shroud ...

24.22b ...and disconnect the wiring plug

24.25 Remove the corner section (Galaxy models)

from the cabin temperature sensor (see illustrations).

Luggage area side panel removal

23 If fitted, remove the rear seat/load area cover.

24 Unbolt and remove the third row seat on the appropriate side, as described in Section 22.

25 Pull the rubber weatherstrip from the tailgate aperture and then prise up the complete tailgate slam panel on S-Max models. On Galaxy models remove the corner section of the slam panel (see illustration).

26 Unclip the cover from the load area side glass panel. Remove the screws and then lower the panel from the headlining. Note that in some cases it will be easier to remove the trim panel if the C-pillar and D-pillar trim panels are partially released first,

27 Remove the C-pillar trim panel and the D-pillar trim panel as described in this Section.

24.29a On galaxy models remove the front ...

24.29b ...and rear screws

28 Remove the access panel and then disconnect the load area lamp (if working on the right-hand side panel) or the 12 volt power outlet if working on the left-hand panel. Disconnecting the 12 volt power outlet is easier if the side panel is partially removed first.

29 On Galaxy models remove the screws from the load area cover mounting bracket and the upper corner (by the D-pillar) (see illustrations).

30 Using a broad plastic trim removal tool release the side panel from the body. On some Galaxy models reach around the panel and disconnect the speaker wiring plug. To fully remove the panel the door step panel must be raised slightly to release the trim clip. Release the seat belt webbing from the panel and then remove the panel to the rear of the vehicle (see illustrations).

31 Recover the metal trim clips from the bodywork, reform them as required and fit them to the side panel. Replace any trim clips that are beyond repair.

Tailgate trim removal

32 Open the tailgate and prise free the upper centre trim, followed by both upper side trim panels (see illustrations).

24.30a Release the panel at the door step

24.30b Work the seat belt webbing free and then ...

24.30c ...fully remove the panel

24.32a Remove the centre section ...

24.32b ...followed by both side sections

24.33 Remove the tailgate lamp

24.36 Remove the end panel

24.37a Remove the screws from the
right-hand side and ...

33 Prise free the tailgate lamp and disconnect the wiring plug **(see illustration)**.

34 Remove the single 'scrivet' from the tailgate interior pull handle.

35 Using a plastic trim tool, work around the panel, releasing the trim clips. Remove the panel and recover any of the metal trim clips that have remained in the tailgate. Reform the metal trim clips and fit them to the trim panel.

Driver's lower facia panel removal

Caution: Disconnect the battery as described in Chapter 5 Section 3 and wait a minimum of five minutes before proceeding, as the drivers knee airbag is removed with the panel.

36 Open the storage compartment and then prise free the drivers door weather seal. Remove the facia end panel **(see illustration)**.

37 Remove the screws from the panel, unbolt the airbag and as the panel is released unclip the diagnostic plug and disconnect the airbag wiring plug **(see illustrations)**.

Refitting

38 Refitting is a reversal of the removal procedure. Where seat belt fastenings have been disturbed, make sure that they are tightened to the specified torque. Renew any broken clips as required.

24.37b ...the left-hand side

24.37c Unbolt the airbag

24.37d Unclip the diagnostic socket as the
facia panel is removed ...

24.37e ...and disconnect the airbag

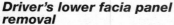

25 Centre console –
removal and refitting

Removal

Note: *The console can be removed with the front seats in position, but it is considerably easier if both front seats are removed first. If the console is being removed to access the heater or AC components removal of both front seat is recommended.*

1 Disconnect the battery as described in Chapter 5 Section 3.

Models with a mechanical handbrake and armrest

2 Using a plastic trim tool, carefully prise up

the main trim panel. Release the gear lever gaiter and the cup holder as the panel is released **(see illustrations)**.

3 Remove the screws and raise the handbrake surround panel slightly. Where switches are fitted to the panel disconnect the

25.2a Prise up and ...

25.2b ...remove the decorative trim

25.3a Remove the screws and…

25.3b …prise up the switch panel

25.3c Push out the switch panel, disconnect the wiring plug…

25.3d …and rotate the panel to remove it

25.4a Remove the forward trim clips…

them and then rotate the panel to remove it from console (see illustrations).

4 On both sides release the trim clips and remove the lower side panels (see illustrations).

5 On the passenger side open the glovebox and remove the screws from the front quarter panel – two from the glovebox and one at the trailing edge of the panel (see illustrations).

6 Repeat the procedure on the driver's and remove the panel (see illustration).

7 Open the rear storage compartment containing the 12 volt power outlet. Lift the

25.4b …and remove the lower side panel

25.5a Remove the front screws..

25.5b …the rear screw and…

25.5c …release the panel

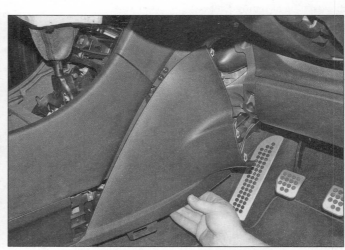

25.6 Remove the driver's side quarter panel

25.7a Remove the 12 volt power outlet

25.7b Remove the single screw and remove the housing to gain...

25.7c ...access to the two hidden screws

25.8a Remove the screws

25.8b Lift out the compartment and disconnect the wiring plugs

25.8c Remove the armrest

compartment slightly and unhook the spring from the base. Rotate the compartment, whilst avoiding damaging the wiring. Remove the screw from the storage compartment housing and then remove the now exposed upper screws (see illustrations).

8 Open the armrest and remove the front screws from the storage compartment. Lift out the compartment, disconnect the wiring plugs and then remove the armrest screws (see illustrations).

9 Working inside the console, disconnect the wiring plugs from the rear 12v power outlet and (if fitted) the USB lead.

10 At both sides remove the outer screws and then remove the inner screws that secure the upper section of the console to the lower. There are 6 screws retaining the upper to the lower, 2 that hold the console to the facia and 2 that locate the console on the support

bracket, forward of the handbrake (see illustrations).

11 The upper section can now be removed by lifting the rear and pulling the console

backwards (see illustration). The main issue is guiding the console over the metal bracket forward of the handbrake – the bracket will pivot to allow the console to pass over it.

25.10a Remove the front screws...

25.10b ...the bracket screws...

25.10c ...the rear screws...

25.10d ...and the side screws

25.11 Removing the centre console

25.13a Release the trim ...

25.13b ...and unclip the gaiter

25.14 Remove the inner panel

25.20 Remove the console

12 If required the lower half of the console can be removed after the handbrake has first been removed as described in Chapter 9 Section 18.

Models with a mechanical handbrake and without and armrest

13 Using a plastic trim tool, carefully prise up the main trim panel. Release the gear lever gaiter as the panel is released (**see illustrations**).

14 Remove the screws and raise the handbrake surround panel slightly. Where switches are fitted to the panel disconnect the them and then rotate the panel to remove it from console (**see illustration**).

15 On both sides release the trim clips and remove the lower side panels.

16 On the passenger side open the glovebox and remove the screws from the front quarter panel (two from the glovebox and one at the trailing edge of the panel).

17 On the driver's side remove the lower facia panel as described in Section 24 and then remove the now exposed screw and remove the quarter panel.

18 Remove the screws from the outer front of the upper section (2 per side) and then remove inboard screws that secure the console to the facia.

19 Remove the remaining inboard screws from the upper section of the console (4 in total) and then guide the upper section past the metal bracket just forward of the handbrake. Remove the front upper section.

20 Remove the remaining screws and remove the rear upper section of the console (**see illustration**).

Models with an Electronic Parking Brake (EPB)

21 Using a plastic trim tool, carefully prise up the main trim panel. Release the gear lever gaiter and the cup holder as the panel is released (**see illustration**).

22 Remove the 2 screws from the switch panel, prise it free and disconnect the wiring plugs.

23 On both sides release the trim clips and remove the lower side panels.

24 On the passenger side open the glovebox and remove the screws from the front quarter panel (two from the glovebox and one at the trailing edge of the panel).

25 On the driver's side remove the lower facia panel as described in Section 24 and then remove the now exposed screws. Remove a single screw from the trailing edge and then remove the quarter panel.

26 Remove the 2 screws from below the heater panel and then (on both sides) remove the 2 outer screws. At the rear of the console remove the bolts.

27 Lift up the console at the rear and disconnect the wiring plugs from the rear 12 volt power outlet and were fitted the USB lead.

28 Disengage the console from the facia by lifting it up slightly. Pull the console back and remove it from the vehicle.

Refitting

29 Refitting is a reversal of the removal procedure.

26 Overhead console –
removal and refitting

Removal

1 Starting at the front edge, carefully prise up the rear section of the console. Disconnect the wiring plug as the panel is removed (**see illustrations**).

2 Remove the screws and lower the main section of the console (**see illustration**).

3 Some Galaxy models have a full length console/storage compartment fitted. Remove

26.1a Insert a screwdriver and unclip the panel

26.1b Disconnect the wiring plug (or plugs)

26.2 Remove the screws

26.3a Remove the lamps followed ...

26.3b ... by the trim piece and ...

26.3c ...then open the compartments and remove the screws

the interior lamps and then with the aid of an assistant supporting the console work along the panel and remove the screws **(see illustrations)**.

Refitting

4 Refitting is a reversal of the removal procedure.

27 Glovebox – removal and refitting

1 Remove the door weatherseal from the A-pillar and then remove the facia end panel **(see illustration)**.
2 Remove the centre console front quarter panel as described in Section 25.
3 Remove the screws from the front of the

glovebox and then remove the hidden bolts from inside the glovebox **(see illustrations)**.
4 Disconnect the wiring plugs as the glovebox is withdrawn **(see illustrations)**. Note that on some models there is a spare wiring plug not connected to anything.
5 Refitting is a reversal of the removal procedure, making sure that the glovebox is located correctly before tightening the bolts.

28 Facia and crossmember– removal and refitting

Note: *Removal of the facia and crossmember is a major undertaking, but will be necessary to access most of the heating and air conditioning components. Make copious notes and take lots of photographs. Label all*

the wiring plugs as they are removed, paying particular attention to the routing and securing of the wiring loom. Whilst removal of the front seats is not essential it is recommended as this greatly improves access.

Fascia

Removal

1 Disconnect the battery as described in Chapter 5 Section 3.
2 Remove the upper section of the centre console as described in Section 25.
3 Remove the glovebox as described in Section 27, and then remove the driver's knee airbag panel (Section 24).
4 With the panel removed, reach up and release the light control switch **(see illustration)**. Disconnect the wiring plug and remove the switch.

27.1 Remove the end panel

27.3a Remove the screws ...

27.3b ... and the hidden bolts

27.4a Disconnect the glovebox lamp and ...

27.4b ... the redundant wiring plug

28.4 Push the switch out from the rear

28.6 Pull out and disconnect the wiring plug

28.7a Remove the screws and …

28.7b … withdraw the panel

28.8 Disconnect the wiring plugs and unclip the loom

28.10 Disconnect the stop/start switch

28.12 Remove the footwell lamps

5 Remove the audio unit as described in Chapter 12 Section 17 and then remove the heater/AC control panel as described in Chapter 3.

6 Pull out the storage compartment from below the heater control panel and disconnect the wiring plug (see illustration).

7 Unscrew and remove the heater control panel and audio unit mounting panel (see illustrations).

8 Disconnect the wiring plugs from the air vent temperature sensors (where fitted) and unclip the wiring loom (see illustration).

9 Remove the steering column shrouds (Section 24) and then remove the steering column as described in Chapter 10.

10 Remove the instrument panel as described in Chapter 12 Section 11 and then disconnect the wiring plug from the stop/start switch (see illustration) wiring loom clip and (where fitted) the keyless entry control module.

11 Release the clip and lower the generic electronic module (GEM) from below the glovebox aperture.

12 On both sides disconnect (or unclip) the footwell lamps (see illustration).

13 Prise off the cover from the central audio speaker and remove the speaker. Prise up the facia mounted tweeters, disconnect them and remove them. (Both procedures are fully described in Chapter 12).

14 Disconnect the wiring plug from the passenger airbag and remove the mounting bolts from the crossmember.

15 By reaching up through the glovebox aperture disconnect the wiring plugs from the bluetooth control module and the Zenon headlight control module – where fitted. Release the wiring loom from the passenger airbag support bracket (see illustrations).

16 At both sides remove the door step panels and then remove the lower A-pillar scuff panels (see illustration).

17 On early models prise out the covers from the ventilation ducts (on the top of the facia) and on later models prise up the upper facia

28.15a Disconnect the wiring plugs from the facia mounted control modules and …

28.15b … then unclip the wiring loom

28.16 Remove the scuff panels (on both sides)

28.17a Unclip the front upper section of the facia (later models) and...

28.17b ...and remove the bolts

28.18a Disconnect the sunlight sensor...

cover. Remove the bolts from both sides **(see illustrations)**.

18 At the left-hand front quarter light disconnect the wiring plug for the sunlight sensor. At the right-hand quarter light disconnect the wiring plug from the audi unit aerial **(see illustrations)**.

19 Remove the facia mounting screws **(see illustrations)**

20 Lastly remove the rearward facing bolts from the A-pillars.

21 Before finally removing the facia check that the wiring loom is free and all necessary components have been removed. With the aid of an assistant, pull back the facia and remove it from the vehicle **(see illustration)**.

Refitting

22 Refitting is a reversal of the removal procedure. On completion, check the operation of all electrical components.

Crossmember

Removal

⚠ **Warning: The air conditioning system must be drained (degassed) before starting work.** *Most garages will have the equipment to do this – and re-gas the system after repairs have been made. Many AC specialist also offer a mobile service as well. Note that it is a criminal offence to knowingly discharge refrigerant to the atmosphere.*
Note: *The crossmember is removed complete with the heater housing.*
23 Remove the facia as described above.

28.18b ...and the aerial lead

28.19b ...the glovebox area...

24 Drain the coolant and have the AC system degassed before starting work. Working under the bonnet disconnect the coolant hoses and the AC refrigerant pipes from the bulkhead.
25 Remove both front doors as described in Section 13.

28.21 Remove the facia

28.26 Unbolt the earth connections

28.19a Remove the screws from the instrument panel area...

28.19c ...and the centre of the facia

26 If not already done so, lower the GEM and then at both sides unbolt the earth connections from the front inner sills **(see illustration)**.
27 Unbolt the gear shift assembly from the front panel **(see illustration)**.

28.27 Unbolt the gear shift assembly (upper bolts shown, lowers hidden)

28.28a Disconnect the various wiring plugs...

28.28b ...release the wiring loom as required and...

28.28c ...then unbolt the front panel...

28.28d ...and remove it

28.29a Unbolt and then...

28 Disconnect the wiring plugs, unclip the wiring loom and remove the front gear shift support panel **(see illustrations)**.

29 Unbolt and then remove the crossmember side support panels **(see illustrations)**.

30 At the left-hand side disconnect the wiring plugs from the GEM and the footwell/wheel arch wiring plugs **(see illustrations)**. (The majority of the wiring loom will be removed with the crossmember and heater box).

31 Mark the position of the crossmember in relation to the A-pillars **(see illustration)**.

32 Remove the blanking plugs and unbolt the long through bolts **(see illustrations)**.

28.29b ...remove the side support panels

28.30a Disconnect the multiplug at the wheel arch and...

28.30b ...at the control module (GEM)

28.31 Use a felt pen and mark around the bolt heads

28.32a Remove the blanking plugs...

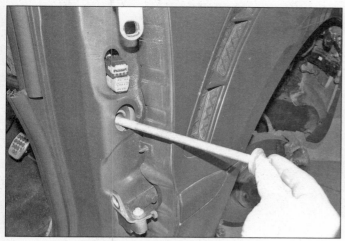

28.32b ...and then remove the bolts

28.34 The crossmember about to be removed

33 Pull back the carpet (in the right-hand footwell) and disconnect the evaporator drain pipe.

34 Remove the A-pillar bolts and with the aid of an assistant pull back the crossmember and lift it over the gear shift assembly and out of the vehicle **(see illustration)**.

29 Wheel arch liner –
removal and refitting

Removal
Front

1 Apply the handbrake. If the wheel is to be removed (to improve access), loosen the wheel nuts. Jack up the front of the vehicle and support it on axle stands (see *Jacking and vehicle support*). Remove the front wheel.

2 Unscrew the bolts securing the liner to the inner wheel arch panel.

3 Remove the bolts and clips securing the liner to the outer edge of the wheel arch and bumper. Withdraw the liner from under the vehicle **(see illustration)**.

Rear

4 Chock the front wheels, and engage 1st gear. If the wheel is to be removed (to improve access), loosen the wheel nuts. Jack up the rear of the vehicle and support it on axle stands (see *Jacking and vehicle support*). Remove the rear wheel.

5 Undo the bolts securing the liner to the outer edge of the wheel arch and bumper.

6 Remove the clips securing the liner to the inner wheel arch, and withdraw the liner from under the vehicle.

29.3 Remove the wing liner

Refitting

7 Refitting is a reversal of the removal procedure. If the wheels were removed, tighten the wheel nuts to the specified torque.

Notes

Chapter 12
Body electrical system

Contents

Degrees of difficulty

Easy, suitable for novice with little experience	**Fairly easy,** suitable for beginner with some experience	**Fairly difficult,** suitable for competent DIY mechanic	**Difficult,** suitable for experienced DIY mechanic	**Very difficult,** suitable for expert DIY or professional

Specifications

System type	12 volt, negative earth	

Bulbs

	Type	Power rating (watts)
Approach light	W5	5
Brake and tail light (S-Max)	P21/5	21/5
Brake light (Galaxy)	P21W	21
Direction indicators	PY21W	21
Direction indicator side repeaters	WY5W	5
Foglamp:		
Front (S-Max)	H8	35
Front (Galaxy)	HB4	55
Rear	P21W	21
Headlight:		
Halogen:		
Dipped	H7	55
Main	H1	55
Gas discharge headlights:		
Dipped	DS2	35
Main	H1	55
Headlight (cornering light)	H1	55
Glovebox light	W5W	5
High-level brake light	W16W/LED	16
Interior light	Festoon	10
Number plate light	C5W	5
Luggage compartment light	W5W	5
Reading light	BA9s	5
Reversing light	P21W	21
Tail light (Galaxy)	W5W	5
Sidelights	W5W	5
Vanity mirror	W5W	5

Torque wrench settings

	Nm	lbf ft
Airbag control unit nuts	8	6
Crash sensor bolts	10	7

1 General information and precautions

1 **Warning:** Before carrying out any work on the electrical system, read through the precautions given in *Safety first!* at the beginning of this manual, and in Chapter 5 Section 1.

2 The electrical system is of 12 volt negative earth type. Power for the lights and all electrical accessories is supplied by a silver-calcium type battery which is charged by the alternator.

3 This Chapter covers repair and service procedures for the various electrical components not associated with the engine. Information on the battery, alternator and starter motor can be found in Chapter 5.

4 It should be noted that prior to working on any component in the electrical system, the battery negative terminal should first be disconnected to prevent the possibility of electrical short-circuits and/or fires – see Chapter 5 Section 3. **Note:** *If the vehicle has a security-coded radio, check that you have a copy of the code number before disconnecting the battery. Refer to your Ford dealer if in doubt.*

2 Electrical fault finding – general information

Note: *Refer to the precautions given in 'Safety first!' and in Chapter 5 before starting work.*

1 The following tests relate to testing of the main electrical circuits, and should not be used to test delicate electronic circuits (such as anti-lock braking systems), particularly where an electronic control unit is used.

2 **Caution:** The electrical system is extremely complex. Many of the ECMs are connected via a 'Databus' system, where they are able to share information from the various sensors, and communicate with each other. Due to the design of the Databus system, it is not advisable to backprobe the ECMs with a multimeter in the traditional manner. Instead, the electrical systems are equipped with a sophisticated self-diagnosis system, which can interrogate the various ECMs to reveal stored fault codes, and help pinpoint faults. In order to access the self-diagnosis system, specialist test equipment (fault code reader/scanner) is required.

General

3 Typically, electrical circuit consists of an electrical component, any switches, relays, motors, fuses, fusible links or circuit breakers related to that component, and the wiring and connectors which link the component to both the battery and the chassis. To help to pinpoint a problem in an electrical circuit, wiring diagrams are included at the end of this Chapter.

4 Have a good look at the appropriate wiring diagram before attempting to diagnose an electrical fault, to obtain a complete understanding of the components included in the particular circuit concerned. The possible sources of a fault can be narrowed down by noting if other components related to the circuit are operating properly. If several components or circuits fail at one time, the problem is likely to be related to a shared fuse or earth connection.

5 An electrical problem will usually stem from simple cause, such as loose or corroded connections, a faulty earth connection, a blown fuse, a melted fusible link, or a faulty relay (refer to Section 3 for details of testing relays). Visually inspect the condition of all fuses, wires and connections in a problem circuit before testing the components. Use the wiring diagrams to determine which terminal connections will need to be checked in order to pinpoint the trouble-spot.

6 The basic tools required for electrical fault finding include a circuit tester or voltmeter (a 12 volt bulb with a set of test leads can also be used for certain tests); a self-powered test light (sometimes known as a continuity tester); an ohmmeter (to measure resistance); a battery and set of test leads; and a jumper wire, preferably with a circuit breaker or fuse incorporated, which can be used to bypass suspect wires or electrical components. Before attempting to locate a problem with test instruments, use the wiring diagram to determine where to make the connections.

7 Sometimes, an intermittent wiring fault (usually caused by a poor or dirty connection, or damaged wiring insulation) can be pinpointed by performing a wiggle test on the wiring. This involves wiggling the wiring by hand to see if the fault occurs as the wiring is moved. It should be possible to narrow down the source of the fault to a particular section of wiring. This method of testing can be used in conjunction with any of the tests described in the following sub-Sections.

8 Apart from problems due to poor connections, two basic types of fault can occur in an electrical circuit: open-circuit, or short-circuit.

9 Largely, open-circuit faults are caused by a break somewhere in the circuit, which prevents current from flowing. An open-circuit fault will prevent a component from working, but will not cause the relevant circuit fuse to blow.

10 Low resistance or short-circuit faults are caused by a 'short'; a failure point which allows the current flowing in the circuit to 'escape' along an alternative route, somewhere in the circuit. This typically occurs when a positive supply wire touches either an earth wire, or an earthed component such as the bodyshell. Such faults are normally caused by a breakdown in wiring insulation, A short circuit fault will normally cause the relevant circuit fuse to blow.

11 Fuses are designed to protect a circuit from being overloaded. A blown fuse indicates that there may be problem in that particular circuit and it is important to identify and rectify the problem before renewing the fuse. Always renew a blown fuse with one of the correct current rating; fitting a fuse of a different rating may cause an overloaded circuit to overheat and even catch fire.

Finding an open-circuit

12 One of the most straightforward ways of finding an open-circuit fault is by using a circuit test meter or voltmeter. Connect one lead of the meter to either the negative battery terminal or a known good earth. Connect the other lead to a connector in the circuit being tested, preferably nearest to the battery or fuse. Switch on the circuit, bearing in mind that some circuits are live only when the ignition switch is moved to a particular position. If voltage is present (indicated either by the tester bulb lighting or a voltmeter reading, as applicable), this means that the section of the circuit between the relevant connector and the battery is problem-free. Continue to check the remainder of the circuit in the same fashion. When a point is reached at which no voltage is present, the problem must lie between that point and the previous test point with voltage. Most problems can be traced to a broken, corroded or loose connection.

⚠️ **Warning: Under no circumstances may live measuring instruments such as ohmmeters, voltmeters or a bulb and test lead be used to test any of the airbag circuitry. Any testing of these components must be left to a Ford dealer or specialist, as there is a danger of activating the system if the correct procedures are not followed.**

Finding a short-circuit

14 Loading the circuit during testing will produce false results and may damage your test equipment, so all electrical loads must be disconnected from the circuit before it can be checked for short circuits. Loads are the components which draw current from a circuit, such as bulbs, motors, heating elements, etc.

15 Keep both the ignition and the circuit under test switched off, then remove the relevant fuse from the circuit, and connect a circuit test meter or voltmeter to the fuse connections.

16 Switch on the circuit, bearing in mind that some circuits are live only when the ignition switch is moved to a particular position. If voltage is present (indicated either by the tester bulb lighting or a voltmeter reading, as applicable), this means that there is a short-circuit. If no voltage is present, but the fuse still blows with the load(s) connected, this indicates an internal fault in the load(s).

Finding an earth fault

17 The battery negative terminal is connected to 'earth': the metal of the engine/ transmission and the car body – and most systems are wired so that they only receive a positive feed, the current returning through the metal of the car body. This means that the component mounting and the body form part of that circuit. Loose or corroded mountings can therefore cause a range of electrical

2.17a Earth connection below the right-hand headlight …

2.17b … on the left-hand chassis member in the engine compartment (under the air filter) …

2.17c … on the transmission (by the gear selector) …

2.17d … on the doorstep inner sills …

faults, ranging from total failure of a circuit, to a puzzling partial fault. In particular, lights may shine dimly (especially when another circuit sharing the same earth point is in operation), motors (eg, wiper motors or the radiator auxiliary cooling fan motor) may run slowly, and the operation of one circuit may have an apparently unrelated effect on another. Note that on many vehicles, earth straps are used between certain components, such as the engine/transmission and the body, usually where there is no metal-to-metal contact between components due to flexible rubber mountings, etc (see illustrations).

18 To check whether a component is properly earthed, disconnect the battery and connect one lead of an ohmmeter to a known good earth point. Connect the other lead to the wire or earth connection being tested. The resistance reading should be zero; if not, check the connection as follows.

19 If an earth connection is thought to be faulty, dismantle the connection and clean back to bare metal both the bodyshell and the wire terminal or the component earth connection mating surface. Be careful to remove all traces of dirt and corrosion,

2.17e … and on the rear inner wing (behind the load area side panel)

2.17f These earths in poor condition were removed, cleaned up …

2.17g … and coated with a special protective lubricant

3.2a Remove the soundproofing...

3.2b ...rotate the fastener anti-clockwise...

3.2c ...and then lower the fusebox

then use a knife to trim away any paint, so that a clean metal-to-metal joint is made. On reassembly, tighten the joint fasteners securely; if a wire terminal is being refitted, use serrated washers between the terminal and the bodyshell to ensure a clean and secure connection. When the connection is remade, prevent the onset of corrosion in the future by applying a coat of petroleum jelly or silicone-based grease or by spraying on (at regular intervals) a proprietary ignition sealer or a water dispersant lubricant.

3 Fuses and relays – general information

Main fuses

1 The fuses are located on a single panel under the passenger's side of the facia, in a fusebox on the left-hand side of the engine compartment and behind the left-hand side load area side panel.
2 Access to the passenger cabin fuses is gained by removing the soundproofing panel, rotating the latch and lowering the fusebox. This gives access to the fuses. The fusebox can be further lowered by unhooking it at the rear **(see illustrations)**.

3 To access the engine compartment fusebox, open the bonnet, release the catches and remove the lid.
4 To access the load area fusebox, lower the third row of seats and open the compartment cover **(see illustration)**.
5 Each fuse is numbered; the fuses' ratings and circuits they protect are listed on the rear face of the cover panel **(see illustration)**. A list of fuses is given with the wiring diagrams.
6 To remove a fuse, first switch off the circuit concerned (or the ignition), then pull the fuse out of its terminals – a pair of tweezers provided specifically for this purpose is fitted on the underside of the engine compartment fusebox cover. The wire within the fuse should be visible; if the fuse is blown the wire will have a break in it, which will be visible through the plastic casing.
7 Always renew a fuse with one of an identical rating; never use a fuse with a different rating from the original or substitute anything else. Never renew a fuse more than once without tracing the source of the trouble. The fuse rating is stamped on top of the fuse; note that the fuses are also colour-coded for easy recognition.
8 If a new fuse blows immediately, find the cause before renewing it again; a short to earth as a result of faulty insulation is most likely. Where a fuse protects more than one circuit, try to isolate the defect by switching on

each circuit in turn (if possible) until the fuse blows again. Always carry a supply of spare fuses of each relevant rating on the vehicle, a spare of each rating should be clipped into the base of the fusebox.
9 Note that some circuits are protected by 'maxi' fuses fitted in the engine compartment fusebox. These fuses are physically much bigger than the normal fuses, and have correspondingly higher ratings. Should one of these fuses fail, have the circuit examined a Ford dealer or specialist prior to renewing the fuse.
10 Two fusible links are fitted to the battery positive lead. These are designed to protect the starter motor and alternator wiring harnesses from damage resulting from a major fault. If either of these two links should fail, do not renew them until the circuit concerned has been examined.

Relays

11 The main relays are located in the and engine compartment fusebox. The location and function of the relays is given on the underside of the fusebox lid.
12 The relays are of sealed construction, and cannot be repaired if faulty. The relays are of the plug-in type, and may be removed by pulling directly from their terminals. In some cases, it will be necessary to prise the two plastic clips outwards before removing the relay.

3.4 The load area fusebox

3.5 The fuse locations are shown on the rear of the lid

13 If a circuit or system controlled by a relay develops a fault and the relay is suspect, operate the system; if the relay is functioning, it should be possible to hear it click as it is energised. If this is the case, the fault lies with the components or wiring of the system. If the relay is not being energised, then either the relay is not receiving a main supply or a switching voltage, or the relay itself is faulty. Testing is by the substitution of a known good unit, but be careful; while some relays are identical in appearance and in operation, others look similar but perform different functions.

14 To renew a relay, first ensure that the ignition switch is off. The relay can then simply be pulled out from the socket and the new relay pressed in.

4 Electrical connectors

1 Most electrical connections on these vehicles are made with multiwire plastic connectors. The mating halves of many connectors are secured with locking clips molded into the plastic connector shells. The mating halves of some large connectors, such as some of those under the instrument panel, are held together by a bolt through the center of the connector.

2 To separate a connector with locking clips, use a small screwdriver to pry the clips apart carefully, then separate the connector halves.

Pull only on the shell, never pull on the wiring harness, as you may damage the individual wires and terminals inside the connectors. Look at the connector closely before trying to separate the halves. Often the locking clips are engaged in a way that is not immediately clear. Additionally, many connectors have more than one set of clips.

3 Each pair of connector terminals has a male half and a female half. When you look at the end view of a connector in a diagram, be sure to understand whether the view shows the harness side or the component side of the connector. Connector halves are mirror images of each other, and a terminal shown on the right side end-view of one half will be on the left side end-view of the other half.

4.5a Most electrical connectors have a single release tab that you depress to release the connector

4.5c Some connectors have two release tabs that you must squeeze to release the connector

4.5d Some connectors use wire retainers that you squeeze to release the connector

4.5f Here's another sliding-lock style connector, with the lock (1) and the release tab (2) on the side of the connector

4.5g On some connectors the lock (1) must be pulled out to the side and removed before you can lift the release tab (2)

4 It is often necessary to take circuit voltage measurements with a connector connected. Whenever possible, carefully insert a small straight pin (not your meter probe) into the rear of the connector shell to contact the terminal inside, then clip your meter lead to the pin. This kind of connection is called "backprobing." When inserting a test probe into a terminal, be careful not to distort the terminal opening. Doing so can lead to a poor connection and corrosion at that terminal later. Using the small straight pin instead of a meter probe results in less chance of deforming the terminal connector. "T" pins are a good choice as temporary meter connections. They allow for a larger surface area to attach the meter leads too.

5 Typical electrical connectors:

4.5b Some electrical connectors have a retaining tab which must be pried up to free the connector

4.5e Critical connectors often employ a sliding lock (1) that you must pull out before you can depress the release tab (2)

4.5h Some critical connectors, like the multi-pin connectors at the Electronic Control Module employ pivoting locks that must be flipped open

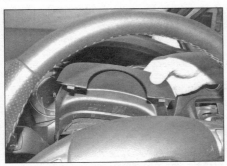

5.2 Rotate the steering wheel and release the upper shroud

5.3a Lower steering column shroud fixings

5.3b Where fitted disconnect the wiring plug from the cabin temperature sensor

5 Ignition switch – removal and refitting

Removal

1 Ensure the battery negative lead has been disconnected as described in Chapter 5 Section 3, then turn the ignition switch to position I.

2 Rotate the steering wheel as necessary to access the column upper shroud retaining clips. Release the clips and remove the shroud (**see illustration**).

3 Undo the bolts and remove the steering column lower shroud (**see illustrations**). Release the steering column adjustment lever to remove the shroud.

4 Disconnect the wiring plug, then depress the clips and remove the ignition switch (**see illustrations**). Do not turn the lock cylinder (key) from position I whilst the ignition switch is removed.

5 Unclip and then remove the key reader coil and then with the key still in position I, insert a thin rod into the hole in the lower part of the cylinder housing. Depress the spring-loaded locking lug, and pull the cylinder from the housing (**see illustrations**).

Refitting

6 Refitting is a reversal of removal. Note that the lock cylinder (key) must be in position I prior to refitting the ignition switch.

6 Switches – removal and refitting

Steering column switches

1 Rotate the steering wheel as necessary to access the column upper shroud retaining clips. Release the clips and remove the shroud (**see illustration 5.2**).

2 Undo the 2 bolts and remove the steering column lower shroud (**see illustration 5.3a**).

5.4a Disconnect the wiring plug

5.4b Release the clips and pull the switch from the lock

5.5a Remove the key reader coil

5.5b The lock/barrel release access point

5.5c Pull the lock cylinder from the housing

6.3a Remove the screws (shown with steering wheel removed for clarity) ...

6.3b ... and slide out the relevant switch

6.6a Disconnect the wiring plugs

Release the steering column adjustment lever to remove the shroud.

3 Undo the bolts and slide the relevant switch from the assembly **(see illustrations)**.

4 If the multifunction switch/rotary contact carrier is to be removed, begin by removing the steering wheel as described in Chapter 10 Section 14.

5 Remove the airbag rotary connector (clockspring) as described in Section 21.

6 Disconnect the wiring plugs, undo the upper and lower fixings and then slide the assembly from the steering column **(see illustrations)**.

7 Refitting is a reversal of removal.

Light switch

8 Remove the driver's side lower facia panel as described in Chapter 11 Section 24.

9 Reach up, squeeze together the switch upper and lower retaining clips, and pull the switch from the facia **(see illustrations)**. Disconnect the wiring plug as the switch is withdrawn.

10 Refitting is a reversal of removal.

Glovebox light switch

11 Open the glovebox, depress the small locking tabs and lower the switch **(see illustration)**. Disconnect the wiring plug.

12 Refitting is a reversal of removal.

Door mirror adjuster

13 The door mirror adjusters are integral with

6.6b Remove the upper screws and then ...

6.6c ... the lower screws

6.6d Slide off the complete assembly

6.9a Reach up behind the facia, squeeze together the light switch clips ...

the window switch assemblies fitted to the door panels.

14 Use a plastic trim tool and prise up

the switch assembly **(see illustration)**. Disconnect the wiring plug.

15 Refit in the reverse order of removal.

6.9b ... and push out the switch

6.11 Squeeze together the clips and lower the switch

6.14 Remove the switch assembly

6.16a Prise up and...

6.16b ...and release the panel

6.17a Disconnect the wiring plug and...

6.17b ...push out the switch

6.19 Release the trim

Facia centre panel switches

16 Working from the outer edge, prise free the switch panel (see illustrations).
17 Disconnect the wiring plug and push out the appropriate switch (see illustrations).
18 Refitting is a reversal of removal.

Sunroof blind control switch

19 Release the upper section of the overhead console (see illustration).
20 Disconnect the wiring plug and push the switch out from the rear (see illustrations).
21 Refit in the reverse order of removal.

Window switches

22 If working on the front door, using a plastic trim tool prise out the switch (see illustration 6.14).
23 On the rear door remove the blanking plug, remove the screw and release the door opener trim panel. Disconnect the wiring plug (see illustrations).
24 Refit in the reverse order of removal.

Courtesy light switches

25 The courtesy lights are controlled by microswitches incorporated into the door locks. The switches are not available separately. If defective, the door lock assembly must be renewed (see Chapter 11 Section 12).

Handbrake warning switch

26 Remove the upper section of the centre console as described in Chapter 11 Section 25.

6.20a Disconnect the wiring plug and...

6.20b ...remove the switch

6.23a Remove the blanking plug...

6.23b ...remove the screw...

6.23c ...disconnect the wiring plug and push out the switch

6.27 Handbrake warning switch

6.34a Remove the rear screw(s) …

6.34b …and the front screw(s)

6.34c Lift out the switch panel

6.37a Disconnect the wiring plug…

6.37b …release the locking tabs and…

27 Undo the single screw using a short (or angled) screwdriver and detach the switch (see illustration).
28 Detach the wiring connector from the switch.
29 Refit in the reverse order of removal.

Brake light switch

30 Refer to Chapter 9 Section 17.

Headlight control/foglamp/instrument illumination

31 These switches are integral with the light switch module. Removal is described earlier in this Section.

Hazard warning switch

32 The switch is part of the facia switch panel. Removal is described earlier in this Section.

Steering wheel switches

33 Remove the driver's airbag as described in Section 21.
34 Undo the screws from the rear of the wheel and from the front. Disconnect the wiring plug as the switch pad is withdrawn (see illustrations).
35 Refitting is a reversal of removal.

Stop/Start switch

36 The switch can only be removed by realising it from the rear – attempting to prise it out from the font will damage the facia. Remove the Audio unit (Section 17).
37 Disconnect the wiring plug and release the switch (see illustrations).

Seat heating switches

38 Where fitted the switches are located

close to the handbrake lever. Remove the trim panel as described in Chapter 11 Section 24.
39 Disconnect the wiring plug and prise out the switch.
40 Refitting is a reversal of removal.

7 Exterior light bulbs – renewal

Note: *This section does not cover bulb renewal on models fitted with gas discharge headlights; refer to Section 10 for renewal details.*
1 Whenever a bulb is renewed, note the following points:
a) *Remember that if the light has just been in use, the bulb may be extremely hot.*
b) *Do not touch the bulb glass with the fingers, as the small deposits can cause the bulb to cloud over.*
c) *Always check the bulb contacts and holder, ensuring that there is clean metal-to-metal contact. Clean off any corrosion or dirt before fitting a new bulb.*
d) *Wherever bayonet-type bulbs are fitted, ensure that the live contacts bear firmly against the bulb contact.*
e) *Always ensure that the new bulb is of the correct rating and that it is completely clean before fitting it.*

Halogen main beam

Note: *Do not handle the bulb glass with bare hands – use a cloth or wear gloves. If the glass becomes contaminated, clean it with*

6.37c …pull out the switch

methylated spirits and dry thoroughly before fitting
2 Remove the headlight unit as described in Section 9.
3 Peel away the plastic cap from the rear of the unit (see illustration).

7.3 Remove the cover

7.4a Pull off the wiring plug

7.4b Release the spring clips …

7.4c …and pull out the bulb

4 Disconnect the wiring plug, unhook the retaining clips and pull out the bulb **(see illustrations)**.

5 Fit the new bulb using a reversal of the removal procedure.

Halogen dipped beam

Note: *Do not handle the bulb glass with bare hands – use a cloth or wear gloves. If the glass becomes contaminated, clean it with methylated spirits and dry thoroughly before fitting*

6 Remove the headlight as described in Section 9.

7 Peel away the plastic cap from the rear of the unit **(see illustration)**.

8 The wiring plug doubles up as the bulb holder. Rotate the complete assembly and pull out the bulb **(see illustrations)**.

9 Fit the new bulb using a reversal of the removal procedure.

Sidelight

10 The front sidelights are mounted in the front fog lights on all models except for S-Max models fitted with daytime running lights. Note that daytime running lights are only fitted from March 2010. On these models the lamp utilises LED type bulbs – if they develop a fault the complete lamp must be replaced (Section 9).

11 On S-Max models remove the trim from the front of the foglight and then unclip the lamp from the bumper housing by releasing the top clip. Unhook the lamp and pull it from the bumper cover.

12 On Galaxy models remove the screws from the base of the bumper cover, tip the top of the lamp forward and pull it out from the bumper.

13 Release the bulbholder from the lamp – there is no need to disconnect the wiring plug. Pull the capless/wedge type pull from the bulbholder.

14 Fit the new bulb using a reversal of the removal procedure.

Front foglamp

15 There are several variations of the front fog lights fitted to the Galaxy and S-max. They all use the same bulb.

16 On S-Max models remove the trim from the front of the foglight and then unclip the lamp from the bumper housing by releasing the top clip. Unhook the lamp and pull it from the bumper cover.

17 On Galaxy models remove the screws from the base of the bumper cover, tip the top of the lamp forward and pull it out from the bumper.

18 Easy access to the bulb is possible after removing the headlight. Disconnect the wiring plug from the bulb **(see illustration)**.

19 Rotate the bulbholder anti-clockwise and pull it from the foglamp **(see illustration)**. Note that the bulb is integral with the bulbholder.

20 Fit the new bulb using a reversal of the removal procedure.

7.7 Remove the cover

7.8a Rotate anti-clockwise to remove the bulb and bulbholder

7.8b Remove the bulb from the bulbholder

7.18 Disconnect the wiring plug

7.19 Remove the foglamp bulb

7.22 Rotate the bulbholder anti-clockwise

7.23 Depress and twist the bulb

7.25 Prise out the lamp

Front direction indicator

21 Remove the headlight as described in Section 9.
22 Rotate the bulbholder anti-clockwise and pull it from the headlight **(see illustration)**.
23 Depress and twist the bulb to remove it from the bulbholder **(see illustration)**.
24 Fit the new bulb using a reversal of the removal procedure.

Direction indicator side repeater

25 Use a small screwdriver and prise open the lamp at the outer edge **(see illustration)**.
26 Pull out the bulbholder and then remove the bulb **(see illustrations)**.
27 Refitting is a reversal of removal.

Approach light

28 Remove the door mirror glass as described in Chapter 11 Section 14.
29 Release the clip and manoeuvre the lamp from the mirror housing **(see illustrations)**.
30 Pull the wedge-type bulb from the bulbholder.
31 Fit the new bulb using a reversal of the removal procedure.

Rear wing mounted combination light

32 The rear wing lamps hold the brake, tail and indicator bulbs. Note that on some later models the lamp may contain non-replaceable LED type bulbs.

7.26a Remove the bulbholder and ...

7.26b ...pull out the wedge/capless style bulb

7.29a Release the retaining clip ...

7.29b ...remove the lamp and pull out the bulbholder

33 Remove the rear light unit as described in Section 9.

34 Remove the screw and then remove the bulbholder **(see illustrations)**.

7.34a Remove the screw and ...

7.34b ...release the bulbholder (Galaxy shown, but the S-Max is similar)

7.35a Push and twist to remove the bulb ...

7.35b ... or simply pull the bulb straight out

7.39a Remove the screws (S-Max shown) ...

7.39b ... and remove the bulbholder

7.39c When replacing a halogen bulb protect the glass – we used a paper towel to hold the bulb

7.40 Remove the number plate light

35 Rotate the relevant bulbholder anti-clockwise and pull it from the light. Where a wedge/capless bulb is fitted pull the bulb straight out **(see illustrations)**.

36 Refitting is a reversal of removal.

Tailgate mounted combination light

37 The tailgate mounted lamp contains the reverse, for and tail light bulbs.

38 Remove the rear light unit as described in Section 9.

39 Remove the screw and remove the bulbholder. Note that some models have a halogen bulb fitted – where fitted do not handle the bulb with bare hands **(see illustrations)**.

Number plate light

40 Open the tailgate and use a small screwdriver to release the lamp **(see illustration)**.

41 Pull the festoon-type bulb (early models) from the contacts. Later models have a wedge/capless bulb fitted **(see illustrations)**.

42 Fit the new bulb using a reversal of the removal procedure.

High-level brake light

43 Later models have LED type bulbs fitted, whilst earlier models use standard bulbs. Models with LED type high level brake light lamps can be identified by the fact that the lamp is screwed in place **(see illustration)**.

44 Remove the lamp as described in Section 9.

45 Disconnect the wiring plug and pull the wedge-type bulb from place.

46 Fit a new bulb using a reversal of the removal procedure.

8 Interior light bulbs – renewal

1 Whenever a bulb is renewed, note the following points:
a) *Remember that if the light has just been in use, the bulb may be extremely hot.*
b) *Always check the bulb contacts and holder, ensuring that there is clean metal-to-metal contact between the bulb and its*

7.41a Twist and pull out the bulbholder and ...

7.41b ... pull out the bulb

7.43 LED type lamps are retained with screws

8.2 Unclip the lamp

8.3a Twist the bulbholder anti-clockwise and remove it

8.3b Pull the wedge/capless type bulb form the bulbholder

8.5 Remove the bulb

8.7 Prise out the lamp

8.8 Remove the bulb

live and earth. Clean off any corrosion or dirt before fitting a new bulb.

c) Wherever bayonet-type bulbs are fitted, ensure that the live contact(s) bear firmly against the bulb contact.

d) Always ensure that the new bulb is of the correct rating and that it is completely clean before fitting it.

Reading lights and courtesy lights

2 Inset a small flat-bladed screwdriver into the slot in the lamp and carefully prise the light unit from place. Galaxy rear combined reading and courtesy light shown, but all the lamps on all models are similar **(see illustration)**.

3 Twist the reading light bulbholder anti-

clockwise and remove it. Pull the wedge type bulb from the holder **(see illustrations)**.

4 Fit a new bulb using a reversal of the removal procedure.

Glovebox light

5 The bulb is part of the switch assembly (see Section 6) and can be removed once the switch is removed **(see illustration)**.

6 Fit the new bulb using a reversal of the removal procedure. Refit the switch

Load area light

7 Use a small screwdriver and prise out the lamp **(see illustration)**.

8 Remove the bulbholder and pull out the bulb **(see illustration)**.

9 Fit the new bulb using a reversal of the removal procedure.

Footwell lights

10 Reach under the facia, and pull the wedge/capless type bulb from the holder **(see illustration)**.

11 Fit the new bulb using a reversal of the removal procedure.

Sunvisor/vanity mirror light

12 Carefully prise the light unit from place **(see illustration)**.

13 Pull the wedge/capless type bulb from the bulbholder **(see illustration)**.

14 Fit the new bulb using a reversal of the removal procedure.

Instrument panel bulbs

15 On all models covered by this Manual, it is not possible to renew the instrument panel

8.10 Pull the footwell light bulb from the holder

8.12 Carefully prise the vanity light lens from place

8.13 Pull the bulb from the holder

9.1 A small screwdriver can be used to release the wiring plug

9.2a Remove the screws...

9.2b ...and lift out the headlight

bulbs individually as they are of LED design and soldered to a printed circuit board. It is not possible to renew a single LED. Where an LED is not functioning, the complete instrument panel must be renewed.

Switch illumination

16 The switches are illuminated by LEDs, and cannot be renewed separately. Refer to Section 6 and remove the switch.

Heater/air conditioning control panel illumination

17 The control panel is illuminated by non-renewable LEDs. If defective, the control panel may need to be renewed.

9 Exterior light units – removal, refitting and beam adjustment

9.6a Open the cover

9.6b Disconnect the wiring plug (Galaxy models)

Headlight unit

Removal

Caution: On models equipped with gas discharge headlights, disconnect the battery negative lead as described in Chapter 5 Section 3, prior to working on the headlights.

1 Disconnect the wiring plug **(see illustration)**.

2 Remove the screws and lift out the headlight **(see illustrations)**. Take care with the front screw as it is easy to drop – ideally remove it with a magnetic screwdriver.

Refitting

3 Refitting is a reversal of the removal procedure. On completion check for satisfactory operation of the lights.

Front foglamp

4 The procedure is as described for bulb renewal in Section 7.

Direction indicator side repeater

5 The procedure is as described for bulb renewal in Section 7.

9.7a Remove the fixings. On S-Max models ...

9.7b ... and Galaxy models

Rear tailgate combination light

6 Open the tailgate and remove the cover **(see illustrations)**.

7 Remove the plastic wingnut fixings **(see illustrations)**.

8 Remove the lamp from the tailgate and on S-max models disconnect the wiring plug **(see illustrations)**.

9 Refitting is a reversal of removal.

Rear wing combination light

10 Open the tailgate and remove the access panel from the load area side trim.

11 Reach up and unscrew the plastic wing

9.8a Disconnect the wiring plug (S-Max models)

9.8b On Galaxy models free the lamp from the locating pegs

9.12a The locating peg on Galaxy models

9.12b Disconnect the wiring plug as the light is removed

9.13a Unscrew the fixings (S-Max models).

nuts. On later S-Max models (with LED lights) the load area side panel will have to be partially (or completely) removed as the plastic wing nuts may have been replaced with standard nuts.

12 On Galaxy models slide the light towards the rear to release it from the locating peg **(see illustrations)**.

13 On S-Max models 3 fixings hold the light in place, with the lower one hard to reach **(see illustrations)**.

Number plate light

14 The procedure is as described for bulb renewal in Section 7.

High-level brake light

15 On models fitted with an LED type light, remove the screws, lower the light and disconnect the wiring plug **(see illustrations)**.

16 On models fitted with standard bulbs, open the tailgate and remove the upper tailgate trim **(see illustration)**.

17 Depress the spring clips and release the light. Disconnect the wiring plug as the light is removed.

Daytime running lights

18 Later models may have Daytime Running Lights (DRL) fitted to the front bumper cover. Theses lamps incorporate LED type bulbs and if faulty the entire lamp must be replaced.

19 Remove the front bumper cover as described in Chapter 11 Section 6.

20 Protect the bumper cover and then disconnect the wiring plug from the DRL. Unclip the lamp from the bumper cover **(see illustration)**.

Beam adjustment

21 Accurate adjustment of the headlight beam on models with standard halogen headlights is only possible using optical beam setting equipment, and this work should therefore be carried out by a Ford dealer or suitably-equipped workshop. All MOT stations have this equipment as correct beam alignment is part of the MOT.

22 For reference, the headlights can be adjusted using the adjuster screws, accessible via the top of each light unit **(see illustration)**.

23 On models fitted with 'Zenon' (HID – High Intensity Discharge) headlights the aim of the beam is controlled by the feedback from the ride height sensors fitted to the front and rear

suspension arms. No attempt should be made to manually adjust these lights – refer to a Ford dealer or suitably equipped garage.

9.13b Remove the light

9.15a Remove the screws, lower the light and…

9.15b …disconnect the wiring plug

9.16 Remove the tailgate trim

9.20 Remove the lamp

9.22 Headlight beam adjustment screws

10.3 Remove the cover

10.4a Release the clip and...

10.4b ...pull out the bulb

10 Xenon gas discharge headlight system – component removal, refitting and adjustment

General information

1 Xenon gas discharge headlights are fitted to some models. The headlights' dipped beam bulbs produce light by means of an electric arc, rather than by heating a metal filament as in conventional halogen bulbs. An electronically-operated shutter is fitted in front of the bulb which angles the light for dipped beam, then re-angles the light for main beam. A conventional halogen bulb is also fitted to augment the main beam light output. The arc is generated by a control circuit which operates at voltages of above 28 000 volts. The intensity of the emitted light means that the headlight beam has to be controlled dynamically to avoid dazzling

other road users. An electronic control unit monitors the vehicle's pitch and overall ride height by sensors mounted on the front and rear suspension, and adjusts the beam range accordingly, using the range control motors built into the headlight units.

 Warning: *The discharge bulb starter circuitry operates at extremely high voltages. To avoid the risk of electric shock, ensure that the battery negative cable is disconnected before working on the headlight units (see Chapter 5 Section 3), then additionally switch the dipped beam on and off to discharge any residual voltage.*

Headlight main beam

2 Remove the headlight as described in Section 9.
3 Peel off the cover from the rear of the headlight (see illustration).
4 Disconnect the wiring plug from the rear of the bulb, then release the retaining clip

and pull the bulb from the reflector (see illustrations). Note how the lugs on the bulb engage with the slots in the reflector. If the bulb is to be refitted, do not touch the glass with the fingers. If the glass is accidentally touched, clean it with methylated spirit.
5 Fit the new bulb using a reversal of the removal procedure.

Headlight dipped beam

Caution: *The dipped beam bulb is under gas pressure of at least 10 bars, therefore it is recommended that protective glasses are worn during this procedure.*
6 Remove the headlight as described in Section 9.
7 Remove the cover from the rear of the headlight and then remove the bulb (see illustrations).
8 Disconnect the wiring plug after the bulb has been removed (see illustrations).
9 Handle the bulb carefully and then remove the locking collar (see illustrations).

10.7a Remove the cover and...

10.7b ...rotate the bulb to remove it

10.8a Use pliers to release the locking clip...

10.8b ...and then remove the wiring plug

10.9a Depress the locking tab...

10.9b ...and remove the collar

10.12a Remove the cover...

10.12b ...disconnect the wiring plug...

10.12c ...release the spring clips...

10 Fit the new bulb using a reversal of the removal procedure.

Cornering lights

11 Some models may also have cornering lights fitted as part of the Zenon headlight system. These bulbs are turned on when the dipped (or main) beam are on and the steering angle is at least 30 degrees (as measured by the steering angle sensor). The bulb is a conventional bulb.

12 Remove the cover, disconnect the wiring plug, release the spring clips and remove the bulb (see illustrations).

Lighting lamp control module

13 If a new module is to be fitted, it must be configured using Ford dedicated diagnostic equipment (IDS). Entrust this task to a Ford dealer or suitably-equipped specialist.

14 The lighting control module is fitted to vehicles with Xenon high-intensity gas discharge lights. The module is located behind the facia above the glovebox.

15 Remove the glovebox as described in Chapter 11 Section 27.

16 Reach up (with difficulty) and disconnect the wiring plug, then remove the screws (again with difficulty) and then remove the module (see illustration).

17 Refitting is a reversal of removal.

Front ride height sensor

Removal

18 The sensor is mounted on the control arm of the left-hand wheel. Apply the handbrake,

10.12d ...and remove the bulb

then jack up the front of the vehicle and support it on axle stands (see *Jacking and vehicle support*). Remove the wheel.

19 Undo the bolt securing the sensor arm bracket to the control arm (see illustrations).

20 Disconnect the wiring plug and unbolt the sensor (see illustration).

Refitting

21 Refitting is a reversal of removal. If a new sensor has been fitted, then a calibration procedure must be carried out. This requires access to Ford diagnostic equipment – entrust this task to a Ford dealer or suitably-equipped specialist.

Rear ride height sensor

Removal

22 The sensor is secured to the left-hand lower control arm and the rear subframe.

10.16 The control module mounting screws

Chock the front wheels, then jack up the rear of the vehicle and support it on axle stands (see *Jacking and vehicle support*).

23 Disconnect the sensor wiring plug, then undo the bolts and remove the sensor, bracket and lever arm assembly.

Refitting

24 Refitting is a reversal of removal. Note that if a new sensor has been fitted, then a calibration procedure must be carried out. This requires access to Ford diagnostic equipment – entrust this task to a Ford dealer or suitably-equipped specialist.

Beam adjustment

25 The basic alignment procedure of the headlights is the same as normal halogen headlights (see Section 9). However, before the procedure is attempted, the ride height sensors must be calibrated using dedicated

10.19a Remove the bolt...

10.19b ...and then unhook the control arm

10.20 Unplug and unbolt the sensor

11.6a Unclip the upper shroud…

11.6b …remove the lower screws…

11.6c …and remove the complete shroud assembly

Ford test equipment. Therefore this task should be entrusted to a Ford dealer or suitably-equipped specialist.

11 Instrument panel – removal and refitting

1 The instrument panel is included in the vehicle's self-diagnosis program. If the instrument panel has a fault, it would be prudent to have the vehicle's fault code memory interrogated by a Ford dealer or specialist, prior to removing the panel.
2 If the instrument panel is being substituted

with a new or exchange unit, the assistance of a Ford dealer or specialist will be required to programme the necessary software, and initialise/adapt the various instrument panel functions.

Removal

3 Disconnect the battery negative lead as described in Chapter 5 Section 3. Wait a minimum of 5 minutes before proceeding.
4 Remove the driver's knee airbag as described in Section 21.
5 Fully extend the steering column, and move it to its lowest position.
6 Unclip the steering column upper shroud.

Remove the lower screws and then remove the shroud (see illustrations).
7 Undo the 2 retaining screws on the lower edge of the instrument panel (see illustration).
8 Using a round ended steel ruler, release the upper retaining clip. The clip is fitted to the facia and must be pushed up to release the instrument panel (see illustrations).
9 Disconnect the wiring plug(s) as the panel is withdrawn (see illustration).

Refitting

10 Refitting is a reversal of removal, but see the note at the beginning of this section.

12 Windscreen wiper components – removal and refitting

Wiper blades

1 Refer to *Weekly checks*.

Wiper arms

Removal

2 If the wipers are not in their parked position, switch on the ignition, and allow the motor to automatically park.

11.7 Remove the screws

11.8a Use a steel ruler to free the top of the panel

11.8b The spring clip with the instrument panel removed and seen from below. Release the clip by pushing in the direction shown

11.9 Disconnect the wiring plug(s)

12.3a Mark the position of the arms

12.3b Pull off the rubber cap...

12.3c ...or lift the cover (rear wiper)

12.3d ...and remove the wiper arm nut

12.3e Remove the arm (rear shown)

12.3f If the arm is hard to remove specialist pullers are availble

3 Before removing an arm, mark its parked position on the glass with a strip of adhesive tape. Prise off the cover and unscrew the spindle nut **(see illustrations)**. Ease the arm from the spindle by rocking it slowly from side-to-side.

Refitting

4 Refitting is a reversal of removal, but before tightening the spindle nuts, position the wiper blades as marked before removal.

Front wiper motor

Note: *There is no physical link between the wiper motors. The left-hand motor is the 'master' and electronically controls (via the GEM) the right-hand motor. When replacing the motor(s) they must have identical part numbers. Where an identical replacement is not available, the motors must be replaced as a matched pair. When replacing the motors, do not install the wiper arms until the motors have been operated, as they will perform an automatic adjustment procedure when first operated.*

Removal

5 Remove the wiper arms as described in the previously in this Section.
6 At the base of both A-pillars remove the small trim panels and then prise free the long A-pillar/Windscreen panels. There is no need to remove the panels completely, just release the lower clips from the inner wing and the cowl panel.

7 Where fitted remove the wiring plug from the cowl panel panel **(see illustration)**.
8 Remove the clips at the front edge, then

12.7 Unclip the wiring plug

12.8b Note how the panel fits at the base of the A-pillars...

pull the windscreen cowling panel upwards to release it from the base of the windscreen **(see illustrations)**. Lift the panel from place.

12.8a Work along the front edge and release the clips

12.8c ...and then remove the panel

12.9a Disconnect the wiring plug and ...

12.9b ...unclip the wiring loom

12.10a Remove the bolts and ...

12.10b ...lift out the motor

12.15a Disconnect the wiring plug ...

12.15b ...and remove the mounting bolts

9 Disconnect the wiring plug and release the loom from the wiper motor **(see illustrations)**.
10 Undo the 3 bolts securing the motor and then remove the wiper motor **(see illustrations)**.
11 If required the lower cowl panel can now be removed. Remove the brake fluid reservoir, place it in a plastic bag and rest it on the engine. Remove the bolts and pull the panel forward to remove it.

Refitting

12 Refitting is a reversal of removal.

Rear wiper motor

Removal

13 Remove the wiper arm.

13.5a Disconnect the wiring plug

13.5b Remove the pump

14 Remove the tailgate trim panel as described in Chapter 11 Section 24.
15 Remove the wiring plug, unscrew the mounting bolts **(see illustrations)** and remove the motor.

Refitting

16 Refitting is a reversal of removal.

13 Windscreen washer system – removal and refitting

Note: *The reservoir fluid level must be regularly topped-up with windscreen washer fluid containing an antifreeze agent, but not cooling system antifreeze – see Weekly checks.*

1 All models are fitted with a front and rear windscreen washer system. Models with Zenon (HID) headlights also have headlight washers.
2 The fluid reservoir is located behind the left-hand corner of the front bumper cover. The windscreen washer fluid pump is attached to the side of the reservoir body. Where headlight washers are fitted a second high pressure pump is also fitted. Access to the reservoir and pump(s) is achieved by removing the front bumper.
3 The tailgate washer is fed by the same reservoir, with a dual output pump.

Washer pump

Removal

4 Remove the front bumper cover as described in Chapter 11 Section 6.
5 The washer pumps (and the fluid level sensor -where fitted) are a push fit in the reservoir. Disconnect the wiring plug – or remove the pump with the wiring plug and disconnect it as the pump is removed. Have a container ready to catch the washer fluid and pull out the pump with a twisting action **(see illustrations)**. Remove the washer pump hoses.
6 A filter is incorporated in the washer pump retaining grommet. Always remove

13.6a Remove the sealing grommet and…

13.6b …check the condition of the filter

13.7 Disconnect the washer hoses as required

the grommet and clean the filter (see illustrations).

7 The supply hoses are attached by rubber couplings to their various connections, and if required, can be detached by simply pulling them free from the appropriate connector (see illustration).

Refitting

8 Refitting is a reversal of removal, but check the reservoir for leaks, before refitting the front bumper cover.

Windscreen washer reservoir

Removal

9 Remove the front bumper as described in Chapter 11 Section 6.

10 On 1.8 and 2.0 litre engine models remove the PCM as described in Chapter 4A Section 12.

11 Disconnect the washer pump wiring plugs and remove the washer hoses.

12 Remove the mounting bolts (see illustration) and lower the reservoir.

Refitting

13 Refitting is a reversal of removal, but check the reservoir for leaks, before refitting the front bumper cover.

Windscreen washer jets

Removal

14 The windscreen washer jets can be adjusted by inserting a pin into the jet and

altering the aim as required. To remove a washer jet, open the bonnet, remove the insulation panel and disconnect the hose from the jet (see illustrations).

15 The rear windscreen washer jet is part of the high level brake light. Remove the high level brake light as described in Section 9, to access the jet. If the jet is faulty the complete lamp must be replaced.

Refitting

16 Refitting is a reversal of removal. Check and adjust the washer jet aim if necessary.

Headlight washer jets

Removal

17 Where fitted, remove the appropriate

13.12a Remove the front bolts…

13.12b …and the upper rear bolt

13.14a Prise out the bonnet insulation panel clips

13.14b Disconnect the wiring plug from the washer jet heater

13.14c Remove the hose…

13.14d …and push out the washer jet

headlight, pull (or push up from below) the washer jet **(see illustration)**.

18 Disconnect the hose and unclip the washer jet **(see illustration)**.

Refitting

19 Refitting is a reversal of removal.

14 Horns – removal and refitting

Removal

1 The horns are located behind the front right-hand bumper cover. Raise the front of the vehicle and support it securely on axle stands (see 'Jacking and vehicle support').

2 Remove the right-hand road wheel and then remove the wing liner.

3 Disconnect the horn wiring plug, undo the mounting bolt and remove the horns from the vehicle **(see illustration)**.

Refitting

4 Refit in the reverse order of removal. Check for satisfactory operation on completion.

15 Central locking system – general information

1 All models are equipped with a central door locking system, which automatically locks all doors and the rear tailgate/boot lid in unison with the manual locking of the driver's front door. The system is operated electronically with motors/switches incorporated into the door lock assemblies. The system is controlled by the Generic Electronic Module (GEM) and the Keyless Vehicle Module (KVM) – where fitted. The GEM and the KVM communicate with the vehicle's other control modules via an information network known as a Databus. Control modules integral with electric window motors receive signals from the GEM via the databus, and directly control the operation of the door locks. The tailgate/boot lid has its own control module, integral with the lock assembly. If any module is renewed, new software for the unit must be downloaded from Ford. Entrust this task to a Ford dealer or suitably-equipped specialist.

13.17 Remove the decorative cover

2 The control unit is equipped with a self-diagnosis capability. Should the system develop a fault, have the control unit interrogated by a Ford dealer or suitably-equipped specialist. Once the fault has been established, refer to the relevant Section of Chapter 11 to renew a door module or tailgate/boot lid lock as applicable.

16 Parking aid components – general, removal and refitting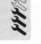

General information

1 The parking aid system is available on all models. Four ultrasound sensors located in the bumpers measure the distance to the closest object behind or in front of the car, and inform the driver using acoustic signals from a buzzer located under the rear luggage compartment trim. The nearer the object, the more frequent the acoustic signals.

2 The system includes a control module and self-diagnosis program, and therefore, in the event of a fault, the vehicle should be taken to a Ford dealer or suitably-equipped specialist who will be able to interrogate the system.

Parking Aid Module (PAM)

Removal

3 The control unit is located behind the right-hand luggage compartment side trim panel. Remove the load area side panel trim as described in Chapter 11 Section 24.

14.3 Horn retaining bolt

16.4 Undo the parking aid module bolts

13.18 Remove the washer jet

4 Undo the 2 retaining bolts, and remove the PAM **(see illustration)**. As the unit is removed, disconnect the wiring plugs.

Refitting

5 Refitting is a reversal of removal.

Range/distance sensor

Removal

6 Remove the relevant bumper as described in Chapter 11 Section 6.

7 Disconnect the sensor wiring plug, then push the retaining clips apart, and pull the sensor from position **(see illustration)**.

Refitting

8 Refitting is a reversal of removal. Press the sensor firmly into position until the retaining clips engage.

Speaker

9 The parking aid warning speaker for models with front parking sensors is located behind the instrument panel – remove the instrument panel as described in Section 11. Remove the screws and and disconnect the wiring plug.

10 The rear speaker is mounted on the right-hand D-pillar trim panel on S-Max models and behind the headlining on Galaxy models.

11 On S-Max models remove the D-pillar trim panel as described in Chapter 11 Section 24.Undo the 2 retaining bolts, and remove the speaker. Disconnect the wiring plug as the speaker is removed.

12 On Galaxy models remove both D-pillar trims as described in Chapter 11 Section 24. Remove the trim panel from the centre seat

16.7 Press apart the clips and pull the sensor from place

17.2 Similar looking release keys are available. Note the curved edge of the correct one

17.5a Carefully prise up the outer edge of the panel

17.5b Disconnect the wiring plugs as the panel is removed

seatbelt roof mounting and then remove the 2 rear fixings from the rear of the roof lining. Lower the lining slightly to access the speaker. Undo the 2 retaining bolts, and remove the speaker. Disconnect the wiring plug as the speaker is removed.

17 Audio/DVD units – removal and refitting

Note: *This Section applies only to standard-fit audio equipment.*
Note: *If a new audio unit is to be fitted, it must be configured using Ford diagnostic equipment (IDS). Entrust this task to a Ford dealer or suitably-equipped specialist.*

Removal

1 Disconnect the battery negative lead as described in Chapter 5 Section 3.

Audio unit (vehicles built up 05/2007, with standard units)

2 A set of 4 audio removal tools will be required (Ford tool number GV3301). These are also widely available in the aftermarket **(see illustration)**.
3 Insert the keys with the long straight side to the outer edge of the unit and release the locking pins.
4 Pull the unit forward and disconnect the wiring and aerial connectors as the unit is removed.

17.7a Undo the fixings and pull the control unit from place

17.7b Disconnect the wiring plugs

Audio unit (vehicles built from 05/2007)

5 Starting at the outer edge, carefully prise the long switch panel from the facia **(see illustrations)**.
6 Remove the gear shift trim panel as described in Chapter 11 Section 25.
7 Undo the fixing from each corner of the audio/heater control trim panel. Pull heater control panel from place, and disconnect the wiring plugs **(see illustrations)**.
8 Remove the main audio mounting screws and then pull the unit forward. Disconnect the wiring plug as the unit is removed **(see illustrations)**.

Audio units (models with DVD SatNav)

9 These units are removed in a similar manner to the standard audio units, except

that the audio removal keys must be used to used to free the unit from the mounting panel after the complete assembly has been removed.

Refitting

10 Refitting is a reversal of removal, but if a new unit has been fitted, suitable software must be downloaded from Ford. Entrust this task to a Ford dealer or suitably-equipped specialist.
11 If 'CODE ----' or 'CODE 0000' is displayed when turning on the audio unit the correct security code must be entered using the radio station preset buttons (0-9). enter the code and then confirm the code by pressing the * (asterisk) or the button between the navigation buttons.

17.8a Remove the fixings

17.8b Pull the unit forward and ...

17.8c ... disconnect the wiring plugs

19.2a Disconnect the wiring plug

19.2b Remove the screws

19.5a Disconnect the wiring plug..

18 Aerial – removal and refitting

1 Removal and refitting of the aerial requires the headlining to be removed. This is an involved task, requiring patience and dexterity. Consequently, we recommend you entrust this task to a Ford dealer or upholstery specialist.

19 Speakers – removal and refitting

19.5b ...and unclip the speaker

19.8 Disconnect the wiring plug

Door speakers

1 To remove a door-mounted speaker, remove the appropriate door trim as described in Chapter 11 Section 9.
2 Disconnect the wiring plug before removing

the speaker. Remove the screws securing the speaker to the door **(see illustrations)**.
3 Refit in the reverse order of removal.

Tweeter speaker

4 Remove the door interior trim panel as described in Chapter 11 Section 9.

5 Disconnect the speaker wiring plug and unclip the speaker **(see illustrations)**.
6 Refitting is a reversal of removal.

Facia mounted speakers

7 To remove the 'tweeters', protect the facia and prise out the speaker using trim tool or similar.
8 With the speaker removed, disconnect the wiring plug **(see illustration)**.
9 To remove the centre speaker (where fitted) prise up the grille to access the speaker **(see illustrations)**.
10 Remove the screws **(see illustration)** lift out the speaker and disconnect the wiring plug.

Third seat row speakers

11 Prise up and remove the grille panel **(see illustrations)**.

19.9a Prise up and...

19.9b ...remove the grille

19.10 Remove the screws

19.11a Use a plastic trim tool and...

19.11b ...remove the grille

19.12 Remove the screws

12 Unscrew the fixings **(see illustration)** and remove the speaker, disconnecting the wiring plug as the speaker is removed.
13 Refitting is a reversal of removal.

20 Airbag system – general information and precautions

⚠ **Warning: Before carrying out any operations on the airbag system, disconnect the battery negative terminal (see Chapter 5 Section 3). When operations are complete, make sure no one is inside the vehicle when the battery is reconnected.**

• **Note that the airbag(s) must not be subjected to temperatures in excess of 90°C. When the airbag is removed, ensure that it is stored the correct way up (pad upwards) to prevent possible inflation.**
• **Do not allow any solvents or cleaning agents to contact the airbag assemblies. They must be cleaned using only a damp cloth.**
• **The airbags and control unit are both sensitive to impact. If either is dropped or damaged they should be renewed.**
• **Disconnect the airbag control unit wiring plug prior to using arc-welding equipment on the vehicle.**

1 A driver's airbag, drivers knee airbag, passenger's airbag side airbags (seat mounted) and overhead curtain airbags are fitted as standard equipment to models in the range. The driver's airbag is fitted to the centre of the steering wheel. The passenger's airbag is fitted to the upper surface of the facia, above the glovebox. The airbag system comprises the airbag unit(s) (complete with gas generators), impact sensors, the control unit and a warning light in the instrument panel.
2 The airbag system is triggered in the event of a direct or offset frontal impact above a predetermined force. The airbag is inflated within milliseconds, and forms a safety cushion between the driver and the steering wheel or (where applicable) the passenger and the facia. This prevents contact between the upper body and the steering wheel, column

and facia, and therefore greatly reduces the risk of injury. The airbag then deflates almost immediately through vents in the side of the airbag. The side airbags and overhead curtain airbags are triggered by side impacts, registered by the sensors fitted to the base of the B-pillars on each side.
3 Every time the ignition is switched on, the airbag control unit performs a self-test. The self-test takes approximately 7 seconds, and during this time the airbag warning light on the facia is illuminated. After the self-test has been completed, the warning light should go out. If the warning light fails to come on, remains illuminated after the initial 7-second period, or comes on at any time when the vehicle is being driven, there is a fault in the airbag system. The vehicle should then be taken to a Ford dealer or specialist for examination at the earliest possible opportunity.

21 Airbag system components – removal and refitting

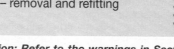

Caution: Refer to the warnings in Section 20 before carrying out the following operations.
1 Disconnect the battery negative terminal (see Chapter 5, Section 3). Wait at least 5 minutes for any residual electrical energy to dissipate before commencing work. **Note:** *If removing the driver's airbag, turn the steering wheel 90° from straight-ahead before, otherwise the steering lock will engage.*

21.6a The locking spring (shown with the airbag removed)

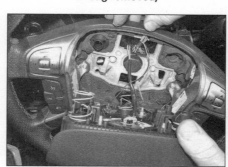

21.6c Lift out the airbag and then ...

Driver's airbag
2 Set the steering wheel and front wheels in the 'straight-ahead' position.
3 Rotate the steering wheel 90° in each direction to access the steering column upper shroud retaining clips.
4 On models built after July 2007 remove the steering column upper shroud as described in Chapter 11 Section 24.
5 On models built up to July 2007 locate the access hole at the base of the steering wheel and insert a flat bladed screwdriver into the hole. Push up on the scredriver and release the spring clip. Lift off the airbag.
6 On models built after July 2007, locate the access holes in the reverse side of the steering wheel. Insert a flat-bladed screwdriver into the hole and with the screwdriver angled away from the steering wheel twist the screwdriver to release the spring from the hook on the steering wheel **(see illustrations)**. Repeat the procedure on the opposite side.
7 On refitting, reconnect the wiring connectors and locate the airbag unit in the steering wheel, making sure the wire does not become trapped, and push the airbag into place to engage the retaining clips. Reconnect the battery negative lead (see Chapter 5 Section 3). Ensure no-one is in the vehicle when the battery is reconnected.

Passenger airbag
8 Remove the glovebox as described in Chapter 11 Section 27.

21.6b The hooks on the steering wheel that retain the airbag

21.6d ...disconnect the airbag wiring plug

21.9 Remove the support bracket

21.10 Remove the mounting bolts

9 Where fitted unclip the wiring loom and then remove the airbag support bracket **(see illustration)**.

10 Disconnect the airbag wiring plug and then remove the mounting bolts **(see illustration)**.

11 Refitting is a reversal of removal. Ensure that the wiring connector is securely reconnected. Ensure that no-one is inside the vehicle. Reconnect the battery negative lead as described in Chapter 5 Section 3.

Airbag wiring contact unit (clockspring)

12 Set the steering in the straight ahead position and remove the steering wheel as described in Chapter 10 Section 14.

13 Fully extend the steering column and then remove the upper and lower steering column shrouds as described in Chapter 11 Section 24.

14 Disconnect the wiring plug from the contact unit and the steering angle sensor (where fitted).

15 If the contact unit is to be refitted, apply tape to lock the unit in position **(see illustrations)**. Do not attempt to rotate the unit.

16 Disconnect the wiring plugs and remove the screws and then slide off the clockspring **(see illustration)**.

17 Ensure the front wheels are still in the 'straight-ahead' position, and the directional indicator stalk is in the off position, then fit the contact unit into position. Tighten the retaining screws.

18 If there is any doubt as to the position of the contact unit (eg, securing tape missing or disturbed), the unit must be centralised as follows:

a) Rotate the clockspring clockwise until resistance is felt.

b) Rotate the clockspring anti-clockwise 2.5 revolutions.

c) Check to see that the yellow roller is visible in the clockspring window. Note that not all clocksprings have this window.

19 The remainder of refitting is a reversal of removal.

Restraint Control Module (RCM)

20 Remove the upper section of the centre console as described in Chapter 11 Section 25.

21.15a Apply tape to secure the rotary contact unit

21.15b Some versions can be locked with a small diameter bolt

21.16a Disconnect the wiring plug...

21.16b ...remove the screws and...

21.16c ...slide off the clockspring

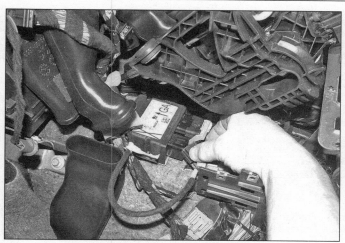

21.21 Disconnect the wiring plugs

21.32 Side crash sensor

21 Release the locking devices and disconnect the wiring plugs for the control unit **(see illustration)**.
22 Undo the retaining bolts and remove the control unit.
23 Refitting is a reversal of removal, ensuring the module is refitted with the arrow mark on the top pointing forwards. Note that if a new module has been fitted, it must be programmed. Entrust this task to a Ford dealer or suitably-equipped specialist.

Driver's knee airbag

24 The airbag is part of the lower facia panel. Removal is described in Chapter 11 Section 24.

Side airbags

25 The side airbags are incorporated into the side of the front and rear seats. Removal of the units requires the seat upholstery to be removed. This is a specialist task, which we recommend should be entrusted to a Ford dealer or specialist.

Head/overhead curtain airbags

26 Renewal of the head airbags/inflatable curtain requires removal of the headlining. This is a specialist task, and should be entrusted to a Ford dealer or specialist.

Crash/lateral acceleration sensors

Front sensor

27 Opent the bonnet. The sensor is located on the inner edge of the bonnet slam panel.
28 Disconnect the wiring plug and unbolt the sensor.
29 Refitting is a reversal of removal.

Side sensors

30 The side sensors are located in the vehicle's B-pillars each side.
31 Remove the B-pillar trim panel (see Chapter 11 Section 24).
32 Disconnect the sensor wiring plug, then undo the bolt and remove the sensor **(see** **illustration)**. Take great care not to damage the sensor wiring harness. Note that the sensor must be handled carefully. Do not refit a sensor that has been dropped or knocked.
33 Refitting is a reversal of removal.

22 Anti-theft alarm system – general information

1 An anti-theft alarm and immobiliser system is fitted as standard equipment. Should the system become faulty, the vehicle should be taken to a Ford dealer or specialist for examination. They will have access to a special diagnostic tester which will quickly trace any fault present in the system.

23 Electronic control modules – removal and refitting

Note: *All of these modules are included in the vehicle's sophisticated self-diagnosis system. Should a fault occur, have the system interrogated using specific diagnostic equipment. Ford's own system (IDS) will be the obvious choice, but many aftermarket alternatives are available. Diagnostic are carried out via the Data Link Connector*

23.0a The diagnostic plug (DLC)

(DLC) located in the driver's side storage compartment **(see illustration)**.

Removal

1 Disconnect the battery negative lead as described in Chapter 5 Section 3.

Generic Electronic Module (GEM)

2 The GEM is integral with the passenger compartment fusebox/central junction box. This module is responsible for the management of the following functions:
a) *Current distribution.*
b) *Headlights.*
c) *Headlight range adjustment.*
d) *Foglamps.*
e) *Sidelights.*
f) *Reversing lights.*
g) *High-level brake light.*
h) *Interior lights.*
i) *Wipers.*
j) *Heated windscreen.*
k) *Cruise control.*
l) *Central locking.*
m) *Anti-theft system.*
n) *Handbrake switch.*
o) *Brake fluid level monitoring.*
p) *Fuel pump.*
q) *Battery charging.*
r) *Databus communications.*
3 Remove the trim panel above the passenger's side footwell **(see illustration)**.

23.3 Remove the trim panel

23.4a Rotate the catch and ...

23.4b ... lower the GEM

23.5 Release the locking catches and disconnect the wiring plugs

4 The GEM is held up by a single fastener. Rotate the catch and lower the GEM **(see illustrations)**. Note that access can be improved if the glovebox is removed first (see Chapter 11 Section 27).

5 Note their fitted positions, and disconnect the wiring plugs as the GEM is withdrawn **(see illustration)**.

6 Unhook and release the GEM from the catches at the rear. Remove the GEM from the vehicle.

7 If a new GEM is to be fitted, the unit must be configured and initialised using Ford diagnostic equipment (IDS). Aftermarket diagnostic tools can not complete this task. Entrust this to a Ford dealer or an independant garage that has invested in the Ford factory tool.

Lighting control module (LCM)

8 This module is only fitted to vehicles equipped with adaptive front lights (AFS) or Xenon high-intensity gas discharge headlights (HID). On models with AFS it controls the movement of the reflectors as the steering is operated, and on models with HID, it controls the range control as the suspension compresses or extends.

9 Renewal of the module is described in Section 10.

Keyless vehicle module (KVM)

10 Where fitted the KVM is is located behind the right-hand load area side panel. On Galaxy models the panel must be removed as described in Chapter 11 Section 24, on S-Max models the KVM is accessible by opening the access panel.

11 Disconnect the wiring plugs and remove the mounting screws.

Refitting

12 Refitting is a reversal of removal. If a new module has been fitted, software will need to be downloaded from Ford. Entrust this task to a Ford dealer or suitably-equipped specialist.

---

24 Fuel filler flap solenoid – removal and refitting

1 Open the fuel filler cap and then remove the right-hand load area trim panel as described in Chapter 11 Section 24.

2 The solenoid is a bayonet fit. Reach up, rotate the solenoid and lower it from rear wing/fuel filler neck. Disconnect the wiring plug **(see illustrations)**.

3 Refitting is a reversal of removal.

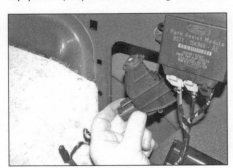

24.2a Lower the solenoid ...

24.2b ... and disconnect the wiring plug

Fuse and relay box in passenger compartment

FUSE/RELAY	VALUE	DESCRIPTION
F1	5 A	Ignition relay Rain sensor
F2	10 A	Fuse box in engine compartment Restraint control unit (RCM)
F3	5 A	Fuse box in engine compartment ABS control unit
F4	7.5 A	Fuse box in engine compartment Accelerator pedal position sensor
F5	15 A	Rear wiper motor
F6	15 A	Fuse box in engine compartment
F7	7.5 A	Fuse box in engine compartment Steering column control unit
F8	5 A	Instrument cluster
F9	15 A	Main beam
F10	20 A	Sunroof
F11	7.5 A	Reversing light relay
F12	-	Not used
F13	15 A	Control unit Front fog light(s)
F14	15 A	Control unit Windscreen washer pump
F15	10 A	Adaptive cruise control
F16	-	Not used
F17	10 A	Ignition relay
F18	5 A	PATS control unit
F19	15 A	Ignition relay Front cigarette lighter
F20	-	Not used
F21	5 A	Control unit Remote control receiver
F22	20 A	Fuel pump
F23	-	Not used
F24	5 A	Fuse box in engine compartment Control unit Ignition switch
F25	10 A	Luggage compartment closing Fuel filler flap relay
F26	5 A	Diagnostic connector Security alarm system
F27	5 A	Climate control unit
F28	5 A	Brake light switch

Fuses and relays

Starting and charging

*1 Up to 29.02.2008
*2 From 01.03.2008
*3 1.8L Duratorq
*4 2.0L Duratorq
*5 2.2L Duratorq
*6 Up to 02.2011
*7 From 03.2011
*8 1.6L Duratorq

Daytime running lamps, trailer socket and turn signal from 03.2010

*1 With Daytime Running lamps
*2 Trailer Socket

Headlamps from 03.2010

*1 Vehicles with Adaptive Front Lighting
*2 Vehicles with High Intensity Discharge Headlamps

CENTRAL JUNCTION BOX

HEADLAMP ASSEMBLY RH

HEADLAMP ASSEMBLY LH

MAIN BEAM

FRONT FOG

INTERNAL HW

HEADLAMP SWITCH

POWER DISTRIBUTION BOX

BATTERY

FRONT FOG LAMP RH

FRONT FOG LAMP LH

ADAPTIVE FRONT LIGHTING MODULE

REAR SUSPENSION VERTICAL POSITION SENSOR LH

FRONT SUSPENSION VETICAL POSITION SENSOR LH

Headlamps up to 02.2010

*1 Vehicles with Adaptive Front Lighting
*2 Vehicles with High Intensity Discharge Headlamps

Rear lamps from 03.2010

*1 Manual transmission

Rear lamps up to 02.2010

*1 Manual transmission

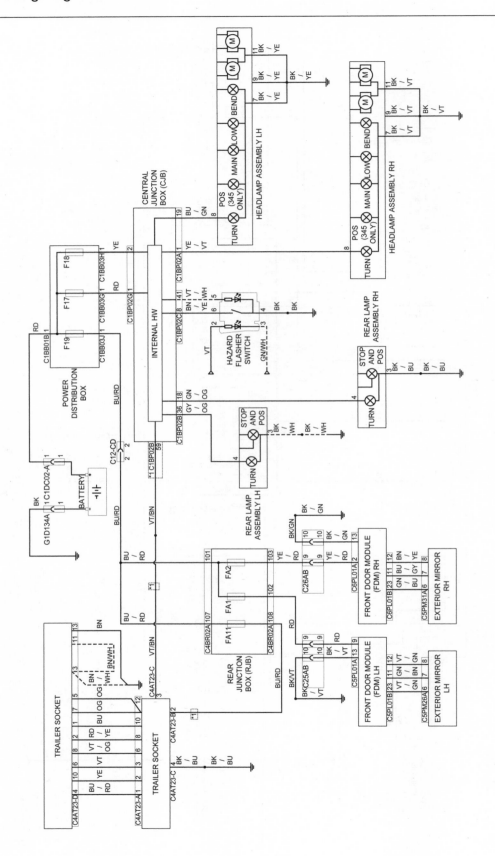

Turn signal, hazard lamps and trailer socket up to 02.2010

*1 Trailer Socket

Vehicles with adaptive front and high intensity discharge headlamps

Vehicles without adaptive front and high intensity discharge headlamps from 03.2010

Interior lights from 03.2008 To 02.2010

*1 LMV

Interior lights from 03.2010 with panoramic roof panel

Interior lights from 03.2010 without panoramic roof panel

Interior lights up to 02.2008

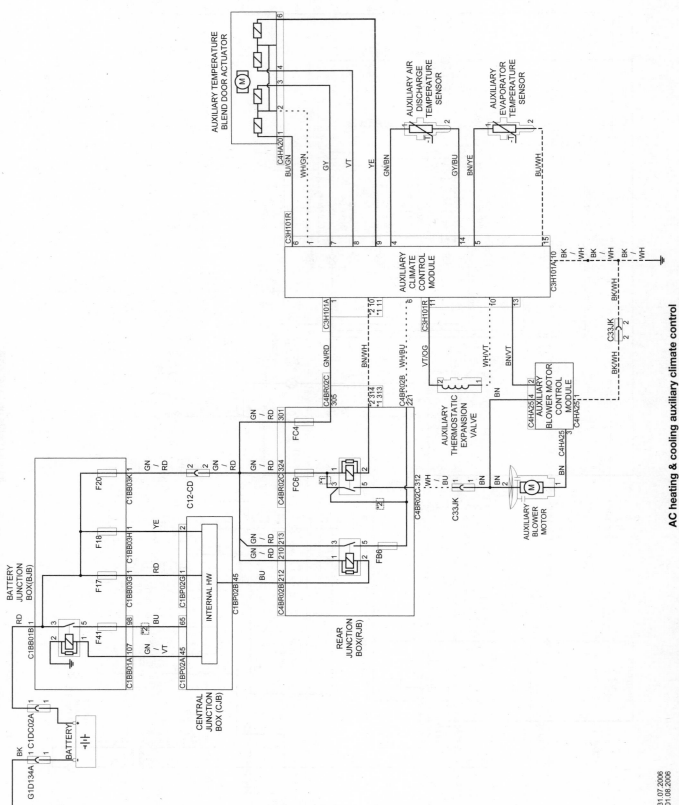

AC heating & cooling auxiliary climate control

*1 From 31.07.2006
*2 From 01.08.2006

AC heating & cooling electric booster heater and fuel fired heater

AC heating & cooling with manual temperature control from 03.2011

AC heating & cooling with manual temperature control up to 02.2011

*1 Up to 02.2008
*2 From 03.2008
*3 1.8L Duratorq
*4 2.0L Duratorq
*5 2.2L Duratorq

AC heating & cooling with with automatic temperature control from 03.2011

AC heating & cooling with with automatic temperature control up to 02.2011

Power windows

*1 Up to 02.2008
*2 From of 03.2008 up to 02.2010
*3 From of 03.2010
*4 Only for LMV

Power windows rear quarter

*1 Up to 02.2010
*2 From 03.2010

Power door locks rear with door module

Power door locks rear without door module

*1 Up to 02.2010
*2 From of 03.2010

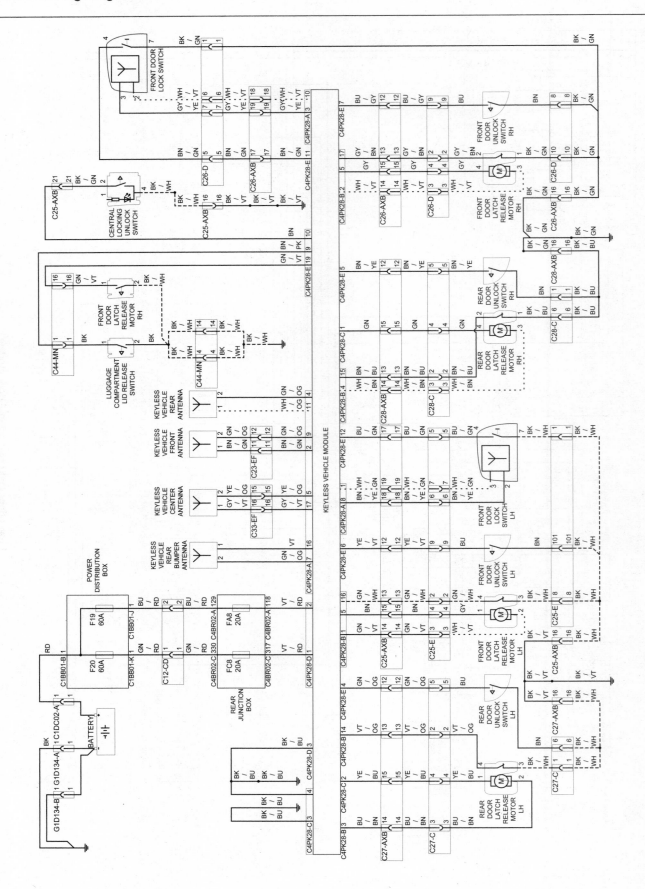

Power door locks remote keyless entry

Wiper washer

*1 Up to 02.2010
*2 From 03.2010

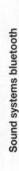

Sound systems bluetooth

*1 Up to 29-02.2008
*2 From 01.03.2008
*3 Cellular Phone

Sound systems from 03.2010

*1 LMV

Sound systems rear passenger entertainment

*1 Up to 02.2010
*2 From 03.2010

Sound systems up to 02.2010

*1 LMV (Luxury multi-purpose vehicle)
*2 Up to 06.2007
*3 From 06.2007 to 02.2008
*4 Up to 02.2008
*5 From 03.2008
*6 With Navigation
*7 With CD
*8 With DVD

Fuel pump

*1 1.8 L Duratorq
*2 2.0 L Duratorq
*3 2.2 L Duratorq
*4 Up to 02.2008
*5 From 03.2008
*6 Emission Requirements: Stage V

Dimensions and weights

Note: *All figures are approximate, and may vary according to model. Refer to manufacturer's data for exact figures.*

Dimensions

Overall length:

    S-Max models . . . . 4772 to 4801 mm

    Galaxy models . . . . 4819 mm

Overall width (including mirrors). . . . . 2154 mm

Wheelbase . . . . 2850 mm

Height:

    S-Max models . . . . 1620 to 1660 mm

    Galaxy models (without roof bars) . . . . 1709 to 1758 mm

    Galaxy models (with roof bars). . . . . 1770 to 1811 mm

Weights

Gross vehicle weight . . . . See Vehicle Identification Plate

Maximum towing weight . . . . See Vehicle Identification Plate

Fuel economy

Although depreciation is still the biggest part of the cost of motoring for most car owners, the cost of fuel is more immediately noticeable. These pages give some tips on how to get the best fuel economy.

Working it out

Manufacturer's figures

Car manufacturers are required by law to provide fuel consumption information on all new vehicles sold. These 'official' figures are obtained by simulating various driving conditions on a rolling road or a test track. Real life conditions are different, so the fuel consumption actually achieved may not bear much resemblance to the quoted figures.

How to calculate it

Many cars now have trip computers which will

display fuel consumption, both instantaneous and average. Refer to the owner's handbook for details of how to use these.

To calculate consumption yourself (and maybe to check that the trip computer is accurate), proceed as follows.

1. Fill up with fuel and note the mileage, or zero the trip recorder.
2. Drive as usual until you need to fill up again.
3. Note the amount of fuel required to refill the tank, and the mileage covered since the previous fill-up.
4. Divide the mileage by the amount of fuel used to obtain the consumption figure.

For example:

Mileage at first fill-up (a) = 27,903
Mileage at second fill-up (b) = 28,346
Mileage covered (b - a) = 443
Fuel required at second fill-up = 48.6 litres

The half-completed changeover to metric units in the UK means that we buy our fuel

in litres, measure distances in miles and talk about fuel consumption in miles per gallon. There are two ways round this: the first is to convert the litres to gallons before doing the calculation (by dividing by 4.546, or see Table 1). So in the example:

48.6 litres ÷ 4.546 = 10.69 gallons
443 miles ÷ 10.69 gallons = 41.4 mpg

The second way is to calculate the consumption in miles per litre, then multiply that figure by 4.546 (or see Table 2).

So in the example, fuel consumption is:

443 miles ÷ 48.6 litres = 9.1 mpl
9.1 mpl x 4.546 = 41.4 mpg

The rest of Europe expresses fuel consumption in litres of fuel required to travel 100 km (l/100 km). For interest, the conversions are given in Table 3. In practice it doesn't matter what units you use, provided you know what your normal consumption is and can spot if it's getting better or worse.

Table 1: conversion of litres to Imperial gallons

litres	1	2	3	4	5	10	20	30	40	50	60	70
gallons	0.22	0.44	0.66	0.88	1.10	2.24	4.49	6.73	8.98	11.22	13.47	15.71

Table 2: conversion of miles per litre to miles per gallon

miles per litre	5	6	7	8	9	10	11	12	13	14
miles per gallon	23	27	32	36	41	46	50	55	59	64

Table 3: conversion of litres per 100 km to miles per gallon

litres per 100 km	4	4.5	5	5.5	6	6.5	7	8	9	10
miles per gallon	71	63	56	51	47	43	40	35	31	28

Maintenance

A well-maintained car uses less fuel and creates less pollution. In particular:

Filters

Change air and fuel filters at the specified intervals.

Oil

Use a good quality oil of the lowest viscosity specified by the vehicle manufacturer (see *Lubricants and fluids*). Check the level often and be careful not to overfill.

Spark plugs

When applicable, renew at the specified intervals.

Tyres

Check tyre pressures regularly. Under-inflated tyres have an increased rolling resistance. It is generally safe to use the higher pressures specified for full load conditions even when not fully laden, but keep an eye on the centre band of tread for signs of wear due to over-inflation.

When buying new tyres, consider the 'fuel saving' models which most manufacturers include in their ranges.

Driving style

Acceleration

Acceleration uses more fuel than driving at a steady speed. The best technique with modern cars is to accelerate reasonably briskly to the desired speed, changing up through the gears as soon as possible without making the engine labour.

Air conditioning

Air conditioning absorbs quite a bit of energy from the engine – typically 3 kW (4 hp) or so. The effect on fuel consumption is at its worst in slow traffic. Switch it off when not required.

Anticipation

Drive smoothly and try to read the traffic flow so as to avoid unnecessary acceleration and braking.

Automatic transmission

When accelerating in an automatic, avoid depressing the throttle so far as to make the transmission hold onto lower gears at higher speeds. Don't use the 'Sport' setting, if applicable.

When stationary with the engine running, select 'N' or 'P'. When moving, keep your left foot away from the brake.

Braking

Braking converts the car's energy of motion into heat – essentially, it is wasted. Obviously some braking is always going to be necessary, but with good anticipation it is surprising how much can be avoided, especially on routes that you know well.

Carshare

Consider sharing lifts to work or to the shops. Even once a week will make a difference.

Electrical loads

Electricity is 'fuel' too; the alternator which charges the battery does so by converting some of the engine's energy of motion into electrical energy. The more electrical accessories are in use, the greater the load on the alternator. Switch off big consumers like the heated rear window when not required.

Freewheeling

Freewheeling (coasting) in neutral with the engine switched off is dangerous. The effort required to operate power-assisted brakes and steering increases when the engine is not running, with a potential lack of control in emergency situations.

In any case, modern fuel injection systems automatically cut off the engine's fuel supply on the overrun (moving and in gear, but with the accelerator pedal released).

Gadgets

Bolt-on devices claiming to save fuel have been around for nearly as long as the motor car itself. Those which worked were rapidly adopted as standard equipment by the vehicle manufacturers. Others worked only in certain situations, or saved fuel only at the expense of unacceptable effects on performance, driveability or the life of engine components.

The most effective fuel saving gadget is the driver's right foot.

Journey planning

Combine (eg) a trip to the supermarket with a visit to the recycling centre and the DIY store, rather than making separate journeys.

When possible choose a travelling time outside rush hours.

Load

The more heavily a car is laden, the greater the energy required to accelerate it to a given speed. Remove heavy items which you don't need to carry.

One load which is often overlooked is the contents of the fuel tank. A tankful of fuel (55 litres / 12 gallons) weighs 45 kg (100 lb) or so. Just half filling it may be worthwhile.

Lost?

At the risk of stating the obvious, if you're going somewhere new, have details of the route to hand. There's not much point in achieving record mpg if you also go miles out of your way.

Parking

If possible, carry out any reversing or turning manoeuvres when you arrive at a parking space so that you can drive straight out when you leave. Manoeuvering when the engine is cold uses a lot more fuel.

Driving around looking for free on-street parking may cost more in fuel than buying a car park ticket.

Premium fuel

Most major oil companies (and some supermarkets) have premium grades of fuel which are several pence a litre dearer than the standard grades. Reports vary, but the consensus seems to be that if these fuels improve economy at all, they do not do so by enough to justify their extra cost.

Roof rack

When loading a roof rack, try to produce a wedge shape with the narrow end at the front. Any cover should be securely fastened – if it flaps it's creating turbulence and absorbing energy.

Remove roof racks and boxes when not in use – they increase air resistance and can create a surprising amount of noise.

Short journeys

The engine is at its least efficient, and wear is highest, during the first few miles after a cold start. Consider walking, cycling or using public transport.

Speed

The engine is at its most efficient when running at a steady speed and load at the rpm where it develops maximum torque. (You can find this figure in the car's handbook.) For most cars this corresponds to between 55 and 65 mph in top gear.

Above the optimum cruising speed, fuel consumption starts to rise quite sharply. A car travelling at 80 mph will typically be using 30% more fuel than at 60 mph.

Supermarket fuel

It may be cheap but is it any good? In the UK all supermarket fuel must meet the relevant British Standard. The major oil companies will say that their branded fuels have better additive packages which may stop carbon and other deposits building up. A reasonable compromise might be to use one tank of branded fuel to three or four from the supermarket.

Switch off when stationary

Switch off the engine if you look like being stationary for more than 30 seconds or so. This is good for the environment as well as for your pocket. Be aware though that frequent restarts are hard on the battery and the starter motor.

Windows

Driving with the windows open increases air turbulence around the vehicle. Closing the windows promotes smooth airflow and

reduced resistance. The faster you go, the more significant this is.

And finally . . .

Driving techniques associated with good fuel economy tend to involve moderate acceleration and low top speeds. Be considerate to the needs of other road users who may need to make brisker progress; even if you do not agree with them this is not an excuse to be obstructive.

Safety must always take precedence over economy, whether it is a question of accelerating hard to complete an overtaking manoeuvre, killing your speed when confronted with a potential hazard or switching the lights on when it starts to get dark.

Conversion factors

Length (distance)

Inches (in)	x 25.4	= Millimetres (mm)	x 0.0394	=	Inches (in)
Feet (ft)	x 0.305	= Metres (m)	x 3.281	=	Feet (ft)
Miles	x 1.609	= Kilometres (km)	x 0.621	=	Miles

Volume (capacity)

Cubic inches (cu in; in^3)	x 16.387	= Cubic centimetres (cc; cm^3)	x 0.061	=	Cubic inches (cu in; in^3)
Imperial pints (Imp pt)	x 0.568	= Litres (l)	x 1.76	=	Imperial pints (Imp pt)
Imperial quarts (Imp qt)	x 1.137	= Litres (l)	x 0.88	=	Imperial quarts (Imp qt)
Imperial quarts (Imp qt)	x 1.201	= US quarts (US qt)	x 0.833	=	Imperial quarts (Imp qt)
US quarts (US qt)	x 0.946	= Litres (l)	x 1.057	=	US quarts (US qt)
Imperial gallons (Imp gal)	x 4.546	= Litres (l)	x 0.22	=	Imperial gallons (Imp gal)
Imperial gallons (Imp gal)	x 1.201	= US gallons (US gal)	x 0.833	=	Imperial gallons (Imp gal)
US gallons (US gal)	x 3.785	= Litres (l)	x 0.264	=	US gallons (US gal)

Mass (weight)

Ounces (oz)	x 28.35	= Grams (g)	x 0.035	=	Ounces (oz)
Pounds (lb)	x 0.454	= Kilograms (kg)	x 2.205	=	Pounds (lb)

Force

Ounces-force (ozf; oz)	x 0.278	= Newtons (N)	x 3.6	=	Ounces-force (ozf; oz)
Pounds-force (lbf; lb)	x 4.448	= Newtons (N)	x 0.225	=	Pounds-force (lbf; lb)
Newtons (N)	x 0.1	= Kilograms-force (kgf; kg)	x 9.81	=	Newtons (N)

Pressure

Pounds-force per square inch (psi; lbf/in^2; lb/in^2)	x 0.070	= Kilograms-force per square centimetre (kgf/cm^2; kg/cm^2)	x 14.223	=	Pounds-force per square inch (psi; lbf/in^2; lb/in^2)
Pounds-force per square inch (psi; lbf/in^2; lb/in^2)	x 0.068	= Atmospheres (atm)	x 14.696	=	Pounds-force per square inch (psi; lbf/in^2; lb/in^2)
Pounds-force per square inch (psi; lbf/in^2; lb/in^2)	x 0.069	= Bars	x 14.5	=	Pounds-force per square inch (psi; lbf/in^2; lb/in^2)
Pounds-force per square inch (psi; lbf/in^2; lb/in^2)	x 6.895	= Kilopascals (kPa)	x 0.145	=	Pounds-force per square inch (psi; lbf/in^2; lb/in^2)
Kilopascals (kPa)	x 0.01	= Kilograms-force per square centimetre (kgf/cm^2; kg/cm^2)	x 98.1	=	Kilopascals (kPa)
Millibar (mbar)	x 100	= Pascals (Pa)	x 0.01	=	Millibar (mbar)
Millibar (mbar)	x 0.0145	= Pounds-force per square inch (psi; lbf/in^2; lb/in^2)	x 68.947	=	Millibar (mbar)
Millibar (mbar)	x 0.75	= Millimetres of mercury (mmHg)	x 1.333	=	Millibar (mbar)
Millibar (mbar)	x 0.401	= Inches of water (inH$_2$O)	x 2.491	=	Millibar (mbar)
Millimetres of mercury (mmHg)	x 0.535	= Inches of water (inH$_2$O)	x 1.868	=	Millimetres of mercury (mmHg)
Inches of water (inH$_2$O)	x 0.036	= Pounds-force per square inch (psi; lbf/in^2; lb/in^2)	x 27.68	=	Inches of water (inH$_2$O)

Torque (moment of force)

Pounds-force inches (lbf in; lb in)	x 1.152	= Kilograms-force centimetre (kgf cm; kg cm)	x 0.868	=	Pounds-force inches (lbf in; lb in)
Pounds-force inches (lbf in; lb in)	x 0.113	= Newton metres (Nm)	x 8.85	=	Pounds-force inches (lbf in; lb in)
Pounds-force inches (lbf in; lb in)	x 0.083	= Pounds-force feet (lbf ft; lb ft)	x 12	=	Pounds-force inches (lbf in; lb in)
Pounds-force feet (lbf ft; lb ft)	x 0.138	= Kilograms-force metres (kgf m; kg m)	x 7.233	=	Pounds-force feet (lbf ft; lb ft)
Pounds-force feet (lbf ft; lb ft)	x 1.356	= Newton metres (Nm)	x 0.738	=	Pounds-force feet (lbf ft; lb ft)
Newton metres (Nm)	x 0.102	= Kilograms-force metres (kgf m; kg m)	x 9.804	=	Newton metres (Nm)

Power

Horsepower (hp)	x 745.7	= Watts (W)	x 0.0013	=	Horsepower (hp)

Velocity (speed)

Miles per hour (miles/hr; mph)	x 1.609	= Kilometres per hour (km/hr; kph)	x 0.621	=	Miles per hour (miles/hr; mph)

Fuel consumption*

Miles per gallon, Imperial (mpg)	x 0.354	= Kilometres per litre (km/l)	x 2.825	=	Miles per gallon, Imperial (mpg)
Miles per gallon, US (mpg)	x 0.425	= Kilometres per litre (km/l)	x 2.352	=	Miles per gallon, US (mpg)

Temperature

Degrees Fahrenheit = (°C x 1.8) + 32   Degrees Celsius (Degrees Centigrade; °C) = (°F - 32) x 0.56

It is common practice to convert from miles per gallon (mpg) to litres/100 kilometres (l/100km), where mpg x l/100 km = 282

Spare parts are available from many sources, including maker's appointed garages, accessory shops, and motor factors. To be sure of obtaining the correct parts, it will sometimes be necessary to quote the vehicle identification number. If possible, it can also be useful to take the old parts along for positive identification. Items such as starter motors and alternators may be available under a service exchange scheme – any parts returned should be clean.

Our advice regarding spare parts is as follows.

Officially appointed garages

This is the best source of parts which are peculiar to your car, and which are not otherwise generally available (eg, badges, interior trim, certain body panels, etc). It is also the only place at which you should buy parts if the vehicle is still under warranty.

Accessory shops

These are very good places to buy materials and components needed for the maintenance of your car (oil, air and fuel filters, light bulbs, drivebelts, greases, brake pads, touch-up paint, etc). Components of this nature sold by a reputable shop are usually of the same standard as those used by the car manufacturer.

Besides components, these shops also sell tools and general accessories, usually have convenient opening hours, charge lower prices, and can often be found close to home. Some accessory shops have parts counters where components needed for almost any repair job can be purchased or ordered.

Motor factors

Good factors will stock all the more important components which wear out comparatively quickly, and can sometimes supply individual components needed for the overhaul of a larger assembly (eg, brake seals and hydraulic parts, bearing shells, pistons, valves). They may also handle work such as cylinder block reboring, crankshaft regrinding, etc.

Tyre and exhaust specialists

These outlets may be independent, or members of a local or national chain. They frequently offer competitive prices when compared with a main dealer or local garage, but it will pay to obtain several quotes before making a decision. When researching prices, also ask what extras may be added – for instance fitting a new valve and balancing the wheel are both commonly charged on top of the price of a new tyre.

Other sources

Beware of parts or materials obtained from market stalls, car boot sales or similar outlets. Such items are not invariably sub-standard, but there is little chance of compensation if they do prove unsatisfactory. in the case of safety-critical components such as brake pads, there is the risk not only of financial loss, but also of an accident causing injury or death.

Second-hand components or assemblies obtained from a car breaker can be a good buy in some circumstances, but this sort of purchase is best made by the experienced DIY mechanic.

Vehicle identification numbers

Modifications are a continuing and unpublicised process in vehicle manufacture, quite apart from major model changes. Spare parts manuals and lists are compiled upon a numerical basis, the individual vehicle identification numbers being essential to correct identification of the component concerned.

When ordering spare parts, always give as much information as possible. Quote the car model, year of manufacture, body and engine numbers as appropriate.

The vehicle identification plate is situated on the drivers side B-pillar **(see illustration)**. The vehicle identification number is also repeated in the form of plate visible through the windscreen on the passenger's side **(see illustration)**.

The engine identification numbers are situated on the front face of the cylinder block, either on a plate, or stamped directly to the centre or side, of the block face. On some models, the engine type is shown on a sticker affixed to the timing belt cover.

Other identification numbers or codes are stamped on major items such as the gearbox, etc.

The VIN plate is mounted on the right-hand door pillar ...

... and on a plate on the facia (visible through the windscreen)

Whenever servicing, repair or overhaul work is carried out on the car or its components, observe the following procedures and instructions. This will assist in carrying out the operation efficiently and to a professional standard of workmanship.

Joint mating faces and gaskets

When separating components at their mating faces, never insert screwdrivers or similar implements into the joint between the faces in order to prise them apart. This can cause severe damage which results in oil leaks, coolant leaks, etc upon reassembly. Separation is usually achieved by tapping along the joint with a soft-faced hammer in order to break the seal. However, note that this method may not be suitable where dowels are used for component location.

Where a gasket is used between the mating faces of two components, a new one must be fitted on reassembly; fit it dry unless otherwise stated in the repair procedure. Make sure that the mating faces are clean and dry, with all traces of old gasket removed. When cleaning a joint face, use a tool which is unlikely to score or damage the face, and remove any burrs or nicks with an oilstone or fine file.

Make sure that tapped holes are cleaned with a pipe cleaner, and keep them free of jointing compound, if this is being used, unless specifically instructed otherwise.

Ensure that all orifices, channels or pipes are clear, and blow through them, preferably using compressed air.

Oil seals

Oil seals can be removed by levering them out with a wide flat-bladed screwdriver or similar implement. Alternatively, a number of self-tapping screws may be screwed into the seal, and these used as a purchase for pliers or some similar device in order to pull the seal free.

Whenever an oil seal is removed from its working location, either individually or as part of an assembly, it should be renewed.

The very fine sealing lip of the seal is easily damaged, and will not seal if the surface it contacts is not completely clean and free from scratches, nicks or grooves. If the original sealing surface of the component cannot be restored, and the manufacturer has not made provision for slight relocation of the seal relative to the sealing surface, the component should be renewed.

Protect the lips of the seal from any surface which may damage them in the course of fitting. Use tape or a conical sleeve where possible. Where indicated, lubricate the seal lips with oil before fitting and, on dual-lipped seals, fill the space between the lips with grease.

Unless otherwise stated, oil seals must be fitted with their sealing lips toward the lubricant to be sealed.

Use a tubular drift or block of wood of the appropriate size to install the seal and, if the seal housing is shouldered, drive the seal down to the shoulder. If the seal housing is unshouldered, the seal should be fitted with its face flush with the housing top face (unless otherwise instructed).

Screw threads and fastenings

Seized nuts, bolts and screws are quite a common occurrence where corrosion has set in, and the use of penetrating oil or releasing fluid will often overcome this problem if the offending item is soaked for a while before attempting to release it. The use of an impact driver may also provide a means of releasing such stubborn fastening devices, when used in conjunction with the appropriate screwdriver bit or socket. If none of these methods works, it may be necessary to resort to the careful application of heat, or the use of a hacksaw or nut splitter device. Before resorting to extreme methods, check that you are not dealing with a left-hand thread!

Studs are usually removed by locking two nuts together on the threaded part, and then using a spanner on the lower nut to unscrew the stud. Studs or bolts which have broken off below the surface of the component in which they are mounted can sometimes be removed using a stud extractor.

Always ensure that a blind tapped hole is completely free from oil, grease, water or other fluid before installing the bolt or stud. Failure to do this could cause the housing to crack due to the hydraulic action of the bolt or stud as it is screwed in.

For some screw fastenings, notably cylinder head bolts or nuts, torque wrench settings are no longer specified for the latter stages of tightening, "angle-tightening" being called up instead. Typically, a fairly low torque wrench setting will be applied to the bolts/nuts in the correct sequence, followed by one or more stages of tightening through specified angles.

When checking or retightening a nut or bolt to a specified torque setting, slacken the nut or bolt by a quarter of a turn, and then retighten to the specified setting. However, this should not be attempted where angular tightening has been used.

Locknuts, locktabs and washers

Any fastening which will rotate against a component or housing during tightening should always have a washer between it and the relevant component or housing.

Spring or split washers should always be renewed when they are used to lock a critical component such as a big-end bearing retaining bolt or nut. Locktabs which are folded over to retain a nut or bolt should always be renewed.

Self-locking nuts can be re-used in non-critical areas, providing resistance can be felt when the locking portion passes over the bolt or stud thread. However, it should be noted that self-locking stiffnuts tend to lose their effectiveness after long periods of use, and should then be renewed as a matter of course.

Split pins must always be replaced with new ones of the correct size for the hole.

When thread-locking compound is found on the threads of a fastener which is to be re-used, it should be cleaned off with a wire brush and solvent, and fresh compound applied on reassembly.

Special tools

Some repair procedures in this manual entail the use of special tools such as a press, two or three-legged pullers, spring compressors, etc. Wherever possible, suitable readily-available alternatives to the manufacturer's special tools are described, and are shown in use. In some instances, where no alternative is possible, it has been necessary to resort to the use of a manufacturer's tool, and this has been done for reasons of safety as well as the efficient completion of the repair operation. Unless you are highly-skilled and have a thorough understanding of the procedures described, never attempt to bypass the use of any special tool when the procedure described specifies its use. Not only is there a very great risk of personal injury, but expensive damage could be caused to the components involved.

Environmental considerations

When disposing of used engine oil, brake fluid, antifreeze, etc, give due consideration to any detrimental environmental effects. Do not, for instance, pour any of the above liquids down drains into the general sewage system, or onto the ground to soak away, as this is likely to pollute your local environment. Many local council refuse tips provide a facility for waste oil disposal, as do some garages. You can find your nearest disposal point by calling the Environment Agency on 03708 506 506 or by visiting www.oilbankline.org.uk.

Note: It is illegal and anti-social to dump oil down the drain. To find the location of your local oil recycling bank, call 03708 506 506 or visit www.oilbankline.org.uk.

The jack supplied with the vehicle tool kit should only be used for changing the roadwheels – see Wheel changing at the front of this manual. When carrying out any other kind of work, raise the vehicle using a hydraulic trolley jack, and always supplement the jack with axle stands positioned under the vehicle jacking points.

When using a trolley jack or axle stands, position the jack head or axle stand head adjacent to one of the relevant wheel changing jacking points under the sills **(see illustration)**. Use a block of wood between the jack or axle stand and the sill.

Do not attempt to jack the vehicle under the sump, or any of the suspension components.

The jack supplied with the vehicle locates in the jacking points on the underside of the sills – see Wheel changing at the front of this manual. Ensure that the jack head is correctly engaged before attempting to raise the vehicle.

 Never work under, around, or near a raised vehicle, unless it is adequately supported in at least two places.

Use a workshop/trolley jack at the points indicated

J46808

Introduction

A selection of good tools is a fundamental requirement for anyone contemplating the maintenance and repair of a motor vehicle. For the owner who does not possess any, their purchase will prove a considerable expense, offsetting some of the savings made by doing-it-yourself. However, provided that the tools purchased meet the relevant national safety standards and are of good quality, they will last for many years and prove an extremely worthwhile investment.

To help the average owner to decide which tools are needed to carry out the various tasks detailed in this manual, we have compiled three lists of tools under the following headings: *Maintenance and minor repair, Repair and overhaul*, and *Special*. Newcomers to practical mechanics should start off with the *Maintenance and minor repair* tool kit, and confine themselves to the simpler jobs around the vehicle. Then, as confidence and experience grow, more difficult tasks can be undertaken, with extra tools being purchased as, and when, they are needed. In this way, a *Maintenance and minor repair* tool kit can be built up into a *Repair and overhaul* tool kit over a considerable period of time, without any major cash outlays. The experienced do-it-yourselfer will have a tool kit good enough for most repair and overhaul procedures, and will add tools from the *Special* category when it is felt that the expense is justified by the amount of use to which these tools will be put.

Maintenance and minor repair tool kit

The tools given in this list should be considered as a minimum requirement if routine maintenance, servicing and minor repair operations are to be undertaken. We recommend the purchase of combination spanners (ring one end, open-ended the other); although more expensive than open-ended ones, they do give the advantages of both types of spanner.

☐ *Combination spanners:*
    Metric - 8 to 19 mm inclusive
☐ *Adjustable spanner - 35 mm jaw (approx.)*
☐ *Spark plug spanner (with rubber insert) - petrol models*
☐ *Spark plug gap adjustment tool - petrol models*
☐ *Set of feeler gauges*
☐ *Brake bleed nipple spanner*
☐ *Screwdrivers:*
    Flat blade - 100 mm long x 6 mm dia
    Cross blade - 100 mm long x 6 mm dia
    Torx - various sizes (not all vehicles)
☐ *Combination pliers*
☐ *Hacksaw (junior)*
☐ *Tyre pump*
☐ *Tyre pressure gauge*
☐ *Oil can*
☐ *Oil filter removal tool*
☐ *Fine emery cloth*
☐ *Wire brush (small)*
☐ *Funnel (medium size)*
☐ *Sump drain plug key (not all vehicles)*

Repair and overhaul tool kit

These tools are virtually essential for anyone undertaking any major repairs to a motor vehicle, and are additional to those given in the *Maintenance and minor repair* list. Included in this list is a comprehensive set of sockets. Although these are expensive, they will be found invaluable as they are so versatile - particularly if various drives are included in the set. We recommend the half-inch square-drive type, as this can be used with most proprietary torque wrenches.

The tools in this list will sometimes need to be supplemented by tools from the *Special* list:

☐ *Sockets (or box spanners) to cover range in previous list (including Torx sockets)*
☐ *Reversible ratchet drive (for use with sockets)*
☐ *Extension piece, 250 mm (for use with sockets)*
☐ *Universal joint (for use with sockets)*
☐ *Flexible handle or sliding T "breaker bar" (for use with sockets)*
☐ *Torque wrench (for use with sockets)*
☐ *Self-locking grips*
☐ *Ball pein hammer*
☐ *Soft-faced mallet (plastic or rubber)*
☐ *Screwdrivers:*
    Flat blade - long & sturdy, short (chubby), and narrow (electrician's) types
    Cross blade – long & sturdy, and short (chubby) types
☐ *Pliers:*
    Long-nosed
    Side cutters (electrician's)
    Circlip (internal and external)
☐ *Cold chisel - 25 mm*
☐ *Scriber*
☐ *Scraper*
☐ *Centre-punch*
☐ *Pin punch*
☐ *Hacksaw*
☐ *Brake hose clamp*
☐ *Brake/clutch bleeding kit*
☐ *Selection of twist drills*
☐ *Steel rule/straight-edge*
☐ *Allen keys (inc. splined/Torx type)*
☐ *Selection of files*
☐ *Wire brush*
☐ *Axle stands*
☐ *Jack (strong trolley or hydraulic type)*
☐ *Light with extension lead*
☐ *Universal electrical multi-meter*

Sockets and reversible ratchet drive

Brake bleeding kit

Torx key, socket and bit

Hose clamp

Angular-tightening gauge

Special tools

The tools in this list are those which are not used regularly, are expensive to buy, or which need to be used in accordance with their manufacturers' instructions. Unless relatively difficult mechanical jobs are undertaken frequently, it will not be economic to buy many of these tools. Where this is the case, you could consider clubbing together with friends (or joining a motorists' club) to make a joint purchase, or borrowing the tools against a deposit from a local garage or tool hire specialist. It is worth noting that many of the larger DIY superstores now carry a large range of special tools for hire at modest rates.

The following list contains only those tools and instruments freely available to the public, and not those special tools produced by the vehicle manufacturer specifically for its dealer network. You will find occasional references to these manufacturers' special tools in the text of this manual. Generally, an alternative method of doing the job without the vehicle manufacturers' special tool is given. However, sometimes there is no alternative to using them. Where this is the case and the relevant tool cannot be bought or borrowed, you will have to entrust the work to a dealer.

- ☐ Angular-tightening gauge
- ☐ Valve spring compressor
- ☐ Valve grinding tool
- ☐ Piston ring compressor
- ☐ Piston ring removal/installation tool
- ☐ Cylinder bore hone
- ☐ Balljoint separator
- ☐ Coil spring compressors (where applicable)
- ☐ Two/three-legged hub and bearing puller
- ☐ Impact screwdriver
- ☐ Micrometer and/or vernier calipers
- ☐ Dial gauge
- ☐ Stroboscopic timing light
- ☐ Dwell angle meter/tachometer
- ☐ Fault code reader
- ☐ Cylinder compression gauge
- ☐ Hand-operated vacuum pump and gauge
- ☐ Clutch plate alignment set
- ☐ Brake shoe steady spring cup removal tool
- ☐ Bush and bearing removal/installation set
- ☐ Stud extractors
- ☐ Tap and die set
- ☐ Lifting tackle
- ☐ Trolley jack

Buying tools

Reputable motor accessory shops and superstores often offer excellent quality tools at discount prices, so it pays to shop around.

Remember, you don't have to buy the most expensive items on the shelf, but it is always advisable to steer clear of the very cheap tools. Beware of 'bargains' offered on market stalls or at car boot sales. There are plenty of good tools around at reasonable prices, but always aim to purchase items which meet the relevant national safety standards. If in doubt, ask the proprietor or manager of the shop for advice before making a purchase.

Care and maintenance of tools

Having purchased a reasonable tool kit, it is necessary to keep the tools in a clean and serviceable condition. After use, always wipe off any dirt, grease and metal particles using a clean, dry cloth, before putting the tools away. Never leave them lying around after they have been used. A simple tool rack on the garage or workshop wall for items such as screwdrivers and pliers is a good idea. Store all normal spanners and sockets in a metal box. Any measuring instruments, gauges, meters, etc, must be carefully stored where they cannot be damaged or become rusty.

Take a little care when tools are used. Hammer heads inevitably become marked, and screwdrivers lose the keen edge on their blades from time to time. A little timely attention with emery cloth or a file will soon restore items like this to a good finish.

Working facilities

Not to be forgotten when discussing tools is the workshop itself. If anything more than routine maintenance is to be carried out, a suitable working area becomes essential.

It is appreciated that many an owner-mechanic is forced by circumstances to remove an engine or similar item without the benefit of a garage or workshop. Having done this, any repairs should always be done under the cover of a roof.

Wherever possible, any dismantling should be done on a clean, flat workbench or table at a suitable working height.

Any workbench needs a vice; one with a jaw opening of 100 mm is suitable for most jobs. As mentioned previously, some clean dry storage space is also required for tools, as well as for any lubricants, cleaning fluids, touch-up paints etc, which become necessary.

Another item which may be required, and which has a much more general usage, is an electric drill with a chuck capacity of at least 8 mm. This, together with a good range of twist drills, is virtually essential for fitting accessories.

Last, but not least, always keep a supply of old newspapers and clean, lint-free rags available, and try to keep any working area as clean as possible.

Micrometers

Dial test indicator ("dial gauge")

Strap wrench

Compression tester

Fault code reader

This is a guide to getting your vehicle through the MOT test. Obviously it will not be possible to examine the vehicle to the same standard as the professional MOT tester. However, working through the following checks will enable you to identify any problem areas before submitting the vehicle for the test.

It has only been possible to summarise the test requirements here, based on the regulations in force at the time of printing. Test standards are becoming increasingly stringent, although there are some exemptions for older vehicles.

An assistant will be needed to help carry out some of these checks.

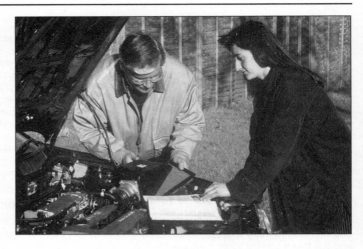

The checks have been sub-divided into four categories, as follows:

1 Checks carried out **FROM THE DRIVER'S SEAT**

2 Checks carried out **WITH THE VEHICLE ON THE GROUND**

3 Checks carried out **WITH THE VEHICLE RAISED AND THE WHEELS FREE TO TURN**

4 Checks carried out on **YOUR VEHICLE'S EXHAUST EMISSION SYSTEM**

---

1 Checks carried out **FROM THE DRIVER'S SEAT**

Handbrake

☐ Test the operation of the handbrake. Excessive travel (too many clicks) indicates incorrect brake or cable adjustment.
☐ Check that the handbrake cannot be released by tapping the lever sideways. Check the security of the lever mountings.

☐ Check that the brake pedal is secure and in good condition. Check also for signs of fluid leaks on the pedal, floor or carpets, which would indicate failed seals in the brake master cylinder.
☐ Check the servo unit (when applicable) by operating the brake pedal several times, then keeping the pedal depressed and starting the engine. As the engine starts, the pedal will move down slightly. If not, the vacuum hose or the servo itself may be faulty.

Footbrake

☐ Depress the brake pedal and check that it does not creep down to the floor, indicating a master cylinder fault. Release the pedal, wait a few seconds, then depress it again. If the pedal travels nearly to the floor before firm resistance is felt, brake adjustment or repair is necessary. If the pedal feels spongy, there is air in the hydraulic system which must be removed by bleeding.

Steering wheel and column

☐ Examine the steering wheel for fractures or looseness of the hub, spokes or rim.
☐ Move the steering wheel from side to side and then up and down. Check that the steering wheel is not loose on the column, indicating wear or a loose retaining nut. Continue moving the steering wheel as before, but also turn it slightly from left to right.
☐ Check that the steering wheel is not loose on the column, and that there is no abnormal

movement of the steering wheel, indicating wear in the column support bearings or couplings.

Windscreen, mirrors and sunvisor

☐ The windscreen must be free of cracks or other significant damage within the driver's field of view. (Small stone chips are acceptable.) Rear view mirrors must be secure, intact, and capable of being adjusted.

☐ The driver's sunvisor must be capable of being stored in the "up" position.

Seat belts and seats

Note: *The following checks are applicable to all seat belts, front and rear.*

☐ Examine the webbing of all the belts (including rear belts if fitted) for cuts, serious fraying or deterioration. Fasten and unfasten each belt to check the buckles. If applicable, check the retracting mechanism. Check the security of all seat belt mountings accessible from inside the vehicle.

☐ Seat belts with pre-tensioners, once activated, have a "flag" or similar showing on the seat belt stalk. This, in itself, is not a reason for test failure.

☐ The front seats themselves must be securely attached and the backrests must lock in the upright position.

Doors

☐ Both front doors must be able to be opened and closed from outside and inside, and must latch securely when closed.

2 Checks carried out WITH THE VEHICLE ON THE GROUND

Vehicle identification

☐ Number plates must be in good condition, secure and legible, with letters and numbers correctly spaced – spacing at (A) should be at least twice that at (B).

☐ The VIN plate and/or homologation plate must be legible.

Electrical equipment

☐ Switch on the ignition and check the operation of the horn.

☐ Check the windscreen washers and wipers, examining the wiper blades; renew damaged or perished blades. Also check the operation of the stop-lights.

☐ Check the operation of the sidelights and number plate lights. The lenses and reflectors must be secure, clean and undamaged.

☐ Check the operation and alignment of the headlights. The headlight reflectors must not be tarnished and the lenses must be undamaged.

☐ Switch on the ignition and check the operation of the direction indicators (including the instrument panel tell-tale) and the hazard warning lights. Operation of the sidelights and stop-lights must not affect the indicators - if it does, the cause is usually a bad earth at the rear light cluster.

☐ Check the operation of the rear foglight(s), including the warning light on the instrument panel or in the switch.

☐ The ABS warning light must illuminate in accordance with the manufacturers' design. For most vehicles, the ABS warning light should illuminate when the ignition is switched on, and (if the system is operating properly) extinguish after a few seconds. Refer to the owner's handbook.

Footbrake

☐ Examine the master cylinder, brake pipes and servo unit for leaks, loose mountings, corrosion or other damage.

☐ The fluid reservoir must be secure and the fluid level must be between the upper (A) and lower (B) markings.

☐ Inspect both front brake flexible hoses for cracks or deterioration of the rubber. Turn the steering from lock to lock, and ensure that the hoses do not contact the wheel, tyre, or any part of the steering or suspension mechanism. With the brake pedal firmly depressed, check the hoses for bulges or leaks under pressure.

Steering and suspension

☐ Have your assistant turn the steering wheel from side to side slightly, up to the point where the steering gear just begins to transmit this movement to the roadwheels. Check for excessive free play between the steering wheel and the steering gear, indicating wear or insecurity of the steering column joints, the column-to-steering gear coupling, or the steering gear itself.

☐ Have your assistant turn the steering wheel more vigorously in each direction, so that the roadwheels just begin to turn. As this is done, examine all the steering joints, linkages, fittings and attachments. Renew any component that shows signs of wear or damage. On vehicles with power steering, check the security and condition of the steering pump, drivebelt and hoses.

☐ Check that the vehicle is standing level, and at approximately the correct ride height.

Shock absorbers

☐ Depress each corner of the vehicle in turn, then release it. The vehicle should rise and then settle in its normal position. If the vehicle continues to rise and fall, the shock absorber is defective. A shock absorber which has seized will also cause the vehicle to fail.

Exhaust system

☐ Start the engine. With your assistant holding a rag over the tailpipe, check the entire system for leaks. Repair or renew leaking sections.

3 Checks carried out **WITH THE VEHICLE RAISED AND THE WHEELS FREE TO TURN**

Jack up the front and rear of the vehicle, and securely support it on axle stands. Position the stands clear of the suspension assemblies. Ensure that the wheels are clear of the ground and that the steering can be turned from lock to lock.

Steering mechanism

☐ Have your assistant turn the steering from lock to lock. Check that the steering turns smoothly, and that no part of the steering mechanism, including a wheel or tyre, fouls any brake hose or pipe or any part of the body structure. ·

☐ Examine the steering rack rubber gaiters for damage or insecurity of the retaining clips. If power steering is fitted, check for signs of damage or leakage of the fluid hoses, pipes or connections. Also check for excessive stiffness or binding of the steering, a missing split pin or locking device, or severe corrosion of the body structure within 30 cm of any steering component attachment point.

Front and rear suspension and wheel bearings

☐ Starting at the front right-hand side, grasp the roadwheel at the 3 o'clock and 9 o'clock positions and rock gently but firmly. Check for free play or insecurity at the wheel bearings, suspension balljoints, or suspension mountings, pivots and attachments.

☐ Now grasp the wheel at the 12 o'clock and 6 o'clock positions and repeat the previous inspection. Spin the wheel, and check for roughness or tightness of the front wheel bearing.

☐ If excess free play is suspected at a component pivot point, this can be confirmed by using a large screwdriver or similar tool and levering between the mounting and the component attachment. This will confirm whether the wear is in the pivot bush, its retaining bolt, or in the mounting itself (the bolt holes can often become elongated).

☐ Carry out all the above checks at the other front wheel, and then at both rear wheels.

Springs and shock absorbers

☐ Examine the suspension struts (when applicable) for serious fluid leakage, corrosion, or damage to the casing. Also check the security of the mounting points.

☐ If coil springs are fitted, check that the spring ends locate in their seats, and that the spring is not corroded, cracked or broken.

☐ If leaf springs are fitted, check that all leaves are intact, that the axle is securely attached to each spring, and that there is no deterioration of the spring eye mountings, bushes, and shackles.

☐ The same general checks apply to vehicles fitted with other suspension types, such as torsion bars, hydraulic displacer units, etc. Ensure that all mountings and attachments are secure, that there are no signs of excessive wear, corrosion or damage, and (on hydraulic types) that there are no fluid leaks or damaged pipes.

☐ Inspect the shock absorbers for signs of serious fluid leakage. Check for wear of the mounting bushes or attachments, or damage to the body of the unit.

Driveshafts
(fwd vehicles only)

☐ Rotate each front wheel in turn and inspect the constant velocity joint gaiters for splits or damage. Also check that each driveshaft is straight and undamaged.

Braking system

☐ If possible without dismantling, check brake pad wear and disc condition. Ensure that the friction lining material has not worn excessively, (A) and that the discs are not fractured, pitted, scored or badly worn (B).

☐ Examine all the rigid brake pipes underneath the vehicle, and the flexible hose(s) at the rear. Look for corrosion, chafing or insecurity of the pipes, and for signs of bulging under pressure, chafing, splits or deterioration of the flexible hoses.

☐ Look for signs of fluid leaks at the brake calipers or on the brake backplates. Repair or renew leaking components.

☐ Slowly spin each wheel, while your assistant depresses and releases the footbrake. Ensure that each brake is operating and does not bind when the pedal is released.

☐ Examine the handbrake mechanism, checking for frayed or broken cables, excessive corrosion, or wear or insecurity of the linkage. Check that the mechanism works on each relevant wheel, and releases fully, without binding.

☐ It is not possible to test brake efficiency without special equipment, but a road test can be carried out later to check that the vehicle pulls up in a straight line.

Fuel and exhaust systems

☐ Inspect the fuel tank (including the filler cap), fuel pipes, hoses and unions. All components must be secure and free from leaks.

☐ Examine the exhaust system over its entire length, checking for any damaged, broken or missing mountings, security of the retaining clamps and rust or corrosion.

Wheels and tyres

☐ Examine the sidewalls and tread area of each tyre in turn. Check for cuts, tears, lumps, bulges, separation of the tread, and exposure of the ply or cord due to wear or damage. Check that the tyre bead is correctly seated on the wheel rim, that the valve is sound and properly seated, and that the wheel is not distorted or damaged.

☐ Check that the tyres are of the correct size for the vehicle, that they are of the same size

and type on each axle, and that the pressures are correct.

☐ Check the tyre tread depth. The legal minimum at the time of writing is 1.6 mm over at least three-quarters of the tread width. Abnormal tread wear may indicate incorrect front wheel alignment.

Body corrosion

☐ Check the condition of the entire vehicle structure for signs of corrosion in load-bearing areas. (These include chassis box sections, side sills, cross-members, pillars, and all suspension, steering, braking system and seat belt mountings and anchorages.) Any corrosion which has seriously reduced the thickness of a load-bearing area is likely to cause the vehicle to fail. In this case professional repairs are likely to be needed.

☐ Damage or corrosion which causes sharp or otherwise dangerous edges to be exposed will also cause the vehicle to fail.

4 Checks carried out on YOUR VEHICLE'S EXHAUST EMISSION SYSTEM

Petrol models

☐ The engine should be warmed up, and running well (ignition system in good order, air filter element clean, etc).

☐ Before testing, run the engine at around 2500 rpm for 20 seconds. Let the engine drop to idle, and watch for smoke from the exhaust. If the idle speed is too high, or if dense blue or black smoke emerges for more than 5 seconds, the vehicle will fail. Typically, blue smoke signifies oil burning (engine wear); black smoke means unburnt fuel (dirty air cleaner element, or other fuel system fault).

☐ An exhaust gas analyser for measuring carbon monoxide (CO) and hydrocarbons (HC) is now needed. If one cannot be hired or borrowed, have a local garage perform the check.

CO emissions (mixture)

☐ The MOT tester has access to the CO limits for all vehicles. The CO level is measured at idle speed, and at 'fast idle' (2500 to 3000 rpm). The following limits are given as a general guide:

At idle speed – Less than 0.5% CO
At 'fast idle' – Less than 0.3% CO
Lambda reading – 0.97 to 1.03

☐ If the CO level is too high, this may point to poor maintenance, a fuel injection system problem, faulty lambda (oxygen) sensor or catalytic converter. Try an injector cleaning treatment, and check the vehicle's ECU for fault codes.

HC emissions

☐ The MOT tester has access to HC limits for all vehicles. The HC level is measured at 'fast idle' (2500 to 3000 rpm). The following limits are given as a general guide:

At 'fast idle' – Less then 200 ppm

☐ Excessive HC emissions are typically caused by oil being burnt (worn engine), or by a blocked crankcase ventilation system ('breather'). If the engine oil is old and thin, an oil change may help. If the engine is running badly, check the vehicle's ECU for fault codes.

Diesel models

☐ The only emission test for diesel engines is measuring exhaust smoke density, using a calibrated smoke meter. The test involves accelerating the engine at least 3 times to its maximum unloaded speed.

Note: *On engines with a timing belt, it is VITAL that the belt is in good condition before the test is carried out.*

☐ With the engine warmed up, it is first purged by running at around 2500 rpm for 20 seconds. A governor check is then carried out, by slowly accelerating the engine to its maximum speed. After this, the smoke meter is connected, and the engine is accelerated quickly to maximum speed three times. If the smoke density is less than the limits given below, the vehicle will pass:

Non-turbo vehicles: 2.5m-1
Turbocharged vehicles: 3.0m-1

☐ If excess smoke is produced, try fitting a new air cleaner element, or using an injector cleaning treatment. If the engine is running badly, where applicable, check the vehicle's ECU for fault codes. Also check the vehicle's EGR system, where applicable. At high mileages, the injectors may require professional attention.

Engine

- [ ] Engine fails to rotate when attempting to start
- [ ] Engine rotates, but will not start
- [ ] Engine difficult to start when cold
- [ ] Engine difficult to start when hot
- [ ] Starter motor noisy or excessively-rough in engagement
- [ ] Engine idles erratically
- [ ] Engine misfires at idle speed
- [ ] Engine misfires throughout the driving speed range
- [ ] Engine hesitates on acceleration
- [ ] Engine stalls
- [ ] Engine lacks power
- [ ] Engine backfires
- [ ] Oil pressure warning light illuminated with engine running
- [ ] Engine runs-on after switching off
- [ ] Engine noises

Cooling system

- [ ] Overheating
- [ ] Overcooling
- [ ] External coolant leakage
- [ ] Internal coolant leakage
- [ ] Corrosion

Fuel and exhaust systems

- [ ] Excessive fuel consumption
- [ ] Fuel leakage and/or fuel odour
- [ ] Excessive noise or fumes from exhaust system

Clutch

- [ ] Pedal travels to floor – no pressure or very little resistance
- [ ] Clutch fails to disengage (unable to select gears)
- [ ] Clutch slips (engine speed increases, with no increase in vehicle speed)
- [ ] Judder as clutch is engaged
- [ ] Noise when depressing or releasing clutch pedal

Manual transmission

- [ ] Noisy in neutral with engine running
- [ ] Noisy in one particular gear
- [ ] Difficulty engaging gears
- [ ] Jumps out of gear
- [ ] Vibration
- [ ] Lubricant leaks

Driveshafts

- [ ] Vibration when accelerating or decelerating
- [ ] Clicking or knocking noise on turns (at slow speed on full-lock)

Braking system

- [ ] Vehicle pulls to one side under braking
- [ ] Noise (grinding or high-pitched squeal) when brakes applied
- [ ] Excessive brake pedal travel
- [ ] Brake pedal feels spongy when depressed
- [ ] Excessive brake pedal effort required to stop vehicle
- [ ] Judder felt through brake pedal or steering wheel when braking
- [ ] Pedal pulsates when braking hard
- [ ] Brakes binding
- [ ] Rear wheels locking under normal braking

Steering and suspension

- [ ] Vehicle pulls to one side
- [ ] Wheel wobble and vibration
- [ ] Excessive pitching and/or rolling around corners, or during braking
- [ ] Wandering or general instability
- [ ] Excessively-stiff steering
- [ ] Excessive play in steering
- [ ] Lack of power assistance
- [ ] Tyre wear excessive

Electrical system

- [ ] Battery will not hold a charge more than a few days
- [ ] Ignition/no-charge warning light remains illuminated with engine running
- [ ] Ignition/no-charge warning light fails to come on
- [ ] Lights inoperative
- [ ] Instrument readings inaccurate or erratic
- [ ] Horn inoperative, or unsatisfactory in operation
- [ ] Windscreen/tailgate wipers inoperative, or unsatisfactory in operation
- [ ] Windscreen washers inoperative, or unsatisfactory in operation
- [ ] Electric windows inoperative, or unsatisfactory in operation
- [ ] Central locking system inoperative, or unsatisfactory in operation

Introduction

1 The vehicle owner who does his or her own maintenance according to the recommended service schedules should not have to use this section of the manual very often. Modern component reliability is such that, provided those items subject to wear or deterioration are inspected or renewed at the specified intervals, sudden failure is comparatively rare. Faults do not usually just happen as a result of sudden failure, but develop over a period of time. Major mechanical failures in particular are usually preceded by characteristic symptoms over hundreds or even thousands of miles. Those components which do occasionally fail without warning are often small and easily carried in the vehicle.

2 With any fault-finding, the first step is to decide where to begin investigations. Sometimes this is obvious, but on other occasions, a little detective work will be necessary. The owner who makes half a dozen haphazard adjustments or replacements may be successful in curing a fault (or its symptoms), but will be none the wiser if the fault recurs, and ultimately may have spent more time and money than was necessary. A calm and logical approach will be found to be more satisfactory in the long run. Always take into account any warning signs or abnormalities that may have been noticed in the period preceding the fault – power loss, high or low gauge readings, unusual smells, etc – and remember that failure of components such as fuses or spark plugs may only be pointers to some underlying fault.

3 The pages which follow provide an easy-reference guide to the more common problems which may occur during the operation of the vehicle. These problems and their possible causes are grouped under headings denoting various components or systems, such as Engine, Cooling system, etc. The general Chapter which deals with the problem is also shown in brackets; refer to the relevant part of that Chapter for system-specific information. Whatever the fault, certain basic principles apply. These are as follows:

4 Verify the fault. This is simply a matter of being sure that you know what the symptoms are before starting work. This is particularly important if you are investigating a fault for someone else, who may not have described it very accurately.

5 Don't overlook the obvious. For example, if the vehicle won't start, is there fuel in the tank? (Don't take anyone else's word on this particular point, and don't trust the fuel gauge either!) If an electrical fault is indicated, look for loose or broken wires before digging out the test gear.

6 Cure the disease, not the symptom. Substituting a flat battery with a fully-charged one will get you off the hard shoulder, but if the underlying cause is not attended to, the new battery will go the same way.

7 Don't take anything for granted. Particularly, don't forget that a new component may itself be defective (especially if its been rattling around in the boot for months), and don't leave components out of a fault diagnosis sequence just because they are new or recently-fitted. When you do finally diagnose a difficult fault, you'll probably realise that all the evidence was there from the start.

Diesel fault diagnosis

8 The majority of starting problems on small diesel engines are electrical in origin. The mechanic who is familiar with petrol engines but less so with diesel may be inclined to view the diesel's injectors and pump in the same light as the spark plugs and distributor, but this is generally a mistake.

9 When investigating complaints of difficult starting for someone else, make sure that the correct starting procedure is understood and is being followed. Some drivers are unaware of the significance of the preheating warning light – many modern engines are sufficiently forgiving for this not to matter in mild weather, but with the onset of winter, problems begin. Glow plugs in particular are often neglected – just one faulty plug will make cold-weather starting very difficult.

10 As a rule of thumb, if the engine is difficult to start but runs well when it has finally got going, the problem is electrical (battery, starter motor or preheating system). If poor performance is combined with difficult starting, the problem is likely to be in the fuel system. The low-pressure (supply) side of the fuel system should be checked before suspecting the injectors and high-pressure pump. The most common fuel supply problem is air getting into the system, and any pipe from the fuel tank forwards must be scrutinised if air leakage is suspected.

Engine

Engine fails to rotate when attempting to start

☐ Battery terminal connections loose or corroded (*Weekly checks*).
☐ Battery discharged or faulty (Chapter 5, Section 2).
☐ Broken, loose or disconnected wiring in the starting circuit (Chapter 5, Section 7).
☐ Defective starter solenoid or switch (Chapter 5, Section 7).
☐ Defective starter motor (Chapter 5, Section 8).
☐ Starter pinion or flywheel/driveplate ring gear teeth loose or broken (Chapter 5, Section 7 and Chapter 6, Section 6).
☐ Engine earth strap broken or disconnected (Chapter 12, Section 2).

Engine rotates, but will not start

☐ Fuel tank empty.Battery discharged (engine rotates slowly) (Chapter 5, Section 2).
☐ Battery terminal connections loose or corroded (*Weekly checks*).
☐ Preheating system faulty (Chapter 5, Section 10).
☐ Air in fuel system (Chapter 4A, Section 7).
☐ Major mechanical failure (eg, timing belt).

Engine difficult to start when cold

☐ Battery discharged (Chapter 5, Section 2).
☐ Battery terminal connections loose or corroded (*Weekly checks*).
☐ Preheating system faulty (Chapter 5, Section 10).
☐ Low cylinder compressions (Chapter 2A, 2B, 2C or 2D).

Engine difficult to start when hot

☐ Air filter element dirty or clogged (Chapter 1, Section 20).
☐ Low cylinder compressions (Chapter 2A, 2B, 2C or 2D).

Starter motor noisy or excessively-rough in engagement

☐ Starter pinion or flywheel ring gear teeth loose or broken (Chapter 5, Section 8 and Chapter 6, Section 6).
☐ Starter motor mounting bolts loose or missing (Chapter 5, Section 8).
☐ Starter motor internal components worn or damaged (Chapter 5, Section 8).

Engine idles erratically

☐ Air filter element clogged (Chapter 1, Section 20).
☐ Uneven or low cylinder compressions (Chapter 2A, 2B, 2C or 2D).
☐ Camshaft lobes worn (Chapter 2A, 2B, 2C or 2D).
☐ Timing belt incorrectly fitted (Chapter 2A, 2B, 2C or 2D).
☐ Faulty injector(s) (Chapter 4A, Section 11).

Engine misfires at idle speed

☐ Faulty injector(s) (Chapter 4A, Section 11).
☐ Uneven or low cylinder compressions (Chapter 2A, 2B, 2C or 2D).
☐ Disconnected, leaking, or perished crankcase ventilation hoses (Chapter 4B, Section 4).

Engine misfires throughout the driving speed range

☐ Fuel filter choked (Chapter 1, Section 19).
☐ Fuel tank vent blocked, or fuel pipes restricted (Chapter 4A, Section 4).
☐ Faulty injector(s) (Chapter 4A, Section 11).
☐ Uneven or low cylinder compressions (Chapter 2A, 2B, 2C or 2D).

Engine hesitates on acceleration

☐ Faulty injector(s) (Chapter 4A, Section 11).

Engine stalls

☐ Fuel filter choked (Chapter 1, Section 19).
☐ Fuel tank vent blocked, or fuel pipes restricted (Chapter 4A, Section 4).
☐ Faulty injector(s) (Chapter 4A, Section 11).

Engine lacks power

☐ Timing belt incorrectly fitted or tensioned (Chapter 2A, 2B, 2C or 2D).
☐ Fuel filter choked (Chapter 1, Section 19).
☐ Uneven or low cylinder compressions (Chapter 2A, 2B, 2C or 2D).
☐ Faulty injector(s) (Chapter 4A, Section 11).
☐ Brakes binding (Chapter 9).
☐ Clutch slipping (Chapter 6, Section 6).
☐ Air filter element clogged (Chapter 1, Section 20).

Engine backfires

☐ Timing belt incorrectly fitted or tensioned (Chapter 2A, 2B, 2C or 2D).

Oil pressure warning light illuminated with engine running

☐ Low oil level, or incorrect oil grade (*Weekly checks*).
☐ Faulty oil pressure switch (Chapter 2A, 2B, 2C or 2D).
☐ Worn engine bearings and/or oil pump (Chapter 2A, 2B, 2C or 2D).
☐ High engine operating temperature (Chapter 3).
☐ Oil pressure relief valve defective (Chapter 2A, 2B, 2C, 2D, 2E).
☐ Oil pick-up strainer clogged (Chapter 2A, 2B, 2C or 2D).

Engine runs-on after switching off

☐ Excessive carbon build-up in engine (Chapter 2A, 2B, 2C or 2D).
☐ High engine operating temperature (Chapter 3).

Engine noises

Pre-ignition (pinking) or knocking during acceleration or under load

☐ Excessive carbon build-up in engine (Chapter) 2A, 2B, 2C, 2D.

Whistling or wheezing noises

☐ Leaking exhaust manifold gasket or pipe-to-manifold joint (Chapter 4A, Section 17, 18).
☐ Leaking vacuum hose (Chapter 4A, Chapter 9).
☐ Blowing cylinder head gasket (Chapter 2A, 2B, 2C or 2D).

Tapping or rattling noises

☐ Worn valve gear or camshaft (Chapter 2A, 2B, 2C or 2D).
☐ Ancillary component fault (coolant pump, alternator, etc).

Knocking or thumping noises

☐ Worn big-end bearings (regular heavy knocking, perhaps less under load) (Chapter 2E).
☐ Worn main bearings (rumbling and knocking, perhaps worsening under load) (Chapter 2E).
☐ Piston slap (most noticeable when cold).
☐ Ancillary component fault (coolant pump, alternator, etc).

Cooling system

Overheating

- ☐ Insufficient coolant in system (*Weekly checks*).
- ☐ Thermostat faulty (Chapter 3, Section 4).
- ☐ Radiator core blocked, or grille restricted (Chapter 3, Section 7).
- ☐ Electric cooling fan or thermostatic switch faulty (Chapter 3, Section 5).
- ☐ Inaccurate temperature gauge sender unit (Chapter 3, Section 6).
- ☐ Airlock in cooling system (Chapter 1, Section 25).
- ☐ Expansion tank pressure cap faulty (Chapter 3, Section 7).

Overcooling

- ☐ Thermostat faulty (Chapter 3, Section 4).
- ☐ Inaccurate temperature gauge sender unit (Chapter 3, Section 6).

External coolant leakage

- ☐ Deteriorated or damaged hoses or hose clips (Chapter 3, Section 3).

- ☐ Radiator core or heater matrix leaking (Chapter 3, Section 7, 9).
- ☐ Pressure cap faulty (Chapter 3, Section 7).
- ☐ Coolant pump internal seal leaking (Chapter 3, Section 8).
- ☐ Coolant pump-to-housing seal leaking (Chapter 3, Section 8).
- ☐ Boiling due to overheating (Chapter 3, Section 1).
- ☐ Core plug leaking (Chapter 2E).

Internal coolant leakage

- ☐ Leaking cylinder head gasket (Chapter 2A, 2B, 2C or 2D).
- ☐ Cracked cylinder head or cylinder block (Chapter 2A, 2B, 2C, 2D or 2E).

Corrosion

- ☐ Infrequent draining and flushing (Chapter 1, Section 25).
- ☐ Incorrect coolant mixture or inappropriate coolant type (*Weekly checks*).

Fuel and exhaust systems

Excessive fuel consumption

- ☐ Air filter element dirty or clogged (Chapter 1, Section 20).
- ☐ Faulty injector(s) (Chapter 4A, Section 11).
- ☐ Tyres under-inflated (*Weekly checks*).

Fuel leakage and/or fuel odour

- ☐ Damaged fuel tank, pipes or connections (Chapter 1, Section 13).

Excessive noise or fumes from exhaust system

- ☐ Leaking exhaust system or manifold joints (Chapter 4A, Section 17, 18).
- ☐ Leaking, corroded or damaged silencers or pipe (Chapter 4A, Section 18).
- ☐ Broken mountings causing body or suspension contact (Chapter 1, Section 11).

Clutch

Pedal travels to floor – no pressure or very little resistance

- [ ] Faulty master or slave cylinder (Chapter 6, Section 3, 4).
- [ ] Faulty hydraulic release system (Chapter 6, Section 5).
- [ ] Broken clutch release bearing or arm (Chapter 6, Section 4).
- [ ] Broken diaphragm spring in clutch pressure plate (Chapter 6, Section 6).

Clutch fails to disengage (unable to select gears)

- [ ] Faulty master or slave cylinder (Chapter 6, Section 3, 4).
- [ ] Faulty hydraulic release system (Chapter 6, Section 5).
- [ ] Clutch driven plate sticking on gearbox input shaft splines (Chapter 6, Section 6).
- [ ] Clutch driven plate sticking to flywheel or pressure plate (Chapter 6, Section 6).
- [ ] Faulty pressure plate assembly (Chapter 6, Section 6).
- [ ] Clutch release mechanism worn or incorrectly assembled (Chapter 6).

Clutch slips (engine speed increases, with no increase in vehicle speed)

- [ ] Faulty hydraulic release system (Chapter 6).
- [ ] Clutch driven plate linings excessively worn (Chapter 6).
- [ ] Clutch driven plate linings contaminated with oil or grease (Chapter 6).
- [ ] Faulty pressure plate or weak diaphragm spring (Chapter 6, Section 6).

Judder as clutch is engaged

- [ ] Clutch driven plate linings contaminated with oil or grease (Chapter 6, Section 6).
- [ ] Clutch driven plate linings excessively worn (Chapter 6, Section 6).
- [ ] Faulty or distorted pressure plate or diaphragm spring (Chapter 6, Section 6).
- [ ] Worn or loose engine or gearbox mountings (Chapter 2A, 2B, 2C or 2D).
- [ ] Clutch driven plate hub or gearbox input shaft splines worn (Chapter 6, Section 6).

Noise when depressing or releasing clutch pedal

- [ ] Worn clutch release bearing (Chapter 6, Section 4).
- [ ] Worn or dry clutch pedal pivot (Chapter 6, Section 2).
- [ ] Faulty pressure plate assembly (Chapter 6, Section 6).
- [ ] Pressure plate diaphragm spring broken (Chapter 6, Section 6).
- [ ] Broken clutch friction plate cushioning springs (Chapter 6, Section 6).

Manual transmission

Noisy in neutral with engine running

- [ ] Input shaft bearings worn (noise apparent with clutch pedal released, but not when depressed) (Chapter 7).
- [ ] *Clutch release bearing worn (noise apparent with clutch pedal depressed, possibly less when released) (Chapter 6, Section 4).

Noisy in one particular gear

- [ ] Worn, damaged or chipped gear teeth (Chapter 7).*

Difficulty engaging gears

- [ ] Clutch fault (Chapter 6, Section 6).
- [ ] Worn or damaged gear linkage (Chapter 7, Section 3).
- [ ] Worn synchroniser units (Chapter 7).*

Jumps out of gear

- [ ] Worn or damaged gear linkage (Chapter 7, Section 3).
- [ ] Worn synchroniser units (Chapter 7).*
- [ ] Worn selector forks (Chapter 7).*

Vibration

- [ ] Lack of oil (Chapter 7, Section 6).
- [ ] Worn bearings (Chapter 7).*

Lubricant leaks

- [ ] Leaking oil seal (Chapter 7, Section 4).
- [ ] Leaking housing joint (Chapter 7).*
- [ ] Leaking input shaft oil seal (Chapter 7, Section 4).

Although the corrective action necessary to remedy the symptoms described is beyond the scope of the home mechanic, the above information should be helpful in isolating the cause of the condition, so that the owner can communicate clearly with a professional mechanic.

Driveshafts

Vibration when accelerating or decelerating

☐ Worn inner constant velocity joint (Chapter 8, Section 4).
☐ Bent or distorted driveshaft (Chapter 8, Section 4).

Clicking or knocking noise on turns (at slow speed on full-lock)

☐ Worn outer constant velocity joint (Chapter 8, Section 4).
☐ Lack of constant velocity joint lubricant, possibly due to damaged gaiter (Chapter 8, Section 4).

Braking system

Vehicle pulls to one side under braking

Note: *Before assuming that a brake problem exists, make sure that the tyres are in good condition and correctly inflated, that the front wheel alignment is correct, and that the vehicle is not loaded with weight in an unequal manner. Apart from checking the condition of all pipe and hose connections, any faults occurring on the anti-lock braking system should be referred to a Ford dealer for diagnosis.*

☐ Worn, defective, damaged or contaminated front or rear brake pads on one side (Chapter 1, Section 9 and Chapter 9).
☐ Seized or partially-seized front or rear brake caliper (Chapter 9, Section 3, 6).
☐ A mixture of brake pad lining materials fitted between sides (Chapter 9, Section 2, 5).
☐ Brake caliper mounting bolts loose (Chapter 9, Section 3, 6).
☐ Worn or damaged steering or suspension components (Chapters 1, 10).

Noise (grinding or high-pitched squeal) when brakes applied

☐ Brake pad friction lining material worn down to metal backing (Chapter 1, Section 9 and Chapter 9, Section 4, 5).
☐ Excessive corrosion of brake disc – may be apparent after the vehicle has been standing for some time (Chapter 9, Section 4, 7).
☐ Foreign object (stone chipping, etc) trapped between brake disc and shield (Chapter 9, Section 4, 7).

Excessive brake pedal travel

☐ Faulty master cylinder (Chapter 9, Section 8).
☐ Air in hydraulic system (Chapter 9, Section 11).
☐ Faulty vacuum servo unit (Chapter 9, Section 12).
☐ Faulty vacuum pump (Chapter 9, Section 20).

Brake pedal feels spongy when depressed

☐ Air in hydraulic system (Chapter 9, Section 11).
☐ Deteriorated flexible rubber brake hoses (Chapter 1, Section 13 and Chapter 9, Section 10)
☐ Master cylinder mountings loose (Chapter 9, Section 8).
☐ Faulty master cylinder (Chapter 9, Section 8).

Excessive brake pedal effort required to stop vehicle

☐ Faulty vacuum servo unit (Chapter 9, Section 12).
☐ Disconnected, damaged or insecure brake servo vacuum hose (Chapter 1, Section 6).
☐ Faulty vacuum pump (Chapter 9, Section 20, 21).
☐ Primary or secondary hydraulic circuit failure (Chapter 9, Section 1).
☐ Seized brake caliper (Chapter 9, Section 3, 6).
☐ Brake pads incorrectly fitted (Chapter 9, Section 2, 5).
☐ Incorrect grade of brake pads fitted (Chapter 9, Section 2, 5).
☐ Brake pads contaminated (Chapter 9, Section 2, 5).

Judder felt through brake pedal or steering wheel when braking

☐ Excessive run-out or distortion of brake disc(s) (Chapter 9, Section 4, 7).
☐ Brake pad linings worn (Chapters 1, Section 9).
☐ Brake caliper mounting bolts loose (Chapter 9, Section 3, 6).
☐ Wear in suspension or steering components or mountings (Chapter 10).

Pedal pulsates when braking hard

☐ Normal feature of ABS – no fault.

Brakes binding

☐ Seized brake caliper piston(s) (Chapter 9, Section 3, 6).
☐ Incorrectly-adjusted handbrake mechanism (Chapter 9, Section 19).
☐ Faulty master cylinder (Chapter 9, Section 8).

Rear wheels locking under normal braking

☐ Rear brake pad linings contaminated (Chapters 9, Section 5).
☐ Rear brake discs warped (Chapters 9, Section 7).

Steering and suspension

Vehicle pulls to one side

Note: *Before diagnosing suspension or steering faults, be sure that the trouble is not due to incorrect tyre pressures, mixtures of tyre types, or binding brakes.*

☐ Defective tyre (*Weekly checks*).
☐ Excessive wear in suspension or steering components (Chapter 10).
☐ Incorrect front wheel alignment (Chapter 10, Section 21).
☐ Accident damage to steering or suspension components (Chapter 10).

Wheel wobble and vibration

☐ Front roadwheels out of balance (vibration felt mainly through the steering wheel) (Chapter 10).
☐ Rear roadwheels out of balance (vibration felt throughout the vehicle) (Chapter 10).
☐ Roadwheels damaged or distorted (Chapter 10).
☐ Faulty or damaged tyre (*Weekly checks*).
☐ Worn steering or suspension joints, bushes or components (Chapter 10).
☐ Wheel nuts loose (Chapter 1, Section 15).

Excessive pitching and/or rolling around corners, or during braking

☐ Defective shock absorbers (Chapter 10, Section 4, 10).
☐ Broken or weak coil spring and/or suspension component (Chapter 10, Section 4, 11).
☐ Worn or damaged anti-roll bar or mountings (Chapter 10, Section 6, 13).

Wandering or general instability

☐ Incorrect front wheel alignment (Chapter 10, Section 21).
☐ Worn steering or suspension joints, bushes or components (Chapter 1, Section 11 and Chapter 10).
☐ Roadwheels out of balance (Chapter 1, Section 11).
☐ Faulty or damaged tyre (*Weekly checks*).
☐ Wheel nuts loose (Chapter 1, Section 11).
☐ Defective shock absorbers (Chapter 1, Section 11).

Excessively-stiff steering

☐ Seized track rod end balljoint or suspension balljoint (Chapter 10, Section 5, 20).

☐ Broken or incorrectly adjusted auxiliary drivebelt (Chapter 1, Section 22).
☐ Incorrect front wheel alignment (Chapter 10, Section 21).
☐ Steering gear damaged (Chapter 10, Section 16).

Excessive play in steering

☐ Worn steering column universal joint(s) (Chapter 10, Section 15).
☐ Worn steering track rod end balljoints (Chapter 1, Section 11 and Chapter 10, Section 20)
☐ Worn steering gear (Chapter 1, Section 11).
☐ Worn steering or suspension joints, bushes or components (Chapter 10).

Lack of power assistance

☐ Broken or incorrectly-adjusted auxiliary drivebelt (Chapter 1, Section 22).
☐ Incorrect power steering fluid level (*Weekly checks*).
☐ Restriction in power steering fluid hoses (Chapter 10, Section 19).
☐ Faulty power steering pump (Chapter 10, Section 19).
☐ Faulty steering gear (Chapter 10, Section 15, 16).

Tyre wear excessive

Tyres worn on inside or outside edges

☐ Incorrect camber or castor angles (Chapter 10, Section 21).
☐ Worn steering or suspension joints, bushes or components (Chapter 10).
☐ Excessively-hard cornering.Accident damage.

Tyre treads exhibit feathered edges

☐ Incorrect toe setting (Chapter 10, Section 21).

Tyres worn in centre of tread

☐ Tyres over-inflated (*Weekly checks*).

Tyres worn on inside and outside edges

☐ Tyres under-inflated (*Weekly checks*).
☐ Worn shock absorbers (Chapter 10, Section 3, 4, 10).

Tyres worn unevenly

☐ Tyres/wheels out of balance (*Weekly checks*).
☐ Excessive wheel or tyre run-out (Chapter 10, Section 21).
☐ Worn shock absorbers (Chapter 1, Section 11).
☐ Faulty tyre (*Weekly checks*).

Electrical system

Battery will not hold a charge more than a few days

Note: *For problems associated with the starting system, refer to the faults listed under Engine earlier in this, Section.*

☐ Battery defective internally (Chapter 5, Section 2).
☐ Battery terminal connections loose or corroded (*Weekly checks*).
☐ Auxiliary drivebelt worn – or incorrectly adjusted, where applicable (Chapter 1, Section 22).
☐ Alternator not charging at correct output (Chapter 5, Section 5, 6).
☐ Alternator or voltage regulator faulty (Chapter 5, Section 5).
☐ Short-circuit causing continual battery drain (Chapter 12, Section 2).

Ignition/no-charge warning light remains illuminated with engine running

☐ Auxiliary drivebelt broken, worn, or incorrectly adjusted (Chapter 1, Section 22).
☐ Internal fault in alternator or voltage regulator (Chapter 5, Section 5).
☐ Broken, disconnected, or loose wiring in charging circuit (Chapter 5, Section 5).

Ignition/no-charge warning light fails to come on

☐ Broken, disconnected, or loose wiring in warning light circuit (Chapter 5, Section 5).
☐ Alternator faulty (Chapter 5, Section 5).

Lights inoperative

☐ Bulb blown (Chapter 12, Section 7, 8).
☐ Corrosion of bulb or bulbholder contacts (Chapter 12, Section 7).
☐ Blown fuse (Chapter 12, Section 3).
☐ Faulty relay (Chapter 12, Section 3).
☐ Broken, loose, or disconnected wiring (Chapter 12, Section 2).
☐ Faulty switch (Chapter 12, Section 6).

Instrument readings inaccurate or erratic

Fuel or temperature gauges give no reading

☐ Faulty coolant temperature sensor (Chapter 3, Section 6).
☐ Wiring open-circuit (Chapter 12, Section 2).
☐ Faulty gauge (Chapter 12, Section 11).

Fuel or temperature gauges give continuous maximum reading

☐ Faulty coolant temperature sensor (Chapter 3, Section 6).
☐ Wiring short-circuit (Chapter 12, Section 2).
☐ Faulty gauge (Chapter 12, Section 11).

Horn inoperative, or unsatisfactory in operation

Horn operates all the time

☐ Horn contacts permanently bridged or horn push stuck down (Chapter 12, Section 14).

Horn fails to operate

☐ Blown fuse (Chapter 12, Section 3).
☐ Cable or cable connections loose, broken or disconnected (Chapter 12, Section 2).
☐ Faulty horn (Chapter 12, Section 14).

Horn emits intermittent or unsatisfactory sound

☐ Cable connections loose (Chapter 12, Section 2).
☐ Horn mountings loose (Chapter 12, Section 14).
☐ Faulty horn (Chapter 12, Section 14).

Windscreen/tailgate wipers inoperative, or unsatisfactory in operation

Wipers fail to operate, or operate very slowly

☐ Wiper blades stuck to screen, or linkage seized or binding (*Weekly checks* and Chapter 12, Section 12).
☐ Blown fuse (Chapter 12).
☐ Cable or cable connections loose, broken or disconnected (Chapter 12).
☐ Faulty relay (Chapter 12).
☐ Faulty wiper motor (Chapter 12).

Wiper blades sweep over too large or too small an area of the glass

☐ Wiper arms incorrectly positioned on spindles (Chapter 12).
☐ Excessive wear of wiper linkage (Chapter 12, Section 12).
☐ Wiper motor or linkage mountings loose or insecure (Chapter 12, Section 12).

Wiper blades fail to clean the glass effectively

☐ Wiper blade rubbers worn or perished (*Weekly checks*).
☐ Wiper arm tension springs broken, or arm pivots seized (Chapter 12, Section 12).
☐ Insufficient windscreen washer additive to adequately remove road film (*Weekly checks*).

Windscreen washers inoperative, or unsatisfactory in operation

One or more washer jets inoperative

☐ Blocked washer jet (Chapter 12).
☐ Disconnected, kinked or restricted fluid hose (Chapter 12).
☐ Insufficient fluid in washer reservoir (*Weekly checks*).

Washer pump fails to operate

☐ Broken or disconnected wiring or connections (Chapter 12, Section 2).
☐ Blown fuse (Chapter 12, Section 3).
☐ Faulty washer switch (Chapter 12, Section 6).
☐ Faulty washer pump (Chapter 12, Section 13).

Electrical system (continued)

Electric windows inoperative, or unsatisfactory in operation

Window glass will only move in one direction

☐ Faulty switch (Chapter 12, Section 6).

Window glass slow to move

☐ Regulator seized or damaged, or in need of lubrication (Chapter 11, Section 11).
☐ Door internal components or trim fouling regulator (Chapter 11, Section 9).
☐ Faulty motor (Chapter 11).

Window glass fails to move

☐ Blown fuse (Chapter 12, Section 3).
☐ Broken or disconnected wiring or connections (Chapter 12, Section 2).
☐ Faulty motor (Chapter 11, Section 11).

Central locking system inoperative, or unsatisfactory in operation

Complete system failure

☐ Blown fuse (Chapter 12).
☐ Faulty ECM (Chapter 12).
☐ Broken or disconnected wiring or connections (Chapter 12).

Latch locks but will not unlock, or unlocks but will not lock

☐ Faulty switch (Chapter 12, Section 6).
☐ Broken or disconnected latch operating rods or levers (Chapter 11, Section 12).
☐ Faulty ECM (Chapter 12, Section 23).

One lock fails to operate

☐ Broken or disconnected wiring or connections (Chapter 12, Section 2).
☐ Faulty motor (Chapter 11, Section 12).
☐ Broken, binding or disconnected lock operating rods or levers (Chapter 11, Section 12).
☐ Fault in door lock (Chapter 11, Section 12)

A

ABS (Anti-lock brake system) A system, usually electronically controlled, that senses incipient wheel lockup during braking and relieves hydraulic pressure at wheels that are about to skid.

Air bag An inflatable bag hidden in the steering wheel (driver's side) or the dash or glovebox (passenger side). In a head-on collision, the bags inflate, preventing the driver and front passenger from being thrown forward into the steering wheel or windscreen.

Air cleaner A metal or plastic housing, containing a filter element, which removes dust and dirt from the air being drawn into the engine.

Air filter element The actual filter in an air cleaner system, usually manufactured from pleated paper and requiring renewal at regular intervals.

Air filter

Allen key A hexagonal wrench which fits into a recessed hexagonal hole.

Alligator clip A long-nosed spring-loaded metal clip with meshing teeth. Used to make temporary electrical connections.

Alternator A component in the electrical system which converts mechanical energy from a drivebelt into electrical energy to charge the battery and to operate the starting system, ignition system and electrical accessories.

Alternator (exploded view)

Ampere (amp) A unit of measurement for the flow of electric current. One amp is the amount of current produced by one volt acting through a resistance of one ohm.

Anaerobic sealer A substance used to prevent bolts and screws from loosening. Anaerobic means that it does not require oxygen for activation. The Loctite brand is widely used.

Antifreeze A substance (usually ethylene glycol) mixed with water, and added to a vehicle's cooling system, to prevent freezing of the coolant in winter. Antifreeze also contains chemicals to inhibit corrosion and the formation of rust and other deposits that would tend to clog the radiator and coolant passages and reduce cooling efficiency.

Anti-seize compound A coating that reduces the risk of seizing on fasteners that are subjected to high temperatures, such as exhaust manifold bolts and nuts.

Anti-seize compound

Asbestos A natural fibrous mineral with great heat resistance, commonly used in the composition of brake friction materials. Asbestos is a health hazard and the dust created by brake systems should never be inhaled or ingested.

Axle A shaft on which a wheel revolves, or which revolves with a wheel. Also, a solid beam that connects the two wheels at one end of the vehicle. An axle which also transmits power to the wheels is known as a live axle.

Axle assembly

Axleshaft A single rotating shaft, on either side of the differential, which delivers power from the final drive assembly to the drive wheels. Also called a driveshaft or a halfshaft.

B

Ball bearing An anti-friction bearing consisting of a hardened inner and outer race with hardened steel balls between two races.

Bearing

Bearing The curved surface on a shaft or in a bore, or the part assembled into either, that permits relative motion between them with minimum wear and friction.

Big-end bearing The bearing in the end of the connecting rod that's attached to the crankshaft.

Bleed nipple A valve on a brake wheel cylinder, caliper or other hydraulic component that is opened to purge the hydraulic system of air. Also called a bleed screw.

Brake bleeding

Brake bleeding Procedure for removing air from lines of a hydraulic brake system.

Brake disc The component of a disc brake that rotates with the wheels.

Brake drum The component of a drum brake that rotates with the wheels.

Brake linings The friction material which contacts the brake disc or drum to retard the vehicle's speed. The linings are bonded or riveted to the brake pads or shoes.

Brake pads The replaceable friction pads that pinch the brake disc when the brakes are applied. Brake pads consist of a friction material bonded or riveted to a rigid backing plate.

Brake shoe The crescent-shaped carrier to which the brake linings are mounted and which forces the lining against the rotating drum during braking.

Braking systems For more information on braking systems, consult the *Haynes Automotive Brake Manual*.

Breaker bar A long socket wrench handle providing greater leverage.

Bulkhead The insulated partition between the engine and the passenger compartment.

C

Caliper The non-rotating part of a disc-brake assembly that straddles the disc and carries the brake pads. The caliper also contains the hydraulic components that cause the pads to pinch the disc when the brakes are applied. A caliper is also a measuring tool that can be set to measure inside or outside dimensions of an object.

Camshaft A rotating shaft on which a series of cam lobes operate the valve mechanisms. The camshaft may be driven by gears, by sprockets and chain or by sprockets and a belt.

Canister A container in an evaporative emission control system; contains activated charcoal granules to trap vapours from the fuel system.

Canister

Carburettor A device which mixes fuel with air in the proper proportions to provide a desired power output from a spark ignition internal combustion engine.

Carburettor

Castellated Resembling the parapets along the top of a castle wall. For example, a castellated balljoint stud nut.

Castellated nut

Castor In wheel alignment, the backward or forward tilt of the steering axis. Castor is positive when the steering axis is inclined rearward at the top.

Catalytic converter A silencer-like device in the exhaust system which converts certain pollutants in the exhaust gases into less harmful substances.

Catalytic converter

Circlip A ring-shaped clip used to prevent endwise movement of cylindrical parts and shafts. An internal circlip is installed in a groove in a housing; an external circlip fits into a groove on the outside of a cylindrical piece such as a shaft.

Clearance The amount of space between two parts. For example, between a piston and a cylinder, between a bearing and a journal, etc.

Coil spring A spiral of elastic steel found in various sizes throughout a vehicle, for example as a springing medium in the suspension and in the valve train.

Compression Reduction in volume, and increase in pressure and temperature, of a gas, caused by squeezing it into a smaller space.

Compression ratio The relationship between cylinder volume when the piston is at top dead centre and cylinder volume when the piston is at bottom dead centre.

Constant velocity (CV) joint A type of universal joint that cancels out vibrations caused by driving power being transmitted through an angle.

Core plug A disc or cup-shaped metal device inserted in a hole in a casting through which core was removed when the casting was formed. Also known as a freeze plug or expansion plug.

Crankcase The lower part of the engine block in which the crankshaft rotates.

Crankshaft The main rotating member, or shaft, running the length of the crankcase, with offset "throws" to which the connecting rods are attached.

Crankshaft assembly

Crocodile clip See Alligator clip

D

Diagnostic code Code numbers obtained by accessing the diagnostic mode of an engine management computer. This code can be used to determine the area in the system where a malfunction may be located.

Disc brake A brake design incorporating a rotating disc onto which brake pads are squeezed. The resulting friction converts the energy of a moving vehicle into heat.

Double-overhead cam (DOHC) An engine that uses two overhead camshafts, usually one for the intake valves and one for the exhaust valves.

Drivebelt(s) The belt(s) used to drive accessories such as the alternator, water pump, power steering pump, air conditioning compressor, etc. off the crankshaft pulley.

Accessory drivebelts

Driveshaft Any shaft used to transmit motion. Commonly used when referring to the axleshafts on a front wheel drive vehicle.

Driveshaft

Drum brake A type of brake using a drum-shaped metal cylinder attached to the inner surface of the wheel. When the brake pedal is pressed, curved brake shoes with friction linings press against the inside of the drum to slow or stop the vehicle.

Drum brake assembly

Glossary of technical terms REF•29

E

EGR valve A valve used to introduce exhaust gases into the intake air stream.

EGR valve

Electronic control unit (ECU) A computer which controls (for instance) ignition and fuel injection systems, or an anti-lock braking system. For more information refer to the *Haynes Automotive Electrical and Electronic Systems Manual.*

Electronic Fuel Injection (EFI) A computer controlled fuel system that distributes fuel through an injector located in each intake port of the engine.

Emergency brake A braking system, independent of the main hydraulic system, that can be used to slow or stop the vehicle if the primary brakes fail, or to hold the vehicle stationary even though the brake pedal isn't depressed. It usually consists of a hand lever that actuates either front or rear brakes mechanically through a series of cables and linkages. Also known as a handbrake or parking brake.

Endfloat The amount of lengthwise movement between two parts. As applied to a crankshaft, the distance that the crankshaft can move forward and back in the cylinder block.

Engine management system (EMS) A computer controlled system which manages the fuel injection and the ignition systems in an integrated fashion.

Exhaust manifold A part with several passages through which exhaust gases leave the engine combustion chambers and enter the exhaust pipe.

Exhaust manifold

F

Fan clutch A viscous (fluid) drive coupling device which permits variable engine fan speeds in relation to engine speeds.

Feeler blade A thin strip or blade of hardened steel, ground to an exact thickness, used to check or measure clearances between parts.

Feeler blade

Firing order The order in which the engine cylinders fire, or deliver their power strokes, beginning with the number one cylinder.

Flywheel A heavy spinning wheel in which energy is absorbed and stored by means of momentum. On cars, the flywheel is attached to the crankshaft to smooth out firing impulses.

Free play The amount of travel before any action takes place. The "looseness" in a linkage, or an assembly of parts, between the initial application of force and actual movement. For example, the distance the brake pedal moves before the pistons in the master cylinder are actuated.

Fuse An electrical device which protects a circuit against accidental overload. The typical fuse contains a soft piece of metal which is calibrated to melt at a predetermined current flow (expressed as amps) and break the circuit.

Fusible link A circuit protection device consisting of a conductor surrounded by heat-resistant insulation. The conductor is smaller than the wire it protects, so it acts as the weakest link in the circuit. Unlike a blown fuse, a failed fusible link must frequently be cut from the wire for replacement.

G

Gap The distance the spark must travel in jumping from the centre electrode to the side

Adjusting spark plug gap

electrode in a spark plug. Also refers to the spacing between the points in a contact breaker assembly in a conventional points-type ignition, or to the distance between the reluctor or rotor and the pickup coil in an electronic ignition.

Gasket Any thin, soft material - usually cork, cardboard, asbestos or soft metal - installed between two metal surfaces to ensure a good seal. For instance, the cylinder head gasket seals the joint between the block and the cylinder head.

Gasket

Gauge An instrument panel display used to monitor engine conditions. A gauge with a movable pointer on a dial or a fixed scale is an analogue gauge. A gauge with a numerical readout is called a digital gauge.

H

Halfshaft A rotating shaft that transmits power from the final drive unit to a drive wheel, usually when referring to a live rear axle.

Harmonic balancer A device designed to reduce torsion or twisting vibration in the crankshaft. May be incorporated in the crankshaft pulley. Also known as a vibration damper.

Hone An abrasive tool for correcting small irregularities or differences in diameter in an engine cylinder, brake cylinder, etc.

Hydraulic tappet A tappet that utilises hydraulic pressure from the engine's lubrication system to maintain zero clearance (constant contact with both camshaft and valve stem). Automatically adjusts to variation in valve stem length. Hydraulic tappets also reduce valve noise.

I

Ignition timing The moment at which the spark plug fires, usually expressed in the number of crankshaft degrees before the piston reaches the top of its stroke.

Inlet manifold A tube or housing with passages through which flows the air-fuel mixture (carburettor vehicles and vehicles with throttle body injection) or air only (port fuel-injected vehicles) to the port openings in the cylinder head.

J

Jump start Starting the engine of a vehicle with a discharged or weak battery by attaching jump leads from the weak battery to a charged or helper battery.

L

Load Sensing Proportioning Valve (LSPV) A brake hydraulic system control valve that works like a proportioning valve, but also takes into consideration the amount of weight carried by the rear axle.

Locknut A nut used to lock an adjustment nut, or other threaded component, in place. For example, a locknut is employed to keep the adjusting nut on the rocker arm in position.

Lockwasher A form of washer designed to prevent an attaching nut from working loose.

M

MacPherson strut A type of front suspension system devised by Earle MacPherson at Ford of England. In its original form, a simple lateral link with the anti-roll bar creates the lower control arm. A long strut - an integral coil spring and shock absorber - is mounted between the body and the steering knuckle. Many modern so-called MacPherson strut systems use a conventional lower A-arm and don't rely on the anti-roll bar for location.

Multimeter An electrical test instrument with the capability to measure voltage, current and resistance.

N

NOx Oxides of Nitrogen. A common toxic pollutant emitted by petrol and diesel engines at higher temperatures.

O

Ohm The unit of electrical resistance. One volt applied to a resistance of one ohm will produce a current of one amp.

Ohmmeter An instrument for measuring electrical resistance.

O-ring A type of sealing ring made of a special rubber-like material; in use, the O-ring is compressed into a groove to provide the sealing action.

O-ring

Overhead cam (ohc) engine An engine with the camshaft(s) located on top of the cylinder head(s).

Overhead valve (ohv) engine An engine with the valves located in the cylinder head, but with the camshaft located in the engine block.

Oxygen sensor A device installed in the engine exhaust manifold, which senses the oxygen content in the exhaust and converts this information into an electric current. Also called a Lambda sensor.

P

Phillips screw A type of screw head having a cross instead of a slot for a corresponding type of screwdriver.

Plastigage A thin strip of plastic thread, available in different sizes, used for measuring clearances. For example, a strip of Plastigage is laid across a bearing journal. The parts are assembled and dismantled; the width of the crushed strip indicates the clearance between journal and bearing.

Plastigage

Propeller shaft The long hollow tube with universal joints at both ends that carries power from the transmission to the differential on front-engined rear wheel drive vehicles.

Proportioning valve A hydraulic control valve which limits the amount of pressure to the rear brakes during panic stops to prevent wheel lock-up.

R

Rack-and-pinion steering A steering system with a pinion gear on the end of the steering shaft that mates with a rack (think of a geared wheel opened up and laid flat). When the steering wheel is turned, the pinion turns, moving the rack to the left or right. This movement is transmitted through the track rods to the steering arms at the wheels.

Radiator A liquid-to-air heat transfer device designed to reduce the temperature of the coolant in an internal combustion engine cooling system.

Refrigerant Any substance used as a heat transfer agent in an air-conditioning system. R-12 has been the principle refrigerant for many years; recently, however, manufacturers have begun using R-134a, a non-CFC substance that is considered less harmful to the ozone in the upper atmosphere.

Rocker arm A lever arm that rocks on a shaft or pivots on a stud. In an overhead valve engine, the rocker arm converts the upward movement of the pushrod into a downward movement to open a valve.

Rotor In a distributor, the rotating device inside the cap that connects the centre electrode and the outer terminals as it turns, distributing the high voltage from the coil secondary winding to the proper spark plug. Also, that part of an alternator which rotates inside the stator. Also, the rotating assembly of a turbocharger, including the compressor wheel, shaft and turbine wheel.

Runout The amount of wobble (in-and-out movement) of a gear or wheel as it's rotated. The amount a shaft rotates "out-of-true." The out-of-round condition of a rotating part.

S

Sealant A liquid or paste used to prevent leakage at a joint. Sometimes used in conjunction with a gasket.

Sealed beam lamp An older headlight design which integrates the reflector, lens and filaments into a hermetically-sealed one-piece unit. When a filament burns out or the lens cracks, the entire unit is simply replaced.

Serpentine drivebelt A single, long, wide accessory drivebelt that's used on some newer vehicles to drive all the accessories, instead of a series of smaller, shorter belts. Serpentine drivebelts are usually tensioned by an automatic tensioner.

Serpentine drivebelt

Shim Thin spacer, commonly used to adjust the clearance or relative positions between two parts. For example, shims inserted into or under bucket tappets control valve clearances. Clearance is adjusted by changing the thickness of the shim.

Slide hammer A special puller that screws into or hooks onto a component such as a shaft or bearing; a heavy sliding handle on the shaft bottoms against the end of the shaft to knock the component free.

Sprocket A tooth or projection on the periphery of a wheel, shaped to engage with a chain or drivebelt. Commonly used to refer to the sprocket wheel itself.

Starter inhibitor switch On vehicles with an automatic transmission, a switch that prevents starting if the vehicle is not in Neutral or Park.

Strut See MacPherson strut.

T

Tappet A cylindrical component which transmits motion from the cam to the valve stem, either directly or via a pushrod and rocker arm. Also called a cam follower.

Thermostat A heat-controlled valve that regulates the flow of coolant between the cylinder block and the radiator, so maintaining optimum engine operating temperature. A thermostat is also used in some air cleaners in which the temperature is regulated.

Thrust bearing The bearing in the clutch assembly that is moved in to the release levers by clutch pedal action to disengage the clutch. Also referred to as a release bearing.

Timing belt A toothed belt which drives the camshaft. Serious engine damage may result if it breaks in service.

Timing chain A chain which drives the camshaft.

Toe-in The amount the front wheels are closer together at the front than at the rear. On rear wheel drive vehicles, a slight amount of toe-in is usually specified to keep the front wheels running parallel on the road by offsetting other forces that tend to spread the wheels apart.

Toe-out The amount the front wheels are closer together at the rear than at the front. On front wheel drive vehicles, a slight amount of toe-out is usually specified.

Tools For full information on choosing and using tools, refer to the *Haynes Automotive Tools Manual*.

Tracer A stripe of a second colour applied to a wire insulator to distinguish that wire from another one with the same colour insulator.

Tune-up A process of accurate and careful adjustments and parts replacement to obtain the best possible engine performance.

Turbocharger A centrifugal device, driven by exhaust gases, that pressurises the intake air. Normally used to increase the power output from a given engine displacement, but can also be used primarily to reduce exhaust emissions (as on VW's "Umwelt" Diesel engine).

U

Universal joint or U-joint A double-pivoted connection for transmitting power from a driving to a driven shaft through an angle. A U-joint consists of two Y-shaped yokes and a cross-shaped member called the spider.

V

Valve A device through which the flow of liquid, gas, vacuum, or loose material in bulk may be started, stopped, or regulated by a movable part that opens, shuts, or partially obstructs one or more ports or passageways. A valve is also the movable part of such a device.

Valve clearance The clearance between the valve tip (the end of the valve stem) and the rocker arm or tappet. The valve clearance is measured when the valve is closed.

Vernier caliper A precision measuring instrument that measures inside and outside dimensions. Not quite as accurate as a micrometer, but more convenient.

Viscosity The thickness of a liquid or its resistance to flow.

Volt A unit for expressing electrical "pressure" in a circuit. One volt that will produce a current of one ampere through a resistance of one ohm.

W

Welding Various processes used to join metal items by heating the areas to be joined to a molten state and fusing them together. For more information refer to the *Haynes Automotive Welding Manual*.

Wiring diagram A drawing portraying the components and wires in a vehicle's electrical system, using standardised symbols. For more information refer to the *Haynes Automotive Electrical and Electronic Systems Manual*.

Note: *References throughout this index are in the form* "**Chapter number**" • "**Page number**". *So, for example, 2C•15 refers to page 15 of Chapter 2C.*

Note: *References throughout this index are in the form* **"Chapter number"** • **"Page number"**. *So, for example, 2C•15 refers to page 15 of Chapter 2C.*

Note: *References throughout this index are in the form "**Chapter number**" • "**Page number**". So, for example, 2C•15 refers to page 15 of Chapter 2C.*

Note: *References throughout this index are in the form* "**Chapter number**" • "**Page number**". *So, for example, 2C•15 refers to page 15 of Chapter 2C.*

Preserving Our Motoring Heritage

< *The Model J Duesenberg Derham Tourster. Only eight of these magnificent cars were ever built – this is the only example to be found outside the United States of America*

Almost every car you've ever loved, loathed or desired is gathered under one roof at the Haynes Motor Museum. Over 300 immaculately presented cars and motorbikes represent every aspect of our motoring heritage, from elegant reminders of bygone days, such as the superb Model J Duesenberg to curiosities like the bug-eyed BMW Isetta. There are also many old friends and flames. Perhaps you remember the 1959 Ford Popular that you did your courting in? The magnificent 'Red Collection' is a spectacle of classic sports cars including AC, Alfa Romeo, Austin Healey, Ferrari, Lamborghini, Maserati, MG, Riley, Porsche and Triumph.

A Perfect Day Out

Each and every vehicle at the Haynes Motor Museum has played its part in the history and culture of Motoring. Today, they make a wonderful spectacle and a great day out for all the family. Bring the kids, bring Mum and Dad, but above all bring your camera to capture those golden memories for ever. You will also find an impressive array of motoring memorabilia, a comfortable 70 seat video cinema and one of the most extensive transport book shops in Britain. The Pit Stop Cafe serves everything from a cup of tea to wholesome, home-made meals or, if you prefer, you can enjoy the large picnic area nestled in the beautiful rural surroundings of Somerset.

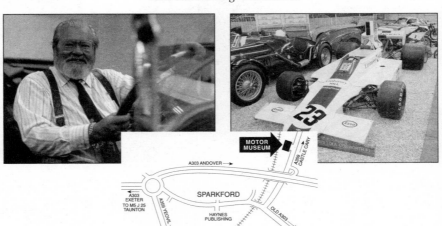

> *John Haynes O.B.E., Founder and Chairman of the museum at the wheel of a Haynes Light 12.*

< *Graham Hill's Lola Cosworth Formula 1 car next to a 1934 Riley Sports.*

The Museum is situated on the A359 Yeovil to Frome road at Sparkford, just off the A303 in Somerset. It is about 40 miles south of Bristol, and 25 minutes drive from the M5 intersection at Taunton.

Open 9.30am - 5.30pm (10.00am - 4.00pm Winter) 7 days a week, *except Christmas Day, Boxing Day and New Years Day*

Special rates available for schools, coach parties and outings Charitable Trust No. 292048